HANDBOOKS

MEXICO CITY

CHRIS HUMPHREY

Contents

Discover Mexico City

Mexico City – also known as La Ciudad, La Capital, México, el Distrito Federal, or simply "De Efe" (D.F.) for short – often astounds first-time visitors with its disarming combination of Old World charm and New World sophistication. The city lures visitors with a long list of superlatives – it's the oldest and highest city in North America, one of the largest in the world, and the only metropolis with three UNESCO World Heritage Sites within its city limits.

Despite its epic sprawl, it can be a remarkably attractive city, in certain areas – the downtown Centro Histórico, lined with colonial mansions and churches; broad, elegant Paseo de la Reforma, lined with office buildings and first-class hotels; the art deco architecture, galleries, and cafés of the Roma and Condesa neighborhoods; and the quiet cobblestone streets of Coyoacán and San Ángel in the south.

Museum-lovers could spend days, even weeks, touring the many exhibits of art, history, archaeology, and popular culture. Architecture enthusiasts can see every kind of building from 2000-year-old pyramids to Latin America's highest skyscraper. And lovers of the good life won't want to miss the fantastic food and the epic, dawn-chasing nightlife for which the city is famous.

But it's the little discoveries that are addictive. A cantina in continuous operation for seven decades, a used bookshop specializing in 19th-

century engravings, street-corner vendors selling blue-corn quesadillas, a colonial-era *plazuela* (little plaza) seemingly lost to all but local inhabitants – all conspire to pull you under the city's spell. It's a city that generously rewards those willing to explore beyond the standard tourist sights.

Crazed? Definitely. But the amazing thing is how well the city works, how it reaches well beyond mere survival. You can zip across town by underground Metro or glide slowly around the Centro Histórico in a *bicitaxi* (pedicab). Dig into a steaming chile-and-cheese tamale served by a sidewalk vendor for $0.35 while standing outside a $200-a-night hotel. Climb aboard a brightly painted *trajinera* (Mexican-style gondola) and disappear down the shaded waterways of Xochimilco. Aztec temples and Catholic cathedrals, punk rockers and mariachi serenaders, poverty-stricken slums and walled villas; they're all part of the phantasmagoric heart of *chilangolandia,* as locals sometimes call Mexico City. The longer you stay, the more intriguing it all seems to become.

Planning Your Trip

▶ WHERE TO GO

Flying into Mexico City for the first time, across what seems to be an endless sea of urbanity, is a daunting experience. But even a first-time visitor shouldn't have too hard a time getting oriented. Almost all the attractions, hotels, restaurants, and other services of interest to visitors are located within an area in the central and southwest part of the city roughly defined on the east by the Calzada de Tlalpan avenue, on the north by Paseo de la Reforma, and the west and south by the Periférico ring highway.

Centro Histórico

If you go to only one place in Mexico City, it should unquestionably be the Zócalo, Mexico City's downtown square, which has been the city's epicenter since the time of the Aztecs. The Zócalo is surrounded by the ruins of the Aztec Templo Mayor (Great Temple), the sumptuous Catedral, the red brick Palacio Nacional, and block after block of colonial palaces and churches, museums, cultural sites, and more.

Alameda Central

Immediately west of the Centro is the Alameda Central, an expanse of trees and grass lined with benches and small plazas, with the massive Palacio de Bellas Artes at one end. The surrounding blocks contain a number of museums worth touring, including the applied arts collection at the Museo Franz Mayer and the new Museo Nacional de Artes Populares. Just south shoppers will find the craft markets at La Ciudadela and Mercado San Juan.

Paseo de la Reforma and Zona Rosa

The broad European-style Paseo de la Reforma avenue housed the city's richest mansions in the late 19th century, which now house embassies and swank restaurants, and are

Palacio Nacional in the Zócalo

IF YOU HAVE...

Zócalo in Centro Histórico

- **A WEEKEND:** Visit Centro Histórico, Alameda, the Museo Nacional de Antropología e Historia, Chapultepec Park, and San Ángel
- **FIVE DAYS:** Add Roma, Condesa, Coyoacán, and Teotihuacán
- **ONE WEEK:** Add another day in the Centro Histórico, and Taxco, Cuernavaca, or Puebla
- **TWO WEEKS:** Add Santa María de la Ribera, Mixcoac, or Tlalpan

surrounded by high-rise bank offices and luxury hotels, with the imposing Monumento a la Revolución nearby. Just south of Reforma are the shops, restaurants, and bars of the Zona Rosa neighborhood.

Chapultepec and Polanco

Chapultepec is a spacious public park in central-western Mexico City centered on a small hill topped by a castle. Right across from Chapultepec is the world-class Museo Nacional de Antropología e Historia, a treasure trove of exhibits on Mexico's rich legacy of indigenous cultures, and nearby are two of the city's best art museums. North of Chapultepec is Polanco, a sort of Rodeo Drive for Mexico City, replete with chic fashion shops and pricey restaurants.

Roma and Condesa

Two of the city's most happening *colonias*, immensely popular with the local and expatriate younger crowds, are the Condesa and Roma. The 1920s-era Condesa is home to hipster cafés, restaurants, and bars in converted art deco–style houses. The more bohemian Roma, built in the late 19th century, has lots of art galleries, coffeehouses, and alternative night spots. Both neighborhoods are great places to walk around, with fine architecture and many tree-filled parks.

Nápoles, Del Valle, and Mixcoac

Tourist destinations in the Nápoles and Del Valle are few, apart from the weird geometric Poliforo Cultural Siqueiros, but many expats find apartments in the middle-class neighborhoods. A bit further south is Mixcoac, a formerly colonial village now surrounded by bustling avenues, with its tranquil stone plaza still intact.

Coyoacán

The plazas and narrow cobbled streets of Coyoacán, once part of huge haciendas and convents, are marvelous places for visitors to stroll and appreciate the neighborhood's

unfurling the Mexican flag in the Zócalo

Ex-Convento del Carmen

relaxed ambience. There are many museums and historical buildings to see, including the Museo Frida Kahlo inside the artist's old house. After all the touring, relax with a drink at one of the many cafés on Coyoacán's twin plazas.

San Ángel

West of Coyoacán is the similar but smaller San Ángel, another former colonial village now surrounded by the ever-growing city. Visitors should stop in the Ex-Convento del Carmen to view an impressive example of colonial architecture, or see the modern art collection at the Museo de Arte Carrillo Gil.

On Saturdays the Bazar Sábado sets up shop on the plaza, offering some of the finest art and handicrafts available in the city.

Greater Mexico City

In southern Mexico City are the famed *chinampas,* the floating gardens of Xochimilco, the breadbasket of the Aztec empire and now a popular destination for boat rides along the ancient canals. Here you'll also find the Museo Dolores Olmedo Patiño, with the largest collection of paintings by Diego Rivera and Frida Kahlo. In the north is the Basílica de Nuestra Señora de Guadalupe, the most sacred shrine in the country.

► WHEN TO GO

Any time of year is a good time to visit Mexico City. Because it is a mainly urban environment, most sights are not particularly weather-dependent. Visiting Mexico City during the April–October rainy season can be wet, so come prepared with an umbrella or rain jacket. Temperatures are cooler in the winter but fairly moderate all year round. Air pollution tends to get a bit worse during the colder, drier winter months

(thermal inversions are not uncommon), but good and bad days are possible throughout the year. In general, pollution is lighter when it's windy.

There's no tourist season per se in Mexico City, but it's often nice to go during Mexican holidays, when many residents are away on vacation and the city is less congested. The Christmas holidays and Semana Santa (Easter week) are great times to visit.

► BEFORE YOU GO

Passports and Visas

Traveling to Mexico City is extremely easy. Visas are granted upon entry to Mexico with no advance arrangements (just bring a passport) for tourists from the U.S., Canada, and nearly 40 countries in Europe and Latin America, meaning you can easily arrange a last-minute trip to D.F. should the mood strike your fancy.

Safety

Mexico City has a well-deserved reputation as a city with a lot of crime, but the truth is that it's no more dangerous than any city in Latin America. Most crime takes place well away from tourist destinations, and tourists can easily stay out of harm's way by sticking to more popular neighborhoods. Most tourist robberies happen when flagging a taxi off the street or getting on a crowded Metro car. Always use a safe *sitio* (radio) taxi, don't bring valuables with you, and watch out for pickpockets and you'll be fine.

Getting There and Around

Aeropuerto Internacional Benito Juárez is the domestic and international airport for Mexico City... and is well past its capacity. Regional airports like Toluca, Puebla, and Querétaro are gearing up for international traffic and may be an option.

Policias charros on patrol in the Alameda

Travel within Mexico City is cheap, efficient, and relatively safe. Metrobús and the Metro system are both convenient and affordable ways of getting around, and a *sitio taxi* can deliver you safely at night. Walking is the best way to see each neighborhood. Driving in Mexico City is an option only for the very brave. If you plan on driving your own car in Mexico, be sure to carry a Mexican liability insurance policy on your vehicle—Mexican authorities don't recognize foreign insurance policies for private vehicles in Mexico.

taxis

Explore Mexico City

▶ THE BEST OF MEXICO CITY

Two days isn't a whole lot of time for one of the biggest cities in the world, but the amount of fun you can have in Mexico City in just a weekend is impressive. It's certainly long enough to get you hooked and start planning your next trip. These days you can purchase last-minute airline tickets from the U.S. sometimes for as low as $250, making D.F. a reasonable alternative to going to New York City, Miami, or San Francisco for the weekend—especially when you factor in lower hotel and restaurant costs.

detail of the Palacio de Bellas Artes

Day 1, Morning

Start in the heart of the city, at the Zócalo, surrounded on all sides by some of the most important monuments in Mexico. Dominating the view is the Catedral Metropolitana, well worth an hour or so to admire both its architectural grandeur and the collection of religious art tucked into the seemingly endless alcoves and side altars. Right next door are the ruins of the Aztec Templo Mayor, along with the Museo del Templo Mayor, which has exhibits on art and artifacts found during its excavation. If you like the look of the red-brick Palacio Nacional, also on the Zócalo, step inside to see Diego Rivera's famous murals. After seeing these three sights at a leisurely pace, you'll be starting to work up an appetite, so walk a couple of blocks west of the Zócalo and stop for an excellent traditional Mexican meal at El Cardenal.

Day 1, Afternoon

After the *comida,* walk west on Calle Tacuba, which dates from Aztec times and is lined with ornate colonial mansions. Across the busy Eje Central avenue, just past the Venetian-style Palacio Postal, is the imposing Palacio de Bellas Artes. Stop in to admire the art nouveau/art deco architecture, the impressive Tiffany glass curtain, and the political murals. Just beyond is the Alameda, Mexico City's first public park, a fine place to take a rest on a bench and watch the world go by. If you've got more energy to spare, finish up the day with a visit to the eclectic applied-arts collection at the Museo Franz Mayer or switch to shopping mode and visit the FONART store, just off the Alameda, or the handicrafts market at

ART LOVERS' TOUR

Casa Lamm

Mexico is filled with explosions of color everywhere, from the wild decals on a minibus to the elaborate and macabre candy decorations for Día de los Muertos (Day of the Dead).

CENTRO HISTÓRICO

The **Palacio Nacional** is home to the well-known Diego Rivera mural. The **Secretaría de Educación Pública** building has more than 100 murals by Rivera covering its three stories. For modern Mexican art, stop into the **Galería SCHP, Museo José Luis Cuevas, Centro de Arte Alternativo Ex-Santa Teresa,** and **Laboratorio de Arte Alameda.**

CHAPULTEPEC AND POLANCO

On Paseo de la Reforma, the **Museo Rufino Tamayo** contains Tamayo's art, as well as works from his private collection. The **Museo de Arte Moderno** showcases Mexican greats from the

20th century. Polanco has a number of high-end art galleries, with works by recent artists.

ROMA AND CONDESA

Galleries like **Nina Menocal** and **Galería OMR** showcase new artists and their openings and are great ways to mingle in the local art world. The **Casa Lamm,** a cultural institute, has exhibits and a number of art courses.

SOUTHERN MEXICO CITY

Coyoacán is home to the **Museo Frida Kahlo,** which features the works and collection of the great artist and wife of Diego Rivera. Her husband's counterpart is the **Museo Estudio Diego Rivera,** in San Ángel. An even larger collection of their work is at **Museo Dolores Olmedo Patiño** in Xochimilco. The **Museo de Arte Carrillo Gil,** also in San Ángel, has a fine collection of Mexico's modernists.

La Ciudadela, just south of the Alameda on Calle Balderas.

Day 1, Evening

With only one weekend night out in Mexico City to live it up, you might as well do it in style. So put on some respectable duds and

head over to Hacienda de los Morales in Polanco, where you can savor sublime Mexican cooking in the refined atmosphere of a 16th-century hacienda. For late-night entertainment, the options are many: salsa dancing, old-school cantinas, hipster lounges, queer clubs, or political cabaret shows. But if you have to pick one place to get a taste of the soul of Mexico City's nightlife, it's got to be Plaza Garibaldi. Make your way through the crowd of revelers mingling with maria-chi musicians crowding this little square in the Centro, and grab a table in the venerable Salón Tenampa. Buy a bottle of your favorite drink, pay one of the roving bands to strike up a classic old *bolero* tune, and join the fun.

Day 2, Morning

You'll be feeling a little groggy, so start off with a solid breakfast. One good option is Café Los Asombros at the El Péndulo book-stores in the Condesa or the Zona Rosa,

unique Condesa architecture

where you can ease into the day with a big omelet filled with spinach, mushrooms, and goat cheese; a tall glass of juice; and an *espresso cortado*. Suitably fortified, head to the world-famous Museo Nacional de Antropología e Historia along Paseo de la Reforma. Don't even think of trying to see all the exhibit halls or you'll be spent for the day. Afterward, deprogram with a walk across the street through the leafy Chapultepec Park, with a short detour up to the hilltop castle/museum to check out the views over the city.

Day 2, Afternoon and Evening

Sunday afternoon is a great time to head down to the former colonial-era village of Coyoacán, in the south part of the city. Amble around the twin plazas, thronged with handicraft vendors and locals out enjoying the weekend. A few blocks away along quiet cob-blestone streets are the houses of the conquis-tador Cortés and his much-maligned lover and interpreter, La Malinche, as well as the Museo Frida Kahlo, dedicated to Mexico's best-known woman artist. After you're done touring, top off your weekend with another good meal—this time at one of the many great restaurants in the hip Condesa district. A good choice is El Zorzal, where you can dig into a juicy Argentine steak with red wine, empanadas, and a big bowl of salad.

▶ A WEEK IN MEXICO CITY

A week is the perfect amount of time for a trip to Mexico City. You'll have plenty of time to tour the major sights and even a few less-fre-quented destinations without running yourself ragged, leaving enough energy to spend a cou-ple of evenings enjoying the city's great night-life. You'll also be able to take a couple of days to visit one of the many towns set amidst the lovely countryside surrounding the capital.

Day 1

Dedicate an entire day to taking in the Centro Histórico, taking the time to explore some of the lesser-known sites. Just north of the Templo Mayor is the Antiguo Colegio de San Ildefonso, a gracefully built religious school from the 16th century that now shows a variety of cultural exhibits; it also has some of first murals by Rivera, Orozco, and the other great painters of the early 20th century decorating the walls. Take a stroll through the Plaza de Santo Domingo to watch the low-budget scribes writing missives for hire on their venerable old printing presses. For an aerial view of the Centro and the rest of the city, pay a nominal fee to ride up to the 38th floor of the Torre Latinoamericana office building, where there is an observation platform.

Day 2

In Chapultepec Park, take in the Museo Nacional de Antropología e Historia, and two top-quality modern art museums—the Museo de Arte Moderno and the Museo Rufino Tamayo. If the park greenery appeals, take the time for a leisurely stroll, perhaps stopping into the zoo or just grabbing a bench by the lake and watching the day go by. After you've had your fill of Chapultepec, spend a couple of hours to tour either the chichi shopping and restaurant district of Polanco, or the more bohemian, relaxed Roma neighborhood, filled with old Porfiriato-era mansions, coffeehouses, and bookstores.

Day 3

The ancient ruins of Teotihuacán, located just northeast of Mexico City, are without doubt the most popular day-trip destination for tourists, and with good reason. This huge city, built by an unknown civilization over 2000 years ago, leaves visitors in awe of the towering pyramids, grand avenues, and stone carvings. The blazing sun and arid landscape can be exhausting, so come prepared with water and a hat. If you've got some energy left on the way back into town, stop off at nearby Acolman, a magnificent early colonial monastery with indigenous motifs carved into the church facade.

Day 4

After being such a dedicated sightseer, a day without any touristy destinations might be in order. One option might be to catch an event of some variety. For example, you could catch a soccer match at one of Mexico City's three stadiums, where you can join in the cheering for the America, Cruz Azul, or Pumas club teams—or, if you're lucky, there might be a national team match. If you'd prefer a slightly more unusual sport, check out *lucha libre,* Mexico's colorful and melodramatic version of professional wrestling. To get yourself some exercise, take a jaunt up to the parks at Ajusco or Desierto de los Leones, where you can breathe crisp mountain air and hike around trails through the pine forest.

Days 5-6

Set aside two days to take an overnight trip to one of myriad destinations in Central Mexico.

Museo Rufino Tamayo

COLONIAL MEXICO CITY

As the crown jewel of the Spanish empire in the New World, Mexico City is filled with monuments to its colonial years. Whether you are interested in the architecture or the history, Mexico City has a wealth of interesting colonial sights to explore.

CENTRO HISTÓRICO

• The **Catedral** and the **Palacio Nacional** are classics of religious and civic architecture.

• For a well-hidden display of religious art in the baroque era, peek into the 18th-century **Iglesia de la Enseñanza** where nine dazzling gold-leafed *retablos* (altar pieces) are crammed inside the small church.

• The **Palacio de Iturbide** and **Casa de los Condes de Heras y Soto** are examples of the old mansions that earned Mexico City its colonial-era sobriquet of *la ciudad de los palacios* (the city of palaces).

• A simple plaque near the altar of the **Iglesia de Jesús Nazareno** marks the final resting place of Hernán Cortés – the Spaniard who conquered Aztec Mexico.

REFORMA AND CHAPULTEPEC

Trace the route of the Spanish soldiers as they fled the city in panic during the *noche triste* (sad night) in 1520 after an attack by the Aztecs.

• Follow Calle Tacuba west from the Zócalo, and once past the Alameda you'll be atop what was once the Aztec causeway across the lake, over which the Spaniards ran for their lives.

• A few kilometers west of the Alameda stands the burned-out trunk of the **Árbol de la Noche Triste** that Cortés leaned against and wept almost five centuries ago when the remaining soldiers reached the mainland to regroup and relaunch their conquest.

• For a taste of how wealthy Spaniards must have lived, take a tour (Sundays only) of the **Casa de la Bola,** an opulent mansion just south of Chapultepec restored with period furniture and decorations.

SOUTHERN MEXICO CITY

• **Coyoacán** offers a taste of what a colonial suburb might have felt like, with narrow cobble-stone streets winding around twin plazas, and with centuries-old churches and houses on all sides.

• **Tlalpan** is situated around a very fine little plaza hidden off backstreets near the highway exit to Cuernavaca.

• In the park of **Desierto de los Leones** is a lovely colonial monastery built as a retreat in the forests by Carmelite monks in the late 18th century.

AROUND MEXICO CITY

• **Puebla** was a key Spanish city during the colonial era and is filled with myriad monuments from that time, including the **Catedral,** one of the finest in Mexico, and the **Biblioteca Palafoxiana** (a library).

• **Cholula** is filled with even more colonial churches.

• **Huejotzingo** is an early 16th-century monastery with fantastical stone carvings.

• Head up to the **Paso de Cortés,** the high pass between the great volcanoes of Popocatépetl and Ixtaccíhuatl, and the vantage point from where Cortés first saw the Aztec capital of Tenochtitlán.

Puebla's Catedral

Everyone will have their own destinations of choice, but one great place to go for first-time visitors is the famed silver city of Taxco, perched precariously on a steep mountainside in the state of Guerrero, a couple of hours south of Mexico City. Apart from shopping for the trademark silver jewelry and other handicrafts, the picturesque town has several museums worth visiting and plenty of restaurants. On your way back to Mexico City the next day, take a short detour to Tepoztlán near Cuernavaca to visit the beautiful convent and hike up to a prehispanic hilltop temple just outside of town.

Taxco

Day 7

Spend your last day in Mexico City in the south of town, touring the colonial-era neighborhoods of Coyoacán and San Ángel, visiting different art and history museums, or just walking around the mansion-lined cobblestone streets and enjoying the ambiance. Any day is a good day to go, but it's worth going on a Saturday for the Bazar Sábado, one of the finest arts-and-crafts markets in the city, held on the plaza in San Ángel. Further south is Xochimilco, where you can rent a *trajinera* to paddle you around the ancient Aztec canals.

▶ INDIGENOUS PAST AND PRESENT

Mexico's indigenous roots and culture are present in every part of D.F.—from the remnants of the ancient Aztec capital in the Centro Histórico to the archaeological and anthropological treasures in the world-renowned Museo Nacional de Antropología e Historia. A visitor could easily spend a week on a tour of just cultural and archaeological sites.

Centro Histórico

The crown of the Centro's Aztec past is of course the Templo Mayor, just off the northeast side of the Zócalo. Walking around the pathways through the ruins feels like—is, really—tapping into Mexico City's very foundation. Inside the adjacent museum are some 7,000 artifacts from the site, including the famous eight-ton circular stone adorned with carvings of the moon goddess Coyolxuahqui. Remnants of the ancient Aztec capital are found in the unlikeliest spots around the Centro, like the serpent's head cornerstone of the colonial palace that houses the Museo de la Ciudad de México. For a taste of indigenous culture, literally, head over to the Fonda de Don Chon, a humble little eatery on a backstreet that specializes in all sorts of well-prepared Aztec delicacies, like *gusanos de maguey* (cactus worms) or *venado con huitlacoche* (deer meat with corn fungus)—definitely for the brave!

Chapultepec

A lengthy stop at the Museo Nacional de Antropología e Historia in Chapultepec is obligatory for those with a strong interest in Mexico's indigenous cultures. If you could

the Basílica de Nuestra Señora de Guadalupe

actually take the time to read and digest all the information in the 23 halls of the vast museum (impossible), you'd be a world-class expert. Outside the museum you can see some of that culture in action, watching the trapeze-like spectacle of the *voladores de Papantla,* costumed indigenous men from Veracruz who swing around a tall pole with ropes around their feet. Just across the street, the hill underneath El Castillo de Chapultepec was a sacred shrine of the Aztecs for the water that sprung from its base, and although you can't see them now, the portraits of Aztec emperors were carved in the hillside, à la Mt. Rushmore.

Southern Mexico City

A couple of millennia ago, the area just south of the national university was the site of the first urban settlement in the Valle de México, Cuicuilco. Although it was destroyed by a volcanic eruption, the ruins of Cuicuilco are still there, poking up out of a hardened lava field right at the intersection of Avenida Insurgentes and the Periférico Sur, easily accessible for a short visit. Further east is Cerro de la Estrella, a small volcanic cone where the Aztecs used to light their 52-year fire, which they believed renewed the world. Nowadays the hill is the site of the city's biggest annual Passion Play reenactment during

Semana Santa (Holy Week). Also worth seeing in the south is the Museo Anahuacalli, built by Mexican painter Diego Rivera to resemble a Mesoamerican pyramid and filled with his collection of prehispanic artifacts.

Northern Mexico City

Not exactly indigenous, properly speaking, the Basílica de Nuestra Señora de Guadalupe, Mexico's most popular religious shrine, nonetheless has a deep connection to Mexico's prehispanic past. It's hard to believe it was a coincidence that *la virgen morena* (the dark-skinned virgin) appeared on the hill of Tepayac, site of the Aztec shrine to the goddess Tonantzin, almost five centuries ago. It's an amazing sight to witness the humble peasants from across Mexico, many of them indigenous, thronging the Basílica, waiting their turn to pray in front of the Virgin. Also in northern Mexico City are two archeological sites, the pre-Aztec piràmide de Tenayuca, dating to at least the 11th century, and the larger Aztec pyramid, Santa Cecilia Acatitlán.

Around Mexico City

Most people will make a beeline to Teotihuacán as their first destination outside the city, as well they should. But the adventurous might want to stop at a much less frequented but surprisingly extensive ruin not far away: the Baños de Nezahualcóyotl, on a mountainside near Texcoco. Other ruins not far from Mexico City include the hilltop city of Xochicalco, near Cuernavaca, and the warrior shrine carved into solid rock outside Malinalco. Those interested in Cuauhtémoc, the last Aztec ruler, might want to make a pilgrimage to Ixcateopan, a remote village in the Guerrero mountains, a two-hour drive from Taxco. This was Cuauhtémoc's birthplace, and if you believe local legend, it is also the place where his body was buried after he was killed by the Spanish.

SIGHTS

Considering its rich culture and eventful history, it's no surprise that Mexico City has an almost overwhelming number of destinations to interest visitors. Start off in the Centro Histórico, the ancient island capital of the Aztecs, where you can walk to the spot where Cortés and Moctezuma met that fateful day in 1519, and then see the result of that meeting a couple of blocks away in the ruins of the Templo Mayor, right next to the Catedral.

There are hundreds of ornate buildings from the colonial era in the Centro and throughout the city, from old monasteries to baroque churches and sumptuous palaces built by silver barons—even haciendas that used to be on farmland but now sit stranded within the city, islands of the past. And there's plenty of ingenious modern architecture to see too, like the modernist buildings at the national university, covered in three-dimensional murals, or a little gem of a house built by architect Luis Barragán, declared a UNESCO World Heritage Site in 2004.

But Mexico City isn't just about seeing monuments and buildings. This is one of the most vibrant cities in the world, with one of the most colorful arrays of cultures and subcultures you're ever likely to run across. Check out the ancient printing presses, where low-budget scribes still write love letters for hire on the Plaza Santo Domingo; listen to sequined mariachis at Garibaldi; or watch the faithful pray at the feet of Mexico's most sacred national symbol, La Virgen de Guadalupe.

Mexico City is a fantastic city to walk in. Basically all the neighborhoods covered in this

© CHRIS HUMPHREY

HIGHLIGHTS

LOOK FOR (TO FIND RECOMMENDED SIGHTS.

(Must-See Square: Since it was founded as the ancient Aztec island capital Tenochtitlán in 1325, the broad, empty **Zócalo** (page 22) has been the epicenter of the city. The square is surrounded by some of the most important monuments in the city, including the Palacio Nacional and the ruins of the Aztec Templo Mayor, but it is truly a showplace for the **Catedral Metropolitana** (page 24).

(Best View: Take an elevator ride up to the top of the 142-meter **Torre Latinoamericana,** located right next to Bellas Artes in the Centro. From the 38th-floor observation deck, with coin-operated telescopes, catch a bird's-eye view of the rooftops of central Mexico City, and if air quality permits, the surrounding mountains (page 31).

(Best Murals: A block north of the Zócalo is the **Antiguo Colegio de San Ildefonso,** where the mural movement began in 1922. Here a group of talented young painters, including Diego Rivera, José Clemente Orozco, and Davíd Alfaro Siqueiros, decorated the walls of this exceptionally beautiful colonial-era building with their murals (page 32).

(Best Museum: One of the finest museums of its kind in the world, the **Museo Nacional de Antropología e Historia** is a seemingly endless collection of indigenous artifacts past and modern, from the huge and austere carved stone Olmec heads to the dazzling artwork of the Zapotecs (page 53).

(Best Hidden Gem: The **Casa Lamm** is a finely-restored late-19th-century mansion in the Roma, once an enclave of the rich and now a favored haunt of artists and bohemians. Take a look at the art gallery and bookstore, or just have a bite to eat at the restaurant and soak up the atmosphere of times gone by (page 59).

(Best Neighborhood Park: In the hip Colonia Condesa, **Parque México** is an oval-shaped Eden of leafy calm, just a couple of blocks from the bustling Avenida Insurgentes. Bring a newspaper or book, grab a coffee at one of the corner cafés, and take a bench on one of the quiet walkways (page 61).

(Best Route for a Stroll: In the center of Coyoacán you'll find lovely cobblestone streets lined with colonial mansions in all directions. One of the best routes is the stroll between two beautiful and quiet little squares, Plaza y Capilla de la Conchita along **Calle de la Higuera** (page 67) and **Plaza Santa Catarina** (page 68).

(Best Artistic Pilgrimage: Iconic artist Frida Kahlo lived most of her adult life in a modest-sized but vibrantly colorful house in Coyoacán, which is now preserved as she left it as the **Museo Frida Kahlo.** Decorating the rooms are not only some of Kahlo's paintings, but also her prodigious collection of folk art and works by other artists, including her husband, Diego Rivera (page 68).

(Best Window to Mexico's Soul: Perched next to the hill of Tepeyac in northern Mexico City is the **Basílica de Nuestra Señora de Guadalupe,** a shrine to Mexico's patron saint, seen in a vision by Aztec Juan Diego in 1531 and now a site of veneration by millions of Mexicans each year. Visiting the 1970s spaceship-like church – complete with conveyer belts to keep the faithful from staying too long beneath the sacred cloak – makes for a unique experience combining the ancient and postmodern (page 74).

(Best Place for a Boat Ride: For a true Mexican-style party, take an afternoon trip down to Xochimilco in the south of the city. Here you can rent a *trajinera* (small boat) that will take you and your friends for a relaxed ride along the tree-lined **canals.** Mariachis float by on their own boats and strike up a cheery tune for a small fee (page 77).

book are excellent for wandering on foot, although moving between them sometimes requires a taxi, bus, or Metro ride. The Centro, Roma, Condesa, San Ángel and Coyoacán are all perfect for strolling through at a relaxed pace, with narrow streets, parks, and plenty of fine historic architecture. And the weather is almost always amenable, with daytime temperatures usually a comfortable 65–75°F (although you might want an umbrella in case of an afternoon shower in the spring–summer rainy season).

TIPS FOR TOURING

Mexico City's 2,240-meter elevation makes it one of the highest capitals in the world. If you're bothered by the altitude, go easy on strenuous activity for the first couple of days. Headaches, mild fatigue, and mild stomach upset may be symptoms of altitude sickness; doctors suggest staying away from alcoholic drinks and eating lightly for those first days.

Two different types of government-sponsored tours provide very good and reasonably priced ways to see the city and learn more about it. The **Turibus** (www.turibus.com.mx) bus service makes circuits frequently throughout

the day among the main tourist neighborhoods in the city on bright-red double-decker buses. A one-day pass costs $11, and you can get on and off as many times as you like. Three-day passes are $19. The buses, which start their circuit right in front of the Auditorio Nacional, run daily 9 A.M.–9 P.M. The full tour takes about three hours, and departures are roughly every half hour.

Paseos Culturales offers informative tours in Mexico City and other parts of the country. The tours are guided by experts in archaeology and history and are run by the Instituto Nacional de Antropología e Historia (INAH, 55/5553-2365 or 55/5553-3822, www.inah .gob.mx). Mexico City trips typically cost $32 per day (8 A.M.–2 P.M.), with transportation, guide, and entrance fee to sites included. Examples of tours include the streets of the Centro Histórico, colonial-era convents in the city, and the Templo Mayor and Palacio Nacional. All the prescheduled trips are in Spanish, but special trips can be arranged with English-speaking guides for groups (minimum 10 people). At last check, information on the tours was only on the Spanish version of the website.

Centro Histórico   Map 1

When the Aztecs first arrived in the Valle de México, they were forced to settle on a small island in the center of the great lake, as the more desirable land on the lake's shores was already populated by other tribes. This small island, known as Tenochtitlán, became the Aztec capital, and later the center of Spanish Mexico. As the centuries passed and the lakes and canals were gradually filled in and covered over, the Centro was physically joined to the rest of the city, but the rough outlines of the old island are still apparent, bordered on the west by the Alameda park, the north by Eje 1 Norte, the south by Avenida Izazaga or San Pablo, and the east by Avenida Circunvalación.

The downtown area, centered on the

broad, wide-open square called the Zócalo, is jam-packed with centuries-old palaces and churches—some crumbling to bits, others renovated—as well as museums, banks, and one of the city's main shopping districts. In any European city, an ancient central area would have long since been renovated, cleaned up, and gentrified, but despite the oft-stated plans of successive city governments, the Centro remains a chaotic place of crowded sidewalks, street vendors, political rallies, tourists both Mexican and foreign, peasants from the countryside, bustling office workers, and who knows who else. Not for nothing do locals jokingly call it the "Centro Histérico" (Hysterical Center).

In 2001, the national and city governments

jointly announced a plan to "rescue" the Centro. While the Centro is still fairly rough around the edges, especially once you get out of the main touristed areas, improvements are noticeable in the years since the plan was announced. But rest assured that the Centro will not soon lose its disheveled charm. This is still a living neighborhood populated by a thriving working-class community renowned throughout Mexico for their street smarts and cynical good humor, and the reputed origin of many classic Mexican slang words. Taxis throng, buses honk, vendors hawk their wares at the top of their lungs, and pedestrians scurry in all directions. And just when you're being overwhelmed with the relentless urbanity of it all, you'll step off the street into the cool, blissfully calm courtyard of some colonial palace covered with marvelous stone carvings and wonder how this spot could be in the middle of such a city.

No matter how short your stay, at least a brief visit to the Centro is obligatory to taste the ambience of Mexico's ancient capital.

History

Until the mid-19th century, Mexico City essentially *was* the Centro Histórico. It was in this roughly 10-kilometer-square area, surrounded by the shallow waters of Lago Texcoco, that the Aztecs first founded Tenochtitlán in the early 14th century, and in turn it was where the Spaniards erected their colonial capital after the conquest in 1521.

The Aztec city was divided into four *calpulli*, self-governing districts grouping several different clans, located in each quadrant of the city. At the intersection of the four districts was the broad central square, flanked by the Templo Mayor complex and the palaces of the Aztec nobility. Four causeways connected the island city to the mainland: Tacuba, to the west; Tenayuca, to the northwest; Tepeyac, to the north; and Ixtapalapa, to the south.

Although the Aztec buildings were utterly destroyed during the Spanish siege, the basic street plan of the old city was nonetheless mostly preserved by Alonso García Bravo, who supervised the construction of the new colonial capital in

1521–1522. The Aztec central square became the new Plaza Mayor, with the government palaces and the Catedral alongside. Many of the wealthier conquistadors built their mansions along Calle Tacuba, to the west of the plaza, while the powerful missionary orders erected huge complexes all over the city. The poor, both mestizo and Amerindian, were left to their own devices to raise ramshackle warrens of shacks to the east and south of downtown (areas more prone to flooding during the annual rainy season).

By the time of independence from Spain, city authorities had relocated the markets from the Plaza Mayor to La Merced, a neighborhood surrounding the convent of the same name a few blocks southeast of the plaza. La Merced remained Mexico's largest marketplace until the Central de Abastos opened in 1992. Commerce also began invading the streets around Plaza Santo Domingo and near Tacuba, northwest of the Zócalo, driving the wealthiest residents to the new "in" street farther south, Plateros, now named Francisco I. Madero.

Armed by the Reform Laws of 1857, which dispossessed the once-mighty religious orders of their properties, city planners ordered the destruction of large chunks of the Centro's many convents and monasteries to lay down new streets such as Cinco de Mayo, Gante, Belisario Domínguez, and others, giving the Centro the street plan it has today.

When Mexico City finally started expanding beyond the boundaries of the original island, and as Lago Texcoco began seriously shrinking in the mid-19th century, the city's elite were not slow to flee the increasingly crowded Centro to the new suburbs. By the end of the Mexican Revolution, in 1920, most of the wealthiest families had long since relocated to the mansions along Paseo de la Reforma or the Roma. The largest merchants and textile producers in La Merced—many of whom were Syrians, Lebanese, and Jews—had by the 1940s moved out to Roma, Condesa, and later Polanco.

The colonial mansions in the Centro were quickly taken over by the flood of new immigrants coming in from the countryside in the boom years after World War II. But rather than

Bus tours are a relaxing and inexpensive way to visit the Centro.

housing one family, as before, the erstwhile palaces now sheltered whole communities. The rent freeze in the 1940s sealed the fate of the Centro, as all the landlords got out as soon as possible and left the buildings to decay.

Successive city governments have promised great things with regard to renovating and rejuvenating the Centro, particularly after it was declared a World Heritage Site by UNESCO in 1987. Progress, however, has been very limited, and city officials are forthright in saying they simply have no money for major work. Much of the downtown area is still inhabited by low-income families and small-scale retail businesses, although the spate of colonial building renovations and an upswing in property values in the Centro may point to the beginnings of a regentrification. But if that does happen—and it's a big "if"—you can be sure the Centro will never lose its manic, magic urban energy.

Orientation

The Centro is a compact area, and its narrow streets and traffic make driving a major headache, so walking is unquestionably the best way to go. Should all the pavement-pounding wear you out, consider hopping onto one of the many bicycle taxis cruising round the Centro; they charge $2–4 to peddle you from one destination to the next.

The sites in this section are divided into five walking tours, the first around the Zócalo and the other four through the neighborhoods in each direction from the Zócalo. Needless to say, readers will have their own ideas of what they would like to visit and should arrange their walks accordingly.

Watching Your Step

Most tourists will likely limit their explorations to the few blocks surrounding the Zócalo and the streets running west toward the Alameda park. Many historic buildings are in this district, and the streets are cleaner and less crowded than in other parts of the Centro. The area southwest of the Zócalo, between Avenidas Madero and Izazaga, is a bit run-down and bustling with small businesses, but it hides a few minor treasures of colonial and 19th-century architecture, and it is generally safe for walking around.

But not too far beyond these areas, the neighborhoods generally take a turn for the dirtier and more crowded. Not all foreign (or even Mexican) visitors will feel comfortable on some blocks to the north of the Zócalo past República de Venezuela, northwest between the Plaza Santo Domingo and Plaza Garibaldi, and east past Loreto and Jesús María. It's not necessarily dangerous to venture out in these directions, in the day at least, but go with your wits about you, and don't hang that expensive Nikon around your neck. It's not a great idea to walk past the north side of Eje 1 Norte (into the Tepito neighborhood, famed as the haunt of smugglers and thieves), east of Eje 1 Oriente Circunvalación, and south of Fray Servando Teresa de Mier. The only reason to venture out this way would be to get a taste of the seamier side of street life in the Centro, as almost all of the main historical sites are close to the Zócalo.

Getting There and Around

If you're not staying in a downtown hotel already, chances are you'll be somewhere near Paseo de la Reforma, Polanco, or another neighborhood to the west and south. The easiest and quickest way to get to the Centro is via Metro to one of the downtown stations: Zócalo (obviously the most central), Allende, Bellas Artes, San Juan de Letrán, Salto de Agua, Isabel la Católica, Pino Suárez, or Garibaldi.

By car, you can reach the Centro Histórico either (from the west) along Paseo de la Reforma, then turning onto Avenida Juárez past the Alameda, and crossing into the Centro on Avenida Madero; or (from the south) by coming up Eje Central Lázaro Cárdenas and taking a right turn (east) on Avenida Madero. It's a bit less expensive to park the car in one of the lots on the south side of the Alameda (for example, on Revillagigedo, Luis Moya, or Dolores Streets) than in lots closer to the Zócalo.

If you come downtown in a taxi, probably the easiest place to get off is at the corner of Juárez and the Eje Central, right in front of the Palacio de Bellas Artes. During the day, traffic can be heavy closer in toward the Zócalo, making it easier to get out and walk.

IN AND AROUND THE ZÓCALO

◖ THE ZÓCALO

Plaza de la Constitución

HOURS: None

COST: Free

METRO: Zócalo

Also called the Plaza de la Constitución, the Zócalo is the second-largest public plaza in the world after Red Square in Moscow. For most of the past two centuries it was lined with trees and grass (as are most plazas in Mexico). Now it's completely empty, save for the flagpole in the center. Although certainly a bit spartan, this massive open square in the very center of one of the most crowded environments on the globe makes a powerful spatial statement. Mexicans regularly fill the plaza for political rallies and protest demonstrations, for concerts, or just to enjoy a sunny afternoon.

The Zócalo has formed the heart of Mexico City since the founding of the original Tenochtitlán in 1325. During the height of the Aztec empire, the space frequently served as a site for dances and celebrations, in addition to being the second most important market in the city. On the northeast corner towered the Templo Mayor, while the palaces of Aztec rulers lined the sides of the plaza. The causeways leading off the island of Tenochtitlán to the north, west, and south began at the plaza and are now paved over by the avenues of República de Brasil, Tacuba, and 20 de Noviembre, respectively.

After the Spanish took over the Zócalo during the colonial years, the import merchants of El Parian market and secondhand traders of El Baratillo flea market filled the space. As in Aztec times, the square remained the city's main meeting place and was a center of constant activity. By the end of the 18th century, the Zócalo was surrounded by the same buildings that flank it today: the Catedral Metropolitana on the north side, the Palacio Virreinal (now Palacio Nacional) on the east, the Palacio del

© ELENA PAPPAS

Aztec dancers, called *concheros* for their shell-covered costumes, perform on the Zócalo.

Ayuntamiento (City Hall) on the south, and the merchants' arcades on the west. The only new building raised since that time is a second city hall building, the easterly of the two, built between 1941 and 1948. Just off the southeast corner of the Zócalo stood the smaller Plaza Volador, which housed a market of its own and also served as the city's bullfighting ring. The Suprema Corte de Justicia (Supreme Court) building now occupies this spot.

The liberal-minded Emperor Maximilian banished the markets and tried to create his vision of a Parisian park in Mexico, replete with tree-lined walks, benches, and a wrought-iron kiosk in the center. With many modifications, the trees remained through the years of Porfirio Díaz, who took pains to cultivate European styles. To achieve its current vaguely social-realist monumental style, the Zócalo was cleared shortly after the 1910–1920 Revolution, perhaps in homage to the Soviet Red Square.

Now a towering flagpole in the center is the square's only ornamentation. In strict military drill, a contingent of goose-stepping guards in full battle gear issue from the Palacio Nacional and then raise (in the morning) or lower (at sunset) a huge Mexican flag daily. The folding of the gigantic tricolor takes a half-dozen soldiers a full 15 minutes to accomplish and is accompanied by a fanfare of drums, bugles, and flugelhorns.

The city government has considered adding a row of trees along one side of the plaza, but that's yet to transpire. Even if it does, the Zócalo is unlikely ever to become just another one of the innumerable tree-lined plazas in Mexican cities, if only because Mexicans love taking advantage of this irresistible void in the center of one of the most populated cities on earth. Every day the plaza gathers a crowd of locals, tourists, street vendors, political activists, beggars, people looking for work, Aztec dancers, clowns, and much else besides.

The **Aztec dancers** perform most days, but always on weekends and also on certain celebration dates: August 13, the day Tenochtitlán fell to the Spaniards; September 21, the fall equinox; November 1 and 2, Días

THE EMPTY PEDESTAL

Shortly after independence from Spain in 1821, Mexico City's central square acquired its popular name, Zócalo, which is also used for the main plazas in many other Mexican towns. Historians agree the name derives from a pedestal (zócalo is an Arabic-derived Spanish word) that stood empty on the plaza for many years in the 19th century, but they disagree on what did or did not stand on the pedestal.

One camp maintains that the mercurial dictator Santa Anna ordered a monument to independence from Spain built in the 1830s, but that in the chaos of his erratic administration, only the pedestal was built.

Others say the pedestal was originally occupied by El Caballito, that peripatetic equestrian statue of Spanish King Carlos IV now standing in front of the Museo Nacional de Arte. The statue was originally erected in the plaza in 1803, but it was hastily removed shortly after the independence movement triumphed, leaving the pedestal behind. Perhaps Santa Anna didn't even get the pedestal built but merely wanted to use the one left behind from El Caballito.

Either way, the pedestal is long gone, but the name remains.

de los Muertos; December 21, the winter solstice; March 21, the spring equinox; and June 21, the summer solstice.

For good, wide-angle views of the square, have a meal at the balcony restaurants of the Hotel Majestic, Holiday Inn, or Artes de México craft store on the west side. The Hotel Majestic won't let you stay just for drinks, unless you're very persuasive and it's not crowded, but the Holiday Inn and Artes de México are more relaxed.

The *portales* (archways) on the southwest side of the plaza often shelter temporary displays of paintings or photography.

The government has installed a tourist information booth on the Zócalo, on the west side of the Catedral (left side as you face it); there you can find maps and other information.

◖ CATEDRAL METROPOLITANA
North side of the Zócalo
HOURS: Daily 7 A.M.-7 P.M.
COST: Free
METRO: Zócalo

In some ways the Zócalo, impressive though it may be, is but a stage for the magnificent Catedral. The government and private palaces pressed up against one another on the other three sides of the plaza seem merely the audience, as it were, to the Catedral's immense architectural performance.

The largest colonial cathedral in the Americas, the current Catedral stands on the site of a more humble chapel built by the Spanish conquistadors in 1524, immediately following the conquest of Tenochtitlán. Intended to symbolically replace the Aztec Templo Mayor, the first church was erected with the rubble of the temple and other buildings destroyed during the Spanish assault.

The rather modest size of Mexico's first cathedral prompted the colonists to develop plans for a structure more suitable to their idea of the city's greatness. Work on the foundations alone took 42 years, and the church would end up taking fully two and a half centuries to complete, from 1573 to 1813.

Because the Catedral took so long to build, different architects and changing architectural fashions left their mark in the building's interior and exterior ornamentation, which include elements of Gothic, baroque, churrigueresque, and neoclassical styles. Despite the apparently eclectic mix, the church's styles come together with remarkable harmony. The north side of the Catedral, facing the plaza, is a perfect example: The exuberant baroque facades of the main church and the adjacent Sagrario chapel seem tempered and balanced by the more austere neoclassical flanking towers and central clock tower, built in the late 18th and early 19th centuries.

BENEATH THE CATEDRAL

Archaeological and geological studies indicate that the Catedral is built over the site of a small spring, which may be why Aztecs chose the location as the center of their city when they first moved to the small island of Tenochtitlán. Thus, the Catedral stands on particularly weak, fissured ground, in what could be construed as unintended Aztec revenge on the Spanish for building the cathedral with stones from their destroyed temple.

Over the centuries the massive weight of the cathedral has forced the ground beneath to compress. The Catedral's slight tilt, easily visible from the opposite side of the Zócalo, indicates how this geologic handicap has placed stress on its structure. Because of the irregularity of the soil, the compression has occurred unevenly, causing some parts of the building to sink more than others.

In a vain effort to halt the subsidence, a steel grid was placed underneath the cathedral's floor in 1940, and when that didn't help, new pilings were sunk to supposedly firmer subsoil 40 meters below the church. That didn't stop the sinking either, and by 1988 government authorities had wrapped the cathedral's columns in metal bands and erected braces and scaffolding to ensure the building didn't collapse outright.

At the same time, architectural engineers began an excavation project beneath the foundation, drilling 32 holes 25 meters deep and carefully digging to the side in selected spots. The theory was to cause "high points" in the subsoil to collapse, and thus allow the cathedral to settle evenly. This was the same technique used at the famously leaning tower of Pisa in Italy.

By late 1999, engineers estimated that different points of the cathedral floor were sinking at a maximum differential of 4-6 millimeters per year, rather than a previously measured 1.8 centimeters. The floor of the building is now about as close to "true" as it was in the 1930s. And as the fissures in the subsoil close, the sinking rate will continue to slow, meaning the cathedral's structure is likely to undergo less stress than in previous years.

As a result of the project, much of the scaffolding that for years impeded the full admiration of one of the greatest examples of Catholic architecture in the world has been removed, although metal supporting bands remain around the columns.

Exterior: Built in the shape of a Latin cross, the cathedral's floor plan measures 109 meters long and 54 meters wide. The rear-facing northern facade was the first to be completed, followed by the eastern and western side facades, all done in Renaissance style, with just a few suggestions of baroque flair. The baroque front facade, finished in 1689, has one principal entrance and two side entrances, each flanked with columns and topped with a sculpted marble relief on the second level. In niches between the columns adjacent to the central portal are statues of St. Pedro and St. Pablo, while St. Andrés and St. Jaime above frame a relief depicting the Asunción de la Virgen (Assumption of the Virgin).

The side towers, measuring 67 meters, were designed by Mexican architect José Damián Ortiz de Castro and completed in 1790, while the central clock tower and dome were finished by Valenciana architect Manuel Tolsá in 1813.

Interior: The cathedral's cavernous interior contains a total of five naves, 14 side chapels, a central choir, and a sacristy, as well as a quantity of artistic detail that is almost impossible to fully absorb.

Upon entering the cathedral, visitors first come upon the golden Altar de Perdón (the Altar of Forgiveness) in the central nave, carved by Andalusian Jerónimo de Balbás. The altar, along with the choir behind it, was damaged in a 1967 fire but has since been restored. The sculpted black Christ at the center of the altar has taken the place of a painting of the Virgen

María, destroyed in the fire. The baroque choir, designed by Juan de Rojas, is made of cedar, while the metal latticework is a mix of gold, silver, and copper; it was cast in China.

The central altar at the front of the Catedral, the Altar de los Reyes (Altar of the Kings), houses a 25-meter-high golden *retablo* (altarpiece) decorated in such ornate baroque complexity that it's difficult for the eye even to begin to notice individual sculptures. The carvings, showing a veritable army of saints, cherubim, and other religious figures, were executed by Jerónimo de Balbás, while Francisco Martínez was responsible for covering the work in gold leaf. Note the odd squared-off *estípite* columns, one of the first uses of churrigueresque elements in Mexico. The two paintings, both by Mexican painter Juan Rodríguez Juárez (1675–1728), depict the Three Wise Men paying homage to the baby Jesús (below) and the Asunción de la Virgen (above).

The 14 side chapels all date from the 17th century. The Capilla de los Ángeles is particularly impressive artistically, with its high baroque altarpiece and painting of San Miguel. The Capilla de San Felipe de Jesús is dedicated to Mexico's first saint, a missionary martyred in Japan, and contains a vase with the remains of Mexican Emperor Agustín de Iturbide (1783–1824), the country's often denigrated leader in defeating the Spaniards in the war of independence.

SAGRARIO

North side of the Zócalo
HOURS: Daily 7 A.M.–7 P.M.
COST: Free
METRO: Zócalo

Adjacent to the main church is the Sagrario, built between 1749 and 1768 by Spaniard Lorenzo Rodríguez. The white sculpted front of the Sagrario, considered by many to be the definitive churrigueresque facade in Mexico (though other art historians place the facade of the cathedral in Zacatecas at the top), is offset by flanking walls made with blocks of deep-red *tezontle*, a volcanic stone. Closed for 10 years for repairs, the Sagrario reopened its doors

in 2001 and now holds regular Masses. The bare, rather unimaginative altars (the originals were destroyed long ago by fire) don't compare to the magnificent exterior. A replica of the Virgen de Guadalupe painting is worth taking a look at, especially if you don't have the time or inclination to make the trip up to see the original at the Basílica de Guadalupe in the north of the city.

TEMPLO MAYOR DE TENOCHTITLÁN

Seminario 8, 55/5542-4943 or 55/5542-4784, www.conaculta.gob.mx/templomayor
HOURS: Tues.-Sun. 9 A.M.–5 P.M.
COST: $4 ($3.50 extra for a video camera); free on Sun.
METRO: Zócalo

At the time Cortés first laid eyes on the Templo Mayor (Teocalli to the Aztecs) in 1519, the holiest shrine in Tenochtitlán had been rebuilt at least six times and consisted of a walled complex of 78 buildings built on different levels, crowned with two tall pyramids. One was intended to symbolize the sacred hill of Coatepec, birthplace of the capricious and violent god Huitzilopochtli, while the other represented the hill of Tonacatepetl and was dedicated to the rain god Tlaloc. Each pyramid, in turn, was crowned with a small temple containing statues of the two gods. The Spanish conquistadors, on first entering the temples, were overwhelmed with righteous disgust at the gloomy atmosphere and insisted to the captive Emperor Moctezuma II that the temples be destroyed.

To the Aztecs, the ritual sacrifices in the temple complex represented a key event in their mythology—namely, when the new god Huitzilopochtli slew his sister Coyolxauhqui, the moon goddess, on Coatepec, and cast her body down to the foot of the hill. Some anthropologists have suggested this myth represented a changeover in Aztec politics from a society dominated by women to one ruled by men.

The rubble of the temple, which was razed during the battle for Tenochtitlán, served as building material for the cathedral and other buildings when the Spaniards rebuilt the city,

AN AZTEC TOMB IN THE TEMPLO MAYOR?

In September 2006, archaeologists made one of the most important discoveries in Mexico City in years. Mexican archaeologist Alvaro Barrera, digging under the western section of the Templo Mayor complex, uncovered an altar depicting the rain god Tlaloc and a 13-foot-high monolith. The altar, which is believed to date to the time of Moctezuma I in the mid-1400s, contains a stucco frieze depiction of Tlaloc as well as another agricultural god.

The 12-ton monolith is believed to be from a couple of decades later, and is covered with deep carvings thought to represent earth god Tlaltecuhtli. Depicted as a woman with huge claws and a stream of blood flowing into her mouth as she squats to give birth, Tlaltecuhtli was believed to devour the dead and then give them new life. The god was so fearsome that Aztecs normally buried her depictions facedown in the earth; this one, however, is faceup. In the claw of her right foot, the god holds a rabbit and 10 dots, indicating the date "10 Rabbit" – 1502, the year of death of Emperor Ahuizotl.

As a result of this discovery, the team believes that the monolith marks the entrance to the tomb of Ahuizotl, who died in 1502 and had ruled when Columbus first arrived in the new world. If so, it would be the first tomb of an Aztec ruler ever found – an extraordinary discovery. Radar tests in the summer of 2007 indicated that four chambers are located underneath the monolith, and hopes are high to uncover a royal tomb.

The complexity of digging down into the chamber, which is flooded with water, and its high importance has led the team to move very slowly. At last report they had not yet opened the chamber. Whatever is inside, this new find suggests that many more Aztec mysteries remain to be uncovered at the Templo Mayor.

---

and the remains of the temple were buried over and mostly forgotten. In 1911, 1933, and 1948, minor archaeological work uncovered remnants of the temple and some sculptures. Then in 1978 workers excavating for the Metro uncovered an eight-ton round rock slab covered with carvings of the moon goddess Coyolxuahqui. The carving is now on display in the temple museum.

This magnificent work of art, found behind the Catedral near the corner of the streets República de Argentina and República de Guatemala, prompted authorities to begin a major archaeological project. After demolishing four city blocks over several years of excavations, archaeologists had uncovered a wealth of artifacts from the Aztec era.

A path leads visitors around the reconstructed foundations of the temple to view sculptures and faded murals. The **Museo del Templo Mayor,** alongside the temple, displays a model of the Aztec city and some 7,000 artifacts found at the site, including life-sized statues of eagle warriors standing menacingly over the skulls of their victims. The museum is an oddly spartan building designed by Pedro Ramírez Vázquez of Museo de Antropología fame.

PALACIO NACIONAL

East side of the Zócalo

HOURS: Daily 9 A.M.–5 P.M.

COST: Free

METRO: Zócalo

Originally one of Hernán Cortés's many residences, this palace of red *tezontle* blocks stands on the site of Aztec Emperor Moctezuma II's castle, on the east side of the Zócalo. Martín Cortés, son of the conquistador, sold the palace to the crown in 1562, after which it became the Palacio Virreinal (Viceregal Palace), the main seat of colonial authority in New Spain. Prochurch, antiviceroy rioters destroyed the first building in 1624, and the current palace was built in 1628. Emperor Maximilian modified it significantly during his brief reign (1864–1867), giving it much of its current European flavor. President Plutarco Elias

fountain inside the Palacio Nacional
© ELENA PAPPAS

Rivera painted a further eight mural panels between 1941 and 1952 to illustrate idealized aspects of Mexico's pre-Hispanic life, and a ninth depicts the arrival of Cortés.

Though the Palacio is the official residence of the Mexican president, recent presidents have opted to spend most of their time in a second residence, known as Los Pinos, in the Bosque de Chapultepec.

Visitors are required to show a photo identification on entering the building. A driver's license will do if you don't want to bring your passport. No flash photography is allowed. The restrooms on the ground floor make a convenient, clean pit stop in your downtown tour.

WEST OF THE ZÓCALO

The corridor of streets between the Zócalo and the Alameda was, during most of the city's post-Aztec history, the Centro Histórico's most posh district. Although the city's wealthy have long since departed this neighborhood, it remains a more upscale area than other parts of the city center, and it is a favorite place for visitors to tour on foot.

While some older buildings have deteriorated or been replaced by poorly made modern structures or parking lots, much of the architecture remains remarkably intact. Because of its storied history and constant development, the buildings in this neighborhood—the colonial churches of La Profesa and San Francisco, the baroque Palacio de Iturbide and Casa de los Azulejos, the neoclassical Palacio de Minería, and the all-over-the-board Palacio Postal—represent a cross-section of the city's architectural styles. The Museo Nacional de Arte is worth a visit, both to admire the fine building and to tour the museum's collection of Mexican art, and several cafés and bars offer places to rest after tromping around. Unlike many other parts of the Centro, these streets are generally safe after dark and are no problem at all during the day.

WALKING WEST ON TACUBA FROM THE ZÓCALO

Calle Tacuba betw. the Zócalo and Eje Central
HOURS: None

Calles ordered the addition of a third floor and further modifications to the facade in 1926.

In 1810 Padre Miguel Hidalgo rang the bell now hanging above the main entrance as he uttered his *grito* (shout) for Mexican independence from Spain in the Guanajuato town of Dolores. President Porfirio Díaz moved the bell to the palace in 1896 and started the tradition of ringing the bell every year on September 15, just before midnight.

Between 1929 and 1935, Diego Rivera painted one of his best-known murals on the walls above the palace's central staircase. Divided into three parts, the mural is Rivera's vision of Mexican history, arranged chronologically right to left. The right-hand panel shows Aztec life before the conquest, while the central wall traces Mexico's history from the brutal conquest and colonial era, through independence from Spain, to the bloody Revolution in 1910–1920. The left-hand mural depicts Rivera's socialist view of Mexico's capitalist milieu and the inevitable workers' revolution yet to come.

On the walls of the 2nd-floor corridor,

EL GRITO

To see the Zócalo at its most vibrant (or most chaotic, depending on your point of view), join the thousands of Mexicans who gather each year to watch the president stand on the balcony of the Palacio Nacional and shout *¡Viva México!* just before midnight each September 15, commemorating Padre Hidalgo's famous launch of the struggle for independence from Spain in 1810.

For the first decades after independence in 1821, Hidalgo was reviled by many (particularly Mexico's elite) as a rabble-rouser, and his ill-fated rebellion was hardly the stuff of official myth. But in 1896 the legendary dictator Porfirio Díaz saw fit to rehabilitate Hidalgo by shouting the first official Grito in Mexican history. According to historians, Hidalgo's original *grito* (shout) was *"¡Vive la Virgen de Guadalupe y mueran los gachupines!"* (Long live the Virgin of Guadalupe and death to the Spaniards!), but Díaz thought it more diplomatic to shout, *"¡Viva México! ¡Vivan los héroes de la Patria! ¡Viva la República!"*

It may seem odd that the Grito happens on September 15 at midnight, when Independence Day is September 16. As it turns out, Don Porfirio took a slight liberty with the dates, since his birthday was September 15.

The Grito has since become one of the main political ceremonies of the year. The scene in the square during and after the Grito is reminiscent of New Year's Eve in Times Square, *a la mexicana*. If you go, be fully prepared to be plastered by the harmless shaving cream everyone is throwing around in jest.

COST: Free
METRO: Zócalo or Allende

Walk from the Zócalo on Calle Tacuba, the route of one of the ancient Aztec causeways that used to leave the island city. One block west, take a one-block detour north on República de Chile to the corner of Donceles to admire one of the finest colonial palaces in the city, the **Casa de los Condes de Heras y Soto.** With exceptionally well-carved reliefs decorating the exterior, the building houses the offices of the Fideicomiso del Centro Histórico, an organization dedicated to restoring the downtown area. Visitors may enter and admire the courtyard Monday–Friday 9 A.M.–6 P.M. Around the corner, the block of Donceles between República de Chile and Palma is a secondhand book emporium of sorts, with around 10 shops on both sides of the street.

Further along Tacuba is the pedestrian street Calle Motolinía. Depending on how much the city government has been cracking down on *ambulantes,* or street vendors, a lively market sometimes fills the block of Motolinía between Tacuba and Cinco de Mayo. Just before Avenida Bolívar, you'll pass the colonial-era **Ex-Convento y Iglesia de Santa Clara,** which now houses the Biblioteca del Congreso (Library of Congress) and is open to the public.

PLAZA MANUEL TOLSÁ

Calle Tacuba just east of Eje Central
HOURS: Plaza has none; Tolsá museum: Tues.–Sun. 10 A.M.–7 P.M.
COST: Tolsá museum $1
METRO: Allende

This small square is flanked by two imposing neoclassical buildings and crowned with a bronze equestrian statue of Spanish King Carlos IV. The statue and one of the buildings are the works of Manuel Tolsá, an architect and artist from Valencia, Spain, who came to Mexico City in 1791 to direct the Academia de San Carlos. On the plaza is the Museo Nacional de Arte, one of the premier colonial art museums in Mexico (see the *Arts and Leisure* chapter for details).

El Caballito (The Little Horse), as the equestrian statue of Spanish King Carlos IV in Roman garb is popularly known, is probably Tolsá's best-known work. The peripatetic *El Caballito* has traveled around the city with some frequency since it was cast in 1803. Originally it stood in the center of the Zócalo, but after independence from Spain it was moved to the courtyard of the national university. Then it was moved again to the mouth of Paseo de Bucareli, west of the Alameda. As the city grew and the statue began to look a bit lost amidst all the traffic, the city moved it to its current location in 1979. The huge bright-yellow sculpture now at the beginning of Bucareli is meant to be an abstract vision of the original, although it's not easy to see the resemblance.

Tolsá was a disciple of a severe though elegant neoclassicism, and he strongly rejected the more ornate baroque styles favored in Mexico City up to that time. Dozens of his works, including buildings, paintings, and his oddly cold neoclassical altarpieces (such as those in the La Profesa and Santo Domingo churches), can be seen throughout the city. The frenetically productive Tolsá also found time to finish the Mexico City and Aguascalientes cathedrals, supervise drainage and running-water projects, and lay out Mexico City's first civil cemetery.

Across the street from *El Caballito* is Tolsá's three-story **Palacio de Minería,** built between 1797 and 1813 to house offices governing the colony's most important industry. The building now serves as the engineering school of UNAM, the national university. On one side is a small museum dedicated to Tolsá's life and work. In the main entrance to the building is a collection of meteorites from around Mexico. Guided tours of the building are conducted in Spanish and run throughout the day on weekends for $2.50.

In a small garden across Palacio and in front of the Museo del Ejército, you'll see three large bronze sculptures of Nezahualcóyotl, Iztcoatl, and Totoquihuatzin—the creators of the Mesoamerican Triple Alliance, which ruled the Valle de México before the arrival of the Spaniards. In the entryway of the museum stands a fourth bronze of the heroic warrior and last Aztec emperor Cuauhtémoc. The sculptures were fashioned by Mexican artist José Faustino Contreras for Mexico's pavilion at the Paris Universal Exposition in 1898. Contreras badly burned his feet with molten bronze as he cast the Cuauhtémoc piece—a gruesome coincidence, considering that the Spanish had burned the feet of Cuauhtémoc in an effort to force him to reveal the whereabouts of hidden gold.

PALACIO POSTAL

Corner of Calle Tacuba and Eje Central
HOURS: Mon.-Fri. 8 A.M.-9 P.M., Sat. 8 A.M.-6 P.M.
COST: Free
METRO: Bellas Artes

Normally a post office wouldn't make it as a tourist destination, but the old Mexico City "postal palace" is an unusual case. At the corner of Eje Central and Tacuba, the building is a Gothic/arabesque palace, with neoclassical, baroque, and art deco elements thrown in for good measure. In a word, eclectic. Designed in 1908 by Italian architect Adamo Boari, who also designed the Palacio de Bellas Artes across the street, the post office is made of a very light, almost translucent stone called *chiluca.* The exterior is covered with all sorts of fine detail, such as the wicked little iron dragon light fixtures and a wealth of stone carving around the windows and at the edge of the roof. The spacious interior is laden with different kinds of marble and much fine metalwork.

CASA DE LOS AZULEJOS

Av. Madero 4, 55/5512-9820
HOURS: Daily 7 A.M.-11 P.M.
COST: Free
METRO: Bellas Artes

Two blocks south of the Palacio Postal on Madero is an exceptionally lovely tile-covered colonial mansion known as Casa de los Azulejos (House of Tiles). Originally built in the 16th century, it wasn't until the mid-18th century that the owners covered the exterior with blue Talavera tile from the state of Puebla. As legend has it, the son of one of the owners added the tiles to live down an insult from his father, who told him he would "never build a house of tiles," meaning that he would never amount to anything. Between 1891 and 1914 the house was home to the Jockey Club, the city's most exclusive social club at the time.

During the Revolution, the Zapatista army occupied the building, and in 1919 Walter and Frank Sanborn opened a soda fountain, the first of what is now the national restaurant chain Sanborns. The atmospheric patio cafeteria inside is a popular place for Mexicans and foreigners alike to have a meal in luxurious surroundings. Take a walk upstairs to view José Clemente Orozco's 1925 staircase mural *Omniciencia* and to see the porcelain art on the upper floor surrounding the patio.

◖ TORRE LATINOAMERICANA

Eje Central at Av. Madero
HOURS: Daily 9:30 A.M.–10:30 P.M.
COST: $5 adults, $4 kids 11 and under
METRO: Bellas Artes

To really get a feel for the immensity of Mexico City, air quality permitting, take an elevator ride to the top of the tallest building in the downtown area. Although not particularly attractive architecturally, the 182-meter-tall

COURTESY OF CONSEJO DE PROMOCIÓN TURÍSTICA DE MÉXICO/IGNACIO GUEVARA

The viewing platform atop the Torre Latinoamericana offers unparalleled views over the Centro.

blue and gray tower, built between 1948 and 1956 at the corner of Eje Central and Avenida Madero, is specially designed to handle the earthquake-prone and flexible subsoil. Avoid weekends, when the small area at the top is packed and you'd be lucky to get an open spot to peer through the fence at the city below. Apart from the views across the valley, the tower affords a unique bird's-eye view of the layout of the downtown area.

IGLESIA Y EX-CONVENTO DE SAN FRANCISCO

Av. Madero at Gante
HOURS: Daily 7 A.M.–8 P.M.
COST: Free
METRO: Bellas Artes

Near the western end of Madero, butting up against the back of the Torre Latinoamericana, are the sad, boxed-in remains of what was one of the greatest convents in Mexico City, San Francisco. Built on the site of Moctezuma II's famed zoo, the Convento de San Francisco and its associated chapels once covered the entire area now enclosed by Bolívar, Madero, Eje Central, and Venustiano Carranza.

After the passing of reform legislation against the Catholic Church in 1857, the Convento de San Francisco, along with other convents in Mexico City, saw their property seized and much of it destroyed to make way for the construction of new roads.

The main Iglesia de San Francisco is actually the third church built on this location, as earlier ones sank in the soft subsoil and had to be torn down. As visitors will notice from the steps leading *down* to the church, the third doesn't appear to be faring much better than the first two.

The church's main facade, dating from 1710, is walled in and thus cannot be seen. Visitors enter by walking through the smaller Capilla de Balvanera, which offers an impressive late baroque facade and a gilded altarpiece dedicated to the Virgin. The main church, with a neoclassical gilded altarpiece and several religious paintings, may be reached through a side door in the Capilla de Balvanera.

Though you wouldn't guess from its uninteresting exterior, the Methodist church at Calle Gante 5 is actually the remains of the San Francisco cloister. The church officials are usually quite friendly and allow visitors to take a look at the old cloister. And on Venustiano Carranza, the Panadería Ideal bakery was built using some of the old walls of the convent. City restoration officials have plans to reconnect some parts of the convent that are now sealed off and open them to the public. Although little progress has been made, a small square has been cleared between the Capilla de Balvanera and the back of the Torre Latinoamerica, which makes a quiet spot to take a rest from touring.

PALACIO DE ITURBIDE

Av. Madero 17
HOURS: Daily 10 A.M.-7 P.M.
COST: Free
METRO: Allende

Continuing down Madero toward the Zócalo leads to a former colonial palace built in 1780 by a Mexico City *alcalde* (mayor), Conde de San Mateo Valparaíso. Fine stone carvings cover the outside of the *tezontle*-block building. Short-lived Mexican Emperor Iturbide occupied the palace in 1822; hence its current name. After serving as a hotel for many years, the mansion was purchased by Banamex and was restored in 1965. It now houses bank offices as well as a free art museum. The revolving exhibits consist mainly of Mexican paintings, sometimes quite interesting, but it's worth looking in regardless to admire the four-story interior courtyard.

NORTH OF THE ZÓCALO

The blocks directly behind the Catedral contain several colonial buildings of note, including the churches of Santo Domingo and the ultrabaroque masterpiece La Enseñanza. The Antiguo Colegio de San Ildefonso, now a museum and cultural center, is worth visiting both to admire what is considered a classic example of colonial architecture and to see the first place where Mexico's renowned muralists began their art revolution in 1922. And the walls of the Secretaría de Educación Pública, housed in a former convent, are covered with more than 100 mural panels by Diego Rivera, making it a must-see for Rivera aficionados.

Those with an interest in the market life in Mexico City might walk farther north to check out Mercado Lagunilla and environs. The name, meaning "little lake," derives from a small lake formerly at this location that divided the Aztec capital city from the neighboring market center of Tlatelolco. If you're feeling particularly brave, head across Eje 1 Norte into the Tepito "thieves' market" (see sidebar, *El Barrio Bravo de Tepito,* in the *Shops* chapter). If you've got a hankering for mariachi, Mexico's national music form, take a walk northwest from the Zócalo to Plaza Garibaldi on the Eje Central to see the many bands hanging out on the square.

While it's no problem walking this area during the day, it's best not to head over this way after dark. You might get away with it around Plaza Santo Domingo, but if you wandered into the streets around Garibaldi or Lagunilla at night you might as well hold out your wallet and save the omnipresent *rateros* ("ratters," or thieves, in Mexican slang) the trouble of asking.

◖ ANTIGUO COLEGIO DE SAN ILDEFONSO

Justo Sierra 16, 55/5792-5223 or 55/5702-6378, www.sanildefonso.org.mx
HOURS: Sun.-Fri. 10 A.M.-6 P.M., Sat. 10 A.M.-9 P.M.
COST: Varies depending on event or exhibition; $1 to just see the murals; free on Tues.
METRO: Zócalo

Running along the north side of the Templo Mayor is the imposing red-brick facade, divided by three baroque portals, of the Antiguo Colegio de San Ildefonso, first begun by Jesuit friars in 1588. Originally it was only a small school, but the Jesuits steadily expanded the building and the number of students until 1767, when the Spanish crown expelled the Jesuit order from New Spain and seized their properties. Shortly thereafter it served as a law

Dancers from the Yucatàn perform at the Antiguo Colegio de San Ildefonso.

© CHRIS HUMPHREY

school and medical school before undergoing a mid-19th-century conversion into the Preparatoria Nacional, which groomed students for the Universidad Nacional.

In 1922, shortly after the end of the Mexican Revolution, idealistic Education Minister José Vasconcelos hired a number of young, then-unknown Mexican artists to paint the walls of the Antiguo Colegio with murals depicting their vision of the revolutionary nation, thus beginning the mural movement that would become so important to 20th-century Mexican art. Diego Rivera, José Clemente Orozco, Davíd Alfaro Siqueiros, Fermín Revueltas, Ramón Alva de la Canal, Fernando Leal, and Jean Charlot all painted different sections of the old school. On several occasions while the painters worked, the school had to be barred and guarded by the police to protect the artists and murals from citizens who disagreed with the artists' sensibilities and leftist ideals.

At the entrance to the Patio Principal (Main Patio), you'll see the first mural painted, Alva de la Canal's *El desembarque de los españoles*

y la cruz plantada en tierras nuevas, depicting the beginning of *mestizaje* (the cultural and genetic mixing of the Spanish and Indian peoples) and the birth of modern Mexico. Directly in front is *Alegoría de la Virgen de Guadalupe,* by Revueltas. The Orozco murals on the walls of the main patio are famed for their intensity, particularly *Cortés y la Malinche,* showing the conquistador and his lover/interpreter naked and holding hands.

In the Anfiteatro Bolívar, an addition built in 1911 at the front of the school and intended to copy the rest of the building's baroque style, Diego Rivera painted his first mural, *La creación.* He had just returned from living in Europe, and the artistic influence of the Old Continent can easily be spotted in the cubist elements and hints of Italian fresco style seen in the mural.

In 1992 the Antiguo Colegio was converted into a museum and cultural center, and it often hosts exhibits and events of cultural interest. On weekends, music and dance groups from around Mexico frequently hold concerts in one of the two large courtyards. A small café on the 2nd floor of the main patio is a fine spot to take a rest and drink in the atmosphere along with refreshments.

CENTRO CULTURAL DE ESPAÑA

Guatemala 18, 55/5521-1925 or 55/5521-1926, www.centroculturalesp.org.mx

HOURS: Tues.-Wed. 10 A.M.-8 P.M., Thurs.-Sat. 10 A.M.-11 P.M., Sun. 10 A.M.-4 P.M.

COST: Free

METRO: Zócalo

For many years this little gem of an early colonial palace right behind the Catedral was a crumbling ruin. But the Mexico City government ceded it to the Spanish government, who in turn undertook a careful and loving restoration of the old *casona.* The two-story narrow house belonged to one of the original conquistadors and had been gradually modified and rebuilt over the centuries, housing lawyers, workshops, and stores of various types. Inaugurated in 2002 by the king of Spain himself, the building now serves as a Spanish-run cultural center. Shows are of both Mexican and Spanish artists and include younger, more experimental artists as well as more established artists. The center has also become something of a hipster spot to go to in the evenings, when there is a bar and often live music or DJs Thursday–Saturday. It's definitely worth a look, both to admire the building and to see what show is currently up. There is a small café upstairs and a gift shop downstairs.

TEMPLO Y PLAZA DE SANTO DOMINGO

Brasil at Belisario Dominguez, 55/5563-0479

HOURS: Daily 8 A.M.-2 P.M. and 4-8 P.M.

COST: Free

METRO: Zócalo

This ancient plaza, three blocks north of the Zócalo, is the site of the first monastery in Mexico and was the second most important square in the city during the colonial period. Today, the Portales de los Evangelistas archways on the south side of the square are lined with low-budget scribes with mechanical printing presses who have been ghost-writing love letters and legal documents since the late 19th century. The center of the plaza contains a statue of independence heroine La Corregidora Josefa Ortiz de Domínguez. A crowd of street sellers usually surrounds the statue, their wares displayed on blankets. It's a lively scene in all, well worth taking a seat and watching the world of Mexico City flow by.

The first church was erected on the square in 1530, then a second in 1556. The existing Templo de Santo Domingo, on the plaza's north side, was built between 1717 and 1736. The baroque facade has statues of San Francisco and San Agustín on either side of the main door, a marble relief of Santo Domingo de Guzmán above, and another relief of the Virgin Mary on the top. Inside is a neoclassical altarpiece sculpted by Manuel Tolsá early in the 19th century to take the place of an earlier baroque piece. The two side *retablos* are done in the ultrabaroque churrigueresque style and date from the early 18th century.

Directly opposite the square is the **Palacio de la Escuela de Medicina.** Built between 1732 and 1736 by Pedro de Arrieta, the same architect who designed Iglesia La Profesa and worked on the Catedral, this palace first housed the dreaded Inquisition Tribunal before becoming a medical school in 1854. Although not dramatic on first glance, Arrieta's corner entrance was considered highly unusual in its time, as were the odd "hanging" arches in the interior courtyard. Visitors can pay $2 to see the medicine museum or just take a quick free look inside to admire the courtyard.

SECRETARÍA DE EDUCACIÓN PÚBLICA

Argentina 28

HOURS: Mon.-Fri. 9 A.M.-5 P.M.

COST: Free

METRO: Zócalo

The Education Secretariat, not to be missed by Diego Rivera fans for its multitude of murals by the master, is housed in two separate but attached buildings: a former customs house at Brasil 31, facing the Plaza Santo Domingo, and the **Ex-Convento de la Encarnación,** with its entrance at Argentina 28. Built in 1729 (against the wishes of the nuns next door, who thought it would block their light), the customs house contains a Davíd Alfaro Siqueiros mural titled *Patricios and Patricidas* (Patricians and Patricide) in its main stairwell. The mural, begun in 1945 and completed in 1971, was continually interrupted by the artist's political work and temporary imprisonment.

While the Siqueiros mural is impressive, it's hard to compete with the ex-convent next door, where 124 Diego Rivera mural panels cover wall space that extends three stories high and two city blocks long. Rivera's work was commissioned by Education Secretary José Vasconcelos, who had been given the convent to serve as the secretariat's offices.

Rivera gave the nicknames Patio de Trabajo (Work Patio) and Patio de Fiesta (Party Patio) for the two courtyards, and filled each with images related to the two themes between 1923 and 1928. The 1st floor of the Patio de Trabajo depicts various industries, as well as religious themes, while the 2nd floor is dedicated to science and intellectual pursuits. Whether because of the topics or some other consideration, the 2nd-floor murals consist of *grisallas,* or gray tones. On the stairwell to the 3rd level is a self-portrait of Rivera.

The bottom level of the second courtyard, true to its nickname, depicts popular festival activities in Mexico, including scenes from Day of the Dead, the Danza del Venado (Deer Dance), and (demonstrating Rivera's socialist beliefs) Labor Day. The murals on the north side of the courtyard were painted by Rivera students Jean Charlot and Amado de la Cueva. Walls on the 2nd floor carry the coats of arms of different Mexican states, painted by Charlot and de la Cueva, while the 3rd floor features some superb Rivera murals dedicated to *corridos,* or traditional storytelling ballads. Particularly noteworthy are *En el arsenal* (In the Arsenal), which shows Frida Kahlo handing out weapons, and *La Balada de Emiliano Zapata* (The Ballad of Emiliano Zapata).

The ex-convent is a quiet, restful place to enjoy the murals, or to take a seat and rest from sightseeing. The chapel of the convent, though reputedly lovely, is closed to visitors.

IGLESIA DE LA ENSEÑANZA

Donceles 104, 55/5702-1843
HOURS: Mon.-Sat. 8 A.M.-8 P.M., Sun. 10 A.M.-5 P.M.
COST: Free
METRO: Zócalo

On your way back to the Zócalo from Plaza Santo Domingo, take a detour left on Donceles to a church with an unusually narrow facade that now exhibits a severe backward tilt because of ground subsidence. Built in the 1770s as the Templo de Nuestra Señora del Pilar—but referred to as La Enseñanza (The Teaching) because it was founded by the Marianists, a teaching order—the former church has an impressive late baroque facade. But the real reason to visit the church is for the nine ultrabaroque gilt *retablos* crammed into the small interior space. Infrequently visited, La Enseñanza is one of the Centro's hidden treasures and merits a few minutes' visit to marvel at the dazzling display inside. The church is packed on the feast day of its patron saint, Pilar, on October 12.

PLAZA GARIBALDI

Eje Central at República de Honduras
HOURS: None
COST: Free
METRO: Garibaldi

Plaza Garibaldi was built in 1850 and then renamed in 1921 in honor of the Italian independence hero who also fought with Francisco Madero in Mexico. The neighborhood square became a nightlife hotspot in the 1920s with the establishment of the Salón Tenampa and its mariachi band led by Cirilo Marmolejo. Because of the success of the bar and the group, the plaza became a magnet for mariachi musicians. Now you can see mariachi bands strolling around Garibaldi looking for clients at all hours of the afternoon or night. On weekend nights, competing groups line Eje Central between the Alameda and Garibaldi, relentlessly chasing down cars that slow down, trying to pick up gigs for private parties (roughly $200 per hour but very negotiable—the groups will arrange their own transport to and from the gig).

Groups will be glad to strike up a tune for you right there on the square for a rather steep $10 per song, perhaps less if you bargain well. Or you can venture into one of the many nearby bars and put back a couple of tequilas to get properly into the spirit of things.

With its facelift to install a parking lot and subway station underneath the square, Garibaldi is not too daunting during the afternoon for the average tourist. It's not uncommon to see a group of foreigners having a couple of beers in one of the taco restaurants and enjoying the activity around them on the northeast corner of the plaza. But if you really want to see Garibaldi in full swing, and you are in the mood for a night of partying *a la mexicana,* show up sometime after 10 P.M. (preferably later) on a weekend night with a group of friends and make your rounds of the bars. Although most bars at Garibaldi see their share of tourists and are generally okay, a couple of dives are to be avoided, so look before you leap. Under no circumstances should you walk on the backstreets around Garibaldi after dark, as you will promptly get robbed. Ask the bar to call you a *sitio* (taxi). If you need to walk back to downtown after dark, walk down Eje Central to Tacuba before turning east toward the Zócalo. (For more information on Garibaldi nightlife, see the *Nightlife* chapter.)

SOUTH OF THE ZÓCALO

Although not as frequented as other parts of the Centro, the blocks between the Zócalo and Avenida Izazaga hide several unique colonial buildings well worth taking a couple of hours to tour. Along Avenida Pino Suárez, which once was the main Aztec road leading south off the island capital, you'll find the Iglesia de Jesús Nazareno. The church is on the spot where Cortés and Moctezuma first met when the conquistadors arrived in Mexico City, and it is also the site of Cortés's tomb. Across the street stands the Museo de la Ciudad, housed in an imposing colonial mansion. Farther south is the Ex-Convento de San Jerónimo, the colonial convent where Mexican poet Sor Juana wrote much of her famed verse, and nearby is the Templo de Regina Coeli, rivaled only by La Enseñanza for the quality of its interior baroque artwork.

Walking south from Avenida Madero, you'll notice the streets start to get a bit shabbier and commercial after Calle Mesones. While walking south of here during the day is no problem, it's best not to venture south of Mesones after dark.

MUSEO DE LA CIUDAD DE MÉXICO
Av. Pino Suárez 30, 55/5542-0487
HOURS: Daily 10 A.M.-6 P.M.
COST: $1.50
METRO: Zócalo or Pino Suárez

Three blocks south of the Zócalo on Avenida Pino Suárez, at the corner of Avenida República del Salvador, sits a colonial-era mansion that now serves as a small city museum. Historians surmise that one of the conquistadors built a house on the site shortly after the conquest, as the building's cornerstone is an impressive serpent head probably taken from the Templo Mayor after its destruction by the Spanish. The Conde de Calimaya ordered the

construction of the current high-baroque mansion in 1781. The richly carved main portal leads to a quiet patio with a fountain on one side, overseen by a stone sculpture of a mermaid strumming a guitar. On the 2nd floor you can see the restored office of one of the 19th-century occupants, as well as a small chapel to the Virgen de Guadalupe with three colonial-era religious paintings.

The museum's permanent exhibit displays some paintings and sketches of the city, but of more interest are the building itself, the rooms upstairs, and the frequently revolving displays of artwork (sometimes surprisingly alternative). Musical and cultural events are often hosted on weekends.

IGLESIA AND HOSPITAL DE JESÚS NAZARENO
Av. República del Salvador at Pino Suárez
HOURS: Mon.- Sat. 7 A.M.-8 P.M., Sun. 7 A.M.-1 P.M. and 5-8 P.M.
COST: Free
METRO: Zócalo or Pino Suárez

The unadorned red-brick Iglesia de Jesús Nazareno, diagonally across Avenida Pino Suárez from the Museo de la Ciudad, is the final resting place of that much-maligned conquistador Hernán Cortés. Perhaps reflecting the less-than-glorious image modern Mexicans have of Cortés, his tomb is marked only by a small plaque at the front of the bare church, to the left of the altar. Legend has it that at the same corner where the church now stands, Aztec Emperor Moctezuma II first met Cortés as the conquistadors rode into Tenochtitlán for the first time. A plaque on the rear of the church, facing Avenida Pino Suárez, commemorates the event. The ceiling of the *coro* (choir seating area) bears a José Clemente Orozco mural, *El apocalipsis.*

Half a block south on Avenida Pino Suárez from the church is the Hospital de Jesús Nazareno, one of the oldest buildings still standing in Mexico City, now hidden by a modern facade. Take a walk through the unremarkable entrance into a tranquil two-story colonial courtyard, filled with plants and a fountain in the center. Past the central staircase, where there is a bust of Cortés, you'll come to a second courtyard. Cortés ordered its construction in 1524 to tend to soldiers who were wounded fighting the Aztecs. Amazingly, the building (much modified since Cortés's time) still functions as a hospital, but tourists are free to walk in and around the courtyards—there's very little activity in the hallways. Judging from the lack of patients, you're probably better off going to one of the better hospitals in Polanco or elsewhere if you have a medical problem.

EX-CONVENTO DE SAN JERÓNIMO

Izazaga 92, 55/5709-4066 or 55/5709-4126,
www.ucsj.edu.mx
HOURS: Mon.-Fri. 10 A.M.-6 P.M.
COST: Free
METRO: Isabel la Católica

It was in this convent, during the late 17th century, where Mexican nun and poet Sor Juana Inés de la Cruz wrote much of her remarkable, passionate verse, and it is under the chapel inside the old convent where she is buried. The remains of the convent have now been converted into a small private university with a humanist focus called the Universidad del Claustro de Sor Juana. Although it's a bit off the usual tourist path, visitors are free to tour the school grounds (particularly the beautiful two-story cloister) and see the old chapel, where Sor Juana and the other nuns of the convent are buried. The chapel is now used for school theater productions and has been mostly stripped of its ornamentation, leaving it eerily bare.

The convent was originally founded in 1585 through the efforts of Isabel de Barrios (daughter of conquistador Andrés de Barrios) and her second husband, Diego de Guzmán. The couple's four daughters and one cousin eventually became nuns in the convent. The chapel, dedicated in 1626, has a somewhat severe Renaissance facade on the north side.

By the middle of the 19th century, when it was closed by the Reform Laws, the convent had at least 200 permanent residents. After the nuns' expulsion, different parts of the convent were used variously as army barracks, a hospital, a stable, a hotel, dozens of private homes, and even a legendary 1940s nightspot called La Smyrna. Prompted by the complaints of people appalled that the burial site of a woman who is practically Mexico's national poet was being thus abused, government authorities intervened and expropriated the property in 1975, and shortly thereafter the university opened.

Visitors should bring some sort of photo identification to leave at the front entrance at Avenida Izazaga 92.

Near the chapel inside the university compound is the **Museo de la Indumentaria Mexicana,** which has rotating displays on traditional Amerindian and mestizo clothing from a large private collection belonging to photographer/folklorist Luis Marquéz Ramay.

TEMPLO DE REGINA COELI

Corner of Bolívar and Regina, 55/5709-2640
HOURS: Daily 8 A.M.-1:30 P.M. and 5-6 P.M.; Wed. open mornings only
COST: Free
METRO: Isabel la Católica

A hidden treasure of religious art in the Centro Histórico, this 17th-century church doesn't look overly spectacular on the outside, although the sculptures and reliefs are attractive enough. But inside, the church houses five separate carved, gilded *retablos,* masterpieces of late baroque colonial art. The principal altar, dedicated to the Regina Coeli and dating to 1671, has an oil painting of the Virgin in the center and a statue of San José with the baby Jesus above. The *estípite* columns, characteristic of the churrigueresque style of the church, are dazzlingly complex. The four side altars are dedicated to the Virgen de la Fuente, Virgen de Guadalupe, Virgen de la Soledad, and San Francisco de Asís.

The Convento de Regina Coeli began construction in 1573, and the church was completed in 1636. As with so many convents, the Regina Coeli was partitioned after the 19th-century Reform Laws, and the eastern part became the Hospital Concepción Beistegui, which is now a run-down senior citizens home.

CASA DEL CONDE MATEO DEL VALPARAÍSO

Isabel la Católica at Venustiano Carranza
HOURS: Mon.-Fri. 10 A.M.-3 P.M.
COST: Free
METRO: Zócalo

A block north of the Templo de San Agustín stands a two-story private palace with a 3rd-story corner tower, built between 1769 and 1772 under the direction of architect Francisco Guerrero Torres. Sculpted reliefs decorate the tower and the area above the main entrance. Originally owned by the same count who built the Palacio de Iturbide on Avenida Madero, this palace is now owned by Banamex and forms part of the bank's central offices.

Visitors can go into part of the old building through a Banamex branch in the adjacent building (itself an amusing modernist retake on the colonial palace, done in *tezontle*-flecked concrete).

EAST OF THE ZÓCALO

In the few blocks behind the Palacio Nacional and Templo Mayor are several important and not frequently visited museums housed in buildings dating from the colonial area. Most of the sites are inexpensive or free and can easily be visited in an hour or two. A very good modern art museum on Academia, three blocks from the Zócalo, is **Museo José Luis Cuevas** (see the *Arts and Leisure* chapter).

It's not recommended that tourists wander too far off—more than about four blocks from the Zócalo—in an easterly direction, toward Avenida Circunvalación or Avenida San Pablo. Although much honest business goes on in these neighborhoods, which form part of La Merced market district, prostitutes patrol the main avenues while more suspicious-looking types walk the backstreets. This is not a place to go around toting a camera and looking lost. But all the sites listed below are close to the Zócalo and quite safe to walk to.

PALACIO DEL ARZOBISPADO

Moneda 4, 55/9158-1245 or 55/9158-1248
HOURS: Tues.-Sun. 10 A.M.-5 P.M.
COST: $1
METRO: Zócalo

Facing the Palacio Nacional from the Zócalo, take the street heading east from the left (north) side of the palace, known as Calle Moneda because the mint was for years located there. On the left side of the street, you'll find the former Palacio del Arzobispado (Archbishop's Palace), now a museum run by the Finance Secretariat. Built in the 1530s, it remained the seat of ecclesiastical authority in Mexico until 1867, when it was seized by the Juárez government along with most other church property.

With the remains of an Aztec palace in the basement, the building is one of the most historic in the city and is worth a visit in its own right, but it also houses a sizeable collection of Mexican art given by artists or collectors to the government in lieu of tax payments. These include works by such greats as Diego Rivera and Rufino Tamayo, as well as contemporary artists such as Benjamín Domínguez and Vicente Rojo. Some rooms also contain modest displays of colonial art and artifacts. Free concerts and theater productions are held every Sunday between noon and 2 P.M.—get there before noon, as it often fills up, and the doors are closed until the show finishes.

CASA DE LA IMPRENTA

Moneda at Licenciado Primo de Verdad, 55/5522-1535
www.cnca.gob.mx/areas.html
HOURS: Mon.-Sat. 10 A.M.-5 P.M.
COST: Free
METRO: Zócalo

In this modest house early colonists cranked up the first printing machine in the Americas in 1536. Apart from a model of the press, the house contains a small exhibit of Aztec artifacts and occasional temporary exhibits.

could spend a few minutes walking around the rambling old building, even if the exhibits aren't of interest. The museum has a good government-run bookstore with plenty of historical and cultural books, postcards, posters, and other assorted trinkets.

ACADEMIA SAN CARLOS

Academia at Moneda, 55/5522-3102
HOURS: Mon.-Fri. 9 A.M.-2 P.M. and 5-8 P.M.
COST: Free
METRO: Zócalo

Once the principal art school in Spanish America, the building of Academia San Carlos began life early in the colonial era as a hospital, but it was occupied by the academy in 1790. To help train sculpture students, master artists made plaster copies of some of the great works of European art, such as *Venus de Milo* and *David,* and these casts line the school's two-story courtyard today. Visitors are free to look inside the school, which is now run by UNAM, the national university. A fee is charged to take pictures. The school frequently mounts art exhibits by young Mexican artists.

IGLESIA DE LA SANTÍSIMA TRINIDAD

Emiliano Zapata at La Santísima
HOURS: Daily 8 A.M.-1:30 P.M. and 5-6 P.M.
COST: Free
METRO: Zócalo

Popularly known simply as La Santísima, this is another little baroque masterpiece tucked away on a scruffy pedestrian backstreet, a couple of blocks east of the Zócalo. The first small hermitage was erected here in 1526, while the current building was constructed between 1755 and 1783. La Santísima is one of the most important churrigueresque churches in the city, along with the Sagrario. The main facade, decorated with busts of the 12 apostles and a symbol of La Santísima Trinidad (the Holy Trinity), is stunning, and the deep relief carvings on the side entrance are also exceptional. The original altarpiece is long gone, so don't worry too much if the church happens to be closed up when you go by.

A hidden colonial gem, Iglesia de la Santísima Trinidad is on a side street just east of the Zócalo.

CASA DE LA MONEDA

Moneda 13, 55/5542-0187,
www.cnca.gob.mx/areas.html
HOURS: Daily 9:30 A.M.-5:45 P.M.
COST: Free
METRO: Zócalo

Just past the north wall of the Palacio Nacional stands a colonial-era building where the silver riches of Mexico's mines were once counted before being sent to the Spanish crown's treasury each year by ship. The building, modified repeatedly over the centuries, served as Mexico's mint from the late 16th century until 1865, when Emperor Maximilian I converted it into a natural history museum. Since 1966 it has served as the **Museo Nacional de las Culturas,** a museum for the cultures of the world. Mexican artist Rufino Tamayo painted the mural in the entranceway. While the permanent exhibit is nothing to write home about, occasional temporary shows can be worth a look. As admission to the museum is free, you

Alameda Central   Map 1

West of Eje Central Lázaro Cárdenas, the older colonial architecture of the Centro Histórico is interspersed with many modern structures, and the city blocks begin to lengthen. Attractions in this area include one of the city's oldest and largest parks, the architectural gem Palacio de Bellas Artes, a small museum housing Diego Rivera's famed mural of the Alameda, La Ciudadela handicrafts market, and assorted smaller plazas and historic churches.

PALACIO DE BELLAS ARTES

Corner of Av. Juárez and Eje Central, 55/5512-2593 ext. 193, www.museobellasartes.artte.com

HOURS: Tues.-Sun. 10 A.M.-9 P.M.

COST: Free to enter the lobby area; $3 admission to the mezzanine and galleries; free on Sun.

METRO: Bellas Artes

Looming over the eastern end of the Alameda Central is the huge, domed Palace of Fine Arts. The white palace, fronted on the south side by a park with marble benches and on the other three by broad avenues, is all the more impressive because of the empty space all around it. Construction began in 1904, during the presidency of Porfirio Díaz, under the supervision of Italian architect Adamo Boari. Boari planned for the building to be a masterpiece of art nouveau architecture, but, frustrated by interruptions wrought by the decade-long Mexican Revolution, he left Mexico in 1916, having completed only the grand facades.

One of Boari's Mexican apprentices, Federico Mariscal, took over the design in 1932 and finished off the interior of the building as well as the impressive cupolas in art deco. The exterior decoration mixes classical Greco-Roman statuary with Aztec motifs such as serpent heads and representations of Aztec warriors, most of it sculpted by Italian artists. The massive marble building is so heavy that it has already settled more than four and a half meters into the old lakebed. The exterior ornamentation of the Palacio has suffered from air pollution and neglect, particularly the copper-laminated cupolas, which are considered the best examples of art deco in Mexico.

For the main auditorium inside, Mexican painter Gerardo Murillo, also known as Dr. Atl, designed a huge stained-glass stage curtain (*cortina de cristal*) depicting the Ixtaccíhuatl and Popocatépetl volcanoes. Tiffany Studios of New York assembled more than a million pieces of glass to realize the design. The building was completed in 1934.

From west to east, the building consists of the entrance vestibule and reception rooms; the large mezzanine and stairwells, beneath the Palacio's three cupolas, plus art galleries; the theater and associated service rooms; and backstage areas and scenery workshops. Only the first two sections are open to the public on a daily basis (except Monday, when Bellas Artes is closed). The theater is reserved for performances—except on Sunday morning, when the public may visit—and the backstage areas and workshops are usually off limits to all but performers and staff.

Aside from admiring the interior architecture, you can visit the 2nd and 3rd floors of the mezzanine to view massive social-political works by Mexico's most famous muralists. Davíd Alfaro Siqueiros's 1944–1945 *Nueva democracia* (New Democracy), on the north wall of the 3rd level, is probably the most striking and clearly designed. Siqueiros's wife served as the model for the bare-breasted, helmeted woman breaking out of chains in the mural. For this painting, which is the central panel of a larger triptych, Siqueiros used pyroxilin, a commercial enamel used for airplanes and automobiles. Four other Siqueiros panels can also be seen on this floor. Diego Rivera's 1934 *El hombre contralor del Universo* (Man, Controller of the Universe) occupies another wall. On the south wall, José Clemente Orozco's 1934–1935 *La katharsis* depicts a confrontation of the mechanistic world with humanity in a swirl of guns, machines, and tortured human faces. Less interesting murals by Rufino Tamayo and Juan O'Gorman cover the remaining walls.

RIVERA AND ROCKEFELLER

When in 1933 Nelson Rockefeller decided he wanted a mural for the new RCA Building at Rockefeller Center, New York, he commissioned Diego Rivera (after receiving refusals from Picasso and Matisse) to carry out the work. Thumbing his nose at the Western world's primary proponent of free enterprise, Rivera chose to depict the modern worker at a symbolic junction of science, industry, capitalism, and socialism in a work provisionally titled *Man at the Crossroads Looking with Hope and High Vision to the Choosing of a New and Better Future.*

Among several influential world personalities portrayed in the fresco – including Edsel Ford, Jean Harlow, and Charlie Chaplin – Rivera included a figure of Russian Communist leader Vladimir Lenin. When Rivera steadfastly refused Rockefeller's request to remove Lenin's portrait, Rockefeller had the entire fresco chiseled off the wall.

In 1934, Rivera reproduced the mural on an interior wall of the 3rd level of the Palacio de Bellas Artes, where it can be seen today under the title *Man, Controller of the Universe*. In the second version he included not only Lenin, but Marx, Engels, and Trotsky. Taking revenge one step further, Rivera added a portrait of John D. Rockefeller Jr. standing in a nightclub and surrounded by sleek women. Just above Rockefeller's head stretches a microscopic view of a swirl of bacteria, said to represent venereal diseases.

On the 2nd floor of the mezzanine you'll see more murals by less-famous Mexican artists Roberto Montenegro, Jorge González Camarena, and Manuel Rodríguez Lozano. Camarena's 1963 *Humanidad librándose* (Humanity Liberating Itself) is especially worth noting. Like Siqueiros, Camarena's approach to color and line was bold and bright, almost psychedelic, but he had a much greater range of technique, which he could turn from abstraction to realism or superrealism. Also on this floor are a couple of galleries used for well-curated temporary exhibits.

The 4th floor of Bellas Artes, the **Museo de Arquitectura,** exhibits building floor plans, photos, and other archived memorabilia related to Mexico City's historic buildings, including many older structures that have disappeared from Roma, Juárez, San Rafael, Tacubaya, and other *barrios* (neighborhoods).

On Sunday mornings visitors are permitted to enter the theater to see the lighted Tiffany glass curtain. Ticket windows downstairs offer advance sales for the Orquesta Sinfónica Nacional (National Symphonic Orchestra) and for the famous Ballet Folklórico (see the *Nightlife* chapter for details). Other concerts and events are scheduled regularly.

Off the main lobby area are a pricey but good gift shop, an excellent bookstore (almost entirely in Spanish), and a tranquil dining area with good-quality meals, strong espresso coffee, and tasty sweet treats.

Right next to the northwest corner of the Palacio is the Metro Bellas Artes subway station. The French government paid for a renovation of the Metro entrance, giving it the full art nouveau treatment like the famed Metro station entrances of Paris.

ALAMEDA CENTRAL

Bordered by Juárez, Hidalgo, Eje Central, and Paseo de la Reforma
HOURS: None
COST: Free
METRO: Bellas Artes or Hidalgo

When the Spanish conquered Tenochtitlán, the area now occupied by the Alameda Central was an Aztec *tianguis* (open-air market). Spanish Viceroy Don Luis de Velasco, as part of a plan to develop what was then the western edge of the city, ordered the construction of the first Alameda—named for the *álamos* (poplar trees) originally planted throughout—between 1592 and 1595. More than 400 years later it is one of the most traditional and well-proportioned city parks in all of Mexico, and it so beloved by Mexicans that parks of all sizes throughout the country take the name "Alameda" in homage.

The original park covered only about half the current area, from the Palacio de Bellas Artes to the park's Hemiciclo de Juárez. The newer western half took the place of an unadorned public square built during the Spanish Inquisition and known as El Quemadero (The Burning Place), as this was where "infidels" were tortured and burned at the stake with much public ceremony. The inquisitors wore special conical hats and yellow shirts emblazoned with devils, flames, alligators, and snakes painted by the top religious artists of the era. By the 1760s, the Inquisition was all but over in Mexico, and in 1770 Viceroy Marqués de Croix ordered the expansion of the park over El Quemadero.

The de Croix expansion was further amplified in 1791 by the Conde de Revillagigedo, who erected a wood fence around the perimeter in an attempt to reserve the park for the exclusive use of the aristocracy. But that didn't last long: The Alameda hosted the main popular celebration of Mexican independence in 1821, and when megalomaniac president Santa Anna rode triumphantly into Mexico City in 1846, he ordered the fountains of the Alameda filled with booze.

A French designer installed five classical fountains inspired by Greco-Roman mythology, and more statuary, both classical and modern, was added in the 19th century. Gas lamps were erected in 1868, to be replaced by electric lighting in 1892, by which time the park had become a popular spot for all classes of Mexicans. Most of what you can see in the park today, from the starburst pathways set around fountains to the band kiosk, dates to the 19th and early 20th centuries.

The Alameda remains a favorite place for local romantics during the week and for a Sunday afternoon stroll with the family. Aside from being a pleasant place to walk and observe Mexican park life at its finest, the park features a couple of monuments worth visiting in and of themselves. Standing at the south side of the Alameda, facing Avenida Juárez, is the **Hemiciclo de Benito Juárez**, a semicircle of eight marble Doric columns joined at the top. Inaugurated by dictator Porfirio Díaz in September 1910, the monument was intended to commemorate 100 years of independence from Spain but wasn't completed till 1919. Four columns stand on each side of a central obelisk topped with a statue of Juárez holding a copy of the Mexican constitution. The mythical Greek goddess Glory places a laurel crown on his head as Victory stands by with brandished sword.

Although any day of the week is a good time for a stroll through the leafy Alameda, the park is at its most festive on Sunday, when many food and trinket vendors set up along the pathways. An excellent children's puppet theater sometimes performs along the north side of the park, toward the Hotel de Cortés, around the middle of the day on Sunday, and occasionally a live symphonic ensemble mounts the kiosk to perform. Check out the *policías charros,* horseback policemen in full black cowboy regalia, complete with a broad sombrero.

During the Christmas season the park is dotted with Santa Claus displays and other Christmas scenery, most of it oriented toward children; between Christmas and January 6, Día de los Reyes, the themes switch to the Three Kings.

Avenida Juárez opposite the south side of the Alameda has undergone major improvements, with the sidewalks widened for pedestrians and formerly vacant lots filled in with luxury hotels.

CHURCHES OF THE PLAZA DE LA SANTA VERACRUZ

Av. Hidalgo opposite the north side of the Alameda
HOURS: Daily 10:30 A.M.-1:30 P.M. and 4:30-6:30 P.M.
COST: Free
METRO: Bellas Artes

This small plaza is surrounded by four small architectural and artistic gems. At the south end of the plaza, which lies a couple of meters below the level of Avenida Hidalgo because of soil subsidence, stands dark **Iglesia de la**

© CHRIS HUMPHREY

Iglesia de la Santa Veracruz, on the Alameda

Santa Veracruz. Reportedly, the original church that once stood here was built by order of chief conquistador Hernán Cortés in 1521 to celebrate the arrival of his ships at Veracruz in 1519, making it the oldest church in Mexico City. The oldest sections of the present structure date to 1730, while the southern facade was redone in 1759 and 1764 in the baroque style. Neoclassical architect Manuel Tolsá—who, ironically enough, abhorred baroque architecture—is entombed inside.

At the opposite end of the plaza, **Iglesia de San Juan de Dios** was completed in 1729 and features a unique concave facade. Inside is a figure of one of the most sought-after saints in the city, San Antonio de Padua. Local myth says San Antonio will help supplicants obtain a fiancé; to win the saint's favor, you must offer only coins obtained from strangers.

The other two colonial buildings, a hospital and a two-story mansion, now house the Museo Franz Mayer and the Museo Nacional de la Estampa (see the *Arts and Leisure* chapter for more information).

MUSEO MURAL DIEGO RIVERA

Corner of Balderas and Colón
HOURS: Tues.-Sun. 10 A.M.-6 P.M.
COST: $1.50
METRO: Hidalgo

Opposite the southwest corner of Alameda Central, facing a smaller garden plaza, a small, modern museum houses the famous Diego Rivera mural called *Sueño de una tarde dominical en la Alameda Central* (Dream of a Sunday Afternoon in the Alameda Central). Rivera created this huge work for the lobby of the Hotel del Prado in 1947–1948. Mexico City's 1985 earthquake damaged the hotel beyond repair, but the mural survived and was moved to this museum built especially to exhibit the work in 1986. Also on display are various photos showing the work in progress, as well as the effects of the quake on the Hotel del Prado.

Dominating the museum's back wall, the 15-by-4-meter mural's park scene portrays many famous Mexican personalities—including Hernán Cortés; Porfirio Díaz; Francisco I. Madero; General Antonio López de Santa Anna (handing the "keys" to Mexico to American General Winfield Scott); and Emperor Maximilian and his wife, Carlota. In the center of the cartoonlike mural, José Guadalupe Posadas, Mexico's most well-known engraver, walks arm in arm with La Calavera Catrina (see Museo Nacional de la Estampa in the *Arts and Leisure* chapter), who is decked out in a feathered hat and serpent-headed boa. To the right of the *calavera* (skeleton) stands Frida Kahlo, holding in her left hand the Taoist yin-yang symbol. A self-portrait of Diego Rivera as a young boy stands in front of Kahlo.

To commemorate the many people who died during the 1985 quake, the Mexico City government established the rectangular **Jardín de la Solidaridad** (Solidarity Garden) in front of the museum. The plaza lies on the former site of the Hotel Regis, which was destroyed during the cataclysm.

TEMPLO DE SAN HIPÓLITO

Corner of Calle de Zarco and Puente de Alvarado, 55/5521-3889

HOURS: Daily 7 A.M.-10 P.M.

COST: Free

METRO: Hidalgo

This church, just across Paseo de la Reforma from the Alameda, was founded a year after the so-called *noche triste* (sad night) of June 30, 1520, when Cortés's Spanish troops came under heavy Aztec attack and were forced to flee the city. Reputedly Cortés vowed to build a church at this spot, the beginning of the Aztec causeway leaving the island, when he returned. A small plaque in a corner of the church courtyard commemorates the infamous event. Cortés returned in 1521, took the city after a three-month siege, razed it, and captured the Aztec Emperor Cuauhtémoc. The church was completely redone in 1577, when America's first mental hospital—Hospital de San Hipólito—was attached.

Worth a brief look is the church's dark *tezontle* and stone three-stage early baroque facade, topped by slender bell towers uniquely twisted so that their corners face toward the front.

PLAZA DE SAN FERNANDO

Puente de Alvarado and V. Guerrero

HOURS: Daily 8 A.M.-3 P.M.

COST: Free

METRO: Hidalgo

Two and a half blocks west of the Templo de San Hipólito, on the north side of Puente de Alvarado, sits the small, narrow landscaped Plaza de San Fernando, with a statue of Mexican independence hero Vicente Guerrero (1782–1831). On the east side is the **Panteón Histórico de San Fernando,** an old cemetery extending from San Fernando's east side. Most of the grave markers—some grand tombs, others mere headstones—date to the 19th century. Revered Mexican president Benito Juárez is interred in a marble tomb surrounded with Greek columns. Atop the tomb is a marble sculpture of Juárez himself, dressed in Greco-Roman robes and dying in his mother's arms. Buried alongside the great

hero are his wife and children. Many of the other gravesites and tombs contain military heroes from the 19th and early 20th centuries, including Vicente Guerrero, Ignacio Comonfort, Melchor Ocampo, Tomás Mejía, and Miguel Miramón.

The **Iglesia de San Fernando** can be seen just beyond the north end of the plaza. Franciscans from Querétaro established the San Fernando church and convent in 1734 to serve as a headquarters for the missionary effort. A century later the convent was badly damaged by an earthquake, and the city razed the ruin in 1862. Around that same time, the convent's surrounding orchards and pasturelands were divided and sold off to create Colonia Guerrero, named, of course, for Vicente. Once an elegant neighborhood, Guerrero is nowadays a bit run-down.

LA CIUDADELA

Plaza Ciudadela at Balderas

HOURS: Park has no hours; Centro de la Imagen Mon.-Fri. 11 A.M.-6 P.M.

COST: Free

METRO: Balderas or Juárez

Built as a tobacco factory in the 18th century, this thick-walled quadrangle served as a military barracks during the Mexican Revolution and is today home to the **Biblioteca de México** (Library of Mexico) (55/5709-1101, www.cnca.gob.mx/areas.html), with a collection of 250,000 volumes of literature, history, and social sciences. The government was considering moving to a new installation, so the library may no longer be here by the time you read this.

In the same building, the **Centro de la Imagen** (55/9172-4724, www.conaculta.gob.mx/cimagen) contains studios, classrooms, a library, and a bookshop—all specializing in photography. The center issues a quarterly journal, *Luna Córnea*, which may be purchased in Imagen's bookshop. They also manage an exhibition space dedicated to Mexican photography.

The complex is located six blocks south of the Alameda Central, on the west side of Avenida Balderas opposite Metro Balderas.

The area surrounding La Ciudadela is sometimes referred to as Plaza de la Ciudadela, although the plaza just north of the complex is also called Plaza José María Morelos. Chess aficionados will find dozens of intent-looking men playing the game of kings under a tent in the park. You can rent a chess set for $0.20 an hour, but if you like to play timed games, bring your own clock because they don't rent them.

On the same side of Balderas, two blocks north at Calle Ayuntamiento, the **Centro Artesanal La Ciudadela,** also called Mercado de Artesanías de la Ciudadela, is one of the better places to buy Mexican handicrafts in the center of the city. (See the *Shops* chapter for further information.)

Just across Avenida Balderas from the Ciudadela market is **Parque Carlos Pacheco,** a small quiet square surrounded by a number of colonial buildings, including the restored **Casa de Cultura of Tamaulipas,** on Calle Pugibet.

Casa de Cultura of Tamaulipas is one of the many restored colonial mansions in the Centro.

© CHRIS HUMPHERY

PLAZA DE SAN JUAN

Betw. Ayuntamiento and Pugibet, four blocks south of the Alameda

HOURS: Mon.-Sat. 9 A.M.-7 P.M., Sun. 9 A.M.-4 P.M.

COST: Free

METRO: Juárez or San Juan Letrán

This renovated small plaza, north of the TelMex tower and west of the Eje Central, was the center of a relatively major market area during the late colonial and early postcolonial eras. In an effort to revitalize the rather run-down neighborhood surrounding Plaza de San Juan, the city government lent money for the restoration of not only the plaza, but adjacent historic buildings and a handicrafts market, **Mercado San Juan,** which sits on the east side of the plaza. The district around the plaza consists mostly of shops selling housing accessories. (See the *Shops* chapter for more information.)

Facing the north end of the plaza is the **Basílica de San José de Nuestra Señora del Sagrado,** a small twin-towered church originally built in 1772 and rebuilt after earthquakes in 1857 and 1985.

Opposite the northwest corner of the plaza stands an imposing republican-era building erected by the **Compañia Cigarrera Mexicana** back when Mexico City was a major tobacco entrepôt. Nowadays the building is subdivided into office space.

The San Juan de Letrán Metro station is only two blocks northeast of the Plaza de San Juan, on the corner of República de Uruguay and Eje Central Lázaro Cárdenas.

TLATELOLCO AND PLAZA DE LAS TRES CULTURAS

Less than a kilometer due north of the Alameda, the Plaza de las Tres Culturas (Plaza of the Three Cultures) is so named because around it are the ruins of an ancient Aztec temple, the renovated 16th-century Iglesia de Santiago Tlatelolco, and a huge 1960s-era apartment complex—thus presenting three cultures in one wide-angle view.

The plaza can be reached by walking about a kilometer or so either from the Garibaldi or

Tlatelolco Metro stations (the latter is a bit closer), or by driving or taking a taxi north on the Eje Central and getting off at the corner of Ricardo Flores Magón. From here the plaza is a short walk through the building complex. While the plaza itself is quite safe, take care walking in the surrounding neighborhood as it can be a bit rough.

History

The plaza sits over the site of Tlatelolco, once a small island appended to Tenochtitlán and the market center of the Aztec empire. Although first settled around A.D. 1000, some 300 years before the founding of Tenochtitlán, Tlatelolco grew in importance when a group of Aztec dissidents, unhappy with the growing empire's power structure, established themselves here in the late 14th century. The island was allowed a degree of autonomy until 1473, when its leaders were executed and the island was annexed by Tenochtitlán.

When Cortés first arrived, Tlatelolco was a massive market complex trading in goods from as far away as Guatemala. Hundreds of products were bought, sold, or bartered (usually the latter) by thousands of people each day. Merchandise was grouped by category in specific areas, and government appointees oversaw the transactions. According to the memoirs of Cortés himself, the market traded more fabrics each day than did the great markets of Granada at that time.

Over the centuries, Tlatelolco has been the location of an unusual number of bloody tragedies. It was here that the fanatical defense of the Aztecs under Cuauhtémoc came to its gory finale, with thousands of Aztecs run through with Spanish steel. The event is commemorated with a plaque in the middle of the plaza. Again in the colonial period, during grain riots in 1692, an unknown number of poor protesters were killed on the square.

But when Mexicans hear the word Tlatelolco today, the first thing they think of is the massacre that took place on the plaza the night of October 2, 1968. In the preceding weeks, a series of student protests had swept Mexico City. While the protests posed no immediate threat to the government, they took place shortly before the 1968 Olympics, and president Gustavo Díaz Ordaz did not want students causing any embarrassing problems. On September 18 the army occupied UNAM, the national university. Students continued to hold smaller demonstrations in different parts of the city and ended up at Tlatelolco the night of October 2. Exactly how the violence started remains a matter of great dispute. The government insisted that protesters had guns and started the shoot-out, while many others hold that gun-toting government agents planted among the protesters provoked the army into opening fire.

However it started, it ended with several hundred protesters dead, and hundreds more wounded and under arrest. The student protests were indeed halted, and the Olympics took place without a hitch, but in the end it was a Pyrrhic victory, for the Tlatelolco massacre was in many ways the birth of the opposition to the long-ruling Institutional Revolutionary Party (PRI). It was this brutal overreaction on the part of the government that, for many Mexicans, unmasked the dictatorship, and it remains a touchstone event for modern Mexico.

As if the violent legacy of 1968 wasn't enough, the government-built Tlatelolco housing complex around the plaza was severely damaged during the 1985 earthquake. The Nuevo León building, residents of which had been complaining for months about evidence of shoddy construction, collapsed in a heap, killing an estimated one thousand people who lived there. Other buildings suffered heavy damage, and to this day the residents are engaged in a long-standing legal battle with the government over the state of the complex.

TLATELOLCO RUINS

Corner of Eje Central Lázaro Cárdenas and Ricardo Flores Magón, 55/5583-0295, www.conaculta.gob.mx/templomayor/tlatelolco.html
HOURS: Daily 8 A.M.–6 P.M.
COST: Free
METRO: Tlatelolco or Garibaldi

The 67 buildings that make up the pre-Hispanic ruins of Tlatelolco are spread across the Plaza de las Tres Culturas, with the largest remaining buildings directly in front of the church. The ruins were originally the ceremonial center for the Tlatelolco—much in the way the Templo Mayor was for Tenochtitlán—and were designed with a similar structure. The remains are, of course, merely the foundations of the original buildings, which would have towered much higher than the adjacent church. The Templo Mayor of Tlatelolco, directly in front of the church, was likely topped with twin pyramids dedicated to Tlaloc and Huitzilopochtli as in Tenochtitlán. One interesting feature is the circular remains of the temple to Ehécatl-Quetzalcóatl, which was the site of important archaeological discoveries; the meanings of the remains are still under debate. Another curious monument is the Templo Calendárico, which contains several glyphs from the Aztec calendar embedded in the walls.

EX-CONVENTO DE SANTIAGO TLATELOLCO
Corner of Eje Central Lázaro Cárdenas and Ricardo Flores Magón

On the southeast side of the ruins stand the colonial church and adjacent Ex-Convento de Santiago Tlatelolco, on the site of the former great market of Tlatelolco that so impressed Cortés and his soldiers. The monastery was one of the first built in Mexico, and was originally constructed in 1527 with the stones remaining from the ruins of the Aztec city. In 1535 it became one of the principal schools where children of Aztec nobility were educated in the ways of Catholicism and the Western world. This was where Fray Bernardino de Sahagún taught and wrote his magisterial 12-volume tome on life in early Mexico, *Historia General de las Cosas de la Nueva España,* one of the most important historical documents of the period. Inside the convent remains the baptismal font of Juan Diego, the former Aztec nobleman who was educated here and had a vision of the Virgen of Guadalupe, Mexico's most important religious figure. The existing convent structure, now part of the Foreign Relations Secretariat, was built in the 1660s, while the unadorned church was built shortly thereafter. The church in front was formerly decorated with two gloriously ornate *retablos* (altar pieces), but they were sacked during the wars of the Reforma in the late 1800s and only a small fragment remains.

Paseo de la Reforma and Zona Rosa   Map 2

Designed by Emperor Maximilian to resemble Paris's famous Champs Élysées, the Paseo de la Reforma (often shortened to "Reforma") is Mexico City's grandest avenue, a broad boulevard that's home to the Bolsa Mexicana de Valores (Mexican Stock Exchange) as well as numerous banks, stock brokerage firms, and office buildings. Foreign visitors will likely find themselves on Paseo de la Reforma at some point during their visit, either on their way to Chapultepec or the Zona Rosa, or to avail themselves of the avenue's many banks, exchange houses, airline offices, hotels, and nearby embassies. South of Reforma lies the Zona Rosa shopping and restaurant district, much frequented by tourists.

The Zona Rosa is still a big shopping and entertainment district, though not as chic as it once was. Many tourists will look around at the chain stores, fast-food restaurants, and beggars and wonder why they came in the first place. That said, the Zona Rosa can be a pleasant place to shop at one of the smart boutiques in the neighborhood, the **Mercado Insurgentes** craft market, or the antiques market. Zona Rosa hotels are of good quality and are conveniently located for touring the city. You'll find music stores and bookshops, gift shops, restaurants, nightclubs, major hotels, airlines, and banks in the area. Many of the shopkeepers in the area speak English; some accept U.S. dollars. Calles Copenhagen and Génova are pedestrian-only streets full of shops and sidewalk cafés. The Zona Rosa is also a center for nightlife, and has become a center for gay nightlife, as evidenced by the

SIGHTS

numerous clubs and bars with the rainbow flag hanging out front.

On the avenue's north side is the imposing Monumento a la Revolución and two interesting and not oft-visited museums, El Chopo and San Carlos. Several blocks north of Reforma, on the north side of Avenida San Cosme (the extension of Avenida Tacuba), are San Rafael and Santa María de la Ribera, two formerly wealthy neighborhoods now on the downside but still replete with historical buildings. The Santa María de la Ribera neighborhood dates from the mid-19th century and was once lined with the mansions of the wealthy. Nowadays Santa María is resolutely lower-middle class, although some predict it will soon be on the upswing, like the Roma. If you've got an extra afternoon for wandering, it's worth taking a stroll through this area to enjoy a corner of Mexico City that isn't visited much by foreigners.

History

Paseo de la Reforma was laid out by Maximilian in the 1860s, and was expanded with Parisian grandeur by the francophile dictator Porfirio Díaz at the turn of the century. Díaz ordered the laying out of a broad central avenue flanked by side lanes (*laterales*), and the city's elite flocked to build their palaces in the new fashionable district. The avenue's *glorietas* (traffic circles) were decorated with monumental sculptures, while the boulevard was lined with 70-odd busts of lesser figures of the late-19th-century elite, most of which are still standing (and which are now accompanied by a series of whimsical modern sculptures).

In the 1950s the cafés and bars in a triangular section of Colonia Juárez bordered by the avenues Insurgentes, Reforma, and Florencia became the gathering spot of choice for the city's cultural elite—including famed writers Carlos Fuentes and Carlos Monsiváis and composer Agustín Lara, to name only three of the most prominent. The district was soon the hip spot to be seen at night, and Mexican newspaper columnists soon christened it the **Zona Rosa** (Pink Zone).

COURTESY OF CONSEJO DE PROMOCIÓN TURÍSTICA DE MÉXICO /IGNACIO GUEVARA

The modernist Torre Caballito marks the start of the Paseo de la Reforma.

Getting There and Around

Distances along Reforma can be far, so it's best to try to arrive fairly close to your destination before walking. By public transport, the easiest way to get there is either via Metro to the Insurgentes stop (for the Zona Rosa); Metro Hidalgo for the eastern end and the Monumento de Colón; and Metro Chapultepec for the avenue's western end, near Chapultepec Park. For destinations close to the Monumento a la Revolución, get off at Metro Revolución, while Santa María de la Ribera and San Rafael are best accessed by the San Cosme Metro station. Those coming from San Ángel or Avenida Insurgentes Sur may come along the Metrobús, and should alight either at the Insurgentes Glorieta or at the stop shortly before or after crossing Reforma. To move along Reforma, hop one of the many *peseros* (minibuses) driving between the Hidalgo Metro station near the Alameda west past the Chapultepec museums to the Auditorio Nacional.

PASEO DE LA REFORMA MONUMENTS

Paseo de la Reforma betw. Bucareli and Chapultepec

HOURS: None

COST: Free

METRO: Hidalgo for eastern end; Chapultepec for western end

The **King Carlos IV statue** that originally marked the start of Reforma has since moved downtown, and in its place stands a bright-yellow modernist interpretation of the horse-riding king—so highly stylized as to be unrecognizable.

Cast in 1877 by French sculptor Charles Cordier, the **Monumento de Colón** still stands despite the best efforts of political protesters, who in an annual ritual sling ropes around the statue and try to pull it down. Once the protesters managed to snap off one of the Great Mariner's thumbs, but the City promptly re-attached it.

At the intersection of the city's two most important avenues, Insurgentes and Reforma, stands a statue of the Aztec Emperor **Cuauhtémoc** (Attacking Eagle), who fought

COURTESY OF CONSEJO DE PROMOCIÓN TURÍSTICA DE MÉXICO/CARLOS SÁNCHEZ

Crystal Reforma building

SIGHTS

in a desperate last stand against the Spaniards before the fall of Tenochtitlán. It is the work of Mexican sculptors Francisco Jiménez and Ramón Agea.

The *glorieta* beyond Cuauhtémoc has a single tall palm tree in the center, while the next one southwest contains Mexico's **Monumento de la Independencia.** This 32-meter-high column, topped with the winged *Ángel de la Independencia,* was formally inaugurated by Porfirio Díaz on September 16, 1910, shortly before his overthrow and the start of the Revolution. The gold-sheathed angel, one of the city's landmark symbols, is the site of frequent political rallies and spontaneous street celebrations whenever the beloved *tricolor* (as Mexico's national soccer team is known) pulls off a victory.

After dodging the traffic to cross Reforma, you can walk up the steps of the monument's base, pass through a door into the foot of the column, and walk around a small passageway wherein the remains of 12 heroes from the independence struggle are stored in three niches: Miguel Hidalgo, José María Morelos, Ignacio Allende, Nicolás Bravo, Mariano Matamoros, Juan Aldama, Mariano Jiménez, Leona Vicario, Vicente Guerrero (whose remains are also supposed to be interred in a tomb at the Panteón Histórico de San Fernando), Francisco Javier Mina, Guadalupe Victoria, and Andrés Quintana Roo. All in all it's a bit spooky, particularly the faceless skull of Hidalgo in the second niche. It's open daily 9 A.M.–6 P.M.; admission is free.

At the westernmost *glorieta* stands a circular fountain and a statue of the Greek goddess **Diana Cazadora** (Diana the Huntress), aiming a bow. Raised in 1942, the naked and voluptuous Diana stirred such a scandal that the sculptor, Juan Francisco Olaguíbel, was forced to add bronze undergarments to her loins. Olaguíbel later confessed he had attached the covering using only three weak solders, and the underwear was removed in 1967. Reputedly at the behest of the prudish wife of one of Mexico's presidents, Diana was again deemed too provocative for such a prominent monument, and the statue was temporarily relocated to a small park off Insurgentes. It was returned to the *glorieta* in 1992.

Punctuating the end of the Reforma business strip is the tallest building in Mexico, and indeed all of Latin America: the 55-story office building **Torre Mayor Chapultepec.** The tower, fronted with a curved wall of grey-green glass and soaring 225 meters high, has a slanted roof that looks for the world like the tip of a flat-head screwdriver. Unfortunately, the building's excellent observation post has closed, and the public currently has no way to access the stupendous views at the top.

MONUMENTO A LA REVOLUCIÓN

Av. Juárez at La Fragua, in Plaza de la República

HOURS: Monument and crypt: Sat.-Sun.
10 A.M.-5:30 P.M.; Museum: Tues.-Sat. 9 A.M.-5 P.M., Sun.
9 A.M.-3 P.M.

COST: Free for monument and crypt; $1 for museum

METRO: Revolución

This massive marble and basalt monument to Mexico's bloody 1910–1920 Revolution was begun by Porfirio Díaz to house his puppet Congress. Designed by a European architect who clearly aimed for an art deco structure, the building ran into massive cost overruns, and once the Revolution began, it was left as an empty hulk and stayed that way for more than 20 years. When the government was on the verge of destroying the unfinished structure, Mexican architect Carlos Obregón Santacilia proposed to convert the shell into a monument to the Revolution.

With the additions of several unsmiling, heroic proletariat statues on the corners, evidently influenced by the socialist realism of Russia and the Eastern Bloc, work was completed in 1938. Crypts within the "feet" of the monument hold the remains of Revolutionary heroes Venustiano Carranza, Francisco I. Madero, Francisco "Pancho" Villa, Plutarco Elias Calles, and Lázaro Cárdenas. It's a little ironic that the five men should end up buried in the same place, as they all despised and plotted against one another.

On weekends, visitors may pass through the

© CHRIS HUMPHREY

The Monumento a la Madre, by artist Luis Ortiz Monasterio, is a legacy of socialist-inspired art in Mexico.

crypt of Plutarco Elias Calles and ride an elevator to the *mirador,* or viewpoint, in the monument's dome. Below the grand ramp running up to the eastern side of the monument lies the **Museo de la Revolución,** where there is a small collection of photos and memorabilia related to the Revolution.

On the northeast side of the plaza, the art deco **Frontón Nacional** contains a wooden court where jai alai—the world's fastest ball game—was played until a 1995 workers' strike closed it down.

A few blocks north of the Monumento, in a busy, slightly run-down neighborhood along Avenida Puente de Alvarado, is the Museo San Carlos art museum (see *Arts and Leisure* chapter for more information).

LA ALAMEDA DE SANTA MARÍA

Dr. Atl and Salvador Díaz Mirón

HOURS: La Alameda has no hours; Santa María's Museo de Geología: Tues.-Sun. 10 A.M.-5 P.M.

COST: La Alameda is free; museum is $1

METRO: San Cosme

The center of Santa María de la Ribera

neighborhood is the lovely Alameda, a leafy, tranquil park with an unusual brightly colored arabesque-style kiosk in the middle, built in 1904. On weekends the park teems with local families out for an afternoon stroll, boys playing soccer, or young couples seeking out a quiet nook. The Alameda is a fine spot, evocative of life in the city from years past.

Santa María de la Ribera was built in the mid-19th century on an old ranch of the same name for wealthy families fleeing the overpopulated and dirty Centro, although nowadays it's a resolutely lower-middle-class neighborhood. If you've got an extra afternoon for wandering, it's worth taking a stroll through this area to enjoy a corner of Mexico City that isn't visited much by foreigners.

On the west side of the Alameda is UNAM's **Museo de Geología** (55/5547-3900), housed in a beautiful old mansion. The displays of meteorites, fossils, and some impressive mammoth skeletons, as well as the opportunity to wander around the old building, are well worth the nominal admission. Check out the imposing art nouveau wrought-iron staircase in the entryway. Guided tours of the museum can be arranged by calling ahead and are even available in English if the museum director (who speaks English) is around.

The unusually designed art museum **Museo El Chopo** is also in Santa Maria (see the *Arts and Leisure* chapter for details).

Chapultepec and Polanco   Map 3

Five kilometers west of the Zócalo along Paseo de la Reforma, Bosque de Chapultepec ("Forest of Chapultepec") is filled with some of the city's finest museums, green grass and trees, small lakes, and plenty of families out for a stroll, especially on Sunday. At the eastern edge of the park, crowning a 60-meter bluff, is the 18th-century Castillo de Chapultepec, a city landmark.

Generations of *capitalinos* have used Bosque de Chapultepec's six square kilometers of trees and meadows to escape the travails of the city. On weekends the grass is covered with families out for a picnic, lovers seeking secluded spots, and all manner of random folks out for a breath of fresh air. During the week the park is usually much more *tranquilo*. The main section of the park is closed on Monday.

Chapultepec is home to one of the finest anthropology museums in the world, the Museo Nacional de Antropología e Historia. Two of Mexico's premier modern art museums, Museo de Arte Moderno and Museo de Arte Contemporáneo Internacional Rufino Tamayo, are located in Chapultepec along Paseo de la Reforma (see the *Arts and Leisure* chapter for details).

Opposite the Paseo de la Reforma from the first section of Chapultepec is Polanco, a Rodeo Drive–style area replete with modern high-rises, hotels, elegant shops, art galleries, embassies, and fine restaurants. Originally land belonging to a colonial silkworm farm known as Hacienda de los Morales, Polanco was subdivided and developed in the late 1930s and early 1940s and was for years the most exclusive neighborhood in Mexico City. Polanco may not have many tourist sites, but if you're after upscale lodgings, top-quality dining, and all the shopping you can handle, this is the place. Just be sure not to forget your wallet.

To the south of Chapultepec is **Tacubaya,** a run-down neighborhood with a couple of interesting museums housed in mansions from the area's more genteel past.

History
The hill and forests of Chapultepec ("Grasshopper Hill" in Náhuatl, the language of the Aztecs) have occupied a special place in Mexican history since the beginning of the Aztec era. On arriving in the Valle de México in the early 13th century from their original homeland in northern Mexico, the small band of Aztecs, unwelcomed

by the valley's other inhabitants, found a temporary home on Chapultepec, and it was there that they held their first "New Fire" ceremony in the valley. Shortly thereafter, the Aztecs suffered their first great defeat on Chapultepec at the hands of the neighboring Tepanecs, who forced the tribe to serve as slave-mercenaries.

Once the Aztecs had emerged from servitude to dominate the valley, Chapultepec became the hunting grounds and summer retreat of successive Aztec rulers. Aztec ally Nezahualcóyotl, the famed poet-king of Texcoco, had his own palace on the hill. In 1465, with the inauguration of the first aqueduct, it also became the principal water supply for the island city of Tenochtitlán. Aztec leaders ordered their likenesses carved into the side of the hill; the fragments of these carvings still exist today, although they are not visible to the public. The caves on the side of the rocky bluff were thought to be the sacred resting place of the last ruler of the Toltecs, whom the Aztecs believed to be their predecessors.

During the Spanish invasion of Mexico, a group of Spanish soldiers attacked an Aztec garrison at Chapultepec in 1521; they then destroyed the aqueduct and cut Tenochtitlán's water supply in preparation for the subsequent siege of the city. The aqueduct was quickly repaired after the conquest, and in 1537 King Carlos V of Spain declared the forests around Chapultepec a protected area for "the good of the population," making it Mexico's first designated nature preserve.

Not that the colonial public was allowed to frolic in the woods, of course: It remained the favored retreat for the Spanish viceroys and governing elite. It was finally turned into a public park by president Lázaro Cárdenas in the 1930s.

Toward the end of the 19th century, the Chapultepec springs that supplied the city with *agua gorda* (literally "fat water," meaning rich in minerals) for more than 400 years finally dried up because of the drainage of the valley's lakes and the sinking level of groundwater. The only remaining traces of Chapultepec's once-great water system are the Baños de Moctezuma, now a concrete pool surrounded by a fence, and the grievously mistreated colonial fountain outside the Chapultepec Metro station, where the aqueduct began. Most of the aqueduct itself was destroyed around the beginning of the 20th century, but 22 of its original 904 arches still stand, looking a bit forlorn, along Avenida Chapultepec near the Sevilla Metro station.

Orientation

Chapultepec Park extends from the eastern entrance on Paseo de la Reforma several kilometers to the west and is bordered on the south by Avenida Constituyentes and on the north (for much of the way at least) by Paseo de la Reforma. The park is divided into three sections: the first closest to downtown and containing most of the museums and sites of interest for tourists, and the second and third west of the Periférico, with an amusement park, children's museum, two restaurants, and plenty of spots for picnics or a jog.

There's a tourist information booth (Tues.–Sun. 9 A.M.–6 P.M.) right in front of the Museo Nacional de Antropología that can help visitors with basic questions in English and Spanish.

Getting There and Around

The first section of Chapultepec is accessible easily enough from the Chapultepec or Auditorio Metro stations. The Chapultepec station works better for El Castillo and the two art museums, while Auditorio is closer to the zoo. The Museo Nacional de Antropología lies more or less midway between the two stations. If you prefer to take a bus, hop one of the *peseros* marked Auditorio near the Hidalgo Metro station, at the western end of the Alameda. These run as far as the Auditorio Nacional.

To get to the second section, catch a *pesero* marked La Feria, Papalote from the Chapultepec Metro station. *Peseros* to the third section also leave from Chapultepec Metro and are marked Panteón Dolores. Several roads cut through the second and third sections, making all the sites there accessible by car. The first section is closed to vehicles.

PRIMERA SECCIÓN

Closest to downtown and with most of Chapultepec's favorite sights, the Primera Sección (5 A.M.–4:30 P.M. Tues.–Sun.) is where most tourists are likely to end up. Here you'll find Cerro Chapultepec itself, crowned by the castle, as well as the zoo and three museums: Museo Nacional de Antropología, Museo de Arte Moderno, and Museo Rufino Tamayo. The grounds around Cerro Chapultepec, particularly to the south toward Avenida Constituyentes, have long shady paths perfect for strolling, cycling, or in-line skating. A small train leaves from near the castle for regular 20-minute narrated (in Spanish) tours around the park for $1. Rent a bicycle to cruise the park near the Paseo de la Reforma entrance for $3.50 per hour.

On the **Lago Mayor** (Bigger Lake) and **Lago Menor** (Smaller Lake), swans and ducks mingle with canoes and rowboats. Rent a rowboat for a paddle around the lake for $1 per hour. The ballet *Swan Lake,* complete with live swans, is presented on an small island in Lago Mayor on weekends in February and March. In the verdant **Jardín de la Tercera Edad** (literally, Garden of the Third Age), the city's senior citizens practice aerobics, yoga, tai chi, and other fitness activities.

On the southwestern edge of the first section, surrounded by extensive grounds, stands the presidential mansion **Los Pinos.** Don't try hopping fences over that way unless you want to cause an international incident.

Bicycles and in-line skates are allowed in the first section of the park, but pets and alcoholic drinks are not.

◖ MUSEO NACIONAL DE ANTROPOLOGÍA E HISTORIA

Paseo de la Reforma, 55/5553-6285 or 55/5553-6554, www.mna.inah.gob.mx
HOURS: Tues.-Sat. 9 A.M.-7 P.M., Sun. 10 A.M.-6 P.M.
COST: $4.50, or $10 with a camera; free on Sun.
METRO: Auditorio

The largest museum in Latin America, and one of the great anthropological museums of the world, the Museo de Antropología is a must-see for most foreign visitors to Mexico City. The museum recounts the crossing of the first hunter-gatherers from Asia onto the North American continent and has magnificent archaeological exhibits from early Mesoamerican societies as well as ethnological displays on Mexico's current Amerindian groups.

Located just west of the Museo Rufino Tamayo, the museum is laid out over two floors, with 23 exhibition rooms. Rooms on the first floor are dedicated to the archaeology of particular geographic areas or cultures throughout Mexican history. Casual visitors may want to skip the first two rooms, which are dedicated to the profession of anthropology and Mesoamerica in general, and move directly to the "Origins" room. Here begins the chronological tracing of different civilizations that grew up in Mexico over the centuries, including Teotihuacanos, Toltecs, Olmecs, Zapotecs, and others, right up to the Aztecs. Many of the finest pieces of pre-Hispanic art anywhere in the world are found in the rooms on this floor. Upstairs, rooms focus on the anthropology and ethnography of different indigenous groups in Mexico today, including the Huichol, Cora, Purépecha, Otomí, Nahua, and different groups from the Sierra de Puebla, Oaxaca, and Gulf of Mexico regions. The exhibits are exhaustively labeled in both Spanish and English, providing a veritable university course of anthropology for those who take the time to read them all.

Apart from its archaeological and anthropological treasures, Pedro Ramírez Vásquez's building itself is an impressive work of art, with its understated exterior and dramatic central patio. In the middle of the patio, a sheer curtain of water flows from a huge overhang supported by a single concrete column. The column is covered with sculpted reliefs depicting events in Mexican history. Out front is a massive sculpture of Tlaloc, the Aztec god of rain; the sculpture came from a mountainside east of Mexico City.

A full day is required to get an adequate tour of the museum, and many people with a serious interest in Mexican history spend two. But

© ELENA PAPPAS

The Aztec rain god Tlaloc stands guard in front of the Museo Nacional de Antropología e Historia.

don't be daunted: If you have just a casual interest in the subject, two or three hours of popping in and out of different halls will give you an excellent taste. Take in the museum's 20-minute orientation film before setting out to tour the five kilometers of walkways, patios, and exhibit halls. If you need to catch your breath, have a snack at the lower-level café or check out the well-stocked bookstore (both English and Spanish titles are available). Rent headsets with taped information (in English or Spanish) for $6—a good value to save your eyes from getting tired due to reading labels all day.

The museum is best avoided on weekends, especially Sundays, when it is usually mobbed. **Note:** No flash photography is allowed. If you don't want to pay the fee, you can check your cameras and anything else not needed at the entrance.

Outside the museum, the vertiginous *voladores* perform daily. These men, who hail from the eastern state of Veracruz, perform their traditional indigenous ceremony, which entails climbing up a tall pole, hanging upside down with their feet attached to a rope, and gradually descending to the ground as the rope unwinds. Those who watch the show should contribute a small amount to the performers. The *voladores* perform throughout the afternoon Tuesday–Sunday.

EL CASTILLO DE CHAPULTEPEC

Primera Sección of Chapultepec
HOURS: Tues.-Sun. 10 A.M.-5 P.M.
COST: $4
METRO: Chapultepec

Standing at attention atop Cerro Chapultepec, the original Castillo was built by Viceroy Bernardo de Gálvez in 1785. While Chapultepec was historically the "weekend" home of Aztecs and viceroys, the previous villas had been on the southern side of the hill, near Chapultepec's spring, while a temple (first Aztec, then Catholic) crowned the hilltop. Evidently Viceroy de Gálvez had defensive considerations in mind when he decided to build atop the hill. As it

© CHRIS HUMPHREY

El Castillo de Chapultepec keeps a watchful eye over the city.

would happen, El Castillo—at that time housing the nation's military college—would be the last, and ultimately unsuccessful, bastion of defense against the U.S. Army during its 1847 invasion of Mexico City.

The castle took its current shape during the brief rule of Emperor Maximilian (1863–1867). Feeling uncomfortable in the tradition-laden Palacio Nacional downtown, Maximilian declared El Castillo to be his official residence, and he and his wife, Carlota, set about remodeling it to their liking during 1865 and 1866 in a vain effort to re-create a little corner of Europe that might shut out the problems of Maximilian's disastrous government. Mexicans heaped criticism on their short-lived emperor for spending so much money on the grand salons, flowered terraces, and rooftop garden.

After Maximilian and Carlota were overthrown by Benito Juárez, the castle was converted to the Mexican presidential residence. In 1876 Porfirio Díaz moved in, and under the dictator the castle's interior reached new heights of sumptuousness. President Lázaro

Cárdenas, disliking the elaborate palace, moved to the more modest residence of Los Pinos in 1939, and the castle became a national history museum.

Perhaps because of its multiple historical roles, El Castillo looks as though it can't decide whether it's a Gothic fortress or a Mediterranean palace. The two-story gray stone building is divided into two distinct sections. The Alcázar, formerly the living quarters of Maximilian and Díaz, is a series of rooms and terraces laid out around a central courtyard. The different rooms are filled with 19th-century furniture, artwork, and musical instruments. The patios, once open to the air, are covered with glass to protect the antiques and art inside.

The more stolid, heavy-looking main wing of the castle houses the **Museo Nacional de Historia** (55/5241-3100, www.mnh.inah.gob .mx), chronicling the nation's turbulent history between conquest and the Revolution. An extensive collection of artifacts, documents, and paintings of modern Mexican history is displayed in 20 rooms on both floors. Among the noteworthy art objects are murals by Juan O'Gorman (of Mexican history), Davíd Alfaro Siqueiros (of Revolutionary leaders), and José Clemente Orozco (of Benito Juárez).

Outside the castle, a side terrace garden makes a quiet place to sit, rest, and admire the views (air quality permitting). Just down the stairs from the terrace is a small, dingy snack shop (good for soft drinks at least).

MONUMENTO DE LOS NIÑOS HÉROES
Primera Sección of Chapultepec, east of the castle
HOURS: None
COST: Free
METRO: Chapultepec

Right below the castle at the foot of Cerro Chapultepec, this six-towered monument commemorates a heroic though ultimately doomed defense of the castle against invading U.S. troops during the Mexican-American War. On September 13, 1847, when it was clear the Americans would take the castle, six military cadets—Juan de la Barrera, Juan Escutia, Fernando Montes de Oca, Vicente Suárez, Francisco Marquéz, and Agustín Melgar— reputedly wrapped themselves in Mexican flags and jumped to their deaths from the castle ramparts rather than surrender. Their deaths are honored by six tall columns, each topped with a black eagle. On September 13, the Mexican president holds a solemn national ceremony honoring the cadets.

Behind the main monument, right up against the edge of the hill, is a smaller monument, a semicircle with paintings of each of the six cadets. Right behind the fence here, archaeologists have made some fascinating discoveries, including Aztec carvings in the rock and burials dating from the era of Teotihuacán, around the time of Christ. At the moment the area is closed to the public.

BAÑOS DE MOCTEZUMA
Primera Sección of Chapultepec, south of the castle
METRO: Chapultepec

Around on the south side of Cerro Chapultepec, following the paved road from behind the Niños Héroes monument,

lie the dilapidated remains of the Baños de Moctezuma. Legend has it Moctezuma once threw treasure into the well on the south side of hill to placate Tlaloc, the Aztec rain god, when the city was flooded. As a result, treasure hunters from across the centuries have dug all around the area—so far, in vain. Even though the baths aren't much to see nowadays, it's worth wandering over that way to enjoy walking in a quieter part of the park.

Just above the *baños* one can see channels cut into the rock where the old springs welled up, supplying Mexico City with much of its drinking water for centuries. Up until the mid-20th century, water still rose here, but it's now long gone.

ZOOLÓGICO DE CHAPULTEPEC
Primera Sección of Chapultepec
HOURS: Tues.-Sun. 9 A.M.-4:15 P.M.
COST: Free
METRO: Auditorio

Chapultepec Zoo houses about 1,600 animals of 270 species, the most famous of which are a family of pandas. As zoos go it's relatively humane, giving most animals plenty of room to roam. If you're tired of walking, take the minitrain from the station in the center of the zoo. Next to the zoo is the park's botanical garden.

Next door is the **Casa del Lago** (55/5211-6093, www.casadellago.unam.mx), a cultural center run by UNAM that often shows art exhibits and holds cultural events.

SEGUNDA SECCIÓN
On the west side of the Periférico highway lies Chapultepec's second section. The main attractions here include a children's museum, an amusement park, and two upscale restaurants: Café del Lago and Café del Bosque. Mexico City residents seeking a place to exercise near the city frequent the meadows and stands of trees to jog and kick a soccer ball on weekends. Just up an old flight of steps in front of the roller coaster are several large, circular old water-storage tanks that have been filled in with dirt and now serve as impromptu soccer fields.

LA FERIA DE CHAPULTEPEC
Segunda Sección of Chapultepec, adjacent to
the Periférico
HOURS: Daily 10 A.M.–9 P.M.
COST: $7
METRO: Constituyentes

This amusement park is in the western section
of the park, on the far side of the Periférico
from El Castillo. It's easy to spot—just look
for the towering *montaña rusa* ("Russian
mountain," as roller coasters are known here).
Coming by car or taxi from downtown, the
best access is to take Avenida Constituyentes
west. After crossing underneath the Periférico,
take the first right into the park, and then right
again, and you'll arrive at the park.

TERCERA SECCIÓN
Past the Panteón Dolores is the newest section
of Chapultepec, added only in the 1970s as the
city expanded to the west. The third section is
a jumble of ravines, meadows, patches of forest, and a few caves, not really developed for
visitors beyond a few picnic tables set up by the
roadside. Aside from the grounds of the horse
club, it's unfortunately not the safest place to
go walking or jogging—better to stick to the
first and second sections.

LIENZO CHARRO
Av. Constituyentes 500, 55/5277-8706,
www.nacionaldecharros.com
HOURS: Varies, usually weekends midday and
afternoon (check website)
COST: Varies, sometimes free

Charreadas—the Mexican equivalent of the
rodeo, but with considerably more finesse and
pageantry—are held in the *charro* ring from
time to time throughout the year.

TACUBAYA
Now an unlovely neighborhood of elevated
highways and rather dirty backstreets south
of Chapultepec, the sorely mistreated Colonia
Tacubaya is one of the oldest settlement areas
in the Valle de México. Although it's certainly
not atop the list for tourists with limited time
in the city, those who have a more leisurely

schedule or who live in Mexico City might like
to spend an hour or two walking around the
Tacubaya for a taste of this unusual corner of
the city. Apart from the Casa de la Bola and the
Museo Casa Barragán described in this section,
the Museo Nacional de la Cartografía—an obscure but interesting army-run museum housed
in a former 16th-century Franciscan convent—
is also in the Tacubaya (see the *Arts and Leisure*
chapter for details).

Tacubaya is situated at the edge of the long-
gone lake, right where several small rivers come
out of the hills; its name derives from an Aztec
word meaning "where one drinks water." The
area was controlled by the Tepanecas when the
Aztecs arrived in the valley, but the intruders
soon saw fit to conquer this strategic location.
After the arrival of the Spanish, Tacubaya became one of the favored places for the colonial elite to live because of its fresh air, clean
water, and myriad orchards. For five years in
the 17th century, when the downtown area was
flooded, it was the colony's capital. Tacubaya
was also the birthplace of Mexican industry, with the construction of mills along the
Becerra, Tacubaya, and de la Piedad Rivers.
Only one mill, the Santo Domingo, still exists
today, but it's located in a private housing development and is not open for visitors.

CASA DE LA BOLA AND PARQUE LIRA
Av. Parque Lira 136, 55/5515-8825 or 55/5515-5582
HOURS: Casa de la Bola: Sun. 11 A.M.–5 P.M., or
by appointment
COST: Casa de la Bola $3; park is free
METRO: Tacubaya

Built in the early 17th century, this lovely
mansion was first the home of Mexico's grand
inquisitor, after which it changed hands frequently over the years before its last owner,
Antonio Haghenbeck y de la Lama, donated it
to the government in the 1940s. Haghenbeck
maintained the two-story house much as it
had looked during the colonial era, supple-
menting the decor with his own unusually
rich tastes, judging from all the fine furniture,
tapestries, and artwork inside. The mansion
offers a magnificent taste of what life was like

in Tacubaya during its era of colonial glory. Step off the noisy avenues through the doors of the Casa de la Bola, and the blissfully calm courtyard and garden will make the city seem a distant dream. Visitors see the house with a guided tour.

The surrounding Parque Lira is a little corner of leafy tranquility amid the avenues of Tacubaya. It is easily reached from Metro Tacubaya or via taxi along Avenida Parque Lira or Avenida Observatorio. At the northern end of Parque Lira is the **Delegación Miguel Hidalgo building,** the administrative offices for this part of the city. Evidently a former colonial hacienda, the sprawling red-brick complex has the **Capilla de Nuestra Señora de Guadalupe** on-site.

MUSEO CASA BARRAGÁN

Av. General Francisco Ramírez 14, 55/5272-4945
HOURS: By appointment only, Mon.-Fri. 10 A.M.-2 P.M. and 4-6 P.M., Sat. 10 A.M.-1 P.M.
COST: $7
METRO: Constituyentes

A museum dedicated to Luis Barragán, one of Mexico's greatest architects, is in a house that Barragán built near Metro Constituyentes—it's well worth a visit for architecture fans. Visitors are taken on guided tours available in Spanish, English, and French. The museum, declared a UNESCO World Heritage Site in 2004, was built in 1947 by Barragán for himself, and is exactly how Barragán left it when he died in 1988. The house's interior is a fascinating display of Barragán's powerful use of simple, unadorned lines and bright primary colors. The rear of the extra-tall main room is covered with a large window facing a small interior garden.

Born in 1902, Barragán was seduced early in his career by the more international styles prominent in Europe, where he lived between the wars. However, he was increasingly influenced by the stylistic traditions of his own country, as well as of the Mediterranean, and by the late 1940s he had developed his own unique vision. In particular his technique relied on imposing walls conceived as pure planes but enlivened with bright colors; he also used natural materials, such as adobe, timber, or even water. He emphasized the importance of gardens as a crucial space and liked to describe himself as primarily a landscape architect.

Roma and Condesa
Map 4

Along both sides of Avenida Insurgentes, roughly between the Zona Rosa on the north and the Eje 3 Sur fast road on the south, are the Roma and Condesa neighborhoods. Roma and Condesa are two of the most happening neighborhoods in the city, filled with young people of all sorts attracted to restaurants, cafés, art galleries, and cosmopolitan nightlife. The Condesa boasts the trendiest restaurant district in the city. They're also both great neighborhoods for strolling around, if you'd like a break from visiting the standard tourist destinations.

ROMA

A tree-lined residential neighborhood between Avenidas Cuauhtémoc and Insurgentes, south of Avenida Chapultepec, the Roma was one of the most upscale areas of the city when it was built in the early 20th century, on land that was originally created out of Aztec-era "floating farms" (*chinampas*) and later was part of Hernán Cortés's land grant. The land was taken from a communal farm in the late 19th century and developed in a few short years with wealthy European-style mansions along broad avenues.

After some decades of decline, accelerated by heavy damage during the 1985 earthquake, Roma has once again become fashionable. Many of the old mansions, left to decay over the decades, have been renovated by newcomers with a taste for the neighborhood's genteel ambience, while others now house cafés and art galleries.

The Roma does not have many tourist sights; most casual visitors will want to walk around the

Roma for an hour or two, visit the Casa Lamm, and have a cup of coffee or a meal in one of a number of good restaurants before returning to their home or hotel. But those who like bohemian-style neighborhoods may want to dally among the bookshops, cafés, and quiet, leafy streets lined with Porfiriato-era mansions.

Since the Roma began its resurgence, it has become Mexico City's premier location for contemporary art galleries. (See the *Arts and Leisure* chapter for gallery listings.)

Because so many writers have lived in the Roma, several important Mexican novels take place in the neighborhood, including *Batallas en el desierto,* by José Emilio Pacheco; *Agua quemada,* by Carlos Fuentes; *Manifestación de silencios,* by Arturo Azuela; and *El vampiro de la colonia Roma,* by Luis Zapata.

The Roma has Metro stations at each of its four corners, clockwise from the northwest: Insurgentes, Cuauhtémoc, Centro Médico, and Chilpancingo. For the Roma Norte, where most visitors will likely be going, Metro Insurgentes is the closest.

AROUND PLAZA RÍO DE JANEIRO
At the intersection of Avs. Puebla and Orizaba
HOURS: None
COST: Free
METRO: Insurgentes

The best place to start a stroll around the Roma is the old heart of the neighborhood, Plaza Río de Janeiro (originally called Plaza Roma), just a few blocks southeast of the Insurgentes Metro station.

Although a couple of remarkably ugly towers now mar the park's skyline, one can still enjoy the graceful mansions around the stately park, with its fountain and a replica of Michelangelo's *David* statue in the center. One building worth a look is **La Casa de las Brujas** (Witches' House), as the Edificio Río de Janeiro is popularly known. It's not hard to spot the striking red-brick castle, built in 1908, on the east side of the park. Note the "face" formed by the windows right on the top floor of the corner tower, and the art deco entranceway, which was added in the 1930s.

A block north of the park, at Orizaba 24 at the corner of Puebla, is the **Casa Universitária del Libro** (Mon.–Fri. 10 A.M.–3 P.M. and 5–8 P.M.), the offices of a small publishing house run by UNAM. During working hours, visitors may sign in and tour a small museum in the renovated mansion, which affords an opportunity to view the lovely wood interior and stained-glass windows of the central atrium.

The blocks between Plaza Río de Janeiro and Álvaro Obregón are dotted with mansions built in the early 20th century, decorated in a variety of eclectic styles. A few noteworthy examples:

Tabasco 133, at the corner of Córdoba: a 1917 mansion with fine iron grillwork and stone carvings over the windows.

Colima 145 at Córdoba: a squat facade with subtle art nouveau stone details.

Colima 168: a Venetian-style palace with pink trim.

Álvaro Obregón and Orizaba: the reserved, elegant Edificio Balmori, overshadowed by a monstrous concrete tower right next door.

Three blocks south of Álvaro Obregón on Orizaba is another tranquil small park called **Plaza Luis Cabrera,** the setting for part of José Emilio Pacheco's classic short story *La batallas en el desierto.*

◖ CASA LAMM
Álvaro Obregón 99 at Orizaba, 55/5514-4899, www.lamm.com.mx or www.galeriacasalamm.com.mx
HOURS: Exhibit space: Tues.–Sun. 10 A.M.–6 P.M.
COST: Free
METRO: Insurgentes

If you have time only for a brief visit to the Roma, at least make sure to take a look around Casa Lamm, a cultural center with an art gallery, bookstore, and restaurant all situated in a beautifully restored 1911 mansion. Whether you're interested in seeing the art exhibits or not, the mansion is worth visiting to get an idea of how people lived in the heyday of the Roma.

It was built by Lewis Lamm, son of one of Roma's founders, but the architect never got around to living there and instead rented it for years to a religious orphanage. In 1939 the house was sold to a private family who lived in

LA ROMITA

The "shameful daughter of the Colonia Roma," as one early chronicler labeled it, La Romita is a tiny corner of the Roma Norte, near the Metro Chapultepec station, with a singularly bad reputation. La Romita was actually the original native village in the area, long predating the building of the Roma (in the late 19th century). In fact, the original Roma developers fought a lengthy battle to try to incorporate what is now La Romita into their neighborhood plans, while the locals resisted tooth and nail.

From this inauspicious beginning, the plaza and little chapel of La Romita were off-limits for the wealthy families of the Roma, who feared getting robbed by La Romita's many *rateros* (thieves). La Romita even boasted two legendary female thieves during the 1930s and 1940s, Plácida Hernández and the ominously named "La Loba" (The She-Wolf).

But the most famed crooks to come out of La Romita managed to take their dirty deeds to another level altogether. During the 1940s a gang known as Los Halcones, led by a thug named Arturo "El Negro" Durazo, controlled part of La Romita's turf. Durazo befriended a more bookish type by the name of José "Pepito" López Portillo and made sure no harm came to the young man.

López Portillo went on to a career in politics and arrived at the presidency (1976-1982). In Mexico one does not forget past favors lightly, so López Portillo made his old protector Durazo the police chief of Mexico City. Thus began a reign of official terror, bringing the routine corruption of the city police to new lows of venality, until El Negro was ousted and imprisoned by the administration of president Miguel de la Madrid.

Los Halcones and their ilk are long gone, but in La Romita their aura somehow lingers. Trying to find the little square and church, just a few meters from Avenida Cuauhtémoc but only reached by a couple of narrow side streets, is no easy task. When you ask a local where the plaza is, the first reply is invariably to warn you about getting robbed. But on one afternoon, the only people in the shady little plaza were a young mother and her baby, and an old man eager to tell a foreign visitor stories of La Romita's legendary past. Of course, there were also three suspicious-looking young men huddled together in the alley next to the church, looking at the visitor with interest...

---

it until 1990, saving the building from the depredations faced by other Roma mansions.

In 1993 Casa Lamm was renovated and opened as a private cultural institute, holding regular events and exhibits. In 1999 it received stewardship of a large collection of art amassed by Mexican media giant Televisa, formerly housed in the now-closed Centro de Arte Contemporáneo. The collection contains hundreds of works by many famed Mexican and international artists, including Sergio Hernández, María Izquierdo, Francisco Toledo, Jasper Johns, Gerhard Richter, Manuel Álvarez Bravo, Tina Modotti, and Guillermo Kahlo (photographer and father of Frida).

Casa Lamm built a new wing in the courtyard to house a small exhibit space (55/5511-0899, www.galeriacasalamm.com.mx) with rotating art displays. The visiting exhibits will continue as well, both in the atrium upstairs in the main house and in the annex. There is no charge to visit the exhibits. Downstairs is the **Biblioteca de Arte** (daily 10 A.M.–7 P.M.), an art library.

On the ground floor of the main house is **Librería Pegaso** (55/5208-0171 or 55/5208-0174, daily 10 A.M.–8 P.M.), one of the most user-friendly bookstores in Mexico City, with free coffee and comfy couches in the middle of the store for relaxing. The store has an extensive selection of titles, many in English, and the art book collection is particularly good. All-day browsing is tolerated.

The Casa Lamm also teaches a couple dozen university-level courses each year on art, literature, music, politics, and society.

Courses cost $200–800 per four-month semester. A program of guided visits to 10 different art galleries in the city over the course of a semester costs $250. Check their website or call for more information.

An odd-looking glassed-in porch structure built into the corner of the old *casona* houses the **Restaurante Lamm,** which has very good international cuisine (see the *Restaurants* chapter for more details).

CONDESA

If there's one neighborhood in Mexico City that can be considered the hip spot in town to live, it would be the Condesa. Until the mid-1980s, this leafy, quiet *colonia* of attractive art deco–era buildings was an upper-middle-class preserve populated predominantly by Jewish families who moved there from the Centro in decades past. Condesa was built in the 1920s on land originally part of a hacienda owned by the Condesa de Miravalle (hence the name); at the time there was nothing on it but open pastures and a defunct horseracing track. Rather than destroy the old racetrack, Mexican developers José Basurto and José de la Lama incorporated the shape into their street plan, giving us the oval Avenida Amsterdam, with Parque México in the middle. Many of the wealthier Catholic and Jewish families still living in the Centro began moving into Condesa in the 1930s and 1940s. The time period is reflected in the architecture, with art deco stylings on some of the older buildings.

The Condesa was not badly damaged in the 1985 earthquake, but many of the older Condesa families joined the exodus to newer suburbs farther west outside of the downtown area. And as with the Roma, the sudden drop in rents and increase in apartment openings led to a recolonization of sorts, this time with actors, gays, artists, journalists, and other bohemian types, who appreciate the local parks, attractive apartment buildings, and many restaurants and bars. The number of restaurants has exploded, and rents have swung up dramatically.

The Condesa is bordered on the east by Insurgentes Sur, on the south by Eje 3 Sur Baja California, on the west by Avenida Patriotismo (a section of the Circuito Interior), and on the north by the Roma Norte. The neighborhood itself is divided in two, the eastern half around Parque México called Hipódromo Condesa (because of the former horsetrack), and the section west of Nuevo León known as the Condesa, which is where most of the restaurants are located. Many people now think of both parts simply as the Condesa.

The closest Metro station for the Hipódromo Condesa is Metro Chilpancingo, while the nearest to the restaurant district in the Condesa is Metro Patriotismo. If you drive to the Condesa, Parque México is a good place to park your car, as spots are usually available. The streets around the restaurant zone are more congested.

One website with lots of information on the Condesa is www.coloniacondesa.com.mx.

◖ **PARQUE MÉXICO**

Av. México, Col. Condesa
HOURS: None
COST: Free
METRO: Chilpancingo

Despite the growing popularity of the Condesa among young Mexicans and foreigners as a place to live and hang out, there's not a whole lot for most visitors to do apart from eating out at one of the (generally pricey) restaurants. But if you feel like seeing something besides colonial churches and museums, you might consider walking around Parque México and the surrounding streets for a couple of hours, or relaxing on a bench with a book or your journal in the park.

The large, oval-shaped park (technically named Parque San Martín), built on the site of a former horsetrack, is filled with remarkably lush, almost tropical vegetation and is a wonderful oasis of clean air in the midst of the city. If you're a runner, you might consider joining the many locals who get their daily exercise jogging, in-line skating, or just walking their dogs around the park. The pedestrian walkway in the middle of Avenida Amsterdam, which forms a larger oval around the park one block away, is also a good place to run.

While the hype of the Condesa as the most pristine art deco neighborhood outside of

© CHRIS HUMPHREY

an old *casona* at the end of Avenida Veracruz in the Condesa

end of the park, right next to the Suburbia department store at the corner of Sonora, is **Edificio Basurto,** named in honor of its architect (José Basurto), who was also one of the developers of the Condesa. For a brief time after its construction in the 1920s, this was the tallest building in Mexico City. It's hard to appreciate the architecture from the outside, but the circular atrium and apartments have clean, crisp lines. Many other art deco and functionalist buildings erected in the 1920s and 1930s can be spotted while walking around Parque México and Avenida Amsterdam.

Parque México is crossed by two streets, Michoacán (in the middle) and Sonora (at the north end). Follow Michoacán four blocks to the west, across Nuevo León and Tamaulipas, and you'll find yourself in the middle of the Condesa restaurant and café zone. Following Sonora west from Parque México will take you across Nuevo León to **Parque España,** a second, smaller park; it's not as nice as Parque México, because it's stranded next to a major avenue. Beyond Parque España is the stately Avenida Veracruz, which is still a bit run-down in places but is quickly being gentrified.

Miami's South Beach is overblown, there are several elegant deco/functionalist apartment houses facing Parque México. Near the north

Nápoles, Del Valle, and Mixcoac   Map 5

Until the 1940s, south of what was then the Río de la Piedad (and is now the Viaducto highway, covering the entubed river), there was nothing but open fields with a few scattered country houses until you reached San Ángel. But with the construction of Avenida Insurgentes, the Nápoles and Del Valle middle-class neighborhoods were developed. Farther south is Mixcoac, a former village which has long since been overtaken by the city though it still has a couple of quiet squares and colonial buildings. Apart from visiting the Polyforum Siqueiros or passing along Insurgentes to get to San Ángel, casual tourists won't find much reason to come down this way.

Metro Chilpancingo is the southernmost Metro station along Insurgentes, so

to get anywhere between the Condesa and San Ángel along Insurgentes, hop onto the Metrobús (a busline with a dedicated lane, going in each direction) at one of the frequent stations along Insurgentes and get off wherever convenient. If you're not sure, the bus driver or fellow passengers can help you pick your stop. Metro Mixcoac, on Avenida Revolución, is a short walk from the Mixcoac neighborhood.

NÁPOLES AND DEL VALLE

South of the World Trade Center along Insurgentes are the Nápoles (west of Insurgentes) and Del Valle (east of Insurgentes) neighborhoods, residential areas developed in the 1950s. At the north end are two major

THE LONG AND NOT SO WINDING ROAD

An appropriately hyperbolic avenue for this city of excess, Insurgentes stretches 28.8 kilometers in length, from Avenida Acueducto de Guadalupe in the northeast, at the start of the highway to Pachuca, across the entire valley to Tlalpan and the highway to Cuernavaca in the south. By one counting (a local one, admittedly), it's the longest avenue in the world.

Lengthy Insurgentes came into being in the 1950s, shortly after the construction of the new university complex south of San Ángel, as the city government linked up dozens of smaller, unconnected roads to form the avenue.

Traffic on Insurgentes is proverbial. One of the jokes going around says the city government should hang strings of garlic on lampposts up and down Insurgentes to improve circulation. The installation of the new Metrobús system, with dedicated bus lanes, and the eradication of the army of *pesero* minibuses, has certainly helped.

While in the United States or Europe such a traffic artery would be given over exclusively to vehicles, millions of pedestrians swarm on and around Insurgentes day and night. It's practically an elongated city in its own right, a sort of urban epiphany, a literal cross-section of Mexico City life. The avenue passes through 60 of the city's 300-odd *colonias* and five of its 16 *delegaciones*. At last count, Insurgentes claimed 217 restaurants, 172 bars, 97 banks, 30 department stores, 12 gas stations, 8 Metro stations, 4 federal secretariat offices, the headquarters of the Institutional Revolutionary Party (PRI), and UNAM (the national university), to name only a few of the most prominent *avenida*-dwellers.

---

stadiums, the **Estadio Azul** for soccer and right next door the **Monumental Plaza de Toros México,** the largest bullfighting ring in the Americas (see the *Arts and Leisure* chapter for more information about both). Farther south, between Eje 6 Sur and Eje 7 Sur, is **Parque Hundido** ("Sunken Park"), a large leafy park along Insurgentes, set below street level. The gravel and dirt paths of the park, lined with about 50 reproductions of pre-Hispanic sculptures, are a good place for a jog—as with Parque México in the Condesa, the trees seem to help keep out the fumes from traffic on nearby Insurgentes.

Across Insurgentes from Parque Hundido is the smaller **Parque San Lorenzo,** another tree-filled park. This one boasts a couple of basketball courts and the 16th-century chapel **Capilla San Lorenzo Mártir** dedicated to San Lorenzo Mártir, with a bare facade and a worn brick bell tower.

POLIFORO CULTURAL SIQUEIROS

Insurgentes Sur 701, 55/5536-4520
HOURS: Daily 9 A.M.-7 P.M.
COST: $1.25 to view the murals; free for the museum

On Insurgentes Sur south of the Viaducto, in the shadow of the monstrous 50-story World Trade Center de México, is this eye-catching, geometric building covered with huge mural paintings inside and out by Mexican artist Davíd Alfaro Siqueiros.

The Polyforum was the brainchild of ex-Revolutionary and later businessman Manuel Suárez y Suárez, who originally conceived of the building for a location in Cuernavaca. But seeing the unique structure and the murals begun by Siqueiros, president Gustavo Díaz Ordaz convinced Suárez to relocate it to its present site.

The 12-sided building was designed to resemble a diamond sitting on four pillars. Inside are eight facets, and three horizontal levels. The first is the entrance, with a small, free museum about the Polyforum, while in the center, but set down a level, is a 500-seat circular theater often used for drama productions.

Upstairs is the main forum hall, frequently used for major events, particularly by the leftist Democratic Revolution Party (PRD), which perhaps feels an affinity for the socialist beliefs expressed in the monumental three-dimensional mural created by Siqueiros inside

© CHRIS HUMPHREY

Mexico City is full of hidden parks and colonial churches, such as Capilla San Lorenzo Mártir in Colonia Del Valle.

the hall, titled *La marcha de la Humanidad* (The March of Humanity). At 11:30 A.M., 12:45 P.M., and 5 P.M. on weekends only, visitors can attend a sound-and-light show ($3.50) narrated by a recording of Siqueiros, describing his vision in the mural.

There's no convenient Metro stop for the Poliforo—best to take the Metrobús along Avenida Insurgentes to get there by public transportation.

MIXCOAC

Another one of the many "lost" neighborhoods populating unlikely corners of Mexico City, Mixcoac is a small oasis of cobblestone streets and colonial buildings hidden between the noisy avenues of Insurgentes and Patriotismo.

The old center of Mixcoac is a remarkably quiet pedestrian area with three interconnecting plazas. Three buildings of note here are the **Casa de Cultura Juan Rulfo,** housed in what was the old Palacio Municipal; the 17th-century **Parroquia de Santo Domingo de Guzmán** church and adjacent convent complex; and the **Universidad Panamericana,** housed in what was an 18th-century textile factory and hacienda. In the archways of a building right opposite the university is **Café Los Arcos,** a sidewalk coffee shop invariably filled with students; it makes a great spot for a soft drink or coffee.

By public transportation, the easiest way to get to Mixcoac is to go by Metro to the Mixcoac station and walk from there. Alternatively it's a short walk from the corner of Insurgentes and Avenida Mixcoac, where there's a Metrobús stop.

INSTITUTO MORA

Plaza Valentín Gómez Farías 12, 55/5598-3777, www.institutomora.edu.mx
HOURS: Mon.-Fri. 8 A.M.-7 P.M., Sat. 8 A.M.-3:30 P.M.
COST: Free
METRO: Mixcoac

The only sight, per se, in the Mixcoac neighborhood is the Instituto Mora, a library specializing in the history of Mexico, Latin America, and the United States. Housed in what was briefly the home of ex-president Valentín Gómez Farías, the library is a wonderful place for anyone interested in history (and who can read Spanish). There's a peaceful garden to sit and read in and a small cafeteria to buy coffee or snacks. In front of the building is a quiet, tree-filled square, and across the street is the colonial-era **Iglesia de San Juan.** To get there, either come from Avenida Extremadura north along Augusto Rodin a couple of blocks, or from Patriotismo (near the Mixcoac Metro stop) walk east along Irineo Paz several blocks. It's several blocks north of the colonial center of Mixcoac.

COURTESY OF CONSEJO DE PROMOCIÓN TURÍSTICA DE MÉXICO/IGNACIO GUEVARA

Poliforo Cultural Siquieros with murals by artist Davíd Alfaro Siqueiros

Coyoacán

Map 6

Eight kilometers south of the Centro, Coyoacán was once a colonial village separated from Mexico City proper by farmland and lakes, and it remains one of the most traditional neighborhoods in the Distrito Federal. The plazas and narrow cobbled streets of Coyoacán, once part of huge haciendas and convents, are marvelous places for visitors to stroll and appreciate the neighborhood's relaxed ambience. Not for nothing was Coyoacán voted the fifth most livable neighborhood in North America (ahead of Rittenhouse, Philadelphia, and behind Camden, Maine—go figure) according to a survey by the Project on Public Spaces.

After the Centro Histórico, Coyoacán might be the most tour-worthy part of the city. Visitors who think that nearby San Ángel is too pricey or "precious" often find Coyoacán more to their taste.

Coyoacán life is centered on its twin main plazas, Jardín del Centenario and Jardín Hidalgo.

On weekends the plazas fill with all manner of street vendors, musicians, and passersby—so many that it can be difficult to find room to walk. Casual tourists may wish to avoid the mad throng on weekends, but it's also when all the handicrafts vendors come out and free concerts on the bandstand take place. Take a break from walking at one of the plaza cafés under brightly colored awnings, while organ grinders play beneath towering Indian laurel trees.

For tourist information, look for the little kiosk in the Jardín del Centenario. At the northwest corner of the plaza is a Banamex, where you can change money or use the ATM if needed.

History

When the conquistadors arrived in Coyoacán in the early 16th century, it was populated by Aztecs, who called the area Coyohuacan, a Náhuatl name meaning "place of coyotes."

Hernán Cortés and his troops were very well received in Coyoacán by the area's earlier inhabitants, the Tepanecas, who resented the oppressive Aztec domination of their homelands. At that time Lago de Texcoco extended all the way south to Coyoacán, and Cortés chose the lakeside port as the spot for his headquarters during the conquest of Tenochtitlán, the Aztec capital. As the reconstruction of the conquered capital was under way, Cortés installed himself in Coyoacán and made it the first capital of New Spain between 1521 and 1523. Coyoacán's current Casa Municipal sits at the north end of Jardín del Centenario on the site of one of Cortés's many former residences.

After Mexican independence from Spain, one of the most notable local historic events occurred on August 20, 1847, when the Convento de Churubusco became the scene of a fierce battle between Mexican troops and invading U.S. forces during the Mexican-American War.

In 1923, the famous Escuela de Pintura al Aire Libre (Open Air School of Painting) was founded in the former Hacienda de San Pedro Mártir, thus establishing Coyoacán as an artists' colony. Later in the 20th century, Coyoacán offered refuge to two world-renowned exiles, Romania's King Carol and Russia's Leon Trotsky.

Coyoacán became part of the Distrito Federal upon the ratification of Mexico's 1857 constitution. The Delegación Coyoacán (much bigger than the colonial neighborhood that tourists visit) extends over 60 square kilometers and is bisected by three waterways, including the channeled Río Churubusco, the partially channeled Río Chiquito, and the Canal Nacional.

Getting There and Around

To get to Coyoacán from the city center, take the Línea 3 Metro to the Miguel Ángel de Quevedo station and hop a *pesero* heading east on Avenida M. A. de Quevedo, telling the driver that you want to get off at Calle Tres Cruces. Walk north along Tres Cruces, which becomes Calle Centenario and reaches the west side of Jardín del Centenario after five blocks. Two other Línea 3 Metro possibilities are the Coyoacán and Viveros stations,

each about a 20-minute walk from the plazas. Another way to combine bus and Metro would be to catch a Línea 2 Metro to the Tasqueña station, southeast of Coyoacán, and from there hop a *pesero* directly to Jardín Centenario, Coyoacán. This takes a little longer but allows you to avoid having to walk into Coyoacán. Most attractions lie within easy walking distance of the two plazas, so you won't find a need for vehicle transport while touring the neighborhood.

JARDÍN HIDALGO AND CASA MUNICIPAL

Bordered by Carillo Puerto, Caballocalco, and B. Domínguez

HOURS: None for square; Casa Municipal Mon.-Sat. 8:30 A.M.-6 P.M.

COST: Free

METRO: Viveros

Coyoacán's lovely *zócalo* (square) is a traditional rectangle centered around a 19th-century kiosk. The kiosk features a stained-glass cupola topped by a bronze republican eagle. Along the north side of the plaza lies the Casa Municipal, which houses local and federal government offices on the site of a former Cortés residence. An attached chapel contains Diego Rosales frescoes narrating local history, while the Sala de Cabildos (Council Hall) features an elaborate mural by the painter Aurora Reyes. Just off the square is the Museo Nacional de Culturas Populares, a cultural museum on Avenida Hidalgo, worth a look to see what the current exhibit is (see the *Arts and Leisure* chapter for details).

PARROQUIA Y EX-CONVENTO DE SAN JUAN BAUTISTA

Jardín Hidalgo

HOURS: Daily 8 A.M.-6 P.M.

COST: Free

METRO: Viveros

Built in 1589 by Dominican friars (and later transferred to the Franciscans), this parish church and former convent looms over the southeast corner of Jardín Hidalgo. The plastered early baroque facade is original, while the interior has been beautifully reconstructed. In one of the church's three naves, the Capilla de Rosario contains an ornate baroque *retablo* from the end of the 17th century.

JARDÍN CENTENARIO

Betw. Carrillo Puerto and Tres Cruces
HOURS: None
COST: Free
METRO: Viveros

This smaller plaza to the west of Jardín Hidalgo is centered around a fountain and bronze sculptures of two coyotes, a reference to the literal meaning of the name Coyoacán. The south side of the verdant plaza is lined with cafés and restaurants, including the well-known Café El Parnaso, considered the perfect place for a philosophical chat over a cup of coffee.

◖ CALLE DE LA HIGUERA

Calle de la Higuera betw. Caballo Calco and Plaza de la Conchita
HOURS: None
COST: Free
METRO: Viveros

Behind the Parroquia San Juan Bautista, this street heading southeast away from the plaza is lined with beautifully renovated colonial homes, including **Casa Colorada,** site of the first Spanish military encampment in the Valle de México.

A little farther southeast, Calle de la Higuera passes the **Plaza y Capilla de la Conchita.** A chapel constructed here in 1521 by order of Cortés was thought to have been the first Christian building in the city. Although officially known as Capilla de la Purísima Concepción, the chapel and surrounding garden are more commonly known by the affectionate nickname La Conchita (The Little Shell). The chapel is thought to be next to the site of ancient freshwater springs.

A controversial piece of Hernán Cortés's past can be found just off Plaza de la Conchita at the **Casa de la Malinche,** the former house of the conqueror's Indian lover/interpreter. A complex woman, originally enslaved by rival

Coyoacán gets its name from coyotes, seen here in statue form in the downtown fountain.

tribes before being taken by Cortés, Malintzin (her Indian name) played a crucial role in the conquest of the Aztec empire, offering Cortés subtle advice along with her interpretations. She is reviled by many modern Mexicans for helping Cortés, to the point that the term *malinchista* refers to any Mexican (but particularly women) who idealizes foreigners and puts down Mexico.

Casa de los Camilos, on the right at the corner of the next block, was built in the 17th century as the residence and hospice of the Camillians, a religious order founded by San Camilo de Lelis (1550–1614), patron saint of hospitals and the sick. The stone-block structure's small, but the unique door, made of black stone, is worth a look.

On the opposite side of the street, the **Jardín Frida Kahlo** is dedicated to the famous Coyoacán painter. A statue of Kahlo contemplates the garden that carries her name. A fountain completes the picture.

Running north along the west side of Jardín Frida Kahlo, tree-shaded **Calle de**

Fernández Leal boasts a string of attractive country mansions and houses built around the beginning of the 20th century and typical of residential Coyoacán.

MUSEO FRIDA KAHLO
Londres 247, 55/5554-5999,
www.museofridakahlocasaazul.org
HOURS: Tues.-Sun. 10 A.M.-6 P.M.
COST: $4.50, $2 for students
METRO: Coyoacán

One of the most popular sights in Coyoacán, the Museo Frida Kahlo is a startlingly blue early-20th-century house in which the world-famous artist was born to a German father and Mexican mother in 1907. Now acclaimed by critics and collectors worldwide, Kahlo painted for years in the shadow of her famed muralist husband, Diego Rivera. She suffered a crippling injury in her early years, and her art suggests a stoic life full of pain and self-absorption. She lived with Rivera off and on for 25 years until her death in 1954. Perhaps because the work she created seems to have transcended her difficult circumstances, Kahlo has become an emblem for contemporary female artists.

A selection of Kahlo's personal art collection is on display—including pre-Hispanic artifacts and Mexican folk art (including jewelry and clothes, most of it inspired by Amerindian designs, which Kahlo herself wore) as well as works by well-known artists José María Velasco, Paul Klee, and, of course, her husband, Rivera. Particularly interesting are Kahlo's self-portraits, which combine her own self-examination along with a fascination with communist ideology and Amerindian folkways. For a larger exhibit of Kahlo's own paintings, head to the Museo Dolores Olmedo in Xochimilco. Kahlo was said to have had a love affair with Leon Trotsky, whose own museum is nearby. The garden at this museum is a quiet spot to sit and write a letter or drink in the atmosphere. A small gift shop and café are on the premises. Cameras aren't allowed inside the museum.

MUSEO LEÓN TROTSKY
Río Churubusco 410, 55/5658-8732
HOURS: Tues.-Sun. 10 A.M.-5 P.M.
COST: $3.50
METRO: Coyoacán

Leon Trotsky's house looks like a fortress—which is the function it served (albeit unsuccessfully) for this exiled Russian bolshevik. Having lost to Josef Stalin in a struggle for rulership over the Soviet Union, Trotsky left the USSR in 1929 under the threat of execution. At the invitation of Diego Rivera and Frida Kahlo, he came to Mexico in 1937 to seek asylum and, after having an affair with Kahlo, he moved to this building, just around the corner from Kahlo's home.

Trotsky lived in justifiable paranoia of Stalin, and seldom left his house, in an effort to protect himself from assassination attempts. But to no avail—in 1940, a Spanish Stalinist named Ramón Mercader convinced Trotsky to allow him in the house and promptly stabbed him with an ice pick as Trotsky looked the other way. The room in which he was killed has been left untouched; every paper and book remains in the same position. Among other artifacts on display are photographs of Trotsky; his wife, Natalia; and Rivera and Kahlo. Some visitors find the veneration expressed by the museum tour guides toward some of Trotsky's daily objects ("This was the spoon he stirred his coffee with!") a bit over the top.

The museum is also headquarters for the **Instituto del Derecho de Asilo y las Libertades Públicas** (IDALP, Institute for the Right of Asylum and Public Liberties), founded in 1990, and for the **Biblioteca Rafael Galván,** housing a collection of books focused on social themes. The IDALP (Viena 45, around the corner from the main museum entrance) organizes occasional expositions, conferences, and art activities.

PLAZA SANTA CATARINA
Francisco Sosa at Tata Vasco
HOURS: None
COST: Free
METRO: Viveros

A few blocks west of Jardín Centenario

along Calle Francisco Sosa is a beautiful small square, fronted by the brightly painted **Capilla de Santa Catarina** as well as several restored colonial-era houses. On one side is the **Casa de Cultura de Coyoacán** (Francisco Sosa 202, 55/5658-7826), which often holds cultural events and art exhibits. It's worth taking a peek in to admire the rambling old hacienda or take a rest in the lush gardens in back. Heading back toward the center of Coyoacán you'll find the **Instituto Italiano di Cultura** (Francisco Sosa 77, 55/5554-0044), also with art exhibits and other events. A couple of short blocks south is another lovely square, Parque Santa Catarina.

VIVEROS DE COYOACÁN

Betw. Universidad, Madrid, Melchor Ocampo, and Pérez Valenzuela

HOURS: Daily 6 A.M.–6 P.M.

COST: Free

METRO: Viveros

These gardens and forests were created in 1907 as the private nurseries (*viveros*) and orchards of Miguel Ángel de Quevedo. Trees from Viveros now populate many other parks in the city, including Parque México and Parque Hundido. Viveros was nationalized under president Venustiano Carranza, and now this wide expanse of green has become a cool park where you might like to go for a walk or a jog to unwind from the surrounding bustle of the city. There's a flower and plant market here as well.

San Ángel

Map 6

During the colonial era, the village of San Ángel attracted wealthy Spaniards who found the pleasant climate and rural ambience perfect for their estates and summer homes. Nine kilometers from the Centro, today it's a posh and attractive suburb that the spreading city has grown to meet. You'll still find cobblestone streets with marvelous old colonial-era homes and haciendas now inhabited by the wealthy. The Saturday art market is a favorite spot for tourists and Mexicans alike to go gift shopping. One of Mexico's best modern Mexican art museums, Museo de Arte Carrillo Gil, as well as the more general Museo Soumaya and the Museo Estudio Diego Rivera, are all a short walk from the center of San Ángel.

San Ángel is easily accessible from downtown via Metro or bus. The closest Metro station to San Ángel is M. A. de Quevedo. From this station, take a *pesero* marked San Ángel. Tell the driver you want to go to Plaza San Jacinto. Or you can take the Metrobús south along Insurgentes from Paseo de la Reforma. Get off at Avenida La Paz—ask the driver to let you know when to get off if you're not sure. The Metrobús ends at San Ángel, but was under construction

to continue south along Insurgentes to UNAM and Cuicuilco, close to Tlalpan.

Driving from central Mexico City, the quickest way to reach San Ángel is either via the Periférico ring highway from Paseo de la Reforma or via Avenida Revolución. Although it has stoplights, Revolución is often faster than the Periférico, especially if traffic is heavy.

PLAZA SAN JACINTO

Av. Madero at San Jacinto

HOURS: None

COST: Free

METRO: M. A. de Quevedo

A short walk up the hill from Avenida Revolución is this fine colonial plaza surrounded by period architecture. Although it's just a couple of blocks from a sea of traffic and asphalt, sitting in one of the relaxed plaza cafés one can still imagine San Ángel as a village far from Mexico City. On Saturday from 9 A.M. to 6 P.M. local artists offer their works for sale, turning the plaza into a *jardín del arte* (art garden) called Bazar Sábado, one of the best art markets in the city. (See the *Shops* chapter for more details.)

The **Iglesia de San Jacinto** on the west

side of the plaza was at one time part of a Dominican monastery built between 1564 and 1614. Notable are the principal *retablo* inside and the carved stone *cruz atrial* (atrium cross) standing in front of the church. The beautiful walled gardens in front of the church are a favorite venue for weekend wedding parties.

A plaque on the square commemorates the execution of Irish-American U.S. soldiers (by order of General Zachary Taylor), who switched sides during the 1847 U.S. invasion to fight for Mexico in religious solidarity with fellow Catholics.

CASA DEL RISCO
Plaza San Jacinto 15, 55/5616-2611
HOURS: Tues.-Sun. 10 A.M.-5 P.M.
COST: Free
METRO: M. A. de Quevedo

Also known as the Casa del Mirador, this late-17th-century house on the north side of Plaza San Jacinto encloses a museum, a library, and two courtyards. The displays at the Museo Colonial Casa del Risco illustrate the fascination with European lifestyles felt by wealthy Mexicans in the colonial era. Upstairs in the Salón Barroco is a display of Mexican baroque art from the 17th century, mostly religious art and furniture. Two rooms feature portraits of European kings and nobility, and another room displays some collected art from the 19th and early 20th centuries. There's one large room downstairs where temporary exhibits of contemporary Mexican artists are mounted. Also in the building is the colonial library **Centro Cultural y Biblioteca Isidro Fabela.**

A large wall fountain in the eastern courtyard is decorated with whole Talavera plates (along with a few Spanish, English, and Japanese ones), interspersed with hand-painted tiles and seashells.

EX-CONVENTO DEL CARMEN
Av. Revolución at Av. La Paz, 55/5616-6622, ext. 110
HOURS: Tues.-Sun. 10 A.M.-4:45 P.M.
COST: $3.50, $7 with video camera
METRO: M. A. de Quevedo

At this Carmelite ex-monastery, built between 1615 and 1626, you'll find a diverse collection of colonial art by such maestros as Cristóbal de Villalpando, Juan Correa, and Juan Becerra, along with colonial furniture displays. Even more notable is the basement crypt containing mummified remains of priests, nuns, and nobility, discovered during a building project. It's well worth walking around the museum to appreciate the convent building and displays. There's a small park in the back where you can rest, providing a quiet little oasis in the busy city.

The adjacent church, built in the usual Latin cross floor plan, contains colonial-era *retablos* of some interest.

PLAZA LORETO
Av. Revolución at Río Magdalena
HOURS: None
COST: Free
METRO: M. A. de Quevedo

A bit south of the center of San Ángel is Plaza Loreto, a shopping mall built in an unusual fashion around what was formerly a colonial-era mill once owned by Hernán Cortés himself. Later, it was the biggest paper factory in Latin America. Apart from the many high-end shops (mainly for clothing, but also music, books, and much else), you'll now find several restaurants and snack shops, as well as a movie theater. Live concerts or performances are often held in the plaza on weekends. Plaza Loreto is also home to a small but interesting art museum, Museo Soumaya, with works by Degas, Renoir, Claudel, and Miró, as well as colonial-era Latin American art (see *Arts and Leisure* chapter for more information).

UNIVERSIDAD NACIONAL AUTÓNOMA DE MÉXICO (UNAM)
Ciudad Universitaria, on either side of Av. Insurgentes Sur north of the Periférico, 55/5622-8222, www.unam.edu.mx
HOURS: Vary
COST: Free
METRO: Universidad

Founded in 1551 by special charter from the king of Spain, Mexico's national university is the oldest university in the Western Hemisphere. The original campus was in Mexico City's Centro, but in the early 1950s it was moved to its present site southwest of the city center. So vast is the present campus—covering 7.3 million square meters, much of it green areas—that it is referred to as the Ciudad Universitaria (University City).

With an enrollment of nearly half a million students and a teaching staff of 25,000, this is the largest campus in the Americas. UNAM has a reputation for teaching left-leaning theories and as a center for political activism. The famed 1968 student riots, which ended in the bloodbath at Tlatelolco, began among students from UNAM. In 1999, a group of students went on strike and closed the university for nine months. The strike was initially triggered by a government plan to raise the miniscule tuition, but it quickly broadened to a more general antigovernment and antiglobalization protest. The strike was eventually broken up when the government sent in the police (a major taboo at the fiercely independent UNAM—the word "Autónoma" in the name refers to its autonomy from the government) in the wee hours of the morning, catching groups of strikers still asleep.

The modern buildings—many covered with elaborate murals—were built between 1950 and 1955 by Carlos Lazo. The campus is divided into two sections, with the northern part containing most of the teaching and research buildings. Sprawling over a huge area of lava fields, the university is laid out in groups of faculties (*facultades*) centered on the **Rectoría** administration building, whose south wall is covered with a three-dimensional David Alfaro Siqueiros mural. Next to the Rectoría is the library, with an impressive Juan O'Gorman mosaic on Mexico's past and future.

In 2007, UNESCO (after much lobbying by Mexico and UNAM) named Ciudad Universitaria as a World Heritage Site, stating that "the campus constitutes a unique example of 20th century modernism integrating urbanism, architecture, engineering, landscape design and fine arts with references to local traditions, especially to Mexico's pre-Hispanic past."

Just south of the Rectoría is the **Museo Universitario de Ciencias y Artes CU** (55/5622-0206, www.muca.unam.mx, Mon.–Fri. 10 A.M.–7 P.M., Sat.–Sun. 10 A.M.–6 P.M.), with free revolving exhibits. Right next to the museum are two bookstores, **El Sótano** and **Librería UNAM.**

Across Insurgentes from the Rectoría complex, the **Estadio Olímpico**—a broad, open stadium designed to mimic one of the many volcanic cones in the area—has a Rivera mosaic over the main entrance. Home to the UNAM Pumas soccer club, the stadium has a reputation for the rowdiest fans in the city. If you go to a game and can understand a bit of Spanish, you'll enjoy hearing the crowd chanting creative (and often profane) songs and mercilessly razzing the opposing team and fans. (Details in *Arts and Leisure* chapter.)

For information about the university, stop in to the **Dirección General de Orientación,** an office on the south side of the large lawn just below the library.

The southern part of the campus is centered on the **Centro Cultural Universitario,** a collection of arts buildings and theaters. Here is the **Sala Nezahualcóyotl,** considered to have the finest acoustics in the country. In the middle of the complex is a café where you can grab some refreshments and the **Librería Julio Torri** bookstore. Just south of the Centro Cultural is the **Unidad Bibliográfica** (55/5622-6814, Mon.–Fri. 9 A.M.–8 P.M.), which houses part of the national library and the **Hemeroteca Nacional,** far and away the most comprehensive collection of newspapers and magazines in Mexico. Next to the library is the **Espacio Escultórico,** a collection of huge, colorful, and bizarre metal sculptures rising out of a field of lava. The maze of trails through the shrubs around the sculptures is a favorite spot for students to go find a quiet nook to read, play music, or even do a bit of rock climbing.

The most direct way to reach University City is by Metrobús traveling on Insurgentes Sur (Insurgentes passes the campus, on the east side of the road, and the stadium, on the west). The bus stops close to both sides, so it's an easy walk to the central part of the campus. Because of the amount of space the university takes up, walking around is feasible only in the north, main section. The closest Metro stop to the central area of campus is Copilco, but it's still a couple of kilometers' walk from there.

SIGHTS

Greater Mexico City   Map 7

The area of greater Mexico City is, in all honesty, a grab bag for everything outside of central Mexico City, rather than a coherent area like the Centro or Coyoacán. Attractions include the shrine to Mexico's patron saint, La Virgen de Guadalupe, several significant Aztec and pre-Aztec ruins, the exotic architecture of the national university, and a number of forested parks in the mountains above the city for spending a day in nature.

NORTHERN MEXICO CITY

Most of northern Mexico City is frankly unattractive, with endless blocks of cinder-block housing or industrial areas. It is, however, the location of Mexico's most famed religious shrine, the Basílica de Nuestra Señora de Guadalupe, as well as two infrequently visited pre-Hispanic temples.

ÁRBOL DE LA NOCHE TRISTE
Avenida México-Tacuba at Cañitas
HOURS: None
COST: Free
METRO: Cuitlahuac or Popotla

On the night of the *noche triste,* June 30, 1520, the Aztecs revolted and expelled the Spanish conquistadors from Tenochtitlán, driving them out of the city in the middle of the night along the Tacuba causeway, killing many and sending the rest fleeing for their lives (hence leading to the name Puente de Alvarado for part of the modern-day road; supposedly the conquistador Alvarado had to use a lance to pole-vault himself over a break in the causeway to escape the Aztecs). The story goes that when the remaining band of conquistadors finally managed to get to the far end of the causeway, on dry land again, Cortés leaned up against a tree and cried. And then—a testament to the will of this ferociously determined soldier—he pulled himself together and asked his company only one thing: Did the carpenter survive? It turns out he had. And so Cortés immediately began his next move, the building of a fleet of brigantines that the Spaniards used to launch an amphibious assault on the city, eventually taking it.

If you can believe it, the tree that Cortés cried against still exists. It's along Avenida México-Tacuba (which is the extension of Avenida Puente de Alvarado/San Cosme), between Metro stations Cuitlahuac and Popotla. The burnt-out, destroyed tree trunk, with a small bust of Cortés nestled inside and surrounded by a metal fence, is not much of a sight to see itself. But anyone with a fascination with Mexican history will feel a shiver at the legendary spot. If you go by Metro, get off at the Popotla station, but better yet, hop a *microbus* (minibus) or take a taxi along Avenida

the modern Basílica de Nuestra Señora de Guadalupe, with the older colonial church in the foreground

COURTESY OF CONSEJO DE PROMOCIÓN TURÍSTICA DE MÉXICO/CARLOS SÁNCHEZ

MYSTERIES OF THE VIRGEN DE GUADALUPE

As the story goes, Mexico City Bishop Juan de Zumárraga refused to believe Juan Diego's story that he had seen the Virgen on December 9, 1531, and demanded further evidence of his vision. On December 12, Juan – a former Aztec nobleman named Cuauhtaoctzin who converted to Catholicism – had a second vision of the Virgen; this time, she was surrounded by roses. This image was miraculously imprinted upon Juan Diego's cloak, and when he brought this to Zumárraga, the bishop was convinced of the miracle. After years of controversy, including a bizarre allegation by former Basilica Abbot Guillermo Shulenburg (of all people) that Juan Diego never existed, Pope John Paul II declared Juan Diego a Catholic saint in 2002.

The vision occurred in Cerro Tepeyac, which coincidentally (or perhaps not) was the site of a temple dedicated to a major Aztec female deity, Tonantzin. Unsurprisingly, most Amerindian inhabitants of Mexico referred to the Virgen as Tonantzin well into the 17th century. It's also curious to note that the first Virgen de Guadalupe shrine was founded in a remote corner of the Spanish province of Extremadura, the home of many conquistadores, including Hernán Cortés. The Extremadura Virgen is also dark and appeared in the 14th century, during the height of the conflict when the Spaniards were reconquering southern Spain from the darker-skinned Moors.

Whatever you make of the unusual coincidences surrounding the apparition, the New World Virgen de Guadalupe was an immediate success with Mexico's Amerindians and dramatically helped the Spanish missionaries with their work of conversion. Over the years la virgen morena ("the dark-skinned virgin," one of Guadalupe's epithets) has grown into the most revered religious figure in Mexico and is considered the protector of all Mexicans – the one who provides hope when all hope is lost. The number of miracles attributed to the icon of the Virgen runs into the many thousands, and her festival day of December 12 is the country's most important religious holiday.

While modern historians are quick to point to the historical situation at the time of the Guadalupe apparition to explain the "miracle," certain aspects of the original's supposedly spontaneous printing of the Virgen are less easy to explain away.

The color image appears to be painted onto a 2.2-by-1-meter piece of ayate – a paper-like cloth made from leaves of the agave using pre-Hispanic technology. While Aztecs used ayate for their codices, it is a very difficult material on which to paint a detailed image such as this. This anomaly alone is in fact one of the elements that convinced many of the validity of the miracle. Furthermore, after 116 years of leaving the cloth in the open, exposed to the elements and the hands of thousands of pilgrims, followed by another 352 years in a glass case, the image has retained most of its unusually brilliant colors. A reproduction done on ayate in the 17th century lasted only 30 years. And despite years of scientific investigation, the origin of the blue and skin-colored pigments remains a mystery.

México-Tacuba and imagine yourself on the ancient Aztec causeway. Along the route you'll see a few old churches, the imposing Colegio Militar, and several old mansions from the years when this was the spot for wealthy residents to have their country homes.

◖ BASÍLICA DE NUESTRA SEÑORA DE GUADALUPE

Plaza de las Américas 1, Col. Villa de Guadalupe, 55/5577-6022, www.virgendeguadalupe.org.mx
HOURS: Daily 7 A.M.–9 P.M.
COST: Free
METRO: Basílica

The church of Mexico's patron saint sees about 15 million visitors a year, and it's by far the most popular religious shrine in the country. It was here that Juan Diego (an Aztec nobleman named Cuauhtaoctzin before converting to Christianity) reported seeing his visions of the Virgen María on December 9 and 12, 1531, on the top of Cerro Tepeyac, a hill not far north of downtown Mexico City.

The first church was a simple chapel built on the hilltop, where Juan Diego lived the rest of his days after his vision. The current hilltop chapel was built at the end of the 17th century, which is also when construction began on the first *basílica* at the foot of the hill. Completed in 1709, by the 1970s the *basílica* was sinking into the soft subsoil and could no longer accommodate the steady stream of pilgrims. So the modern *basílica,* designed by Pedro Ramírez Vásquez (of Museo Nacional de Antropología fame), was constructed in 1976 and is now the main place of worship at the site.

Whatever your religious proclivities, there's no denying that the latest *basílica* has all the mystical aura of an airport terminal. For a slightly surreal religious experience, take a conveyor-belt ride behind the altar to see the image of the Virgen. The conveyor belt was put there so there wouldn't be a traffic jam of the reverent below the image. The succession of faithful is an amazing cross-section of Mexican life, from the most humble countryside indigenous campesino to upper-class

Mexico City residents. A religious art museum at the rear of the older 18th-century *basílica* contains oil paintings and sculptures of the colonial period, including works by such famed masters as Cabrera, Villalpando, Correa, and Echave.

The original chapel at Tepeyac, built on the hilltop in the late 17th century over the site of the old temple to the Aztec mother goddess Tonanztin, is reached by a walking path that winds up through the hillside gardens.

In the days running up to December 12, the highways around Mexico City are filled with a steady stream of pilgrims walking or bicycling along the side of the road on their way to the *basílica*. The night of the 12th is a crowded spectacle almost beyond imagining, a unique focus of Mexico's spiritual and national character. Unless you wish to pay your respects to the Virgin, or you have a particular fascination with checking out a huge crowd *a la mexicana,* it's best to avoid the *basílica* during most of the month of December.

Technically, the range of hills north of Tepeyac, known as the Sierra de Guadalupe, are protected as a national park. Unfortunately the hills are almost totally denuded of trees and would make for fairly desolate hiking. Because some of the neighborhoods surrounding and creeping up the sides of the hills are poor and rough, it's not recommended to venture into the range.

The easiest way to reach the *basílica* is to take the Metro to the Basílica station and walk the short distance to the church. The gardens and pathways leading up to the hilltop chapel are a relaxing place for a stroll.

PIRÁMIDE DE TENAYUCA

San Bartolo Tenayuca
HOURS: Tues.–Sun. 10 A.M.–4:45 P.M.
COST: $3

On the northern edge of Mexico City, in the state of Mexico suburb Tlalnepantla, stands a pre-Aztec pyramid known as Tenayuca. Two parallel stairways climb the large, wide base and lead to temples on top. The site was occupied since at least the 11th century, and six structures were raised here, each built over the other at 52-year intervals. Studies of the ruins indicate that the site was occupied by Teotihuacáns at one point in time. The nicely landscaped grounds have a small museum.

To get to Tenayuca, go to the Metro La Raza station, then switch to a *pesero* marked Pirámide.

PIRÁMIDE SANTA CECILIA ACATITLÁN

Callejón del Tepozteco Santa Cecilia Acatitlán
HOURS: Tues.-Sun. 10 A.M.-4:45 P.M.
COST: $3

A little farther north of Tenayuca in a *colonia* known as Santa Cecilia is the more interesting, but less visited, pyramid of Acatitlán. In the Náhuatl language, Acatitlán means "place between the reeds," no doubt in reference to a time when the environs of Mexico City were much wetter. This archaeological site dates to the late postclassic period (A.D. 1300–1521) and is thought to have been a ceremonial center where Tlaloc and Huitzilopochtli, the Mesoamerican gods of rain and war/sun, respectively, were worshipped. The adjacent Parroquia de Santa Cecilia bears a large number of stones taken from the pyramid's base; with the arrival of the Spanish, Amerindian temples were usually ransacked, and the materials were used for building Spanish churches and colonial houses.

The temple that tops the small, steeply sloped pyramid is one of the only intact pyramid temples in Mexico and is considered the most authentically restored. The first archaeological exploration of this site was carried out in 1923, and in 1961, archaeologist Eduardo Pareyón restored the pyramid's foundation. The work of this Mexican researcher has special merit, because he reconstructed the upper temple that crowns the foundation after carrying out extensive research on the codices and archaeological materials (such as clay scale models) available. You can climb the steep steps to the top and walk inside the temple to see how these rooms were constructed, with wooden roofs, panels with embedded nails, an entrance with a wooden lintel, a bench, and a mezzanine or loft inside. On the outside, the temple is flanked by ceremonial arms. The entrance displays a carved sacrificial stone.

INAH-sponsored plaques on the grounds chronicle the history and architecture of Acatitlán in Spanish, English, and Náhuatl. Near the entrance to the grounds, the **Museo de la Escultura** contains sculpture from the late postclassic period. Many of the carved stone figures on display represent flora and fauna, which no doubt had a direct relation to the Mesoamericans' daily lives. Anthropomorphic art in the museum tends toward the gruesome; a large stone receptacle, for example, is decorated in relief with various elements and symbols of human sacrifice— hearts and severed arms, hands, and ears, which no doubt went into the stone bowl as offerings to Aztec gods. The museum building itself is a former Porfiriato home made of simple stone block and brick. A few rooms have been set aside to exhibit rustic antique furniture of the era, representing how the more common people lived.

To get there from Tenayuca, either hop a taxi or get on a bus heading north along the Tenayuca–Santa Cecilia road, and ask the driver where to get off.

SOUTHERN MEXICO CITY
CERRO DE LA ESTRELLA

Off Calzada Ermita-Iztapalapa, via Av. Rojo Gomez
HOURS: None
COST: Free
METRO: Cerro de la Estrella

In the midst of Iztapalapa, a sprawling and dirty region in the southeastern part of the capital, a conical volcano rises up from the valley floor. This was the ancient sacred site where the Aztecs performed the New Flame ceremony that marked the beginning of each 52-year cycle in their calendar. Nowadays the mountain, which is technically protected as a national park, is the location of Mexico's biggest annual Passion Play, an elaborate reenactment of Jesus's crucifixion every Easter. The event attracts literally hundreds of thousands of people from across Mexico and the globe—quite a chaotic scene. If you go see it, take good care to watch out for pickpockets, as they are rife in the crowds.

Since 2004, archaeologists have been working at the top of the mountain, slowly uncovering the remains of an ancient pyramid long predating the Aztecs. The pyramid, which is only partially uncovered out of respect for the Holy Week ceremony which takes place on the site, appears to measure roughly 500 feet on each side and 60 feet high. Archaeologists estimate that it was built around A.D. 500, and was abandoned 300 years later, leading them to believe it was linked to the huge city at Teotihuacán northeast of Mexico City, which was abandoned at about the same time.

For most of the year Cerro de la Estrella is a quiet, somewhat unkempt park with lots of graffiti but with superlative views out across the eastern and southern parts of the valley and of the surrounding volcanos. The entrance road goes part of the way up the hill to a parking lot and small, not very interesting museum, and from there, it's another 30 minutes' walk up to the top. The path passes through groves of eucalyptus trees, along with a whole lot of exercise equipment improvised out of tree trunks and similar materials used by local low-budget health enthusiasts. On top are the remains of a reconstructed Aztec pyramid and a white cross. It's best to go on weekends, when there are lots of people around. The nearest Metro stop is Cerro de la Estrella, and from there it takes about 20 minutes to walk to the museum and parking lot. If you're driving, look for the entrance off of Eje 8 Sur Calzada Iztapalapa.

CUICUILCO

Just south of the intersection of Insurgentes and Periférico Sur, 55/5606-9758
HOURS: Mon.-Sat. 9 A.M.–5 P.M.
COST: $2.50
METRO: Insurgentes Metrobús

Only a few round ruins remain to be seen of the structures at Cuicuilco that once housed a settlement of 20,000. The city was built in approximately 600 B.C. and the ceremonial center was active 600–200 B.C. The main "pyramid" (actually a rare circular-shaped platform) measures 118 meters in diameter and 18 meters tall and was topped with a ceremonial altar. Volcán Xitle, which looms to the south, buried the base of the pyramid, along with the rest of the ceremonial center, with lava. Much of the lava has been removed, making it possible to see the construction of the pyramid. Excavations continue around the base of the pyramid.

Take a look at the small museum nearby for information about the people and a few artifacts found at the site, along with descriptive paintings. Note the image of the fierce fire and volcano god. Guided visits (in Spanish) are available Monday–Friday 9 A.M.–1 P.M. There's no Metro stop nearby, but it's easy to get here from the Universidad station—take a bus marked Cuicuilco traveling south on Insurgentes. The Insurgentes Metrobús was being extended from UNAM to Copilco, and should be operational by the time this book is in stores.

TLALPAN

Betw. Insurgentes Sur, Viaducto Tlalpan, and Av. San Fernando
HOURS: None
COST: Free

For a taste of what Coyoacán and San Ángel might have looked like in decades past, consider taking a trip down to the old center of Tlalpan. It's a bit off the beaten path—hard to find amidst a maze of streets located just south of the Periférico highway, not far from where the Cuernavaca highway comes into the city—and there's not much in the way of sights per se. But those who make the trip will enjoy the odd feeling of being in a small colonial town (which is of course what Tlalpan was until not too long ago) hidden away in the middle of Mexico City. There are a couple of restaurants right around the plaza with well-prepared meals, offering a convenient excuse to make the trip. Tlalpan is also a particularly relaxed place to come during the September 15 Independence Day celebration, which is a mob scene in the Centro.

The epicenter of Tlalpan is the **Plaza de la Constitución,** an especially lovely square; it's not very big but is filled with tall trees, creating a verdant canopy. A kiosk punctuates the middle, with benches on all sides invariably filled with locals passing the day in this time-honored Mexican fashion. On the east side of the plaza is the **Iglesia de San Agustín de las Cuevas,** surrounded by well-kept gardens and lawn. On the south side of the square is the grey stone neoclassical municipal building, with the front wall under the archways covered by historical murals. Behind the municipal building, in the same block, is the **Mercado de la Paz,** a large, airy market built in the old style: fun to wander around and also good for low-priced food if you're on a budget. Far better though, if you can afford it, is to sit down and eat in style at either the Argentine steak house **1900** on the north side of the plaza, or at **La Jaliscience,** a traditional cantina with very well-cooked Mexican classics (see the *Restaurants* chapter for more details).

Without your own car, the easiest way to get to Tlalpan is by taxi, which can take anywhere from 30 minutes to two hours (but usually a bit under an hour) from the central part of the city, depending on traffic. By public transport, catch a *pesero* from either Izazaga or Tasqueña metro stops. Look for buses with signs in the front window that say Centro de Tlalpan.

XOCHIMILCO

According to the Códice Ramírez, Xochimilco ("place where flowers grow") was originally founded on an island in Lago de Xochimilco in A.D. 919 by a Náhuatl-speaking tribe that called themselves Xochimilcas. Semi-independent of the Aztecs, they fought many wars with neighboring tribes before the Spanish conquest. Today, the central *colonia* of Xochimilco serves as a living museum for pre-Hispanic Mexico City, conserving

the ancient canals and *chinampas* (floating gardens) of a long-lost lifestyle. Hiring a boat to cruise the canals and have a floating party is a favorite weekend pastime for Mexico City residents.

Downtown Xochimilco is a bustling area centered around a colonial-era square, and well worth walking around to get a flavor of this working-class part of the city. You'll find a big market (Mercado Xóchitl) and many streets lined with vendors hawking all manner of goods. Because it's so far from downtown, Xochimilco is not frequented by foreign tourists. Expect at least an hour each way between Xochimilco and central Mexico City—transport is lengthy and slow, either by rail or by car.

For a local culinary treat, try a *tlapique,* a very large tamale (steamed corn dough) stuffed with fish, chicken, nopal cactus, *chile de árbol,* and the Mexican herb epazote. You can find stands selling them at the boat docks.

Xochimilco has a **tourist office** just off the main plaza (Calle Pino, 55/5676-0810 or 55/5676-8879, daily 9 A.M.–8 P.M.); some English is spoken. There's also a tourist booth at the Nativitas Embarcadero (55/5653-5209).

Xochimilco is 24 kilometers southeast of the Zócalo. Take Metro Línea 2 as far as Tasqueña, then board the Tren Ligero (light train, or streetcar) to the Xochimilco station (20–30 minutes). If you're driving, avoid Sunday, when traffic in Xochimilco can be very heavy. In fact traffic getting in and out of Xochimilco can be terrible any day, so the Tren Ligero is the best bet.

◖ CANALS

Docks are along Calle Violeta
HOURS: Boats usually run daily 8 A.M.-8 P.M.
COST: $14 per hour for a 12-person boat; $16 per hour for an 18-person boat
METRO: Xochimilco light rail station

The Xochimilco canals are a popular spot for locals and visitors alike to rent colorful *trajineras turísticas,* drinking and picnicking onboard for an afternoon while the boatmen propel the craft down the canals with a long pole. Although prices are posted and are the same for each boat, it is sometimes possible to negotiate cheaper rates, especially during the week. Each of these boats has a name—usually a woman's name, such as Lupita or Julieta—so if you have a favorite it's easy to find the same boat and boatman on subsequent visits. An hour's rental is the minimum, but it's better to spend two or three hours to get farther out into the canals, see more, and have a more relaxing time. Be sure to confirm the price *before* you board. Also, give the boat a look; some are nicer than others.

Several embarcaderos (docks) are located close to the center of town and the Tren Ligero station, including Caltonga, Salitre, Belem, and others, located along Calle Violeta. Further away is Embarcadero Nativitas, reached either by walking for 30 minutes or so, taking a short taxi ride, or hopping on any bus driving along Calle Violeta. Ask the bus driver to let you off close to Nativitas (two blocks' walk from the bus stop).

Food service is available on all the boats for around $2–3 per dish. Of course it wouldn't be Mexico without live music—musicians float by on their own boats, and, like the price of boat hire, the rates are regulated and publicly posted: A mariachi number costs $7 (a bargain compared to Plaza Garibaldi), a *norteña* song is $5, marimba $3, and *salterio* (Mexican zither) or *acordeón* $3.

Most visitors see only a small portion of the 189 kilometers of canals comprising Xochimilco, usually amidst a number of other party boats full of revelers. But in the farther reaches of the canals reside at least 150 species of endemic birds and another 70-odd migratory species that dally here in the winter months. The birds can be best seen on some of the quieter canals, where mariachi and radio music is prohibited to leave the birds (and a few humans!) in peace to enjoy the pastoral surroundings. During the week, it's almost empty, so visit then if you want a peaceful ride. On the other hand, if you want to see how the Mexicans most enjoy Xochimilco, the weekend would be the time to go.

PARROQUIA DE SAN BERNARDINO DE SIENA

Violeta at Pino

HOURS: Daily 10 A.M.–1 P.M. and 4–8 P.M.

COST: Free

METRO: Xochimilco light rail station

In the center of town, not far from the main docks, rises this enormous parish church, founded by Franciscans in 1535 and inaugurated in 1590. The strong, stable architectural style has been described as "military monastic," with plain buttressed walls and ornate *portadas* (doorways). Exterior decoration mixes Greco-Roman, Gothic, and native motifs, while the interior of the attached convent shows Moorish influences. Inside, the principal *retablo* and 12 side *retablos* are authentic late 16th-century jewels of art.

COURTESY OF CONSEJO DE PROMOCIÓN TURÍSTICA DE MÉXICO/CARLOS SÁNCHEZ

In Xochimilco, live mariachi bands float by on their own boats, playing song requests for tourists.

AZTEC HYDROPONICS

Long before the Spanish arrived in Mexico, the Xochimilcas had developed an imaginative solution to the difficulties of farming in the Valle de México. As the low-lying lake water could not easily be directed to the higher land on the islands and shoreline of Lago de Xochimilco, the Aztecs brought the soil to the lake and – assembling reeds, tree limbs, and soil – built the floating islands (the word *chinampa* means "terrain fenced by sticks"), on which they planted their crops. The bottom soil proved to be extremely fertile, yielding two or three harvests a year, and as more *chinampas* were created, the lake was broken into a series of canals. Early European visitors often referred to Xochimilco as "the Venice of Mexico," although the setting is far more rural and agricultural than Venice.

The Spaniards spared Xochimilco after the conquest because the area produced much of the city's food. Vegetables and flowers continue to grow on the *chinampas* today, and floriculture is the region's principle source of income. **Mercado Xóchitl** in the center of town, **Mercado de Plantas Madreselva** in the south of town, and **Mercado de Flores, Plantas y Hortilizas** next to the Parque Ecológico are the main plant markets. Native flora can be seen along the banks of the canals, including bulrushes, pepper trees, camphor, *jarilla*, *toloache*, and Mexican poppy.

Of the estimated 40,000 *chinampas* found in Xochimilco at the beginning of the 18th century, only 15,000 were left when the 20th century began. Canoe vendors began serving snacks to weekend visitors around 1920, followed quickly by the first restaurants on the embarcaderos. Around this same time, traditional *trajineras*, poled barges used for transporting local cargo along the canals, were transformed into tour boats by the addition of seats, tables, tarp roofs, and flower-festooned facades (nowadays heavily painted, wired-together bunches of bulrushes). In 1987 UNESCO named Xochimilco a World Heritage Site to publicize its cultural importance. However, UNESCO has threatened to rescind the designation because of constant urban encroachment. In part because of UNESCO's prodding, the city government announced plans in 2005 to invest $17 million in restoring natural areas, but time will tell how effectively the resources are used.

PARQUE ECOLÓGICO DE XOCHIMILCO (PEX)

Periférico Sur at Canal de Cuemanco
HOURS: Tues.-Sun. 9 A.M.-6 P.M. in summer;
Tues.-Sun. 10 A.M.-4 P.M. in winter
COST: $3 adults, $1 over age 60, $0.50 under age 12
METRO: Xochimilco light rail station, then by taxi

This educational/recreational park got its start in 1989 as part of the Ecological Rescue Plan for Xochimilco, an ambitious strategy to include water reclamation, agricultural reactivation, and historical and archaeological studies—all based on the traditional *chinampero* systems.

PEX covers about 300 hectares distributed into three areas, including the 13-hectare Mercado de Flores, Plantas y Hortilizas—reportedly the largest horticultural market in Latin America and the third-largest in the world. A second part, the 67-hectare Deportivo Ecológico Cuemanco, is dedicated to water sports, leaving the 189-hectare Parque Ecológico de Xochimilco, or PEX.

About a quarter of the PEX consists of lakes, *ciénegas* (underground springs), and canals. Wide gravel and asphalt walking paths wind through the park, making this a great place to get some exercise and relatively fresh air. One path leads through the flower-lined Paseo de las Flores. In addition to viewing natural and cultivated flora, visitors have a good chance of spotting herons, cormorants, egrets, ducks, and other waterfowl.

If you don't want to walk, a truck-pulled

"train" takes visitors around the park frequently throughout the day. *Trajineras* are available on weekends. Guards patrol the park, and it seems to be a very safe place to get out for some exercise.

The best way to get to the park, located a couple of kilometers from downtown Xochimilco (too far to walk), is to take a taxi. The entrance is found by taking Avenida División del Norte to the Glorieta de Vaqueritos traffic circle, then turning onto the side road (not the main highway) of the Periférico ring highway, and looking for signs. The park entrance has a colorful painted arch similar to those decorating the canal boats.

RESTAURANTS

Coming to Mexico City for the sole purpose of dining your time away here, with maybe a little sightseeing in between meals, is a perfectly legitimate excuse for a trip. The variety of different cuisines available in D.F. is astounding, from the perfect hole-in-the-wall taco joint with the flaming habanero sauce where you can stuff yourself and wash it all down with an ice-cold beer for $3, to Asian-Mexican fusion dishes like shrimp with wasabi and tequila sauce served in a sleek glassed-in dining room surrounded by Mexico City power brokers. Traditional cuisine from every region in Mexico abounds in D.F., such as *cochinita pibil* (tender pork dish) from the Yucatán, moles from Oaxaca and Puebla, and seafood Veracruz or Mazatlán style, flown in fresh daily from the coast. There are Spanish tapas bars, world-class French cuisine, sushi restaurants, and Argentine steak houses that seem to open every week.

The quality and number of higher-end Mexican and international restaurants in Mexico City has been increasing dramatically. These sorts of places were so rare until 20 years ago that they could survive with mediocre, expensive food and snooty waiters. No longer. The growing number of Mexicans with enough disposable income to dine out regularly has led to a proliferation of restaurants catering to their clients' more international tastes and openness to seeing traditional Mexican food reinvented in unexpected ways.

The Condesa district, not far south of Paseo de la Reforma, was the epicenter of this culinary renaissance starting in the early 1990s,

COURTESY OF CONSEJO DE PROMOCIÓN TURÍSTICA DE MÉXICO/INDUSTRIA 3

HIGHLIGHTS

LOOK FOR [TO FIND
RECOMMENDED RESTAURANTS.

[**Best Cantina:** A tough choice in this city of endless cantinas, but for a superlative combination of atmosphere and food, you can't go wrong with **Bar La Ópera** in the Centro. Where else can you sit in cozy, dark wooden booths, eat a steaming seafood paella, and listen to a pair of strumming guitarists – in the same room where Pancho Villa left a bullet in the ceiling (page 84)?

[**Best Sugar Fix:** For Mexico's tastiest sweet treat, head directly to the legendary **Churrería El Moro** in the Centro to feast on these addictive pastries dunked in hot chocolate (page 84).

[**Best Traditional Mexican:** An impossible choice, but **El Cardenal** in the heart of the Centro is a great place to start. Try their famed *chiles en nogada*, or the beef in chipotle sauce (page 87).

[**Best Hangover Helper:** A little too much tequila last night? Proceed directly to **La Polar**, a cantina where you can wolf down a steaming bowl of *birria* (a hearty meat stew) along with a bunch of other bleary-eyed folks on weekends (page 93).

[**Best Caffeine Fix:** For a bit of tradition with your java, head to **La Habana.** The bare tables are always filled with journalists and literary types poring over newspapers with cigarettes and coffee underneath huge 1950s-era photos of Havana, Cuba. If you really want a jolt, try the wickedly strong *café campechano* (page 93).

[**Best Colonial Atmosphere:** A perennial favorite for tourists and Mexicans alike, **Hacienda de los Morales** is a mansion built in the 16th century on farmland now in the middle of the Polanco district. The dining rooms are set around lovely patios and gardens, and the Mexican cuisine is excellent – try the succulent *cabrito*, kid goat (page 97).

[**Best Place to Eat-and-Be-Seen:** Really anywhere in the center of the uber-hip Condesa restaurant district will do, but **Garufa** is one of the best. Grab a sidewalk table to watch the crowds of beautiful people while you savor a creative pasta dish (page 101).

[**Best *Comida Corrida*:** You'll find little eateries serving inexpensive lunchtime set meals in all corners of the city, but one particularly good spot to try out this Mexican standby is **La Tecla,** a low-priced but high-quality restaurant in the Roma near the Zona Rosa (page 105).

[**Best Seafood:** About the finest seafood in the city is served at **Contramar,** a high-end restaurant in the Roma open for lunch only. The deep-fried shrimp tacos make a great starter, and for a main course try the juicy *filete contramar*, a fish fillet served on a wooden platter with four different sauces (page 106).

[**Best Taco Joint:** Choosing one taco joint out of the thousands in Mexico City is a cruel task, but you could definitely do worse than **El Tizoncito.** Grab a stool and order a few *tacos al pastor* carved off a spit and topped with a slice of pineapple (page 106).

when cafés and restaurants gradually took over part of what had been a quiet residential neighborhood. But the Condesa is just the most concentrated; you'll find creative new restaurants in Polanco, Roma, the Centro, Coyoacán, San Ángel, and elsewhere.

The turnover is high in restaurants of all types and all price ranges, but that's because the demands of the clients are high too, as in New York or any other great dining city. If a restaurant—whether they serve humble *comidas corridas* (set meals) or inch-thick cuts of Argentine beef—has been around more than three years and it's still got a crowd during meal hours, it's bound to be good. It's an eater's market.

WHEN TO EAT

Capitalinos used to have two kinds of breakfasts, an early one, called *desayuno*, eaten shortly after rising, and a second, called *almuerzo,* that was usually taken about 11 A.M. Nowadays most people just have one breakfast, whenever they get up and go. The multicourse main meal of the day, *la comida* (although called *almuerzo* in many other parts of Latin America) is usually somewhere between 2 and 5 P.M. The *comida* is where Mexicans pack on most of the day's calories. The large afternoon *comida* will sustain most Mexicans till at least 8 P.M. or so, when it's time for *cena,* traditionally a light evening meal usually consisting of *pan dulce* (Mexican pastries) with tea or coffee. While the light evening meal is still eaten by many Mexicans, an increasing number have a heartier dinner, especially in Mexico City.

WHERE TO EAT

At the more humble end of the dining scale comes the venerable **puesto,** or street stand, most often located in areas where there's lots of foot traffic, like outside a Metro station. The most common *puesto* is of course the omnipresent taco stand, but those selling *tortas,* an inexpensive Mexican-style sandwich, are a close second.

Another economical choice is any **lonchería** or **comedor,** which are small, café-style places that usually serve *almuerzo* (late breakfast or early lunch) and *comida* (midday meal). Hours are typically 11 A.M.–5 P.M., and the staple is invariably an inexpensive *comida corrida* with some variety: a beverage, an entrée or two to choose between, side dishes, and dessert with coffee. Travelers often become completely hooked and find themselves becoming connoisseurs of the best *corrida* eateries in their vicinity.

Taquerías, logically enough, are simple sit-down eateries (sometimes with stools only) specializing in tacos. In Mexico City you can often spot a *taquería* by a spit of meat at the

PRICE KEY

$ Most entrées less than $5

$$ Most entrées between $5-15

$$$ Most entrées more than $15

entrance for making *tacos al pastor* (marinated pork), a local favorite.

More formal meals are available at **restaurantes,** which tend to serve *platos fuertes* (main dishes) rather than *antojitos* (snacks). Male, uniformed waiter service and the use of tablecloths often distinguish *restaurantes* from simpler venues.

One of the most convivial places for an evening meal in Mexico City is the **cantina.** Unlike in many other towns in Mexico, the cantinas of Mexico City often welcome both women and men. Food at cantinas can be very good and relatively inexpensive, and service is often exemplary. Some cantinas offer free *botanas* (snacks) when you order drinks for a couple of hours in the afternoon and (sometimes) early evening.

ORDERING AND PAYING

You really don't need that much Spanish to get by in a Mexican restaurant. Stating what you want, and adding *"por favor"* (please), will usually do the trick (e.g., *"dos cervezas, por favor"* (two beers, please). The menu is called *el menú* or *la carta.* As a last resort, you can always point to what you want on the menu.

La cuenta is the bill. A tip (*propina*) of 10–15 percent is expected at any restaurant with table service; look to see if it's already been added to the bill before placing it on the table. In small *comedores, fondas,* or *taquerías,* tips are not expected.

RESTAURANTS

Centro Histórico
Map 1

RESTAURANTS

Downtown Mexico City is crammed with restaurants of all types, with plenty of choices for travelers in all price ranges. The emphasis among almost all of the Centro eateries is Mexican (as opposed to international) cuisine in all its myriad variations, varying from some great hole-in-the-wall taco joints to veritable pageants of traditional Mexican dishes served in renovated colonial mansions.

CANTINAS

☾ BAR LA ÓPERA $$

Av. Cinco de Mayo 10, 55/5512-8959

HOURS: Mon.-Sat. 1-11:30 P.M., Sun. 1-5:30 P.M.

METRO: Bellas Artes

For a little history with your meal or cold *cerveza,* stop in this historic bar. The dark baroque cavern of a place has huge mirrored booths big enough to hold large parties of revelers (or conceal couples deep in the recesses). Musicians often play in the evenings. The menu is large and the food is good. Try the seafood paella or the *favada asturiana,* a hearty Spanish meat-and-bean dish. They also have a set menu of the day during the afternoon meal.

LA MASCOTA $$

Mesones 20

HOURS: Daily noon-11 P.M.

METRO: Isabel la Católica

This downtown cantina is well-lit and friendly, comfortable for foreigners and Mexicans alike. They serve *botanas,* snacks offered free with drinks during the late afternoon, or multicourse fixed meals. Most people come for the free *botanas,* usually a choice of seven different plates like meatballs in chipotle sauce or *carnitas.*

SALÓN CORONA $$

Bolívar 24, 55/5512-9007

HOURS: Daily 9 A.M.-11:30 P.M.

METRO: Allende

For a *torta* or shrimp cocktail, and a mug of cold beer to wash it down, drop into the Corona, a family restaurant/cantina in business since 1928. Large *tarros* (mugs) of draft Corona—light, dark, or mixed together (*campechana*)—cost $1.50. The *caldo de camarón* (shrimp stew) comes in a glass and is excellent. This is a very popular spot on Sunday afternoons, when many other downtown spots are closed, and anytime there's a soccer game on TV.

COFFEE AND SWEETS

CAFÉ EL PASSAJE $

Gante 6

HOURS: Mon.-Sat. 9 A.M.-9 P.M.

METRO: Bellas Artes

Just off Madero, this pleasant coffee shop serves espresso drinks and sweet treats. The tables, some set up on the pedestrian-only street and some inside, are a fine place to sip a cup and read one of the international or Mexican papers sold at the café. The name is from an adjacent shop-filled passageway through a building.

CAFÉ LA SELVA $

Bolívar 31

HOURS: Daily 8 A.M.-10 P.M.

METRO: Allende

This downtown branch of a well-known Mexican coffee chain serves a good, strong cup of java at its collection of small tables in the cool courtyard of a two-story colonial house.

☾ CHURRERÍA EL MORO $

Eje Central 42 betw. Uruguay and V. Carranza

HOURS: Daily 24 hours

METRO: San Juan Letrán

For a late-night treat, head for the 1935-vintage El Moro for some excellent churros, deep-fried sugary pastries meant to be dipped in hot chocolate before eating. Warning: Churros can be very addictive.

CHILANGO COOKING

Although most dishes commonly served in Mexico City have culinary origins outside the capital, a few have been claimed as the city's own. One common dish in this category is *barbacoa*, lamb that has been wrapped in *maguey* leaves and slowly pit-barbecued. Some restaurants serve *barbacoa* with a *salsa borracha*, a sauce made with chiles and *pulque* (fermented cactus sap).

Another *capitalino* dish is *budín azteca*, in which tortillas, chicken, puréed tomatillos, roasted chiles, cheese, and various seasonings are baked in a *cazuela*, or earthenware bowl – basically a casserole version of *chilaquiles*. Economic necessity in the infamous market ghetto of Tepito gave birth to *migas*, literally "crumbs," made by frying broken pieces of dried tortilla with eggs, onions, chiles, and whatever else is available.

Caldo tlalpeño, originally from the village of Tlalpan, now a suburb of southern Mexico City, is a very popular soup made by stewing chicken in a broth flavored with chipotles (smoked jalapeños) and served with garnishes of cilantro and avocado. This smoky-flavored *caldo* has become a menu standard throughout Mexico.

Street vendors sell a wide variety of foods that originated in the Mexican countryside but which have taken on their own Mexico City style. *Tacos al pastor*, made with layers of meat marinated in orange-red *adobo* sauce and cooked on a vertical spit, have become so ubiquitous in the capital that *al pastor* is now considered a D.F. specialty. On many street corners in the Centro, you'll also see steel washtubs filled with steaming tamales that tend to be larger than those you might encounter in Mexican villages. Served with a hot cup of *atole* – a drink made with cornmeal – a Mexico City tamal makes a filling breakfast for only around $0.70. Other common street foods, especially in the Centro, include *huaraches* and *sopes*, which are both types of a thicker tortilla covered with beans, cheese, and often some type of meat topping.

PASTELERÍA IDEAL $

West of Eje Central on the north side of República de Uruguay
HOURS: Daily 7 A.M.–8 P.M.
METRO: San Juan Letrán

Founded in 1927, the original Ideal may be the ultimate Mexican bakery. It's worth a visit just to see the marvelous cakes on display and the seemingly endless variety of *pan dulce*. Right next door is the similar Pastelería El Globo.

PANADERÍA Y PASTELERÍA VASCONIA $

Tacuba at Palma
HOURS: Daily 7 A.M.–8 P.M.
METRO: Allende

It's hard to miss this huge bakery a couple of blocks from the Zócalo. Pick up a tray and tongs and serve yourself, then sit down and have some coffee at one of the tables inside. Try the *oreja* (ear), a spiral-shaped crunchy and sugary pastry.

MEXICAN

BEST WESTERN HOTEL MAJESTIC $$

Madero 73 at Monte de Piedad, 55/5521-8600
HOURS: Daily 8 A.M.–11 P.M.
METRO: Zócalo

Umbrella-shaded tables at this rooftop hotel restaurant look out over the Zócalo, affording good views of the Catedral, Sagrario, Palacio Nacional, and the twice-daily flag ceremonies in the center of the plaza. Prices are moderate, considering the view, and the food is quite respectable if not the most exciting in the capital (the real attraction is the view). The *pollo almendrado* (chicken baked in a tasty almond sauce) and *crema de queso Sonora* (a rich Sonoran cheese soup) are both hearty and good. If you're just dropping by for dessert, try the *crepas de cajeta al tequila* (crepes in a goat-milk caramel and tequila sauce).

© CHRIS HUMPHREY

trays of fresh sweet bread at a downtown panadería

BISQUETS OBREGÓN 🟢🟢
Madero 29
HOURS: Daily 7:30 A.M.–10 P.M.
METRO: Zócalo

Bisquets Obregón is a favorite example of the gradually disappearing *bisquet* restaurant or *café chino*—operated by Chinese families and once popular in the 1940s and 1950s in Mexico City. This one is a branch of the famous diner in the Roma neighborhood. On weekends there's often a line for tables, a testament to the reliable, reasonably priced meals. Breakfasts are a particular favorite. The coffee is served Veracruz-style, with a waiter filling your cup with coffee to the desired level, then topping it off with warm milk.

CAFÉ EL POPULAR 🟢🟢
Cinco de Mayo 10
HOURS: Daily 8 A.M.–1 A.M.
METRO: Bellas Artes

El Popular is another old *bisquet* café, with an unspectacular but reliable menu. The branch of El Popular near the Zócalo (Cinco de Mayo 50, open 24 hours daily) is smaller and has more character, though you may have to wait briefly by the cash register for an open table.

CAFÉ LA BLANCA 🟢
Cinco de Mayo 40
HOURS: Daily 7 A.M.–11 P.M.
METRO: Allende

The simple tables and Formica counter at this 1930s-vintage café are always filled with men poring over newspapers while sipping coffee. The reliable though unexceptional menu focuses on Mexican specialties at very reasonable prices (one of the main attractions). Breakfasts are a good deal here. Lithographs on the walls depict Mexico City of yesteryear.

CAFÉ TACUBA 🟢🟢
Tacuba 28, 55/5521-2048
HOURS: Daily 8 A.M.–11 P.M.
METRO: Allende

Set in a converted 17th-century colonial mansion, this popular restaurant has been in operation since 1912. It's so well-known there's even a famous Mexican rock band named in its honor. The restaurant seems to be resting on its laurels a bit (I've heard a couple of poor reviews), but it generally still serves well-prepared traditional Mexican meals amid historic ambience. One good choice, *cuatro cositas* (four little things), comes with a large, moist, and tasty tamal filled with cheese and fresh *epazote,* an *enchilada Tacuba* (chicken rolled up in a corn tortilla bathed in a house sauce), rice, beans, and guacamole. Be prepared to wait for your meal as the service can be terrible.

COOX HANAL 🟢
Isabel la Católica 83, 55/5709-3613
HOURS: Daily 9 A.M.–5 P.M.
METRO: Isabel la Católica

If you'd like to try *comida yucateca* (food from the Yucatán region), head over to this breakfast and lunch joint always bustling with locals gobbling down inexpensive specialties such as *sopa de lima* (lemon soup), *panuchos* (fried tortilla filled with beans and topped with chicken and onions), or *papadzules* (tortilla with eggs and tomato sauce). It's invariably packed around the 3 P.M. lunch rush.

🄲 EL CARDENAL 🌑🌑

Palma 23, 55/5521-8815, www.elcardenal.com.mx
HOURS: Mon.-Sat. 8 A.M.-7 P.M., Sun. 9 A.M.-6 P.M.
METRO: Zócalo

The Cardenal is a longtime Mexico City classic, serving traditional Mexican meals such as sea bass in barbecue sauce or beef tips in chipotle sauce, as well as a number of seasonal specialties like *chiles en nogada* (chiles stuffed with a mix of shredded beef, raisins, olives, and almonds, bathed in a cream and nut sauce, available Aug.–Sept.) and *bacalao* (Cod fish, avail. Nov.–Dec.) at very reasonable prices, considering the quality. The restaurant has three floors of quietly elegant dining rooms.

FONDA DE DON CHON 🌑🌑

Regina 160, 55/5542-0873
HOURS: Mon.-Sat. noon-6 P.M.
METRO: Merced

Culinary adventure-seekers after a taste of exotic pre-Hispanic cuisine, including *gusanos de maguey* (cactus worms), *venado con huitlacoche* (deer meat with corn fungus), and other Aztec delicacies, should not miss a trip to this famed eatery southeast of the Zócalo. Even Mexican presidents and other politicos stop by once in a while, to prove they are "down with the people." The surrounding neighborhood is a bustling commercial neighborhood and rather run-down, so watch your step heading over this way.

HOSTERÍA SANTO DOMINGO 🌑🌑

Belisario Dominguez 72, 55/5510-1434
HOURS: Daily 9 A.M.-10 P.M.
METRO: Allende

How many restaurants can you go to that have been in operation for 150 years? The Santo Domingo, located just off the plaza of the same name, has been serving classic Mexican dishes since 1860. The *chiles en nogada* are considered by some to be the best in the city, and the *mole poblano* is also legendary. Some have complained about uneven food quality, but it still attracts a steady clientele. Musicians frequently

serenade diners. On weekends expect a long wait for a table, particularly during the middle of the afternoon.

LA CASA DE LAS SIRENAS 🌑🌑🌑

Av. República de Guatemala 32, 55/5704-3345
or 55/5704-3225
HOURS: Mon.-Sat. 11 A.M.-11 P.M., Sun. 11 A.M.-7 P.M.
METRO: Zócalo

La Casa de las Sirenas makes an excellent choice for a relaxing (though not cheap) midday meal while sightseeing. The restaurant, located behind the Catedral, serves well-prepared Mexican classics such as *mole poblano, chiles en nogada,* and *pozole.* It's on the 2nd and 3rd floors of a colonial-era mansion; the 2nd-floor patio is favored by Mexico City politicians who work in the Centro and are fond of taking their power lunches here. They have an excellent tequila selection also, if you are in need of a digestif after your meal.

LOS GIRASOLES 🌑🌑🌑

Tacuba 8 at Calle Xicotencatl, 55/5510-3281
HOURS: Tues.-Sat. 1 P.M.-midnight, Sun.-Mon. 1-9 P.M.
METRO: Allende

Another "power lunch" favorite is a formal restaurant frequented by senators and their staff from the federal Senate next door. The menu offers some interesting *nueva cocina* specialties, such as *tacos de pato* (duck tacos) and trout cooked in *mezcal* sauce, as well as Mexican classics like *mole poblano, chiles en nogada,* and *escamoles* (this last a rather unusual Mexican specialty: ant eggs).

MEXICO VIEJO 🌑🌑

Tacuba 87, 55/5510-3748
HOURS: Mon.-Sat. 8 A.M.-9 P.M., Sun. 8 A.M.-6 P.M.
METRO: Zócalo

This is a popular restaurant for tourists visiting downtown, and although it may not be the most traditional restaurant in the Centro, it covers the bases adequately and has a spacious, peaceful dining room in an old building on the northwest corner of the Zócalo. The extensive menu (available in English) offers specialties such as *crepas huitlacoche* and *chilaquiles con*

the original Sanborns cafeteria inside the Casa de los Azulejos in the Centro

© CHRIS HUMPHREY

pollo. It also has a reasonably priced *comida del día* (meal of the day), and good breakfasts.

SANBORNS $$

Av. Madero 4, 55/5512-9820
HOURS: Daily 7 A.M.–11 P.M.
METRO: Bellas Artes

While most Sanborns locations feel somewhat like a Mexican-style Denny's, the historic original restaurant on Madero is an exception. Set in the two-story courtyard of the Casa de los Azulejos, a 16th-century palace covered in blue tiles, the spacious restaurant is always packed with businessmen, politicians, tourists, and others. The Mexican menu is unexceptional but hygienic and reasonably priced.

MIDDLE EASTERN
AL ANDALUZ $$

Mesones 171, betw. Las Cruces and Jesús María,
55/5522-2528
HOURS: Daily 9 A.M.–6 P.M.
METRO: Pino Suárez

Al Andaluz is considered by some to have the best Middle Eastern food in the city, but it's tucked into a busy, scruffy commercial district about seven blocks southeast of the Zócalo. The restaurant, which caters principally to the Arab community that dominates much of the neighborhood textile trade, is hidden in a cozy, renovated two-story colonial house, an oasis from the surrounding streets. Specialties include baba ghanoush, *shwarma,* hummus, and *kepa bola* (this last a mix of wheat, ground beef, and onion). Top off your meal with a cup of strong Arab coffee. Prices are very reasonable and the quality is excellent. Because of the location, Al Andaluz is not frequented by tourists, and visitors will have the feel that they've happened upon a secret hideaway not meant for outsiders, but not unfriendly to them either. All in all an unusual but worthwhile experience.

EL EHDEN $$

Venustiano Carranza 148, 2nd fl.
HOURS: Daily 1–6 P.M.
METRO: Zócalo

This restaurant, run by a Lebanese woman and her Mexican husband, first opened three blocks southeast of the Zócalo and now has a second branch (at Gante 11) on a quiet pedestrian street near the Eje Central. They serve a wide selection of Middle Eastern dishes, including stuffed grape leaves, hummus, falafel, baba ghanoush, tabouli, and more. Prices are reasonable

© ELENA PAPPAS

fresh pineapple for sale in front of the Sagrario, on the Zócalo

early-20th-century building. Open only for lunch, the Casino's restaurant serves an excellent Spanish-style *comida del día* with five dishes, as well as a selection of specialties from the menu. The Casino is particularly popular on weekends.

TACOS, *TORTAS*, AND SNACKS
EL REY DEL PAVO ⑤
Palma 32
HOURS: Mon.-Sat. 11 A.M.-6:30 P.M.
METRO: Zócalo
Turkey lovers should stop in for a bite at the "King of Turkey," where you can get a full meal for $3–4, or tasty turkey *tortas* topped with guacamole for $1.40 each in a funky but clean cafeteria-style restaurant.

GILI POLLOS ⑤
Corner of Cinco de Mayo and Isabel la Católica
HOURS: Daily noon-8 P.M.
METRO: Allende
This modest corner eatery offers delicious and inexpensive roast chickens and chicken tacos, with stools for the clients. Those familiar with Iberian Spanish slang will catch the off-color pun in the name.

LONCHERÍA VASCONIA ⑤
Corner of Tacuba and Palma
HOURS: Mon.-Sat. 7:30 A.M.-9 P.M., Sun. 7:30 A.M.-8 P.M.
METRO: Zócalo
This small cafeteria, attached to the bakery of the same name, serves *tacos al pastor* and roast chicken; it's a good place for a quick, inexpensive bite to eat.

TACO INN ⑤⑤
Tacuba 10
HOURS: Daily 8 A.M.-11 P.M.
METRO: Allende
This somewhat fast-food-style taco restaurant, at the east end of Plaza Manuel Tolsá near the Museo Nacional de Arte, serves tacos and other *antojitos* at slightly higher-than-normal prices (for tacos). Perhaps they're not the most traditional tacos, but they are tasty and hygienic.

in both branches, but the Venustiano Carranza one is a bit cheaper.

SEAFOOD
EL DANUBIO ⑤⑤
Uruguay 3, just off Eje Central, 55/5512-0912
HOURS: Daily 1-10 P.M.
METRO: San Juan Letrán
This refined spot is the place to go for top-quality seafood downtown at mid-range prices. In past years it had a good claim to the best seafood in the city, and though others have since surpassed it, the Danubio is still reliable. The weekday multicourse *comida corrida* (served 2–6 P.M. only) is a solid value at $14.

SPANISH
CASINO ESPAÑOL ⑤⑤
Isabel la Católica 31, 55/5521-8894
HOURS: Daily 1-6 P.M.
METRO: Allende
A gathering place for Spaniards living in Mexico, and lovers of Spanish food, the Casino Español is housed in a sumptuous

The steaming *café de olla,* served in ceramic mugs, is excellent.

VEGETARIAN
SUPER SOYA ⑤
16 de Septiembre 79
HOURS: Mon.-Sat. 9 A.M.-8 P.M., Sun. 9 A.M.-7 P.M.
METRO: Allende
This chain of health food stores/lunch counters, with three branches downtown (the other two locations are at Brasil 11 and Bolívar 31-A), serves vegetarian *tortas, comidas corridas,* and juices at low prices, and also sells a variety of vegetarian and health products.

VEGETARIANOS DEL CENTRO ⑤
Filomeno Mata 13 near Cinco de Mayo, 55/5510-0113
HOURS: Mon.-Sat. 8 A.M.-8 P.M., Sun. 9 A.M.-8 P.M.
METRO: Allende
Decent vegetarian meals can be found at this diner-like restaurant. A fixed vegetarian menu is served every day, or you can order dishes à la carte, including stuffed avocados, baked potatoes, and lots of egg dishes, all at low prices.

Alameda Central   Map 1

The neighborhoods around the Alameda are not particularly well-known for notable eateries, with a few exceptions noted here. Apart from these, budget travelers will find plenty of street *taco* and *torta* stands, as well as numerous *comida corrida* restaurants scattered around, catering to the working-class folk looking for low-priced lunches. One particularly good area to look for cheap eats is along Avenida Balderas and in the streets around Mercado San Juan, south of the Alameda.

CANTINAS
LA ÚNICA DE GUERRERO ⑤⑤
Guerrero 258 at Marte, 55/5526-6839
HOURS: Mon.-Sat. 10 A.M.-10 P.M., Sun. noon-8 P.M.
METRO: Hidalgo or Guerrero
Since 1933 "La U de G," as it is locally known, has preserved a legacy of culinary tradition that many other city cantinas aspire to. Popular with writers and intellectuals, the cantina dispenses good *caldo de camarón* (shrimp stew), as well as its trademark *cabrito al horno* (kid goat) and plenty of other cantina favorites besides, but no free *botanas.* Live *salterio* (Mexican zither) music is played from 3 P.M. onward, with an emphasis on sad *valses* (waltzes). To find it, go a block south of Avenida Ricardo Flores Magón on Guerrero, turn right (west) at Martes, and look for the cantina at the southwest corner of the intersection. Although the cantina itself is very safe, the surrounding Guerrero neighborhood is not, so its best to get a taxi there and ask the waiters to call one for you when it's time to go.

SALÓN LA VICTORIA ⑤⑤
Magnolia 3 at Eje Central Lázaro Cárdenas, 55/5526-3667
HOURS: Mon.-Sat. noon-11 P.M., Sun. noon-8 P.M.
METRO: Garibaldi
La Victoria, another traditional cantina a couple of blocks south of Plaza Garibaldi on the opposite side of the Eje Central, specializes in regional dishes from many parts of Mexico. It offers a choice of seven daily platters. Best to take a taxi from here when leaving as the neighborhood is not the best.

MARKETS
MERCADO SAN JUAN ⑤
Betw. Ayuntamiento and Pugibet
HOURS: Daily 7 A.M.-5 P.M.
METRO: San Juan Letrán
Those really pinching their pesos can choose from a variety of inexpensive *comidas corridas* served at simple lunch restaurants in this neighborhood market, which also has a good

selection of handicrafts for sale. The market four blocks south of the Alameda is well-known as selling some of the more exotic foods available in Mexico City, like obscure herbs and imported meats and cheeses.

MEXICAN
CAFÉ DEL PALACIO $$

At Av. Juárez and the Eje Central, inside Bellas Artes
HOURS: Daily 11 A.M.-7 P.M., or later during evening shows
METRO: Bellas Artes

The café inside Bellas Artes is a lovely place to relax after an afternoon of touring, either for a full meal or just a dessert and espresso. Despite the good quality and elegant ambience, prices are quite reasonable. A *menú* including an appetizer, main course (such as grilled red snapper or steak), salad, and drink costs $16. If you just want a snack, try a pâté, quiche, or *cazuelitas de salpicón* (a dish of beans, shredded beef, onion, potato, lettuce, olive oil, and vinegar).

EL CARDENAL $$

Hotel Sheraton, Alameda at Juárez 70, 55/5518-6632, www.elcardenal.com.mx
HOURS: Mon.-Sat. 8 A.M.-7 P.M., Sun. 9 A.M.-6 P.M.
METRO: Hidalgo

This classic Mexico City restaurant from the Centro has a branch in the lobby of the Sheraton, offering international visitors who don't wish to leave the plush confines of the hotel a chance to taste excellent traditional Mexican cuisine. The modern dining room doesn't quite have the same timeless atmosphere of the original restaurant on Calle Palma (see listing in *Centro Histórico* section), but the meals are equally good.

FONDA SANTA ANITA $$

Humboldt 48, 55/5518-4609
HOURS: Daily 1:30-6 P.M.
METRO: Hidalgo

Hidden away a couple of blocks southwest of the Alameda is this low-key traditional Mexican restaurant offering tasty home-cooked standards at inexpensive to moderate prices. The multicourse *comidas corridas* are an excellent value at $6 with a choice of entrée, served in a cheerfully decorated dining room. The Fonda is open for lunch only.

RESTAURANTS

Paseo de la Reforma and Zona Rosa   Map 2

Restaurants in the Zona Rosa and around Reforma are generally more upscale than in the Centro Histórico or Alameda Central, and prices are accordingly higher. Visitors can choose from several international cuisine styles as well as upscale Mexican fare. But those on a budget need not fear: Lower-priced meals can be found in the surrounding neighborhoods, particularly at the markets and in little *comida corrida* eateries. McDonald's, KFC, Starbucks, and other chains have outlets in the Zona Rosa for those desperate for a taste of Americana.

ARGENTINE
QUEBRACHO $$

Río Lerma 175, 55/5208-3999
HOURS: Daily 1-11 P.M.

Located on a pleasant block with several sidewalk cafés is this very good and reasonably priced Argentine restaurant popular with the middle-class crowd who work and live in the Cuauhtémoc neighborhood north of Reforma. The tender *arrachera* steak for $11 is a reliable choice, and try the cream-of-spinach side dish.

ASIAN
DAIKOKU $$

Río Pánuco 170 at Río Nilo, 55/5525-6520
HOURS: Daily 1-11 P.M.

If you're looking for Japanese cuisine, this spot

COOKING METHODS

Entrées, whether meat, poultry, or seafood, are most commonly prepared in one of the following styles:

adobo, adobada – marinated or stewed in a sauce of vinegar, chiles, and spices; often reddened by the addition of annatto seed extract

a la parrilla – broiled or grilled

a la veracruzana – seafood, often *huachinango* (red snapper), cooked with tomatoes, onions, chiles, and olives

albóndigas – meatballs

al carbón – charcoal-grilled

al mojo de ajo – in a garlic sauce

al pastor – slowly roasted on a vertical spit

al vapor – steamed

asado – grilled

barbacoa – pit-roasted

con arroz – with rice

empanizada – breaded

encebollado – cooked with onions

enpapelada – baked in parchment

frito – fried

guisado – in a spicy stew

horneado – baked

machacado – mashed or chopped up

rostizado – roasted

a couple of blocks north of Reforma is a reliable option. Japanese expats living in Mexico City say the sushi and sashimi is some of the best in the city.

LUAU'S ⓈⓈ

Niza 38, 55/5525-7474

HOURS: Mon.-Sat. noon-11 P.M., Sun. noon-6 P.M.

METRO: Insurgentes

This Zona Rosa restaurant serves decent Cantonese food amid an amusingly kitsch decor. House specialties include *cha siu* (barbecued pork) and the ever-popular *chow mein cantonés*. The hearty multicourse set meals are a good value.

SUSHI ITTO ⓈⓈ

Hamburgo 141, 55/5525-2635

HOURS: Daily 1-10:30 P.M.

METRO: Insurgentes

This fast-food-style restaurant whips up (very quickly) sushi of the mass-produced variety, but it's hygienic, and the miso soup is tasty. It's a decent place for a quick meal on the go, but don't have high expectations.

BASQUE

TEZKA ⓈⓈⓈ

Hotel Royal Zona, Amberes 78, 55/5228-9918, ext. 5067

HOURS: Mon.-Fri. 1:30-11 P.M., Sat. 1:30-6 P.M.

METRO: Insurgentes

For those who don't know, the Basque region in northwest Spain and southwest France is known for its fierce independent streak, unusual language, and top-notch food. Tezka is an upscale hotel restaurant specializing in Basque cuisine. Be prepared to drop a pretty penny here, but the quality is superb, with specialties such as venison ($25), lamb in coffee ($25), or a tasting menu for $40. The chef learned his trade in the legendary Basque food mecca, San Sebastián.

CANTINAS

BOHEMIO'S ⓈⓈ

Londres 142, 55/5514-0790

HOURS: Mon.-Sat. 1 P.M.-1 A.M.

METRO: Insurgentes

In the center of the Zona Rosa is this somewhat upscale cantina that stays entertaining and rowdy nonetheless, with live Mexican music and many pitchers of light and dark Kloster beer swinging among the crowded tables. The food is traditional Mexican and of good quality. Try the *tampiqueña*, a piece of tender beef served with guacamole, a couple of enchiladas, and other fixings, for $10.

CANTINA LATINO ⓈⓈ

Antonio Caso 17, 55/5564-0800

HOURS: Mon.-Fri. 11 A.M.-midnight, Sat. 11 A.M.-6 P.M.

METRO: Revolución

Behind the Hotel Meliá Reforma is a large bar/restaurant with high-backed wooden booths popular for business lunches. The menu has a heavy emphasis on meats, including *arrachera* steaks, *cabrito*, *chistorra* (a type of spicy sausage), and a selection of Spanish hams and sausages (no free *botanas* here). There is also a full bar.

◖ LA POLAR **$$**

Guillermo Prieto 129, at Circuito Interior, 55/5546-5066
HOURS: Daily 9 A.M.–midnight, until 2 A.M. Fri.
METRO: San Cosme

For very possibly the best *birria* in Mexico City, stop off at this classic old-style cantina in the San Rafael neighborhood. The several rooms are usually filled with crowds of Mexicans enjoying their legendary bowls of *birria*, a stew of shredded lamb in a spicy broth, served with tortillas, onion, salsa, and avocado. *Birria* is famed as a hangover cure, to which the bleary-eyed crowds on Saturday and Sunday around noon can attest. La Polar also has beer on tap, and entertainment is provided by roving *norteña* and mariachi bands. It also serves *birria* to go from a take-out window. It's best to come by taxi.

COFFEE AND SWEETS

◖ LA HABANA **$$**

Morelos 62, 55/5535-2620
HOURS: Mon.–Sat. 8 A.M.–midnight
METRO: Juárez

At the corner of Avenida Cuauhtémoc and Morelos, at the eastern edge of the Reforma area, is this venerable coffeehouse and restaurant, frequented by generations of journalists working in the surrounding blocks. La Habana is a wonderful spot to enjoy a strong cup of coffee at your leisure. Ground or whole-bean Veracruz coffee can be purchased to go. The restaurant also offers set menus for both breakfast and lunch. I'm a huge fan of the *huevos con machaca* (eggs with dried, shredded beef in a spicy sauce with flour tortillas on the side) for breakfast, but there are plenty of other options. The Formica and plastic decor comes straight from the 1950s, along with the old photos of Cuba on the walls. Legend has it that a young Fidel Castro planned his return to Cuba on the legendary ship *Granma* sitting at the tables here.

FRENCH

CHAMPS ÉLYSÉES **$$$**

Paseo de la Reforma 316, betw. Estocolmo and Amberes, 55/5533-3698
HOURS: Mon.–Sat. 1–11 P.M.
METRO: Insurgentes

This Zona Rosa standby is frequently recommended for its exemplary foie gras and *confit de pato* (duck confit). Attached to the restaurant is a deli with fresh baguettes and a selection of French wines and other specialties.

CORDON BLEU **$$$**

Havre 15, 55/5208-0660
HOURS: Mon.–Sat. 9 A.M.–6 P.M.
METRO: Insurgentes

The Casa de Francia, a cultural organization run by the French embassy, has a good restaurant, and the setting—with an outdoor patio—is more relaxed and informal than the other Zona Rosa French eateries (although the prices are equally steep). The foie gras is a tasty appetizer, and for a main course the *buñuelos de camarón* (breaded shrimp) are also recommended. When you're done eating, take a stroll through the adjacent art gallery, which has rotating exhibits of French artists. Upstairs is the **Medioteca** (Mon.–Sat. 10 A.M.–8 P.M.) with French books, movies, newspapers, and magazines.

LES MOUSTACHES **$$$**

Río Sena 88, 55/5533-3390
HOURS: Mon.–Sat. 1–11:30 P.M.
METRO: Insurgentes

A very posh restaurant in a converted old *casona* (old mansion), Les Moustaches has top-notch service and authentic French food, although you certainly pay for the quality. Specialties include duck in a green-olive sauce and chicory-leaf salad with goat cheese. Soft piano music adds to the ambience. It's located a block and a half north of Reforma, near the British embassy.

RESTAURANTS

INTERNATIONAL
CAFÉ MANGIA ❸❺
Río Sena 85
HOURS: Mon.-Fri. 8 A.M.-6 P.M.
METRO: Insurgentes

This bright, modern-looking lunch spot is difficult to classify, but well worth visiting if you're tired of *tortas* and *comidas corridas* for lunch. The deli-style restaurant caters to the local office-and-embassy crowd with breakfasts such as croissants stuffed with egg, cheddar cheese, avocado, and bacon, or eggs scrambled with gruyère cheese, for $2–5. Italian sandwiches are $4–8. They also have daily set meals, often with some type of pasta.

MARKETS
MERCADO CUAUHTÉMOC ❺
Río Lerma betw. Río Sena and Río Danubio
HOURS: Mon.-Fri. 6 A.M.-6 P.M., Sat.-Sun. 7 A.M.-4 P.M.
METRO: Insurgentes

Directly behind the U.S. embassy is this regular neighborhood market. The food stands inside serve tasty *comidas corridas* for $2–4 and *antojitos* for $1–3.

MERCADO INSURGENTES ❺
East of Florencia betw. Liverpool and Londres
HOURS: Mon.-Sat. 9 A.M.-7 P.M., Sun. 10 A.M.-3 P.M.
METRO: Insurgentes

This Zona Rosa market is mainly dedicated to handicrafts, but one corner of the market has a number of relatively hygienic *comida corrida* stands where a meal will set you back around $4.

MEXICAN
FONDA DEL REFUGIO ❸❺
Liverpool 166, 55/5525-8128
HOURS: Mon.-Sat. 1 P.M.-midnight, Sun. 1-10 P.M.
METRO: Insurgentes

An all-time Zona Rosa favorite, Fonda del Refugio prepares traditional Mexican dishes such as *chiles en nogada* and *tacos de huitlacoche*, along with imaginative daily specials such as *albóndigas chipotle* (meatballs with chipotle chile sauce) in the quiet, relaxed ambience of a two-story colonial house. The restaurant displays the folk art collection of the late Judit van Beuren, a writer who founded the restaurant in the 1950s. If you have a hard time with the Spanish menu, ask for the English version.

RESTAURANTE EL MIXTECO ❺
At Thomas A. Edison and Lotería Nacional
HOURS: Mon.-Fri. 1-4 P.M.
METRO: Hidalgo

This little hole-in-the-wall spot specializes in cuisine from the Mixtec region of Oaxaca, including *tlayuda* (a tortilla with salsa, onions, shredded beef, and special sauce), *tazajo* (a beef or shrimp dish), and exotica such as *chapulines* (grasshoppers). It offers a *comida corrida* with a fresh-squeezed fruit drink for $4.50.

SEAFOOD
LOS ARCOS ❺❺
Liverpool 104 at Niza, 55/5525-4408,
www.restaurantlosarcos.com.mx
HOURS: Mon.-Sat. noon-10 P.M., Sun. noon-8 P.M.
METRO: Insurgentes

Half a block off of Insurgentes, in the ground floor of a converted house, is a branch of the well-known seafood restaurant chain from the northwestern state of Sinaloa. The interior is colorful and usually not so crowded, and the staff are tourist-friendly.

MARISCOS DEL CAMARONERO ❺
Ignacio Ramírez 21B
HOURS: Mon.-Sat. 10 A.M.-10 P.M.
METRO: Revolución

This clean and inexpensive little eatery just north of Reforma serves tasty shrimp and fish tacos, ceviche, and seafood cocktails.

RESTAURANTE EL DELFÍN ❺
Arriaga 7
HOURS: Daily 10 A.M.-7 P.M.
METRO: Revolución

A few blocks past the Monumento a la Revolución is this seafood spot patronized by locals and serving inexpensive fare. Don't expect a lot of frills—just Formica tables bustling with working-class folk enjoying the tasty snacks and meals.

STEAK
ANGUS $$$
Copenhague 31, betw. Hamburgo and Reforma, 55/5208-2828
HOURS: Daily 1 P.M.–midnight
METRO: Insurgentes

A perennial favorite with the big-spending business crowd, Angus will certainly sate your craving for meat in short order. Even the potatoes come with ham in them. The waitresses, dressed in skimpy Santa Fe–style cowgirl outfits, seem puzzled that one could want a plain potato.

VEGETARIAN
YUG $$
Varsovia 3 at Paseo de la Reforma, 55/5533-3296
HOURS: Mon.-Fri. 7 A.M.-10 P.M., Sat. 8 A.M.-8 P.M., Sun. 1-8 P.M.

This well-established vegetarian restaurant goes beyond the standard health-store ambience of most D.F. veggie options to serve vegetarian crepes, potato latkes, and a variety of fruit and vegetable juices.

Chapultepec and Polanco
Map 3

As with hotels in this zone, Chapultepec and Polanco restaurants tend to be upscale and pricey, but they offer excellent quality. Reservations are recommended for many of these spots, particularly during the afternoon meal hours, and most credit cards are accepted.

ARGENTINE
EL ZORZAL $$
At Presidente Mazaryk and Anatole France, 55/5280-0111
HOURS: Mon.-Thurs. 1-11 P.M., Fri-Sat. until midnight, Sun. until 7 P.M.
METRO: Polanco

Near the center of the original shopping district in Polanco is El Zorzal, with tasty Argentine food. The *corte criollo* ($12), a thick, juicy steak, is delicious, as are the spinach-and-cheese empanadas ($4). The original branch of the restaurant is in Condesa; this one is located on the triangular corner set back from the intersection.

RINCÓN ARGENTINO $$$
Presidente Mazaryk 177, 55/5254-8744
HOURS: Daily 1-11 P.M.
METRO: Polanco

Opened by an Argentine soccer star who played in Mexico for years, Rincón Argentino has some of the best Argentine food in the city, with succulent steaks, sausages, pastas, and wines. The cavernous log cabin–style restaurant is always packed.

ASIAN
CHEZ WOK $$$
Tennyson 117, 55/5281-2921
HOURS: Mon.-Sat. 1:30-4:45 P.M. and 7:30-11 P.M., Sun. 1:30-4:45 P.M.
METRO: Polanco

For those after authentic Chinese cuisine, never mind the bill, Chez Wok is the place. On the 2nd floor of a converted house at the corner of Presidente Mazaryk you can savor a superb Peking duck, steak in orange sauce, and many other specialties from the extensive menu. Most meals are meant to be shared among two to six people. Dim sum is served on weekends only.

NANDA-YO $$$
Alejandro Dumas 105, 55/5281-8973
HOURS: Mon.-Wed. 1:30-11 P.M., Thurs.-Sat. 1:30 P.M.-1:30 A.M., Sun. 1:30-6 P.M.
METRO: Polanco

This upscale Japanese eatery is housed in a sleek building and features the ever-popular food conveyer belts. An extensive menu offers sushi, sashimi, tempura, and other Japanese specialties. The *samurai tempura,* with sea bass, crab, shrimp, cheese, avocado, cucumber, and salmon eggs, is a popular choice, as is the *kakiague*, with vegetable tempura, crab, cheese, avocado, and chile.

RESTAURANT TANDOOR 💲💲
Copernico 156 at Leibniz, 55/5203-0045
HOURS: Mon.-Sat. 1-11 P.M., Sun. 1-7 P.M.
METRO: Chapultepec

Here you'll find Pakistani and Indian dishes at reasonable prices in a quiet house near the Hotel Camino Real. Mexicans apparently find the taste of Indian food rather odd, as the place usually contains only foreign customers, and not very many, either. But quality, thankfully, remains high. The chicken tandoor is the house specialty, and vegetarians will love the *palak paneer*, a tasty spinach-and-cheese dish. Service is excellent.

COFFEE AND SWEETS
THE COFFEE BAR 💲
Presidente Mazaryk
HOURS: Mon.-Sat. 8:30 A.M.-10 P.M., Sun. noon-10 P.M.
METRO: Polanco

If you need a caffeine injection to revive you after your touring, stop in at one of the two locations (Temistocles at Presidente Mazaryk and Moliere at Presidente Mazaryk) of this coffee shop, located at either end of the main center of Polanco. The espresso is strong, the selection of sweet treats is extensive, and you'll find plenty of room to relax and recharge your batteries. The Temistocoles branch also has a large selection of magazines and newspapers, including some in English.

DINERS
KLEIN'S RESTAURANT 💲💲
Presidente Mazaryk 360B betw. Alejandro Dumas and Anatole France, 55/5281-0862
HOURS: Mon.-Sat. 8 A.M.-midnight, Sun. 9 A.M.-midnight
METRO: Polanco

This is about the closest you'll come to a New York diner in Mexico (and it isn't all that close, either). Klein's serves moderately priced sandwiches and meals. The *enchiladas verdes,* with either chicken or cheese, are

a filling treat for $6, and the burgers aren't bad either. It's usually packed for the 2–4 P.M. midday meal.

FRENCH
AU PIED DE COCHON 💲💲💲
Presidente Inter-Continental Hotel, Campos Eliseos 218, 55/5327-7756
HOURS: Daily 24 hours
METRO: Auditorio

Fans of wonderfully rich French cuisine will be pleased to discover this high-end restaurant in the Presidente Inter-Continental Hotel. Should you get out of a nightspot and find yourself craving a sublime French onion soup ($6) or pig's feet in béarnaise sauce ($13) at ungodly hours of the morning, now you know where to go.

LE CIRQUE 💲💲💲
Camino Real Hotel, Av. Mariano Escobedo 700, 55/5263-8881
HOURS: Mon.-Sat. 1 P.M.-midnight, Sun. 2-5 P.M.
METRO: Chapultepec

This is another top-notch French restaurant in a Polanco hotel, serving a tasty and filling three-course meal for $37. Or you can order from the menu: Try the rack of lamb ($38) and top it off with *fantasia del abuelo* (grandpa's fantasy), a crème brûlée topped with nuts, coffee ice cream, and hot chocolate.

INTERNATIONAL
CAFÉ BISTRO MP 💲💲💲
A. Bello 10, 55/5280-2506 or 55/5281-0592
HOURS: Mon.-Sat. 1:30 P.M.-midnight, Sun. 1:30-6 P.M.
METRO: Auditorio

An unusual mix of Asian and Latin cuisine is the specialty at this chic, upscale restaurant located between Campos Eliseos and Reforma. Enjoy dim sum, pizza, entrecôte with wasabi, or Thai sirloin with tamarind and mangoes in a sleek, modern dining room decorated with Asian art. They also host live jazz Monday and Wednesday evenings 9–11 P.M., and have a DJ Thursday–Saturday later in the evening.

ITALIAN
IL PUNTO 🪙🪙🪙
Emilio Castelar 213B, 55/5280-3623
HOURS: Mon.-Sat. 1 P.M.-midnight, Sun. 1-6 P.M.
METRO: Polanco

One of the best Italian restaurants in town, Il Punto specializes in pizzas baked in a wood oven ($17–20), *farfalle tequila* (pasta and shrimp with a tequila cream sauce, $10), and *canelones Il Punto* (round pasta stuffed with tuna and a tomato cream sauce, $10).

L'OSTERÍA DEL BECCO 🪙🪙🪙
Goldsmith 103, 55/5282-1059
HOURS: Mon.-Sat. 1 P.M.-midnight, Sun. 1-6 P.M.
METRO: Polanco

For high-end Italian food in a super-chic atmosphere, this is the place to go. The elegant dining room—complete with a glassed-in wine room where you can sip fine Italian reds at the perfect temperature, and be seen by all while doing so—is invariably thronging with businessmen, diplomats, and the city's wealthy, especially on Friday nights. The cuisine is vaguely northern Italian, but mixed with many Mexican ingredients. Among the many excellent main-course options is the *paglia e fieno al ragu d'anatra,* handmade naturally green pasta served with a duck-based bolognese sauce.

NON SOLO PASTA 🪙🪙
Julio Verne 89, 55/5280-9706
HOURS: Mon.-Sat. 1 P.M.-1 A.M.
METRO: Polanco

A bit less stuffy than most Polanco restaurants, with more of a corner trattoria feel, Non Solo Pasta is in the center of the Polanco commercial district. Run by a friendly French expat, this is a reasonably priced spot to have a glass of wine and pasta in a low-key environment.

MEXICAN
CAFÉ LOS ASOMBROS 🪙🪙
Alejandro Dumas 81, 55/5280-4111
HOURS: Mon.-Fri. 8 A.M.-11 P.M., Sat.-Sun. 10 A.M.-11 P.M.
METRO: Polanco

Located inside the El Péndulo bookstore, Café Los Asombros serves creatively (and literally)

named dishes, like beef *el pre-socrático* or *ensalada de pollo Neruda.* The restaurant is popular for lunch and breakfast with Mexican classics like *chilaquiles* and *huevos a la mexicana* prepared with quality ingredients. Service is invariably slow, but with plenty of books and music to browse, what's the rush?

🌙 HACIENDA DE LOS MORALES 🪙🪙🪙
Vázquez de Mella 525, 55/5281-4703 or 55/5281-4554
HOURS: Daily 1 P.M.-midnight

This superlative restaurant next to the Periférico is housed in a hacienda dating from the 16th century and was originally a silk-producing farm (hence the name—from *moral,* the mulberry tree groves in which the worms lived) in what was then a rural area west of Mexico City. The city has long since surrounded the hacienda, but this oasis of colonial calm is renowned for its Mexican cuisine, good service, and beautiful gardens. Well-prepared Mexican specialties include *chiles en nogada* (meat-stuffed poblano chiles in a cream and nut sauce), shrimp in tequila sauce, and *cabrito norteño* (Northern Mexican–style barbecued goat). The clientele tends to dress up to dine here, so don't come in shorts and a T-shirt.

VILLA MARÍA 🪙🪙
Homero 704, 55/5203-0306
HOURS: Mon.-Sat. 1:30 P.M.-midnight, Sun. 1:30-7 P.M.

Another very good traditional Mexican restaurant in Polanco is Villa María. Start off with the delectable *infladitas,* a sort of miniquesadilla, or the *sopa capilla* with *queso panela,* corn, and squash flowers. The *arrachera* steak is a popular main course. Live mariachi musicians stroll among the tables during dinner—be sure to specify a table well away from them if you want to talk!

SEAFOOD
CAFÉ DEL LAGO 🪙🪙🪙
Segunda Sección of Chapultepec Park, 55/5515-9586
HOURS: Mon.-Sat. 7:30 A.M.-11 P.M., Sun. 10:30 A.M.-4 P.M.
METRO: Auditorio

After walking through an entranceway that seems part of an elegant spaceship, you'll be seated in the spacious dining room, with one glass wall facing Chapultepec Lake, right in the middle of the park. The restaurant is a favored haunt of Mexican politicians and others from the elite set seeking a quiet place to hold their negotiations. The contemporary Mexican menu emphasizes seafood. Reservations are required.

LOS ARCOS ⑤⑤⑤

Torcuato Tasso 330, just off Presidente Mazaryk, 55/5254-5624

HOURS: Mon.-Sat. noon-10 P.M., Sun. noon-8 P.M.

METRO: Polanco

A Mexico City branch of the famed Sinaloa seafood restaurant, Los Arcos has fresh fish flown in daily. Be ready to drop an easy $20–30 per person with drinks, but rest assured your stomach will thank you profusely. Try the house specialty appetizer, *callo de hacha,* a scallop dish. The *huachinango al mojo de ajo* (red snapper cooked in garlic) is always a reliable choice.

TACOS, *TORTAS,* AND SNACKS
EL REY DEL TACO ⑤

Virgilio 10

HOURS: Daily 9 A.M.-8 P.M.

METRO: Polanco

Right in the heart of the Polanco neighborhood, with chi-chi restaurants and high-end clothing stores just around the corner, is this old-school taco joint. You won't find many Polanco residents eating here. Instead, the crowd consists of the men and women who clean their houses and care for their lawns, hankering after tacos of *carnitas* (braised pork) and *campechana* (mixed beef and *longaniza,* a pork sausage spiced with chiles).

LAS TORTUGAS ⑤

Presidente Mazaryk 249 at Arquimedes, 55/5280-1290

HOURS: Daily 9 A.M.-11 P.M.

METRO: Polanco

Those after a quick *torta* or *comida corrida* in Polanco can head over to this popular lunchtime cafeteria. They're not the cheapest *tortas*

in Mexico City, but they are hearty and hygenically prepared. Las Tortugas delivers within Polanco.

YAMIL ⑤

Virgilio 9

HOURS: Daily 1-6 P.M.

METRO: Polanco

Grab an inexpensive Lebanese-style snack of stuffed grape leaves, falafel, or *tacos árabes* (tacos with meat cut from a rotating spit) at this little spot right in the middle of the Polanco shopping area.

WEEKEND BRUNCH
CAFÉ DEL BOSQUE ⑤⑤⑤

Segunda Sección of Chapultepec Park, 55/5516-4214

HOURS: Sat.-Sun. 8 A.M.-6 P.M.

METRO: Constituyentes

This Chapultepec Park restaurant is open all week, but is particularly popular among the moneyed set for its weekend brunches (morning breakfast buffet $15, afternoon lunch buffet $21). One tasty breakfast option is the *omelette azteca* stuffed with jam, nopal cactus (spikes removed, rest assured!), and *tostadas.* The prime rib is a popular choice for lunch.

JW GRILL ⑤⑤⑤

JW Marriott Hotel, Andrés Bello 29, 55/5999-0000

HOURS: Sat.-Sun. 9:30 A.M.-3 P.M.

METRO: Auditorio

Even if you're not staying in Polanco but feel like a decadent splurge, especially after an intensive night of partying, the weekend buffet here is a great way to greet the day. A mimosa is included in the price to subdue that hangover if it starts getting any ideas.

LA HUERTA ⑤⑤⑤

Hotel Camino Real, Av. Mariano Escobedo 700, 55/5263-8888

HOURS: Sun. 11:30 A.M.-5 P.M.

METRO: Chapultepec

The Camino Real is another brunch option, serving a buffet with a huge array of cheeses, smoked fish, cold cuts, and half a dozen main dishes to choose from.

Roma and Condesa   Map 4

Starting in the early 1990s, high-end restaurants have proliferated in the Condesa neighborhood. The epicenter is near the intersection of Vicente Suárez and Michoacán, where you'll find a dozen places to choose from, but eateries have also opened on nearby streets such as Tamaulipas, Montes de Oca, and Nuevo León, and a handful of others near Parque México. Emphasis is definitely international—several taco joints still occupy the neighborhood, but the real attraction is the more upscale places. It's gotten to the point where local residents are getting annoyed by all the traffic on weekends, with people coming from across the city to dine in what is now one of the hippest parts of town. Many restaurants have sidewalk dining, which makes a lovely way to spend a couple of hours tucking into a fine meal and a bottle or two of wine with some friends. The nearby Roma neighborhood also has some very good restaurants, although not as many as the Condesa.

ARGENTINE
EL ZORZAL $$

Tamaulipas at Alfonso Reyes, 55/5273-6023
HOURS: Sun.-Thurs. 1:30-11 P.M., Fri.-Sat.
1:30 P.M.-midnight
METRO: Patriotismo
Specializing in hearty cuts of imported steak (the *corte criollo* and the *arrachera* are both top-notch)—as well as sublime spinach-and-cheese empanadas, large salads, pastas, and wines—is this small Argentine bistro. A full meal with wine runs $20–35, depending on how much you indulge—well worth it for the superb quality.

QUEBRACHO $$

Atlixco 93, 55/5211-5918
HOURS: Sun.-Thurs. 1-11 P.M., Fri.-Sat. 1 P.M.-midnight
METRO: Patriotismo
Another good choice for Argentine steaks and empanadas is this eatery just off the main restaurant strip in the middle of the Condesa. It's a simple set-up, but the service is good and the

location a bit off the main "restaurant row" means it's often easier to get tables during busy times. They also have a branch near Paseo de la Reforma.

ASIAN
SUSHI KAITEN $$

Plaza Villa de Madrid 22 at Oaxaca, 55/5511-8390
HOURS: Mon.-Sat. 1:30-11 P.M., Sun. 1:30-6 P.M.
METRO: Sevilla
This sleek, modern place on a corner in the midst of a well-populated restaurant center (called Fuente de los Cibeles) in the Roma is a trendy spot for sushi. Take a seat at one of the diner-style booths, order your sushi rolls, and watch it be delivered on the slow-moving conveyer belts right to your table. Try the "moori," with breaded shrimp, crab, mango, and avocado, or the "astroboy," a spicy crab tempura with asparagus and cheese.

CANTINAS
LA AUTÉNTICA $$

Corner of Álvaro Obregón and Av. Cuauhtémoc
HOURS: Daily 11 A.M.-11 P.M. (closing hours vary)
METRO: Cuauhtémoc
La Auténtica is exactly what its name suggests: a classic cantina of the old school, with uniformed waiters bustling around to keep the many clients well supplied with hearty traditional Mexican food and bountiful drinks to wash it down. If you're really hungry, try the monster *molcajete,* a huge bowl brimming with chorizo, beef, beans, and cheese, or the thick pork tenderloin. Service is great, the ambience is convivial, and wandering guitarists play tunes for a nominal fee.

LA COVADONGA $$

Puebla 121, 55/5533-2701
HOURS: Mon.-Fri. 1 P.M.-2 A.M.
METRO: Insurgentes
Walking into this cavernous room with a bar at one end and a couple dozen tables populated mostly by men playing dominoes, you

RESTAURANTS

Dominos is the main occupation at La Covadonga, but the Spanish-style food is worth a visit, too.

could be forgiven for questioning this guidebook author's taste. But sit down and order a drink, and you'll start to appreciate the vibe. There is usually an assortment of artists and random other people from the Roma here, as the place has become oddly hip. Women will feel quite comfortable, unlike at some cantinas. Covadonga has an extensive menu filled with reasonably priced Spanish-style fish and meat dishes, appetizers such as *tortilla española*, soups, salads, and a midday set meal ($8). The paella is excellent, and so is the service by the uniformed waiters. The liquor selection is extensive.

COFFEE AND SWEETS

CAFÉ D'CARLO ⑤
Orizaba 115
HOURS: Mon.-Fri. 8 A.M.-10 P.M., Sat. 8 A.M.-9 P.M.
METRO: Insurgentes
This is a great little hole-in-the-wall Roma coffee shop with a few tables on the sidewalk, often filled with an interesting assortment of artist-hipster types, longtime Roma residents, and occasional expats sipping a strong espresso. They also serve light meals and sweet snacks.

CAFÉ LA SELVA ⑤
Vicente Suárez 38D, 55/5211-5170
HOURS: Daily 9 A.M.-10:30 P.M.
METRO: Patriotismo
This is the central Condesa branch of a socially conscious café chain serving only organically grown coffee from Chiapas collectives. It even has a branch in Atlanta, Georgia. The java is wickedly strong.

CAFÉ TAPANCO ⑤
Orizaba 161, 55/5564-2274
HOURS: Mon.-Thurs. 8 A.M.-11 P.M., Fri.-Sat. 9 A.M.-11 P.M., Sun. 9 A.M.-10 P.M.
METRO: Insurgentes
Café Tapanco is another Roma café serving very tasty and inexpensive breakfasts and light meals along with the coffee. Popular with local artists, this friendly café often has art displays on the wall and live events like poetry readings or acoustic music.

CAFEMANÍA 💲
Av. México 123 at Ixtaccíhuatl, 55/5264-0577
HOURS: Daily 9 A.M.–11 P.M.
METRO: Chilpancingo
This little corner coffee shop right on Parque México is a great spot to while away the hours while sipping espresso and reading a newspaper or chatting with friends. I should know—I used to live around the corner and spent many a day here. Apart from coffee drinks, it also serves light meals and pastries.

VILLAGE CAFÉ 💲
Tamaulipas 99, 55/5211-0346
HOURS: Mon.-Sat. 8:30 A.M.–11 P.M., Sun. 11 A.M.–11 P.M.
METRO: Patriotismo
This is a funky little café closer to the main restaurant district in the Condesa. Check out the Beatles memorabilia and stacks of old magazines. Seating is available in two quiet rooms or at outdoor tables.

INTERNATIONAL
BARRACUDA DINER 💲💲
Nuevo León 4A, 55/5211-9480
HOURS: Daily 24 hours
METRO: Sevilla
If you've got a craving for a retro-lounge/diner complete with burgers and milkshakes, but with a decidedly hipster, upscale vibe, the Barracuda might fit the bill. Sit either at the long bar or one of the booths with vinyl seats and take your pick among the sandwiches, burgers, breakfasts, and other treats. One good burger is the Redneck, with bacon, cheddar cheese, and barbeque sauce ($8). It's a refreshing change from tacos for a late-night munchie.

BISTROT MOSAICO 💲💲
Michoacán 10, 55/5584-2932
HOURS: Mon.-Sat. 1–11:30 P.M., Sun. 1–5:30 P.M.
METRO: Chilpancingo
A deli-restaurant with a distinctly European feel, Bistrot Mosaico serves snacks like *tortilla de patatas* (potato and egg pie), quiche lorraine, goat cheese salad, corned beef sandwich, and various fish, meat, and pasta dishes. Prices are high, unsurprising considering the upscale clientele, but so is the quality.

🍸 GARUFA 💲💲
Michoacán 93, 55/5286-8293
HOURS: Sun.-Thurs. 1–11 P.M., Fri.-Sat. 1 P.M.–1 A.M.
METRO: Patriotismo
Garufa was one of the first of the trendy restaurants in Condesa, and still considered one of the best, with tables inside and on the sidewalk—perfect for people-watching. Among the excellent pastas are cannelloni with spinach or corn and *fettucini hindú*, chicken breast in a tangy yogurt-and-ginger sauce over a bed of pasta. The steaks are great too.

IXCEL 💲💲💲
Medellín 65, 55/5280-4055
HOURS: Mon.-Tues. 1:30 P.M.–midnight, Wed.-Sun. 1:30 P.M.–2 A.M.
METRO: Insurgentes
In a converted old Roma mansion, this former nightclub is now a hip, popular upscale restaurant, still with something of a club feel to it. The Blue Room upstairs is particularly lounge-like, if that's what you're looking for. The food is an eclectic mix of Mexican and international, including grilled shrimp with couscous, ravioli stuffed with spinach and goat cheese, duck-meat tacos with plum sauce, and Vietnamese spring rolls. It's best to call ahead for a table, particularly on weekends.

RESTAURANTE LAMM 💲💲💲
Álvaro Obregón 99 at Orizaba, 55/5514-8501,
www.lamm.com.mx
HOURS: Tues.-Fri. 8 A.M.–midnight, Sat. 9 A.M.–2 A.M., Sun. 9 A.M.–6 P.M.
METRO: Insurgentes
This architectural curiosity, housed in the Casa Lamm Cultural Center, consists of a modernist glass-and-wood-framed patio jutting into the courtyard of a 1890s stone mansion. The high-end Mexican and international cuisine is of very good quality. Choose between several kinds of pastas ($6–8), fresh tuna in tamarind sauce ($17), or giant shrimps with coconut sauce ($25).

bueno, bonito, y barato: tacos for 30 cents each

© CHRIS HUMPHREY

ROJO BISTROT $$

Corner of Parras and Amsterdam, 55/5211-3705

HOURS: Mon.-Thurs. 2-11 P.M., Fri.-Sat. 2 P.M.-midnight

METRO: Sevilla

Rojo Bistrot is a relaxed European-style café with an airy dining room as well as sidewalk seating in a quiet residential area of the Condesa. Subdued lighting and well-chosen music give a pleasing intimate feel, and there's a small bar also. The *magret de pato,* duck in black cherry sauce with potatoes ($13), is a popular choice.

ITALIAN
LA PIAZZA $$

Corner of Guanajuato and Orizaba, 55/5264-5556

HOURS: Mon.-Sat. 1:30-11 P.M., Sun. 1:30-7 P.M.

METRO: Insurgentes

On Roma's tranquil Plaza Luis Cabrera, La Piazza serves good, if not superlative, Italian cuisine in a pleasingly relaxed ambience. If the night is balmy, take a table out on the sidewalk.

MARKETS
MERCADO MEDELLÍN $

Betw. Medellín, Campeche, Monterrey, and Coahuila

HOURS: Daily 8 A.M.-5 P.M.

METRO: Chilpancingo

While Condesa has a market on the corner of Calles Tamaulipas and Michoacán, it's small and fairly pricey, which is no surprise considering the neighborhood. Far better is the Mercado Medellín in the Roma Sur. A spacious, well-lit market with mountains of fresh produce, Medellín is known for its excellent seafood, sold in bulk and cooked in the many market restaurants. Shrimp cocktails are a tasty treat for a mere $2. This market is also famed for selling special ingredients from the southeastern region of the Yucatán, including *achiote* and fresh banana leaves.

MEDITERRANEAN
CAPÍCUA $$

Nuevo León 66, 55/5211-5280

HOURS: Mon.-Sat. 1 P.M.-1 A.M.

METRO: Patriotismo

This tapas bar is popular with the chic Condesa

set, who sit in the sleek, postmodern atmosphere with glass walls and metal chairs chatting and nibbling on the wide selection of tasty cooked snacks. Some excellent options (far too small, which means you will order several) include the *croquetas de jamñn serrano* (a ham tart), the lamb ribs in mint, or the ever-popular *tortilla espaóola* (a Spanish-style omelet).

LA PATA NEGRA $$

Condesa Cinema at north end of Tamaulipas, 55/5211-5563
HOURS: Sun.-Tues. 1 P.M.-1 A.M., Wed.-Sat. until 2 A.M.
METRO: Patriotismo

Just about across the street from Capícua is another ragingly popular tapas bar, this one with a slightly less austere feel. It's frequented as much for people-watching as for the food and drink, which are good and not overly expensive. *Bocatas* (mouthfuls) cost $6 and smaller tapas like garlic mushrooms run $3.50. Expect crowds most nights.

TIERRA DE VINOS $$$

Durango 197, 55/5208-5133, www.tierradevinos.com.mx
HOURS: Mon.-Tues. 11 A.M.-6 P.M., Wed.-Sat. 11 A.M.-1 A.M.
METRO: Sevilla

For probably the best wine selection anywhere in the city, stop in at the aptly named Tierra de Vinos located just off the Fuente de los Cibeles traffic circle in the Roma. Hard to spot because of its nondescript facade, the restaurant offers a vast array of different wines from around the world and serves superb Mediterranean cuisine (the chef is Catalán) to accompany it. They have an extensive selection of tapas, as well as full meals such as salmon with spinach or breast of veal, each with suggested wines. The menu changes frequently. The restaurant sometimes hosts intimate jazz concerts, with the ticket (often around $60) including a complete meal with wine.

MEXICAN

AJO Y CEBOLLA $$

Fernando Montes de Oca at Cuautla
HOURS: Mon.-Fri. 1- 5 P.M.
METRO: Patriotismo

Comida corrida connoisseurs will appreciate this simple little lunch joint serving set meals during the week. Each meal includes a pitcher of *agua de sabor* (watery fruit drink), a starter snack, soup, salad or potato dish, choice of main course (usually two or three options), dessert and coffee.

BISQUETS OBREGÓN $$

Álvaro Obregón and Mérida
HOURS: Daily 7 A.M.-midnight
METRO: Insurgentes

Roma remains a holdout for the classic Mexico City *café chino,* coffee shop–style restaurants originally started by Chinese owners, often known as *"bisquits"* because of one of their trademark snacks. The most famous of them all (and now a citywide chain), is Bisquets Obregón. Because of the popularity of the original 1950s-style restaurant, a McDonald's-style multistory Bisquets is now open across the street. Both serve a large menu of inexpensive Mexican meals (breakfasts are a good deal), as well as the mandatory *bisquets* and chop suey. The excellent coffee is served in the Veracruz style with the waitress bringing two pitchers, one of coffee and the other of warm milk, and you tell her to stop as you like. A block west on Álvaro Obregón at Córdoba are the two branches of **Café Paris** (daily 7:30 A.M.–midnight, mains $2–5), another longtime Roma favorite with bright-purple booths and a similar menu to Bisquets Obregón.

CAFÉ LOS ASOMBROS $$

Av. Nuevo León 115 at Vicente Suarez, 55/5286-9493
HOURS: Mon.-Fri. 8 A.M.-11 P.M., Sat.-Sun. 10 A.M.-11 P.M.
METRO: Patriotismo

This quiet café in another location of El Péndulo bookstore offers meals in a fittingly refined atmosphere. Breakfasts here are particularly good, and on weekend mornings it often has live classical music to aid your digestion. While the food is very good, service is often slow, so don't come in a hurry.

RESTAURANTS

ANTOJITOS

This word literally means "little whims," thus implying "snacks" to many people. However, the word also refers to any food that can be ordered, served, and eaten quickly – in other words, Mexican fast food. Visitors who identify these terms with dishes at Mexican restaurants in their home countries are sometimes confused by the different shapes and forms they may take in Mexico. Tacos can be rolled as well as folded, and enchiladas can be folded or stacked as well as rolled; shape is irrelevant. An enchilada (literally, "chilied") is any *antojito* made with a tortilla dipped or cooked in a chile sauce; an *entomada* (or *entomatada*) is the equivalent made with tomatoes, while the *enfrijolada* is the same made with a thin bean sauce.

COMMON ANTOJITOS

alambre – a stir-fry of sorts, with chopped beef, onions, peppers, and bacon and served with tortillas

birria – lamb or goat stew in a sauce spiced with chiles, cinnamon, cloves, cumin, and oregano

burrito – a flour tortilla rolled around meat, beans, or seafood fillings; rare in Mexico City

carnitas – braised pork, chopped into thin slices and eaten with tortillas, guacamole, and various salsas

cecina – a type of cured beef pounded flat and served with beans, fresh cheese, avocado, nopal cactus, and corn tortillas

chalupa – a crisp, whole tortilla topped with beans, meat, etc. (also known as a tostada); or a thicker, canoe-shaped cornmeal tortilla filled with the same

chile relleno – a mild poblano chile stuffed with cheese, deep-fried in egg batter, and covered with a sauce of tomatoes, onions, and chiles

chimichanga – tortilla (usually flour) with beans, ham, and cheese

enchilada – a corn tortilla dipped in chile sauce, then folded or rolled around a filling of meat, chicken, seafood, or cheese and baked in an oven

enfrijolada – same as enchilada except dipped in a sauce of thinned refried beans instead of chile sauce

entomatada – same as enchilada except dipped in a tomato sauce instead of chile sauce

FLOR DE LIS 💲💲
Huichapán 17, 55/5286-2229
HOURS: Daily 8:30 A.M.–5 P.M.
METRO: Sevilla

In operation in Condesa since 1918, this simple cafeteria is a great place to enjoy a top-quality tamale stuffed with mushrooms or chicken and green chiles ($2.50 each), or an assortment of other Mexican dishes at mid-range prices.

FLORA LOUNGE 💲💲
Corner of Michoacán and Nuevo León
HOURS: Mon.-Fri. 10 A.M.-11 P.M., Sat. 10 A.M.-midnight
METRO: Chilpancingo

This corner eatery in the center of the Condesa has a slightly upscale, hipster vibe to it, but serves reasonably priced and healthy lunches and dinners. The midday multicourse *comida corrida* is a good value at $5–6. The menu also offers a variety of salads, soups, and light meals.

LA BUENA TIERRA 💲💲
Corner of Michoacán and Atlixco
HOURS: Sun.-Thurs. 8 A.M.-11 P.M., Fri.-Sat. 8 A.M.-12:30 A.M.
METRO: Patriotismo

This is one of the most popular spots in the heart of the Condesa restaurant district, both for its prime location and the extensive menu of creative and healthy (including several organic) dishes. Popular choices are the *flor de jamaica* (a type of flower) tacos as a starter, and salmon in a citrus sauce of orange, mango, and tamarind for a main course. Vegetarians and meat lovers alike will find many options here.

flauta – a small corn tortilla roll, usually stuffed with beef or chicken and fried

gordita – a small, thick corn tortilla stuffed with a spicy meat mixture; a common street-vendor offering

huarache – literally, "sandal"; a large, flat, thick oval-shaped tortilla topped with fried meat and chiles; a common street-vendor offering

machaca – a northern dish of dried, shredded beef served with flour tortillas and guacamole, or also sometimes mixed in with scrambled eggs as a hearty breakfast

menudo – a thick soup made with cows' feet and stomachs (and less commonly, intestines) and garnished with *chiles de árbol*, oregano, and fresh chopped onion; reputedly a sure hangover cure

pancita – the Mexico City equivalent of *menudo*

picadillo – a spicy salad of chopped or ground meat with chiles and onions (also known as *salpicón*)

pozole – hominy stew made with pork or chicken and garnished with radishes, oregano, onions, chile powder, salt, and lime

quesadilla – a flour tortilla folded over sliced cheese and grilled; some cooks can add *chiles rajas* (pepper strips), *flor de calabaza* (squash flower), *champiñones* (mushrooms), or *huitlacoche* (a trufflelike fungus that grows on fresh corn) on request

sincronizada – deep-fried corn tortilla with beans, ham, and cheese, topped with guacamole

sope – a small, thick, round corn cake with dimpled edges, topped with a spicy meat mixture and crumbled cheese

taco – a corn tortilla folded or rolled around anything and eaten with the hands; *tacos al pastor*, made with thin slivers of spit-cooked pork marinated in reddish *adobo* sauce, are the most popular Mexico City variation

tamal – cornmeal dough (*masa*) wrapped in a corn husk and steamed; sometimes stuffed with cheese, chile strips, corn, olives, pork, or turkey; popularly seen on street corners (plural: tamales)

torta – a Mexican-style sandwich made with *pan telera*, a large, flat roll; *jamón* (ham) and *pollo* (chicken) are common

RESTAURANTS

LA TECLA ❶❷
Durango 186A, 55/5525-4920
HOURS: Mon.-Sat. 1 P.M.-midnight, Sun. 1-6 P.M.
METRO: Insurgentes

La Tecla is one of the best all-Mexican restaurants in Roma. Prices are reasonable, too; a *menú de degustación* (tasting menu) is available Monday through Thursday nights for just $8. The daily *comidas corridas* for both lunch and dinner are an excellent value. Main dishes include trout, steak with roquefort cheese and *huitlacoche,* or squash flower stuffed with goat cheese in a chipotle sauce.

LAS ARRACHERAS ❶❷
Vicente Suarez 110 at Mazatlán
HOURS: Daily 1:30-8 P.M.
METRO: Patriotismo

If you're in the mood for a hearty, meat-based

meal but don't want to spend a whole lot of money, stop in at this unpretentious eatery in the Condesa. It serves reasonably priced, good-quality *arrachera* steaks, as well as very tasty *alambres,* a stir-fry of sorts with chopped steak, green peppers, onions, and a bit of bacon for flavor, eaten with tortillas. The green salsa here, made with green tomatoes, avocado, and habanero, is hot and tasty.

LOS TAMALES EMPORIO ❶
Álvaro Obregón 154, 55/5574-2078
HOURS: Mon.-Sat. 8 A.M.-9 P.M., Sun. 9 A.M.-5 P.M.
METRO: Insurgentes

For an inexpensive and reliable (if unspectacular) Mexican restaurant serving breakfast, lunch, and dinner, as well as its namesake tamales (only $1.50 each), head to this spot in the middle of the Roma. Try the *oaxaqueño,* with mole and chicken; the *chiapaneco*, with mole, chicken, olives, almonds, plums, egg, and pepper; or the *yucatecos*, with gouda cheese, strips of green poblano peppers, and *guajillo* chile sauce.

SEAFOOD
CERVECERÍA 💲💲
Corner of Tamaulipas and Vicente Suarez
HOURS: Mon.-Tues. 1 P.M.-midnight, Wed.-Sat.
1 P.M.-2 A.M., Sun. 1-8 P.M.
METRO: Patriotismo

This dimly lit corner spot in the heart of the Condesa seems more like a bar than a restaurant (as its name, which means "brewery," suggests), but serves a selection of excellent and well-priced seafood snacks and light meals. The seafood tacos (try the *combinado,* one fish and one shrimp) are addictive, as is the *tostada de atun* (thin-sliced tuna strips on a crunchy tortilla shell). Let's hope they maintain their current high standards.

🍴 CONTRAMAR 💲💲💲
Durango 200, 55/5514-9217 or 55/5514-3169
HOURS: Daily 1-6 P.M.
METRO: Sevilla

For very possibly the finest seafood in Mexico City, head directly to Contramar for lunch (no dinner here). They serve outstanding seafood in a bright, airy dining room bustling with waiters. Start with the delicious *tacos de camarón* ($7), stuffed with minced shrimp and more reminiscent of an Asian-style spring roll than a taco, then move on to the succulent *filete Contramar* ($20), served on a wooden platter and lightly coated with sauce. No reservations are accepted, so show up and expect to wait a bit for a table.

LA EMBAJADA JAROCHA 💲💲
Jalapa at Zacatecas, 55/5584-2570
HOURS: Daily at 3 P.M., closes at 2 A.M. Thurs.-Sat.,
earlier other nights
METRO: Insurgentes

This long-running popular Roma restaurant doesn't have any of the chic style of the Condesa, but is a classic in its own right. The name translates as "the Veracruz Embassy," and they specialize in seafood cooked in the styles of this eastern coastal state. *Huachinango* cooked in a variety of ways runs $15, as does a large order of lobster tacos. Live tropical music serenades diners Thursday through Sunday.

TACOS, *TORTAS,* AND SNACKS
🍴 EL TIZONCITO 💲💲
Campeche and Cholula
HOURS: Sun.-Thurs. noon-3 A.M., Fri.-Sat.
noon-4:30 A.M.
METRO: Patriotismo

With two locations two blocks away from one another—one a stool-and-bar, eat-and-run affair (at Campeche and Tamaulipas), and this more formal sit-down restaurant—El Tizoncito is a taco phenomenon in Mexico City, now with branches across the city. At each you'll find delicious *tacos al pastor* ($0.70 each) and a variety of other *antojitos*, along with beer and soft drinks. Prices are a bit higher than most *taquerías*, but the food is reliably hygienic and service is swift. Be sure to leave a couple of pesos tip to the grill man who made your tacos.

HOLA'S 💲
Amsterdam 135 at Michoacán
HOURS: Mon.-Sat. from early morning until
around 4 P.M.
METRO: Chilpancingo

At this hole-in-the-wall spot you'll find a wide variety of delicious and inexpensive ($0.75 each) taco fillings already prepared and served from large ceramic bowls. They even serve a couple of vegetarian tacos, believe it or not—one with spinach, and the other with squash and corn. There's a constant line of clients standing around the "taco bar" in the afternoon, calling out orders to the cheerful servers, who scoop out the fixings into fresh tortillas and add grated cheese and beans if you like.

TACOS ÁLVARO O. 💲
Av. Álvaro Obregón near Jalapa
HOURS: Daily from early afternoon until 3 A.M.
METRO: Insurgentes

This is a good taco option in the middle of the

Roma. Try the tasty and filling *alambre*, a mix of grilled beef with green peppers, onions, and bacon served with a pile of tortillas ($3.50).

TAQUERÍA EL GRECO 🟢🟢
Michoacán 54 near the corner of Nuevo León
HOURS: Mon.-Sat. 2-10 P.M.
METRO: Chilpancingo
The *taco árabe* with pita bread ($3–5) is a popular Mexican culinary fusion of Middle Eastern and Mexican, as the regular crowds in this little restaurant will attest. Lean pork is cooked on a spit, then sliced off and crisped further on the grill below before going into the various tacos and *tortas* served here. The *tortas* with cheese ($3) are a good, filling value—ask them to put the guacamole sauce on it for extra fire. If there's no room at the half-dozen small tables, you can order from the man in charge of cutting the meat and eat them right there on the sidewalk.

TORTA STAND 🟢
Av. Álvaro Obregón and Córdoba
HOURS: Mon.-Sat. until late afternoon
METRO: Insurgentes
Grab an inexpensive *torta* of *milanesa* (breaded pork) or chicken ($1.20) and fresh-squeezed juice to wash it down at this clean, well-run street stand in the middle of the Roma.

VEGETARIAN
LETTUZZE 🟢
Av. Mexico 67
HOURS: Mon.-Sat. 1-7 P.M.
METRO: Chilpancingo
A modest lunchtime restaurant in a converted house right on Parque México, Lettuzze has vegetarian *comidas corridas* for $5, as well as nonvegetarian ones for a bit more, and baguette sandwiches for $4.50.

RESTAURANTS

Nápoles, Del Valle, and Mixcoac   Map 5

These residential neighborhoods in the center of Mexico City are stocked with all manner of eateries, mainly catering to the middle-class tastes of the locals. While most aren't particularly noteworthy, there are several places that could be of interest to foreign visitors, especially a couple of Asian restaurants.

ASIAN
BLOSSOM 🟢🟢
San Francisco 360, corner of Luz Saviñon, 55/5523-8516
HOURS: Mon.-Sat. 1-11 P.M., Sun. 1-6:30 P.M.
Here you'll find some of the better Chinese food in Mexico City, in the quiet, residential Del Valle neighborhood south of the Roma. The zippy *filete mongol* steak, with chile and spices, runs $10, while the sumptuous *pescado blossom* (fried red snapper with shrimp and vegetables in a sweet-and-sour sauce) will set you back $17. The restaurant has set lunch and dinner meals costing $17.

NAGAOKA 🟢🟢
Arkansas 38, 55/5543-9530
HOURS: Tues.-Sat. 1-10 P.M., Sun. 1-7 P.M.
In a converted house on a quiet side street in the Nápoles neighborhood, Nagaoka has recommended Japanese cuisine. After walking in past the stands of bamboo at the entrance, take a seat in the peaceful dining room and enjoy the excellent sushi, *teppanyaki* (stir-fried beef and vegetables), and other dishes.

CANTINAS
BAR MONTEJO 🟢🟢
Benjamín Franklin 261 at Nuevo León
HOURS: Mon.-Sat. 10 A.M.-midnight
METRO: Chilpancingo
This bar in the southern part of the Condesa offers a full bar, inexpensive and good-quality *comida yucateca* (Yucatán cuisine), and even a couple of tasty, full-bodied *yucateca* beers—Montejo and León. The service is exemplary.

RESTAURANTE EL CANDELERO 🟡🟡

Insurgentes Sur 1333, Col. Mixcoac, 55/5598-9008

HOURS: Thurs.-Sat. 1:30 P.M.-midnight, Sun. 1:30-6 P.M.

METRO: Insurgentes Metrobús

El Candelero is an interesting updated version of a traditional Mexican restaurant/cantina, set amidst vaguely Gothic decor. Grab a table in the cozy bar or in the high-ceilinged, spacious central area and order from the menu of excellent-quality Mexican specialties while enjoying the strains of the roaming mariachi or *trío* bands. It's a good spot for late-night eats and drinks *a la mexicana,* especially if you are near this area of Insurgentes.

ITALIAN
BELLINI'S 🟡🟡

Av. Insurgentes Sur at Filedelfia, Col. Nápoles, 55/5628-8304 or 55/5628-8305

HOURS: Mon.-Sat. 1 P.M.-1 A.M., Sun. 9 A.M.-11 P.M.

METRO: Insurgentes Metrobús

For haute cuisine in the most literal sense, try this restaurant on the 45th floor of the World Trade Center de México, the country's second-highest building. Sweeping views over the city accompany respectable and surprisingly moderately priced Italian food. Apart from Italian favorites such as *fettucine tres quesos* (with provolone, manchego, and roquefort cheeses), the restaurant also features an international array of dishes such as Latin American ceviche, English-style prime rib, and French foie gras. The Sunday brunch (9 A.M.–2 P.M., $20) is bountiful. Jackets and ties are required for men.

Coyoacán

Map 6

This neighborhood in southern Mexico City—a mix of bohemian, working class and upper crust—offers some of the capital's finest and most traditional dining options.

ASIAN
DAO 🟡🟡🟡

Av. México 59, 55/5554-9000

HOURS: Mon.-Sat. 1:30-11 P.M., Sun. 1:30-6 P.M.

METRO: Viveros

A stylish, high-end place, Dao prepares flavorful pan-Asian dishes presented with maximum color and flair. Try the bed of *camarones* (shrimp) served with dozens of peppers, or the *painapurru,* chicken with *chile de árbol* served over half a pineapple. Reservations are recommended.

CANTINAS
CANTINA LA GUADALUPANA 🟡🟡

Caballo Calco facing Jardín Hidalgo, 55/5554-6253

HOURS: Mon.-Thurs. 10 A.M.-9:30 P.M., Fri.-Sat. 10 A.M.-midnight

METRO: Viveros

The venerable Guadalupana, now in a location a block from the old place, has been around for decades and is one of the city's most traditional and popular *cantinas familiares* (family cantinas). Foreigners both male and female will feel quite comfortable here. The full menu covers all the Mexican standards.

COFFEE AND SWEETS
CAFÉ EL PARNASO 🟡🟡

Carrillo Puerto 2, 55/5554-2225

HOURS: Mon.-Fri. 9 A.M.-10 P.M., Sat-Sun. 9 A.M.-11 P.M.

METRO: Viveros

For intellectual stimulation over a cappuccino, head to El Parnaso, a cluster of wrought-iron tables just outside the ground floor of an old three-story colonial near the southeast corner of Jardín del Centenario. The attached bookstore offers tomes covering all subjects, mostly in Spanish, as well as music CDs. If you're after more than just a coffee, try the empanadas, filled with your choice of tuna, spinach, ground beef, or other fillings, or share a *plato combinado* piled with empanadas, *tortilla española* (thick egg and potato omelet), cheeses, and *pan dulce* (sweet bread).

An ice cream vendor displays his wares.

CAFETERÍA MOHELI ⓢ

Francisco Sosa just west of Jardín del Centenario
HOURS: Daily 8 A.M.–10 P.M.
METRO: Viveros

A good place to get away from the plaza scene a bit, this coffee shop is, like El Parnaso, a popular place for those addicted to both books and caffeine. Apart from the java, Moheli also serves a good selection of sandwiches, salads, and meals at reasonable prices.

EL JAROCHO ⓢ

Calle Cuauhtémoc 134 at Allende
HOURS: Daily 9 A.M.–10 P.M.
METRO: Viveros

This tiny spot north of Jardín Hidalgo serves some of the best Mexican-style coffee in Mexico City. It's easy to spot: Look for the line of people patiently awaiting their cup—mostly longtime neighborhood residents—or lounging around the street corner drinking and chatting about politics, the weather, or life in general. There is no seating inside the small shop, which has been serving fresh-roasted coffee since 1953. You can buy whole-bean coffee by the kilo and half kilo here, as well as *tortas.*

PANADERÍA EL GLOBO ⓢ

Corner of Caballo Calco and Av. Hidalgo
HOURS: Mon.–Sat. 8 A.M.–7 P.M., Sun. 10 A.M.–5 P.M.
METRO: Viveros

Opposite the east side of Coyoacán's Jardín Hidalgo is one of Mexico City's best bakeries. Founded in 1884, El Globo now has several branches in the capital, and this is one of the fancier ones; most of the pastries come prewrapped, and there's a section dedicated to *pan rustico europeo* (rustic European breads).

INTERNATIONAL
FABIO'S ⓢⓢ

Upstairs at Allende 15, 55/5554-7961
HOURS: Daily 8 A.M.–10 P.M.
METRO: Viveros

Opposite the north end of Jardín Hidalgo, Fabio's serves a mid-range Mediterranean and Italian menu that includes pizzas, olive and eggplant appetizers, a Lebanese platter, and

RESTAURANTS

fresh produce

pastries. The restaurant has a balcony overlooking the park, which makes for good people-watching during your meal.

MARKETS
MERCADO COYOACÁN 💲

Three blocks north of Jardín Hidalgo off Calle Allende
HOURS: Daily 7 A.M.–5 P.M.
METRO: Viveros

At this bustling neighborhood market you'll find a string of *marisquerías,* countertop purveyors of fresh seafood. Popular choices include *tostada de ceviche* (crisp corn tortillas topped with ceviche), *pulpo en su tinta* (octopus cooked in its own ink), and *sopa de mariscos* (seafood soup). One particularly good place is the **Jardín del Pulpo,** at the corner of Allende and Malintzin, with ceviche and fried fish at reasonable prices. Other *comedores* are sprinkled throughout the market, and most are very clean. Off to one side of the market there's also a *sección comidas,* where you'll find big *cazuelas* bubbling with *pancita,* Mexico City's answer to *menudo.*

MEXICAN
FONDA EL MORRAL 💲💲

Allende 2
HOURS: Fri.-Sat. 8 A.M.–midnight, Sun. 8 A.M.–10 P.M.
METRO: Viveros

This popular restaurant with a tile facade specializes in regional dishes from different areas of Mexico. Have a complete breakfast ($5), *antojitos* ($3–5), or entrées of fish, fowl, and beef ($8–15), all served with tasty handmade tortillas in a colorful and festive environment. Fonda El Morral is just north of Jardín Hidalgo and is only open Friday–Sunday.

LAS LUPITAS 💲💲

Francisco Sosa at the corner of Plaza Santa Catarina
HOURS: Mon.-Fri. 9 A.M.–5 P.M. and 7-11 P.M., Sat.-Sun. 9 A.M.–11 P.M.
METRO: Viveros

A neighborhood legend, Las Lupitas has attracted visitors from across the city for years to munch on the tasty, inexpensive northern Mexican specialties in a colorful tiled dining room about six blocks west of Jardín del Centenario. Try the *enchiladas potosinas* (cheese and onion enchiladas in a tortilla prepared with *ancho* chile in the dough), one of the specialties.

LOS DANZANTES 💲💲💲

Jardín del Centenario 12, 55/5658-6451
HOURS: Sun.-Thurs. noon-11 P.M., Fri.-Sat. noon-1 A.M.
METRO: Viveros

The Swiss-trained chef's lyrical way with food lives up to the name of this plaza-side restaurant, which means "the dancers." The menu emphasizes Mexican fusion cuisine, offering such house specialties as *fettuccine con salsa de jitomate, ostiones ahumados, y chile pasilla* (fettucine topped with a sauce of smoked oysters, tomato, and chocolate-colored dried chiles) and *pechuga rellena de queso con salsa de cabuches* (chicken breast filled with cheese and covered with the fruit of the barrel cactus). The plush bar offers a wide selection of high-quality tequilas. Prices are high, but this is one of the more culinarily interesting restaurants in the city, so foodies should find it a worthwhile splurge. They offer plaza-side tables as well as indoor seating on the ground floor of a two-story colonial-style mansion.

MIDDLE EASTERN
EL SHEIK $$

Madrid 129, 55/5659-3311
HOURS: Daily 8 A.M.-7 P.M.
METRO: Viveros

A few blocks northwest of Jardín Hidalgo, El Sheik serves specialties such as hummus and tabouli ($3.50) or a mixed plate of goodies for $12. Although it caters to a mostly wealthier crowd (and is priced accordingly), the dining room is a fairly unpretentious place, popular for lunch.

TACOS, TORTAS, AND SNACKS
EL TIZONCITO $$

Aguayo and Cuauhtémoc
HOURS: Sun.-Thurs. noon-2 A.M., Fri.-Sat. noon-4 A.M.
METRO: Viveros

This branch of the famed Condesa restaurant, in the bottom floor of an imposing colonial mansion, offers a delicious variety of tacos and other *antojitos* along with beer and soft drinks. Prices are a bit higher than in most *taquerías,* but the food is very reliable. The *tacos al pastor,* marinated meat cooked on a spit, are the house specialty.

PEPE COYOTES $

Av. Hidalgo, half a block off the Jardín
HOURS: Daily 8 A.M.-2 A.M.
METRO: Viveros

At this simple little eatery you'll get filling tacos at reasonable prices and savory *pozole* (corn and meat stew) also. Not a lot of frills here, but the food is hearty and well prepared, and a good value.

QUESADILLA STANDS $

Half block east of Jardín Hidalgo, on the north side of Calle de la Higuera
HOURS: Daily 8 A.M.-5 P.M.
METRO: Viveros

Those unafraid of food sold from street stands should stop by this cluster of semi-indoor stands serving quesadillas with your choice of cheese, cheese with pepper strips, cheese with beans, potato, *panza* (beef stomach), *sesos* (cow brains—yes, believe it), *huitlacoche* (corn fungus—believe that too), mushrooms, *flor de calabaza,* and chicken or beef *tinga* (spicy stew), along with *sopes* and tostadas with choice of toppings. It's all under one roof; plain cheese quesadillas start at $0.60 each. Also on hand are delicious *flautas* (rolled, deep-fried tortillas with meat filling) and *pozole.*

URUGUAYAN
ENTRE VERO $$

Jardín del Centenario 14C, 55/5659-0066
HOURS: Mon.-Fri. 1:30-11 P.M., Sat.-Sun. until midnight
METRO: Viveros

This South American restaurant right on the southern edge of Jardín del Centenario offers such delectables as a grilled vegetable platter with radicchio, eggplant, and zucchini, first grilled and then baked ($8); great pizzas ($10–14); and the standard steaks, empanadas, and pastas.

San Ángel

Map 6

Restaurants in relatively upmarket San Ángel tend to be substantially pricier than those in Coyoacán.

COFFEE AND SWEETS
CHURROS EL CONVENTO ❸

Av. Revolución just off Av. La Paz

HOURS: Mon.-Fri. 9 A.M.-1 A.M., Sat.-Sun. 9 A.M.-midnight

METRO: M. A. de Quevedo

This tiny little shop, next to Ex-Convento del Carmen, serves an endless stream of addictive churros (a sweet Mexican pastry) and hot chocolate to an appreciative crowd of clients. Churros make for an excellent afternoon snack to regain energy after touring the neighborhood.

FRENCH
CLUNY ❸❸

Av. La Paz 57, 55/5550-7350

HOURS: Mon.-Sat. 1 P.M.-midnight, Sun. 1-10 P.M.

METRO: M. A. de Quevedo

Cluny, just across Avenida Revolución from the center of San Ángel, serves a selection of delectable crepes to local francophiles. You can choose between "salty" crepes, with ingredients such as chicken, corn, cheese, and *huitlacoche;* or sweet ones with strawberries and cream or caramel and nuts. It also has very good salads.

MEXICAN
FONDA SAN ÁNGEL ❸❸

San Jacinto 3, 55/5550-1641

HOURS: Mon.-Sat. 9 A.M.-midnight, Sun. 10 A.M.-9 P.M.

METRO: M. A. de Quevedo

Right on Plaza San Jacinto in a two-story colonial building, the Fonda San Ángel has a lovely ambience and well-prepared Mexican dishes. One culinary attraction is that instead of choosing from the menu, you can pick a meat and your own mix of 15 different sauces to go with it. The *arrachera* (tender flank steak) with *pimiento* (pepper) sauce is one excellent choice, or the waiters can help you pick another combination to suit your tastes. It's a good place to have a drink after a hot Saturday morning of shopping.

SAN ÁNGEL INN ❸❸❸

Diego Rivera 50, 55/5616-0973 or 55/5616-1527

HOURS: Mon.-Sat. 1 P.M.-1 A.M., Sun. 1-10 P.M.

METRO: Barranca del Muerto

Built in the 17th century as an opulent Carmelite monastery, and later home to Spanish viceroys—and, briefly, Emperor Maximilian and his wife, Carlota—the justifiably famed San Ángel Inn has seen a variety of guests over its three centuries, including Santa Anna and his troops, and, during the Revolution, Emiliano Zapata and Pancho Villa. Today, though still called San Ángel Inn, it's a restaurant only, with no overnight guests. The traditional Mexican food is sublime though pricey (especially the drinks, which add up fast), and the dining room is often crowded.

SEAFOOD
LA CAMELIA ❸❸

Madero 3, 55/5616-4668

HOURS: Mon.-Wed. noon-9 P.M., Thurs.-Sun. 10 A.M.-11 P.M.

METRO: M. A. de Quevedo

The long-running La Camelia, located right on the plaza, serves excellent Mexican seafood dishes. Try the red snapper with a green sauce made with *hoja santa* (special herb) and cilantro for $18, or *tostada camellia* with either shrimp, octopus, or fish ceviche for $5. The seafood buffet for $12 from 2–5 P.M. on Wednesday, Friday, Saturday, and Sunday is a very good value considering the quality.

Greater Mexico City Map 7

While most visitors will seek out food in the main neighborhoods described in this guide, the quiet colonial neighborhood of Tlalpan, southeast of Coyoacán, has a fine little square around which are tucked a number of sidewalk cafés and restaurants. It's a ways off the main tourist track, but if you go that way, the restaurants below are definitely worth a look.

ARGENTINE
RESTAURANTE 1900 $$
Hidalgo on the plaza, 55/5573-3693
HOURS: Tues.-Sat. 1:30-11:30 P.M., Sun. 1:30-7 P.M.

This very popular eatery on the north side of the Tlalpan plaza has a small, simple dining room invariably bustling with diners. The *bife de chorizo* ($27) is the star of the menu, but there are a number of other less expensive and still very hearty steaks, as well as a very good *pizza mediterranea* with shrimp and calamari ($14).

CANTINAS
LA JALISCIENCE $$
Plaza de la Constitución 6
HOURS: Mon.-Sat. noon-11 P.M.

On the southeast side of the Tlalpan square is this traditional old cantina, the name of which means "the lady from Jalisco," and the place features swinging doors, sturdy wooden tables, uniformed waiters, and roving musicians. It's great for a drink and a meal in classic Mexican style. They have a rather unusual (for a cantina) house specialty: *tortas de bacalao* (cod sandwiches).

COFFEE AND SWEETS
CAFÉ LA SELVA $
Corner of Hidalgo and Madero, on Plaza de la Constitución
HOURS: Daily 8 A.M.-11 P.M.

Right on the northeast corner of the plaza is a branch of the Chiapas organic coffee shop chain, with strong and politically correct coffees as well as pastries and light sandwiches.

RESTAURANTS

NIGHTLIFE

Maybe it's the fact that living in such a determinedly urban environment already seems unhealthy, but Mexico City residents are unquestionably prone to excess. They like to have fun often, and tend to do it for several hours, if not days, at a time. Most parties really don't get going until after midnight, and if the vibe is right, staying up until the morning light is not uncommon—and not just for 20-year-olds, either.

The varieties of nightlife options in Mexico City are prodigious. Martinis with the slick set, tequilas in a decades-old cantina, salsa dancing in one of the legendary *salones,* or banging heads with an underground rap/punk band are only the more standard options. The more exotically inclined might consider a late-night visit to an old-school *bar de ficha,* where clients buy dances by the ticket, or a transvestite dance review, or an after-hours club thumping with house music until daybreak. You are limited only by your tastes and budget.

Whatever taste appeals, consider making an effort to hear some live music. Mexican music claims a rich heritage, from the traditional folk *chileñas* of the southwestern states to the Latino ska of Mexico City. Because of Mexico's position between the United States and the rest of Latin America, an unusually vibrant cross-fertilization results in an astonishing variety of musical styles that only an ethnomusicological survey could adequately convey.

While Mexico City has a fantastically vibrant music nightlife, it also has a fairly high rate of club turnover, due both to the vagaries of changing tastes as well as an increased propensity by

© GUILLAUME COPART MULLER/WWW.GCMPHOTO.COM

HIGHLIGHTS

LOOK FOR **(** TO FIND RECOMMENDED NIGHTLIFE.

(**Best Pool Hall:** Most Mexico City pool halls are a little on the gritty side, but **Billares Malafama** in the Condesa is a far cry from that, with a dozen tables packed with a younger crowd, a cozy lounge to wait for a table, plenty of drinks to fuel the fun, and groovy music on the stereo (page 115).

(**Best Traditional Cantina:** Of the hundreds of cantinas in this town, **La Guadalupana** in Coyoacán is a great choice. Popular with tourists and Mexicans alike, this old-school cantina has exemplary service, reliable food, and wandering musicians to strike up a tune in front of your table (page 120).

(**Best Folkloric Dance Performance:** With its performances taking place in the ornate Palacio de Bellas Artes, **Ballet Folklórico de Amalia Hernández** is an impressive display of choreographed traditional dances from around Mexico, with elaborate costumes and great music (page 127).

(**Best Salsa Dancing:** It might be tough to squeeze in among all the sweaty bodies, but if you can find room, **Mama Rumba** is well worth it for a taste of live Cuban music and serious hip-shaking, fueled by many *mojitos*. (page 129).

(**Best Night *a la Mexicana*:** There's really no better way to plumb the depths of a night in D.F. than to spend a couple of hours (preferably past midnight) in Plaza Garibaldi. Make your way through the throngs of revelers and mariachis out on the square and grab a table at the convivial **Salón Tenampa,** where the mariachi phenomenon began in the 1920s (page 130).

(**Best Rock Club:** At last check, the hippest club to tap your feet to the latest *rock en español* band was **Pasagüero** in the Centro. Head over on a weekend night to see which band might become the next Café Tacuba or Botellita de Jeréz (page 134).

NIGHTLIFE

city authorities in recent years to shut places down for code violations. Well-established places are almost certain to stay in business for years to come, but there's always a chance that newer places won't survive. Call ahead to make sure a hip new hotspot still has its doors open.

Bars and Clubs

BILLIARDS

Shooting pool is a favorite pastime (mainly for men) in Mexico City, as it is throughout Latin America. The game of choice at most Mexican billiard parlors is *pool,* wherein balls 1–15 are lined up around the sides of the table and are sunk in order. Several players, rather than just two, can play at the same time (as in the common U.S. game cutthroat). Second in popularity is *ocho bola,* or eight-ball, played much like it is in the United States. Less popular but still common are *carambola* tables, which feature three balls and no pockets; you use one ball to strike the other two, but only after it has touched three rails of the table.

(BILLARES MALAFAMA

Michoacán 78, 55/5553-5138

HOURS: Mon.-Wed. 10 A.M.-midnight, Thurs.-Sat. 11 A.M.-1 A.M., Sun. noon-midnight

COST: $8 an hour per table

METRO: Patriotismo

Map 4

Right in the center of the Condesa in a converted warehouse, Malafama is extremely popular with the local hipsters, and with good reason. There are a dozen well-maintained pool tables, a large area with tables and a bar if you aren't playing, great music, and plentiful drinks. Come in the afternoon or early evening to avoid a wait, or sit and watch the crowd with a beer until a table opens up, enjoying the music. The charge is two hours for the price of one before 4 P.M.

CAFECITO DEL BILLAR
Orizaba 99, 55/5207-8441
HOURS: Mon.-Fri. 11 A.M.-11 P.M., Sat. 4-11 P.M., Sun. 4-10 P.M.
COST: $3 an hour per table
METRO: Insurgentes
Map 4

This is a traditional, no-frills Mexican pool hall, with local men drinking beer and shooting Mexican pool beneath fluorescent lights. The tables are in good condition, with both pool and *carambola* tables, and chess and backgammon sets are available also.

UPS & DOWNS
Isabel la Católica 83, 55/5709-1539
HOURS: Mon.-Sat. 10 A.M.-10 P.M.
COST: $3 an hour per table
METRO: Isabel la Católica
Map 1

Most pool halls downtown are not in the greatest condition, and this one is not an exception. However it's a safe spot comfortable for foreigners, and you can also get great *yucateco* food downstairs at Restaurant Coox Hanal.

CANTINAS

Mexico City's many cantinas are wonderful places to toss back a few *tragitos* (swallows; i.e., drinks) with friends while listening to the music of strolling *trovadores* (music groups) and munching on the ever-present *botanas* (snacks). The variety of cantinas in Mexico City is staggering, but in almost all you can expect relatively simple decor (sometimes wood paneling and booths, sometimes linoleum floor and unadorned tables), uniformed waiters, music, food, and of course plentiful drinks. A favorite way to spend an afternoon is sitting with some friends for a few drinks in a cantina, feasting

on the *botanas* that come free with each drink. And we're not talking about salted peanuts here, but meatballs in chipotle sauce, quesadillas, and cheese-filled pastries. *Botanas* are only served during the afternoon meal hour (Mon.–Fri. 2–6 P.M.). Since most true cantinas serve food, you'll find several cantina listings in the *Restaurants* chapter. If a band walks by your table, and you agree to hear a tune, you are expected to pay a bit afterwards. Although some of Mexico City's older bars, especially working-class ones, are men-only hangouts, women will feel comfortable in all the places listed in this section, along with most cantinas in middle-class neighborhoods.

Despite the trepidation that might come over a foreigner stepping into an old neighborhood cantina, most clientele and staff are very polite and friendly to new visitors. Should you attract some unwarranted company, the best thing to do is to be friendly, and hail a waiter to come over and help you out. The waitstaff in most cantinas are exemplary compared to other Mexican restaurants and bars. As well, prices are not the cheapest and the bill can add up quickly, especially if you start drinking shots of good tequila. Check the price list beforehand to know what you're getting into.

BAR LA ÓPERA
Av. Cinco de Mayo 10, 55/5512-8959
HOURS: Mon.- Sat. 1-11:30 P.M., Sun. 1-5:30 P.M.
METRO: Bellas Artes
Map 1

La Ópera is a more traditional, upscale bar in the Centro, where Pancho Villa left bullet holes in the ceiling while riding around inside on his horse during the Revolution. The cantina was built with plenty of wood and huge booths big enough to hold large groups for a tasty dinner ($6–12) or just drinks. Musicians often wander from table to table in the evenings, adding to the ambience. It's an atmospheric spot for a couple of drinks.

BOHEMIO'S
Londres 142, 55/5514-0790
HOURS: Mon.-Sat. 1 P.M.-1 A.M.

METRO: Insurgentes

Map 2

Bohemio's is a lively little cantina that serves pitchers of beer to a crowd of middle-class Mexicans most nights (especially weekends) around their dozen or so tables and bar. The food is Mexican standards, well prepared. It's one of the more relaxed bars in the middle of the Zona Rosa.

CANTINA DE LOS REMEDIOS

Corner of Río Tiber and Río Lerma, Cuauhtémoc, 55/5208-8922

HOURS: Daily 2 P.M.-1 A.M.

METRO: Insurgentes

Map 2

This slightly yuppieish cantina is in a spacious building located a block north of Reforma and is favored by the middle-class office workers from nearby businesses. Wash down tasty *botanas* with reasonably priced (especially during 6–10 P.M. happy hour) drinks in a convivial atmosphere, with sports on the TVs and guitarists strumming from table to table.

CENTENARIO

Vicente Suarez 42

HOURS: Mon.-Sat. noon-1 A.M.

METRO: Patriotismo

Map 4

Right in the center of the Condesa restaurant district is this old-school cantina, a remnant from years past before the neighborhood got so trendy. The crowd is certainly a bit more gentrified than the old days, with a few tables of hipsters taking a break from the scene in the trendy restaurants on the surrounding streets, but there's still a contingent of regulars, strolling musicians, and men playing dominoes. The tequila is not cheap, but the waiters are attentive and amiable.

EL CANDELERO

Insurgentes Sur 1333, 55/5598-9008

HOURS: Mon.-Sat. 1:30 P.M.-2 A.M., Sun. 1:30-6 P.M.

METRO: Insurgentes Metrobús

Map 5

Down Insurgentes Sur between Condesa and

San Ángel is this baroque-styled restaurant and bar. Choose between sitting in the cozier bar or at a table in the high-ceilinged, spacious central area and enjoy the strains of the roaming mariachi or *trío* bands. Perhaps not worth going out of your way for, but certainly a decent place to stop by for late-night drinks as well as good, traditional Mexican food if you are in the vicinity.

LA AUTÉNTICA

At Álvaro Obregón and Av. Cuauhtémoc, 55/5564-7588

HOURS: Daily 10 A.M.-11 P.M., although closing time can vary widely depending on the number of clients

METRO: Cuauhtémoc

Map 4

A well-run, traditional cantina in the Roma, La Auténtica might look a little daunting from the outside, but take the plunge and grab a seat and you will soon feel quite comfortable. Uniformed waiters bustle to and fro keeping the many clients well supplied with hearty traditional Mexican food and bountiful drinks to wash it down. The service is great, the ambience is friendly, and wandering guitarists play tunes for a nominal fee.

LA COVADONGA

Puebla 121, 55/5533-2701

HOURS: Mon.-Fri. 1 P.M.-2 A.M.

METRO: Insurgentes

Map 4

To see a classic example of a decidedly uncool place suddenly become hip, take a visit to this well-kept cantina/restaurant near the Plaza Río de Janeiro, housed in a cavernous room with a fine old bar at one end and a couple dozen tables populated mostly by men playing dominoes. Many artists and art-scene followers converge at Covadonga after an exhibit opening in the neighborhood to enjoy a few drinks and the good Spanish and Mexican food.

NIGHTLIFE

THE LIQUID HEART OF MEXICO

Tequila is a pallid flame that passes through walls and soars over tile roofs to allay despair.

Álvaro Mútis, *Tequila: Panegyric and Emblem*

Mexico's national drink has been in production since at least the time of the Aztecs. The Aztecs in fact called themselves Mexicas in direct reference to the special spiritual role mescal – tequila's forerunner – played in their culture via Mextli, the god of agave (the desert plant from which mescal and tequila are derived). These names, as interpreted by the Spanish, eventually yielded "Mexico."

The first true distillers of mescal – as opposed to pre-Hispanic forms of fermented maguey juice such as *pulque* – are thought to have been the Filipinos who accompanied the Spanish to Mexico aboard the famous Manila galleons. Although modern historians once assumed the distilling technique for tequila came from Europe, tequila stills – now as in the past – copy Southeast Asian rather than European methods of distilling, eschewing the familiar coiled piping for a simple distillation dome over the boilers.

In 1795, King Carlos IV granted the first legal concession to produce tequila to Don José María Guadalupe Cuervo. The liquor's name was taken from the Ticuila Indians of Jalisco, who mastered the technique of baking the heart of the *Agave tequiliana weber,* or **blue agave,** and extracting its juice, a process employed by tequila distilleries today. Native to Jalisco, this succulent is the only agave that produces true tequila as certified by the Mexican government. All liquors labeled "tequila" must contain at least 51 percent blue agave distillates. Contrary to the myth that all true tequila must come from Tequila, Jalisco, Mexican law enumerates specific districts in five different Mexican states where tequila may be legally produced.

Despite the fact that tequila sales are booming today, much of the tequila-making process is still carried out *a mano* (by hand). In the traditional method, the mature heart of the tequila agave, which looks like a huge pineapple and weighs 50–150 pounds, is roasted in pits for 24 hours, then shredded and ground by mule- or horse-powered mills. After the juice is extracted from the pulp and fermented in ceramic pots, it's distilled in copper stills to produce the basic tequila, which is always clear and colorless, with an alcohol content of around 40 percent.

True "gold" tequilas are produced by aging the tequila in imported oak barrels to achieve a slightly mellowed flavor. The *reposado,* or "rested," type is oak-aged for at least two months, while *añejo,* or "aged," tequila must stay in barrels at least a year. Inferior "gold" tequilas may be nothing more than the silver stuff mixed with caramel coloring – always look for *reposado* or *añejo* on the label if you want the true gold.

Dozens of tequilas populate the shelves of liquor stores and bars in Mexico. José Cuervo and Sauza are the two brands best known to most foreigners. A step up is Jimador, Cazadores, and Centenario, which are decent for mixing but not so hot straight up. Some of the better makes include Las Trancas, Don Julio, La Perseverancia, Tesoro de Don Felipe, Patrón, and my personal favorite for flavor and price, Herradura. Herradura uses 100 percent agave, while the less-expensive brands are only 51 percent. If it's 100 percent, it will say so on the bottle. Cuervo produces a high-end limited-edition tequila called Reserva de la Familia that is pricey and superb.

Drink tequila straight up from a tall, narrow shot glass (*caballito*). Licking a few grains of salt before taking a shot and sucking a lime wedge afterward makes it go down smoother, but when it comes to a good tequila, try it *solo*. An old tequila standby is the much-abused margarita, a tart Tex-Mex cocktail made with tequila, lime juice, and Cointreau (usually substituted with Controy or triple sec in Mexico) and served in a salt-rimmed glass. More popular than margaritas among Mexican drinkers is a sort of Mexican highball, mixing tequila with 7-Up, Squirt, or (for a real wake-up call) Red Bull.

MESCAL AND THE WORM

The distillate of other agave plants – also known

WWW.123RF.COM/SHANE MORRIS

Tequila is derived from the blue agave cactus, grown in central-western Mexico near the city of Guadalajara.

as magueys or century plants – is called mescal (sometimes spelled "mezcal"), not to be confused with the nondistilled mescal – *pulque* – prepared in pre-Hispanic Mexico. The same roasting and distilling process is used for today's mescal as for tequila. (Actually, tequila is a mescal, but no drinker calls it that.) Although many states in Mexico produce mescal, the best is said to come from the state of Oaxaca.

The caterpillar-like grub or *gusano de maguey* (maguey worm) at the bottom of a bottle of mescal lives on the maguey plant itself. They're safe to eat – just about anything pickled in mescal would be – though not particularly appetizing. Maguey worms are often fried and eaten with fresh corn tortillas and salsa – a delicious appetizer.

PULQUE

Let some maguey-cactus sap ferment and you have *pulque*, an ancient Mexican drink infused with more mystique than even tequila. Usually served in rustic establishments called *pulquerías*, the nutty-flavored, somewhat viscous liquid has an alcohol level comparable to beer and is said to be loaded with protein, vitamins, and minerals. *Pulquerías* are men-only establishments where outsiders are sometimes viewed with mild but real suspicion; it's best to enter with a regular. In the nearby states

of Tlaxcala, Hidalgo, and México, you will also find the occasional *ambulante* (street vendor) selling the beverage, often blended with fruit or nut extracts to produce a colorful display of bottles.

Before the arrival of the Spanish, Aztec priests drank *pulque* – Mexico's first alcoholic beverage – only during religious rituals. Spanish colonization and later Mexican independence secularized and democratized the consumption of *pulque*, and by 1883 Mexico City denizens were imbibing 100,000 tons of the inebriating liquid. Under Porfirio Díaz, consumption in the capital tripled, as huge haciendas in nearby Apam, Soltepec, Omestuco, Otumba, Apizaco, and Guadalupe dedicated themselves to cultivation of the agave plant and *pulque* production. By 1905 Mexico City boasted well over a thousand *pulquerías* – one for every 300 residents. The popularity of *pulque* waned considerably after World War II, when *capitalinos* became more accustomed to beer, brandy, and tequila.

The method for making the ancient drink has varied little over the last thousand years. When an agave or *maguey* is about to flower, a *tlachiquero* (harvester) slices the top off the plant and scoops out the middle of the plant's heart (often referred to as the *piña* for its pineapple-like shape). The sweet sap of the plant will naturally accumulate in the resulting hollow. Several times daily the *tlachiquero* collects this *aguamiel* (literally, "honey water") by inserting a long tube into the hollow and siphoning the juice into a shoulder-slung sack. One *maguey* will continue to produce *aguamiel* for two or three months before drying up. Left to stand, the sweet juice will ferment on its own into *pulque*, but the process is usually helped along by adding *madre* ("mother," previously fermented *pulque*), which will turn the entire batch into *pulque* in just one day. The results must be drunk within 24 hours, before the beverage goes bad.

NIGHTLIFE

Dominos are a favorite pastime in many Mexico City cantinas.

LA FAENA

V. Carranza 49, 55/5510-4417
HOURS: Sun.-Thurs. noon-10 P.M., Fri.-Sat. noon-2 A.M.
METRO: San Juan Letrán
Map 1

This rather unusual high-ceilinged bar/restaurant pays homage to the *fiesta brava,* bullfighting. Stylish old bullfighting costumes fill the glass cases around the room. It often has tacky live music and, amusingly enough, some nights it gets taken over by hipsters holding alternative music events or just sitting around drinking. It's an interesting, offbeat place to have a couple of drinks, set in a beautiful though decrepit colonial-era building.

LA FLOR ASTURIANA

Puente de Alvarado 80, near the Monumento a la Revolución, 55/5535-4353
HOURS: Mon.-Sat. noon-11 P.M.
METRO: Revolución
Map 2

"The Asturian Flower" is a low-key neighborhood cantina with tasty *botanas* free with the drinks in the late afternoon. There is live music Wednesday through Friday from 5 P.M. onward. It's a quiet spot for early-evening drinks and snacks, particularly if you're staying at one of the nearby budget hotels.

🄲 LA GUADALUPANA

Caballo Calco at Jardín Hidalgo, 55/5554-6253
HOURS: Mon.-Sat. 10 A.M.-midnight
METRO: Viveros
Map 6

This very popular *cantina familiar* (family cantina) in Coyoacán first opened its doors in 1932, although it moved to its current location just a couple of years ago. It manages to still be authentic (complete with boozy locals) and comfortable for most foreigners. The full menu covers all the Mexican standards. Prices are a bit higher than in most cantinas.

LA MASCOTA

Mesones 20
HOURS: Daily noon-11 P.M.
METRO: San Juan Letrán
Map 1

This downtown cantina is well-lit and

friendly, comfortable for foreigners and Mexicans alike. They offer *botanas* or multi-course fixed meals. Most people come for the free *botanas,* usually a choice of seven different plates like meatballs in chipotle sauce or *carnitas* (braised pork).

DANCE CLUBS AND LOUNGES

Because of both the current spate of club closures by city authorities and the generally very fast turnover of clubs among the trend-conscious crowd, attempting to list currently hip dance clubs and bars is a dangerous task. Those in this section seem to have withstood the test of time, and hopefully, they will be around for some time. But to be sure, it's a good idea to take a look at club listings in current magazines and newspapers to check on the latest hot spots. The weekend pullout section of the daily newspaper *Reforma* has a good club list with descriptions of what to expect, as does the Mexico City *Chilango* magazine, including a section in English.

Also worth looking for are occasional outdoor concerts, with big bands like Manu Chao and Los Tigres del Norte playing in the Zócalo, and less-known bands in smaller parks like Parque México in Colonia Condesa.

A.M.

Upstairs in the old Condesa Cinema building at the corner of Tamaulipas and Juan Escutia
HOURS: Thurs.-Sat. 11 P.M.-7 A.M.
COST: $10
METRO: Patriotismo or Sevilla
Map 4

At last report this was one of the trendiest after-hours clubs in central Mexico City, but with fickle D.F. trends don't be surprised if it no longer is when you read this. But one never knows, and if it does stay at its present level it would be worth checking out. A.M. is quite the decadent super-late-night scene, with groovy music, lots of really attractive wealthy people, and copious drinks (and probably much else besides). It's right around the corner from the Pata Negra bar in the Condesa.

CIBELES

Plaza Villa de Madrid 17, 55/5208-2029
HOURS: Tues.-Sat. 7 P.M.-close
COST: No cover
METRO: Sevilla
Map 4

The upscale and massively trendy Cibeles bar takes its name from the traffic circle it is situated on, the Fuente de los Cibeles (itself named after the plaza of the same name in Madrid). A combination of leather couches, chandeliers, wicker chairs, and flocked wallpaper with exposed brick walls gives the place a retro-eclectic atmosphere. Oven-fired pizzas and fruity martinis don't come cheap but they are tasty. On Thursday, Friday, and Saturday nights you will nearly always need a reservation.

EL ÁREA

Rooftop of Hotel Hábita, Av. Mazaryk 201, 55/5282-3100
HOURS: Daily until all hours
COST: No cover
METRO: Polanco
Map 3

This modernist bar looks like a transplant from Miami to the roof of a Polanco hotel. The jet-set clientele lounge and admire each other in relaxing sofas outside, and videos are projected on a nearby building's wall. The same owners run Condesa D.F., another very hip hotel located in the Condesa neighborhood, and their upstairs bar El Patio is similarly popular with the flashy crowd. Entertainment celebrities visiting town are often spotted at one of the two places.

EL HIJO DEL CUERVO

Jardín Centenario 17, 55/5658-7824
HOURS: Mon.-Wed. 5-11 P.M., Thurs.-Sun. 1 P.M.-1 A.M.
COST: No cover
METRO: Viveros
Map 6

If you're in the south of the city looking for a night out, it's hard to go wrong with the ever-popular El Hijo del Cuervo. This large bar located right on Jardín Centenario is invariably packed with more upscale Coyoacán denizens, especially on weekends.

NIGHTLIFE

NIGHTLIFE

EL MITOTE

Amsterdam 33, 55/5211-9150, www.elmitote.com
HOURS: Tues.-Sat. 8 P.M.-1 A.M., Sun.-Mon. 1 P.M.-2 A.M.
COST: No cover
METRO: Sevilla
Map 4

El Mitote is more relaxed and less pretentious than many Condesa nightspots, a chilled out little bar set around several small rooms in an old Condesa house just off Parque México. The music—usually jazz or alternative rock—is kept at a volume that still allows for conversation with friends around the various stools and chairs.

LA BODEGUITA EN MEDIO

Cozumel 37, 55/5553-0246
HOURS: Mon.-Wed. 1-11 P.M., Thurs.-Sat. 1 P.M.-1 A.M., Sun. 1-5 P.M.
COST: No cover
METRO: Sevilla
Map 4

For those who know the famed Havana bar of the same name, don't get too excited. There's no dancing here—the place is just a relaxed restaurant and bar where you can order *mojitos* and enjoy the small band that wanders from table to table.

LA PATA NEGRA

At the corner of Tamaulipas and Juan Escutia, 55/5211-5563
HOURS: Sun.-Tues. 1 P.M.-1 A.M., Wed.-Sat. 1 P.M.-2 A.M.
COST: No cover
METRO: Patriotismo or Sevilla
Map 4

For a taste of the Condesa in-crowd, stop by this hugely popular Spanish-style tapas bar that can get packed later in the evening with Condesa hipsters, all milling around looking beautiful with their drinks and food. The bar has a large selection of mixed drinks.

LA PERLA

República de Cuba 44
HOURS: Usually Thurs. and Fri. until 4 A.M. or so, but hours and days vary
COST: $4
METRO: Allende
Map 1

For a taste of underground nightlife in Mexico City, hit La Perla. Normally there is techno/house music on Thursday and a mixed bag of random music and events on Friday and Saturday. There are frequently transvestite shows on Friday nights, which get packed with a mostly straight crowd; it's best to arrive before 10 P.M.

NON SOLO BAR

Álavaro Obregón 130, Roma, 55/5574-8795
HOURS: Mon.-Sat. 8 P.M.-2 A.M.
COST: No cover
METRO: Insurgentes
Map 4

This laid-back place is in the Roma on the 2nd floor of a modest Italian restaurant, Non Solo Pasta. There is usually a DJ spinning house music or something similarly groovy.

PERVERT LOUNGE

Uruguay 70, 55/5510-4454
HOURS: Wed.-Sat. 11 P.M.-5 A.M. or so
COST: $6
METRO: Zócalo
Map 1

The long-running Pervert in the Centro has truly withstood the test of time, keeping a young crowd dancing until the wee hours for well over a decade now. It's perhaps not quite the "in" place that it once was, but it has a reputation for great music.

REXO

Saltillo 1 at Nuevo León, 55/5553-1300
HOURS: Mon.-Fri. 1 P.M.-2 A.M.
COST: No cover
METRO: Patriotismo
Map 4

An upscale spot favored by the well-dressed set in the Condesa, Rexo is in a sleek glass-and-metal structure, with the bar downstairs to the left and tables distributed around different levels of the post-modern-feeling place.

RIOMA

Insurgentes Sur 377, 55/5584-0613
HOURS: Wed.-Sat. 11:30 P.M.-close
COST: $12
METRO: Chilpancingo
Map 4

One still popular late-night dance club in the Condesa is Rioma. Don't be put off by the strange entrance, which looks like a parking garage. The club reputedly was owned years ago (in a very different permutation, no doubt) by famed Mexican comedian Cantinflas.

GAY AND LESBIAN

Mexico City has a vibrant queer subculture. It may not be as out in the open as in Europe or the United States, but it's a lot more apparent than in much of Latin America. The capital's queer scene is replete with hangouts of all different styles, from old-time gay cantinas to techno discos to drag dance revues. Pamphlets such as "La Otra Guia" or "Sergay" have listings of current clubs and can be picked up at several of the places written up below. Most of these clubs welcome women as well as men, although the women will be heavily outnumbered. For more information, check the Internet: www.sergay.com.mx has information in English and Spanish, while www.saldelcloset.com/homopolis is a good resource (in Spanish) for events and information about gay life in Mexico.

In the Mexico City queer scene you may observe a class, race, and social divide. A lighter-skinned, upper-class clientele tends to frequent the more expensive clubs, while middle- and lower-class folks who are more likely to live with their families, perhaps in the closet, frequent the cheaper joints.

Many gays and lesbians live in the Colonia Condesa neighborhood, and a stroll through its streets or around the ellipse of Parque México is a pleasant way to spend a couple of hours. There are several gay-owned eateries in the Condesa restaurant. The Zona Rosa has become a gay nightlife district, as evidenced from the many rainbow flags you'll see around the neighborhood. The streets of the Zona Rosa are a major cruising zone for gay men on weekend afternoons and evenings.

If after all this hedonism you are missing something spiritual in your life, you'll be welcome at Mexico City's only gay church, the **Instituto de la Comunidad Metropolitana** (Norte 77, No. 3218, in Azcapotzalco, 55/5556-2172 or 55/5396-7768). It is an ecumenical chapel in the house of Father Jorge and Father Rodolfo, two priests who have been partners for more than 20 years. Mass is on Sunday at 10 A.M., 12:30 P.M., and 7 P.M. and lasts about two hours. Take the Metro to Cuitlahuac station, and from there take a taxi to the address.

BUTTERGOLD

Izazaga 9 at Eje Central, 55/5761-1861 or 55/5761-1351
HOURS: Fri.-Sat. 10 P.M.-close
COST: $6
METRO: Salto de Agua
Map 1

This is the reincarnation of the former Butterflies club, and the basic style is the same as before. The big club holds one of the city's best drag revues, and it is always packed on Friday and Saturday nights.

CANTINA VIENA

República de Cuba 3
HOURS: Daily until late
COST: No cover
METRO: Bellas Artes
Map 1

The Viena is a working-class gay bar near the Eje Central that looks just like any other Mexican cantina you might see, even down to the fact that men are the only clients. It gives a taste of what Mexico City gay life was like in years past, when acting overtly gay was not an option. There are a few other gay bars nearby, some of them extremely seedy. Be wary in the dark streets when arriving and departing. Right next door is the similar Cantina Oasis.

NIGHTLIFE

NIGHTLIFE

EL ANSIA

Insurgentes Sur 1391, 55/5615-9841
HOURS: Thurs. 9 P.M.–close, Fri.–Sat. 10 P.M.–close
COST: Free Thurs. 9–11 P.M., $7 otherwise
METRO: Mixcoac
Map 5

This is an intriguing club where on Thursdays, if you so choose, you may wear a numbered badge allowing potential beaux to leave notes for you in the corresponding message box. Friday and Saturday are more regular DJ dance nights. And for the cowboy in you, the last Friday of every month is rodeo night, complete with *grupera* music, a mechanical bull, and lots of men in leather.

EL TALLER/EL ALMACÉN

Florencia 37, 55/5533-4984 or 55/5207-0727
HOURS: Daily from early evening until late
COST: $6 Thurs.–Sun., free Mon.–Wed.
METRO: Insurgentes
Map 2

El Almacén is a longtime favorite, located in a semi-industrial sort of space on the west side of the Zona Rosa, with popular tunes, videos, strippers, and lots of men on the make. Tuesday and weekend nights are particularly strong. This is also a good place to find out about other "in" spots. Downstairs in the same building, connected via a stairway from the men's bathroom in El Almacén, is El Taller, a dance club favoring techno and remix pop tracks.

GAYTA

Amberes 18 at Reforma
HOURS: Daily until late
COST: No cover
METRO: Insurgentes
Map 2

This little café and bar is popular with both men and women for the chilled-out atmosphere and even more chilled frozen drinks, which come with amusingly obscene names and dramatic colors. It's a good place to have a drink or coffee, connect with others, and gear up for dancing later on in the evening elsewhere.

LIPSTICK

Amberes 1, 55/5514-4920
HOURS: Wed.–Sat. 10 P.M.–4 A.M.
COST: $7 Wed., $12 Thurs.–Sat.
METRO: Insurgentes
Map 2

Located in the upper floor of an old mansion right on the corner of Amberes and Paseo de la Reforma, Lipstick is one of the most popular mainly (but not exclusively) lesbian venues in the city. The dance floor is packed most nights with ladies dancing to mainly pop music, with videos on the wall and the windows flung open wide to let in the breeze.

LIVING

Paseo de la Reforma 483, 55/5286-0069, www.living.com.mx
HOURS: Fri.–Sat. 10 P.M.–close
COST: $10–15
METRO: Chapultepec
Map 2

This is *the* spot to be for a Saturday-night dance party. The cavernous club, located on Reforma just next to the Torre Mayor skyscraper, has great DJs, wild dancers and performances, laser light shows, dry-ice smoke—the works. The main room pulsates with driving electronica beats, and there's also a pop room for dancing to English and Spanish hits. Head out to the small terrace overlooking Reforma if you need a break from dancing and a breath of air.

TOM'S LEATHER BAR

Insurgentes Sur 357, 55/5564-0728, www.toms-mexico.com
HOURS: Tues.–Sun. until late
COST: cover $8
METRO: Chilpancingo
Map 4

You won't find much leather here, but it's definitely a more dressed-down sort of place than other D.F. gay clubs, with plenty of men in blue jeans and T-shirts drinking beers. There are also strippers, porn videos, a dark gothic interior, a backroom, and eclectic music—the only gay bar where you might croon along with Ella Fitzgerald singing "Summertime."

VIP CABARETITO

Londres 104, 55/5208-2305, www.cabaretito.com
HOURS: Wed.-Sun. 7 P.M.-close
COST: Wed. usually no cover, then variable
on weekends
METRO: Insurgentes
Map 2

The Cabaretito is a Zona Rosa gay institution, popular with both men and women. Wednesday is DJ night, while an erotic show is held most other nights. Thursday is usually for women only.

PULQUERÍAS

Bars serving *pulque,* a weirdly viscous and alcoholic fermented juice of the agave plant, could be found on virtually every street corner in the city before World War II. Nowadays they are few in number, though a few classics hold on. Pulquerías tend to be humble establishments, so don't come expecting the same quality as cantinas—the "bathroom" is usually an open drain against the back wall, barely partitioned off. There is a predominantly male clientele in pulquerías and the environment is not always welcoming for women. One pulquería I went to that has since closed had a curious little booth of sorts near the entrance to the bar, which was for women who might want a drink, but who weren't allowed to come into the main bar area.

PULQUERÍA HERMOSA HORTENSIA

North side of Plaza Garibaldi
HOURS: Wed.-Mon. 5 P.M.-2 A.M.
METRO: Garibaldi
Map 1

Probably the most convenient place for tourists to sample *pulque* is this venerable spot right on Plaza Garibaldi. Although not the most traditional *pulquería* in the city, the Hermosa Hortensia is a relatively safe place to try the drink. However take care walking in the surrounding area after dark—best to take a taxi.

PULQUERÍA LAS DUELISTAS

Aranda 30 betw. Ayuntamiento and Puente de Peredo
HOURS: Mon.-Sat. 9 A.M.-9 P.M.
METRO: San Juan Letrán
Map 1

This spot, next to Mercado San Juan in the Centro, a few blocks south of the Alameda, has been serving *pulque* for more than 50 years. Especially good are the *curados* (*pulque* mixed with fruit or nut extracts). The *rockola* (jukebox) specializes in José Alfredo Jiménez, one of the great *ranchera* singers.

TEQUILARÍAS

Although tequila is served in virtually every bar or cantina in the city, a few places make a point of providing a full range of Mexico's better tequilas. Because of the emphasis on quality, these can be pricey places to drink, but if you fancy yourself a tequila aficionado—or if you mean to become one—*tequilerías* are a must. In addition to the usual Jimador, Herradura (their *reposado* is my personal favorite), and Cazadores, you'll find such illustrious brands

the joys of a well-stocked bar...

© EMILIA GOMEZ

NIGHTLIFE

as Garañón, Los García, Don Jesús, El Tesoro de Don Felipe, Pura Sangre, Los Corrales, Dos Amigos, Tres Mujeres, Sombrero Negro, Don Leoncio, Cimarrón, Misión Imperial, Don Tacho, Las Iguanas, Bambarria, Los Tres Alegres Compadres, La Cava del Villano, Tenoch, Las Trancas, Reserva del Patrón, Zafarrancho, El Grito, Los Valientes, Chamuco Reposado, and many more.

MARÍA BONITA
Av. Mariano Escobedo 700, Col. Anzures, 55/5203-2121
HOURS: Mon.-Sat. 5 P.M.-1 A.M.
METRO: Chapultepec
Map 3

If you're not the type to venture out to cantinas but you'd like to sample some high-end tequila, head to this bar in the luxurious Hotel Camino Real, which pours more than 120 kinds of tequila. If straight tequila isn't to your liking, the bartenders will mix up tequila cocktails, including a *margarita azul,* tequila sunrise, *cucaracha,* iguana, *chilango, México lindo,* or a *tecama.* Bolero *tríos* wander the floor, and there are assorted free *botanas.*

SALONES TEQUILA DE LA CASA DE LAS SIRENAS
República de Guatemala 32, 55/5704-3273
HOURS: Mon.-Thurs. 1-11 P.M., Fri.-Sat. 1 P.M.-2 A.M.,
Sun. 1-6 P.M.
METRO: Zócalo
Map 1

Behind the Catedral Metropolitana in the Centro, La Casa de las Sirenas occupies three rooms of a beautiful old mansion built of volcanic stone. At last report, the bar offered more than 120 labels of tequila. Service includes all the elements for tackling your assignment: salt, *chile piquín,* and limes. It's a pleasingly refined ambience to sample some fine tequila, and the food is excellent if you're hungry.

SALÓN ESPAÑA
Luis González Obregón 25 at República de Argentina, 55/5702-1719
HOURS: Mon.-Sat. 10 A.M.-11:30 P.M.
METRO: Zócalo
Map 1

Despite its name, this cantina is devoted to Mexico's national drink. In a section of the former *convento* of La Enseñanza (see the *Sights* chapter), you'll find more than 215 brands of tequila costing $3–20 per glass. Don't be deterred by the less-than-impressive entryway; the interior is clean and orderly. Three or four different free *botanas* are served daily, along with a menu of traditional *antojitos* (snacks) and a *comida corrida* (set meal) costing only $5.

Live Music

CABARET
While cabaret and vaudeville are not overly popular in Mexico City, there are a couple of well-established venues for this sort of act. You'll need proficient Spanish and a decent awareness of Mexican politics and society to catch most of what the performances are about, but even if your Spanish isn't so hot, shows can be entertaining for the music and spectacle.

EL BATACLÁN
Popocatépetl and Amsterdam, 55/5511-7390
HOURS: Most shows Fri. and Sat. at 9 or 10 P.M.
COST: $20
METRO: Insurgentes
Map 4

This small performance space, on the second floor of a beautiful old neighborhood mansion, hosts a varied mix of performances, sometimes music and sometimes theater and vaudeville-type shows. If you get the chance, look for a show by **Astrid Hadad** (www.astridhadad.com for her schedule), a superlative performer who manages to artfully combine biting social and political commentary with respectful takeoffs of Mexico's *rancheras* and *boleros*. Hadad is worth seeing for her stage sets and costume changes alone, and her backing band is excellent. When she's not traveling the world on tour, she frequently plays at El Bataclán on weekend evenings. Stop in for a drink and/or a Cuban-style meal downstairs at La Bodega after the show, and listen to the small group playing Cuban *son*.

EL VICIO

Madrid 13, 55/5659-1139, www.lasreinaschulas.com
HOURS: Vary; shows usually start at 9:30 P.M.
COST: Usually $10-15
METRO: Viveros
Map 6

A more varied lineup can be found at this venue in Coyoacán, an incarnation of the long-running El Hábito. The leaders of El Vicio are *Las Reinas Chulas* ("The Beautiful Queens"), a comedy/cabaret troupe of four women who joined forces with political satirist Jesusa Rodríguez. Shows range from political comedy to monologues to music performances.

FOLKLORIC MUSIC AND DANCE

Música folklórica, ethnic folk music, has its roots at the local level in Mexico's rural areas, with differing *son* or song forms and instrumentation tied to particular regions of Mexico, such as the *sandunga* in Oaxaca, *jarabe* in Jalisco, *jarana* in Yucatán, *danzón* in Veracruz, or *huapango* in Tamaulipas and San Luis Potosí. Such song forms are for the most part restricted to regional festivals or, in Mexico City, at shows staged for the benefit of tourists.

◖ BALLET FOLKLÓRICO DE AMALIA HERNÁNDEZ

Palacio de Bellas Artes at Eje Central and Av. Juárez, 55/5529-9320 or 55/5529-9321, www.balletamalia.com.mx
HOURS: Wed. 8:30 P.M. and Sun. 9:30 A.M. and 8:30 P.M.
COST: $30-50, depending on seating
METRO: Bellas Artes
Map 1

This troupe, founded by Hernández and now managed by her daughter Norma López Hernández, has accumulated 76 folk dances from around Mexico that have been choreographed for Mexico City and foreign tastes into 40 separate "ballets." The costuming, settings, and music for these performances are superb. Some of the choreography—such as the "Aztec" dances—are by nature highly speculative but also among the most dramatic. Each performance consists of ten separate dances, with an intermission. Performances at Bellas Artes are offered only two days a week. They sometimes play at the Teatro Hidalgo across the street also. Although the Amalia Hernández troupe is the most well known and is the permanent Bellas Artes troupe, other folkloric dance companies, such as the Compañia Nacional de Danza Folklórica, perform at Bellas Artes and elsewhere in the city.

GRUPERA

This northern Mexican music (hence it's other name, *norteña*), an accordion-driven adaptation of polka, is hugely popular throughout the country. The lyrics, often about the exploits of famous drug runners, give it a rebel edge. Although Mexico City is not a huge center for *norteña*, there are several places to see a live show.

SALÓN CALIFORNIA

Calz. Tlalpan 1189, Col. Portales, 55/5672-3317
HOURS: Sun. only from 6 P.M.
COST: $8
METRO: Portales
Map 7

Salón California, in the Portales neighborhood well south of the Centro, is better known for its tropical-music dancing, but it has a *grupera* night every Sunday until very late (don't these people have work to do?). It's close to the Portales Metro stop on the blue line.

NIGHTLIFE

BAR LINGO

botanas – snacks (often free with each drink in a cantina)
cantinero/cantinera – bartender
casco – "helmet," empty bottle
cerveza – beer
chela – beer (slang)
chupar – to drink (slang)
con hielo – with ice
copa – glass (for wine)
copita – "little cup," a drink
envase, botella – bottle
hasta atrás – drunk
hasta las chanclas – drunk
la cruda – "the crude," hangover
pedo – drunk (off-color slang)
sin hielo – without ice
tarro – mug (beer)
tragito – "little swallow," a drink
una fría – "a cold one"
vaso – glass (for most drinks)

SALÓN PACÍFICO
Bucareli at Morelos, 55/5592-2778
HOURS: Fri.-Sat. 9 P.M.-3:30 A.M.
COST: $6 men, $2 women
METRO: Hidalgo
Map 2

The best place in town to see live *grupera* and dancing is this longtime dance hall just off Paseo de la Reforma, the modestly named "Catedral de la Quebradita" (after the popular *grupera* dance step). The house band, La Perla Sinaloense (The Pearl from Sinaloa), alternates with visiting acts. Be prepared for cowboy hats and boots and some acrobatic dancing.

JAZZ AND COFFEEHOUSES
Jazz music in Mexico is still somewhat incipient, or at the least not very popularized. Other than the Latin jazz of hard-swinging Cuban bands in the city, it's difficult to find straight-ahead jazz ensembles in D.F. The Zinco club in the Centro Histórico is far and away the best in the city—let's hope they stay open, and encourage others to follow their lead.

BAR ZINCO
Motolinia 20 at Cinco de Mayo, 55/5512-3369 or 55/5518-6369
HOURS: Wed.-Sun. starting around 10 P.M.
COST: Wed. usually free, $10-30 other nights depending on the band
METRO: Bellas Artes
Map 1

This funky lounge is built in the vault of a bank right in the middle of the Centro and comes complete with red velvet curtains and a smoky bar. Jazz varies widely, from a group of 60-year-old Germans playing Dixieland to a young Mexican singer channeling Lena Horne. The bar even serves up very tasty *arrachera* (flank steak) tacos on blue-corn tortillas, if you're craving some bar food *a la mexicana*. It's well worth a visit for jazz fans visiting Mexico City.

CENTRO CULTURAL ESPAÑA
Guatemala 18 right behind the Catedral, 55/5521-1925 or 55/5521-1926, www.centroculturalesp.org.mx
HOURS: Thurs.-Sat. usually 9-11 P.M., sometimes later depending on the event
COST: No cover
METRO: Zócalo
Map 1

The Spanish Cultural Center, housed in a lovingly restored 17th-century colonial palace right in the heart of the Centro, holds numerous cultural and music events on weekend evenings at no cost, making it a popular place for younger intellectual types. Sometimes there's a DJ, sometimes a live band, and frequently there's jazz or acoustic music. The bar has a comfortable vibe, and the crowd is usually interesting.

NEW ORLEANS
Av. Revolución 1655, 55/5550-1908, www.neworleansjazz.com.mx
HOURS: Music most days, usually starting 8 P.M.
COST: $4-8 for regular nights, up to $20 for special events
METRO: Barranca del Muerto
Map 6

The New Orleans has been around since 1972 doing their best to promote jazz in Mexico City. They have several jazz bands that play a regular gig on different nights of the week, ranging from blues to Dixieland to Latin jazz and boleros. Sundays is usually an invited band, and special concerts occur regularly. They also have a full restaurant. It's located right in front of the flower market in San Ángel, on Avenida Revolución.

LATIN DANCE

From the lower Gulf of Mexico coast, Afro-Caribbean styles, from rumba to reggae, have made serious inroads in the Mexico City music and dance scene. Tropical *cumbias* from Colombia and salsa from New York and Puerto Rico have also become standards in the capital, along with the Dominican specialties merengue and *bachata*. All of these Afro-Caribbean forms are generally referred to as *música antillana* (music from the Antilles) or *música tropical*. Although Mexico City is not considered a hot spot for tropical-music dancing (nothing like Puerto Rico, Cuba, the Dominican Republic, or Colombia), the *chilangos* are no strangers to the dance floor. Aficionados will find a few clubs dedicated to tango and flamenco.

BAR ARRABALERO

Corner of Marsella and Dinamarca, 55/5524-4864
HOURS: Fri. 9 P.M.-close
COST: $8
METRO: Insurgentes
Map 2

For live tango music and some excellent dancers, check out Arrabalero, located adjacent to the Posada Viena hotel in Colonia Juárez near the Zona Rosa. Classes are on Fridays in the early evening (to piped-in music) and then the live band starts later on the same night. There are frequently classes at 7 P.M. on other nights also; check with the bar for the latest schedule.

BARFLY

First floor of Plaza Mazaryk, betw. La Fontaine and A. France
HOURS: Tues.-Sat. 10 P.M.-close
COST: $14
METRO: Polanco
Map 3

Polanco is more known for its hipster Miami-style bars and clubs, but it does boast one decent Cuban-style dance club, where the wealthier crowd struts their stuff on the dance floor to a live band. Despite being in a shopping center, it has a comfortable, dimly lit ambience.

GITANERIAS

Oaxaca 15, 55/5514-2027, www.gitanerias.com
HOURS: Thurs.-Sat., first show at 11:30 P.M., second at 1:30 A.M.
COST: $12
METRO: Insurgentes
Map 4

Flamenco music has a small but strong following in the capital. One club serving up hot flamenco in the Roma is Gitanerias, established in 1947 and going strong ever since. The large building belies the cozy, almost cavelike interior, with dim lighting and comfortable seating. Apart from the weekend regular flamenco shows, Gitanerias often hosts special events, such as Arab or Caribbean dance shows.

GRAN LEÓN

Querétaro 225, 55/5564-7110 or 55/5584-5956
HOURS: Tues.-Sat. 9 P.M.-3:30 A.M.
COST: $5
METRO: Insurgentes
Map 4

More or less across the street from Mama Rumba in the Roma, and not quite as chic, is the Gran León, originally established by the same people who ran the famed Bar León in the city center. The live bands keep the crowd swinging their hips until the wee hours with salsa and merengue tunes. Tuesday is *danzón* night, dedicated to a dance from Veracruz. Seating is available in the main hall downstairs by the dance floor or in the smaller balcony. Check out the egg-carton soundproofing on the walls and the fake palm trees.

☾ MAMA RUMBA

Querétaro 230 at Monterrey, 55/5564-6920
HOURS: Wed.-Sat. until very late
COST: $7
METRO: Insurgentes
Map 4

This hugely popular Cuban bar has live *son*

(sort of a Cuban proto-salsa) band nightly, a lively crowd, and plenty of *mojitos*. Although the club has expanded to cope with the crowds, Mama Rumba is still packed every weekend, and it can be difficult to get a table or find space on the packed dance floor. Reservations are a good idea.

SALÓN CALIFORNIA

Calz. Tlalpan 1189, 55/5672-3317
HOURS: Fri.-Sun. until late
COST: $4-6
METRO: Portales
Map 7

The self-proclaimed "Palacio de Baile" (Palace of Dance) of Mexico City is in the Portales neighborhood well south of the Centro. It's another old-style traditional dance hall where the clients take their dancing seriously. Bad dancers can't hide behind inebriation either, as they don't serve any alcohol. Saturday night is usually the best salsa, while Sunday sees a raging *grupera* party.

SALÓN LOS ÁNGELES

Lerdo 206, betw. Ricardo Flores Magón and Estrella, Col. Guerrero, 55/5597-5181
HOURS: Tues.-Sun. 8 P.M.-midnight
COST: $5
METRO: Garibaldi
Map 1

At this old-school dance hall north of the Alameda (and not in a particularly safe area; best to come and go in a taxi), the sign over the door reads *"Quién no conoce Los Ángeles, no conoce México"* (Who doesn't know Los Angeles, doesn't know Mexico), a tribute to Salón Los Ángeles' long-standing place in the hearts of dancing *chilangos*.

SALÓN MÉXICO

Pensador Mexicano 11 at San Juan de Dios near the Alameda, 55/5518-0931
HOURS: Thurs.-Sat. 9 P.M.-3:30 A.M.
COST: $4-6
METRO: Bellas Artes
Map 1

The venerable Salón México is another example of an old-style tropical dance club, the *salón de baile* (dance salon), which reached its peak between the 1930s and 1950s in Mexico City and has managed to hang on into the 21st century. Made famous by the Mexican film of the same name, it was remodeled and reopened in 1993. The spacious club hosts large bands playing salsa, merengue, and sometimes *danzón*, and attracts a wide selection of Mexicans from different social classes and age groups.

PLAZA GARIBALDI

This little square along the east side of Eje Central Lázaro Cárdenas, a few blocks north of Bellas Artes, has been one of the main centers of traditional Mexican nightlife in the capital since the 1920s, when Cirilo Marmolejo and his mariachi band first took up residence at the Salón Tenampa. Marmolejo is long gone, but legions of fellow mariachis still fill Garibaldi every day and night. A foreign visitor interested in experiencing a night of partying *a la mexicana* should go to Garibaldi forthwith, preferably on a Friday or Saturday evening from about 11 P.M. onward. Just make sure you get a *sitio* (radio) cab or other type of safe ride home afterward, as the gangs of *rateros* (thieves) lingering in the back streets a couple of blocks from Garibaldi are almost as famous as the mariachis themselves. The main square, however, is quite safe.

While Garibaldi is in true form mainly at night, tourists may enjoy coming by on a sunny afternoon, having a beer and a couple of tacos at one of the little restaurants on the square's north side, and watching the mariachis ply their trade. A group will gladly strike up an impassioned tune for you right then and there on the square, but it's not cheap—usually $10 for a song, although sometimes you can convince them to play two for the price of one.

◖ SALÓN TENAMPA

North side of Plaza Garibaldi, 55/5526-6176
HOURS: Sun.-Thurs. until 3 A.M., Fri.-Sat. until 4 A.M.
COST: No cover
METRO: Garibaldi
Map 1

The legendary Tenampa, where it all started at Garibaldi decades ago, is still going strong,

MARIACHI TRIVIA

- The word mariachi comes from the French word *mariage* (marriage). The music first became popular at weddings during the French occupation of Mexico (1862-1867).

- Mexico's first nationally known mariachi ensemble was headed by Concho Andrade in the 1920s.

- A traditional troupe features 10 performers — four violinists, three guitarists (actually *guitarrón*, guitar, and *vihuela*), and three trumpet players.

- The male mariachi's tight-fitting silver-studded costume is inspired by Mexican *charro* (horseman) suits.

- About 20 percent of all mariachi musicians are women, whose trademark *coronela* or *china poblana* outfits feature embroidered blouses and long, billowing, brightly colored skirts.

and is a great place to spend a lively evening with much music, alcohol, and merriment. The best bet is to go with a group and commandeer a table or two. If you have a group, buying an entire bottle is a better value than buying lots of individual drinks. Although you don't have to hire bands all night, it's worth paying for a couple of songs from one of the many bands that will walk by. Be sure to confirm the price beforehand. If you really get lit up, by the end of the night you may find yourself paying someone with a little hand electric machine to give your group a collective shock, until one person lets go and breaks the current. Sounds ridiculous, but after the fourth tequila, it starts to seem positively sensible.

Two other favorite mariachi bars on the east side are **Guadalajara de Noche** and **Nuevo México Típico** (both daily 8 P.M.–2 A.M., later on weekends). On the south side adjacent to Eje Central is **Tropicana** (daily 9 P.M.–4 A.M.).

RANCHERAS, CORRIDOS, AND BOLEROS

The most popular song forms among the middle class and among the older generation in Mexico City are *rancheras* (similar to American country and western), *corridos* (Mexican ballads), and boleros. This music become very popular in the 1940s and 1950s, with *trío* bands such as Los Panchos and Los Diamantes. At any bar, cantina, or restaurant where *trovadores* (strolling musicians) play, you'll hear plenty of music of this sort. In most bars or cantinas, you can expect to pay about $3 for a song played by a guitar *trío* at your table. If you're not sure which Mexican tune to pick, ask for anything by Mexican composer Agustín Lara.

LA CASA DE PAQUITA LA DEL BARRIO
Zarco 202, 55/5583-8131
HOURS: Thurs.-Sat. nights
COST: $10
METRO: Guerrero
Map 1

To see a more formal show of *boleros* (or a slightly ironic version of one, at any rate), check out the legendary Paquita la del Barrio, who has her own modest club in Colonia Guerrero. The club is in a relatively sketchy neighborhood after dark, so be sure to come and go by radio taxi. It's for the more adventurous only. Paquita—who is getting on a bit in years—continues the Lola Beltrán tradition of castigating men for their abuse of love through dramatic boleros. She occasionally performs at larger venues around the city, such as the Teatro Metropolitán, and is sometimes on tours around Mexico, so best to call ahead or at least have the taxi waiting to make sure the club is open when you go.

ROCK EN ESPAÑOL

Mexico City was an unquestioned epicenter of the reinvention of rock music with a distinctly Latin style in the 1980s, and continues to be an incubator of more bands than anywhere else in the country. Appropriately for such a city, *chilango* rock bands tend to have a fairly frenetic, often ska/punk edge to

NIGHTLIFE

© GUILLAUME COPART MULLER/WWW.GCMPHOTO.COM

A Mexican party isn't a party unless the mariachis play.

them, although there's plenty of more heavy industrial groups, rappers, bohemian singer-songwriters, and more.

Tickets and schedules for shows at larger venues are best found through TicketMaster (55/5325-9000, www.ticketmaster.com.mx).

ALICIA

Cuauhtémoc 91, 55/5511-2100,
www.myspace.com/foroalicia
HOURS: Thurs.-Sat. 9 P.M.-close
COST: $5-7
METRO: Cuauhtémoc
Map 4

A bare room with a small stage, Alicia can pack in a few hundred enthusiastic young patrons on a good night. Many Mexican bands, mostly but not exclusively from Mexico City, play here regularly. Usually three acts play each night. The telephone works only intermittently, so you're better to either checking their webpage, come by, or keep an eye out for the posters plastered all over the city advertising concerts.

AUDITORIO NACIONAL

Paseo de la Reforma 50, 55/5280-9250,
www.auditorio.com.mx
HOURS: Days and times vary
COST: Usually $30-150 depending on seating
METRO: Auditorio
Map 3

Built in 1950 following the design of architects Teodoro González de León and Abraham Zabludovsky, this 10,000-seat venue is a striking concrete modernist geometric structure opposite the big Polanco hotels on Paseo de la Reforma. Originally designed to host athletic events and conventions, it was converted into its current use as a concert hall in 1990. It has since hosted innumerable major music shows, including many of the major rock bands touring in Mexico as well as classical music, ballet, opera, and even beauty pageants (Miss Universe 1993 and 2007).

BULLDOG

Rubens 6 at Av. Revolución, 55/5331-4381,
www.bulldogcafe.com

© GUILLAUME COPART MULLER/WWW.GCMPHOTO.COM

Rock concert venues range from hole-in-the-wall alternative clubs to huge stadiums.

HOURS: Thurs.-Sat. usually
COST: Cover varies according to event
METRO: Mixcoac
Map 5

Located in the Mixcoac neighborhood, south of Condesa and just north of San Ángel, Bulldog is housed in a bright white converted arabesque mansion. The atmosphere is laid-back and unpretentious, and the cover is usually a lot more for men than women. The club has hosted numerous international bands looking for a D.F. venue, including the Strokes and Red Hot Chili Peppers, to name a couple.

HARD ROCK CAFÉ

Campos Eliseos 278 at Paseo de la Reforma, 55/5327-7101, www.hardrock.com
HOURS: Bar and restaurant daily 1 P.M.-1 A.M., music Thurs.-Sat. from 10:30 P.M.
COST: No cover
METRO: Auditorio
Map 3

The Hard Rock is always reliable, thought not exactly cutting edge, as should be expected from an international chain. The club, very close to the Auditorio Metro station, consists of a main restaurant/bar area and a separate small auditorium for live concerts. Tickets are also available through TicketMaster (55/5325-9000, www.ticketmaster.com.mx).

EL PÉNDULO

Nuevo León 115, 55/5286-9493, www.pendulo.com
HOURS: Varies, but usually Fri. and Sat. nights
COST: Cover varies according to event
METRO: Patriotismo
Map 4

The bookshop El Péndulo in Condesa has an interestingly constructed two-story space around an intimate stage, and frequently hosts small concerts of major bands in a coffeehouse atmosphere. Call or check their website for upcoming shows, or just walk by and look at the big sign on their building, where upcoming acts are posted.

PALACIO DE LOS DEPORTES

Av. Río Churubusco at Viaducto, 55/5237-9999,
www.ticketmaster.com.mx

HOURS: Varies according to event
COST: Varies according to event
METRO: Velódromo
Map 7

Larger *rockero* shows, particularly by major international groups touring in Mexico like White Stripes, Bon Jovi, Lenny Kravitz, and others, are often held at the "Sports Palace." The strange geodesic arena was originally built for the 1968 Olympics. Major concerts are also sometimes held at the outdoor **Foro Sol** in the adjacent Autódromo Hermanos Rodríguez car racetrack.

PASAGÜERO

Motolinia 33, 55/5521-6112, www.pasaguero.com

HOURS: Days vary; shows usually start around 9 P.M.
COST: Varies, but usually $10–20 for well-known band
METRO: Bellas Artes
Map 1

At last report the trendiest rock club was Pasagüero, located in the heart of the Centro, an unusual location for a hip nightspot. The smaller venue is reputedly favored by some bands that can play bigger spaces (like Monterrey's Kinky), but who occasionally prefer a more intimate space to better *convivir* with the audience. The club also hosts regular art shows and events.

VIVE CUERVO SALÓN

Lago Andrómaco 17 near Moliere, 55/5255-1496 or 55/5255-5322

HOURS: Days and times vary
COST: Cover varies according to the event
Map 7

Formerly known as Salón 21, the Vive Cuervo Salón is now only open for special events, but it often has excellent shows. International groups such as the Kaiser Chiefs and Travis have played here. The cavernous club is located just north of Polanco in a nondescript area not well served by public transport. It's best to come in a taxi.

SHOPS

Mexico City has been an entrepôt of trade for many centuries—even before the legendary markets of Tlatelolco that so dazzled the Spanish conquistadors with produce from across the Aztec empire sold in orderly stalls under vigilant imperial guards. Markets still thrive today all over this huge city, selling anything you can imagine, and they are joined by the luxury shops of Polanco with the latest imported fashions, high-end department stores, block-long strips of stores in the Centro specializing in books, electronics, or musical instruments, and street vendors handing a 75-cent bouquet of divine-smelling gardenias through your car window as you're waiting at a red light. If you want it in D.F., you can buy it.

Mexican craft art is some of the most colorful and collectible in the world, with a dizzying assortment of styles from the many different regions of the country. It's a rare foreign visitor who doesn't dedicate part of their trip to purchasing Mexican art or handicrafts, and with good reason. Favorite choices include Puebla's Talavera ceramic and tile, animal masks from Guerrero, silver jewelry from Taxco, and copperware from Michoacán, to name just a few. Venues to buy craft art range from specialized markets to high-end shops. Apart from the places discussed in this chapter, consider taking a shopping trip to one of the cities and towns around central Mexico. (For details on these and other shopping destinations outside Mexico City, see the *Excursions from Mexico City* chapter.)

HIGHLIGHTS

LOOK FOR (TO FIND
RECOMMENDED SHOPS.

(**Best Bookstore:** Other bookstores may have a more comprehensive section of Spanish-language literature, but **El Péndulo** has the best overall selection of books in English and Spanish, as well as a decent music section and a great coffee shop to boot (page 139).

(**Best Punk Rock Market:** At **Mercado El Chopo,** a Saturday street market just off Avenida Insurgentes Norte, aficionados of loud music, outrageous hair styles, and lots of piercings and tattoos will feel right at home (page 140).

(**Best Art Market:** Housed in a colonial-era building off San Ángel's main square, **Bazar Sábado** might be the best place in the country to buy artwork. This Saturday market gathers several dozen of the finest artisans in the city. Prices are not cheap, but the paintings and crafts available are well worth it (page 145).

(**Best Quality Handicrafts:** If you're looking for top-quality handicrafts, never mind the price, head to one of the government-run **FONART** stores. They carry some of the finest, well-made traditional artwork you can find anywhere in Mexico, including ceramics, jewelry, and weavings (page 147).

(**Best Budget Handicrafts:** A maze of little walkways, **La Ciudadela** market has more than a hundred little shops selling all kinds of handicrafts. These aren't necessarily the most finely crafted goods available, but prices are low (bargaining is expected) and the huge selection makes it an easy place to buy some last-minute gifts (page 147).

(**Best Flea Market:** Lining the sidewalks of several streets just north of the Centro every Sunday morning is **La Lagunilla Flea Market,** with an incredible assortment of old books, furniture, and collectibles from years past, all to be had for a negotiable price (page 150).

(**Best Place to Buy Tequila:** There's any number of stores with extensive tequila selections in Mexico City, but **La Naval** has been around since the 1930s and tops the list (page 154).

(**Best Herbal Remedies:** Looking for a love potion to charm someone or a talisman to ward off bad luck? Then head directly to the bustling **Mercado Sonora.** This isn't a tourist destination, but it is an amazing spectacle, with squawking birds (many of them endangered species) and all sorts of mysterious powders and liquids (page 157).

SHOPPING DISTRICTS

In reality, just about all of Mexico City is a shopping district, as visitors will quickly see on any drive through the city. Anywhere a stop light holds up traffic, you'll find indigenous women with babies strapped on their back (known as *marías*) selling *chicles* (chewing gum). Open areas of sidewalk are invariably colonized by *ambulante* (street vendor) stands stocked with pirated DVDs, low-priced clothing, or other cheap consumer goods. And it's a rare Metro car that doesn't have someone wandering through hawking herbal remedies or ballpoint pens in some weirdly distinctive (and loud) repetitive chant.

Most visitors will find themselves shopping in a few neighborhoods that are convenient to tourist destinations and hotels, and that carry the types of goods foreigners are most likely to want to buy.

The tradition of shopping at local markets remains strong in Mexico City. Almost every part of the city has a covered market building open every day except Sunday, selling all manner of domestic goods, clothes, and fresh food. Many are known for carrying specialty goods as well, most notoriously the "witchcraft" market, Mercado Sonora. And even neighborhoods that don't have their own market building will usually have a designated day of the week where a street is blocked off and an open-air market holds court throughout the day. Market shopping, with the constant chatter among stall keepers and the give and take with customers, is a much more pleasurable and sociable experience than waiting in mind-numbing checkout lines at grocery or department stores.

Centro Histórico

The narrow streets of the Centro have always been and remain one of the prime shopping areas of the city. While formerly luxury items along with lower-priced goods were sold here, nowadays it's almost exclusively the latter, with pricier wares now found elsewhere in the city. An interesting feature of the Centro—similar to many other big, old cities—is that certain blocks have become informally colonized by stores carrying one type of good, making it easy to compare prices and quality. These include second-hand booksellers and photography shops on Donceles; musical instruments on Bolívar; computers and stereo equipment on República de Uruguay; household appliances on Artículo 123; jewelers on Madero; sporting goods on V. Carranza; and bicycles on Avenida San Pablo. Just south of the Centro is the well-stocked handicrafts market of La Ciudadela, a popular stop for tourists.

Tepito

On the northern edge of the Centro, on the north side of Eje 1 Norte, is the commercial neighborhood of Tepito. For literally centuries Tepito has been home to sellers of second-hand, smuggled, or even stolen goods. While it's a fascinating neighborhood, it's not particularly safe. One relative exception is Sunday's La Lagunilla Flea Market for antique goods—well worth visiting for those who like to poke around unusual street markets.

Zona Rosa

In the 1950s the Zona Rosa—located just south of Paseo de la Reforma near Insurgentes—grew up as a bohemian area of cafés and nightlife, but it has become much more of a commercial center aimed at tourists and middle-class Mexicans. Many handicrafts and antiques shops are located here, as well as a good daily craft market. There are also a couple of mini-malls with fancier shops selling books, clothing, and music.

Polanco

The wealthy neighborhood of Polanco in western Mexico City (in particular, the main drag of Av. Presidente Mazaryk) is *the* high-end shopping neighborhood in the city. Here you'll find all the latest international designer boutiques and several art galleries, along with plenty of pricey restaurants and cafés. Be prepared to drop a pretty peso.

Condesa

This hipster neighborhood just west of Insurgentes and south of the Zona Rosa is known more for its restaurants and cafés than for shopping. But some very trendy clothing and interior design shops have opened, catering to the young urban crowd with interesting and unusual fashion options. There are also a couple of excellent bookstores in the area.

Coyoacán and San Ángel

These two southern Mexico City neighborhoods are sort of mini-towns in their own right, with all manner of necessities for sale. But both are also known for an excellent selection of handicrafts and Mexican art for sale in shops and markets. The Bazar Sábado Saturday art market in San Ángel is about the best in the city. Wealthier shoppers will find numerous high-end boutiques on Calle Altavista in San Ángel.

Books and Music

BOOKSHOPS

Mexico City is, along with Buenos Aires, one of the two great literary capitals of Latin America. Innumerable writers, both Mexican and expatriate, have spent their productive careers in the city, including Carlos Fuentes, Octavio Paz, Juan Rulfo, Chilean Roberto Bolaño, and even the world-famous Colombian Gabriel García Marquéz. Thus it comes as no surprise that visitors will find numerous well-stocked bookstores throughout the city. Many of the larger bookstore chains, particularly El Péndulo and Gandhi (with several branches each) carry novels and nonfiction in English, French, and Italian as well. Whether buying books in Spanish or other languages, be prepared for some sticker-shock—even paperback editions of recently published books will set you back an easy $20, and often more.

Apart from the stores listed below carrying new books, bibliophiles will find clusters of used bookshops in a couple parts of the city. The best-known area is along Calle Donceles in the Centro, principally on the block between Palma and República de Brasil, just a couple of blocks from the Catedral Metropolitana. The selections are entirely in Spanish, but book lovers will enjoy trolling through the stacks. **Librería Hermanos de Hoja** is good for art books; **El Mercader de Libros** has a large general-interest selection; and **El Laberinto,** across the street, is also good hunting grounds. In the Roma along Avenida Álvaro Obregón is a string of stores with both new and used books. Two right next to each other are **Através del Espejo** (A. Obregón 118A), and **Librería Ático** (A. Obregón 118B).

AMERICAN BOOKSTORE

Bolívar 23, 55/5512-6350
HOURS: Mon.-Sat. 10 A.M.-7 P.M.
METRO: Bellas Artes
Map 1

The American Bookstore used to be the best place to get English-language books in Mexico City. Though the size of its collection has slimmed down, you'll still find a decent collection of English-language novels, travel guides, and history books, as well as technical books on engineering, software, finance, and more.

CENTRO CULTURAL BELLA ÉPOCA

Tamaulipas at Benjamín Hill, 55/5276-7110, www.fondo deculturaeconomica.com/BellaEpoca/BellaEpoca.asp
HOURS: Sun.-Thurs. 9 A.M.-11 P.M., Fri.-Sat. 9 A.M.-midnight
METRO: Patriotismo
Map 4

The Bella Época, housed in a beautifully re-done old cinema of the same name, is the best overall Spanish-language bookstore in the city. The interior is very light and spacious, with plenty of comfy chairs to read in as well as a coffee shop. The store, which opened in 2006, thus far has only a small selection of books in English, all classics. The French and Italian sections are larger.

CONACULTA BELLAS ARTES

Corner of Av. Juárez and Eje Central, 55/5512-2593, www.librosyarte.com
HOURS: Daily 10 A.M.-9 P.M.
METRO: Bellas Artes
Map 1

The bookstore on the ground floor of the Palacio de Bellas Artes in the Centro is chock-full of mostly Spanish-language books, but also some in English. The focus is on art, but there's a sizeable nonfiction section on history, culture, and tourism in Mexico City and Mexico. Most of Mexico City's larger art museums contain similar bookshops, all run by the government cultural institute Conaculta.

EL PARNASO

Carrillo Puerto 2, 55/5658-3195
HOURS: Daily 9 A.M.-10 P.M.
METRO: M. A. de Quevedo or Viveros
Map 6

A stalwart for southern Mexico City's intellectual

crowd, El Parnaso was founded in 1980 in a colonial-era building right on the corner of Jardín del Centenario in the center of Coyoacán. The two-story bookstore carries mainly Spanish-language fiction and nonfiction (especially the latter), but also has a selection of books in English, French, and Portuguese. Attached is a popular café, an excellent place to settle in with a book and a coffee and watch the world go by on the plaza.

◖ EL PÉNDULO

Av. Nuevo León 115, Condesa, 55/5286-9493, www.pendulo.com
HOURS: Mon.-Fri. 9 A.M.-11 P.M., Sat. 9 A.M.-midnight, Sun. 9 A.M.-10 P.M.
METRO: Chilpancingo
Map 4

El Péndulo started as a long-running respected bookstore in the Condesa, and has branched out to other parts of the city like Polanco (Alejandro Dumas 81, 55/5280-4111) and Zona Rosa (Hamburgo 126, 55/5208-2327). The selection of Spanish-language books, both fiction and nonfiction, is very good. The Polanco branch, in particular, has an excellent English fiction selection, mixing both classics and contemporary novels. Each store has a restaurant and coffee shop inside, and the Condesa branch also holds occasional music performances.

LIBRERÍA FRANCISCO JAVIER CLAVIJERO

Córdoba 43, 55/5514-0420
HOURS: Mon.-Fri. 9 A.M.-6 P.M., Sat. 9 A.M.-2 P.M.
METRO: Insurgentes
Map 4

Run by the government's Instituto Nacional de Antropología e Historia (INAH), this bookstore specializes in books and magazines related to Mexican history, archaeology, and culture. The majority of books are published by the INAH itself, but they also carry works by other publishers related to these topics, almost entirely in Spanish. As well, you'll find the latest bulletins of INAH's work, and a selection of reproductions of jewelry, carvings, and other archaeological discoveries found in Mexico.

LIBRERÍA GANDHI

Av. Juárez 4, 55/5510-4231, www.gandhi.com.mx
HOURS: Mon.-Fri. 10 A.M.-9 P.M., Sat.-Sun. 11 A.M.-8 P.M.
METRO: Bellas Artes
Map 1

In the Centro Histórico, Gandhi rivals El Péndulo as the best all-around bookshop for both English- and Spanish-language books in Mexico City. All their branches have extensive selections of fiction, nonfiction, books for children, and travel guides. Gandhi also sells books on CD as well as a good selection of music. Particularly unusual for Mexico is the assortment of American jazz and also hard-to-find Mexican folk music, especially from the local label Discos Corasón. Gandhi has several other branches, including one in Coyoacán (Av. M. A. de Quevedo 134, 55/5661-0911) that features an upstairs café, and a second shop in the Centro (Madero 32, 55/2625-0606).

LIBRERÍA PEGASO

Casa Lamm, Orizaba 99, 55/5208-0171, www.casalamm.com.mx/libreria.html
HOURS: Mon.-Sat. 11 A.M.-8 P.M., Sun. 10 A.M.-7 P.M.
METRO: Insurgentes
Map 4

The cultural center Casa Lamm in the Roma has one of the best art bookstores in the city, Librería Pegaso. It's in the basement floor of a lovingly restored late-19th-century mansion (take a look at the stained-glass windows around the door at the top of the main staircase). The quiet store is laid out in several rooms, with couches and even free coffee for visitors to peruse books at their leisure. Pegaso also has sections on literature, poetry, history, philosophy, esotericism, feminism, and sexuality, as well as a children's room with books, toys, and teaching materials.

MUSIC

Mexico is without doubt one of the most musical countries on the planet, with an incredible array of styles ranging from mariachi to ranchera to *trío* to traditional *son huasteca* to punk rock, and much else besides (see the *Background* chapter for more information on

SHOPS

© CHRIS HUMPHREY

Two CDs selling for US $1.50? Probably pirate copies.

Mexican music). If you like the sounds you will inevitably hear constantly blaring out from taxis, buses, shop stereos, and on the street, consider stopping into one of the places listed here to pick up something to listen to when you get home. For aficionados of traditional folk music, keep an eye out for CDs by Discos Corasón (www.corason.com), an independent Mexican label that has recorded many artists from around the country, preserving part of the country's musical heritage. Corasón eventually went on to record some of the greats from Caribbean music too, and co-produced the legendary Buena Vista Social Club album with Ry Cooder.

◖ MERCADO EL CHOPO

Along Aldama in Col. Buena Vista
HOURS: Sat. 10 A.M.–5 P.M.
Map 2

Just north of Centro Artesanal Buena Vista on the same street, the *rockero* street market of El Chopo is *the* place for Mexican punks, rockers, and alternative types to hang out and look for music. Expect to bump through crowds of young folks adorned with wild haircuts, heavy makeup, extensive piercings, and plenty of leather. It's in a warehouse district behind the Buenavista train station on Insurgentes Norte; take the Metro to the Buenavista station, then walk up Eje 1 Norte to Calle Aldama, turn left (north), and follow the crowd of rockers into the market area. More than 200 vendors sell all kinds of Mexican and Latin rock cassettes and CDs, with sections that specialize in thrash metal, hard-core punk, and rarities such as out-of-print Three Souls in My Mind (El Tri) records with psychedelic covers. Bootleg live cassettes are also available and even tolerated by many Mexican artists (Joselo Rangel, of the band Café Tacuba, says it was on the basis of the number of bootlegs sold at El Chopo that they got their first record contract). Rock paraphernalia—T-shirts, jewelry, tattoo artistry, even hair-dyeing stands—are also on hand.

MIXUP

Isabel la Católica and Madero, www.mixup.com.mx
HOURS: Mon.-Sat. 9 A.M.-midnight, Sun. 9 A.M.-10 P.M.
METRO: Zócalo
Map 1

Mixup is the best Mexican-owned music chain in the city, with a huge selection of Mexican and international music of all conceivable varieties. They also carry DVDs, iPod accessories, video games, and any other kind of digital entertainment you can think of. The store has 30 branches in the Mexico City area, including at Génova 76, between Liverpool and Londres in the Zona Rosa; Galerías Insurgentes in Colonia Del Valle; and at Plaza Loreto in Colonia San Ángel.

TOWER RECORDS

Pabellón Altavista, Calzado al Desierto los Leones 52, 55/5616-5270, www.towerrecords.com.mx
HOURS: Daily 11 A.M.-9 P.M.
METRO: Barranca del Muerto
Map 6

This international chain appears to be closing its doors in parts of the United States, but their Mexico City stores are still going strong. The store has a wide selection from all genres of Mexican and international music.

Tower is obviously best-known for its music selection, but they also carry a selection of books and magazines in English. While not large, the book section stocks many popular fiction and nonfiction choices, and everything from Octavio Paz to Aztec histories.

Clothing

Those after the latest in expensive fashion clothing and accoutrements can sate themselves easily, either heading to department stores like Palacio de Hierro and Liverpool or to the high-end boutiques along Avenida Presidente Mazaryk in Polanco, Mexico's equivalent of Rodeo Drive. Many smaller shops in the center of the Condesa cater more to the urban hipsters.

Although most modern clothing shops don't merit a description in this guide, there are a couple of stores worth noting that have more of a unique Mexican flavor in their fashions.

CARMEN RION

Michoacán 30-A, 55/5264-6179,
www.carmenrion.com.mx
HOURS: Mon.-Fri. 11 A.M.-8 P.M., Sat. noon-6 P.M., Sun. noon-4 P.M.
METRO: Chilpancingo
Map 4

This high-end designer manages to combine international fashion with Mexican styles in a unique way. The designer's loose-fitting, flowing clothing, often done in solid pastel colors, looks classy and sexy at the same time. Most clothing is for women, but men will find some updated versions of the Mexican *guayabera* shirt as well. The store, right on Parque México in the Condesa, also sells stylish jewelry, some made of natural materials, and unusual accessories such as crocheted bikinis.

GRYPHO

Ensenada 6, near Vicente Suárez, 55/5212-0283,
www.grypho.com
HOURS: Mon.-Thurs. 11 A.M.-8 P.M., Fri.-Sun. 11 A.M.-9 P.M.
METRO: Patriotismo
Map 4

Right in the heart of the Condesa restaurant district is this clothing boutique, carrying fashions designed by the company founded in 1996 by designer Mauricio Olvera and a group of collaborators. They initially sold clothing principally through other large stores and also directly to some well-known Mexican musicians, like Alejandra Guzmán and the groups La Ley and Sentidos Opuestos. The brand doesn't incorporate traditional Mexican styles per se, but is definitely a unique local take on urban hipster outfits.

SHOPS

PINEDA COVALIN

Campos Eliseos 215, 55/5280-2179,
www.pinedacovalin.com
HOURS: Mon.-Sat. 10 A.M.-8 P.M., Sun. 11 A.M.-2 P.M.
Map 3

This unusual design company, founded by two Mexican designers in collaboration with the government's anthropology and history institute, takes its inspiration from all things Mexican. You'll find patterns based on pre-Hispanic designs, colonial motifs, colors of the Mexican landscape, and modern Mexican artists. Where else could you find a tie decorated with *The Two Fridas,* one of Kahlo's most famed paintings? Items sold include handbags, ties, scarves, shoes, linens, and jewelry. Apart from their boutique in Polanco, Pineda Covalin goods are also sold by two small stores in the international terminal of the Mexico City airport, by gates 25 and 31.

SOMBREROS TARDAN

Plaza de la Constitución 7, 55/5512-3902,
www.tardan.com.mx
HOURS: Mon.-Sat. 10 A.M.-7 P.M.
METRO: Zócalo
Map 1

For one of the largest selections of men's hats you'll find in Mexico, step into this shop right on the Zócalo, originally founded (if you can believe it) in 1847. They've got a huge variety of well-made *sombreros* ranging from formal city hats to cowboy hats.

Department Stores

LIVERPOOL

Venustiano Carranza 92, 55/5133-2800,
www.liverpool.com.mx
HOURS: Daily 11 A.M.-9 P.M.
METRO: Zócalo
Map 1

Mexico's first major department store, Liverpool was first founded in 1847 to sell clothing, and in 1872 took the current name, as much of the merchandise was imported from the British port of Liverpool. Liverpool has 42 stores nationwide, of which nine are in Mexico City. Much of the brand-name goods are imported, and are usually a bit more expensive than you'd expect for the same product in the United States. Other locations convenient for visitors are in Col. Del Valle (Insurgentes Sur 1310, 55/5480-1300) and Col. Polanco (Mariano Escobedo 425, 55/5328-6400).

PALACIO DE HIERRO

Av. 20 de Noviembre, 55/5728-9905,
www.elpalaciodehierro.com.mx
HOURS: Mon.-Sat. 11 A.M.-8 P.M., Sun. 11 A.M.-7 P.M.
Map 1

Similar to Liverpool but a bit more upscale, with only nine stores in the country (five in Mexico City), Palacio de Hierro was established in the late 1800s and took its name ("Iron Palace")

SHOPPING LINGO

While most words used for shopping in Mexico are the same as elsewhere in Latin America, a few words are unique to the country.

un abarrotes – small general store, usually selling groceries, snacks, cigarettes, etc.
ambulante – street vendor
fayuca – smuggled goods
ganga – a deal
llevar – literally "to take", but often used as "to buy," as in "llévatelo," or "take it." "Para llevar" is "to go" (as in a coffee)
regatear – to bargain
remate – on sale
tianguis – market (derived from an Aztec word)
tlapelería – hardware store, also sometimes called *ferretería*

SHOPS

SANBORNS ALL OVER

Multiple generations of Mexican families have grown up with Sanborns department stores – and their attached restaurants – during the more than 100 years the company has been in existence. With well over a hundred branches throughout the Mexican republic, Sanborns has set the standard for Mexico-based retail chains and still enjoys a higher profile than any franchise.

It all began in 1903, when American brothers Walter and Frank Sanborn founded the Farmacia Americana in Mexico City to fill a perceived market for international pharmaceuticals in a nation where most people still relied on herbal remedies.

Around 1919 the Sanborn brothers moved their growing business into the prestigious Casa de los Azulejos (House of Tiles) in the Centro Histórico and expanded services to include a pharmacy, gift shop, curio shop, and elegant tea salon – thus creating Mexico's first department store.

Today the typical department store operated by Sanborn Hermanos S.A. (owned by Carlos Slim, the richest man in Latin America) integrates the services of a Mexican restaurant, bar, and large retail store with departments offering books, magazines, games, sweets, jewelry, fashion accessories, arts and crafts, audio and video equipment, baked goods, and, of course, a pharmacy. Newer on the scene has been the establishment of Sanborns Café outlets, which focus on food service only. Menu choices and prices at all Sanborns restaurants tend to be the same, a consistency that Sanborns regulars – Mexican businesspeople, upper-middle-class families, and tourists – have come to count on.

from its original building, which was the first steel construction in Mexico City. Their ubiquitous advertising slogan, "Soy totalmente Palacio" ("I'm totally Palacio") gives an idea of the chi-chi image they like to portray. Apart from the downtown store, other convenient Palacios are found in Coyoacán (Av. Coyoacán 2000, 55/5422-1900) and Polanco (Moliere 222, 55/5283-7200).

SANBORNS

Av. Madero 4, 55/5512-9820
HOURS: Daily 7 A.M.-11 P.M.
METRO: Bellas Artes
Map 1

Sanborns is a middle-class general store/department store found all over the city (and in fact the country) in just about every kind of busy neighborhood. It's a reliable place to pick up basics such as personal grooming items, standard pharmaceutical products, books and magazines, and household electronics. Each Sanborns has a cafeteria restaurant with reasonably priced Mexican fare, always distinguished by the winged and colorful costumes of the waitresses and reliably hygienic food. There are several dozen Sanborns across the city; just ask around and you'll inevitably find one not too far off.

MALLS

As with department stores, malls are not exactly top of the list for visitors to Mexico. But those who are staying in the city for a longer period of time, or who happen to be looking for a number of high-end shops in one place, may find occasion to patronize one of these bastions of consumerism. Many years ago malls basically did not exist in Mexico, but they have been springing up with remarkable rapidity, and are now found not only in wealthy neighborhoods, but also in middle- and even working-class parts of the city. Below are just a few mall options, chosen mainly for their convenience to neighborhoods frequented by foreign visitors and (in the case of Santa Fé) for sheer size.

CENTRO SANTA FÉ

Av. Vasco de Quiroga 3800, 55/3003-4300,
www.centrosantafe.com.mx
HOURS: Sun.-Fri. 11 A.M.-8 P.M., Sat. 11 A.M.-9 P.M.
Map 7

Santa Fé is the largest mall in Mexico, with

SHOPS

more than 300 businesses distributed over three floors. Shops include major national and international department stores, clothing outlets, even auto dealers. It's a massive temple to high-end consumption, and a place to come with a well-stuffed wallet as you won't find discount shops here. After you get worn out with all the shopping, you can refuel at one of the numerous bars and restaurants, and—if you can believe it—practice your drive at a golf range. There's also a huge cinema complex.

GALERÍAS INSURGENTES

Parroquia 194, 55/5545-1000,
www.galeriasinsurgentes.com.mx
HOURS: Daily 11 A.M.-8:30 P.M.

Map 5

Located on Av. Insurgentes just south of Eje 7 Sur, in the Del Valle neighborhood, Galerías Insurgentes is the largest mall near downtown, with more than 125 shops over three floors. Apart from the eclectic assortment of stores selling jewelry, toys, clothing, and electronics (and one excellent cigar shop), there are a Liverpool and Sanborns department stores as well as a cinema and several fast-food restaurants. The large clock above the main entrance is reputedly the largest in Mexico.

PLAZA INSURGENTES

Insurgentes Sur at San Luis Potosí, 55/5230-3971
HOURS: Daily 11 A.M.-8:30 P.M.

Map 4

In the Roma neighborhood not far south of Reforma is this small mall, centered around Sanborns and Sears department stores. There are several other shops and a six-screen Cinemex movie theater too.

PLAZA LORETO

Altamirano 46, 55/5616-3332
HOURS: Daily 11 A.M.-8 P.M.

Map 6

Notable if only for the unique historical background of the building, Plaza Loreto was originally a flour mill owned by Martín Cortés, son of the famed conquistador. It later became a textile and then paper factory, which closed its doors in the 1980s. The building was thoroughly renovated in the 1990s and reopened as a high-end mall of sorts, although not in the bland style most mall-goers are accustomed to. The boutiques (no big department stores around here) are arranged around restored brick buildings and courtyards in a tasteful style, and there's even a very good art museum, Museo Soumaya, on the premise. All in all, it's a more cultured shopping experience than most.

Handicrafts

Shopping for a selection of Mexico's famed craft art (called *artesanías* in Spanish) is a popular pastime for many visitors to the city, and with good reason. Mexico City gathers handicrafts from all across this sprawling, culturally diverse country, making it possible to buy everything from spooky indigenous masks from Guerrero, *guayabera* shirts from Yucatán, silver jewelry from Taxco, and woven baskets from Nayarit all in one market or store, often at very reasonable prices.

To get an idea of the huge variety of handicrafts made in Mexico, take a visit to the Museo Nacional de Artes Populares just south of the Alameda, or the government-run FONART store right on the Alameda. Both have a wide selection of good-quality material with information about where and how they are made. They also sell craft art themselves, although often at slightly higher prices (but usually better quality) than elsewhere in the city. More detailed information on Mexican popular art can be found in the *Artes de México* magazines, often for sale in book and art stores around the city or available at www.artesdemexico.com.

Apart from the shops and markets listed here, visitors may wish to shop for handicrafts in several cities and towns in the vicinity of Mexico City, like Puebla, Taxco, or Tepoztlán (see the *Excursions from Mexico City* chapter for details).

ARTS AND CRAFTS MARKETS
ARTE MEXICANO PARA EL MUNDO
Monte de Piedad 11, 55/5518-0300, www.arte-mexicano.com.mx
HOURS: Mon.-Tues. 9 A.M.-5 P.M., Wed.-Sun. 9 A.M.-8 P.M.
METRO: Zócalo
Map 1

Conveniently located right on thewest side of the Zócalo in a six-story colonial-era building, this store opened its doors in 2005, and carries traditional and contemporary craft art from 20 states, along with one of the better

baskets woven from henequen, produced in the southern Mexican state of Yucatán

COURTESY OF CONSEJO DE PROMOCIÓN TURÍSTICA DE MÉXICO/IGNACIO GUEVARA

collections of books on popular art. There are also rotating exhibitions focusing on different regions of the country. Prices are not the cheapest, but the workmanship is reliably good, unlike what you may find in the craft markets. They also have a terrace restaurant on the sixth floor, where you can enjoy a bite to eat with views over the Zócalo.

◖ BAZAR SÁBADO
Plaza San Jacinto 11
HOURS: Sat. 10 A.M.-7 P.M.
METRO: Barranca del Muerto or M. A. de Quevedo
Map 6

This is one of the finest craft and art markets in the city, where talented artisans sell handcrafted items such as jewelry, pottery, leather, and clothing. If you're looking for fine workmanship and artistry, more than can be found at the regular crafts markets like La Ciudadela, make a point to come to San Ángel on a Saturday to see what's on offer. The market is around the interior courtyard of a 17th-century stone edifice adjacent to the park. Some of the more successful artists selling the highest-quality crafts maintain regular shops here. Spurred by the success of the market, artists without a stall inside have taken to spreading out their wares across the plaza, making the entire area one big art market. Bargaining is not well received inside the main market, but is more accepted outside.

CALENDAR STANDS
Filomeno Mata at Tacuba
HOURS: Mon.-Sat. 10 A.M.-5 P.M.
METRO: Bellas Artes
Map 1

Two booths selling traditional Mexican calendars, including reproductions of the late Jesús Helguera's colorful idealized scenes of early-20th-century Mexico and the ubiquitous Aztec warriors bending over swooning Aztec maidens, can be found on either side of Callejón de Filomena Mata.

SHOPS

MEXICO'S WORLD OF HANDICRAFTS

The array of folk art and handicrafts produced around Mexico is truly phenomenal, certainly one of the most varied of any country in the world and a testament to the artistic spirit, craftsmanship, and creativity of the Mexican people. And Mexico City, the country's commerce center, is an excellent place to shop for *artesanías* from Sonora to Chiapas to Quintana Roo. To get an inkling of the full range of arts and crafts in Mexico, visit the Museo Franz Mayer and Museo Nacional de Culturas Populares, both near the Alameda park (see the *Arts and Leisure* chapter for more information).

Mexican Indians still produce pre-Hispanic-style textiles such as the *huipil* (sleeveless tunic) and *quechquemitl* (close-shouldered cape) in the states of Morelos, Guerrero, Oaxaca, and Chiapas, and on the Yucatán Peninsula. Another *yucateco* specialty, the cool *guayabera* shirt worn by men in the tropics worldwide, is made in Mérida.

Mexico's famous *rebozos* (shawls) come from San Luis Potosí, while the finest serapes and *jorongos* (ponchos) are made in Saltillo and Zacatecas, amid Mexico's largest wool-producing region.

Among the many types of embroidered, woven, and beaded shoulder bags produced throughout Mexico, those of the Huichol in Jalisco, Nayarit, and Durango are the most popular. Also often sought are bright, psychedelic Huichol yarn paintings.

The states of Zacatecas, Durango, Nuevo León, and Tamaulipas produce the finest *charreada* costumery – sequined sombreros, embroidered *charro* jackets, and tight-fitting trousers studded with *conchos* (shells).

A wide range of plant materials are used to fashion Mexican baskets, including palm strips, agave fibers, grass, pine needles, and henequen. High-quality baskets (*cesta, canasta*) are handwoven by the Seri, Yaqui, and Papago Indians of Sonora; the Tarahumara of Chihuahua; and the Mixtecs of Oaxaca.

Rural Mexicans and Amerindians make and wear an incredible variety of hats, from the wavy-brimmed but stiff Texas-style headgear in Chihuahua to the flat-brimmed, round-crowned sunbusters of the Yucatán. A Mexican hat blocker can reshape just about any woven, natural-fiber hat to fit your head.

Wood-carving thrives as a folk art applied to everyday housewares as well as decorative objects. Orangewood combs from Oaxaca, guitars from Michoacán, and cedar *rebozo* boxes from San Luis Potosí are some of the more notable wood arts. Many different Indian cultures throughout Mexico fashion finely carved and lacquered wooden masks for use in tribal ceremonies; most of the masks seen in souvenir shops are knockoffs produced by carvers in Guerrero or Michoacán.

Retablos, religious paintings on wood or tin, are commonly found near religious centers. Lacquered gourds and boxes from Guerrero, Michoacán, and Chiapas represent Mexico's finest lacquerwork.

Alebrijes are brightly painted, fantastically shaped animal-like sculptures carved of wood or fashioned from papier-mâché. The very first *alebrijes* were created in Mexico City by Pedro Linares, who created the figures after they appeared to him in a series of dreams, or nightmares, during a long illness. Seeing that the figures sold well among tourists and collectors, residents of Oaxaca later took up the craft and today the pieces are available throughout Mexico.

Glasswork is a popular purchase in Mexico for foreign tourists. Most handicrafts shops carry a variety of colored or tinted glass sets.

© CHRIS HUMPHREY

classic old-style Mexican calendar art for sale in the Centro

CENTRO ARTESANAL BUENA VISTA

Aldama 187, Col. Buena Vista
HOURS: Daily 9 A.M.–5 P.M.
METRO: Buenavista
Map 2

Several blocks north of Reforma and east of Avenida Insurgentes Norte, near the old Buenavista railroad station, this sprawling market in a high-ceilinged warehouse contains an incredibly large selection of everything made or sold in Mexico, much larger than the better-known Ciudadela and with some goods of better quality (if you look). The only drawback is that it's pretty well off the beaten tourist track. The best option for getting there other than by taxi is to go via Metro to the Buenavista station and walk a couple of blocks. Don't walk toward Insurgentes from the Metro, walk the other way (east)—there's a huge sign over the building that's easy to spot.

MERCADO DE ARTESANÍAS COYOACÁN

Felipe Carillo Puerto 25
HOURS: Daily 11 A.M.–7 P.M.
METRO: Viveros
Map 2

There's a huge craft market in Coyoacán on weekends; it's perhaps not quite as refined as Bazar Sábado in nearby San Ángel but is quite good nonetheless and is certainly less pricey. It's located just off Jardín del Centenario, and you can go in either through the Sanborns or off Calle Aguayo. The market started off relatively modest, but it seems to be getting bigger each year. Jardín del Centenario is also packed with a variety of vendors (adding to the pedestrian traffic jams) on the weekends. A group of Huichol indigenous people from northwestern Mexico sell their traditional handicrafts from the south side of the square, just in front of the Entre Vero restaurant.

FONART

Av. Juárez 89, 55/5521-0171, www.fonart.gob.mx
HOURS: Mon.-Sat. 10 A.M.–7 P.M.
METRO: Hidalgo
Map 1

In terms of handicrafts stores (as opposed to markets), one of the best places to start is the government-run FONART shop near the Alameda; it's a combination handicrafts museum/store. The merchandise—silver, onyx, pottery, baskets, textiles, and more—is of excellent quality; prices are nonnegotiable and fairly steep. There's a slightly larger FONART branch in the southwestern part of the city in Colonia Mixcoac (Patriotismo 691, 55/5093-6000, Mon.–Sat. 9 A.M.–8 P.M., Sun. 10 A.M.–7 P.M.).

LA CIUDADELA

Balderas at Ayuntamiento
HOURS: Daily 10 A.M.–6 P.M.
METRO: Balderas
Map 1

A few blocks south of the Alameda, La Ciudadela is the best all-around place in the Centro if you're looking for a great variety of Mexican handicrafts in one place. In addition to all the usual trinkets, Ciudadela's complex

SHOPS

of vendor booths is especially good for leather goods, ceramics, silver jewelry, and blankets. The quality here is not always the best, so if you are after a top-quality handicraft be sure to look closely, and don't be surprised if you don't find the level of workmanship you are after. For example, although several stalls sell hammocks, it's impossible to find the tightly woven and large-sized hammocks you'll find sold on the coasts. Toward the southern end of the market, almost an annex to the main complex, is a luthier's shop with lots of handmade guitars. Bargaining is expected. Balderas is the nearest Metro station. Parking is available, on the side street adjacent to the market.

La Ciudadela is actually the large building (originally a tobacco factory) opposite a small park from the market. Along Calle Balderas, on the edge of the park, is a sidewalk **flea market** with all sorts of random goods for sale, including music, used clothing, and handicrafts.

MERCADO INSURGENTES

Betw. the Liverpool and Londres off Florencia
HOURS: Mon.-Sat. 10 A.M.-5 P.M.
METRO: Insurgentes
Map 2

This large (over 200 stalls) indoor handicrafts market is popular among tourists for its convenient location in the heart of the Zona Rosa. You'll find much of the same merchandise here as at La Ciudadela, although prices can be a bit higher. Bargaining is expected. The many food stands on the side of the market are great for inexpensive lunches.

MERCADO SAN JUAN

Betw. Ayuntamiento and Pugibet
HOURS: Mon.-Sat. 9 A.M.-7 P.M., Sun. 9 A.M.-4 P.M.
METRO: San Juan de Letrán
Map 1

Also known as Mercado de Artesanías Xochicalco or La Casa de las Flores, this renovated handicrafts market on the east side of Plaza de San Juan stands on the site of one of Mexico City's oldest colonial-era markets. It reopened in 1999 as a cooperative venture among Mexican artisans, but it's still feeling its way in terms of quality. Prices

are good, especially if you bargain, but the selection is not quite as varied as at La Ciudadela. The adjacent food market is also worth a visit.

MERCADO VASCO DE QUIROGA

Insurgentes Sur at Camino a Santa Teresa, Tlalpan
HOURS: Daily 10 A.M.-6 P.M.
METRO: Universidad, then by bus south to Tlalpan
Map 7

This market, named after a Spanish priest famed for teaching wood-working skills to indigenous craftsmen in the colonial period, started out as just a few stalls but has evolved into a full-scale market selling all variety of handmade wooden furniture. Here you can get just about any type of furniture you want, out of a variety of woods including bamboo, pine, oak, mahogany, and more (almost all natural woods, very few processed materials), at very reasonable prices. If you don't see what you are looking for, the craftsmen there will happily build it for you in a few days if you leave a deposit and clear instructions. Delivery service is easily arranged to all parts of the city, for a nominal extra fee.

MUSEO NACIONAL DE ARTES POPULARES

Revillagigedo at Independencia, 55/5510-2201, www.map.org.mx
HOURS: Tues.-Sun. 10 A.M.-5 P.M.
METRO: Juárez
Map 1

This popular art museum opened in 2006 and is located in an art deco building just south of the Alameda. It houses an excellent collection of art works from across the country, including a spectacular *árbol de la vida* ("tree of life") from Metepec, state of Mexico. The gift shop is jam-packed with all manner of crafts for sale, including sculpture, textiles, toys, lacquerware, silver art, wood carvings, glass, leatherwork, and weavings. As with the FONART stores, prices are a bit higher here than the markets, but so is the quality.

CERAMICS AND TILE

Mexico boasts an astounding number of potters and pottery styles. Among the most highly valued by collectors are polychromatic Pueblo-style ceramics from Chihuahua's Casas Grandes area, green-glazed pots from Michoacán, rainbow-hued vessels and black Zapotec jars from Oaxaca, and Puebla's famous tin-glazed Talavera plates and bowls. Potters emigrating from Talavera de la Reina in Spain settled in Puebla, where they fashioned majolica-inspired pottery that became known as Talavera. Although the best pieces still hail from Puebla, much Talavera today comes from potters' workshops in Dolores Hidalgo, in the state of Guanajuato. Usually the place of origin will be marked on the bottom of the piece, but after a while you may be able to tell the difference without checking the inscriptions.

Smaller ceramic pieces fashioned into brightly colored human and animal shapes—some functioning as candelabras or receptacles, others purely decorative—are everyday folk art throughout the country.

The enamel used to color-finish some Mexican ceramic products may contain lead. This doesn't usually pose a health problem for decorative pieces, but if you plan to use Mexican pottery as cooking or eating utensils, you should buy articles *sin plomo* (without lead) to avoid accidental lead ingestion. Nowadays many Mexican ceramicists create lead-free products whose characteristics surpass those of traditional enamelware and which are available at accessible prices. As recommended by FONART (Fondo Nacional para el Fomento de las Artesanías), such pieces may be marked EBT-SP, signifying *esmalte baja temperatura sin plomo* (low-temperature enamelware without lead).

Two higher-end ceramics shops are listed here, but a wider selection of less expensive ceramics can be found in the many handicrafts stores and markets listed elsewhere in this chapter.

LAS ARTESANÍAS

Oscar Wilde 29, 55/5280-9515,
www.lasartesanias.com.mx
HOURS: Mon.-Sat. 10 A.M.-8 P.M., Sun. noon-6 P.M.
METRO: Polanco
Map 3

A high-end craft shop in the middle of the Polanco shopping district, Las Artesanías has a wide variety of products, but is particularly good for different kinds of ceramics, including from the state of Guanajuato and the famous Talavera from Puebla. They also carry lacquerware from Guerrero, *azulejo* tile from Puebla, and blown glass from Mexico City and the state of Jalisco. Prices are high, but shoppers can be confident of good-quality products.

URIARTE TALAVERA

Calz. Santa Catarina, 55/5550-5915,
www.uriartetalavera.com.mx
HOURS: Mon.-Fri. 11 A.M.-7 P.M., Sat. 11 A.M.-2:30 P.M.
METRO: Barranca del Muerto
Map 6

Top-quality (and pricey) Talavera ceramics from Puebla can be bought in San Ángel, in a small shop near the San Ángel Inn selling the work of the famed Puebla workshop. Uriarte was first established in 1824 in Puebla, and continues to use designs from as far back as the 16th century. As well, the famed workshop has collaborated with modern Mexican artists such as Francisco Toledo and José Luis Cuevas. They are formally registered as a producer of Talavera under strict quality-control rules established in the early 1990s, to combat increasing low-quality fake Talavera. There's also a store in the Santa Fé shopping center in western Mexico City (Local 350, 55/5257-0123).

FLEA MARKETS AND ANTIQUES

Antiques-hunting is not high on the list of most tourists coming to Mexico, but those with a passion for objects from the colonial or post-colonial eras will find several shops and markets to prowl. The streets of the Zona Rosa neighborhood near Paseo de la Reforma contain many small antiques shops with colonial and European books, art, and coins. Those with a more adventurous disposition may also want to visit the second-hand flea markets in La Lagunilla and Colonia Roma.

If you happen across someone trying to sell you a pre-Columbian artifact, don't even think

EL BARRIO BRAVO DE TEPITO

Tepito is, with no exaggeration, the most famous neighborhood in all of Mexico. This relatively small area just north of the Eje 1 Norte from the Centro is the legendary poor neighborhood of thieves, drug dealers, prostitutes, street gangs, and world-champion boxers; and of the most bravado-filled *cabrones* (an offensive word for "tough guys" or "jerks") you'll ever run across.

But most of all, it is the land of commerce, Mexico City's ultimate capitalist neighborhood. Here you can find just about anything in the thousands of small shops and market stands lining the labyrinth of narrow streets and alleys. Or you can, at least, if you ask the right people, carry yourself well, and are discrete. Some of the merchandise for sale in Tepito is stolen, and some is simply secondhand, but most of it is *fayuca*, imported goods smuggled over the U.S. border free of taxes and sold for very low prices. The authorities have been raiding Tepito literally since colonial times, to no avail, as any trip through the thriving market will immediately tell you.

Tepito was, according to most historical accounts, a small market area in the time of the Aztecs, and the name is thought to come from the Náhuatl term *tepitoyótl* meaning small neighborhood (although an amusingly literalist version has it deriving from *"te pito,"* or "I blow the whistle on you"). During the colonial era, when the Crown's monopoly on trade made smuggling a major industry, Tepito's location near the main northern gate to the city made it the perfect place to sneak goods in and out.

The protectionist PRI-led governments that governed Mexico from the 1930s to the 1990s, with their tight restrictions on imported goods as a way to boost domestic production, was a huge boon to the *fayuqueros* of Tepito. It was during this time that the neighborhood began to gain its national fame. A number of Mexican boxing greats came out of Tepito in the 1950s and 1960s, the first being Raúl "El Ratón" Macías, one of 15 children of a Tepito shoemaker, who became bantamweight (53.5 kilos) world champion in 1953. He was a humble man who was favored by the PRI and prone to saying he owed everything "to my manager and the Virgin of Guadalupe." Much more in the Tepito style was Rubén "El Púas" Olivares, who became world champion in a fight in Los Angeles in 1969, and then became an antiestablishment hero who liked to smoke weed and listen to rock music; he also openly criticized the PRI and the Catholic Church.

One ex-boxing trainer, asked by a journalist why he thought Tepito had produced so many great boxers, didn't mince his words. "Well, the neighborhood is a battleground...."

about buying it—you will get in serious hot water with the authorities.

CENTRO DE ANTIGÜEDADES PLAZA DEL ÁNGEL

Bordered by Hamburgo, Florencia, Londres, and Amberes
HOURS: Shops daily 10 A.M.-8 P.M.; market Sat.-Sun. 10 A.M.-4 P.M.
METRO: Insurgentes
Map 2

This semi-enclosed market area and surrounding shops inside a large pink building brings together more than 30 stores selling antique furniture, paintings, art objects, silver, and other articles—much of it high-end goods from the 19th century. Most shops can arrange shipping anywhere in the world. Some shops have more erratic hours. On Saturday and Sunday, a flea market in antiques, typically featuring more than 100 exhibitors, convenes in the open hallways of the plaza.

◖ LA LAGUNILLA FLEA MARKET

Several blocks along and east of Paseo de la Reforma at the corner of Eje 1 Norte
HOURS: Sun. all day
METRO: Garibaldi
Map 1

On Sunday a flea market, or *mercado de pulgas,*

We all live in *vecindades* [several houses built around a communal patio], so the little kids are fighting there right from the start. And then when they're a little older, they go out on the streets ready to fight whomever. Everyone around here knows the phrase: *'camarón que se duerme, ahí lo plancharon'* ["the shrimp that sleeps just got flattened"]."

This last phrase sounds funny, but even more so when you know that it's a typically *tepiteño* twist on the original, more poetic *"camarón que se duerme, se lo lleva el corriente"* (the shrimp that sleeps gets taken by the current).

Tepito – which does not technically exist as a *colonia*, or official city demarcation – was the subject of a number of movies during Mexico's golden era of cinema and was even the setting of one of the all-time classics in urban anthropology, Oscar Lewis's *Children of Sánchez* (1961).

Appropriately for a barrio of this character, the favored saint is rather low on the Vatican's list of approved objects of veneration. The Santa Muerte (Saint Death) is a life-sized statue of the skeleton of a woman carrying a scythe in one hand, often wearing a feathered hat, and bedecked in jewelry. The cult of the Santa Muerte is followed across the country by thieves, drug runners, and other underworld types, but only in Tepito do they openly hold Santa Muerte ceremonies (once a month, at midnight, on the aptly named Calle Bravo – "Brave Street") and parade the statue through the streets. As one Tepito merchant told a reporter, "We are all hard people, and we live hard lives. But she accepts us all. She understands us because she is a *cabrona* like us." In 2007, newswires reported that the Santa Muerte had gotten a makeover of sorts: The scythe and skull have been replaced with a woman with dark hair and a shawl.

When Mexico's economy began to open up to international trade again in the 1990s, the *fayuca* of Tepito no longer earned as much money. Creative *tepiteños* continue wheeling and dealing, branching out into pirated videos and CDs, rip-offs of brand-name clothing, and, increasingly, drug dealing. Police raids still come and go, and contraband merchandise and drugs are impounded, but Tepito goes on, hard and fast as always. When director Tony Scott was filming *Man on Fire* with Denzel Washington in Mexico City, he thought it would be the perfect place for some of the "mean streets" scenes. And indeed they would have been, but maybe a little too much so: The city authorities refused to guarantee the safety of the film crew, so they moved elsewhere.

known as La Lagunilla sets up on the *lateral* (side lane) along the east side of Paseo de la Reforma just north of the Eje 1 Norte, and on a few side streets heading east into the Tepito neighborhood from Reforma. Although the prices are not as rock-bottom as they once were, it's a great place to wander around for an hour or two and check out the heaps of old books, toys, silverware, movie posters, antique and not-so-antique furniture, as well as all manner of other paraphernalia spread out on the streets and sidewalks. The side streets are crowded but safe, although common sense suggests you won't want to be dangling high-priced cameras around your neck or flashing wads of bills. Don't walk east past the market, as the streets head into the rough neighborhood of Tepito.

ROMA FLEA MARKET

Álvaro Obregón betw. Frontera and Orizaba
HOURS: Sat.-Sun. late morning to late afternoon
`Map 4`

If you want a taste of a flea market but don't want to walk near the rough neighborhood of Tepito, walk around the weekend street market along the pedestrian median (called a *camellón*) in the middle of Avenida Álvaro Obregón in the Roma. This is a very low-key, positively civilized market. Most vendors make little effort

The weekend flea market in Roma is small and not as hectic as other markets.

to flog their wares but are happy to talk if you ask questions. The market is small, and prices are a little higher than elsewhere, but it's nice to walk through, even if you don't buy anything. Part of the merchandise consists of antiques and collectibles, as in La Lagunilla, but you'll also find artists selling their paintings and a number of different handicrafts. It makes a good excuse to visit the Roma, a lovely neighborhood in which to spend half a day.

A few blocks away, in Colonia Doctores, another flea market sets up on Saturday mornings in a large park right along Avenida Cuauhtémoc, just north of Avenida Álvaro Obregón. This is more like Lagunilla, with piles of old collectibles, much of it junk but with some treasures hidden in their midst.

JEWELRY

Well-crafted silver (*plata*) jewelry is plentiful and relatively inexpensive throughout Mexico. The finest work comes from Taxco, Guanajuato, and Zacatecas. Look for ".925" stamped into silver products; this means they're 92.5 percent silver, the highest quality. You'll also come across *alpaca,* an alloy of copper, nickel, and zinc that looks like silver and costs a third to a half less than the real thing.

The best gold (*oro*) jewelry is said to come from Oaxaca, where Zapotec women regard gold adornments as the most important source of portable wealth. Most pieces are fashioned from 12-carat gold, though some may feature 24-carat plating.

Elaborate earrings, bracelets, and necklaces strung together from semiprecious or nonprecious materials such as turquoise, amber, beads, bone, and onyx have been popular throughout Mexico since the artist Frida Kahlo painted herself wearing pre-Hispanic jewelry. Though fashioned mostly in the central and southern states, this jewelry is sold all over the country.

Apart from the stores listed in this section, shoppers will also find jewelry in many of the handicrafts stores and markets listed throughout this chapter. Numerous generic jewelry shops using international designs can be found lining Avenida Madero in the Centro (which used to be called Av. Plateros, or "Silversmith Street") and on Avenida Presidente Mazaryk in Polanco. The ones in the Centro are, unsurprisingly, less expensive.

MINERALIA
Madero 28, 55/5518-2047, www.mineralia.com.mx
HOURS: Mon.-Sat. 10:30 A.M.-7 P.M.
METRO: Allende
Map 1

An unusual shop, Mineralia carries a wide variety of precious and semi-precious stones used in making jewelry, as well as numerous fossils. Stones are sold as individual pieces, or put together in decorations or jewelry (like necklaces). The store is worth walking into just to admire the beautiful colors of the many kinds of stone. If you've ever had a strong desire to learn how to mount precious stones onto jewelry, the company's Colonia Roma store (Av. Oaxaca 131, 55/5533-1411) offers hour-long classes.

NACIONAL MONTE DE PIEDAD
Monte de Piedad 7, 55/5278-1700 or 55/5278-1800, http://dns.montepiedad.com.mx
HOURS: Mon.-Fri. 8:30 A.M.-6 P.M., Sat. 8:30 A.M.-1 P.M.
METRO: Zócalo
Map 1

On the west side of the Zócalo, this government-run pawnshop (whose name means Mountain of Mercy) has for more than two centuries offered low-interest loans to the needy. In times of economic crisis, people line the surrounding blocks waiting to put their jewelry, musical instruments, and other personal possessions in hock for a loan.

Monte de Piedad sits over the site of one of Cortés's many palaces, which in turn was built on the remains of Moctezuma I's residence. Cortés's huge original palace, which covered several city blocks, was divided up and sold in 1615, and the current structure was built in 1775 by Pedro Romero de Terreros, owner of the fabulously wealthy Regla silver mines near Pachuca. After independence from Spain, the government took over the building. The shop sells all manner of second-hand pawned objects, including

occasionally interesting antiques, but the great majority is jewelry of all types.

Lining the sidewalk along the same block as Monte de Piedad are dozens of men and women standing in front of private pawn shops, their windows filled with jewelry and trinkets, calling out to the passing crowd *"¿Algo le vende?"* (Something to sell?).

PORTALES DE LOS MERCADERES
Plaza de la Constitución betw. Cinco de Mayo and Madero
HOURS: Vary, but closed on Sundays
METRO: Zócalo
Map 1

This section of archways on the Zócalo has drawn jewelry merchants since the earliest years of the colony, and they are still going strong. Many shop owners have representatives out on the street, looking to get people to sell secondhand jewelry in their shops instead of taking it to the nearby Monte de Piedad pawnshop. Most of the jewelry here is of standard design and not particularly "Mexican" per se, but you can occasionally find some unique Taxco-style designs, and prices are often very good. Gold and silver is also sold by the gram in many shops.

TANE
Presidente Mazaryk 430, 55/5282-6200, www.tane.com.mx
HOURS: Mon.-Fri. 10 A.M.-7 P.M., Sat. 11 A.M.-7 P.M.
METRO: Polanco
Map 3

This is considered one of the finest silver shops in Mexico, with prices to match. Designs are classy and original, although not with any particular Mexican flavor. Apart from the regular line of earrings, rings, bracelets, and necklaces, they also carry special lines of artwork in silver by artists such as Javier Marín and Sergio Hernández. Apart from the Polanco store, other locations convenient for tourists include Avenida Álvaro Obregón 99 in Colonia Roma (in the Casa Lamm), 55/5207-5483; and Santa Catarina 207 in Colonia San Ángel, 55/5616-1198.

SHOPS

Liquor and Tobacco

Mexico City offers an abundance of places selling *licores* and *vinos,* especially those many varieties of tequila for which Mexico is so famous. Finding good-quality mescal (a cousin of tequila, with a smokier flavor and the worm in the bottom of the bottle) is more of a challenge, as the best stuff is made in the state of Oaxaca.

Cigar smokers will be pleased to learn that the city has many shops specializing in *puros* (cigars), including Mexico's best brands (made in the Veracruz region of Las Tuxtlas) as well as the ever-popular Cubans. Apart from the shops mentioned here, most of the upscale hotels and several shops at the airport sell cigars from Cuba, Mexico, and elsewhere in Latin America (cigars from the Dominican Republic and Honduras can be very good).

Note: Bringing Cuban cigars to the United States is a violation of the American trade embargo against Cuba. If U.S. customs finds a couple of cigars during an inspection of your luggage, the usual practice is to confiscate them, nothing more, although you're legally liable for a very stiff fine. When I got nabbed with three lovely Romeo y Julieta Churchills, I pleaded in vain with the customs agent that they were for a wedding celebration, but he was unsympathetic and shredded them before my eyes. If you try to smuggle in a full box or more, you might be in for real trouble. Also be aware that a great many "Cuban" cigars sold in Mexico and elsewhere are fake.

LIQUOR AND WINE
LA EUROPEA
Ayuntamiento 21, 55/5512-6005,
www.laeuropea.com.mx
HOURS: Mon.-Sat. 10 A.M.-8 P.M.
METRO: San Juan Letrán
Map 1

La Europea was one of the first stores in Mexico City to sell imported gourmet food and drink, and has since expanded to have 28 stores nationwide. The original store is still at Ayuntamiento, near the Mercado San Juan. They have about the most complete selection of different liquors to be found in the city, although neither the downtown nor Polanco (Arquimedes 119, 55/5280-2205) branches have as large a selection as their mega-store near the Toreo, north of Polanco (Rodolfo Gaona 86, Col. Lomas de Sotelo, 55/5580-5096).

LA NAVAL
Av. Insurgentes Sur 373 at Michoacán, 55/5584-3500
HOURS: Mon.-Sat. 8 A.M.-9 P.M.
METRO: Chilpancingo
Map 4

La Naval is one of the best places to buy fine-quality alcohol by the bottle in central Mexico City. The store has been around since the 1930s, when the Condesa neighborhood was first built, and has a great selection of tequilas and wines, although the prices are not the cheapest. They also carry some high-end microbrew-style Mexican beers, such as Casta (made in Monterrey), and excellent cheeses, meats, cigars, and other delicacies.

MUNDO GOURMET
Av. Revolución 1541, 55/5616-7386,
www.mundogourmet.com.mx
HOURS: Mon.-Sat. 9 A.M.-8 P.M., Sun. 11 A.M.-3 P.M.
METRO: Barranca del Muerto
Map 6

This large shop in San Ángel caters to the wealthier residents of southern Mexico City with a superlative selection of wines from Mexico and around the world. Yes, Mexico does produce wine—almost entirely in the northern state of Baja California, including Cabernet Sauvignon, Tempranillo, Shiraz, Chardonnay, and Sauvignon Blanc. The store has a wide selection of high-quality cheeses, meats, and other deli goods, and also holds events and courses on wines.

SHOPS

TOBACCO
LA CASA DEL FUMADOR
Galerías Insurgentes, Parroquia 194, 55/5627-8313
HOURS: Daily 11 A.M.–8 P.M.
METRO: Insurgentes Metrobús
Map 5

This well-stocked shop is located in the bottom floor of the Galerías Insurgentes mall, on Insurgentes Sur just south of Eje 7 Sur. Step into their walk-in humidor to choose from their many varieties of Cuban, Mexican, and other cigars, at reasonable prices. They have a wide variety of smoking accoutrements and specialty cigarettes too.

LA CASA DEL HABANO
Plaza Mazaryk on Av. Mazaryk, 55/5282-1046
HOURS: Daily 11 A.M.–8 P.M.
METRO: Polanco
Map 3

This shop, located in a mini-mall in the wealthy neighborhood of Polanco, is a bit pricier than most (not surprising, considering the location), but they have a decent selection of stogies from around Latin America, especially Cuba. There's another branch of the store in San Ángel in the Plaza Loreto shopping center (Altamirano 46, 55/5616-1430).

PUROS DE LA ROMA
Zacatecas 184, betw. Monterrey and Tonalá, 55/5264-4076
HOURS: Mon.–Fri. 9 A.M.–6 P.M.
METRO: Insurgentes
Map 4

This small shop in the Roma neighborhood is an old-school tobacco shop, serving the neighborhood for years and at relatively reasonable prices. They carry a good selection of Cuban, Dominican, and Mexican cigars of various sizes, as well as some smoking accessories.

PUROS VALLE DE MÉXICO
Zacatecas 172, 55/5584-0239
HOURS: Mon.–Fri. 9 A.M.–6 P.M., Sat. 9 A.M.–5 P.M.
METRO: Insurgentes
Map 4

Just a few doors down from Puros de la Roma is another cigar shop, this one exclusively carrying Mexican cigars from the San Andrés valley in the eastern Mexican state of Veracruz. Types of cigars here include Montecruz (the best and most expensive), Mina de Veracruz, Churchill, and Quetzalcoáatl. They are happy to sell individual cigars or in bulk, with wood, glass, or cardboard boxes available.

Public Markets

CENTRAL DE ABASTOS DEL DISTRITO FEDERAL (CEDA)
Canal Churubusco and Canal Apatlaco, www.ficeda.com.mx
HOURS: Daily 24 hours
METRO: Aculco
Map 7

Covering about four square kilometers, La Central de Abastos ("Supply Center") is said to be the "heart" that pumps the food into that great "body" that is Mexico City and the surrounding Valle de México. An armada of up to 17,000 cargo trucks docks at this huge complex each day, handling an estimated 30,000 tons of fruits and vegetables that represent no less than 40 percent of Mexico's national harvest, along with 3,600 tons of dry groceries and other provisions. Although not a mainstream tourist attraction by any means, if you're struck with an odd desire to see the largest food market in the country, this is it.

CEDA was founded in 1982 to supply food wholesale and retail services that had outgrown Mercado La Merced in the north, and purportedly to create more cooperative and equitable leasing opportunities for vendor and *bodega* (warehouse) space. In the southeast part of the complex, a nine-hectare seafood section called La Nueva Viga displays virtually every kind of

SHOPS

fish from all over the country, far more than any one Mexican port.

In addition to the 2,000-odd food stalls, the central corridors of the *bodegas* contain 18 banks, along with a number of small businesses—truck repair shops, tire shops, stationery stores, post and telegraph offices, travel agencies, pharmacies, bakeries, medical clinics, record stores, moneychangers, restaurants of all types, beauty shops, perfume stores, video stores, dry cleaners, clothing stores, tortilla factories—in short, everything essential to maintain this city within a city.

MERCADO COYOACÁN

Three blocks north of Jardín Hidalgo off Calle Allende
HOURS: Daily 7 A.M.–5 P.M.
METRO: Coyoacán or Viveros
Map 6

If you're in the south of the city, this bustling market is a great place to stock up on fresh fruits, vegetables, meats, or other domestic necessities. It's a classic, busy yet low-key neighborhood market, worth a visit to see the way many Mexico City residents still shop. If you're hungry while there, stop in at one of the many *marisquerías,* countertop purveyors of fresh seafood. Popular choices include *tostada de ceviche* (crisp corn tortillas topped with ceviche), *pulpo en su tinta* (octopus cooked in its own ink), and *sopa de mariscos* (seafood soup).

MERCADO LA MERCED

Bordered by Santa Escuela, General Anaya, Rosario, and Cerrada del Rosario, Col. Merced Balbuena
HOURS: Daily 6 A.M.–6 P.M.
METRO: La Merced
Map 1

One of the largest retail and wholesale markets in Mexico, La Merced covers several blocks just north of Avenida Fray Servando Teresa de Mier and just east of Avenida Circunvalación, near the Ex-Convento de la Merced (from whence it got its name). First built in 1890, La Merced was for many decades the city's principal marketplace and was the centerpiece of a bustling commercial neighborhood. It's divided into several sub-markets for particular types of

goods, some dedicated to retail and others to wholesale. The original location was chosen because of the system of canals that arrived to the Centro from the southern part of the city, where much of the agricultural goods were produced. In 1982 the city inaugurated the Central de Abastos farther south, and it soon superseded La Merced in the wholesale business. But La Merced is still going strong, and many *capitalinos* still consider it the quintessential Mexico City market. It's a unique place to visit, and generally quite safe, but take care in walking the rough streets around the market.

MERCADO MEDELLÍN

Bordered by Medellín, Campeche, Monterrey, and Coahuila
HOURS: Daily 8 A.M.–5 P.M.
METRO: Chilpancingo
Map 4

This neighborhood market in the Roma Sur is spacious and well-lit, with dozens of stands piled high with fresh produce, as well as stalls selling shoes, clothing, and domestic supplies. It's a very pleasant place to shop, with the friendly merchants steering you where to find whatever it is you are seeking. Mercado Medellín is known for its excellent seafood, sold in bulk and also cooked in the many market restaurants. Shrimp cocktails are a tasty treat for a mere $2.50. As with most markets, the best fresh produce is to be found earlier in the day.

MERCADO DE PLANTAS CUEMANCO

Periférico Sur at the corner of Canal Nacional, Col. Ciénega Grande, Xochimilco
HOURS: Daily 9 A.M.–5 P.M.
METRO: Xochimilco light rail station, then by taxi
Map 7

The southern part of the city around Xochimilco has for centuries been the valley's breadbasket, with farmers growing all manner of produce on the legendary *chinampas,* or floating gardens, along the region's canals. In 1992, the Mexico City government started a project to rescue a neglected area of *chinampas,* creating an ecological park and building what has become the largest flower market in Latin America, and the third-largest in the world (after ones in Holland and Canada). The 13-hectare market, stocked with flowers as well as herbs, fruit trees, and medicinal plants, is not often visited by foreigners, but it certainly makes a colorful and unusual destination, and can be combined with a trip to the adjacent ecological reserve, Parque Ecológico de Xochimilco (see the *Sights* chapter for more details).

A smaller (but still considerable) plant market in Xochimilco that's easier to visit by public transportation is Mercado Madreselva, right next to the docks (*embarcaderos*) in Nativitas, a couple of kilometers from the center of Xochimilco, reached by bus or inexpensive taxi.

MERCADO SAN JUAN
Betw. Ayuntamiento and Pugibet
HOURS: Daily 7 A.M.–5 P.M.
METRO: San Juan Letrán
Map 1

This neighborhood market, four blocks south of the Alameda, is legendary for selling some of the most obscure and exotic foods available in the city, imported and domestic. Here you can find (should you care to) unusual meats like snake, armadillo, lion, buffalo, and snails, obscure cheeses from across the globe, and specialty herbs and chiles from around Mexico.

⟨ MERCADO SONORA
Av. Fray Servando Teresa de Mier at Calz. de la Viga
HOURS: Daily 8 A.M.–5 P.M.
METRO: La Merced
Map 1

Across Avenida Fray Servando Teresa de Mier from Mercado La Merced is Mercado Sonora, the so-called "witches' market." Mexicans flock here to buy herbal remedies, love potions, special candles, talismans, and other assorted psycho-spiritual balms. Visitors can take part

a busy side street near Mercado La Merced, in the Centro Histórico

© CHRIS HUMPHREY

in a *limpia* ("cleansing") ceremony, complete with herbs, lotions, burning incense, and much chanting by a *brujo* (witch). The market also does a booming illegal trade in endangered plants and animals, for which it is routinely raided by the police.

MERCADO XÓCHITL
Bordered by Madero, 16 de Septiembre, Guerrero, and Morelos
HOURS: Daily 5:30 A.M.–6 P.M.
METRO: Xochimilco light rail station
Map 7

This traditional municipal market in Xochimilco, founded in 1957, stocks everything from fresh produce to clay, leather, and cane *artesanías*. It's southwest of the Parroquia, just off the main Xochimilco plaza.

SHOPS

ARTS AND LEISURE

In their relentless quest for diversion, *capitalinos* have turned their city into a world-class font of art and leisure for virtually every taste. Whether you're into modern art museums, avant-garde theater, gallery exhibitions, cult cinema, mariachi bands, festivals, parades, or *charreadas,* you'll find some part of the city dedicated to every form of expression. If all that city living has you in need of some recreation, fear not—there's a myriad of ways to sate the craving. Mexico City has numerous parks and gyms within the city for those after a jog or workout, and plenty of venues to watch sports if you're more of a spectator.

While the suggestions in this chapter should give you plenty to start with, there's a whole lot more going on just waiting to be discovered by those who choose to explore. A good place to start is the entertainment listings of local newspapers and magazines, especially *Tiempo Libre* and *Chilango*. One website full of cultural events around the city is www.defecito.com.

HIGHLIGHTS

LOOK FOR 【 TO FIND RECOMMENDED ARTS AND ACTIVITIES.

【 **Best Modern Art Museum:** Mexico City has a number of top-notch modern art museums, but one of the best is **Museo de Arte Carrillo Gil** in San Ángel. You'll find a comprehensive collection of Mexico's greatest artists of the last 100 years, including Rivera, Siqueiros, Tamayo, and Toledo, as well as newer, more experimental artists (page 166).

【 **Best Diego and Frida Museum:** It's a bit out of the way, but for fans of Mexico's most famous artist couple, the trip down to Xochimilco to the **Museo Dolores Olmedo Patiño** is well worth it. Housed in a lovely 16th-century hacienda surrounded by lush gardens, this museum was created by Olmedo out of her personal collection of works by Rivera and Kahlo (page 167).

【 **Most Unusual Art Gallery:** Not every city has an art gallery run by the tax man, but D.F. does. Right behind the Catedral is the **Galería SCHP,** which shows an eclectic selection of works donated by Mexican artists in lieu of their tax bill (page 170).

【 **Best Place to Go for a Jog:** The Primera Sección (First Section) of **Chapultepec Park** is criss-crossed with paths through grassy meadows, groves of trees, and around a couple of small lakes – an ideal and safe place for a run away from all the traffic. Better to come during the week, though, as the park fills up on weekends (page 182).

【 **Best Hiking and Mountain Biking:** On the slopes of El Ajusco mountain, outdoor enthusiasts will be happy to find **San Nicolás Totolapan,** a community-managed forest reserve. For a nominal fee, hikers and bikers can roam over 150 kilometers of well-maintained and guarded trails, or take guided naturalist walks for a bit more (page 187).

【 **Strangest Place to Go Rock Climbing:** Amidst the gritty streets of an industrial neighborhood in northern Mexico City is a most unexpected find: **Parque Ecológico El Cantil,** a wall of 25-meter cliffs offering dozens of great top-rope and even a few trad routes ranging in difficulty from 5.8–5.12 (page 189).

【 **Least P.C. Way to Spend the Afternoon:** Foxhunting may be a thing of the past in Britain, but bullfighting is alive and well here in Mexico. It's definitely not for everyone, but it is certainly a most unusual, ritualistic spectacle. The big shows are held at the **Monumental Plaza de Toros México** (page 191).

【 **Best Place to Lay a Wager:** For a lazy afternoon of sipping drinks and betting on the ponies, head out to **Hipódromo de las Américas.** With bets allowed as low as a dime, you don't need to be a big spender to participate (page 192).

【 **Best Place to Watch Mexican Wrestling:** Lucha libre is Mexico's answer to professional wrestling, and the best place to see it is at **Arena México.** Outlandishly costumed fighters perform crazy acrobatic stunts to the cheers of an enthusiastic crowd (page 194).

【 **Best Fútbol Stadium:** The 120,000-seat Estadio Azteca is quite a spectacle if you can grab a seat for a national team match, but for most regular league games, the better bet is the lively **Estadio Olímpico** in the national university (page 196).

The Arts

MUSEUMS

As one of the principal cultural centers in Latin America, Mexico City has dozens of noteworthy museums covering all manner of topics, from colonial art to historical themes to maps and geology. The majority of museums are about some aspect of arts and culture. Most museums only charge a small admission, usually a couple of dollars, and many are free on Sundays. Apart from those listed below, a few of the most important museums (such as the Museo de Antropología e Historia, for example) are described in the *Sights* chapter.

Centro Histórico Map 1
MUSEO DEL EJÉRCITO
Corner of Tacuba and Gante
HOURS: Tues.-Sat. 10 A.M.-6 P.M., Sun. 10 A.M.-4 P.M.
COST: Free
METRO: Bellas Artes

This museum, in a former Bethlehemite hospital and chapel in the Centro across from the Palacio de Minería, is dedicated to the soldiers of Mexico. The museum contains armor worn by Spanish conquistadors and Aztec soldiers, plenty of old pistols and rifles, and other assorted military paraphernalia from across the centuries. There's no entrance fee, so it's worth taking a quick look inside if you're in the area, if only to admire the interior of the old church. The museum also boasts a café and gift shop, attended by extremely efficient young soldiers.

MUSEO DEL ESTANQUILLO
Isabel la Católica 26 at Madero, 55/5521-3052, www.museodelestanquillo.com
HOURS: Wed.-Mon. 10 A.M.-6 P.M.
COST: Free
METRO: Allende

This most unusual and highly entertaining museum is the personal collection of Carlos Monsiváis, a famed chronicler of Mexico City life over the past four decades, from elite culture to life on the streets. His collection of essays, *Los Rituales del Caos,* is a classic portrayal of the city. The highly irreverent collection surveys D.F.'s recent social and physical evolution through sketches, photos, advertisements, comics, bone carvings, and much else besides. The museum is housed in one of the most ornate buildings on Madero, the original La Esmeralda jewelry store, built in the late 19th century. Guided tours are available. Labels are all in Spanish, although English-speaking guides are sometimes available on weekends.

MUSEO JOSÉ LUIS CUEVAS
Academia 13, 55/5522-0156 or 55/5542-6198, www.museojoseluiscuevas.com.mx
HOURS: Tues.-Sun. 10 A.M.-5 P.M.
COST: $1, free for students with ID
METRO: Zócalo

This unusual modern art museum two blocks behind the Palacio Nacional was established by one of Mexico's preeminent sculptors, José Luis Cuevas. Housed in the remodeled 16th-century Convento de Santa Inés, the museum mounts new exhibits every month or two that are drawn from the artist's private collection, which he donated to create the museum. The collection contains works by Mexican artists Francisco Toledo, Vicente Rojo, and Arnold Belkin, among others, as well as by foreign artists such as Pablo Picasso, Leonora Carrington, and Roberto Matta.

Erotica, found in a room draped in ominous black curtains on the 1st floor, contains a small display of rather tame erotic sketches by Cuevas. Several impressive Cuevas sculptures are placed throughout the museum. Particularly striking is the eight-meter-high bronze sculpture of a female figure that Cuevas designed especially for the center patio, titled *La giganta* (The Giantess).

To find the museum, walk up Calle Moneda from the Zócalo to the corner of Academia, turn left, and look for a bright red metal sculpture marking the entrance.

MUSEO NACIONAL DE ARTE

Tacuba 8, 55/5130-3459 or 55/5130-3460,
www.munal.com.mx

HOURS: Tues.-Sun. 10:30 A.M.-5:30 P.M.

COST: $3, $1.50 students, free Sun.

METRO: Bellas Artes

This austere gray palace on the north side of
Calle Tacuba—originally built as the Palacio de
Comunicaciones—was finished in 1910 under
the supervision of Italian architect Silvio Contri
and was converted into a museum in 1982. The
building's cool, beautiful interior houses an
overview of Mexican art dating from the early
colonial period to the mid-20th century. Among
the notable artists featured are colonial painters
Miguel Cabrera, Cristóbal Villalpando, and Luis
Juárez; 19th-century painters Juan Cordero,
José María Velasco, and Ramón Sagredo; and
the 20th century's Diego Rivera, Frida Kahlo,
Rufino Tamayo, and others. Guide service is
free and sometimes available in English.

MUSEO NACIONAL DE LA CHARRERÍA

Izazaga at Isabel la Católica, 55/5512-2523

HOURS: Mon.-Fri. 11 A.M.-5 P.M.

COST: Free

METRO: Isabel la Católica

Another one of the Centro's offbeat museums,
this two-story building housed in a former
16th-century Benedictine convent is dedicated to Mexico's passion for the *charreada* (a
show of horsemanship). The humble little museum contains a few displays of the famed outfits worn by *charros* (horsemen) from Mexico,
Spain, Argentina, and Venezuela, along with
a collection of swords, saddles, and guns. A
.44-caliber pistol once owned by Pancho Villa
is the only labeled display. Historical inscriptions placed throughout the museum are written in Spanish, English, and even French.

MUSEO NACIONAL DE LA ESTAMPA

Hidalgo 39, 55/5510-4905

HOURS: Tues.-Sun. 10 A.M.-6 P.M.

COST: $2

METRO: Bellas Artes

Estampa means "print" in Spanish, and this
museum is filled with a large collection of
printmaking paraphernalia, from the clay
seals and agave leaves of pre-Hispanic times
to modern metal plates. There are also many
displays of the prints themselves. Among the
most interesting are those that were used to illustrate books and periodicals before the pop-
ularization of photography. The latter include
works by Manuel Manilla (1830–1890) and
José Guadalupe Posadas (1852–1913), both of
whom were famous satirical newspaper illustra-
tors in the late 19th century.

The etchings of Aguascalientes native
Posadas often feature variations of the *calavera*
the skeleton figure associated with Mexico's
Day of the Dead celebration. His most famous
calavera engraving, *Catrina*, depicts a skeleton
wearing an expensive lady's hat ("Catrina" is
an old-fashioned slang word used to refer to a
well-dressed aristocratic woman) and is on display here, as is his noted Don Quijote skeleton.
Great muralists Rivera and Orozco, who hung
around his studio when they were novice artists, revered Posadas as the first truly Mexican
artist in the country's history.

Alameda Central **Map 1**

LABORATORIO DE ARTE ALAMEDA

Dr. Mora 7, 55/5510-2793,
www.artealameda.inba.gob.mx

HOURS: Tues.-Sun. 9 A.M.-5 P.M.

COST: $1, free Sun.

METRO: Hidalgo

On the Alameda, in what was formerly a museum
for colonial art, is the "Alameda Art Laboratory."
This space for young artists is run by Instituto
Nacional de Bellas Artes (INBA). Rotating exhibits of experimental modern art (video is prominent) are on display. Guided tours of the gallery
are available for free, in Spanish only.

MUSEO FRANZ MAYER

Av. Hidalgo 45 opposite the Alameda, 55/5518-2266,
www.franzmayer.org.mx

HOURS: Tues.-Sun. 10 A.M.-5 P.M., Wed. until 7 P.M.

COST: $3.50, $1.70 students, free for those over 60
and under 12 years old

METRO: Bellas Artes

On the north side of the Alameda, in the Plaza de

la Santa Veracruz, this eclectic museum housed in a 16th-century former hospital contains the carefully and tastefully displayed applied-arts collection of German financier-philanthropist Franz Mayer. The fine selection, which extends to two floors, includes 16th- through 19th-century Mexican ceramics, antique *rebozos* (Mexican shawls), religious articles, furniture, textiles, silver and gold pieces, clocks, and even full *cocinas poblanas* (tiled Puebla-style kitchens)—a real treat for fans of Mexican culinary history. The museum contains a few canvases by European Renaissance artists as well, plus temporary exhibitions of often excellent quality. A courtyard café toward the back of the museum is a quiet spot for reflection and refreshment.

MUSEO NACIONAL DE ARTES POPULARES

Revillagigedo at Independencia (NW corner), 55/5510-2201, www.map.org.mx
HOURS: Tues.-Sun. 10 A.M.-5 P.M., Thurs. until 9 P.M.
COST: $4
METRO: Juárez

This welcome addition to downtown Mexico City's museum collection is dedicated to the country's popular arts and crafts. Opened in 2006, the Museo de Artes Populares is housed in a renovated 1928 art deco building just south of the Alameda. The permanent exhibit, covering two floors, contains a myriad of sculpture, textiles, toys, lacquerware, silver art, wood carvings, glass, leatherwork, weavings, and much else besides. There's a spectacular *árbol de la vida* ("tree of life") from Metepec, state of Mexico. The other two floors are dedicated to temporary exhibits, a gift shop, and a small coffee shop.

Paseo de la Reforma [Map 2] and Zona Rosa

MUSEO CASA DE CARRANZA

Río Lerma 35, Col. Cuauhtémoc, 55/5546-6494
HOURS: Tues.-Sat. 9 A.M.-7 P.M., Sun. 11 A.M.-3 P.M.
COST: $3
METRO: Insurgentes

This French-inspired mansion two blocks north of Reforma was the last home of

The Museo Nacional de Artes Populares has fine craft work from across the country, like this angel made in Taxco.

COURTESY OF CONSEJO DE PROMOCIÓN TURÍSTICA DE MÉXICO/CARLOS SÁNCHEZ

Mexican revolutionary leader Venustiano Carranza, who stayed here for six months before his execution in Puebla on May 7, 1920. Carranza's widow was granted the house after the Revolution, and in 1942 she in turn converted it into a museum commemorating her husband. Art, period furniture, and memorabilia from Carranza's life fill the various rooms. One particularly interesting piece is an ambiguous Carranza portrait by Mexican painter Dr. Atl (Gerardo Murillo).

MUSEO DE GEOLOGÍA

Jaime Torres Bodet 176, on the Alameda in Col. Santa María de la Ribera, 55/5547-3900
HOURS: Tues.-Sun. 10 A.M.-5 P.M.
COST: $1
METRO: San Cosme

On the square of the little-visited Santa María de la Ribera neighborhood is UNAM's Geology

Museum, housed in a beautiful old mansion. The displays of meteorites, fossils, and some impressive mammoth skeletons, as well as the opportunity to wander around the old building, are well worth the $1 admission charge. Check out the imposing facade with archways below and columns above, and the sweeping art nouveau wrought-iron staircase in the entryway. Guided tours of the museum can be arranged by calling ahead and are even available in English if the museum director (who speaks English) is around.

MUSEO EL CHOPO

Dr. Enrique González 10, Col. Santa María de la Ribera, 55/5546-5484, www.chopo.unam.mx
HOURS: Tues.- Sun. 10 A.M.-2 P.M. and 3-7 P.M.
COST: $0.70
METRO: San Cosme

The Eiffelesque structure of girders and glass now housing El Chopo was originally built in Germany and was moved to Mexico in pieces. It first served as the Japanese pavilion at an industrial exposition in 1910 and then was moved to its current site to become a natural history museum. UNAM, the national university, took over the building in 1973 and uses it as a forum for revolving shows of modern art, mostly by younger Mexican artists. Occasional theater shows are also staged in the cavernous interior, which boasts wonderful light from all the colored stained glass. A small café at the museum serves coffee and snacks. At the rear of the museum is the **Cinematógrafo del Chopo,** run by UNAM and showing art movies daily.

The museum is a block from the intersection of Insurgentes and San Cosme (look for the iron towers).

MUSEO SAN CARLOS

Av. Puente de Alvarado 50, 55/5566-8342
HOURS: Wed.-Mon. 10 A.M.-6 P.M.
COST: $2.30, $1 extra for cameras, $4 extra for video
METRO: Revolución

On the corner of Puente de Alvarado and Ramos Arizpe, amidst a row of otherwise drab buildings, stands an anomalous neoclassical palace that was once the home of the Marqués de Buenavista, and now houses an art museum. Although the original building plans have been lost, it's thought to have been the work of that omnipresent Valencian architect and artist Manuel Tolsá. The rooms of the former mansion, around the unusual oval-shaped courtyard, now house a remarkable collection of early European artworks, including Gothic Spanish and Dutch paintings from the 13th and 14th centuries, Italian Renaissance works including some by Tintorreto, as well as later baroque and romantic art up to the 19th century—about 2,000 paintings in all. Works by foreign masters who taught at the San Carlos school, such as Eugenio Landesio and Pelegrín Clavé, are also included.

King Carlos IV donated much of the art to the Academia de San Carlos when the art school opened in the late 18th century. Originally housed in the academy building in the Centro, these sculptures and paintings served as models for students learning their chosen medium. The collection was opened to public viewing during the last years of the Spanish colony, thus establishing the first public art museum in the Americas. When the quantity of visitors began to overwhelm the art school in the Centro, many of the finest works were moved to the current museum, which doesn't see a whole lot of traffic. It's a great place to look at works by some of the European masters without the crowds.

Chapultepec and Polanco Map 3
MUSEO RUFINO TAMAYO

Paseo de la Reforma at Gandhi, 55/5286-5889, www.museotamayo.org
HOURS: Tues.-Sun. 10 A.M.-6 P.M.
COST: $2
METRO: Chapultepec

The Tamayo was created by one of the great Mexican painters of the 20th century, a Zapotec Indian born in Oaxaca in 1899. Heavily influenced by his indigenous roots, Rufino Tamayo gained fame in the 1950s (when he was living in New York) for his dramatic use of colors, particularly the earth tones from his native state. In 1981, he and his wife, Olga, donated this museum along with a fabulous collection of modern art, consisting of his works plus the works of Salvador Dalí, Max Ernst, Gunther Gerzso, Alberto Giacometti, Willem de Kooning, René Magritte, Joan Miró, Andy Warhol, and many others. Tamayo died in 1991 at the age of 91.

A modernistic red sculpture sits in front of the odd, bunkerlike building of concrete and white marble, hidden away amid a stand of trees. World-class traveling exhibits change frequently in the 10 halls around a central patio. The museum installed a cyberlounge in 2001, dedicated to art on the Internet. The museum is east of the Museo Nacional de Antropología, on Paseo de la Reforma.

MUSEO DE ARTE MODERNO

Primera Sección of Chapultepec, 55/5553-6233, www.cnca.gob.mx
HOURS: Tues.-Sun. 10 A.M.–6 P.M.
COST: $2
METRO: Chapultepec

Mexico's top public modern art museum is in the first section of Chapultepec Park, just about opposite Reforma from the Tamayo Museum, and has a wide ranging collection of Mexican art from recent decades. This dark glass building, designed by Pedro Ramírez Vásquez of Museo de Antropología fame, looks a bit drab on the outside, but inside are four spacious, well-lit exhibition halls off a broad central stairway. Three rooms are dedicated to rotating exhibits of sometimes excellent quality (a fine show of Cartier-Bresson photography is one recent example), while the fourth displays selections from the museum's permanent collection, including Mexican greats Diego Rivera, José Clemente Orozco, Rufino Tamayo, Manuel Álvarez Bravo, and Dr. Atl. One of the galleries contains Frida Kahlo's largest work, *Las Dos Fridas,* in which twin portraits of the artist are joined by arteries looping from the exposed hearts of each figure. Also notable are some 1920s paintings by Ángel Zárraga.

MUSEO DEL NIÑO

Segunda Sección of Chapultepec, adjacent to the Periférico, 55/5237-1881, www.papalote.org.mx
HOURS: Mon.-Fri. 9 A.M.–1 P.M. and 2-6 P.M., Sat.-Sun. 10 A.M.–2 P.M. and 3-7 P.M.
COST: $3 adults, $2.50 children, free for kids under two
METRO: Constituyentes

Popularly known as El Papalote, this excellent interactive children's museum is a bright-blue oddly shaped building just south of the amusement park at the edge of the Periférico. On the premises are 380 "touch, play, and learn" exhibits on science, the human body, communications, and other subjects. The museum has limited capacity, meaning you may have to wait (usually not long) before being allowed into the museum. Tickets can also be bought in advance through TicketMaster (55/5325-9000, www.ticketmaster.com.mx).

MUSEO NACIONAL DE LA CARTOGRAFÍA

Av. Observatorio at Periférico, Col. Tacubaya
HOURS: Mon.-Sat. 10 A.M.–6 P.M., Sun. 10 A.M.–4 P.M.
COST: $1
METRO: Tacubaya

Seemingly lost amid a sea of concrete and traffic in Colonia Tacubaya is a former Franciscan convent dedicated to San Diego, built in 1590 and now housing the national map museum. The red domed building with a simple facade and a small park shaded with palm trees out front has seen a turbulent history. It was taken over by the Dominicans in the late 17th century and then closed in 1827 by the government because the convent authorities had supported the Spaniards against the Mexican independence movement. During the U.S. invasion in 1847, the church was the site of a prisoner exchange between the Mexicans and the victorious Americans. It was briefly reopened as a church in the late 19th century but was taken over by the government in 1918.

Nowadays the building houses a fascinating museum of maps (fascinating if you like maps, that is) and is run by the Mexican military. Inside are copies of old codices and many maps

Gaba
tus dos fine
dau fine
Castramos
MUCA Roma (Colonia)
Bdir
Zacatecas 43 —
Samecs niña
Tonala

COURTESY OF CONSEJO DE PROMOCIÓN TURÍSTICA DE MÉXICO/IGNACIO GUEVARA

The bright-blue Museo del Niño has hundreds of interactive displays for kids.

of colonial and more recent Mexico City and the country as a whole, as well as mapmaking gear, such as compasses, cameras, projectors, and GPS instruments, all housed amid the bare walls of the old church. For an idea of Mexico City's prodigious growth, check out the satellite photo showing how the city has changed over 110 years.

MUSEO SALA DE ARTE PÚBLICO DAVÍD ALFARO SIQUEIROS

Tres Picos 29, Polanco, 55/5203-5888
HOURS: Tues.-Sun. 10 A.M.-6 P.M.
COST: $1.50
METRO: Auditorio

Fans of the Mexican muralist movement may want to stop in at this small museum dedicated to Davíd Alfaro Siqueiros, one of the three best-known muralists (along with Diego Rivera and José Clemente Orozco). Here, in a private house donated by the artist shortly before his death in 1974, you'll find a permanent exhibit of his art, as well as temporary exhibits of other contemporary art.

Roma and Condesa Map 4

MUSEO UNIVERSITARIO DE CIENCIAS Y ARTES ROMA (MUCA ROMA)

Tonala 51 at Colima, Roma Norte, 55/5511-0925, www.muca.unam.mx
HOURS: Mon.-Fri. 10 A.M.-5 P.M.
COST: Free
METRO: Insurgentes

Just off Avenida Insurgentes in the Roma Norte is a national university–run art space housed in a fine old Porfiriato-era mansion. Several rooms exhibit works of different Mexican and international artists; they are often very good and usually fairly experimental. Although technically a museum, it's actually more like a gallery/alternative art space. There's also a small art bookstore and a coffee shop.

Coyoacán Map 6

MUSEO NACIONAL DE CULTURAS POPULARES

Av. Hidalgo, half block northeast of Plaza Hidalgo
HOURS: Tues.-Thurs. 10 A.M.-6 P.M., Fri.-Sun. 10 A.M.-8 P.M.

COST: Donation requested

METRO: Viveros

This fascinating museum, founded in 1982, is dedicated to Mexico's astoundingly diverse artistic and cultural expressions. Sometimes the shows can be very interesting, like one on Día de los Muertos art from throughout the country. Visitors will encounter displays of both traditional and modern handicrafts, along with live demonstrations. Special courses and fairs with gastronomic or handicraft themes are also frequently hosted here. A cafeteria offers refreshment, while shops purvey a variety of books, magazines, and posters. One of the posters for sale in the shop is a lovely black-and-white photo of the church and plazas of Coyoacán a century ago, surrounded by farmland and countryside.

MUSEO NACIONAL DE LAS INTERVENCIONES

20 de Agosto at General Anaya, 55/5604-0699,

www.inah.gob.mx/Museos/delasintervenciones/

index_museo_intervenciones.html

HOURS: Tues.-Sun. 9 A.M.-6 P.M.

COST: $3.50

METRO: General Anaya

For a country that has been sorely treated by invading countries (one of its great holidays, Cinco de Mayo, commemorates one winning battle in a war Mexico lost), it's only appropriate that one of the best historical museums would be dedicated to invasions. The museum, two kilometers from the center of Coyoacán, is in the 17th-century **Ex-Convento de Churubusco,** where Mexican General Pedro Anaya surrendered his sword to U.S. forces in 1847. The museum's 13 rooms chronicle invasions of Mexico on the part of Spain in 1829, France in 1838, and the U.S. in 1846–1847, 1914, and 1916. Administered by INAH, the museum also hosts temporary historical exhibitions, cultural extension courses, roundtable discussions, conferences, and other educational/cultural activities.

In addition to weaponry, flags, paintings, lithographs, maps, photos, and documents, the casual visitor can admire large-scale dioramas depicting various battles against French and U.S. forces. The museum is of particular interest to history buffs, and all sides are treated fairly and without animosity in the displays. A plaque commemorates a group of Irish American soldiers from Texas known as the St. Patrick's Battalion, who switched sides during the 1847 invasion, in large part because of their religious affinity with the Mexicans. Those who survived the battle for Mexico City were executed by the Americans.

San Ángel Map 6

MUSEO DE ARTE CARRILLO GIL

Av. Revolución 1608, 55/5550-6260,

www.macg.inba.gob.mx

HOURS: Tues.-Sun. 10 A.M.-6 P.M.

COST: $1.50, $0.90 students, free for children under 12 and on Sun.

METRO: Barranca del Muerto

One of Mexico's finest modern art museums, the Carrillo Gil is housed in a slick building in San Ángel. Along with an excellent collection of works by Mexican greats such as Rivera, Siqueiros, Tamayo, and Toledo, the museum also shows more experimental current Mexican and international artists. They have more than 1,700 works in their permanent collection, based on the donated works of Dr. Alvar Carrillo Gil, a businessman from Yucatán who collected Mexican art. The museum is a 10-minute walk from Plaza San Jacinto north along Avenida Revolución.

MUSEO ESTUDIO DIEGO RIVERA

Av. Diego Rivera, at the corner of Altavista, 55/5550-1189

HOURS: Tues.-Sun. 10 A.M.-6 P.M.

COST: $1

METRO: Barranca del Muerto

Rivera lived and worked for a time with his wife, Frida Kahlo, in this unique dwelling designed by architectural prodigy Juan O'Gorman in 1928. Rivera's life and work (reproductions only) are depicted on the ground floor of this tightly spaced functionalist structure, while the upper floor is arranged as it might have been when Rivera was still in residence, complete with unfinished paintings on easels.

MUSEO SOUMAYA

Plaza Loreto, Av. Revolución and Río Magdalena, 55/5616-3731, www.soumaya.com.mx
HOURS: Thurs.-Mon. 10:30 A.M.-6:30 P.M., Wed. 10:30 A.M.-8:30 P.M.
COST: $1, $0.50 students, free seniors and children under 12, free for all Sun.-Mon.
METRO: M. A. de Quevedo

The Plaza Loreto shopping center in San Ángel is home to this private museum with a varied and interesting collection, including several sculptures by Rodin and paintings by Degas, Renoir, Camine Claudel, and Miró. There's also a modest collection of colonial-era Latin American art, as well as two murals by modern Mexican painter Rufino Tamayo. The museum offers free guided tours of the museum (in Spanish) on weekends at noon. Plaza Loreto, an unusual mall of sorts in the refurbished remains of what was first a colonial-era mill once owned by Hernán Cortés himself, and later the biggest paper factory in Latin America, is itself worth a look around.

Greater Mexico City Map 7
MUSEO ANAHUACALLI

Calle de Museo 150, Col. San Pablo Tepetlapa, 55/5617-4310
HOURS: Tues.-Sun. 10 A.M.-2 P.M. and 3-6 P.M.
COST: $3
METRO: Xotepingo light rail station

Mexican muralist Diego Rivera designed and built this bizarre Mesoamerican pyramid–inspired museum of volcanic stone to contain his prodigious collection of pre-Hispanic treasures. The museum displays 60,000 artifacts from the Zapotec, Toltec, Teotihuacán, Veracruz, Mixtec, and Aztec cultures. Upstairs a studio holds many personal belongings and sketches of Rivera, offering a window on this legendary artist's personal life. On the top floor is a terrace offering views out over the city.

The museum is in Colonia San Pablo Tepetlapa, southeast of Coyoacán, in the direction of Xochimilco. By car or taxi, follow Avenida División del Norte south from Avenida Miguel Ángel de Quevedo until you reach Calle de Museo, about a 20-minute drive. The easiest way to get there on public transportation is to go to Tasqueña Metro station and catch the *tren ligero* south to the Xotepingo stop. From there, walk 10 minutes along Avenida División del Norte until it crosses Calle de Museo.

◀ MUSEO DOLORES OLMEDO PATIÑO

Av. México 5843, Col. La Noria, 55/5555-1221 or 55/5555-0891, www.museodoloresolmedo.org.mx
HOURS: Tues.-Sun. 10 A.M.-6 P.M.
COST: $3
METRO: La Noria light rail station

The best place to view Frida Kahlo's work is this palatial stone hacienda formerly owned by Dolores Olmedo Patiño, a wealthy lifelong friend and supporter of Diego Rivera (not to mention an occasional model for his paintings). Olmedo donated a large part of her own house as a museum dedicated to Rivera and Kahlo. The building, the lovingly restored 16th-century Hacienda La Noria, is worth a visit in and of itself, even if it weren't for the collection of more than 600 pre-Hispanic artifacts and pieces of native art, and works by Rivera (127 pieces) as well as Frida Kahlo. Although the Kahlo collection numbers only 25 pieces, this is the largest single private collection of the painter's work. Not all pieces are displayed at any given time, however.

Rivera's collection is large and varied, starting from one of his earliest paintings in Europe imitating then-current styles, *La Noche en Ávila* from 1907, a night landscape. Ten years later comes *En las Afueras de Toledo* (Los Viejos), a large multi-level scene with hints of the monumental muralist style to come. For an idea of the artist's humor and self-deprecation, see the self-portrait as a frog, carved as a table. Interspersed among Rivera's work are numerous pre-Hispanic and colonial pieces too, many from the state of Oaxaca.

After passing through several rooms displaying the technical brilliance and controlled style of Rivera, stepping into the single hall of Kahlo's work is a shock. The paintings are much more directly powerful than Rivera's, much more surreal also, with strong evident influence of Dalí, among others. Several are

DIEGO AND FRIDA

Mexico City in the 1920s stood on the threshold of a new era. In the socialist-inspired aftermath of Mexico's 1910–1920 revolution, the newly created government decided that public works of art could play an important role in restoring a nationhood tattered by civil war. Commissioned to create a number of murals at the National Preparatory School at the University of Mexico in 1922, painter Diego Rivera took on the task of conceiving a new art medium that avoided a Eurocentric orientation and instead celebrated Mexican heritage from early Mesoamerica through the Revolution. Rivera, who spent much of his youth in Paris where he counted Picasso, Braque, Gris, Modigliani, and Derain among his friends, was joined by a number of other similarly commissioned Mexican artists. In a public tract issued by the group in 1922, fellow muralist Davíd Alfaro Siqueiros urged Mexican artists to "repudiate so-called easel painting and every kind of art favored by the ultra intellectual circles, because it is aristocratic, and praise monumental art in all its forms, because it is public property."

The soon-to-be-dubbed Mexican Modernist School abandoned the solemn and detached art of Europe and instead embraced bold New World imagery full of color and human activity. Looking for a medium beyond the confines of canvas and church porticoes, they settled on the vast, undecorated walls of Mexico's governmental edifices. Like the Aztecs and Maya of earlier eras, who painted on the walls of their temples and tombs, the Mexican muralists left their public buildings awash with color. And instead of creating portraits of Spanish aristocrats, they glorified the everyday lives of the contemporary Amerindian population; in place of Franciscan friars fingering rosaries, they painted peasants tilling the soil.

Although many Mexican artists participated in the muralist movement, three names quickly came to the fore in Mexico City: Diego Rivera, Davíd Alfaro Siqueiros, and José Clemente Orozco. One of Rivera's earliest mural efforts emblazoned the courtyard of the Secretaría de Educación Pública with a series of dancing Tehuanas (natives of Tehuantepec, in Southern Mexico). This four-year project went on to incorporate many other contemporary Amerindian themes, and it eventually encompassed 124 frescoes that extended three stories high and two city blocks long. Such prodigious output, along with the predominance of native elements, had a profound effect on the Mexican art scene.

But as famous as the Mexico City murals made Rivera and his colleagues, a star-crossed romance with a teenaged National Preparatory School student named Frida Kahlo drew Rivera into a living tableau that for much of the world has symbolized the 20th-century Mexican art milieu, seemingly for all eternity. Kahlo and Rivera married in 1929 and nearly overnight became a charismatic, celebrated couple on the art and society circuit around Mexico, the United States, and Europe. Their tumultuous relationship and Rivera's notorious infidelity only seemed to propel their mythic status. "I have suffered two accidents in my life," Kahlo is quoted as saying in the Malka Drucker biography, *Frida Kahlo: Torment and Triumph in Her Life and Art.* "One in which a streetcar ran over me at age 18. The other is Diego."

The aftermath of the streetcar accident, which included more than 30 surgical procedures and 28 plaster corsets designed to support her damaged spine, forms a recurring theme in Kahlo's famous self-portraits.

But more than the sometimes tortuously clinical details in these *autoretratos*, it's her iconic facial features – the batwing eyebrows; the stern, roselike mouth; and secretive, sidelong glance fixed on the viewer – that one most remembers. A pronounced sexual ambiguity is also often present. In one portrait she suggests androgyny by merging her face with Diego's, while another portrays Kahlo sporting shorn hair and a man's suit and tie. In a now-famous family photo from 1926, her hair is pulled back tightly, and she again is dressed like a man.

In spite of her preference for personal rather than overtly political themes, Kahlo's work formed a central part of the Mexican renaissance in its employment of native Mexican elements. Many of her paintings show an influence rooted in the tradition of Mexican religious folk culture, yet in a sense her work was postmodernist, since she didn't completely turn away from traditional European presentation concepts. In *The Little Deer* (1946), Kahlo superimposed her head on the body of a stag (once again blending genders), whose body is pierced by numerous arrows. The painting recalls the martyrdom of St. Sebastian – a popular European theme in medieval religious art – while evoking the *danza del venado*, a mythic deer-hunting dance ritual common among Amerindian tribes throughout Mexico.

Although she didn't participate in public works of art like the muralists – in her physical condition she could hardly be expected to mount scaffolds – Kahlo in her own way became just as influential in her promotion of Mexican cultural nationalism. She decorated her home not with European and American art and accessories, but with Mexican handicrafts and folk art. Rivera and his colleagues typically dressed in the European fashions of the day, while Kahlo, though born of a German immigrant father, most often wore Amerindian dresses, shawls, and jewelry. Although she was born in 1907, she usually gave 1910 – the year the Mexican Revolution began – as her birth date.

Kahlo died in 1954, and Rivera followed her three years later. Of all the Mexican artists who have worked in the 20th century, Diego and Frida are the most loved and remembered. In spite of the dynamic couple's original living-legend status, over the last decade, Kahlo's international reputation has grown beyond that of her contemporaries, as well as that of Rivera.

Where to See Art by Diego and Frida: The more famous of Rivera's murals are all located in the Centro: the Palacio Nacional, the Secretaría de Educación Pública building, and Museo Mural Diego Rivera, on the Alameda. In Coyoacán is the Museo Frida Kahlo, which is more about the artist's life than her own art collection.

The largest collection of works by both Rivera and Kahlo is the Museo Dolores Olmedo, housed in a gorgeous colonial hacienda in the southern neighborhood of Xochimilco – well worth the trip. The Museo de Arte Moderno holds a permanent exhibit of Kahlo's most famous work in Mexico, *The Two Fridas*, as well as several paintings by Rivera. The Museo Carrillo Gil in San Ángel also has works by both artists. Rivera has two museums dedicated to him: the Museo Estudio Diego Rivera in San Ángel, where the artist lived and worked, and the Museo Anahuacalli, a bizarre pyramid-type structure full of his collection of pre-Columbian artifacts.

unnervingly graphic and illustrate the horrific pain the artist was afflicted with following her accident early in life.

Well worth a brief look are the several rooms where Olmedo herself lived, which house an astounding collection of mainly Asian artwork, furniture, gorgeous elaborate ivory carvings, shimmering blue glass chandeliers, and photos of Olmedo with an endless parade of important people.

The 6,000-square-meter Hacienda La Noria (originally built as the San Juan Evangelista Tzomolco hermitage in the 16th century) also displays colonial objects and furniture. The surrounding grounds, which together with the main building encompass 37,000 square meters, are beautifully landscaped with native trees and plants. You may also see Mexican turkeys and a few unique Xoloitzcuintle dogs, a rare pre-Hispanic canine species that is small, dark, and hairless—a rather spooky-looking creature.

To reach the museum by public transport, take the Metro to the Tasqueña station and then board the *tren ligero* (light rail) from the metro station to La Noria streetcar terminal (fourth from the end of the line, about 20–25 minutes from Tasqueña). From here, walk west along Avenida Guadalupe Ramírez till you come to a large three-way intersection, a distance of around 100 meters, and then make a sharp left (southeast) onto Antiguo Camino Xochimilco. After another 300 meters or so, you'll come to the museum on your left, at the intersection with Avenida México. The museum is very close to the training grounds of the Cruz Azul soccer team, which can help when asking directions.

GALLERIES

Mexico City used to be second-best to Guadalajara when it came to art, but those days are changing fast. New galleries are opening regularly, and more and more international artists are seeing D.F. as a place to be. The **Festival del Centro Histórico,** held in three weeks in March, includes a major art show. The Roma and Polanco neighborhoods, in particular, are where most art galleries are found. Check the website www.arte-mexico.com for an excellent listing of galleries with upcoming openings. The following sections highlight some of the best-known galleries in the city, carrying both Mexican and international art.

Centro Histórico   `Map 1`

Although the Centro is not a major art destination, the Finance Ministry's gallery is worth a look if you are in the area.

◖ GALERÍA SCHP

República de Guatemala 8
HOURS: Daily 10 A.M.–5:30 P.M.
METRO: Zócalo

If you're a starving artist and you owe Mexico's government some back taxes, you may have a work in this gallery run by the Finance Ministry. It's housed in a colonial building right behind the Catedral. Here artists whose tax payments are delinquent may erase their tax debt by donating works of art. Those interested in seeing an eclectic collection of Mexican modern art might want to take a glance inside to see what's on display.

A peacock strolls the grounds of the Museo Dolores Olmedo Patiño in Xochimilco.

Chapultepec and Polanco `Map 3`

Polanco is the home to some of Mexico City's finest art galleries, with both Mexican and international modern art. In general, the more established artists are found in Polanco's galleries, unlike the Roma galleries, which tend to work with newer artists. On the opposite (south) side of Chapultepec Park from Polanco is Mexico City's oldest art gallery, Galería de Arte Mexicano.

GALERÍA ALFREDO GINOCCHIO

Arquimedes 175, 55/5254-8813, www.praxismexico.com
HOURS: Mon.-Fri. 10 A.M.-7 P.M., Sat. 10 A.M.-3 P.M.
METRO: Polanco

This is Mexico's branch of the Praxis galleries, begun in Buenos Aires in 1978 with the intention of promoting Latin American art, and now with galleries in Santiago, Lima, São Paulo, Miami, and New York. The Mexico City gallery recently renamed itself in honor of the man who founded it in 1988, but the mission is the same as always. Here you'll find more experimental work by Mexican and Latin American artists such as Mónica Dower, Graciela Fuentes, and Alejandro Pintado.

GALERÍA DE ARTE MEXICANO

Gob. Rafael Rebollar 43, Col. San Miguel Chapultepec,
52/5272-5696, www.artegam.com
HOURS: Mon.-Fri. 10 A.M.-7 P.M.
METRO: Juanacatlán or Constituyentes

Founded in 1935, the Galería de Arte Mexicano was Mexico City's first art gallery, with early shows by some of Mexico's greats such as Rivera, Kahlo, Orozco, Covarrubias, Tamayo, and others. Located in a residential neighborhood roughly between Chapultepec Park and the Condesa neighborhood, just off Avenida Constituyentes, the gallery continues to show both well-established masters as well as newcomers like Paula Santiago, Rafael Cidoncha, and Magali Lara. Apart from regular shows, they also have the most complete library of Mexican art in the city, as well as numerous art books for sale.

GALERÍA ENRIQUE GUERRERO

Horacio 1549A, 55/5280-2941,
www.galeriaenriqueguerrero.com
HOURS: Mon.-Fri. 10 A.M.-2:30 P.M. and 5-7 P.M., Sat. 11 A.M.-2 P.M.
METRO: Polanco

Although a relatively new gallery (established in 1997), Enrique Guerrero calls itself a "consolidated avant-garde" gallery, if that's not a contradiction in terms. It focuses on more established Mexican artists, such as famed muralist José Clemente Orozco and surrealist Remedios Varo, as well as international stars like Robert Mapplethorpe and Louise Nevelson, although they do work with a stable of younger Latin artists such as Santiago Borja and Olga Adelantado.

GALERÍA LÓPEZ QUIROGA

Aristótles 169, 55/5280-6218
HOURS: Mon.-Fri. 10 A.M.-7 P.M., Sat. 10 A.M.-2 P.M.
METRO: Polanco

Another high-end Polanco gallery, López Quiroga has been in business since 1980 and has held shows for many of the greats of Latin American art, including legendary Oaxacan painters Francisco Toledo, Vicente Rojo, and Rufino Tamayo; Brazilian photographer Sebastiao Selgao; Mexican-born Gunther Gerzo; and Chilean painter Roberto Matta. The gallery also sells volumes of poetry decorated with drawings by well-known artists.

Roma and Condesa `Map 4`

Since the Roma began its resurgence during the late 1980s and 1990s, it has become Mexico City's premier location for contemporary art galleries. Most galleries hold regular opening parties; call or check websites for information on upcoming exhibitions.

GALERÍA FLORENCIA RIESTRA

Colima 166, Roma Norte, 55/5514-2537,
www.galeriaflorenciariestra.com.mx
HOURS: Mon.-Fri. 10 A.M.-7 P.M., Sat. 10 A.M.-1 P.M.
METRO: Insurgentes

This gallery, housed in a lovely 1908 Porfiriato mansion, was begun in the 1980s to help promote younger Mexican artists, and has since evolved into space for modern artwork as well as antiques. The main rooms downstairs focus on contemporary Mexican painting and photography. Upstairs, several rooms are crammed with an eclectic collection of colonial art and antiques. The owners also have a second gallery in San Miguel de Allende.

GALERÍA OMR

Plaza Río de Janeiro 54, 55/5511-1179 or 55/5207-1080, www.galeriaomr.com
HOURS: Mon.-Fri. 10 A.M.-3 P.M. and 4-7 P.M., Sat. 10 A.M.-2 P.M.
METRO: Insurgentes

Housed in an imposing stone mansion right on Roma's Plaza Río de Janeiro, OMR was founded in 1983 and carries both Mexican and international contemporary art (mainly paintings and sculpture) in a converted mansion, with frequent group shows and openings. The gallery usually sponsors six to eight new shows per year. Among the better-known artists working with OMR are Laureana Toledo, Pablo Vargas Lugo, and Gabriel Acevedo Velarde.

GALERÍA 13

Orizaba 92, Roma Norte, 55/5525-6077, www.galeria13.com
HOURS: Mon.-Fri. 10 A.M.-6 P.M.
METRO: Insurgentes

For a glance at some of the more experimental art coming out of Mexico City, stop by this gallery in the Roma dedicated to younger artists. The quality can be all over the place, but that's what you get with new artists. The openings here can be quite entertaining and less stuffy than at some of the other galleries.

NINA MENOCAL

Zacatecas 93, 55/5564-7209 or 55/5564-7443, www.ninamenocal.com
HOURS: Mon.-Fri. 9 A.M.-7 P.M., Sat. 10 A.M.-3 P.M.
METRO: Insurgentes

Nina Menocal is owned by Cuban expatriates and carries contemporary Latin American art, with an emphasis on young Cuban artists. This gallery, opened in 1990, was one of the first to show the new Cuban artists of the 1980s, such as Tomás Sánchez, Glexis Novoa, and Félix González Torres. Although they continue to work with younger Cuban artists, nowadays they show art from across Latin America, and are also involved in the Basel contemporary art festival.

THEATER

Mexico City is rich in live theater. The weekly *Tiempo Libre* is a good source of information on theater, typically devoting a dozen pages to what's playing and where. Listings are also in the weekend sections of several newspapers (*Primera Fila*, printed on Friday by *Reforma*, is particularly good). The Consejo Nacional para la Cultura y las Artes (Conaculta, the National Council for Culture and the Arts) funds many plays. You can find the latest information on Conaculta shows at www.conaculta.gob.mx/Cartelera. Listed below are only the main drama venues; many smaller production companies are found throughout the city.

TEATRO DE LOS INSURGENTES

Av. Insurgentes Sur 1587, 55/5598-6894 or 55/5611-4253, www.ticketmaster.com
HOURS: Shows usually Thurs.-Sun.
COST: $20-60 depending on seats
METRO: Barranca del Muerto
Map 7

This large theater in the south of the city was built in 1953 at the behest of President Miguel Alemán, and was decorated with a mural on the history of the theater by Diego Rivera (note Cantinflas, the Mexican comedian, portrayed as taking from the rich to give to the poor). Here you'll find some of the more major dramatic productions (often imported from Broadway) put on in Mexico City, usually with big-name national or international actors. One such show was a production of *Victor/Victoria* with Mexican actress Daniela Romo in the lead.

TEATRO HELÉNICO

Av. Revolución 1500, 55/5662-2945 or 55/5662-7535, www.helenico.gob.mx
HOURS: Shows are held most days at 8:30 P.M. during the week and in the afternoons on weekends
COST: $10–15 for most shows
METRO: Barranca del Muerto or Coyoacán
Map 6

One of the most active theaters in Mexico City today is this 450-seat space (divided in two levels) in southern Mexico City, in the former Hellenic Cultural Center that was taken over by the government cultural institute in 1990. Apart from the main theater, which shows a wide variety of shows throughout the year, there is also a small space known as *La Gruta* (The Cave) where more experimental shows are put on for a smaller audience.

Teatro de los Insurgentes, one of the city's premier drama venues, is decorated with a mural by Diego Rivera.

TEATRO JUAN RUIZ ALARCÓN

Insurgentes Sur 3000, at UNAM's Centro Cultural Universitario, 55/5665-6583, www.teatro.unam.mx
HOURS: Days and times vary, but shows are usually Thurs.-Sun.
COST: $10, $5 students
METRO: Universidad
Map 6

The national university bases their dramatic productions out of this theater (and the adjacent smaller Foro Sor Juana Inés de la Cruz) right in the middle of the university complex, just off Insurgentes. Here you'll see anything from a remake of *Peer Gynt* or a Shakespeare production alternating with plays written by university students. Teatro Santa Catarina (Plaza Santa Catarina 10, Coyoacán, 55/5658-0560) is also linked to UNAM's theater program, and information on shows can be found at the same website.

CINEMA

Like other megalopolises—such as New York, London, or Tokyo—Mexico City boasts a thriving cinema scene, with many world-class cinema facilities for viewing commercially distributed films (both international and Mexican), as well as institutes and clubs where films and filmmaking are dissected, critiqued, studied, and treated as a serious art form.

Film fans will find plenty of *cines* (cinemas) and *cineclubes* (film clubs) to choose from for an evening's entertainment, any night of the week. Many cinemas screen first-run American films, typically of the blockbuster genre, along with Mexican reels of all kinds.

Foreign-language films—most of them American, with lesser numbers of French, German, and Italian—are almost always projected in the original language, with Spanish subtitling. Ticket prices differ depending on the neighborhood and the movie house. Even branches of the same cinema chain will vary their admission prices according to the location. Compared to cinema-going in other world capitals, viewing first-run international films in modern Mexico City facilities for $4 (the standard price) is already a bargain, but

CINE MEXICANO

Mexico's first cinema opened on Avenida Plateros (now Avenida Madero) in Mexico City on August 16, 1896, a few months after the Lumière brothers had premiered their famous cinematic projection system in Paris. *Capitalinos* took to the silver screen with great enthusiasm; statistics indicate that by 1902 Mexico City boasted more than 300 cinemas and 1,000 separate screenings per year.

Popular Mexican films run the gamut, from drama to comedy to action pictures, with a high number of what might be called "cops and cowboys" films, which focus on struggles between Mexican police agencies and *narcotraficantes* (drug traffickers). As in the *narco-corridos* that celebrate the exploits of Robin Hood–like drug smugglers in song, such movies often extol smugglers' honor over police corruption. *Lucha libre* (professional Mexican wrestling, in which the opponents wear full head masks) films make up another curious subgenre of Mexican film. The longest-lasting of these is a series of B horror/detective films featuring El Santo, Mexico's most famous *luchador,* with such titles as *Santo contra los zombies* (Santo Against the Zombies), *Santo contra las mujeres vampiro* (Santo Against the Vampire Women), and *Santo: la leyenda del enmascarado de plata* (Santo: The Legend of the Silver Masking). Other Mexican productions have inserted masked wrestlers into all sorts of movie formulae.

In the 1940s and 1950s, Mexican films went through a high point known today as *la época de oro* (the golden age) for the quality of films produced. This was the era of great singer/actors such as Pedro Infante and Jorge Negrete, the dazzling actresses Maria Felix and Dolores del Río, and legendary comedian Cantinflas. Of the many top directors of the era, two of the best-known are Emilio "El Indio" Fernández and Alejandro Galindo, and cinematographer Gabriel Figueroa is considered one of the best ever in Mexico.

Mexico's cinematic tradition slipped in the 1960s and 1970s, with only a few classics shot during these years. An exception was the work of the father of cinematic surrealism, Luis Buñuel. Born in Spain in 1900, Buñuel moved to Mexico in the 1940s and directed some of his greatest cinematic works in his adopted homeland, including *Los olvidados* (1950), *Él* (1955), and *El ángel exterminador* (1962), before dying in Mexico City in 1983.

Another watershed art film made in Mexico, *El Topo* (1971), sees a nameless gunfighter travel from one bizarre village landscape to another in what could be a surreal version of a Kurosawa or Sergio Leone/Clint Eastwood epic. Alejandro Jodorowsky (Chilean-born but a Mexican resident) directed the film, wrote the story, composed most of the music, and designed both sets and costumes. Both Buñuel and Jodorowsky were major influences on American director David Lynch.

Ariel de Oro (the Mexican equivalent of the Oscar) winner *Cronos*, directed in 1992 by Guadalajara native Guillermo del Toro, employs del Toro's trademark insect imagery and fondness for religious relics to create a story of a Mexican antiques dealer who comes upon a strange scarablike mechanism that promises eternal life yet leads to the inevitable tragic end. Del Toro no longer works in Mexico, but has continued to create spectacularly intense, dream-like movies such as *Pan's Labyrinth* (2006) and the surreal comic book humor and pathos in *Hellboy* (2004).

A more international hit was 1992's *Like*

Water for Chocolate (Como agua para chocolate). Based on Laura Esquivel's recipe-studded novel of love, lust, and gustation, and adapted for the screen by her director husband, Alfonso Arau, the film is considered one of the most successful transitions of Latin American literature's magic realism to the screen. Chocolate was filmed in Piedras Negras, Coahuila, near the U.S.-Mexico border. Two other films shot in la frontera that have become cult international hits include action thrillers El Mariachi (1992) and Desperado (1995), both directed by Mexican American Richard Rodriguez on shoestring budgets.

In 1995 El Callejón de los milagros (Alley of Miracles) not only won Mexico's Ariel de Oro but became the most critically acclaimed film in Mexican history, earning 49 cinema awards around the globe. Loosely based on a novel by renowned Egyptian author Naguib Mahfouz and directed by Jorge Fons, the film paints a complex portrait of the interwoven lives of a cantina owner, a tarot card reader, a prostitute, and a small-time landlady in downtown Mexico City. Like several other Mexican art films, it was produced by the Universidad de Guadalajara with support from the Instituto Mexicano de Cinematografía (Mexican Institute of Cinematography, or IMCINE) and Fondo de Fomento a la Calidad Cinematográfica (Fund in Support of Cinematic Quality).

Mexican cinema seems to be on the upswing again, with several excellent releases that have done well both in Mexico and abroad. The 1999 film La ley de Herodes (Herod's Law), directed by Luis Estrada, is an extremely entertaining political satire which, for the first time in Mexican movies, explicitly skewered the then ruling PRI party, as well as the now ruling PAN, the Catholic church, and much else besides.

But the real international breakthrough came with the brilliant Amores perros (dubiously translated in the English release as Love's a Bitch), filmed in 2000 by Alejandro González Iñárritu. The harrowing, at times painfully realistic, movie follows the stories of three groups of Mexico City residents whose lives are brought together by a horrific car accident. By far the most moving of the stories is of a lower-class youth (played by Gael García Bernal, in his breakthrough role) who falls in love with his brother's wife, and who begins to make money by bringing his pet rottweiler to underground dog fights. The movie won more than 30 prizes around the world and was nominated for an Oscar for best foreign film. Shortly thereafter came 2002's Y tu mamá también (2002), directed by Alfonso Cuaron and also starring García Bernal along with Diego Luna and Maribel Verdu.

Some more recent releases include the hugely popular crime thriller Nicotina (2003) starring Diego Luna and El misterio de trinidad (2003), a treasure-hunting story that won several film awards in Mexico and Spain. Luna and García Bernal teamed up to produce 2007's Cochochi, a resolutely non-Hollywood-style movie about two Tarahumara (Raramuri) boys from the Copper Canyon country in northern Mexico, starring two indigenous youths with no acting experience in the lead roles. This new stripped-down style can also be seen in Luz silenciosa (2007), a low-budget film directed by Carlos Reygadas, short on narrative and long on extended thoughtful takes, about the Mennonite community in northern Mexico, also filmed with amateur actors who are themselves Mennonites.

you can do even better if you attend showings before 6 P.M. (when there is a slight discount most days of the week) or on Wednesday, when most movie theaters offer half-price tickets. In general the theaters in Polanco have the best projection and sound systems—and the highest prices.

Below are listed only a few noteworthy cinemas—look in *Tiempo Libre* magazine or the daily newspapers for complete listings of first-run shows. At least two local chains maintain their own websites, complete with addresses and phone numbers for all cinema outlets, ticket prices, and the titles of current film screenings: www.cinemex.com and www.cinepolis.com.mx.

CINEMATOGRÁFICA UNIVERSITARIA

Centro Cultural Universitario, Insurgentes 3000, Ciudad Universitaria in UNAM, 55/5665-0709, www.filmoteca.unam.mx
HOURS: Vary
COST: $2, $1 students
METRO: Universidad
Map 6

UNAM, the national university, has a major film program which includes several theaters with an ongoing program of unusual Mexican and international films. The two main theaters are at the university itself, in the south of the city. In addition, UNAM runs screening rooms at the Museo El Chopo (Dr. Atl 37, Col. Santa María La Ribera, 55/5546-1245) and at the Antiguo Colegio de San Ildefonso (San Ildefonso 43, Col. Centro, 55/5792-5223). Check newspapers or the website for listings of upcoming movies.

CINEMEX CASA DE ARTE

Anatole France 120 in Plaza Mazaryk, 55/5280-9156, www.cinemex.com
HOURS: Vary
COST: $5 adults, $4.50 seniors or children under 12, $3 Wed.
METRO: Polanco
Map 3

Cinemex is the largest movie theater chain in Mexico City, with nearly 40 theaters in the city, as well as in Guadalajara, Toluca, and elsewhere. You can expect good-quality picture and sound, clean seats, plenty of junk food to gorge on, and a series of really annoying ads to sit through before the movie starts. While most Cinemex theaters show the standard Hollywood blockbusters, the Casa de Arte in Polanco shows more offbeat, alternative movies, frequently from elsewhere in Latin America. Other branches convenient for tourists include: **Cinemex Plaza Insurgentes** (San Luis Potosí 214 at Insurgentes Sur, Col. Roma, 55/5264-7079), **Cinemex Real** (Colón 17, Col. Centro, 55/5512-7718), **Cinemax Manacar** (Insurgentes Sur 1457, Col. Mixcoac, 55/5611-5256), and **Cinemex Loreto** (Altamirano 46, Col. Tizapán San Ángel, 55/5550-0914).

CINETECA NACIONAL

Av. México Coyoacán 389, 55/1253-9300, www.cinetecanacional.net
HOURS: Vary
COST: $3, $1 students
METRO: Coyoacán
Map 6

The Cineteca is a national government organization created in 1974 to promote film culture. The Cineteca building, located in Coyoacán, contains seven projection rooms (from the 500-seat Jorge Stahl theater to the tiny 40-seat Alejandro Galindo theater), which means several different films are screened every night of the week. Here you can see everything from experimental new Mexican short films to retrospectives of Jim Jarmusch or Akira Kurosawa. Also on the premises are a library and bookstore. For the latest schedule, see *Tiempo Libre* or the Friday arts section of *Reforma*. Classes in film history, such as "La historia de México, vista a través del cine" (The History of Mexico Viewed Through Cinema) and "Cine y literatura" (Cinema and Literature) are offered on weekday nights and on Saturday.

Festivals and Events

Like Mexicans around the country, *capitalinos* love a fiesta. Any occasion will suffice as an excuse to hold a celebration, from a birthday or promotion to a chile harvest. Add to all the civic possibilities the vast number of Mexican Catholic religious holidays, and there's potential for some kind of public fiesta at least every week of the year, if not all 365 days. Besides the national religious holidays, there are feast days for 115 Catholic saints per year—that's 9 or 10 each month. Any pueblo or *colonia* (neighborhood) named for a saint will usually hold a fiesta on the feast day of its namesake. Individuals named for saints will often host parties on their *día de santo* (saint's day).

The primary requisites of a fiesta are plenty of food (especially tamales, considered a festive dish), liquid libations, music, and dancing. More elaborate celebrations include parades, exhibitions, *charreadas,* and occasional fireworks.

Some of the more memorable yearly events and public holidays observed in Mexico City are highlighted here by month. Actual dates may vary from year to year, so be sure to check with the appropriate tourist office in advance. Apart from the annual events, Mexico City hosts frequent festivals of all kinds, including film, cooking, music, and much else besides. Check www.dfiestaeneldf .com for upcoming events.

JANUARY
DÍA DE LOS REYES MAGOS

January 6, and not Christmas, is King's Day—traditionally the day of giving presents to children in Mexico, although many families now give presents on Christmas. Nativitas, a neighborhood of Xochimilco in the south of Mexico City, holds an elaborate party in honor of the day, with costumed "kings" filling the shoes of children with candies and toys. Several dances are also held, along with food and music.

MARCH AND APRIL
FERIA DE LA FLOR
MÁS BELLA DEL EJIDO

For over two centuries the southern Mexico City neighborhood of Xochimilco—famed for its canals, floating gardens, and flowers—has celebrated its floriculture with a grand festival. Events include cooking demonstrations, exhibitions of agriculture, cattle, and handicrafts, and a contest for the best-decorated *trajinera* (gondola). The highlight is choosing the "Most Beautiful Flower," a beauty contest amongst local young women. Dates vary from year to year.

FESTIVAL DE MÉXICO EN
EL CENTRO HISTÓRICO

This two-week cultural celebration, held in the Centro each April since 1985, features concerts, theater performances, art exhibits, seminars, dance, gastronomical events, and activities for children. Many colonial-era buildings downtown host different events. This festival usually coincides with an especially beautiful time of the year in Mexico City when the jacaranda trees are in full bloom. Exact dates vary from year to year; call 55/5277-9757 or check online at www.festival.org.mx.

FERIA DE NIEVES

An ice cream festival is held every year, usually in the beginning of April, in Santiago Tulyehualco in Xochimilco. The festival, held over the course of a week, hosts exhibitions and sale of ice creams and *nieves* (Mexican ices), from the usual favorites to more exotic flavors including mole, tequila, and nopal. Some are even reported to be medicinal. The 2007 edition was inaugurated with the presentation of a new ice cream flavor, *chinelo,* which consists of strawberry, coconut, nuts, raisins, and a bit of pineapple. Sounds interesting! Dates vary from year to year.

MÉXICO ARTE CONTEMPORÁNEO

Since 2004, Mexico City has had its own contemporary art festival, better known as MACO (www.femaco.com). Every year in late April, the festival organizes coinciding openings by dozens of Mexican and international galleries (80 in 2008). MACO is fast becoming one of the most important showcases for Mexican art, and is also a fun time for mixing in the art world scene.

SEMANA SANTA

Easter week, or Holy Week (usually in April, sometimes in late March), is second only to Christmas as the most important holiday period of the year in Mexico. One of the most prominent Semana Santa customs is breaking *cascarones,* colored eggs stuffed with confetti, over the heads of friends and family. Besides attending Mass on Good Friday and Easter Sunday, many Mexicans take this opportunity to go on vacations. Mexican beach resorts can be overcrowded this week with a large influx of both Mexicans and North Americans.

The Passion Play is reenacted at Ixtapalapa, a *colonia* nine kilometers southeast of the Zócalo. A young man portrays Christ and a young woman becomes Mary—both must be locally born virgins. On Good Friday, crowds gather in Ixtapalapa's central plaza to watch the Christ figure suffer mock beatings and a real crown of thorns. Then the young man must drag a 80-kilogram wooden cross for a distance of four kilometers to the summit of Cerro de la Estrella, a hill considered sacred since the pre-Hispanic era. There he will be tied to the cross and ritually "crucified" before his attendants carry him back down the hill (and to a hospital to make sure he's still healthy). The entire procession is followed by literally hundreds of thousands of people, so be prepared for quite a crowd (and a few pickpockets) if you go.

Smaller Passion plays are also played out on Thursday and Friday in Cuajimalpa (western Mexico City, near the highway exit to Toluca) and Milpa Alta (far southern Mexico City, toward Cuernavaca). As well, on Holy Thursday thousands of children gather outside the downtown Catedral dressed in finery

COURTESY OF CONSEJO DE PROMOCIÓN TURÍSTICA DE MÉXICO/CARLOS SÁNCHEZ

Mexico City residents re-enact *The Passion Play* in the Ixtapalapa neighborhood during Semana Santa (Easter week).

and carrying baskets of fruit and food, to be blessed by the priest.

MAY
CINCO DE MAYO
This festival commemorates the defeat of an attempted French attack on Puebla, east of Mexico City, on May 5, 1862, by an improvised Mexican defense, including a Zacapoaxtla indigenous regiment, which fought with particular ferocity. The French invasion eventually succeeded, but the battle is nonetheless celebrated with gusto by Mexicans. It features music, dance, food, and other cultural events. This has become a more important festival for Mexicans living in the United States, but it is still celebrated in Mexico also. In the capital, a small hill next to the airport called El Peñon is the site of a curious reenactment of the battle, with local men dressing up as the French and Mexican sides. This is a somewhat scruffy working-class neighborhood, and many tourists would not feel comfortable attending.

JULY
DÍA DE LA VIRGEN DEL CARMEN
This colorful festival takes place every year in San Ángel on July 16, the Day of the Virgin of Carmen, in the Ex-Convento del Carmen on Avenida Revolución. Various groups of dancers and musicians congregate in the convent courtyard and hold performances, including one group called Los Concheros, who play a mandolin made out of the shell of an armadillo. Devotees of the Virgen del Carmen make solemn processions into the church to deposit floral offerings on the altar.

DÍA DE SANTIAGO
The fiesta for St. James' Day is held in the Plaza de las Tres Culturas on July 25, where a great number of groups gather to perform their folkloric dances, wearing traditional costumes. Fireworks, art exhibits, and a handicrafts market are also on hand. The event takes place throughout the day and into the evening.

AUGUST
COMMEMORATION OF THE DEFENSE OF MEXICO AND THE FALL OF TENOCHTITLÁN
On August 13 at the Plaza de las Tres Culturas in Tlatelolco, the handsomely costumed *concheros* (dancers dressed in shell costumes) and many other groups entertain with dances to celebrate the temporary victory of the Aztecs over the Spaniards before the fall of Tenochtitlán. Aspects of the celebration are also held on elegant Paseo de la Reforma, in the Zócalo, and in front of the monument to Cuauhtémoc—the Aztec Emperor who led his armies in defense of the city.

SEPTEMBER
FIESTA PATRIA DE LA INDEPENDENCIA
Sometimes called *diez y seis* (sixteen), since it falls on the 16th, Mexican Independence Day celebrates the country's independence from Spain, as proclaimed (a decade or so ahead of actual independence, as it turned out) in 1810 by Father Hidalgo in the town of Dolores, Guanajuato. Festivities begin on the 15th and last two days, with fireworks, parades, *charreadas* (costumed horse riders), music, and folk dance performances. Activities in Mexico City are centered on the Zócalo, where at 11 P.M. on the 15th, the president of Mexico and the crowds congregated on the square below call out Father Hidalgo's cry for independence—*El Grito*—followed by singing the national anthem. There is a huge parade through the Centro Histórico on the 16th. This is a Times Square New Year's Eve–type scene, so be prepared for major crowds.

NOVEMBER
DÍA DE LOS MUERTOS
The Day of the Dead is Mexico's third most important holiday and corresponds to Europe's All Saints' Day except that it's celebrated on the first and second of November instead of only the first. Some of the festivities are held in cemeteries, where children clean the headstones and crucifixes of their deceased relatives (*los difuntos*) and play games unique to

COURTESY OF CONSEJO DE PROMOCIÓN TURÍSTICA DE MÉXICO/IGNACIO GUEVARA

whimsical Día de los Muertos figurines

this fiesta. In some areas the faithful spend an entire day and night beside the family graves. Roadside shrines throughout Mexico are laid with fresh flowers and other tributes to the dead. Offerings of *pan de los muertos* (bread of the dead) and food and liquor are placed before family altars on behalf of deceased family members, along with papier-mâché or sugar skulls (*calaveras*) and skeletons. Short plays are occasionally performed in local theaters or large cemeteries, especially the melodrama *Don Juan Tenorio,* in which a murderer finds redemption through his victim's ghost. The best-known Día de los Muertos celebration in Mexico City is held in the village of Mixquic, in the Tlahuac district in the hills in the south of the city. Here, villagers prepare elaborate shrines to their deceased relatives, and leave their doors open for two days so that passers-bys will visit. At 4 p.m. on November 2, the entire village joins a procession to the cemetery, where they then stay past midnight. The view over the cemetery from the church bell tower is spectacular. Colorful remembrances, with smaller crowds, are also held in San Lucas Xochimanca (Ixtapalapa), Santa Cecilia Tepetlapa (Xochimilco), and San Antonio Tecómitl (Milpa Alta). Festivities also take place on the Zócalo downtown, with a competition for the best shrines as well as music and dance.

DÍA DE LA REVOLUCIÓN

The anniversary of the 1910 Revolution is an official holiday. In Mexico City, expect a variety of civic ceremonies, topped off with parades by the military downtown in the Zócalo, as well as smaller parades by sporting teams, union members, and children's school groups.

DECEMBER
DÍA DE NUESTRA SEÑORA DE GUADALUPE

The feast day of the Virgin of Guadalupe, Mexico's patron saint, is one of the most important in the country. On the days and weeks leading up to the 12th, groups of pilgrims

La Virgen Morena, "the dark-skinned Virgin", is Mexico's most revered saint.

can be seen walking toward the Basílica de Guadalupe in northern Mexico City. Special Masses are held that day throughout Mexico, and in Mexico City the area around the basilica is packed with many thousands of pilgrims. The festival in Mexico City begins with the faithful—usually led by a well-known Mexican performer—singing "Las Mañanitas," Mexico's traditional birthday song, in honor of the Virgen, followed by numerous special dances. The nearest Sunday to the 12th also features special events, such as mariachi Masses, food booths, and games.

LAS POSADAS

Beginning on December 16 Mexicans hold nightly *posadas*—candlelight processions terminating at elaborate, community-built nativity scenes—in commemoration of the Holy Family's search for lodging. The processions continue for nine consecutive nights. Other activities include piñata parties where children break open hanging papier-mâché figures filled with small gifts and candy.

Churches large and small hold continuous Christmas Masses beginning at midnight on the 24th (Día de la Natividad, or Christmas) and throughout the 25th.

Las Posadas culminates on January 6, which is Día de los Santos Reyes (literally, Day of the King-Saints), referring to the story of the Three Wise Men. On this day Mexican children receive their Christmas gifts, and family and friends gather to eat a wreath-shaped fruitcake called *rosca de reyes* (wreath of the kings) baked especially for this occasion. Hidden inside each *rosca* is a small clay figurine (*muñeco*) that represents the infant Jesus. While sharing the *rosca* on this day, the person whose slice contains the *muñeco* is obliged to host a *candelaria,* or Candlemas party, on February 2 for everyone present.

At the *candelaria*—which commemorates the day the newborn Jesus was first presented at the temple in Jerusalem—the host traditionally displays a larger Christ-infant figure and serves tamales and *atole,* a thick, hot corn drink flavored with fruit or chocolate.

Recreation

For an adventurous outdoor experience, consider heading up to one of the forested parks south and west of the city for a long hike or mountain bike ride, or visit one of the several rock climbing destinations in or near the city. Those more inclined toward spectator sports will find plenty to keep them entertained, too. Soccer, or *futból* as it's called here, is the ruling passion in Mexico, and Mexico City has three stadiums where you can watch local league games and the national team. Baseball also has a following in D.F., as does bullfighting (not for the squeamish!), horseracing, and *lucha libre*, as the colorful professional wrestling is known here.

Many more recreation options in central Mexico can be found in the *Excursions From Mexico City* chapter.

CITY PARKS

Mexico City is a fairly relentless urban environment, but there are a number of parks within the city that provide a bit of green respite from the smog and noise. These parks are frequented by residents of all ages and classes, and are quite safe for a stroll or jog during the day. However, it's best not to go into these parks after dark.

☰ CHAPULTEPEC PARK

Betw. Paseo de la Reforma and Av. Constituyentes
HOURS: Tues.-Sat. 5 A.M.-4:30 P.M. for the Primera Sección; no hours for other two sections
METRO: Chapultepec, Auditorio, Constituyentes
Map 3

The roads and pathways of the Primera Sección (First Section) of Chapultepec Park are quiet, safe, and well away from traffic for jogging, walking, or in-line skating. The Segunda (Second) section is more extensive, although not as easy to get to and without as many pathways. Adjacent to the amusement park in the second section are three large circular stone structures, formerly water storage tanks that have since been filled in with dirt and are now

often used as playing fields for pickup games of soccer and (occasionally) Ultimate Frisbee. The Tercera (Third) section is more isolated and consequently not as safe. Directly behind the Anthropology Museum, across Avenida Gandhi, is a small forested park with a one-kilometer jogging path that is marked every hundred meters.

PARQUE HUNDIDO

Av. Insurgentes between Eje 6 Sur and Eje 7 Sur
HOURS: None
METRO: Insurgentes Metrobús
Map 5

Parque Hundido ("Sunken Park," officially called Parque Luis Urbina), a large leafy park along Insurgentes, is set below street level. The gravel and dirt paths of the park, lined with about 50 reproductions of pre-Hispanic sculptures, are a good place for a jog. As with Parque México in the Condesa, the trees help keep out the fumes from traffic on nearby Avenida Insurgentes. Across Insurgentes from Parque Hundido is the smaller Parque San Lorenzo, another tree-filled park. This one boasts a couple of basketball courts where ballers can occasionally get a pickup game.

PARQUE MÉXICO

Av. México
HOURS: None
METRO: Chilpancingo
Map 4

This large, oval-shaped park in Colonia Condesa, built on the site of a former horserace track and formally known as Parque San Martín, is filled with remarkably lush, almost tropical vegetation, and it is a wonderful oasis of clean air in the midst of the city. Join the many locals who get their daily exercise jogging, in-line skating, or just walking their dogs around the park. Beware the tiled walkways when it rains as they are slippery. The pedestrian walkway in the middle of Avenida

Amsterdam, which forms a larger oval around the park one block away, is also a good place to run.

VIVEROS

Bordered by Universidad, Madrid, Melchor Ocampo, and Pérez Valenzuela
HOURS: Daily 6 A.M.–6 P.M.
METRO: Viveros
Map 6

Originally the private orchards of Miguel Ángel de Quevedo, Viveros was founded in 1907 and nationalized after the Revolution to become the country's first official plant nursery (*vivero*). It's a very popular park for neighborhood folk out for a stroll or jog, especially during the early morning and late afternoon. The dirt road around the park is about two kilometers long. Open yoga and tai chi classes are often held in the park also.

HEALTH AND FITNESS

Most neighborhoods have several less-expensive gyms that cater to the nonwealthy, where you can often get in for $10 or so for a single visit. Most have just standard weight equipment and exercise machines, and usually a sauna and/or steam room. Asking around at your hotel is a good way to start looking. Yoga, pilates, and other newer exercise styles are growing very fast in Mexico City, and are offered in the private gyms listed below as well as specialized centers.

GOLD'S GYM

Homero 440, 55/5203-4385,
www.goldsgympolanco.com.mx
HOURS: Mon.–Fri. 6 A.M.–10 P.M., Sat. 8 A.M.–4 P.M., Sun. 11 A.M.–2 P.M.
COST: $20 per day for non-members
METRO: Polanco
Map 3

The venerable Gold's Gym is not quite as luxurious as Sport City (no pool, for example), but they do have a good setup of cardio machines and weights to get in a good workout, as well as a steam bath.

JUNIOR CLUB

Sindicalismo 3, 55/5516-8101
HOURS: Daily 6 A.M.–6 P.M.
COST: Membership only
METRO: Chilpancingo
Map 5

Although not of use to those visiting Mexico City, long-term expats may want to consider joining the Junior Club in Colonia Condesa. It's not cheap at $750 inscription and $115 a month, but they have an amazing 50-meter outdoor swimming pool as well as 14 tennis courts, steam bath and sauna, full weight and cardio room, and a fine cafeteria.

SPORT CITY

Miguel de Cervantes Saavedra 397, 55/5580-0716, www.sportcity.com.mx
HOURS: Mon.–Fri. 5 A.M.–11 P.M., Sat. 8 A.M.–6 P.M., Sun. 9 A.M.–3 P.M.
COST: $45 a day for non-members, or $20 a day as a guest of a member
METRO: Polanco
Map 3

About the best gym available with daily rates for visitors is Sport City, with five locations throughout Mexico City. It's far from cheap, but they do have 25-meter swimming pools, all variety of exercise equipment, and a steam room and sauna. A monthly membership is $450. All the clubs offer many types of exercise classes also, including yoga, pilates, and aerobics.

YOGA DEL SUR

Av. San Jerónimo 263, 55/5550-3536, www.yogadelsur.com.mx
HOURS: Classes daily, times vary
COST: $16 for drop-in classes, less with membership and packages
METRO: Barranca del Muerto
Map 6

Yoga del Sur, based on the Iyengar method, is one of the better-respected Hatha yoga centers in Mexico City. Apart from the numerous classes for all levels, they also offer a variety of special workshops and teacher trainings. Many other yoga centers of different styles are also around the city—the best way to find them is to start out searching on the Internet. The oldest yoga teaching center in the city, located in Lomas de Chapultepec and thus not that convenient for many tourists, is the Yoga Center (55/5520-6895, www.yogacenter.com .mx), also with drop-in classes available.

HIKING AND MOUNTAIN BIKING

After a lengthy dose of Mexico City, visitors and expatriates will likely feel the need for a counterbalancing dose of fresh air and nature best found in southern and western Mexico City. The mountains forming the southwest corner of the valley are home to four parks and one community-run nature preserve, perfect for picnicking, hiking, and mountain biking. The parks enclose pine and oak forests from about 2,500 meters to the top of the hills marking the edge of the Valle de México, well over 3,000 meters in places. Visitors from low altitudes could notice shortness of breath, dizziness, or headaches—don't be shy about heading back down the hill if you feel these symptoms.

Note: While the places described below are generally quite safe, robberies have occurred in more remote areas. Those who stick to welltrod trails with other people around will have no problems whatsoever, but should you decide to venture further afield, it's worth asking around among locals or park officials what the current situation is like.

AJUSCO

Camino al Ajusco
HOURS: None
COST: Free
Map 7

The volcanic peak of El Ajusco (3,930 meters) looms over the southern end of the Valle de México, visible to anyone looking down Avenida Insurgentes to the south on a semiclear day. Easily reached from downtown, the fields around the base of Ajusco are popular for weekend picnickers, who make good use of the soccer fields, horseback riding, dirtbike tracks, and many small rustic restaurants.

Be sure to stop for some food at one of the many small stands selling mushroom soup, quesadillas, *barbacoa,* and other munchies in the grassy meadows along the roadside. The Camino al Ajusco access road makes a complete circuit around the volcano, a popular route for road bikers.

Hiking to the top of Cerro El Ajusco is a stiff but not too lengthy hike—doable if you're reasonably fit and acclimatized (the top is well over 12,000 feet). The only drawback is that it's not the safest place to wander around— more than a few robberies have been reported in the forests around Ajusco over the years. If you go on weekends, when there are plenty of folks around, it should be no problem. But it's best not to go during the week, and never go hiking alone (it's dangerous for accidents more than for robberies).

To get to the start of the hike, take the Camino al Ajusco around the west side of the mountain to the highest point of the road, right at the place where a paved side road branches off toward Toluca. Opposite the turnoff, poke around at the edge of the forest and you'll find a trail leading to the top of the peak in a one- or two-hour steep climb. Be sure to bring enough warm clothes, as the mountaintop is frequently chilly and the weather is unpredictable. Don't underestimate the altitude either; it can really hit you.

To reach Ajusco by car, get on Periférico Sur and look for the turnoff to Reino Aventura amusement park (there are lots of signs). The road, also called Camino al Ajusco, winds steadily uphill, past the amusement park on the left, through several kilometers of gradually less urban neighborhoods into fields and forest at the base of Volcán Ajusco. By public transport, the easiest way is to go to Metro Tasqueña; from there, take the light rail (*tren ligero*) to the Estadio Azteca stop. Here look for a *pesero* marked Ruta 39, which goes up to Ajusco for $0.50. The last one back down to the city leaves Ajusco around 9 P.M. Alternatively, you can catch a *pesero* at Metro Universidad and transfer to the Route 39 bus.

DESIERTO DE LOS LEONES

Camino al Desierto
HOURS: Park daily 7 A.M.-6 P.M.; monastery Tues.-Sun. 10 A.M.-7 P.M.
COST: $1 for cars into the park (free if you come by bus); $0.50 entrance to monastery

Map 7

Decreed Mexico's first national park in 1917, Desierto de los Leones is neither a desert nor populated with lions, but is a pine and oak forest covering almost 1,529 hectares of mountainside and centered on the remains of an early-18th-century Carmelite monastery. Picnickers frequent the groves and gardens around the semiruined monastery, while hikers and mountain bikers roam the dirt roads and trails in the hills above. The woods around Desierto de los Leones are well patrolled, particularly on weekends, making it safe for hiking and biking.

Desiertos were Carmelite monasteries first built in Spain in forests, meant to isolate the monks from the travails of urban life. The name is thought to be an allusion to Christ's 40 days in the desert. Started in 1606, Desierto de los Leones was the first such monastery built in the Americas. An earthquake destroyed the original building in 1711, and the current monastery was erected in 1722. The Carmelites moved away in 1801 to their present location in Mt. Niscongo above Tenancingo, in the state of Mexico.

Although there were likely some mountain lions in the area when the monastery was in operation, the second half of the monastery's name is thought to derive from the León family, who acted as the order's representative in affairs with the Spanish crown for many years.

Today the old monastery is a museum. Parts are a bit decrepit, but the main building is in good condition and features a lovely chapel. One large room has been converted into a restaurant, open for breakfast and lunch. On Sundays a crowd is usually milling around the hallways, but the gardens behind have quiet, restful corners. Dotting the woods around the monastery are 8 of the original 10 hermitages.

Although most visitors limit themselves to walking around the grounds of the monastery and nearby woods, those seeking a more energetic hike or mountain bike ride should look for the turnoff to **Cruz Blanca**, 0.8 kilometer up the road from the monastery in the direction of San Ángel, on the right-hand side. A 1.5 kilometer hike up a dirt road, past a forest workers' camp, will take you to a guard station and picnic area, and from here, dirt roads continue further into the forest, uphill along a river valley. Continuing straight uphill will eventually (roughly two hours, or less if you hoof it) come out at the top of the mountain ridge forming the southwest corner of the Valle de México.

From the top of the pass, other dirt tracks head off farther to the west and south, good for mountain bike adventurers. If you stay left at the pass and continue down, staying left all the way, you'll come out at the forest camp on the dirt road between the monastery and Cruz Blanca—a wicked ride. Other roads from the pass lead to Los Dinamos and Ajusco. Although these are fun roads for riding if you like to explore, they pass through more isolated stretches of forest and are thus a bit more risky in terms of running into the odd *bandito* (bandit). If you come up this way, plan for a long day, and bring water, some food, and a sweater or jacket in case of cold. The return ride to Cruz Blanca is also a great downhill ride.

Another option, involving less altitude gain but still plenty of time in the woods, is found a kilometer or so above Cruz Blanca, where there's a open area next to the river, often full of people resting. Here a side trail crosses the river, climbs uphill briefly, then meets an old dirt road that has been closed off, winding along the side of the hills, without gaining or losing altitude for perhaps a couple of kilometers, finally coming out at Valle de los Conejos, near La Marquesa (described next). This is a great place for bike riding or a long hike in the woods. About halfway out along the road is an army camp. At the far end of the road is a great downhill mountain bike track leading to the Malinalco highway at Valle de los Conejos, near La Marquesa. Several other single-tracks descend from this dirt road and eventually come out on the Mexico City–Toluca highway, not far from La Marquesa.

Camino al Desierto runs from the Toluca highway near the neighborhood of Cuajimalpa to San Ángel. Unless you're in the south of the city, the best way in for those driving motor vehicles is via the Toluca highway. From the south, the quickest route is to drive up Camino al Desierto from its junction with the Periférico Sur, at Calle Altavista in San Ángel. A bus runs from the Barranca del Muerto Metro station up to the monastery on Saturday and Sunday only 6 A.M.–5 P.M. Hiring a taxi from the city would cost $10–15 or so.

LA MARQUESA

Either side of Mexico City–Toluca highway, roughly
30 km west of Mexico City and 30 km east of Toluca
HOURS: None
COST: Free
Map 7

Just as the Mexico City–Toluca highway crosses the pass leaving the valley and starts its descent into the state of Mexico, the road passes through Parque Nacional La Marquesa, in a high valley surrounded by pine forest. Here visitors can find plenty of space to stretch out a blanket, kick around a soccer ball, mountain bike, buy fresh trout, and generally laze around and enjoy the clean, fresh air and greenery. The forests above La Marquesa, particularly around Valle de los Conejos or Valle del Potrero (open grassy meadows in the southern part of the park), are filled with great trails for hiking, mountain biking, or horse riding. Horses can be rented at Valle de los Conejos or Valle del Potrero for about $10 an hour. It's best to check with locals before wandering off, as robberies have been reported in the past. Rock climbers will be glad to hear of a rock pitch called Peñasco de los Perros, in the northwest part of La Marquesa (see *Rock Climbing* later in this chapter for details).

If you feel the stomach rumbling when at La Marquesa, be sure to enjoy local specialties such as *barbacoa* (pit-baked sheep meat), *sopa de hongo* (mushroom soup), and *quesadillas de flor de calabaza* (squash flower and cheese in a corn tortilla), as well as fresh rabbit and trout, served at the innumerable roadside restaurants.

La Marquesa is easy to reach. By car, take either Avenida Constituyentes or Paseo de la Reforma west out of the city, and continue on either the free or toll road toward Toluca. You'll see the turnoff to the park shortly after crossing the highest part of the road. To get to La Marquesa without a car, catch a *pesero* bus at either Tacubaya or Juanacatlán Metro stations up to the park for $2, taking 45–75 minutes, depending on traffic. The last bus returns to Mexico City at around 8 P.M. As well, you can go to the Observatorio bus station and catch an intercity bus to Tenancingo, Malinalco, or Chalma, and get off at La Marquesa.

LOS DINAMOS

Camino a los Dinamos de Contreras
HOURS: None
COST: Free
Map 7

A deep gorge in the southwest corner of the Valle de México, Los Dinamos comprises 2,293 hectares of communally protected forest and offers some of the most challenging rock climbing in the Mexico City region. The name refers to four power generators (*dinamos*), only two of which are still in operation, along the narrow Río Magdalena valley.

While the meadows and forest along the valley make a fine spot to pass a sunny afternoon biking on the single-track trails, the forest is best enjoyed on weekends, when mounted police from the Magdalena Contreras *delegación* patrol the area. The area around the Segundo (Second) Dinamo, in particular, has been cleaned up and turned into an ecological park that's quite safe on weekends. But it's best not to wander too far from the beaten path, particularly in the forest above the Cuarto (Fourth) Dinamo, as robberies have been reported in the past. Nearby is some very good rock climbing (see next section for details).

To reach Los Dinamos by car, take the Periférico Sur to the Magdalena Contreras exit, just west of the Ajusco exit. Follow the signs to Contreras and Los Dinamos through Santa Teresa and Magdalena Contreras to the edge of the forest, three kilometers from the Periférico. A paved road continues up the left side of the valley, reaching the Segundo Dinamo in three kilometers and the Cuarto Dinamo four kilometers farther. By public transport, look for the *microbuses* to Contreras from the Miguel Ángel de Quevedo or Copilco Metro stations. Get off at the end of the line, a small square faced on one side by food and handicrafts shops and on the other by the 18th-century Santa María Magdalena Contreras chapel, with a fine gilded *retablo*. From this square, special buses continue farther up the road on weekends only, stopping just short of the Cuarto Dinamo. During the week, visitors have to walk or hire a taxi from the Contreras bus stop.

◖ SAN NICOLÁS TOTOLAPAN

Km 11.5 on the Camino al Ajusco, 55/5630-8935, www.parquesannicolas.com.mx

HOURS: Mon.-Fri. 8 A.M.-4:30 P.M., Sat.-Sun. 7 A.M.-4:30 P.M.

COST: $2

Map 7

This local *ejido* (communal farm) has cordoned off about 2,300 hectares of hillside adjacent to Ajusco (and accessed via the same road) and is crossed with over 150 kilometers of dirt roads and trails, ranging in altitude from 2,700 to 3,740 meters at its highest point, Montaña Nezehuiloya. The *ejido* patrols the forest, making it totally safe for hiking and mountain biking. Some trails are for bikes only, others for hikers only, and some are for both. Bikes are usually available for rent on weekends at the park, but get there early if you want to get one, as they go fast. The park is often held up as a model for other ecotourism projects in Mexico involving local communities. Guided trips (in Spanish) oriented toward local flora and fauna and the community's reforestation work are available. Contact the park for more information. This is an excellent place for those after a taste of the high-altitude forests of central Mexico in a safe environment.

ROCK CLIMBING

Rock climbing has not reached the fanatical level in Mexico that it has in the United States, Europe, and elsewhere, but a determined and ever-growing community of climbers has established several areas with well-defined, often bolted climbs. There's an interesting non-elite (in fact, anti-elite) subculture of urban climbing in Mexico. To get a taste of it, head to El Cantil climbing park (described later in this section), or wander around the lava fields of Ciudad Universitaria at the national university, in an area called the Espacio Escultorio (Sculpture Space). Another place I went to once was a series of volcanic cliffs right in the middle of a neighborhood of working-class buildings in Copilco, near the university, which was slightly surreal but lots of fun.

Intrepid climbers will find many more routes in Parque Nacional El Chico, near Pachuca in Hidalgo (see the *Excursions from Mexico City* chapter for more information). Another place reported to be good for climbing and camping (though I've never been personally) is Jilotepec, in the state of Mexico northwest of Mexico City. For information on these destinations, and much else about climbing, head to one of Mexico City's climbing shops or the rock-climbing gym and ask around. Wherever you go climbing, don't forget to bring sunscreen, as the sun can be scorching at this altitude.

Gear, Courses, and Guided Trips

Two shops in Mexico City with a high-quality range of climbing gear are **Vertimania** (Patriotismo 899, Col. Mixcoac, 55/5615-5229, www.vertimania.com.mx) and **El Séptimo Grado** (Fernando Montes de Oca 61, Col. Condesa, 55/5553-3777, www.elseptimo grado.com). Less expensive and more generic equipment can be found at **Mochilazo** (55/5239-5485, www.mochilazo.com.mx), which offers rock climbing courses and guided trips. The courses are $250 per person for a six-session course, culminating in climbing the six-pitch Peñon de Bernal (transport not included). One-day trips near Mexico City run

GREEN HOLDOUTS

Amazingly enough, 37 percent of Mexico City's territory (the city proper, not the entire valley) still consists of open land, mostly in the southern parts of the capital. Pine and oak forests cover 18 percent of the city, while cultivated lands make up 13 percent, and 6 percent serves as pasture land, meadows, or city parks.

The remaining forests in Mexico City are almost entirely concentrated in the Milpa Alta, Tlalpan, and Magdalena Contreras delegations, on the steep mountains and narrow gorges in the south and southwestern parts of the valley. These forests are crucial for the continued health of the valley, as the trees help generate oxygen, and their roots collect desperately needed groundwater to replenish the dwindling aquifers.

Unfortunately, the forests have not fared well and face eventual extinction from clandestine logging and the continual encroachment of *paracaidistas* (parachutists), squatters who take up residence on the hilly outskirts of the city as if dropped from above.

But the effects of Mexico City's air pollution on the forests have been worse still. The winds in the valley blow from northeast to southwest, thereby sweeping much of the airborne pollution right into these forests. After decades of accumulating heavy metals and other toxins, the immune defenses of the forests have weakened, opening them up to repeated infestations by burrowing insects and other pests.

Between hunting and pesticide spraying, the pests' only natural predator, the woodpecker, has been driven to virtual extinction. The other technique used to prevent the pests from spreading has been to fell swaths of infested trees. Some observers claim such actions are a veiled attempt to justify logging for profit.

One stubborn local environmentalist, Dr. Luis Manuel Guerra, has taken on the lonely task of trying to reintroduce woodpeckers to the forests. Other efforts include the development of naturalist activities in the forests of Ajusco, Los Dinamos, La Marquesa, and Desierto de los Leones, offering economic incentives to local people to help protect the forests. One great example of this is the community-run park of San Nicolás Totolapan near Ajusco, worth a visit to learn more about Mexico City's imperiled forests and what is being done to help save them.

$45 per person for a group of six (transport not included).

ESCALÓDROMO CARLOS CARSOLIO

Técnicos Mexicanos 18, Col. Santa María Ticomán, 55/5752-7574, www.escalodromo.com
HOURS: Tues.-Fri. 2-10 P.M., Sat. 9 A.M.-7 P.M., Sun. 9 A.M.-5 P.M.
COST: $6 day pass; $2.50 to rent shoes and $2 to rent harness
METRO: Indios Verdes, then by bus
Map 7

Near the Instituto Politécnico Nacional, in the north part of Mexico City, is the best rock climbing gym in town, with 1,200 square meters of climbing walls. For the first visit, equipment is provided free of charge; after that, either bring your own or rent. Four-hour introductory classes are available for $27. The easiest way to get there is from Metro Indios Verdes; take any *colectivo* marked Ticomán. Get off at the Restaurant Galeón Español—the gym is directly behind the restaurant.

LOS DINAMOS

End of Camino Magdalena Contreras
HOURS: None
COST: Free
Map 7

Some of the most challenging sport routes (no top-ropes possible here) in the Mexico City area are found at Los Dinamos, a narrow gorge in the southwest part of the Valle de México. Much of the rock face on the western side of Los Dinamos gorge is covered with dozens of climbing routes, many of them bolted. Routes range mostly from 5.9 to 5.12B, with lots of cracks and overhangs. They're all single pitch, some quite run out between bolts, ranging usually between 20 and 30 meters in height. The cliff directly opposite the Segundo Dinamo parking lot is dotted with climbers every weekend. More bolted routes are found downriver by the Primer Dinamo, while the climbs up at the Cuarto Dinamo are mostly bolt-free for the trad climbers out there.

Climbers have generally not had problems with theft at Los Dinamos (although hikers and bikers have), but its best to keep an eye out when climbing here.

Look for the road to Los Dinamos turning off the Periférico highway not far past San Ángel, posted for Magdalena Contreras. Catch buses from Metro stations Miguel Ángel de Quevedo or Copilco to Contreras, and from there either catch buses to the park (on weekends) or take a taxi (during the week).

◖ PARQUE ECOLÓGICO EL CANTIL

Av. Ticoman, near the Politécnico Nacional off Insurgentes Norte
HOURS: Tues.-Sun. 8 A.M.-6 P.M.
COST: Free (apart from tip to guard if you leave your car in the parking lot)
METRO: Indios Verdes, then by bus
Map 7

The best climbing in Mexico City itself—in fact a thoroughly bizarre place to find such good cliffs—is at El Cantil, very close to the climbing gym described earlier. This park, built around a ring of exposed rock jutting up out of the valley floor, is located in a dirty, semi-industrial neighborhood in northern Mexico City. The extensive climbing area has several dozen bolted, top-rope, and trad routes ranging from 5.8 to 5.12, some fully 25 meters high. I was told the rock is volcanic, but it's smooth and hard, nothing like the hardened lava climbing in the south of the city. It's popular on weekends and is a great place to come if you don't have enough time to get outside of the city.

The entrance to the park is watched over by a policeman, who makes sure everyone signs in. Kudos to whichever city official thought of that, because climbers feel quite safe in what would otherwise be a sketchy neighborhood for such things. The policeman also keeps an eye on the small parking lot, and it's customary to give him a small tip ($1 or so) if you park there. To get there, drive or take a taxi up Avenida Insurgentes Norte, and turn on Avenida Ticoman. The park is right near Cinemex Ticoman. By public transport, take the Metro to Indios Verdes and hop on any *colectivo* (minibus) marked Ticomán.

PEÑASCO LOS PERROS

Near village of Salazar, La Marquesa National Park
HOURS: None
COST: Free
Map 7

This rocky outcrop near La Marquesa park on the road between Mexico City and Toluca is a great place for beginning and intermediate climbers to set up some top-ropes of varying difficulty, ranging up to 30 meters in length.

© CHRIS HUMPHREY

doing the balancing act up a delicate 5.10 at Parque Ecológico El Cantil in northern Mexico City

Most of the routes are also bolted, if you want to practice your sport leads. A 60-meter rope is needed to top-rope some of the harder and longer routes.

Facing the base of the cliff, a scramble up a narrow trail to the right leads to the top, where you'll find several anchors, as well as a few boulders to rope off of if you don't trust the anchors. Bring plenty of anchor rope, as you may have to hang the anchor to get the climbing rope all the way down to the ground, especially if you only have a 50-meter rope. Facing the rock from the bottom, the crack to the left is the easiest climb (a 5.7), while the few farther to the right have more difficult entries and are more like 5.8–5.11. A dozen quick draws will be plenty to lead all the routes. The most difficult route is the farthest to the right.

On weekends you may well have to wait your turn. Los Perros is very popular because it's easy to reach and suitable for novice climbers. It's better to come during the week if possible, when you'll likely have the place to yourselves. Be sure to take a long break at the top to enjoy the views out across the mountain peaks and forests.

To get there by car, drive past La Marquesa 2.4 kilometers farther toward Toluca, to a turn-off on the right, leading another 0.8 kilometer to the village of Salazar. From the village, ask for the road to Los Perros. Take this dirt track heading north into a valley and, after arriving at a fork (1.6 kilometer from the beginning of the track), take the right-hand turn and you'll be facing Los Perros, a couple of hundred meters away across a field. Leaving the car in a dirt lot to the left of the road, right at the base of the outcrop (there appear to be no problems with theft here), walk up a steep trail into the pine forest to the base of the 25–35 meter pitch. Without a car, visitors can get to Los Perros by taking a *pesero* (green-and-white bus) marked Salazar from Metro Juanacatlán to the town, and from there, either walking or taking a taxi out to the rocks. It's also possible to take local buses to Toluca from the Observatorio bus station and get off at the turn to Salazar, but be sure not to get on an express Toluca bus, which won't stop.

SPECTATOR SPORTS

For general information on Mexican sports, nothing can top *El Afición*, a daily newspaper sold at any newsstand and devoted to all types of professional athletics, but principally to the sacred orb, *fútbol*.

Baseball

Although it can't quite compare to soccer, *béisbol* is extremely popular in Mexico, particularly in the northern part of the country but also in D.F. Mexico has two leagues, the Liga del Pacífico, which plays in the northwestern part of the country, and the Liga Mexicana de Béisbol, which fields teams pretty much everywhere else. The Liga Mexicana has 16 teams, including the Diablos Rojos of Mexico City. Formerly the Tigres played in town also, but because of falling attendance, they now play in Puebla, which is a shame—their venerable old stadium in Mexico City was a great place to watch a game. For more information, see the league website at www.lmb.com.mx.

FORO SOL

Col. Ciudad Deportiva, 55/5639-8722, www.diablos.com.mx

HOURS: Sun. games at noon; on other days either 4 or 6:30 P.M.

COST: $1-7 depending on seats

METRO: Ciudad Deportiva

Map 7

The Diablos Rojos—perennial playoff contenders—play at the Foro Sol, which seats 26,000 spectators and is in Ciudad Deportiva, right at the junction of the Viaducto and the Circuito Interior, on the eastern side of the city. Tickets are a bargain for an afternoon of kicking back, watching a game, and having a beer. The season is between March and July, with the playoffs in August.

Bullfighting

Alternately called *la corrida de toros* (the running of bulls), *la fiesta brava* (the brave festival), *la lidia de toros* (the fighting of bulls), or *sombra y sol* (shade and sun, in reference to the stadium seating), the bullfight can be perceived as a sport, an art, or a gory spectacle of animal cruelty, depending on the attitude of the observer. To the aficionado, the *lidia* is a ritual drama that rolls together courage, fate, pathos, and death in one symbolic event. No matter how you may feel toward the bullfight, it is undeniably an integral part of Mexican history and culture.

◖ MONUMENTAL PLAZA DE TOROS MÉXICO

Agusto Rodín 241, Colonia Ciudad de los Deportes, 55/5563-3961, www.plazadetorosmexico.com.mx
HOURS: Sat. or Sun. 4 P.M.
COST: $5-6 for general admission, up to $50 for seats close to the ring
METRO: San Antonio, or Insurgentes Metrobús
`Map 5`

Often referred to as Plaza México, Mexico City's bullfighting stadium is the largest and best-outfitted in the world. Begun in 1944 as part of a huge sports complex that was to include a bullring, soccer stadium, tennis courts, *frontón* (jai alai court), and restaurants, the project was suspended after the *corrida* and soccer stadiums were finished. The plaza was inaugurated on February 5, 1946, with a *cartel* (program) that featured the legendary Luis "El Soldado" Castro, Manuel "Manolete" Rodríguez, and Luis Procuna. The stadium, just west of Insurgentes Sur, can hold over 40,000 spectators.

Monumental Plaza de Toros México's main bullfighting season is in the winter (Nov.–Feb.), with full-fledged matadors pitted against the largest and most ferocious bulls. May to September is reserved for *novilladas,* in which *novilleros* (novice bullfighters) fight *novillos*—younger, smaller bulls.

It's usually a good idea to buy tickets for a *corrida* in advance if possible, since it's not unusual for an event to sell out (in which case you might still be able to buy a ticket— at higher prices—from a scalper, or *revendedor*). Spectator sections are divided into the *sol* (sunny side) and *sombra* (shaded side), then subdivided according to how close the seats are to the bullring itself. The *sol* tickets aren't bad, since the *corrida* usually doesn't begin until

around 4 P.M.; bring a hat, sunglasses, and sunscreen, plus plenty of pesos for beverages (tequila and beer are usually available, along with soft drinks).

Ticket offices are open to special pass holders Thursday and Friday only; the general public must buy their tickets Saturday–Sunday 9:30 A.M.–1 P.M. and 3:30–7 P.M. Check the website for scheduling details.

Charreada

Decreed the national sport of Mexico in 1933 by presidential edict, the *charreada* (rodeo) is more popular in Mexico than bullfighting. *Charreadas* are staged in skillet-shaped *lienzos charros* (*charro* rings) by private *charro* associations to demonstrate equestrian and ranching skills, much like the U.S. counterpart, which was inspired by the *charreada.* Though open to everyone, *charrería* (the *charro* art) is a rather expensive pastime, requiring the maintenance of trained horses and elaborate clothing, somewhat analogous to polo in the Anglo world.

Unlike in American rodeo, *charros* and *charras* (gentleman and lady riders) compete for team, not individual, awards. Each team fields six to eight people, who singly or in combination perform a series of nine *suertes* (maneuvers or events); upon completion of all *suertes,* the team with the most points wins. *Charreada* points are usually scored for style rather than speed. Live mariachi music adds drama and romance.

The **Museo Nacional de la Charrería** (Izazaga and Isabel la Católica, 55/5512-2523) can tell you where to find *charreadas* in or near the capital, or you can check with the Mexico City tourist office.

LIENZO CHARRO

Av. Constituyentes 500, 55/5277-8706, www.nacionaldecharros.com
HOURS: Varies, usually weekends midday and afternoon
COST: Varies, sometimes free
`Map 3`

Charreadas are held in the *charro* ring from

BULLFIGHTING IN MEXICO

Mexico City's first bullfight took place in the Plaza Mayor (as the Zócalo was then called) on August 21, 1529, to commemorate the eighth anniversary of the fall of Tenochtitlán. Between 1554 and 1810, bullfights were held in the adjacent Plaza Voladores (currently the Supreme Court building). By the 18th century, they were also held on the south side of the Alameda, and in the 19th century, at the now defunct Plaza de Toros San Diego, near the current site of the Monumento a la Revolución.

EL TORO

The bulls used in the ring, *toros de lidia* (fighting bulls), are descendants of wild Iberian bulls that for more than four centuries have been bred especially for their combative spirit. They're not trained in any way for the ring nor goaded into viciousness, but as a breed, they are naturally quick to anger. The fighting bull's neck muscles are much larger than those of any other cattle breed in the world, making the animal capable of tossing a torero and his horse into the air with one upward sweep.

Bulls who show an acceptable degree of bravery by the age of two are let loose in huge pastures in Zacatecas, San Luis Potosí, or Guanajuato to live as wild beasts until they reach four years, the age of combat. By the time *el toro* (the bull) enters the ring, he stands around 127 centimeters high at the withers (the highest part of the bull's back) and weighs 500 kilograms or more. (The mea-surement is higher at the shoulder, but bulls aren't measured there, because the neck muscle expands to varying degrees when the bull is preparing to attack.)

EL TORERO

The bullfighter is rated by his agility, control, and, as surprising as it may seem to the uninitiated, his compassion. The torero who teases a bull or who is unable to kill it quickly when the moment of truth arrives is considered a cruel brute. In order to be judged a worthy competitor by the spectators, he must excel in three areas: *parar*, or standing still as the bull charges (as opposed to stepping away from the bull, even as little as an inch) – only the cape and the torero's upper body should move; *templar*, or timing and grace – the movements must be smooth, well timed, and of the right proportion; and *mandar*, or command, the degree to which he masters the entire *lidia* through his bravery, technique, and understanding of the bull, neither intimidating the animal nor being intimidated by it.

Standard equipment for the torero is the *capote de brega*, the larger cape used in the first two-thirds of the *lidia;* the *muleta*, a smaller cape used during the final third; the *estoque*, or matador's sword; and the *traje de luces*, or suit of lights, the colorful torero's costume originally designed by the Spanish artist Goya.

LA LIDIA

The regulated maneuvers, or *suertes*, followed time to time throughout the year, located in the third section of Chapultepec park.

Horse Racing

Horse racing has a lengthy history in Mexico City—dating at least from 16th century reports of races around the Zócalo—but at the moment only one track operates within the city.

◖ HIPÓDROMO DE LAS AMÉRICAS

Av. Industria Militar, 55/5387-0600, www.hipodromo.com.mx
HOURS: Thurs. 5:30-10 P.M. and Fri.-Sun. 3-8 P.M.
COST: $2 general admission, $5 for box/mezzanine seating
Map 7

This 1.5-kilometer oval course is a diverting place to spend an afternoon, tipping drinks in one of the various bars, watching the horses and riders parade around and race, and of course placing a few bets to keep the excitement up. The officials in a bullfight date from 18th-century Spain. Anywhere from four to eight bulls may appear in a *corrida* (though there are typically six), and one torero is on hand for every two bulls scheduled. The order of appearance for the toreros is based on seniority. Toreros who have proven their skills in several bullfighting seasons as *novilleros* (novice fighters) are called *matadores de toros* (bull killers). Ordinarily each torero will fight two bulls; if he is gored or otherwise put out of action another torero will take his place, even if it means facing more than his allotment of bulls.

Each *lidia* is divided into three *tercios*, or thirds. In *el tercio de varas*, the bull enters the ring and the matador performs *capeos*, a cape maneuver that doesn't expose the matador's body to the bull's horns but is meant to test the bull or lead it to another spot in the ring. He then "lances," a cape maneuver that exposes the matador's body to the horns and brings the bull closer to him, while two horsemen receive the bull's charge with eight-foot *varas*, or lances. The *varas* have short pyramid-shaped points that are aimed at the bull's neck muscle but do not penetrate very deeply on contact.

In *el tercio de banderillas*, the bull's shoulders receive the banderillas – 26-inch wooden sticks decorated with colored paper frills, each tipped with a small, sharp, iron barb. They can be placed by the matador himself or more often by hired assistant toreros (called banderilleros when performing this function). Placed in pairs, up to six banderillas may be stuck into the bull, varying in number and position according to the needs of the individual animal.

The final round of the *lidia* is called *el tercio de muerte*, the third of death. The main activity of this *tercio* is *la faena*, the work, involving cape and sword, during which a special set of passes leads to the killing of the bull. For the first two *tercios* there is no time limit; for the last, however, the matador has only 15 minutes within which to kill the bull, or else he is considered defeated, and the bull is led from the ring (where it is killed immediately by the plaza butcher).

In a good *faena*, a matador will tempt fate over and over again, bringing the bull's horns close to his own heart. The time for the kill arrives when the bull has so tired from the *faena* that it stands still, forelegs squared as if ready to receive the sword. Then, with his cape the matador must draw the bull into a final charge while he himself moves forward, bringing the sword out from under the cape, sighting down the blade, and driving the blade over the horns and between the animal's shoulders. A perfect sword thrust severs the aorta, resulting in instant death. If the thrust is off, the matador must try again until the bull dies from one of the thrusts.

If the matador has shown bravery and artistry, the crowd will let him know with its applause; an unusually dramatic performance will see lots of hats and flowers thrown into the ring.

---

at the betting windows are usually all too happy to explain the general betting rules to a novice. The minimum bet is $0.10. The Hipódromo is just west of the Periférico, beyond Polanco in Colonia Lomas de Sotelo. By public transport, get off at either Chapultepec or Auditorio Metro stations and look for buses marked Hipódromo driving west on Paseo de la Reforma.

Lucha Libre

"Free Fight" is Mexico's answer to professional wrestling, and has a strong tradition in the country—to the point that a *lucha* fighter even had a film career in the 1950s. (See sidebar *Lucha Libre* for more information.)

ARENA COLISEO

República de Perú near República de Chile, 55/5526-1687, www.cmll.com
HOURS: Tues. 8:30 P.M., Sun. 5 P.M.
COST: $3-5
METRO: Garibaldi
Map 1

The Coliseo is a bit more run-down and not

as large as the Arena México; a trip here is definitely an adventure. The crowd seems a bit rowdier, perhaps because of the proximity to the rough neighborhood of Tepito, but foreign visitors will quite safe, as long as they sit well back from the ring to avoid flying bodies and the occasional chair. Take care coming and going from the Coliseo as this is not a very safe part of town.

◖ ARENA MÉXICO
Dr. LaVista and Dr. Lucio, Col. Doctores,
55/5588-0508
HOURS: Fri. 8:30 P.M.
COST: $5-7
METRO: Cuauhtémoc
Map 2

The best place in central Mexico City to catch a *lucha libre* match is at the Arena México on Friday night. This "Catedral de la Lucha" has been in business for more than 50 years and is still going strong; there are usually four or five matches per evening. Although the neighborhood around the arena is not the best (watch out after dark), inside it's surprisingly clean and welcoming. Although beer is for sale, the crowd does not tend to get overly inebriated here, and you'll see plenty of younger kids with their fathers (and occasionally their mothers too) enjoying the spectacle.

Soccer

Soccer (or *fútbol,* as it's called here) is by far Mexico's favorite sport, and sports fans may want to catch a league game during the two-part winter-summer seasons—one between August and January and the other between March and June. Tickets cost $5–15, depending on the seat, and are best bought at the stadium ticket office the day before the game, or the same day. If the tickets sell out (although they usually don't), a vociferous crew of *revendedores* (scalpers) can be found selling tickets for a small markup. It's also possible to buy tickets for most games through TicketMaster (55/5325-9000, www.ticketmaster.com.mx), which can be picked up at any Liverpool department store or Mixup music store.

Often the best matches to watch are the big rivalries, such as the *Superclásico* each season between the Chivas of Guadalajara and Mexico City's América, and the cross-town match between the city's two most popular teams, América and Cruz Azul. In recent years the Pumas, Cruz Azul, Atlas of Guadalajara, Los Diablos Rojos of Toluca, and América have consistently been among the best and most fun teams to watch, although that can change quickly.

Attending a match in Mexico is a remarkably relaxed affair, especially for those accustomed to European football matches. Fans from opposing teams often sit right next to each other and exchange mock-angry commentary throughout the game. Actual fights among fans are very rare, though like most fans in the world, they take great glee in flinging whatever they can onto the field, particularly rolls of toilet paper.

Among the several Internet sites related to Mexican soccer are www.femexfut.org.mx (the official league site), www.futbolmundial.com .mx (general information), www.seleccion mexicana.com.mx (national team), www.esmas .com/clubamerica (Águilas del América), www .pumasunam.com.mx (Pumas de UNAM), www.chivasdecorazon.com.mx (Chivas de Guadalajara), and www.cruz-azul.com.mx (Cruz Azul). If you poke around, you'll find some hilarious sites dedicated to trashing the Águilas del América, who are sort of the Real Madrid of Mexico: They are by far the richest and most hyped team, but they are also the most hated in the country.

ESTADIO AZTECA
Calzada de Tlalpan 3465, Col. Santa Ursula,
www.esmas.com/clubamerica
HOURS: Vary
COST: Most games $5-15
METRO: Estadio Azteca light rail station
Map 7

The massive Azteca (sometimes known as "el Coloso de Santa Ursula") is Mexico's largest stadium. It's located in the southern part of the city, home of Las Águilas del América and

LUCHA LIBRE

Outrageously camp, surreally choreographed, wildly acrobatic, or just plain silly: Whatever your opinion of *lucha libre*, the sport's popularity among Mexicans is undeniable. Filling wrestling auditoriums big and small across the country to watch local amateurs or international stars from as far afield as Japan and Scotland, more live spectators watch *lucha libre* in Mexico than any other sport, including soccer.

Bouts are often rowdy affairs, with the wrestlers strutting about the ring and gesticulating or shouting to the excited fans as the opening bell draws near. Once the fight begins, spectators, including housewives, children, and the elderly, cram closer to shout encouragement or abuse at the heaving hulks. In the smaller auditoriums particularly, they can save themselves the effort as the sweating combatants – complete with tights, masks, and capes – many times end up grappling with each other in the front and sometimes even the back rows of seating.

The fights are hammily staged, but that doesn't mean that the sweat, and sometimes blood, is not real, or that the blows are not hard. Equally, the spectacular agility of the wrestlers, especially the lighter weights, is impressive. Professional wrestlers are frequently injured, occasionally seriously. Broken necks are rare but not unheard-of. Wrestlers are not usually well paid, and all but the very best also have day jobs.

Wrestlers divide into two categories, the clean-cut *técnicos* and the surly *rudos*, roughly corresponding to the good guys and the bad guys respectively. The idea is that the *técnicos* are better looking, more skillful, and just plain decent types. The *rudos* are more ruthless and frequently "cheat" in a crude and highly visible fashion. Whacking opponents over the head with various props is a predictable crowd-pleaser. Referees are also routinely strangled, poked in the eye, or dumped out of the ring by *rudos*. Both *técnicos* and *rudos* have no shortage of fans.

© KEITH DANNEMILLER

A working-class sport, *lucha libre* is often looked down on by Mexico's elite. *Lucha libre* venues are usually down-at-the-heel places with a distinctly blue-collar clientele, and that's part of the charm. Nevertheless, *lucha libre's* influence is so pervasive in Mexico that it has even crept into politics and onto the big screen. Famously, Superbarrio is a Mexico City activist who first donned wrestling attire in the 1980s to campaign against poverty and bureaucratic corruption. Meanwhile, El Santo, the archetypal *técnico* and Mexico's most popular grappler back in the 1950s and 1960s, made a series of cheesy lead appearances in eponymous low-budget flicks that many camp aficionados still regard as classics.

For more information (in Spanish) about *lucha libre*, including upcoming events, see the official website at www.cmll.com.

– Contributed by Simeon Tegel

Los Rayos de Necaxa (both owned by media giant Televisa). The national team also plays most of its important matches here. This concrete monster has no frills at all, and is unnervingly vertical—spectators seeing a game from the cheap seats almost feel like you can fall right onto the field. Call for times or check in the sports section of local papers for upcoming games. The massive iron sculpture presiding over the stadium entrance is called *Red Sun* and is one of American artist Alexander Calder's more famous pieces.

ESTADIO AZUL

Just off Insurgentes Sur at Holbein, Col. Ciudad de los Deportes, www.cruz-azul.com.mx
HOURS: Vary
COST: Most games $5-15
METRO: San Antonio, or Insurgentes Metrobús
Map 5

The closest stadium to downtown Mexico City is this semi-sunken mid-sized stadium right next to the Plaza México bullfighting ring. This is home to the Cementeros de Cruz Azul, the second-most popular team in the city after América. The small size and central location make this a good choice for someone looking to get a flavor of Mexican *fútbol*.

� ESTADIO OLÍMPICO

Insurgentes Sur just south of Eje 10 Sur at Ciudad Universitaria, www.pumasunam.com.mx
HOURS: Vary
COST: Most games $5-15
METRO: Universidad
Map 6

Also in the south is this unusually designed stadium, home to the UNAM Pumas. The stadium is meant to look like one of the many volcanic cones in this part of the valley and has a Diego Rivera fresco over the entrance. The UNAM Pumas is frequently one of the better teams in Mexico, and is known for fielding relatively young players (although not from the UNAM—students do not play on the team). Going to see a Pumas game at Estadio Olímpico is always good fun, as the *porras* (fan clubs) of the Pumas are well known for their elaborate and often hilarious (and profane) chants.

HOTELS

Places to stay in Mexico City run the gamut, from spartan hostels to no-nonsense business hotels to plush inns in historic surroundings. In the expensive to premium categories, you can pretty well request and receive any service you desire. In the shoestring and budget classes, make sure you know what you're getting before moving in. If it's important to you to have a window, look before accepting a room. Check for security, too—is there a safe deposit box or some similar place to leave your valuables while touring? Though the weather in Mexico is usually mild, it can get cold at night in the winter; check for heat or ask for plenty of blankets. In the summer, it can get warm on occasion, so consider looking for air-conditioning or a fan.

Hotels likely to be frequented by foreigners are concentrated in a few areas, mainly in the Reforma/Zona Rosa/Centro Histórico area and along busy boulevards radiating from the center. Most travelers on a tight budget opt to stay in the less expensive and centrally located hotels downtown and near the Monumento a la Revolución. Downtown and near Paseo de la Reforma has a good supply of mid-range and higher-priced hotels, while the real luxury spots are found mostly in Chapultepec/Polanco. The Roma and Condesa neighborhoods, two of the more happening parts of town these days, have a couple of new places worth considering but are ripe for more rooms. Coyoacán and San Ángel could also use some convenient accommodations—there's nothing available within 10 blocks of the center of either area, due to strict zoning regulations.

HIGHLIGHTS

LOOK FOR ◖ TO FIND RECOMMENDED HOTELS.

◖ **Best Budget Accommodation:** Hugely popular with the backpacker crowd, **Hostal Moneda** in the heart of the Centro is well-known for its inexpensive but clean dorm rooms and slightly more expensive private rooms. It's a great spot to meet other travelers, too (page 199).

◖ **Best Mid-Range Downtown Hotel:** If you're staying in the Centro and want a bit of luxury at a reasonable price, **Hotel Catedral** is a good choice. Conveniently located just off the Zócalo, the Catedral has comfortable rooms and efficient service (page 200).

◖ **Most Socially Aware Hotel:** Near the Monumento a la Revolución, the **Casa de los Amigos** is a Quaker-run hostel that rents out dorm beds to all sorts of interesting travelers, including many who are socially active in non-governmental organizations in Latin America. You can meet some interesting people cooking up dinner in the communal kitchen (page 203).

◖ **Most Relaxed Hotel:** In a quiet neighborhood just north of Paseo de la Reforma is **Casa González,** a cluster of little buildings spread out across a grassy yard. This inexpensive little inn is a lovely oasis in the middle of the city, where you can wind down from the day on their patio (page 204).

◖ **Best Luxury Hotel:** There are a number of world-class hotels in Mexico City, but the **Hotel Four Seasons** is the *crème de la*

crème. Rooms here are homier than most luxury spreads, which is perhaps why it's favored by the international business crowd. The courtyard is a popular breakfast spot for local politicians and power brokers (page 206).

◖ **Most Artistic Hotel:** Designed by architect Ricardo Legorreta, the **Camino Real Mexico City** is a truly bizarre cubist structure. As you wander the spacious hallways, check out the art works by Rufino Tamayo, Alexander Calder, Pedro Coronel, Davíd Alfaro Siqueiros, and Gunther Gerzo (page 206).

◖ **Best Chic Hotel:** Housed in a lovely mansion in the Condesa, the chic **Condesa df** is an innovative hotel with all the modern amenities, favored by Mexican and international jet-setting hipsters. Rooms are distributed around the sides of a triangular-shaped building, with a rooftop deck and a dining area in the central patio (page 210).

◖ **Most Historic Luxury Hotel:** Built in a Porfiriato-era mansion in the Roma neighborhood, **La Casona** has only 30 rooms, each decorated with period furniture and lacy curtains. It's a relaxed, quiet alternative to the busier high-rise hotels along Paseo de la Reforma (page 210).

◖ **Best Apartment-Hotel: Suites Coyoacán** in southern Mexico City is perfect for visitors looking for an apartment set-up, complete full kitchen, housekeeping, and excellent service (page 210).

CHOOSING AN ACCOMMODATION
Rates

Accommodation values, surprisingly, are among the best of any city in Mexico, probably because competition is keen. The more expensive hotels along Reforma or in Polanco generally have a range of prices for different types of clients and time/date of stay, and the prices quoted in this chapter are the most expensive, last-minute rates. Even in the priciest hotels you can often get some kind of a discount,

especially at certain times of the year, if you arrive late at night, or if the hotel isn't filled. Rates are also invariably much lower over the weekend for expensive hotels. A few more possibilities: American Automobile Association (AAA) members generally can get 20 percent off. If you carry a business card, ask for a business discount. If you make reservations from the airport hotel desks, they frequently offer packages for a little less than the going rates. Or just ask for a discount after they quote a price. It won't always work, but occasionally discounts come to those who ask. More up-scale hotels often have better rates available on their website.

At hotels in the Centro Histórico or at tourist-oriented hotels anywhere in the city, there's no difference between weekend and weekday stays.

Whatever the walk-in rate, you can occasionally bargain the price down at mid-range and less-expensive hotels, except during peak periods such as Christmas or Easter. When checking in, inquire whether the room rate includes breakfast—occasionally it does. Asking for a room without breakfast (*sin desayuno*) is an easy way to bring the rate down, or simply ask if there's anything more inexpensive available (*"¿Hay algo más económico?"*). You can usually count on finding cheaper breakfasts outside the hotel.

Taxes and Surcharges

Unless otherwise noted, the prices listed in this guide do not include the 15 percent IVA (value added tax) and 2 percent city lodging tax. Some of the more expensive hotels also tack on a 10 percent service charge. Be sure to ask, before checking in, whether tax and service are included in quoted rates.

Centro Histórico   Map 1

You'll find plenty of hotels in the Centro to suit almost any price range, particularly in the area from the Zócalo west to Eje Central. Budget travelers in particular will find a number of good deals to choose from, all conveniently located, including at least four hostels. All are well managed and receive good reviews from the backpacker crowd. Those looking for a bit more pampering have a few decent options, but for a top-quality luxury hotel, head to the Zona Rosa or Polanco.

UNDER $15

HOSTAL AMIGO
Isabel la Católica 61, 55/5521-3464,
www.hostalamigo.com
METRO: Isabel la Católica

The owners of Hostal Moneda, unable to expand their facilities, opted to open another hostel with similar services and prices to their original lodging. As at Hostal Moneda, guests will find English-speaking staff, Internet access, lockers, walking tours of the city, and inexpensive dorm rooms. No private rooms are available.

HOSTAL MEXICO CITY
Brasil 8, 55/5512-3666 or 55/5512-7731,
www.mexicocityhostel.com
METRO: Zócalo

One of the newer hostels downtown is half a block north of the Catedral, housed in a renovated colonial building. Apart from the low-priced dorm rooms, private rooms are also available for $20–30 d. It was also a bit easier at last report to get a room here compared to the other downtown hostels, because it's not yet as well known.

◖ HOSTAL MONEDA
Moneda 8, 55/5522-5803, www.hostalmoneda.com.mx
METRO: Zócalo

This popular spot, just a block east of the Zócalo, is invariably full of backpackers from across the globe crashing in the dorm rooms (four beds—and hence easy to take over with a group of friends traveling together) or the pricier ($35–39) double rooms with private bath. Prices are lower for Hostelling International members. Downstairs is a kitchen, washing area, and Internet station, and on the roof is a small terrace café with great views. The owners also offer package deals including tours of the city and environs. Breakfast is included in prices.

HOSTEL CATEDRAL
República de Guatemala 4, 55/5518-1726,
www.hostelcatedral.com
METRO: Zócalo

Literally right behind the Catedral, this

hostel is slightly more upscale than the Hostal Moneda, with 204 beds in dorm-style rooms with wooden floors, lockers, and new furniture. Private rooms are $37–55, more for ones with views over the Catedral. Coin washing machines and a small kitchen are available for guests. Downstairs is a pool hall, Internet café, travel agency, and patio restaurant. A buffet breakfast is included in the room price. Best to reserve ahead for dorm rooms, and necessary for private rooms. HI or International Student I.D. cards get discounted prices.

HOTEL BUENOS AIRES
Motolinía 21, 55/5518-2104
METRO: Allende
The venerable Buenos Aires occupies an ancient two-story colonial building just off Cinco de Mayo. The rooms are surprisingly decent, considering how tattered the outside of the building looks. All rooms have TVs and high ceilings.

HOTEL ZAMORA
Cinco de Mayo 50, 55/5512-1832
METRO: Allende
This downtown cheap hotel is a stalwart among the backpacker crowd, with 36 rooms in four stories around a small interior patio. The tiled building is kept clean, but is often noisy. For this price don't expect luxury. Rooms with private bath are a bit more expensive ($16).

$15-30
HOTEL ISABEL
Isabel la Católica 63, 55/5518-1213,
www.hotel-isabel.com.mx
METRO: Isabel la Católica
Four blocks southwest of the Zócalo in a rambling old five-story building across from the Templo de San Agustín, the Isabel is very popular with young foreign travelers. The 74 rooms have high ceilings, private or shared baths, TV, and phone. Exterior rooms are less stuffy than interior rooms but also noisier. A restaurant and bar are on the premises, and the

staff speaks English. Rooms cost a bit less with shared bathroom.

HOTEL LAFAYETTE
Motolinía 40, 55/5521-9640
METRO: Allende
On a pedestrian street three blocks west of the Zócalo, the Lafayette is a rather unattractive modern structure on the corner of 16 de Septiembre, but its TV-equipped rooms are a fair value and popular with many low-budget Mexican tourists. The interior rooms are a bit claustrophobic, but the exterior ones are well lit, and the pedestrian-only street is quiet after dark. Laundry service is available.

HOTEL MONTE CARLO
República de Uruguay 89, 55/5521-2559
METRO: Zócalo or Isabel la Católica
Just behind the massive Templo San Agustín, this hotel offers 60 rooms housed in what used to be part of the Augustinian convent. With the interior makeover (pink paint-job and all), it's hard to notice the colonial flavor, but the rooms do have high ceilings. Famed authors D. H. Lawrence and Somerset Maugham both stayed here in the early 20th century. Parking is available.

HOTEL PRINCIPAL
Bolívar 29, 55/5521-1333, www.hotelprincipal.com.mx
METRO: Allende
Four blocks west of the Zócalo in an older four-story stone building is another young traveler favorite, with clean rooms with TV and phone and lower prices if you're willing to share a bathroom. The rooms are nothing to write home about but they serve their purpose for cheap lodgings, and the central courtyard with leafy plants makes for a pleasing, well-lit interior. The hotel also has a spacious dining room with well-priced, decent meals.

$30-50
HOTEL CATEDRAL
Donceles 95, 55/5518-5232, www.hotelcatedral.com
METRO: Zócalo
Behind the Catedral Metropolitana, and half

a block from Templo Mayor, is this clean, modern, and very comfortable place with a friendly and helpful staff. The hotel features a good restaurant and bar, as well as a travel agency and Internet access—all on the ground floor. Another major plus: All local calls are free, and you can make data as well as voice calls, unlike at many Mexico City hotels that cost much more. One drawback is the traffic on Donceles in front of the hotel, which can be quite thick during rush hour; keep this in mind if you're planning to catch a taxi to the airport or bus station. Junior suites run $70 d.

HOTEL GILLOW

Isabel la Católica 17, 55/5510-2636, www.hotelgillow.com
METRO: Zócalo

Run by the same owners as the Hotel Catedral, the Gillow has 103 clean if somewhat characterless carpeted rooms, each with private bath, TV, and some rather dodgy color schemes, that don't quite match the promise of the more ornate wood-paneled lobby. The hotel is conveniently located just off the Zócalo, and the restaurant is good.

$75-110

TULIP INN RITZ MEXICO

Madero 30, 55/5130-0169, www.tulipinnritzmexico.com
METRO: Allende

The downtown Ritz is perhaps not as luxurious as its name might suggest, but its not a bad deal with 120 recently remodeled rooms with carpets, cable TV, in-room modems, free local phone calls, bathtubs, and lock boxes.

The seven-floor hotel has a rooftop terrace restaurant with room service available. A buffet breakfast is included in the price.

OVER $110

BEST WESTERN HOTEL MAJESTIC

Av. Madero 73, 55/5512-8600, U.S./Canada 800/528-1234, www.majestic.com.mx
METRO: Zócalo

The Majestic's 84 rooms are small and service is not the best, but the location on the Zócalo is hard to beat. Rooms facing the square cost more. The patio restaurant is a fine spot for a meal overlooking the square, whether or not you're staying at the hotel. The five-story interior atrium of this colonial-era building is quite the ornate display, decorated with tile, glass, and wood and a large stone fountain in the center. Children under 12 stay for free. There's no Internet access at the hotel.

HOLIDAY INN

Av. Cinco de Mayo 61, 55/5130-5130, toll-free in Mexico 800/990-9999, www.holidayinn.com
METRO: Zócalo

Also right on the west side of the Zócalo and located in a colonial-era building, with its entrance on Cinco de Mayo, this hotel has 110 rooms that are a bit cramped but well stocked with new furniture and accoutrements, and the service is very good. Like the adjacent Hotel Majestic, the Holiday Inn has a rooftop patio restaurant, a good spot for a bird's-eye view of the square. High-speed Internet access is available in rooms for those with their own computer.

HOTELS

HOTELS

Visitors will find a number of hotel options in different price ranges near the Alameda, particularly on Avenida Juárez and the blocks just to the south. The massive Sheraton on Juárez—the most luxurious hotel in the downtown, built in 2002—provided a major boost to the area, which was formerly a bit rundown. Now it's a good choice for those who plan on touring the Centro, but prefer not to be stuck in the middle of the busy streets. Budget travelers won't find many places to suit their price range here, as most hotels tend to be mid-range and up.

$15-30
HOTEL CONDE
Pescaditos 15, 55/5521-1084
METRO: Juárez

This hotel's clean, bright, and efficient rooms with tile baths are a good value for those who would like to stay near the Alameda. The lounge includes an upright piano, TV, and several sofas for relaxing. Parking is available. The hotel is conveniently close to the San Juan and Ciudadela craft markets.

HOTEL SAN DIEGO
Luis Moya 98, 55/5510-3523
METRO: Salto de Agua

The 87-room San Diego is an affable and affordable option on Luis Moya. The street boasts a number of these medium-sized cheapies. This one is a bit farther south from the Alameda then the others, and the surrounding streets are somewhat on the scruffy side. The San Diego offers room service and a central garden.

$30-50
HOTEL FLEMING
Revillagigedo 35, 55/5510-4530,
hotelfleming@prodigy.net.mx
METRO: Juárez

This mid-range hotel near the Alameda is a good value, with 80 spotless rooms, ample parking, and a decent coffee shop. Internet is available in a room downstairs from the lobby

(free if you have laptop, or $1 for 15 minutes if not) but not in guest rooms. Junior suites with hot tubs are available for a bit extra ($46).

HOTEL MARLOWE
Independencia 17, 55/5521-9540,
www.hotelmarlowe.com.mx
METRO: Juárez

With a modern facade and a welcoming sculpture-and-cactus garden just off the Alameda, the Marlowe offers 100 rooms and 20 suites, including some with terraces, and free wireless Internet. The off-pink carpeted rooms are low on ambience but fully functional and a decent value for the price.

$50-75
HOTEL METROPOL
Luis Moya 39, 55/5510-8660
METRO: Juárez

Another good value two blocks south of the Alameda, the Metropol has 160 modern, clean rooms with telephones and new color TVs, and hotel service is generally good. There is a restaurant/bar and travel agency, as well as room service. Wireless Internet is free in all rooms.

HOTEL SAN FRANCISCO
Luis Moya 11, 55/5521-8960
METRO: Juárez

This refreshing combination of modern convenience and Mexican decor is half a block from the Alameda's southern esplanade. The hotel's lobby boasts bright, modern Mexican murals and rustic seating. The rooms, including suites with large balconies (some with Alameda views), are spacious and tasteful. Internet is available in the lobby for $1 per 20 minutes.

OVER $110
FIESTA INN
Av. Juárez 76, 55/5130-2900, U.S. 800/343-7821,
www.fiestainn.com
METRO: Juárez

Right next door to the huge Sheraton on the

Alameda is the more modest and less visible Fiesta Inn, with 140 rooms on four floors, done up in cheerful colors. The hotel has a restaurant, bar, and gym. A room designed for disabled guests is also available. Rooms have free wireless Internet, and there's also a business center with computers available. There's a parking lot for guests, although it costs an extra $4.50 a day.

SHERATON CENTRO HISTÓRICO

Av. Juárez 70, 55/5130-5300, U.S./Canada 800/325-3535, www.sheratonmexico.com
METRO: Juárez

Dominating the southwest corner of the Alameda is the towering Sheraton, built in 2002. The 457-room hotel, with a stylish modernist facade, was one of the first private concerns to sign on to the city government's efforts to revitalize the Alameda and Centro neighborhoods. The thoroughly modern, comfortable rooms offer high-speed Internet connection, flat-screen television with video games, and the suites have whirlpool tubs and kitchenettes. The hotel also has a fitness center, a wine bar and a lobby bar, and business and convention centers—and even a heliport. The Cardenal restaurant in the lobby is a new branch of one of Mexico City's best traditional eateries.

Paseo de la Reforma and Zona Rosa   Map 2

Because of its central location, the availability of services, and the relatively easy access to transportation, the Reforma/Zona Rosa area makes a good base from which to tour Mexico City. Many hotels in the Zona Rosa and on Reforma fall toward the higher end of the scale, but numerous attractive midrange accommodations can be found just off Reforma, both near the Monumento de Colón and behind the U.S. embassy. One thing to keep in mind is that the Reforma hotels are usually several blocks from the closest Metro station, Insurgentes. Budget travelers will find plenty of low-priced hotels of varying quality in the few blocks between the Monumento a la Revolución and Avenida Puente de Alvarado, near the Revolución Metro station.

UNDER $15

◀ CASA DE LOS AMIGOS

Ignacio Mariscal 132, 55/5705-0521, www.casadelosamigos.org
METRO: Revolución

This unusual hostel, near the Monumento a la Revolución, is run by Quakers and often serves as a base for people doing social work in Mexico and Central America. Don't worry, they don't proselytize, and it can be a good place to meet some very interesting travelers.

Alcohol is not allowed in the hostel. Reception closes at 10 P.M., so arrive before that on your first night. Guests may also use the kitchen, which can help save pesos. There is a minimum stay of two days and a maximum stay of 15 days per month. Low-priced private rooms are also available, ranging from $13 to $35 depending on amenities.

HOTEL OXFORD

Ignacio Mariscal 67, 55/5566-0500
METRO: Revolución

Near the Casa de los Amigos but of a very different social milieu, the Oxford serves as a part-time brothel, but it remains popular with backpackers because it offers reasonably clean, inexpensive rooms. It has a decent, funky little bar inside for late-night drinks, and occasional inebriated guitarists play melancholy *trío* laments.

$15-30

HOTEL EDISON

Thomas A. Edison 106, 55/5566-0933
METRO: Revolución

One block from the Monumento a la Revolución, the Edison is a modest, inexpensive hotel. Each of the carpeted rooms has a writing desk, TV, telephone, and chairs with well-worn cushions. Check your mattress, as some are mushy. Parking is available. Internet is available for a fee in a room off the lobby.

$30-50
ⓒ CASA GONZÁLEZ
Río Sena 69 at Río Lerma, 55/5514-3302

METRO: Insurgentes

This small inn consists of a cluster of colonial and postcolonial houses close to the U.S. and British embassies. The owner and his family still live in one wing, and staying here is a little like staying in an old, rambling home. The separate buildings, each painted a cheerful white with blue trim and containing several rooms, are situated around a landscaped courtyard. Several of the 22 rooms have their own little patios, which make lovely spots to sit outside, relax, and listen to the birds sing. The rooms near the street are a bit noisier and hence less expensive. Off-street parking isn't available at the hotel, but there's a public pay lot next door. Wireless Internet access is available for those with a laptop, as is a hotel computer. It's best to call ahead for reservations.

HOTEL CORINTO
Vallarta 24, 55/5566-6555

METRO: Revolución

This 10-story, 155-room hotel is one block south of the Monumento a la Revolución. The modern rooms are a bit on the small side but comfortable and a good value, with a tiled bath, TV, and phone. Parking is available, and the hotel also has a small pool. Wireless Internet is available in the lobby and bar, but not in rooms.

$50-75
HOTEL BRISTOL
Plaza Necaxa 17, 55/5208-1717,
www.gsevilla.com.mx/bristol/esp

METRO: Insurgentes

Just behind the U.S. embassy, three blocks from Paseo de la Reforma and near the Zona Rosa, this hotel has 148 thoroughly modern rooms with air-conditioning and large TVs. The rooms are quite functional, despite being housed in a dramatically unattractive, seven-story featureless box building. Top-floor penthouse suites cost considerably more than the regular rooms. Amenities include a restaurant, bar, free parking, and an efficient staff. Wireless Internet and computers are available for guest use.

HOTEL DEL PRINCIPADO
Londres 42, 55/5533-2944

METRO: Insurgentes

Located in a residential neighborhood conveniently located near the Zona Rosa, Colonia Roma, and Paseo de la Reforma, the Principado has 50 modern rooms decorated in a rather bland but functional style. Management is very efficient and helpful, the breakfast buffet is hearty, and free wireless Internet is available in all rooms. The hotel is right next to the well-known Clínica Londres medical center.

HOTEL MARÍA CRISTINA
Río Lerma 31, 55/5566-9688,
www.hotelmariacristina.com.mx

METRO: Insurgentes

A couple of blocks north of Reforma, the 150-room María Cristina is a reliable hotel in a four-story colonial-style building featuring interior gardens and frequented by midrange travelers. The large suites are a decent value, and each is furnished with a wet bar. The attached coffee shop is popular with guests and nonguests alike. The hotel bookshop has a good selection of international magazines. Wireless Internet is available in most rooms and the lobby.

MI CASA
General Prim 101, 55/5566-6711

METRO: Insurgentes

Mi Casa is a good option for those who want to do their own cooking. The apartment-hotel is located about halfway between the Zona Rosa and the Alameda with 27 modern rooms equipped with full kitchens. It's located about halfway between the Zona Rosa and the Alameda. No Internet service is available.

$75-110

HOTEL CASA BLANCA

La Fragua 7, 55/5096-4500, fax 5096-4510, U.S./
Canada 55/800/905-2905,
www.hotel-casablanca.com.mx

METRO: Revolución

The 12-story Casa Blanca is very popular with mid-range travelers and international tour groups. It's a modern hotel with 270 pastel rooms, each with wall-to-wall carpeting, firm mattresses, subdued fluorescent lighting, marble-tiled baths, purified water on tap, comfortable chairs and tables, and air-conditioning. A small rooftop pool and bar overlook the city. Wireless Internet is available for an extra charge.

HOTEL IMPERIAL

Paseo de la Reforma 64, 55/5705-4911,
www.differentworld.com/mexico

METRO: Juárez or Hidalgo

For a bit of Old World style with modern comforts, check out the gold-domed Imperial, in a triangular building right next to the Monumento de Colón on Paseo de la Reforma, well located in between the Alameda and the Zona Rosa. The 60 spacious rooms, distributed around a Guggenheim-style multi-level interior atrium, are comfortable and well kept. The hotel restaurant specializes in Spanish cuisine, and also has a very good breakfast buffet. Wireless Internet is available in all rooms.

HOTEL POSADA VIENA

Marsella 28 at Dinamarca, 55/5566-0700,
www.posadavienahotel.com

METRO: Insurgentes

Another good mid-range hotel option in the Juárez neighborhood, conveniently located close to the Zona Rosa, Paseo de la Reforma, and Colonia Roma, the Posada Viena caters to U.S. tourist families and groups. The rooms are done up in colorful, slightly kitschy style with lots of Mexican decorations, but they are also spacious and well equipped and have firm mattresses. Prices are a tad high for what's offered, but discounts are frequently available. Breakfast is included in the price.

OVER $110

FIESTA AMERICANA

Paseo de la Reforma 80, 55/5140-4100,
www.fiestaamericana.com

METRO: Juárez

In front of the Monumento de Colón on Reforma, the venerable Fiesta Americana does well with the middle-class business crowd. The huge hotel contains over 600 rooms on 25 floors, with a dedicated executive floor and higher-end suites also available. Rooms are large and comfortable, with wireless Internet access. There's a 24-hour business center and gym, and the Santa Clara restaurant has a good reputation for quality Mexican food.

GALERÍA PLAZA

Hamburgo 195, 55/5230-1717, www.brisas.com.mx

METRO: Insurgentes

A luxury favorite near the Zona Rosa, a couple of blocks south of Paseo de la Reforma, the

the gold-domed Hotel Imperial on Paseo de la Reforma

HOTELS

Galería Plaza has 440 rooms. The hotel looks like a large office building from the outside, but each elegantly decorated room has modern dark wood furniture, marble bathroom, and all the amenities. Choose between a modest cafeteria or a higher-end international restaurant for eating options, and there's a gym facility with two modest-sized rooftop outdoor pools too, one for laps and one just to splash around.

☾ HOTEL FOUR SEASONS

Paseo de la Reforma 500, 55/5230-1818, toll-free in Mexico 800/906-7500, www.fourseasons.com/mexico
METRO: Sevilla

This is the premier high-end choice for international businesspeople in Mexico City, with the extremely attentive service and full amenities they expect. In an eight-story neocolonial building at the western end of Reforma, close to Chapultepec, the rooms are unusually homey, filled with plants and comfortable furniture, and the café in the spacious, green courtyard is a lovely spot for breakfast. The hotel restaurant is frequented by politicos and businessfolk negotiating deals or hobnobbing with journalists. For those really after some pampering, in-room massage and facial service is available.

HOTEL MARQUIS REFORMA

Paseo de la Reforma 465, 55/5229-1200, U.S. 800/235-2387, Canada 877/818-5011, www.marquisreforma.com.mx
METRO: Sevilla

A pink granite-and-glass structure on the western section of Reforma, with hints of art deco lines, this hotel contains 208 rooms and 84 suites with soft-toned modern styling and vaguely antique-looking furniture. All rooms have data ports, faxes, and wireless Internet, and cell phone rental is available. Female guests can choose to room on a floor reserved for women only. On the premises are the international restaurant La Jolla, a bar, and a gym with sauna and hot tub.

Chapultepec and Polanco   Map 3

The area around Chapultepec and Polanco has some of the finest and most expensive hotels in the city, favored by many businesspeople and wealthier tourists. Low-budget travelers won't find anything in their price range here.

OVER $110
☾ CAMINO REAL MEXICO CITY

Av. Mariano Escobedo 700, 55/5263-8888, U.S./ Canada 800/722-6466, www.caminoreal.com/mexico
METRO: Chapultepec

A short distance from the edge of Chapultepec Park, the Ricardo Legorreta–designed Camino Real fills its unique whitewashed cubist building with a flamboyant selection of modern art, including a Rufino Tamayo mural in the lobby and masterworks elsewhere by Alexander Calder, Pedro Coronel, Davíd Alfaro Siqueiros, and Gunther Gerzo. Wandering around the palatial corridors of the five-story main building, lined with banquet halls and bars, one could be forgiven for forgetting that it's a hotel. The 713 airy rooms, decorated in solid colors, are practically hidden in the corners of the hotel, which also boasts three swimming pools, four rooftop tennis courts (illuminated for night play), and an excellent health club. The hotel has several restaurants and bars to choose from, including a branch of Le Cirque, one of the best French restaurants in Mexico.

CASA VIEJA

Eugenio Sue 45, 55/5282-0067, www.casavieja.com
METRO: Polanco

A change from the high-powered high-rise hotels that populate Polanco and Chapultepec, though even more pricey, the Casa Vieja is a converted late-19th-century mansion well

COURTESY OF CAMINO REAL MEXICO CITY

poolside oasis at the Camino Real Mexico City

located in the center of Polanco along a quiet side street. The 10 rooms all have a kitchen, stereo, fax machine, desk, and satellite TV and are decorated in Mexican style with bright solid colors, tiles, woven rugs, and wooden furniture. Corporate rates and other discounts are frequently available. Service is personalized and very attentive.

FIESTA AMERICANA GRANDE

Mariano Escobedo 756, 55/5281-1500, toll-free in Mexico 800/504-5000, U.S. 800/343-7821, www.fiestaamericana.com

METRO: Chapultepec

A complement to the venerable Fiesta Americana on Paseo de la Reforma, this sleek hotel with a round turret on one corner tower houses 203 rooms and 14 suites, with a full spa, business center, and three executive floors. It's geared more to business travelers rather than tourists, with an emphasis on efficiency rather than luxury. Many rooms have their own exercise bike, and some have lovely views over Chapultepec Park.

HOTEL HÁBITA

Av. Presidente Mazaryk 201, 55/5282-3100, www.designhotels.com

METRO: Polanco

A member of Small Luxury Hotels and Design Hotels, Hábita is done up in an ultramodern style, with lots of glass and sleek styling. Each of the 36 carpeted rooms is elegantly simple, with futons and a small terrace. Suites are only slightly larger than the regular rooms. Each room has direct Internet data ports, and the hotel has a business/conference center. On the roof is a glassed-in exercise room and open-air pool, as well as a popular hipster lounge bar called El Área. The restaurant downstairs is very good and often frequented by nonguests.

HOTEL NIKKO MÉXICO

Campos Eliseos 204, 55/5283-8700, U.S./Canada 800/645-5687, www.hotelnikkomexico.com.mx

METRO: Auditorio

Just off Paseo de la Reforma, opposite the first section of Chapultepec Park, the 38-story

HOTELS

Hotel Nikko México is one of the several luxury hotels found in the upscale Polanco neighborhood.

tower of the Nikko is visible from much of the city on a clear day, along with its two neighboring luxury hotel towers of the Marriott and Inter-Continental. The Nikko boasts a complete business center, health club with pool and tennis courts, a golf driving range, several restaurants and bars, and a wealth of other amenities. The 745 rooms are rather standard-looking, considering the price, but service is top-notch.

JW MARRIOTT

Andrés Bello 29, 55/5999-0000, U.S./Canada
888/813-2776, www.marriott.com
METRO: Auditorio

A half block from the Nikko and Presidente, the Marriott is considered by many to have the best rooms of the "big three" hotels near Chapultepec Park. It has 300 rooms and 20 suites on 26 floors, and a reputation for excellent service. The gym and spa have all the expected amenities, along with a roof-top outdoor heated swimming pool. There are three restaurants to chose from, and a bar with (nice!) more than 100 tequilas on offer. Rooms are done up in a warm, homey style, a refreshing change from the more bland modern rooms in many high-end hotels, and all come with requisite wireless Internet access.

PRESIDENTE INTER-CONTINENTAL MEXICO CITY

Campos Eliseos 218, 55/5327-7700, U.S./Canada
800/327-0200, www.interconti.com
METRO: Auditorio

Right next door to the Nikko and Marriott, the Inter-Continental was built in 1977, making it the oldest of the park hotels. A multistory pyramid lobby topped with an immense skylight never fails to impress. The 660 rooms, though not exceptional, are well equipped, and executive suites equipped with Internet connections and fax machines are available. The hotel has a "gourmet center," with seven restaurants featuring different world cuisines, including the superlative Au Pied de Cochon French restaurant, open 24 hours a day, and the Balmoral tea room, with English-style high tea and snacks.

Roma and Condesa
Map 4

As Roma and Condesa have for many years been a bit off the tourist track, not a lot of hotel options are to be found in these neighborhoods. But the section of Álvaro Obregón between Insurgentes and Cuauhtémoc, Roma's main drag, has a few decent lower-priced hotels to choose from. There are only three higher-end places here, but they are all very nice in their own way, making this area an alternative to the posh hotel districts of Reforma or Polanco.

$15-30

HOTEL COLONIA ROMA

Jalapa 100, at Álvaro Obregón, 55/5584-1396

METRO: Insurgentes

The bright-pink Colonia Roma is nothing special, but acceptable for those on a budget and conveniently located to tour the Roma and Condesa neighborhoods. The 50 small carpeted rooms each have TV and telephone.

HOTEL MONARCA

Álvaro Obregón 32, 55/5584-0461

METRO: Insurgentes

A slight (very slight) step up in quality from the Colonia Roma is the nearby Monarca, an unattractive five-story building which has inexpensive and decent rooms. It's popular among middle-class Mexicans and is a reasonable option for those on a budget who want to stay in the neighborhood.

$30-50

HOTEL LISBOA

Av. Cuauhtémoc 273, 55/5574-7088, toll-free in Mexico 800/710-2856, www.hotellisboa.com.mx

METRO: Hospital General

A bit out of the way at the southeastern edge of the Roma, near the Hospital General Metro station, the Lisboa offers 130 rooms in a retro, 1970s-looking white eight-story tower. Rooms are unremarkable but functional and well maintained. The more expensive rooms have balconies facing south across the city, but the

traffic noise from Avenida Cuauhtémoc below detracts a bit from the view.

HOTEL MILAN

Álvaro Obregón 94, 55/5584-0222

METRO: Insurgentes

The Milan has a remarkably ugly facade, but the rooms are modern and very livable. The hotel has a restaurant/bar and parking. Wireless Internet is available in all rooms.

HOTEL PARQUE ENSENADA

Álvaro Obregón 13, 55/5208-0052, www.hotelensenada.com.mx

METRO: Insurgentes or Cuauhtémoc

This is an excellent mid-range hotel in the Roma Norte, with 140 comfortable carpeted modern rooms, each equipped with bedside fan, small fridge, TV, and phone. Free wireless Internet is available, and there's a small business center and restaurant too. The hotel staff is efficient and friendly.

HOTEL ROOSEVELT

Insurgentes Sur 287, 55/5208-6813

METRO: Insurgentes

Right on Insurgentes but with easy walking access to Parque México in the Condesa, this hotel has 75 modern motel-like rooms, each with cable TV and telephone. It doesn't have a lot in the way of character, but it's the lowest-priced hotel option in the Condesa at last report. A reasonably priced coffee shop and parking garage are on the ground floor.

$50-75

CASA DE LA CONDESA

Plaza Luis Cabrera 16, 55/5574-3186 or 55/5584-3089, www.extendedstaymexico.com

METRO: Insurgentes

A relatively new place in the Roma, wonderfully located right on the quiet little Parque Luis Cabrera, Casa de la Condesa rents out apartment-style units with fully equipped kitchens and daily housekeeping. Choose

HOTELS

Condesa df

OVER $110
◖ CONDESA DF

Av. Veracruz 102, 55/5241-2600, www.condesadf.com

METRO: Chapultepec

A great addition to Mexico City's hotel market, Condesa df is run by the same owners as Hotel Hábita, in Polanco. A fine triangular-shaped *casona* (old mansion) built on a corner property just off Parque España in the Condesa has been intriguingly remodeled to house 24 rooms and 16 suites, all done in a sleek, minimalist style. The top-floor rooms have patios and are more expensive. Also upstairs is a steam room and hot tub, while the restaurant (with excellent food) is in the building's central patio. The staff is bilingual and very efficient. The hotel bar is a favorite watering hole for the hipster crowd, both Mexican and foreign.

◖ LA CASONA

Durango 280, 55/5286-3001,
www.hotellacasona.com.mx

METRO: Sevilla

In a residential area of the Roma neighborhood, convenient to Reforma, Polanco, and Condesa but on a quiet side street, La Casona is housed in a lovingly refurbished late-19th-century mansion. The small but luxurious hotel contains a very good café-restaurant, a gym, services for business travelers, and 30 rooms filled with wooden writing desks and lacy curtains.

between the smaller studio apartments or the full-size units with separate dining, living, and bedrooms. Rooms on the higher floors facing the park, with porches and hammocks, are great but cost more ($94 d). Wireless Internet is available in all rooms.

Coyoacán

Map 6

This part of the city has a major dearth of good hotels, with none at all in the central area because of zoning laws. In recent years some city officials, backed no doubt by the local business community, have attempted to change the laws, but as yet the residents have successfully resisted the change. While it makes it hard on the tourists, it certainly keeps the neighborhood more pleasingly residential. If you really want to stay in the area, there are a couple of acceptable (but not cheap) nearby hotels.

OVER $110
◖ SUITES COYOACÁN

Av. Coyoacán 1909, 55/5534-8353,
www.suitescoyoacan.com

METRO: Coyoacán

Technically in the Colonia Del Valle but very close to Coyoacán, Suites Coyoacán feels more like a private housing compound than a hotel. Designed for people with extended stays in Mexico City, each of the hotel's nine suites comes equipped with a high-speed Internet connection, full kitchen, direct telephone, and reserved parking. The more expensive suites also come with a VCR, stereo sound system, and microwave. The hotel has 24-hour security and can arrange for taxis and laundry service. All in all, it's a very comfortable, relaxing place to stay, and service is excellent.

Greater Mexico City

Map 7

Whenever possible, avoid staying near the Mexico City airport, as rooms are far less of a value than what you can get a mere 20 minutes' drive away in the city. There's only one vaguely acceptable mid-range option near the airport, while the others are all high-end, and not very good values at that.

$30-50
HOTEL AEROPUERTO
Boulevard Aeropuerto 380, 55/5785-5888 or 5785-5851
METRO: Terminal Aéreo
This is the closest decent low-priced hotel to the airport, just across the Circuito Interior highway. To get there on foot from the airport, walk all the way past the domestic terminal, follow the street around to the left past the Metro station entrance, and cross the Circuito Interior via the nearby pedestrian bridge—it's about a 15-minute walk. The hotel, with 52 basic rooms with TVs and telephones, is right on the far side of the bridge. It's definitely no great shakes, but if you're pinching pesos and want to stay near the airport, this is about the best you'll find.

HOTEL FINISTERRE
Calz. de Tlalpan 2043, 55/5689-9544
METRO: Tasqueña
About the only decent moderately priced choice in this area is the modern, characterless Finisterre, located not far from the Tasqueña Metro and bus stations. The 128 rooms are functional but nothing to write home about. Really the only thing making this place worth mentioning is its location reasonably close to Coyoacán.

$75-110
HOTEL ROYAL PLAZA
Parroquia 1056, Colonia Santa Cruz Atoyac, 55/5605-8943, toll-free in Mexico 800/009-1000, www.hotelroyalplaza.com.mx
METRO: Tasqueña
Located just off Avenida Universidad a few blocks north of the Circuito Interior, the Royal Plaza is the only upscale hotel in this area. The 130 rooms are all spacious and well appointed (although the artwork over the beds is of dubious taste). The hotel has both a cafeteria and a more formal restaurant, and it offers babysitting services to those traveling with small children. It's about a 15-minute drive (depending on traffic) to the Terminal Sur bus station and 10 minutes to the center of Coyoacán.

OVER $110
AIRPORT HILTON
In airport terminal, tel./fax 55/5133-0505, www.hilton.com
METRO: Terminal Aéreo
This Hilton is built on top of the international terminal—take the elevator up to the 4th floor, and you will be in the lobby. The 129 rooms all have a separate phone line for computers and free wireless Internet. Carlos' Place Bar is a good place to sip a drink, watch planes take off and land, and also keep track of incoming flights if you are waiting for someone. It's pricey for what you get, but that's to be expected for the convenience of staying in the airport terminal.

CAMINO REAL AEROPUERTO
Puerto México 80, 55/3003-0033, www.caminoreal.com
METRO: Terminal Aéreo
Connected to the domestic terminal (near Sala

HOTELS

B) via a pedestrian bridge, the Camino Real is a 583-room monster of a hotel with a pleasant, leafy lobby. Guests (and the general public, for $10) have access to a full health club and indoor pool. The hotel has four restaurants, a pizza parlor, a bar, a 24-hour café, and a 24-hour business center. Rooms are mediocre for the price, but more spacious then the Hilton and about the best available around the airport. It's certainly nothing compared to the Camino Real in the city.

FIESTA INN AEROPUERTO

Boulevard Puerto Aéreo 502, 55/5133-6600, www.fiestaamericana.com

METRO: Terminal Aéreo

Right opposite the airport terminal, the Fiesta Inn's 324 rooms are nothing special, but serve their purpose and are somewhat less expensive than the other two high-end options. There's a convenient shuttle from the terminal to the airport running 24 hours a day, and wireless Internet is free in the hotel.

EXCURSIONS FROM MEXICO CITY

Roads radiate from Mexico City in all directions, providing ample opportunities for daytrippers and weekenders to explore the region. This chapter covers the major cities and sights within about two or three hours' drive from Mexico City, maximum; many destinations are not more than an hour away.

It's amazing how much variety you'll find in central Mexico, just a short trip from the capital. Several different pre-Hispanic ruins, most notably Teotihuacán but also more obscure sites like Malinalco, Cacaxtla, and the Baños de Nezahualcóyotl, are easy day trips, as are jewels of colonial architecture like the Catedral in the city of Puebla, the 15th-century monastery at Huejotzingo, and the colonial art museum in Tepozotlán.

Leaving the city to the east, west, or south,

the scenery is dramatic, with highways winding up the steep mountains flanking the Valle de México, passing through pine-forested parks dotted with lakes and meadows. These are favorite spots for *chilangos* (capital dwellers) to escape for a day of fresh air. Don't forget to pull over at the highway stops lined with little restaurants selling mushroom soup, *tacos de cecina* (cured-meat tacos), and some of the best blue-corn *quesadillas* you're ever likely to have.

Adventure-sport enthusiasts will be gratified to hear that they can risk life and limb in a variety of entertaining ways, including rock and ice climbing, mountain biking, paragliding, and hang gliding. There are also endless kilometers of quiet mountain paths for hiking, and quiet walks through patches of forest

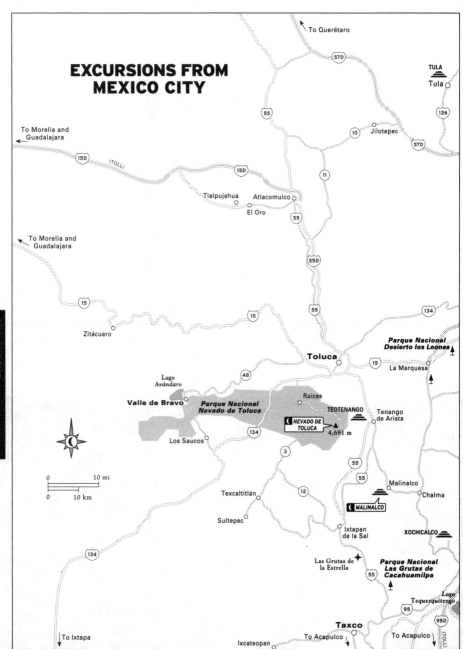

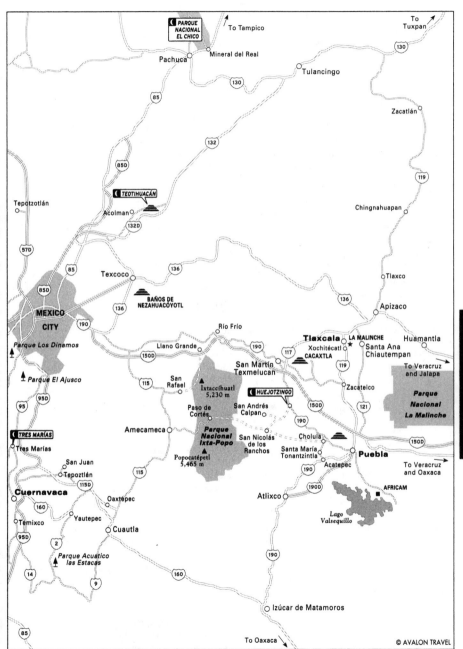

© AVALON TRAVEL

HIGHLIGHTS

LOOK FOR ◖ TO FIND RECOMMENDED SIGHTS, ACTIVITIES, DINING, AND LODGING.

◖ **Most Impressive Ruins:** Right outside of Mexico City stands one of the greatest pre-Hispanic cities in all the Americas, **Teotihuacán,** dominated by the towering Pyramid of the Sun. This ancient city housed 200,000 people at its height, rivaling its contemporary, Rome (page 217).

◖ **Best Place to Pitch a Tent:** In the hills outside of Pachuca, **Parque Nacional El Chico** is full of idyllic meadows in the pine forest, perfect for pitching a tent. This safe area is full of trails for taking walks or bike rides and old mining villages to explore. The adventurous can even find guides to take them rock climbing on the mountaintop cliffs (page 229).

◖ **Best Roadside Food:** Up at **Tres Marías,** a village in the mountains between Mexico City and Cuernavaca, hungry travelers can feast on scrumptious *antojitos* in one of the dozens of little restaurants lining the road. Try a *quesadilla* with *flor de calabaza* (squash flower), a taco of *cecina* (cured, flattened beef), or a *sopa de hongo* (mushroom soup), all at criminally low prices (page 237).

◖ **Best Views by Car:** As long as there's no snow, follow the dirt road winding up to the extinct crater of **Nevado de Toluca** (4,691 meters). Enjoy the fantastic views across the mountains of central Mexico, or if you are motivated, hike up to the crater rim (page 255).

◖ **Best Hidden Getaway:** There's a myriad of little-known towns to explore near Mexico City, but **Malinalco** is particularly charming. Tucked into a narrow, lush valley, this *pueblo* has a huge and beautiful early colonial monastery right in the middle, and an unusual pre-Hispanic temple cut into a nearby mountainside (page 257).

◖ **Best Arts and Crafts:** The silversmiths of Taxco are second to none, but for overall variety of *artesanías,* the shops and markets in and around Puebla are better. Take a walk through **El Parian,** a market housed in a former 18th-century warehouse, thronged with stalls selling Talavera pottery, woven indigenous *rebozos* (shawls), silver cowboy accoutrements, and *alebrijes* (animal-like sculptures carved of wood or fashioned from papier-mâché) (page 282).

◖ **Best Colonial Monastery:** Built by one of the first Catholic missionaries to arrive in Mexico in the early 16th century, the monastery **Huejotzingo** near Puebla is a spectacular amalgam of the spiritual art of both Spanish Catholicism and indigenous traditions. The elaborate artwork decorating the stone facade contains many pre-Hispanic symbols. Inside, the *retablo* (altarpiece) is one of the loveliest in Mexico (page 288).

literally blanketed with monarch butterflies in their winter home.

But be sure to take the time to enjoy a day (or three, or ten) *puebleando,* a wonderful Mexican verb meaning something like "wandering around small towns." Dozens of towns and villages dot the countryside, some with little hidden treasures like a gorgeous baroque chapel or a 17th-century hacienda converted into a museum. Others don't offer anything in particular to do but are nonetheless fine places to stroll through the town market to buy a *torta* and fresh fruit juice, then head over to the *zócalo* (main square) and sit down on a bench to take in the atmosphere along with your snack, remembering in a flash exactly what it is you love about Mexico.

When leaving from or returning to Mexico City from visiting the destinations in this chapter, choose your times carefully. Nothing's worse than having a lovely, relaxing weekend in some bucolic spot, and then getting caught in endless Sunday-afternoon traffic on your way back to the city, leaving you even more frazzled and stressed than when you left! Friday afternoons leaving town and Sunday afternoons and evenings returning are the worst, so if you can schedule your trip to avoid these times, you'll be happier.

GUIDED TRIPS

While many visitors will want to organize trips on their own, the Mexican government Instituto Nacional de Antropología e Historia (INAH) offers various trips every weekend to destinations around Mexico City. The trips, called Paseos Culturales de INAH, typically cost $33 per day (8 A.M.–8 P.M.), with transportation, guide, and entrance fee to sites included. All the prescheduled trips are in Spanish, but special trips can be arranged with English-speaking guides for groups (minimum 10 people). For more information, contact the INAH office in the Museo Nacional de Antropología (55/5553-2365 or 55/5215-1003, www.inah .gob.mx). Information on the tours was at last report only in the Spanish version of the website, not the English version.

One private tour operator with a variety of different trips throughout central Mexico is **Rebozo Ecoturismo** (55/5550-9080, www .marlene-ehrenberg.com.mx). This company is focused as much (if not more) on cultural tourism, with trips geared around certain town festivals or markets, or to see different kinds of local dances or taste local cuisines.

For guided outdoor-adventure trips around Mexico City or central Mexico look to www .amtave.org, the website of the Mexican Association of Adventure Tourism and Ecotourism, with links to many different adventure-travel guide companies and lots of other good information besides. **Mochilazo** (55/5239-5485, www.mochilazo.com.mx) is one company geared toward younger adventure travelers, with all sorts of trips available, including rock climbing and nature hikes around Mexico City and more adventurous trips farther afield in central Mexico. Two recommended outfits for mountain bike trips are **Mountain Bike Mexico** (55/5846-0793, www.mtbmexico .com) and **Solo Montaña** (55/5678-1151, www .ruedapormexico.com.mx), both of which offer trips of various lengths and difficulties.

North of Mexico City

EXCURSIONS

◖ TEOTIHUACÁN

Little is known about the people who built the ancient city of Teotihuacán, one of the largest, most impressive archaeological sites in the Americas. During the city's heyday it was Mesoamerica's most powerful social and political hub. The structures were built between 100 B.C. and A.D. 250, accommodating as many as 200,000 people and forming the largest and most sophisticated city in the Western Hemisphere, comparable with its contemporaries in the Roman Empire. During its height, the influence of the Teotihuacano empire was felt throughout Mesoamerica. Whatever civilization produced Teotihuacán lasted roughly until the 7th century A.D., but despite its obviously complex technology left behind no writing system or any other hints as to who built the city. It is clear from the types of artifacts excavated within the pyramids and temples that the builders of Teotihuacán were a heavily

militarized society, not unlike the later Toltecs and Aztecs. More than 1,200 human skeletons have been discovered amid the ruins, all of them thought to have been sacrificial victims.

Archaeologists believe a four-chambered lava-tube cave in the Valle de Teotihuacán prompted the choice of location for the construction of the original monuments. Considered places where gods and ancestors emerged, as well as doors to a magical underworld, caves played an important role in Mesoamerican religion. Teotihuacán's Pyramid of the Sun was built directly over the cave in the 2nd century A.D.

The site flourished until about A.D. 750, when it was abandoned and set afire. Some researchers suggest the calamity may have been a war between Teotihuacán and Cacaxtla, a smaller contemporary city in nearby Tlaxcala. Over the centuries, pyramids, citadel, temples, palaces, plazas, and paved streets remained deserted

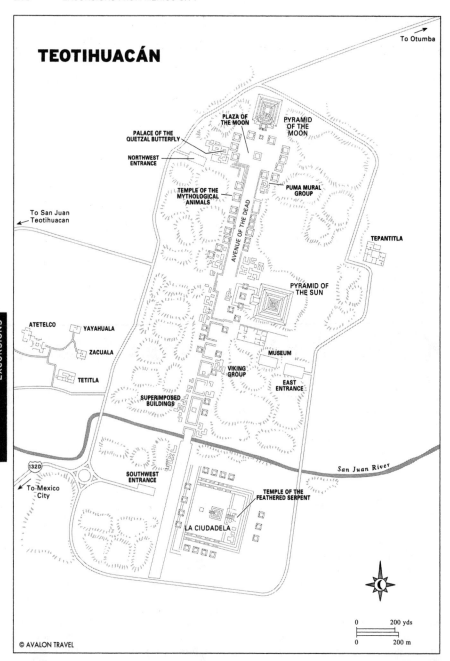

TEOTIHUACÁN

To Otumba

PLAZA OF THE MOON

PYRAMID OF THE MOON

PALACE OF THE QUETZAL BUTTERFLY

NORTHWEST ENTRANCE

TEMPLE OF THE MYTHOLOGICAL ANIMALS

PUMA MURAL GROUP

To San Juan Teotihuacan

AVENUE OF THE DEAD

TEPANTITLA

PYRAMID OF THE SUN

ATETELCO

YAYAHUALA

ZACUALA

TETITLA

MUSEUM

VIKING GROUP

EAST ENTRANCE

SUPERIMPOSED BUILDINGS

San Juan River

132D

To Mexico City

SOUTHWEST ENTRANCE

TEMPLE OF THE FEATHERED SERPENT

LA CIUDADELA

0   200 yds
0   200 m

The ruins so amazed the Aztecs that they called it Teotihuacán, "place where gods are born."

© GUILLAUME COPART MULLER/WWW.GCMPHOTO.COM

and forgotten until the Aztecs arrived in A.D. 1200. Recognizing the site's formidable history, the Aztecs named the ruins Teotihuacán, or "place where gods are born." The Aztecs used Teotihuacán as a pilgrimage center; according to Aztec legend, the sun, moon, and universe itself were created here. Though awestruck by the city's size, the Aztecs probably knew less about the site than we know today.

The most visited archaeological site in Mexico, it is also among the world's most researched and excavated archaeological sites—loved to death, according to some. Even though it is a national icon and a major center of tourism, government support has been ambivalent and commercial exploitation of Teotihuacán has been ongoing. UNESCO has designated the ruins a World Heritage Site, and the World Monuments Fund added them to its list of the world's 100 most endangered monuments in 1998, noting that a permanent conservation program and tourist management plan are badly needed.

In 2004, despite protests, retail giant Wal-Mart opened a discount store a kilometer from the pyramids site, in the town of San Juan Teotihuacán. INAH says the building poses no threat to the site.

La Ciudadela (The Citadel)

Across from the visitors center is a fortress-like enclosure in the geographic center of the city, measuring about 400 meters on each side and with estimated room for 100,000 people. Archaeologists surmise that this area, called the Main Plaza, may have been the designated place for many ritual performances. At the southeast end of the plaza is the famed **Templo de Quetzalcóatl,** a striking construction decorated with amazing stone carvings of serpent heads. Although not as tall as either the Sun or Moon Pyramids, the elaborate carvings on the Templo de Quetzalcóatl attest to its ritual importance. While the sculptures on three sides of the pyramid have been destroyed, a protective platform built by the Teotihuacanos themselves (for unknown reasons) on the front has protected the artwork on that side.

The remains of 137 people were found

buried here. They were apparently sacrificed, their hands tied behind their backs, during the construction of the pyramid. Scholars believe they were killed as part of a warfare cult that was regulated by the position of Venus in its 584-day celestial cycle. Many of these individuals wore collars made of imitation human jawbones with teeth carved from shell, as well as several real maxillae and mandibles. The corpses were placed in pits with more than 2,100 pieces of worked shell and numerous obsidian blades and points.

Next to the pyramid are two large palaces that may have been living quarters or offices for the city's rulers.

Calzada de los Muertos (Avenue of the Dead)

This causeway, now probably about half the length it was in the city's heyday, runs north–south between the visitors center (at the south end) and the Pyramid of the Moon (at the north end). It received its ominous name from the Aztecs, who apparently believed the structures lining the causeway contained the graves of giants who had died and become gods. Modern archaeologists instead believe these buildings were ancient residential complexes.

Pirámide del Sol (Pyramid of the Sun)

This is one of the largest, most impressive pyramids in the world. As it now stands, the pyramid (actually five stepped platforms) measures 225 meters on each side and just under 70 meters in height. Two tunnels burrowed by modern researchers into the core of the pyramid, however, indicate that it was first 215 meters on each side and 63 meters high and was later enlarged to its current height. The hike up is steep and—on the frequent dusty, hot days—exhausting. Take your time, but be prepared for some fantastic views on a clear day. The stark, unadorned lines of the pyramid add a certain austere grandeur to the imposing structure. A temple once stood atop the pyramid, but it has long since been destroyed.

© ELENA PAPPAS

sculpture detail, Teotihuacán

In 1971, a long stairway was discovered that ended in a four-chamber lava cave 100 meters long under the pyramid. Archaeologists believe the cave was considered by the city's builders to be a sacred entryway to another world, which is why they chose the location to build their largest pyramid.

Pirámide de la Luna (Pyramid of the Moon)

At the north end of the Calzada de los Muertos is the Pyramid of the Moon, centered on the Plaza of the Moon, which along with the Main Plaza at the Ciudadela was one of the principal ritual areas in the city. Built later than the other principal monuments in the city, the Pyramid of the Moon is 46 meters high and not as steep a climb as the Pyramid of the Sun, but the views over the city and surrounding countryside are still great. When approaching the pyramid along the Avenida de los Muertos, note how the outline of the structure mirrors that of Cerro Gordo, the mountain behind it.

TEOTIHUACÁN'S VIOLENT PAST

For many years, archaeologists had theorized that Teotihuacán was a relatively peaceful society, especially compared to the bloody excesses of the later Aztecs. In part this was because of the lack of artistic depictions glorifying human sacrifice and war. But excavations underneath the 1,900-year-old Pyramid of the Moon by a Mexican-Japanese-American team are changing that view.

In 1999, a burial chamber containing what may be the remains of a retainer of an early Teotihuacán ruler was discovered in the Pyramid of the Moon by an excavation team led by American and Mexican archaeologists. Inside the chamber, which has been dated to 150 B.C., the team found the skeleton of an adult male who had been bound and sacrificed. Surrounding the skeleton were more than 400 burial offerings, including obsidian and greenstone figurines, ceremonial obsidian blades and spear points, pyrite mirrors, and conch and other shells, along with the remains of eight hawks or falcons, two jaguars, a wolf, a puma, and various serpents, all of which may have been buried alive. The buried individual is thought to be a royal attendant of some kind.

Further excavations through successively earlier levels of the construction of the pyramid have led to further spectacular finds, many with indications of militaristic and sacrificial rituals associated with political and religious power. Five tombs in total have been uncovered, the last (in 2004) of which included 12 sacrificial human remains (all with hands bound and 10 which were decapitated) as well as sacrificial animals associated with war such as wolves, jaguars and eagles. All in all, the archeologists believe it must have been a terrifyingly bloody spectacle.

Researchers have long speculated about any possible links between the Teotihuacanos and the apparently totally separate Mayan civilization further south. One of the earlier tombs, discovered in 2002 at the Pyramid of the Moon, deepened the mystery by revealing links with the Maya: three ceremonially arranged bodies buried with jade jewelry of Mayan design.

The Pyramid of the Moon excavations are complete, but the tantalizing evidence they unearthed suggests that the city has many secrets yet to reveal.

EXCURSIONS

Visitors Center

Back at the south end of the site, the visitors center holds a museum, several craft shops, a bookstore, a restaurant, and restrooms. The 2nd-floor restaurant enjoys a captive audience so is a bit overpriced. The museum is worth visiting to see the scale model of the city at its height.

Tips and Information

Wear good walking shoes—the Avenue of the Dead alone stretches about four kilometers. A hat, sunblock, and water are musts to carry with you. Remember, you are at an altitude of 2,300 meters; unless you're accustomed to this, take the steep stairs slowly. The best time of day to visit the site (594/956-0052, daily 8 A.M.–6 P.M., $4.50, free for Mexicans on Sun.) for pictures and peace is 8 A.M., when the ticket-takers open

the gate. The tour buses start arriving around 10 A.M. Weekends are the busiest, especially on Sunday, when admission is free. A parking fee is also charged. For more information on the history and archaeology of the site, see the websites http://archaeology.asu.edu/teo or http://astro.temple.edu/~dcm/teo.htm.

Getting There and Away

The ruins lie about 50 kilometers northeast of Mexico City. To get there by bus from Mexico City, look for the sign Autobuses Sahagun at the northwest end of the Terminal Central del Norte. Buses leave the terminal every 30 minutes 5 A.M.–6 P.M.; the trip to Teotihuacán takes about an hour. You want the bus marked Los Pirámides, otherwise you may end up at the nearby city of San Juan Teotihuacán. To return to the city, catch your bus at the entrance gate of the museum. The last bus leaves the main entrance at 6 p.m. Buses also leave every 15 minutes from outside the northwest entrance.

If you're driving from Mexico City to Teotihuacán, you have a choice of toll-free México 132D or the toll road (*cuota*) México 85D. The toll road usually has lighter traffic and is quicker. Taking a taxi is a reasonable option, especially if you are going with a group of people.

Acolman

Along the free road to Teotihuacán from Mexico City, and easily visible from the toll road, is the 16th-century Augustinian church and monastery complex of Acolman (595/957-1644, daily 9 a.m.–6 p.m., $3), noted for its fine plateresque facade and the churchyard cross in front, carved with a mix of Catholic and Amerindian motifs. Inside the cloister are a series of religious murals. The fortresslike monastery makes a great stop-off while visiting Teotihuacán, especially if you've got your own car. By public transport, you can either take the local (not direct) bus between San Juan Teotihuacán and Indios Verdes Metro stop in Mexico City, or hop a *colectivo* (small bus) from Teotihuacán ruins headed toward Ecatepec and alight right next to the monastery for $0.80.

TEXCOCO

A large, dusty town northeast of Mexico City, on what used to be the eastern shores of the nearly vanished Lake Texcoco, Texcoco is not much to see itself, but it has three interesting sites to visit nearby, little seen by foreigners: Molino de Flores, Universidad de Chapingo, and the Baños de Nezahualcóyotl. Texcoco was founded originally around A.D. 1200 by the Toltecs and later became the seat of the Acolhua empire, which was one of the principal allies of Aztecs. The city reached its height under Acolmiztli Nezahualcóyotl (1402–1472), the famed king of Texcoco. Not only was he a brilliant poet (his translated verse remains powerful even to modern readers), but he was also a budding monotheist and a superlative engineer. It was Nezahualcóyotl who designed the complex of dams controlling the interlocking lakes of the valley, which were destroyed by Cortés during the conquest. Because of Texcoco's importance, Augustinian monks established one of the first missions in Mexico nearby at Acolman, just off the highway to Teotihuacán.

The hills to the east of Texcoco, forming part of the Valle de México, remain a heavily indigenous area, populated by Nahua farming communities. In many of these villages, the residents still don't speak Spanish. Ruins from the pre-Hispanic era are found all over this little-explored region. San Miguel Coatlinchan, a village in the hills southeast of Texcoco, is the original site of the Tlaloc statue that now sits outside of the Museo Nacional de Antropología. Although the statue was taken decades ago, the villagers are still reputed to be extremely angry that their rain god was stolen by the government. A 16th-century church and convent in town is worth a visit. Another nearby village with many ruins around is San Luis Huexotla.

Nowadays Texcoco is a primarily agricultural town, and to celebrate that, the town holds the annual **Feria del Caballo.** The party is held just before Easter (Semana Santa). This blowout bash, known as "La Cantina Más Grande de México" (The Biggest Bar in Mexico), features horse shows, bullfights, lots of good food, and very loud *ranchera* music.

To get to Texcoco, take Primera Plus or one of several other bus lines leaving basically constantly from the TAPO eastern terminal in Mexico City. The 15-minute ride costs $2. By car, take the Circuito Interior, and look for the exit to Texcoco (marked Via Rápida Texcoco) just north of the airport. The toll costs $2 but is definitely worth it rather than struggling through the maze of back roads and slums on the free road.

Universidad de Chapingo

Three kilometers south of Texcoco is this university, one of the premier agricultural schools in the country. The university, started in 1923, is not a particular attraction in itself, although

EXCURSIONS

the grassy grounds are nice enough. But in one of the main buildings is the **Capilla Riveriana** (595/952-1500, www.chapingo.mx, Mon.–Fri. 10 A.M.–3 P.M., Sat.–Sun. 10 A.M.–5 P.M. $3 for foreigners, $1 for Mexicans), a chapel painted by famed Mexican muralist Diego Rivera between 1924 and 1927. The socialist proclivities of Rivera are much in evidence here, with hammer-and-sickle symbols throughout the murals. Also prominent is an earth mother theme, possibly a nod to the school's agricultural focus. Check out the wooden doors at the entrance, carved by Abraham López according to a design by Rivera. A guide offers a complete tour of the chapel and the adjacent building (a hacienda dating from 1690) for free during the week, and there are audio guides for rent on weekends for $1. Check out the pre-Hispanic stone carving in the entrance to the hacienda. To get to the university from Texcoco, hop a *microbus* (small bus) from downtown for $0.50, or take a taxi for about $3.

Parque Nacional Molino de Flores

The ruins of this 16th-century hacienda (Mon.– Fri. 9 A.M.–2 P.M., Sat.– Sun. 11 A.M.–5 P.M.), three kilometers east of Texcoco in a small, tree-filled valley, is now a park frequented on weekends by local folks. The old hacienda was originally built in 1567 to produce cloth, and 20 years later it became a wheat mill. The mill passed through a variety of hands over the next centuries and continued functioning until the 1910–1920 Mexican Revolution. It was expropriated by the government in 1937.

Some of the hacienda buildings have been restored, while others remain in ruins, but all are very beautiful and well worth a visit to get an idea of what life might have been like on a hacienda. Free guided tours are available in Spanish only. The park is mobbed on weekends, so it's best to come during the week. Taxis from downtown Texcoco cost $2.50, or you can hop a bus for $0.50.

Baños de Nezahualcóyotl

These ruins (daily 10 A.M.–5 P.M., free), surprisingly impressive considering how little-known they are, cover a hill just above the town of San Nicolás, about six kilometers east of Texcoco. Whether they were built by Nezahualcóyotl himself is not certain, but one can be sure he made use of them. To get to the ruins, formally known as Zona Arqueológica de Tetzcotzinco, take a bus ($1) or a taxi ($3.50) from Texcoco to San Nicolás. By car, follow the road to Molino de Flores; just before arriving at the park, look for a right turn continuing uphill. From this junction it's three kilometers to San Nicolás. There is no gate per se, and when I went there was no one watching over the site, either. I had no problems and saw nobody threatening, but it's probably better to come on weekends when there are other visitors around.

Right at the entrance to San Nicolás, a dirt road to the right leads to a modern public swimming pool (where you can leave your car if you came in one). Just behind the parking lot, a dirt road leads uphill; it quickly becomes a footpath. Passing a carved cave, you will come to a rebuilt staircase leading

EXCURSIONS

© CHRIS HUMPHREY

Baños de Nezahualcóyotl, near Texcoco just east of Mexico City

to the first stone bath, facing west over the valley. Here you can continue uphill to more baths or take side paths winding around the hillside. Wherever you go, you'll find carved stones and baths all over the place. On the back (east) side are the reconstructed ruins of a major temple built into the hillside, as well as the remains of a causeway and aqueduct leading up into the mountains. More ruins are found continuing east. Visiting these ruins makes for a great alternative day trip from Mexico City instead of going to the same tourist destinations as everyone else. On your way back down, you might consider taking a refreshing dip in the public pool for $3 adults, $2.50 kids under 12.

TEPOTZOTLÁN

Known for its magnificent churrigueresque convent and church, Tepotzotlán also holds a cobbled-street colonial city center—mostly unspoiled either by modernization or chic restorations—and the country's largest and most complete colonial history museum. Very popular with Mexico City tourists, the small town makes a good day-trip destination from Mexico City, about an hour away (43 kilometers) by bus from the Terminal del Norte. If you're driving up from the capital, take México 57D about 37 kilometers north toward Querétaro. The well-marked turnoff to Tepotzotlán lies just before the tollbooth.

Templo de San Francisco Javier and Plaza Hidalgo

The single-towered Spanish church and the attached convent form the nucleus of the town's tourist attractions. The simple early baroque side *portada* (entry) facing the main street corresponds to the first stage of the construction of the church, 1670–1682, and is topped by a niche containing an image of San Ignacio de Loyola. The front entry facing the Plaza Hidalgo is classic late baroque, or *churrigueresco,* and was crafted between 1760 and 1762. This much larger facade consists of many *estípites* (sculpted columns) filled with saints—I lost count at 22. San Francisco

sombreros for sale in front of the Templo de San Francisco Javier

Javier, of course, stands in the main niche, right above a rosette window.

Sunday is a very popular time to visit the plaza and church, not just for Mass but to avail oneself of the food vendors who fill the plaza in front. The plaza and area surrounding the church and convent were restored by INAH in 1993–1994.

Museo Nacional de Virreinato

This large, impressive museum (55/5876-0245, www.munavi.inah.gob.mx, Tues.–Sun. 9 A.M.–5:45 P.M., $4.30, free Sun.) occupies a magnificent ex-convent that once served as a Jesuit college of Indian languages. The convent chapels, cloisters, library, refectory, kitchen, and other spaces were constructed between 1606 and 1767, and the overall three-story stone structure is considered an excellent model of the evolution of Spanish colonial architecture in Mexico. Even if you're not especially interested in the art contained in the museum, the convent architecture alone—with its thick walls, winding passageways, arched cloisters, and heavy wood-paneled doors and windows—is worth seeing. On the 3rd floor is a terrace overlooking the town.

Several areas of the building conserve the convent's original art, which was extensive in and of itself, and in 1964, when INAH converted the ex-convent into a national museum, the collection was further enriched with religious art pieces from the Catedral Metropolitana in Mexico City. A few rooms are devoted to the history of Mexico's conquest, with displays of Spanish armor and weaponry. Other rooms contain an extensive collection of colonial textiles, including a display of religious garments worn by monks, nuns, and priests. There's no shortage of gold and silver, and you'll see vestments woven with these precious metals, plus candlesticks, chalices, and crucifixes of silver and gold inlaid with precious stones. Also worth noting are the collections of religious calligraphy, furniture, porcelains, and ceramics.

The selection of religious paintings rivals that of the Museo Nacional de Arte in Mexico City, added to which is an ample supply of religious sculpture. A capilla doméstica (domestic chapel, meant for the use of convent residents only) on the ground floor contains exquisite retablos (altarpieces) and religious paintings.

Restaurants
On the upper floor of the old convent attached to the church, **La Ostería del Convento de Tepotzotlán Restaurant Bar** (mains $4–6) offers pre-Hispanic-style delicacies such as gusanos de maguey (cactus worms) and escamoles (ant larvae), as well as such familiar central Mexican dishes as chiles en nogada (stuffed chiles in a nut sauce), crepas de huitlacoche (corn fungus crepes), queso fundido (Mexican-style fondue), caldo tepotzotlán (a local soup), and fajitas de pollo (chicken fajitas), plus a long list of tequila brands.

At the opposite end of the plaza in front of the church is a row of restaurants, including **El Rancho Restaurante Bar.**

Food vendors on Plaza Hidalgo, in front of the Templo de San Francisco Javier and the Museo Nacional del Virreinato, sell huaraches (corn snack in the shape of a sandal, hence the name) and other antojitos (snacks) as well as pulque curado (fermented cactus juice).

Shops
If you're setting up house in Mexico City, Tepotzotlán is a good place to look for rustic wooden furniture, custom wrought iron, and terra-cotta pottery. Opposite the plaza in front of the church are a few artesanía (artisan) shops.

TULA ARCHAEOLOGICAL SITE
Tollan, today known as Tula, was founded in the 10th century, after the decline of Teotihuacán and well before the arrival of the Aztecs. Evidence suggests that refugees from Teotihuacán caused a rapid increase in Tula's population. It is possible that the city was the capital of the Toltec-Chichimeca Empire. And though this was a powerful nation, it never grew as large as Teotihuacán. At its peak, archaeologists believe, Tollan covered an area of 13 square kilometers and held a population of 60,000.

Scholars believe Tollan was engulfed in a great fire that destroyed much of the city, and by A.D. 1125, the empire began to decline. Sacked and looted by outsiders, Tollan was abandoned before A.D. 1200. The Aztecs, who arrived in the Valle de México shortly thereafter, considered the Toltecs their imperial and cultural ancestors, not unlike how the Romans viewed the ancient Greeks.

Little is left of the once-great city (Tues.–Sun. 10 A.M.–6 P.M., $3.30), which is not as frequently visited as nearby Teotihuacán. Despite the dusty desolation of the place, locals (and a few foreign New Age disciples) claim the site emits spiritual forces. The main attraction of Tula is the **Pyramid of the Morning Star,** or Templo de Tlahuizcalpantecuhtli. The top of the pyramid is the resting place for four massive stone warriors known as the **Atlanteans,** for which Tula is famed. Each warrior is 4.6 meters tall, wears a butterfly-shaped breastplate and feathered headdress, and holds an atlatl (spear thrower) in one hand. Around the sides of the pyramid are reliefs of eagles eating human hearts, as well as coyotes, jaguars, and imaginary creatures.

Other structures at the site feature carvings of snakes, skeletons, and richly dressed nobles. If you look closely, you can see remnants of the paint that once covered the carvings. A ball court here is identical in size to one at the archaeological site of Xochicalco, in Morelos. Some speculate that this is the original Mesoamerican ball court, where the game was conceived.

The site entrance fee includes parking and entrance to a small museum. Vendors sell soft drinks and souvenirs. A tourist information module provides some basic information Tuesday–Sunday 9 A.M.–4 P.M. next to the Municipal Palace of the nearby town of Tula, also known as Tula de Allende.

Restaurants

If you're planning a day trip to Tula and are looking for a quick bite on the walk to the ruins, try **Pizzas In/Out** (Melchor Ocampo 20, mains $2–5). The restaurant serves good Mexican food, hand-tossed pizzas, and a dozen different types of burgers. There's another location on Hidalgo between Moctezuma and Zaragoza.

Taquería Parrillada Country (Melchor Ocampo in front of Pizzas In/Out, mains $2–6) serves tacos, burgers, and good Mexican cuisine in a down-home setting with checkered tablecloths and friendly service. The restaurant's second location faces the town plaza between Leandro Valle and Hidalgo.

Across the street from Hotel Catedral is **Chicas Tortas,** a lively sandwich shop with loud music that's open into the evening.

Cafetería-Nevería Campanario (Zaragoza across from the church) is an excellent choice for well-made coffee, drinks, or a light meal.

For a more local experience, head to the **Plaza del Taco,** a cavernous "taco mall" on the corner of Colegio Militar and 5 de Mayo. Vendors operate individual stalls selling various specialty tacos—but don't expect anything fancy; this is strictly wooden benches and meat-laden tortillas.

Helados Bing (Melchor Ocampo betw. Hotel Sharon and the pizzeria) is an ice-cream shop that also sells snacks, soft drinks, and good coffee.

Hotels

Most visitors to Tula are day-trippers from Mexico City, but if you have a keen interest in exploring the archaeological site, or if you're just looking to stay in a place where tourists rarely spend the night, Tula has several options.

$15-30

Near the center of town, **Hotel Cuellar** (Cinco de Mayo23, 773/732-2920, www.hotelcuellar .com, $25 s, $30 d) offers 48 basic, small but clean rooms that open onto a brick-laid parking area and garden. **Hotel Catedral** (Zaragoza 106, 773/732-0813, $30 s/d) offers similar-quality rooms with cable TV, parking, and an open street-front lobby.

$50-75

The most modern rooms in town are to be found at **Hotel Sharon** (Callejon de la Cruz 1, 773/732-0976, $58 for room with two double beds). A large facility with banquet areas and restaurant, the hotel has 120 rooms and helpful staff, and is less than 10 minutes' walk from the archaeological site.

Getting There and Away

Autotransportes Valle del Mezquital (55/5567-6791 in Mexico City and 773/732-9600 in Tula, www.gvm.com.mx) runs buses to Mexico City's Terminal del Norte for Tula every 30 minutes, 7 A.M.–9 P.M.; the fare is $4.50. The bus will drop you off in town; you can either walk the three kilometers to the site (about 15–20 minutes), flag a cab, or take the minibus marked "Tlahuelilpan." You might want to make arrangements with your cab or the minibus to be picked up for the return to town. The last bus to Mexico City leaves Tula at 8 P.M.

If you're coming by car, take México 57 from Mexico City toward Querétaro. At Tepotzotlán it becomes a toll road, México 57D. Continue till you see signs on the right directing you to Tula; this road is México 126, which takes you right through town. Look for signs directing you to Las Ruinas; from town the sign says Parque Nacional Tula.

PACHUCA

The state capital of Hidalgo lies in the Sierra Madre Oriental, an important part of Mexico's silver belt. Mining has driven the local economy since before the Spanish arrival in 1534, and it continues to be the most important industry. The hills above the city have been worked off and on for centuries and are riddled with mine shafts and ancient slag heaps. The region still produces more than a million ounces of silver a year.

Most visitors find themselves in Pachuca either to visit Fototeca, Mexico's national photography archive, or because they're on their way to Parque Nacional El Chico.

Around the Centro

Pachuca is a town of narrow, twisting streets climbing steep hillsides. Though not brimming with architectural treasures, it's worth spending a couple of hours strolling around the *centro.*

The center of town is the broad **Plaza de la Independencia,** punctuated by the 40-meter-high **Torre del Reloj** (Clock Tower), decorated with four carved statues and a carillon imported from Austria. The **Casa Colorado,** built in the 18th century, is now the city's law court, while the 17th-century **Las Casas** formerly served as a hall for storing the *quinta real,* or royal fifth—the percentage of the area's mined wealth automatically owed to the Spanish crown.

At the modern **Palacio de Gobierno** (in the civic center a few blocks from the Plaza de la Independencia) you'll find a statue of Benito Juárez by Juan Leonardo Cordero and murals by Pachucan painter Jesús Becerril.

South of the plaza and west of the civic center, **Parque Hidalgo** is a favorite Sunday haunt for Pachucans out for a stroll, vendors, and mariachis. On Avenida Guerrero near Salazar is the large enclosed **Mercado de Barreteros.**

Centro Cultural de Hidalgo/Fototeca

A 10-minute walk southeast of the Plaza de la Independencia leads to the former monastery of San Francisco, which has seen many different residents during its 400-year existence, including monks, horses, and criminals. The Conde de Regla, who made a fabulous fortune in local silver mines, is buried in the adjoining church. Today the Instituto Nacional de Antropología e Historia (INAH) runs a fine group of museums in the old ex-convent.

The **Museo Regional de Historia** (771/714-3989, Tues.–Sun. 10 A.M.–6 P.M., free) displays archaeological and ethnological artifacts representing the Huastec, Aztec, Toltec, Otomi, and northern Amerindian cultures. You'll see displays of folk art, crafts, everyday utensils, and traditional dress.

On the 2nd floor of the ex-convent is the **Museo Nacional de Fotografía** (771/719-1274 or 771/714-3653, museodelafotografia@inah .gob.mx, same hours as the Museo Regional, free, guided tours Tues. and Fri. by appt.), a small but interesting collection of historical Mexican photography, from early daguerreotypes to Antonio Casasola's famed Revolution-era pictures to the work of modern photographers such as Graciela Iturbide and Nacho López.

In the same building as the photography museum but with a separate entrance is **Fototeca** (771/714-3653, www.sinafo.inah.gob.mx, Mon.–Fri. 8 A.M.–3 P.M.), where INAH has cataloged 1.2 million photographs on computer and can search for them by photographer, date, location, or subject. The Fototeca will make high-quality 8-by-10-inch prints of any of its photographs for $34, plus reprint permission fees if required. It's best to call ahead and arrange an appointment so a staff member can help you run a search. If you have the information needed, photos can be ordered by phone and delivered to you by courier for an additional charge.

Restaurants

Pachuca's regional food specialties include *mixiotes,* tamale-type ingredients baked in maguey leaves; *barbacoa,* lamb wrapped in maguey leaves and baked underground; and *escamoles,* fried ant eggs. The large numbers of British miners who lived in Pachuca at the end of the 19th century introduced *fútbol* (soccer) to Mexico and also brought with them the tradition of pasties. Here called *pastes,* these little pies stuffed with minced meat and vegetables are found all over Pachuca and surrounding towns. They make a great inexpensive midday snack.

A number of small cafés surround the town center. On the side of the Plaza de la Independencia at Matamoros is **Restaurante La Blanca** (daily 8 A.M.–11 P.M.), a cafeteria-style restaurant with inexpensive meals and snacks.

Excellent homemade tacos, with nine fillings to choose from, can be found at the cozy **Mesón de Los Ángeles Gómez** (Guerrero 723, just up from the Plaza Juárez, Mon.–Sat. 9 A.M.–11 P.M.). During the day you can buy breakfasts, *comidas corridas* (set meals), and snacks, and it starts serving tacos in the evening. **Hotel Noriega** also has a decent dining room.

Helados Santa Clara at the side of the square on Matamoros, and another branch on Allende, serves good ice cream, sweets, and even a decent espresso.

Hotels
$15-30
Two blocks below the plaza, **Hotel Noriega** (Matamoros 305, 771/715-1555, $20 s, $25 d) offers 40 large, clean rooms in an old colonial building, popular with the occasional young traveler who comes to Pachuca. Though not as nice as the Noriega and a bit more expensive, **Hotel de los Baños** (just off the plaza at Matamoros 205, 771/713-0700, $23 s, $27 d) also has decent low-priced rooms.

$30-50
On the square is **Gran Hotel Independencia** (Independencia 116, 771/715-0515, $40 s/d, $45 d with two beds), remodeled in 2001. Each of the 35 simple, brightly painted rooms around the spacious open patio has a phone and TV. The rooms in the front of the building have a small balcony.

$50-75
Hotel Emily (Hidalgo at the corner of Plaza de la Independencia, 771/715-0849, $49 s, $66 d) is one of the better places in the town center (though still nothing special), with a restaurant and parking.

Over $110
Out on the highway exit to Mexico City is **Hotel Fiesta Inn** (Carr. México–Pachuca Km 85.5, 771/717-0700, rooms start from $150, call for promotional rates), a modern hotel with an adjoining nine-hole golf course. The hotel has a restaurant and bar, and guests have access to a gym, tennis courts, and a pool at a nearby health club.

Practicalities
The municipal tourist office (ground floor of the Torre del Reloj on Allende, 771/718 4454, Mon.–Wed. 9 A.M.–3 P.M., Thurs.–Sun. 10 A.M.–6 P.M.) offers a selection of decent printed information, but only in Spanish. The **state tourist office** (Av. Revolución 1300, 771/711-4150 or 771/718-4454) is a fair way out of the center of town and not convenient for pedestrians.

The post office is at Juárez and Iglesias. There's a *lavandería* (laundry) at Centro Comercial Constitución L-14, and an Internet café on Calle Doria.

Several banks in the *centro* will change money and have internationally connected ATM machines.

The Hospital General is on Avenida Madero, on the road toward Tulancingo, while Farmacia del Pueblo is at Matamoros 205.

From Mexico City, México 85D (toll road) is a good way to get out of Mexico City quickly, and the toll to Pachuca costs $4. To get to Pachuca's **central bus station,** hop the city bus that leaves from in front of the tourist office on Allende. Several lines run buses all day between the Pachuca terminal and Mexico City's Terminal del Norte ($5). **Ovni** offers frequent buses 7 A.M.–7 P.M. to Tula ($5). **ADO** (771/713-2910) runs four buses daily to Poza Rica ($11) and two daily to Tampico ($27). **Estrella Blanca** (771/713-2747) departs every hour for Querétero ($14). The same company (but a different phone number for information, 771/719-1131) also runs the direct bus to the Mexico City airport 15 times daily for $9. **Primera Plus** (771/713-3303) offers frequent buses to Puebla ($8), as well as two daily to Jalapa ($14) and Veracruz ($20).

◖ PARQUE NACIONAL EL CHICO

In the hills above Pachuca is Parque Nacional El Chico, a densely pine-forested park covering 2,700 hectares, with campsites, hiking and mountain-biking trails, and fishing holes. El Chico has a reputation for being exceptionally safe and *tranquilo* (tranquil), an attractive place to enjoy the outdoors, and camp if you like, close to Mexico City. Just remember to bring warm clothes as it can get surprisingly chilly, especially at night if you're sleeping in a tent. Within the park is the old mining village of Mineral del Chico, perched on a mountain plateau high above Pachuca, with beautiful views. For more information, see the park website at www.parqueelchico.gob.mx.

Rock Climbing

El Chico is best-known among Mexicans as one of the premier rock climbing playgrounds near Mexico City (not to be confused with Potrero Chico, a much larger rock-climbing area near the northern city of Monterrey), with several dozen bolted routes up the many rock formations in the park. Most routes rate 5.7–5.9. The two hardest routes are 5.12. **La Ventana,** the 150-meter tower reaching the highest point in the park, has three routes up it ranging between 5.8 and 5.10.

A fine place to start looking around for climbing routes and to talk to other climbers is the parking lot around the **Albergue Alpino Las Ventanas,** a hostel of sorts where you can crash with a sleeping bag on weekends, on the south side of the main road running through the park. Right behind the building is a rock formation aptly named **La Botella** (the bottle), a 40-meter free-standing rock with a couple of 5.7–5.8 routes. Behind La Botella are cliffs with dozens of bolted routes of varying difficulty.

One good place to inquire about local guides for rock climbing and bungee jumping is **Restaurante Las Güeras** (Morelos s/n, 771/715-2941) in Mineral del Chico.

Camping, Hiking, and Biking

Apart from rock climbing, the park is a wonderful place to wander about in the forest, breathe the crisp clean air, and enjoy the views. Several small valleys make great campsites, and locals charge around $2 for permission to pitch a tent. You can also leave your car at the Albergue parking lot for $1.50 and hike up to pitch a tent on the ridge above, with a lovely view overlooking the park and surrounding countryside. The Albergue itself has 50 simple cots in a dormitory room on weekends only for $10 per person—to make reservations, call the Pachuca office at 771/715-6686 or write to aalpino@parqueelchico.gob.mx. Just across the road is a small restaurant and store, also open weekends only. Remember to take warm clothing. Cabins ($40) and platforms for tents ($15) are also available at the campsites of Dos Aguas, Conejos, and Los Cedros—see the park website for more information.

Mountain bikers will also find a couple of decent trails descending different sides of the hill from the area around the Albergue. One great (though slightly hairy, especially if it's wet) trail descends from the south side of the main road, shortly before reaching the Albergue coming from Pachuca, and comes out after a steep and fast ride to a small reservoir by the village of **Estanzuela.** From here you can ride the paved road a couple of steep kilometers back up to the Albergue.

Other trails head downhill from the north side of the road near the Albergue through the woods to Mineral del Chico, and then return uphill on the paved road to the Albergue. Still more trails are located near the campsites of Dos Aguas, Conejos, and Los Cedros, for a nominal charge of $3.

Restaurants

The food market in Mineral del Chico is a great place to have breakfast, lunch, or a snack, and it claims with some justification to have the best view of any market in the country. Try the beef-and-onion-stuffed *pastelitos, mole rojo, arroz con leche,* or chiles rellenos.

Two restaurants in Mineral del Chico that offer unadorned but well-cooked meals for around $6 are **Las Güeras** (Morelos s/n, 771/715-2941, daily 9 A.M.–8 P.M.) and **La Morenita** (Jardín Hidalgo 25, 771/715-2055, Mon.–Sat. 9 A.M.–10 P.M., Sun. until 6 P.M.). Las Güeras is also a good place to find guides for rock climbing and bungee jumping.

Hotels

In Mineral del Chico, **Posada El Amanecer** (Morelos 3, 771/715-4812, $70 s/d) has rooms in a converted convent. Pay a bit more and get a lovely wood-burning fireplace— well worth it on those cold nights. The hotel also has a restaurant.

At Km 19 of the Pachuca–Mineral del Chico road, just before the entrance to Mineral del Chico on the left-hand side, is **Hotel Paraíso** (771/715-5654, $150 s/d), a modern hotel with good services and panoramic views of the rivers in the valley below.

You can also find a number of houses renting rooms or entire cabins in the area at the state government website, http://turismo.hidalgo.gob.mx; click on "Haciendas y Casas R."

Practicalities

To get to El Chico by car, take the highway leaving Pachuca toward Tampico. About 15 minutes from the city you'll see a paved road angling off to the left, clearly marked El Chico. Turn here and continue driving several kilometers into the park. This road continues all the way through the middle of the park to the town of **Mineral El Chico,** an attractive mining village that has become a favorite weekend spot for Pachucans.

Regular minibuses run between Mercado Benito Juárez in Pachuca and Mineral del Chico; the fare is about $1 for the whole ride, or less to get dropped off at the Albergue. The last minibus descends from the park to Pachuca at 7 P.M. In Pachuca, catch the buses at the north end of town, where the Viaducto turns into the highway leading to Tampico. Buses also leave the central bus station in Pachuca for Mineral del Chico three times a day.

Cuernavaca

Nicknamed the "City of Eternal Spring" for its balmy climate, Cuernavaca was first founded as a city of the Tlahuica people, named Cuauhnáhuac (Place at the Edge of the Forest). It fell quickly to Spanish swords in 1521 and was granted to Cortés by the Spanish crown as one of his *encomiendas* (feudal-style land grants).

Cortés was the first of many Mexico City residents to keep a vacation home in Cuernavaca; his was built out of the ruins of the city pyramid.

Many of Mexico's most powerful politicians and businesspeople have built luxury villas here for their weekend getaways. While you won't see much of Cuernavaca's wealthy residents, who are safely ensconced behind their mansion walls, the city center area is a very popular day trip for Mexico City residents, and it is mobbed on weekends and national holidays.

The city also hosts about 20 Spanish-language schools and a correspondingly large contingent of foreign-language students.

If you read Malcolm Lowry's *Under the Volcano* and hope to find the village of Quauhnahuac in which the fictional consul passes a singular day, you will be disappointed. With a population of more than one million, Cuernavaca has grown dramatically in the past few decades, adding several kilometers of nondescript concrete neighborhoods surrounding the colonial city center.

One website with information on Cuernavaca and the state of Morelos is www.morelos-travel.com.

Orientation

Although Cuernavaca covers a lot of territory

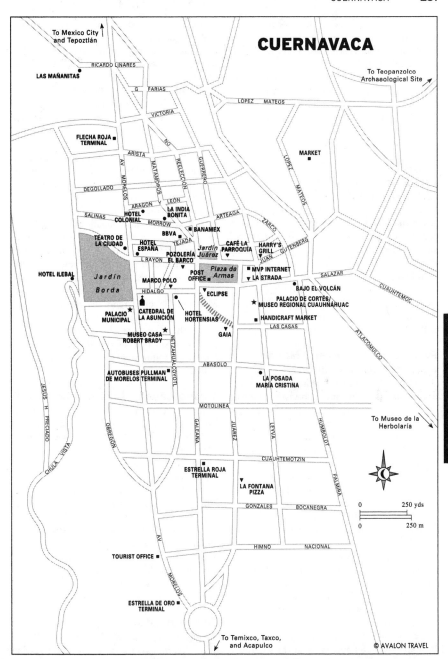

CUERNAVACA

To Mexico City and Tepoztlán

To Teopanzolco Archaeological Site

LAS MAÑANITAS

RICARDO LINARES

G   FARIAS

VICTORIA

LÓPEZ   MATEOS

FLECHA ROJA TERMINAL

ARISTA

DEGOLLADO

SALINAS

ARAGON   LEÓN

HOTEL COLONIAL

LA INDIA BONITA

MORROW

ARTEAGA

BBVA   BANAMEX

TEJADA

TEATRO DE LA CIUDAD

HOTEL ESPAÑA

POZOLERÍA EL BARCO

Jardín Juárez

CAFÉ LA PARROQUIA

HARRY'S GRILL

L RAYON

Jardín Borda

MARCO POLO

HIDALGO

POST OFFICE

Plaza de Armas

MVP INTERNET

LA STRADA

BAJO EL VOLCÁN

SALAZAR

HOTEL ILEBAL

ECLIPSE

PALACIO MUNICIPAL

CATEDRAL DE LA ASUNCIÓN

HOTEL HORTENSIAS

PALACIO DE CORTÉS/ MUSEO REGIONAL CUAUHNÁHUAC

HANDICRAFT MARKET

LAS CASAS

MUSEO CASA ROBERT BRADY

GAIA

ABASOLO

AUTOBUSES PULLMAN DE MORELOS TERMINAL

LA POSADA MARÍA CRISTINA

MOTOLINEA

To Museo de la Herbolaría

ESTRELLA ROJA TERMINAL

CUAUHTEMOTZIN

LA FONTANA PIZZA

GONZALES   BOCANEGRA

0   250 yds

0   250 m

TOURIST OFFICE

HIMNO   NACIONAL

ESTRELLA DE ORO TERMINAL

To Temixco, Taxco, and Acapulco

MARKET

LÓPEZ   MATEOS

ZARCO

GUTENBERG

SALAZAR

CUAUHTEMOC

ATLACOMULCO

JESUS H. PRECIADO

CHULA VISTA

OBREGON

NETZAHUALCOYOTL

GALEANA

JUÁREZ

LEYVA

HUMBOLDT

PALMIRA

AV. MORELOS

MORELOS

© AVALON TRAVEL

EXCURSIONS

these days, most places of interest to visitors are within easy walking distance of the two adjacent central squares, the Plaza de Armas and Jardín Juárez.

If possible, avoid visiting Cuernavaca on weekends, when the city center is invariably crowded with Mexico City tourists. If you do come on a weekend, be prepared for tremendous traffic returning to Mexico City on Sunday afternoon and evening.

SIGHTS
Plaza de Armas and Jardín Juárez

Plaza de Armas is the larger of the two plazas in the center of town. The tree-lined plaza is continually bustling with locals and visitors sitting on the many benches, reading papers, chatting with friends, or just watching the world go by.

Next to the plaza, smaller Jardín Juárez features a late-19th-century kiosk designed by French architect Alexandre Gustave Eiffel, of Eiffel Tower fame.

Palacio de Cortés and Museo Regional Cuauhnáhuac

Begun by Cortés in 1522, this austere, intimidating structure has more the look of a fortress than a luxury palace—a reminder that the Spaniards lived in fear of Indian uprisings in the early colonial era. Cortés lived between here and his palaces in Mexico City until 1540, when he returned to Spain. Since then, the building has served variously as a prison and the state legislature and now contains a museum of colonial and pre-Hispanic artifacts.

After viewing the museum collection, head upstairs to see the Diego Rivera mural on the 2nd floor, tracing the history of Cuernavaca from the Spanish invasion to the present. The mural was paid for by U.S. ambassador Dwight Morrow, who kept a house in Cuernavaca during his three years in Mexico. On the ground floor are the barely visible remains of the ancient pyramid destroyed by Cortés to build the palace.

The palace (777/312-8171, Tues.–Sun. 10 A.M.–7 P.M., $4.50) stands at the southeast end of the Plaza de Armas. A shop on the premises offers an excellent selection of books on history, as well as some art and travel in Mexico; it's open 11 A.M.–7 P.M.

Catedral de la Asunción

Opposite the Jardín Borda at the corner of Hidalgo and Morelos, Catedral de la Asunción (777/312-1290, daily 8 A.M.–8 P.M.) was built by Spanish architect Francisco Becerra, under Cortés's orders, beginning in 1529. Becerra, who also designed the Palacio Cortés, gave the church a similarly intimidating, unadorned facade. Keep an eye out for the ominous-looking skull and crossbones over the main entrance, as well as a dramatic, Japanese-style painting inside depicting the martyring in Japan of Mexico's first saint, missionary San Felipe de Jesús. The painting (artist unknown) was discovered during remodeling work in the 1950s. For a taste of Catholicism with a singularly Mexican flavor, attend the mariachi Mass Sunday at 10:30 A.M. or 8 P.M.

On the other side of the cathedral courtyard is the smaller **Templo del Tercer Orden,** a newer baroque-style church with an ornate gilded altarpiece.

Museo Casa Robert Brady

Originally part of the cathedral cloister, the Museo Casa Robert Brady (Netzahualcóyotl 4, 777/314-3529, Tues.–Sun. 10 A.M.–6 P.M., $3) is an unusual private art museum containing the collection of an American who lived in Cuernavaca for 24 years but who had an eye for works of art from around the globe. The house, known as Casa de la Torre, contains an eclectic collection of more than 1,000 works of native art from the world over, as well as colonial antiques and a number of paintings by well-known artists such as Frida Kahlo, Rufino Tamayo, and Miguel Covarrubias. Spanish-speaking guides are available all day, but call in advance for tours in English.

Jardín Borda

Silver-mining empresario José de la Borda built this mansion and surrounding garden

(777/318-1038, Tues.–Sun. 10 A.M.–5:30 P.M., $3 adults, $1.50 children, free Sun.), which also served briefly as a holiday home for Emperor Maximilian and his wife, Carlota. Several of the rooms the ill-fated couple used have been restored and now house a small museum and occasional art exhibits.

The artificial "lake" is perhaps less lovely than in its former glory days, but the gardens are a lush haven in which to relax in the middle of the city. The entrance is on Morelos at Hidalgo, across from the cathedral.

Next door stands the pretty 18th-century **Iglesia de Nuestra Señora de Guadalupe,** which is also burial place of José de la Borda.

Palacio Municipal

Adjacent to Jardín Borda, this 19th-century town hall contains a museum (Morelos 265, Mon.–Fri. 9 A.M.– 6 P.M., free) displaying 20 paintings by Salvador Tarazona, each depicting a different facet of Morelos history (with a heavy emphasis on pre-Hispanic life).

La Casa del Olvido and Museo de la Herbolaría

This small house and garden (Matamoros 200, 777/312-3108, daily 9 A.M.–5 P.M., free) about 1.5 kilometers southeast of the town center received its nickname, "The House of Forgetting," because of a brief stay by Emperor Maximilian in the summer of 1866. For a few short weeks here, Maximilian consorted with Margarita Lefuisamo Sedano, the gardener's wife, avoiding his own fiercely ambitious wife Carlota, and the unpleasant realities of his precarious situation as leader of Mexico. Maximilian hadn't really wanted to come to Mexico in the first place (Carlota convinced him to do so), and once here, he managed to alienate everyone with his well-intentioned but ill-planned liberal ideas. He was deposed and executed the following year. Who can blame him for coming to this little spot and wishing it would all go away, if only for a short while?

Today the house holds a modest museum devoted to traditional indigenous medicine.

Teopanzolco Archaeological Site

In what is now the neighborhood of Colonia Vista Hermosa northeast of the city center, you can see the remains of a Tlahuica pyramid, with an Aztec pyramid built around it (daily 10 A.M.–5 P.M., $3.50). The first pyramid was built around A.D. 1200, while the second was still in progress when Cortés appeared on the scene. The site is located on Avenida Teopanzolco, cross street Usumacinta, close to Avenida Río Mayo. To get there, hop a Ruta 4 *combi* (minibus) from Avenida Morelos in the city center.

RESTAURANTS

While not known for any particular regional cuisine, Cuernavaca has a large selection of quality Mexican and international restaurants catering to visitors and part-time residents.

Coffee and Sweets

For breakfast and light meals, or just a cup of strong coffee, check out **Café La Parroquía** on the east side of Jardín Juárez, with tables out on the sidewalk.

Mexican

About a block from the *zócalo,* **Pozolería El Barco** (I. Rayon 5F, 777/313-2131, daily 11 A.M.–midnight) specializes in *pozole,* a flavorful hominy stew with your choice of pork or chicken (vegetarian upon request). Home delivery is also available.

Las Gaoneras (Av. Domingo Diez 1880, daily 1–9 P.M.) is a popular restaurant for its hearty meat cuts, *chiles en nogada,* soups, and other tasty Mexican cuisine, located a short taxi ride north of downtown.

A classic old-time Cuernavaca restaurant that first opened its doors in 1933, **La India Bonita** (Dwight Morrow 15, 777/318-6967, Tues.–Thurs. 8 A.M.–10 P.M., Fri.–Sat. 9 A.M.–11 P.M., Sun. 9 A.M.–6 P.M.) is named in reference to Emperor Maximilian's reputed lover. Favorite dishes include the *India Bonita* soup with squash flower and corn and the *cecina de Yecapixtla,* pork meat pounded flat and served with beans, fresh cheese, avocado, nopal cactus, and corn tortillas.

Just off the *zócalo* is **Gaia** (Benito Juárez 102, 777/312-3656, lunch and dinner Tues.–Sat., lunch only Sun.), serving good-quality contemporary Mexican cuisine with a Mediterranean touch at mid-range prices. The restaurant is housed in a beautiful old colonial mansion that was once owned by the legendary Mexican comedian Mario Moreno, better known as Cantinflas (English-speakers may remember him as David Niven's sidekick in *Around the World in 80 Days*), who supposedly convinced artist Diego Rivera to paint the mural in the swimming pool. Try the portobello mushroom stuffed with spinach, corn, and pepper as an appetizer, or the salmon in a sauce of apricots and chipotle.

Las Mañanitas (Ricardo Linares 107, 777/314-1466, daily noon–5 P.M. and 7–11 P.M.) serves tasty (though pricey) food and cocktails on a very relaxing terrace overlooking the hotel gardens. It always has a fresh seafood meal of the day, as well as other specials.

International

An upscale Chinese option, complete with a garden and reflecting pools, is **Log Yin** (Morelos 46, Col. Acapatzingo, 777/312-4142, Mon.–Thurs. 1–10 P.M., Fri.–Sat. 1–11 P.M., Sun. 1–8 P.M.), with specialties such as pork or vegetable dim sum or spicy shrimp with baby corn, mushrooms, and nuts. To get there, take a short taxi ride or 15-minute walk southeast from downtown along Avenida Atlacamulco, looking for Calle Morelos on the right side.

La Strada (Salazar 38, 777/318-6085, Mon.–Thurs. 1:30–11 P.M., Fri.–Sat. 1:30 P.M.–midnight, Sun. 2–6 P.M.), in a 300-year-old building at the rear of the Palacio de Cortés in the city center (go to the left of the building and then almost to the bottom of the stairs), serves very respectable Neapolitan-style Italian food at moderate prices. Specialties include calamari in white wine and *medaglioni La Strada,* beef in red wine with purple onion.

Another popular Italian restaurant is **Marco Polo** (Hidalgo 30, right in front of the cathedral, 777/312-3484 or 777/318-4032, www.marco-polo.com.mx, Mon.–Thurs. 1–10:30 P.M., Fri.–Sat. 1 P.M.–midnight, Sun. 1–10 P.M.). The upstairs dining room is always packed with customers, often foreigners, enjoying the relaxed ambience and decent food. It serves a good cappuccino to top off your meal too. Don't go in a rush, as service is less than stellar.

At **La Fontana Pizza** (Calle Benito Juárez 19, downtown; and Av. Morelos Sur 900, Col. Las Palmas, 777/310-1527, daily noon–midnight) you can go in and enjoy pizza, pasta, or *troncos* (baked sandwiches)—or have your food delivered.

NIGHTLIFE

The pedestrian street Fray Bartolomé de las Casas has several outdoor bars popular with young folks both local and foreign to gather, shoot the breeze, and have a drink. A few of the places, such as **Eclipse,** have live music of varying quality.

Longtime nightlife stalwart **Barba Azúl** (Prado 10, 777/322-4282) has been remodeled and continues to draw the crowds for the thumping techno music and impressive light show. It charges a cover of $10; drinks are $4–7 each. Latin music lovers should drop in at **Zúmbale** (Bajada de Chapultepec 13, Col. Chapultepec), east of downtown off Avenida Plan de Ayala, where a live band keeps the salsa dancers swinging Thursday to Saturday. A newer Latin music spot, one of a nationwide chain, is **Mambo Café** (Vicente Guerrero, Col. Nueva Italia, 777/313-5813), with dancing Wednesday through Saturday after 10 P.M. There's no cover Wednesday and Thursday, and also dance classes those nights 8–10 P.M. It's located north of downtown, and is best reached by taxi. Popular among the younger American visitors is **Harry's Grill** (Gutemberg 5 in the center of town, 777/312-7679), with loud music parties, especially on Thursdays, as well as satellite television for international sporting events. It's another in the Anderson chain of restaurants throughout tourist spots in Mexico.

Live performances of music and theater are often staged at the **Teatro de la Ciudad** (Morelos and Rayon), the **Teatro Ocampo** (on the *zócalo*), and **Jardín Borda.** Ask at the tourist office for upcoming shows.

RECREATION

Golf

The city's several golf courses are all private, although some of the higher-end hotels can arrange access for you. Expect to pay from $65 weekdays and up to $180 on weekends for greens fees. Local courses include **Club de Golf de Cuernavaca** (Vivero 1, Col. Club de Golf, 777/314-0248, www.golfcuernavaca. com), **Club de Golf Los Tabachines** (Carr. México–Acapulco Km 93.5, 777/314-3999), and **Club de Golf Santa Fe** (www.santafegolf .com.mx), on the highway to Acapulco, about 20 minutes south of Cuernavaca.

Tennis

Many of the more expensive hotels in Cuernavaca have courts, and two public courts can be found on Domingo Diez. You can also rent courts by the hour at **Tennis Palace** (Paseo del Conquistador 903, Col. Lomas de Cortés, 777/313-6500, $10 per hour) and **Calinda Racquet Club** (Francisco Villa 100, 777/101-0350, $20 per person, for the time you want).

Water Sports

Eight kilometers down the free highway toward Taxco, **Temixco** (777/325-0355, 9 A.M.–6 P.M. daily, $15 adults, $12 kids up to 1.25 meters tall) is a *balneario* (Mexican bathing resort) with pools everywhere you look. It has 22 pools, filled with slides and other water games, as well as a wave pool. It's lots of fun on a hot day, especially for kids. The resort occupies a former hacienda that started as a sugar plantation owned by Martín Cortés, son of Hernán, and then served as a fort during the Mexican Revolution. Vestiges of the old hacienda are still seen around the complex. The Ruta Temixco *combi* from Calle Galeana in Cuernavaca will take you there. If you're driving, follow the toll highway toward Acapulco and turn off at the Las Brisas exit.

HOTELS

As a longtime holiday city, Cuernavaca has a wide range of hotel options, from modest-but-decent rooms near the plaza to luxury spreads on the outskirts of town. If you plan on coming to town over a weekend, or especially during a *puente* ("bridge," or a three- or four-day holiday weekend), it's best to make reservations a couple of weeks in advance to be sure of having a room. Prices tend to the expensive side because of Cuernavaca's popularity with both foreign and Mexican visitors.

$15-30

Hotel Colonial (Aragón y León 104, two blocks from the *jardín*, 777/318-6414, $24 s/d, $35 d with two beds) is nice for the price. However, rooms vary widely in quality, so look first. All rooms have a TV.

$30-50

Hotel Hortensias (Hidalgo 13, 777/318-5265, $27 s, $31 d) is a small family-run hotel in the center of town set around an interior court-yard; rooms have cable TV.

A large, friendly place, with a restaurant inside, is **Hotel España** (Morelos 190 at Rayon, 777/318-6744, $30–50 s/d). The 30 tile-floored rooms are spacious and airy, with fans and TV.

$75-110

On a quiet street up against Jardín Borda, **Hotel Ilebal** (Chula Vista 7, 777/318-2725, $75 s, $85 d) has 35 rooms with TVs, WiFi, safe deposit boxes, and terraces. The hotel has a friendly, helpful staff and a hot tub and pool for guests.

Named in honor of the Malcom Lowry novel set in a fictionalized Cuernavaca, **Bajo El Volcán** (Av. Humboldt 119, 777/312-4873, www.tourbymexico.com/bajoelvolcan, $80 s/d) has 28 tiled rooms; some have terraces. The patio features a medium-size pool. Rooms in the newer section of the hotel boast a view of the river and fields. Breakfast is included with the price of room.

Over $110

Just east of the Mexico City highway, **Hacienda de Cortés** (Plaza Kennedy 90, Atlacomulco, 777/316-0867, www.haciendade cortes.com, rooms from $240) is just what it purports to be: an old hacienda built by the legendary conquistador, on the outskirts of

Cuernavaca just off the highway to Tepoztlán. Occupied briefly during the Revolution by the equally legendary Emiliano Zapata, and later destroyed, the hacienda lay in ruins until the 1970s, when it was restored to its current form, with 23 rooms. The gardens and outdoor pool make a great spot to relax.

The cozy 14-room **Posada María Cristina** (Blvd. Juárez 300, one block from the Palacio de Cortés, 777/318-5767, www.maria-cristina.com, $135–170 s/d) offers colonial atmosphere with amenities including a swimming pool, lovely gardens, and an excellent restaurant. Suites with king-sized beds and hot tubs are available.

Camino Real Sumiya (Colonia José Parras, in Jiutepec, near the highway exit to Tepoztlán and Cuautla, 777/329-9888, U.S./Canada reservations 800/7-CAMINO, www.caminoreal.com, $140 s/d, $365 junior suite, $465 master suite) offers a taste of Asia here in central Mexico. The main part of the hotel was carried across the ocean in pieces from Japan under the direction of heiress Barbara Hutton, whose fine art collection graces the walls of the Kabuki Theater. The hotel has 163 rooms looking onto acres of Japanese-style gardens and walking paths. One restaurant, **La Arbolera** (daily 7 A.M.–11 P.M.) features an international menu, while the other, **Sumiya** (Wed.–Sun. noon–midnight), is highlighted by excellent Japanese cuisine.

Las Mañanitas (Ricardo Linares 107, 777/314-1466, www.lasmananitas.com.mx, $320–450 s/d), a 15-minute walk from the city center, is considered one of the best hotels in Mexico. The verdant grounds, in addition to the resident peacocks and other tropical birds, feature an elegant swimming pool and plenty of intimate nooks to sit and enjoy the refined ambience. The relaxing hotel bar is a great place to unwind even if you're not staying at the hotel. The hotel has only 20 suites, and service is superb. Only American Express credit cards are accepted.

PRACTICALITIES
Information and Services
The Morelos state tourist office (Av. Morelos Sur 187, 777/314-3872 or 777/314-3920, Mon.–Fri. 8 A.M.–5 P.M., Sat.– Sun. 10 A.M.–3 P.M.) stocks lots of literature in English, including information on the city's language schools and archaeological sites. The website www.morelostravel.com offers a wide variety of helpful information in Spanish.

The city runs small tourist booths in the bus stations (daily 10 A.M.–5 P.M.), but with limited information. Staff at the municipal tourism office in the Palacio Municipal on the plaza are also helpful and armed with up-to-date information.

The main post office (Mon.–Fri. 8 A.M.–7 P.M., Sat. 8 A.M.–1 P.M.) is on the south side of the plaza, next to the government palace.

Bancomer, on the Jardín Juárez, and Banamex, on Matamoros at Arteaga, just north of the Jardín Juárez, exchange dollars or travelers checks at good rates.

Hospital General (Domingo Diez at Guadalajara, 777/311-2209 or 777/311-2210) has some English-speaking doctors, and is located a short taxi ride northeast of downtown. **Farmacia Cuernavaca** (Dr. Gómez Azcarte 200, right next to the Hospital General, 777/311-4111) is open 24 hours.

Cuernavaca has dozens of language schools. For a complete list of schools and prices, contact the local tourist office. Prices start around $250 per week for one-on-one classes or $135 for classes with five people.

Four of the better-known schools are **Center for Bilingual Multicultural Studies** (Apdo. Postal 1520, Cuernavaca, Morelos 62000, 777/313-0402, U.S. 800/932-2068, www.spanishschool.uninter.edu.mx); **Cuauhnáhuac Escuela Cuernavaca** (Apdo. Postal 5–26, Cuernavaca, Morelos 62051, 777/312-3673 or 777/318-9275, U.S. 713/292-1614, www.cuauhnahuac.edu.mx); **Cemanahuac** (San Juan 4, Colonia Las Palmas, 777/318-6407, www.cemanahuac.com); and **Spanish Language Institute** (800/552-2051, www.langlink.com), run by Language Link of Peoria, Illinois.

Getting There and Away
If you're coming from Mexico City, you'll leave from the southern part of that city either by

México 95 *libre* (free) or 95D *cuota* (toll). For the most part the two run parallel to each other, but the narrow, truck-filled free road takes considerably longer, often more than two hours. The toll road, which costs $6, is a fine open highway.

Four different bus companies serve Cuernavaca, each from a separate terminal.

Autobuses Pullman de Morelos has two terminals in Cuernavaca: one in the center of town, at the corner of Abasolo and Netzahualcóyotl, 777/314-3650; and a large, efficient station at Casino de la Selva, northeast of the *centro,* at Plan de Ayala 102, 777/318-4638. The company runs buses to Mexico City's Terminal Tasqueña every 15 minutes 4:30 A.M.–9:40 P.M. for $7, or Executive Service (with coffee and cookies) for $9. A direct bus to the Mexico City airport (20 daily) costs $12.

Estrella de Oro (Morelos Sur 900, 777/312-3055), whose terminal is 1.5 kilometers from the center of town, also has frequent buses to Mexico City for the same price. It also has regular departures to Acapulco ($24), the last one leaving at 10:30 P.M. If you don't want to flag a taxi, take a local bus going up the hill on Morelos; you can get off at the city center.

Flecha Roja/Estrella Blanca (Morelos 503 at Arista, 777/312-8190) has buses to Taxco ($5, 12 buses daily) and Mexico City ($7, 20 buses daily).

From its terminal about eight blocks from the city center, **Estrella Roja** (Galeana 401 at Cuauhtemotzín, 777/318-5934) runs buses to Cuautla and Puebla 6 A.M.–7 P.M. for $5 and $14, respectively.

To get to Tepoztlán, hop one of the frequent-but-slow buses leaving from the market on Avenida López Mateos, just northeast of the city center.

Getting Around

It's easy to get around Cuernavaca on foot; most of the main tourist attractions are within walking distance of the center of town. Local buses to different parts of the city cost about $0.30. Street taxis are inexpensive and usually quite safe, but after dark, it is advisable

to call a *sitio* (radio) taxi. Two reliable services are **Radio Taxis Ejecutivos** (777/322-1200 or 777/322-1202) and **Radio Taxis Excelencia** (777/382-0931 and 777/382-3101). Taxi prices increase after sunset.

Car rental agencies in town include **Hertz** (Av. Emiliano Zapata 611, Col. Tlatenango, 777/313-1607); **Solar Auto** (Av. Benito Juárez 45, Col. Las Palmas, 777/312-2588); and **Deguer Rent-A-Car** (Av. Morelos Sur and Galeana, Col. Las Palmas, 777/318-5466).

NEAR CUERNAVACA
◖ Tres Marías

Whichever road you take out of Cuernavaca, be sure to make a snack stop at Tres Marías, a roadside village high in the mountains; it's famed for excellent *cecina* (flattened, cured beef), *sopa de hongo* (mushroom soup), quesadillas, and other Mexican treats. At Tres Marías is a turnoff east to a mountain lake park called **Laguna de Zempoala,** a popular forested picnic spot for weekenders from the city.

Xochicalco Archaeological Site

About 42 kilometers southwest of Cuernavaca, this hilltop ruin was once a city populated by at least 10,000 people. Archaeologists place the apogee date at A.D. 700, a time when the lights were going out in so many other cultures of Mexico. Scientists continue to find hints of Olmecs, Toltecs, and Maya among the ruins.

The most outstanding structure here is the **Pyramid of the Plumed Serpent,** marked by intricate geometric patterns and stone reliefs of sinuous serpents and men with plumed headpieces. On the back side of the main acropolis is a tunnel leading to a cave used by the priests of Xochicalco as a kind of subterranean observatory; a long vertical shaft dug by hand let full sunlight into the cave only on two days a year, when the angle of the sun was perfectly aligned with the shaft. The priests used these fixed dates as a reference point to check the accuracy of their calendar. Locals insist that if you put your hand in the ray of sun on those two days, you can see the bones in your hand—but good luck getting through the crowds in the cave on

the hilltop ruins of Xochicalco, southwest of Cuernavaca

those two days to test the theory! Guides waiting at the entrance to the tunnel will give you an informative tour. They don't charge a fee, but tips are expected.

Be sure to bring water and a sun hat, especially if you go in the dry season, as the ruins (777/374-3090, daily 9 A.M.–5 P.M., $4.50) can get scorching hot. Views across the surrounding mountains from the hilltop are lovely. Admission includes entrance to a small museum (at the parking lot) that provides background on the site; you'll appreciate the ruins more if you visit the museum first. If you want to bring a video camera in, you'll pay an extra $3.50.

To reach Xochicalco from Cuernavaca by car, drive south on México 95 or 95D to the turnoff past the town of Alpuyeca. Continue past the town of El Cabrito and turn north on the paved road (signed Xochicalco). To get to Xochicalco via public transport, catch a **Pullman de Morelos Laser** bus from Cuernavaca to Coatlan, and from here take a $2–3 taxi up to the ruins. Alternatively, hop a second-class bus from the Cuernavaca market directly to the ruins for a mere $1. The last bus returns to Cuernavaca from the ruins at 6 P.M.

Lago Tequesquitengo

About 40 minutes south of Cuernavaca off the highway to Acapulco, this lake is a favorite among locals for picnicking, swimming, and waterskiing. To get there without a car, take a bus with Pullman de Morelos from Cuernavaca to Jojutla, and take a short taxi from there to "Tequis," as it's commonly known.

Parque Acuático Las Estacas

A great spot for cooling off on a hot afternoon, especially during the week when it's not so crowded, is this water park (734/345-0077 or 734/345-0159, in Cuernavaca 777/312-4412, www.lasestacas.com, $21, $13 for kids under 1.25 meters, free for kids under 0.9 meters), five kilometers from the small town of Tlaltizapán. Built around a small, crystalline river draped in jungly flora, with grassy meadows to relax on, Las Estacas has been the scene of several Mexican and U.S. movies, including one of the Tarzan series (1967) and *Beat* (2000), with Kiefer Sutherland and Courtney Love.

To get there, take a Pullman de Morelos bus from Cuernavaca ($2) or from Terminal Tasqueña in D.F. ($7 direct) to the town of Jojutla, and from there take either a minibus or taxi to Las Estacas. By public transportation the trip can be quite slow, especially the minibus part. If you're driving, take the highway to Cuautla from Cuernavaca, and at the town of Yautepec turn south to Jojutla–Tlaltizapán.

It's possible to camp at the park for $30 per person the first night, and $10 for each subsequent night—not exactly a bargain. Hotel rooms are available also, for considerably more (around $100 per person).

The nearby town Tlaltizapán was the general headquarters of Emiliano Zapata during the Mexican Revolution. The building now holds the **Museo de la Revolución del Sur** (Museum of the Southern Revolution). Nearby is an impressive 17th-century sugar hacienda, **Ex-Hacienda de San Francisco Temilpa,** worth a visit if you're coming this way.

Tepoztlán

Tucked into a lush valley up against a wall of cliffs about 30 kilometers northeast of Cuernavaca, Tepoztlán enjoys a ruggedly beautiful setting. It is the mythical birthplace of the Mesoamerican god Quetzalcóatl, and the town is steeped in Indian tradition. Older residents still speak Náhuatl, and the town's biggest festival of the year (the night of September 7 and the following day) honors Ometochtli, the god of *pulque,* drunkenness, and fertility.

For centuries a sleepy little village, Tepoztlán has in recent years developed into both a favorite weekend getaway for Mexico City residents and a budding artist community with a vaguely hippie/New Age feel. Although the people of Tepoztlán (frequently shortened to "Tepotz" by the weekender crowd) seem content enough with all the cafés, art shops, and weekend visitors, they keep tourism on their own terms. When wealthy developers tried to build a golf course outside of town in 1995, residents decided that was too much. They deposed the town government that had backed the project, organized a committee to run the town, and eventually saw the project canceled. If you ask Mexicans about this, either from D.F. or from Morelos, no one seems surprised. Tepoztecos are known to have plenty of spunk and character, especially those who live in smaller villages in the hills around Tepoztlán.

The town center of Tepoztlán turns into one big market on weekends. The many shops sell all variety of jewelry, art, and clothing from around the world, while locals sell Mexican handicrafts in outdoor stalls on the streets and in front of the church.

The **Auditorio Ilhuicalli** (Av. 5 de Mayo, 739/395-0673) can give information about *danza folklórica* (folkloric dance), concerts, and other musical events, which take place most weekends and holiday periods. The official state tourism website (www.morelostravel .com) includes some information on the town under the "destinos" link.

Orientation

A small town nestled into one end of a narrow valley, Tepoztlán itself is quite easy to negotiate on foot. The main road leading into Tepoztlán from Cuernavaca and Mexico City is called Avenida Cinco de Mayo until after it passes the town square, where it becomes Avenida del Tepozteco, dead-ending at the beginning of the trail up to a small pyramid in the hills. The pyramid, perched on a shoulder of one of the mountains directly behind town, can be seen from the town center.

Branching off Cinco de Mayo to the right (east) next to the plaza, Avenida Revolución descends past the church and out of town on the free road toward Oaxtepec.

EXCURSIONS

SIGHTS

Apart from the church and pyramid described below, among the town's main tourist activities are shopping in the weekend handicrafts market or simply enjoying a walk around town. (For information on hikes in the nearby hills, see *Near Tepoztlán*.)

Capilla de Nuestra Señora de la Asunción

Tepoztlán's imposing church and adjacent Dominican monastery seems more like a castle than a religious complex, reflecting the tenuous situation of the Spanish missionaries when the church was built in the mid-16th century. Although it is simply decorated inside, the church's facade is adorned with interesting sculptures of both Spanish and Amerindian designs. The Christmas midnight Mass, held in the candlelit courtyard thronged with villagers from the surrounding hills, is a lovely experience even for non-Catholics.

A Dominican monastery, **Ex-Convento de la Natividad** (Tues.–Sun. 10 A.M.–5 P.M., free) has been restored and now serves as a regional museum with five rooms.

Museo Arqueológico Colleción Carlos Pellier

This small museum (Pablo González 2, Tues.–Sun. 10 A.M.–6 P.M., $1) at the rear of the church houses a tasteful though poorly displayed collection of pre-Hispanic pottery from Totonac, Aztec, Maya, Zapotec, and Olmec cultures, from the collection of poet Carlos Pellier.

Pirámide de Tepozteco

Perched on a ledge in the hills 400 meters above Tepoztlán (and over 2,000 meters above sea level) is a 10-meter-high pyramid dedicated to Ometochtli, the Aztec god of plenty and the legendary creator of *pulque*. The pyramid itself is not much to see, but the chance to hike up into the hills and catch views of the Tepoztlán valley below make it well worth the trip.

From the town square it's a hike of about two kilometers to the pyramid (daily 9:30 A.M.–6 P.M., $3.50). To find the start of

the trail, just follow the town's main street past the square toward the hill and you'll run right into it. Although plenty of nonathletes make their way up the narrow and at times steep 1.2-kilometer trail, be prepared for a good hour's workout. Wear sturdy shoes and avoid weekends, or you'll feel as though you're hiking up with the entire population of Mexico City.

RESTAURANTS

Budget travelers should check out the *mercado* (market), where several *loncherías* (lunch restaurants) offer healthy and inexpensive *comidas corridas* (set meals). One of the stalls even offers a vegetarian meal. Or for a light snack, choose from the piles of magnificent produce grown in this lush region. The avocados are particularly sublime.

At the end of Avenida del Tepozteco, right at the foot of the hills in a house set amidst a jungle of trees and plants, is **Restaurant Axitla** (739/395-0519 or 739/395-2555, Wed.–Sun. 10 A.M.–7 P.M.). It's well worth the 10-minute walk from the square for the extensive menu of tasty, reasonably priced meals, both Mexican and international. Specialties include *chile jaral*, a wide chile pepper stuffed with shredded beef and raisins, and lamb cooked in a zucchini sauce. All dishes come with a tasty salad. You can dine in the pink high-ceilinged dining room overlooking the trees and river, or alfresco. A lone guitar player adds to the atmosphere weekend lunchtimes. Special arrangements can be made ahead of time for groups to eat after regular closing time.

For classic, well-prepared Mexican specialties, go to **Colorines** (Av. al Tepozteco, three blocks north of the plaza, 739/395-0198, Mon.–Fri. 9:30 A.M.–7:30 P.M., Sat.–Sun. 8:30 A.M.–8 P.M., mains $4–6). The ambience is colorful and cheerful, and the food is authentic, hearty, and moderately priced. It has the added advantage of being open throughout the week, unlike many local restaurants.

The classiest restaurant in town is **El Ciruelo** (Zaragoza 17, behind the market, 739/395-1203 or 739/395-1037, Wed.–Thurs. 1:30–6 P.M., Fri.–Sat. 1–11:30 P.M., Sun. 1–7:30 P.M., mains

$8–12), which features an outdoor patio with views of the mountains, an elegant atmosphere, and creative cuisine. Dishes include *enchiladas de pato* (duck enchiladas), chicken breast in mole and plum sauce, beef fajitas with nopal, and chiles rellenos stuffed with seafood and bathed in a goat-cheese sauce. The bill can run up quickly, especially with drinks and desserts.

Far at the other end of the glamour spectrum, but a gem of its own kind nonetheless, is the shabby little **Pulquería Alejandro Gómez** (Av. Del Tepozteco 23, closes 8 P.M. or thereabouts), where the daring can sample *pulque* either *natural* (plain) or *curado* (flavored in a number of ways, including *betabel,* or beet, and *avena,* or oat) for only $0.70 cents a cup. Despite the lamentable condition of his customers stumbling over steps and bumping into doorposts, the owner Gómez is a great source of information on this curiously viscous fermented cactus beverage, and his *pulque* tastes (and feels!) good.

HOTELS

If you don't have a reservation on the weekend, it's unlikely you'll find a room in Tepoztlán. During the week it's usually no problem to show up without reservations, at least at the less-expensive hotels.

Camping

About three kilometers west of town, against the foot of the mountains, you can pitch a tent at **Mextitla** (739/395-0068, www.tepoz.com.mx/meztitla) for $7.50 per person. Showers and food are available, as are tent rentals and guide services for hiking. The hills behind the camp are a popular spot for hiking and rock climbing.

$15-30

At the bottom end of the price scale is the conveniently located **Hospedaje Mely** (Av. Cinco de Mayo25, 739/395-3719, $22 for 2 people, $32 for 4). The friendly family rents out eight spartan but relatively clean rooms—three with two beds. It often has space even on weekends.

Another mid-range option is **Posada Sarita**

(Allende 26, 739/395-0635, www.geocities .com/tepoz_sarita, $40 s/d), three blocks south of the square, with simple rooms with bathrooms and cable TV located in a closed-in grassy area with shady trees.

$75-110

A major step up is the family-run **Posada Ali** (Netzahualcóyotl 2C, 739/395-1971, $80 s/d with breakfast), a rustic little place with decent rooms that have increased in price along with the town's tourism.

Over $110

Hotel Nilayam (Calle de las Industrias 6, 739/395-0523, toll-free in Mexico 800/221-5903, www.nilayam.net, $120 s/d) offers a full health spa with massage, sauna, pool, and *temazcal* (an Aztec sauna). Rooms in the large concrete (not overly attractive) building are modern and clean, and prices include a buffet breakfast at the vegetarian restaurant.

By far the best hotel in town is **La Posada del Tepozteco** (Paraíso 3, a block above the square, 739/395-0010, www.posadadeltepozteco .com, $180 s/d with breakfast). Many of the 20 rooms and seven suites offer great views overlooking town and valley. The garden patio is a supremely pleasant place to sip a drink and contemplate the beautiful scenery. This is a fine place to come and enjoy a meal with a view, even if you don't stay in the hotel.

In the village of Amatlán, at the eastern edge of the Tepoztlán valley, is **Hostal de la Luz** (Carr. Tepoztlán–Amatlán Km 4, 739/395-3374, www.hostaldelaluz.com, $230 per night including breakfast and certian activites such as meditation). It's a high-end spa offering concerts, workshops, and yoga included in the price, along with three meals. The conference complex offers lovely views, which guests can contemplate in meditation chairs set in bay window alcoves, and it blends appealingly with the environment.

PRACTICALITIES

The two-lane free road between Cuernavaca and Tepoztlán, which passes through farmland

and several villages, takes about a half-hour to drive. Most auto-equipped tourists coming to Tepoztlán from Mexico City take the Cuernavaca toll highway ($6), turning off before Cuernavaca onto a branch toll road west to Tepoztlán ($1.90). It's also possible to drive to or from Mexico City via a lesser-known but lovely highway, which cuts across the mountains east of Tepoztlán and arrives in Xochimilco. The drive takes considerably longer than on the toll road, but if you're not in a hurry, the forests and mountain views are worth it. Be prepared for heavy traffic from Mexico City to Tepoztlán on Friday afternoons, and even worse going the other way on Sunday afternoons.

Autobuses Pullman de Morelos (Av. 5 de Mayo, 739/395-0520, in Mexico City 55/5549-3505) runs regular buses every 40 minutes to and from Terminal Tasqueña in Mexico City 8 A.M.–7:30 P.M. for $7. The best option is to catch more-frequent buses to and from the *caseta* (tollbooth) above town, for the same price. The ten-minute taxi to and from the *zócalo* will cost you 15 pesos, or less if you share with more travelers. You rarely have to wait even 10 minutes to hop any passing first-class bus headed for Mexico City.

NEAR TEPOZTLÁN

Forming the dramatic backdrop to Tepoztlán is the **Sierra del Tepozteco,** a jagged formation covered in dense vegetation. Above and behind the Sierra del Tepozteco rise the volcanic mountains forming the southern part of the Valle de México, which in this region is protected as the **Parque Nacional Corredor Chichinautzin.** Both ranges offer plenty of hiking opportunities for the adventurous.

The local company **Foliah Tours y Aventuras** (Av. Revolución 60, 739/395 7232, www.foliah.com) offers naturalist-oriented hiking, horseback riding, and caving tours in the mountain countryside around Tepoztlán. Prices range from $30 to $50 per person per trip, depending on the size of the group, with all transport and food included, and usually last a half day. Their guides are very knowledgeable about local flora and fauna as well as

local indigenous traditions, including herbal healing and *limpias,* or "cleansings."

San Juan

Perched on a high plateau in the Tepozteco mountains, San Juan is a Náhua town of farmers surrounded by pine forest, about 10 kilometers by road from Tepoztlán. San Juan is a good place to take a walk in the woods, either farther up into the national park or down to Tepoztlán; ask around in town for good places to go hiking. Following an old set of railroad tracks between Mexico City and Cuernavaca, passing through San Juan, is one recommended route.

To Tepoztlán, one can either follow the old railbed down from San Juan, then turn off on a path down to the Tepozteco pyramid, or go farther east from San Juan to the next valley, where a trail descends to the Mextitla campground just outside of Tepoztlán. Either hike would take a couple of hours—ask for directions in San Juan to find these trail entrances.

Those interested in trying a traditional Náhua sauna (*temazcal*) should consider trying the one in San Juan. Run by several Náhua women in a local community center, the *temazcal* is open on Saturday only, from early morning until early afternoon. The ladies are very friendly and helpful—if you speak some Spanish they'll tell you a great deal about the tradition of the *temazcal*. Clothing is optional, and visitors may get in or out of the large, mud-baked chamber as often as they like. Bathers are wrapped in blankets afterward and even served a bowl of delicious vegetable soup. The experience is perhaps not for everyone, but it's definitely interesting and physically rewarding. The cost is $14 per person.

Buses run between Tepoztlán and San Juan every hour or so and cost about $0.50, while a taxi runs around $3.

Amatlán

Another town that serves as a good place to start hiking into the mountains is Amatlán, at the far eastern edge of the Tepoztlán valley. Amatlán has in recent years become a favorite spot for artists and alternative-lifestyle types from Mexico City and elsewhere to build houses. There's a hotel catering to this crowd as well. It's possible to hike from Amatlán up several different trails to different points in the Sierra Tepozteco, with great views of the valley and of Volcán Popocatépetl to the east.

However, it is wise to stick to main trails, don't go alone, and keep your wits about you, as robberies have occurred.

Regular *combis* leave Tepoztlán for Amatlán ($0.50), or you can take a taxi for $3–5, depending on how rich you look.

Taxco

Soon after Cortés founded Taxco in 1529, the Spaniards discovered silver here and began mining in earnest. One of the city's hills, Cerro Barmeja, holds what was known as the King's Shaft, supposedly the oldest Spanish mine on the continent. The Taxco mines yielded vast quantities of silver—most of the early colony's supply came from here. But the veins were worked over so completely and efficiently that the city soon became a silver ghost town. It remained so for centuries, until American William Spratling opened a workshop in 1929 and began creating attractive original silver art designs. Since then the city has served as the locus of the most skilled silversmiths in Mexico, which accounts for its nickname as the "silver city." Most of the workshops found within the city are welcoming to foreign visitors, and will gladly demonstrate the entire silversmithing process at no cost—although of course with the hope that you'll buy something when they're done.

SIGHTS

The city itself is built on and between seven hills covered by a maze of cobblestone streets. The steep, narrow streets climb up, down, and about, twisting in and out of the hilly landscape and occasionally opening up to reveal intimate plazas and cooling fountains. You need to watch your step when exploring this city on foot, as there's barely room for both cars and pedestrians on the steep, windy streets. Visitors with physical disabilities may have a rough go of it.

Although the maze of streets can be confusing at first, most of the main sites, as well as shops, hotels, and restaurants, are all close to the center of town. The main drag, a section of the México–Acapulco highway, is Avenida Presidente John F. Kennedy, also known by locals as Avenida de los Plateros. The main part of town is basically uphill from Avenida Kennedy, so if you get lost, just go downhill to reorient yourself.

Taxis are cheap in Taxco, with a normal fare within the city not exceeding $1.50. If you need to call for a cab service in advance, drivers with **Sitio Cuauhtémoc** (762/622-7444) work around the clock. Another service can be located at 762/622-0600.

Iglesia Santa Prisca

A fine example of churrigueresque architecture and art, the church is a study in 18th-century detail, with an ornate pink facade punctuated by two steeples and a tiled dome. The oval relief on the facade depicts the baptism of Jesus. On the inside, you will see twelve magnificent altars of hand-carved wood, covered with 22-carat gold leaf. In a room at the back are magnificent paintings by Miguel Cabrera—a famed Zapotec Indian colonial artist—amid a bewildering assortment of gold leaf, sculptures, and nooks. One painting is said to be unique in the world for its depiction of the birth of the Virgin Mary.

The church (open daily) took seven years to complete and was paid for by rich miner José de la Borda. At the back is a small museum shop (Mon.–Sat. 9 A.M.–7 P.M., Sun. 10 A.M.–5 P.M.).

Plaza Borda

A shady spot under ancient laurel trees, Plaza

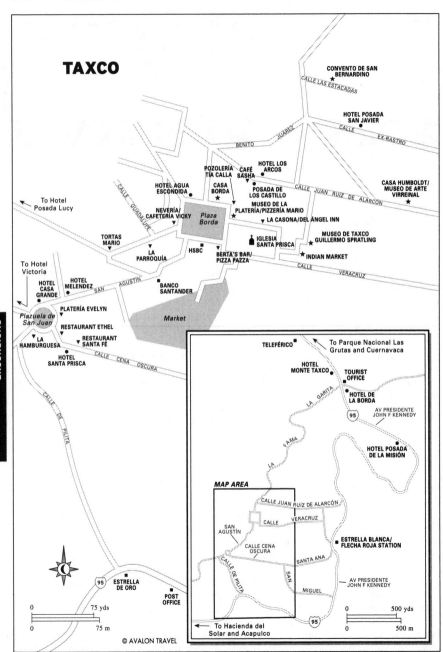

TAXCO

© AVALON TRAVEL

Borda is a rare flat spot in the center of town. Bordering the square are Iglesia Santa Prisca and some lovely old buildings containing a variety of gift shops—look for colorful woven baskets, Guerrero masks, local paintings, and of course silver. The plaza also holds court to an array of restaurants, which are generally mediocre and overpriced but have glorious views.

Museo de Taxco Guillermo Spratling

The two top floors of this museum (Delgado 1, 762/622-1660, Tues.–Sat. 9 A.M.–6 P.M., Sun. 9 A.M.–3 P.M., $2.70), on Plazuela Juan Ruíz de Alarcón behind Iglesia Santa Prisca, house a fine collection of pre-Hispanic art from Guerrero and central Mexico, gathered by famed silversmith William Spratling during his years in Mexico. Downstairs is an exhibit hall for temporary art displays.

Museo de la Platería

Aficionados of Taxco silver should pay a visit to this small museum next to the Iglesia Santa Prisca (Plaza Borda 16, Mon.–Sat. 10 A.M.–2 P.M. and 3–6 P.M., $1), which briefly traces the history of silver mining and craftsmanship in Taxco, and in Mexico as well. Several of William Spratling's most famed designs are on display here. The museum, which is run by a Taxco silversmith, has labels in Spanish only.

Casa Humboldt and Museo de Arte Virreinal

Originally built in the late 18th century as a private home, this meandering building (Calle Juan Ruíz de Alarcón 6, a block and a half from the plaza, 762/622-5501, Tues.–Sat. 10 A.M.–6 P.M., $1.50) served as a guesthouse in later years and reputedly was where Baron Alexander Von Humboldt stayed when he came through Taxco in the 19th century. Now it's an interesting religious art museum.

Casa Borda

Right next to the Iglesia Santa Prisca on the plaza is this mansion (daily 10 A.M.–7 P.M.) built for the Borda family in the mid-18th century.

graphic wood carvings inside Iglesia Santa Prisca

COURTESY OF CONSEJO DE PROMOCIÓN TURÍSTICA DE MÉXICO

EXCURSIONS

Now it's the town Casa de la Cultura (House of Culture), often hosting shows by local artists. It houses a small café on the 1st floor that serves breakfast and lunch at reasonable prices.

Town Market

Beside the Iglesia Santa Prisca, this market is chockablock with stalls hawking all manner of food, herbal remedies, and clothes. Some of the streets are so steep, you feel you could navigate them more safely sliding down on your behind than walking.

"Indian" Market

Directly behind Santa Prisca, near the entrance to the Spratling Museum, is a cheerful, cluttered market run by Indians who descend on Taxco from their villages in the hills above and from far around the state. This offers the best bargains for strands of semiprecious stones, lacquered boxes and trays, grimacing jaguar and angel masks, wooden salad bowls, and brightly painted pottery, and some textiles are sold for a fraction of their going price in Mexico City. It's open daily until about 5 P.M.

The Teleférico (Cable Car)

At Los Arcos, at the north end of town, a Swiss-built cable car takes passengers up 240 vertical meters to the top of a bluff overlooking the city. The cable car runs daily 8 A.M.–7 P.M.; the fare is $3 round-trip, $2 for children. Views are predictably spectacular. At the top you'll find the pricey Hotel Monte Taxco, with a restaurant, disco, bar, shops, gym, spa, pool, horseback riding, and a golf course.

Rancho Spratling

The former workshop of William Spratling and current studio of some of Taxco's finest craftsmen is well worth the half-hour trip south of town. Directly off México 95 at Km 177.5, the ranch (Mon.–Sat. 8 A.M.–1 P.M., free) includes the accessible workshop where fine silver is crafted by artisans, a museum depicting Spratling's life, and a showroom of work.

RESTAURANTS
Mexican and International

A small dining room and seemingly endless patio corners confront the visitor at **La Casona** (Celso Muñoz 4, 762/622-1071, daily 8 A.M.–8 P.M., mains $8–12). Located beside the Iglesia Santa Prisca, the restaurant offers a panoramic view of Taxco.

Restaurant El Adobe (Plazuela de San Juan, 762/622-1416, 8 A.M.–midnight daily, mains $6–10) is also good and a bit less expensive, with specialties such as *queso adobo* (melted cheese with herbs and veggies) or the *enchiladas oaxaqueños.*

Del Ángel Inn (Celso Muñoz 4, 2nd fl., 762/622-5525, ext. 2, daily 8 A.M.–10:30 P.M., mains $9–16), formerly a 10-room guesthouse, is now an elegant culinary haven. Steaks and meat-oriented dishes stand out in this patio restaurant, though vegetarian Mexican meals are also available.

White tablecloths will greet you at **La Parroquia** (Plazuela de Los Gallos 1, 762/ 622-3096, daily 9 A.M.–10:30 P.M., mains

$10–15), as well as a menu replete with international favorites and Mexican specialties.

La Pagaduría del Rey (Colegio Militar 8, 762/622-0075, daily 1:30–9:30 P.M., mains $8–20) is a hacienda-style restaurant just north of the city center. A serene setting both indoors and out, the high-end restaurant serves everything from fettuccine to filets.

La Ventana de Taxco (Hacienda del Solar, about seven minutes south of town on the highway to Acapulco, 762/622-0587, daily 8 A.M.–10 P.M., mains $8–15), with one of the best views in town, gets high marks from *Bon Appétit* magazine. The homemade chicken ravioli is a house specialty. Reservations are recommended, especially on weekends.

Pizza

The best pizza in town is at **Pizza Pazza** (Calle Arco 1, 762/622-5500, daily 10 A.M.–midnight, $3–10 per pizza), next to the church on the plaza. Apart from the excellent and reasonably priced pizzas, the menu includes pastas and other Italian dishes. Do your best to get a window seat for a good view of the plaza.

Pizzería Marios is in an indoor square at Plaza Borda 1. The menu includes cheese fondue, good-sized pies, and spaghetti dishes. A terrace faces the plaza.

Tacos, Tortas, and Snacks

The cozy **La Hamburguesa** (Plazuela de San Juan 5, 762/622-0941, Thurs.–Tues. 8 A.M.–midnight, burgers $3–5, mains $7–11) serves cheap burgers and tacos *al pastor* (pork cooked on a vertical spit), as well as complete meals. The piano bar gets lively in the evenings.

Lovers of *pozole* (a hearty stew with a base of hominy) will be thrilled to find the **Pozolería Tía Calla** (Plaza Borda 1, downstairs, on the left facing Santa Prisca church, 762/622-5602, $4 a bowl), probably the best eatery in town. In addition to the huge, inexpensive bowls of green, red, or white pozole, you can choose from other authentic Mexican fare at friendly prices.

For more than 40 years, **Restaurant Santa Fé** (Hidalgo 2, just down from Plazuela de San Juan, 762/622-1170, daily 8 A.M.–10 P.M., mains

$5–7) has been serving good, inexpensive food. Check out the *comida corrida* for $6.

Restaurant Ethel (Plazuela de San Juan 14, 762/622-0788, daily 9 A.M.–9 P.M., mains $5–7) charges similar prices for *comidas corridas* and specializes in good *antojitos*.

Nevería/Cafetería Vicky (daily 8 A.M.–10 P.M.) has a balcony that faces Plaza Borda. It's a great place to go for a coffee drink or ice cream. The restaurant also serves affordable tacos, burgers, and beer.

For *tortas*, go to **Tortas Mario** on Callejón de las Delicias (*tortas* $1–2), where the cook-owner will help you practice your Spanish.

NIGHTLIFE

Taxco's most alternative bar is **Cafe Sasha** (opposite Hotel Los Arcos in Calle Juan Ruiz de Alarcón, daily 8:30 A.M.–1 A.M.). A decent restaurant by day, at night Cafe Sasha becomes a hip place to sink tequilas and listen to reggae, drum 'n' bass, and world music. They have live music on Sundays.

Berta's Bar (next to the Santa Prisca church and adjacent to Pizza Pazza, 762/622-0172, 11 A.M.–8 P.M.) is something of a local institution and a great place to meet locals and travelers alike. It was opened in the 1930s by Berta, a Taxco resident, for whom a specialty house drink—made with tequila, honey, lime, and mineral water—is named.

If you get the urge to play pool while in Taxco, one spot is **La Estación.** The bar and burger joint is one floor below El Corcel Negro, at Cuauhtémoc 8, between Plaza Borda and Plazuela de San Juan.

FESTIVALS AND EVENTS
Semana Santa

The Holy Week festival begins on the week before Easter. On Palm Sunday, the first procession begins in the nearby village of Tehuilotepec, with an image of Jesus placed on the back of a donkey and carried to Taxco. Candlelight processions take place in town every following night, with hooded *penitentes* making their peregrination (many flagellating their backs raw, or carrying heavy bundles of brambles) to the Iglesia Santa Prisca. On Holy Thursday, in front of Santa Prisca, the Last Supper is performed by the locals, and the major procession takes place from 11 P.M. until the early hours. After that things calm down, although there are other, smaller processions on Saturday morning and Sunday.

Fiesta Alarconia

The last three weekends in May are devoted to a festival honoring Taxqueño Juan Ruíz de Alarcón, a writer during the colonial era. Art exhibits, band concerts, Alarcón plays, and other cultural presentations take place all over town.

Feria Nacional de la Plata

The last week in November each year is dedicated to Taxco's most famous product, crafted silver. Hundreds of artists enter a contest overseen by a panel of judges, who choose what they consider to be the year's best silverwork. This is a great opportunity to see some of the country's most creative silver craftsmanship.

SHOPS

Taxco offers some of the finest silver creations in Mexico and has dozens of silver shops. The bulk of the town's shops are in the city center, and while the ones closer to the plaza tend to be more expensive, these are also some of the best or more original. When buying a piece, always look for the ".925" stamp on the back, which ensures authenticity, and be sure to spend some time comparing prices before buying. You can find bargain-basement prices at the market on the corner of the plaza (to the left as you exit Santa Prisca), but don't expect quality workmanship there. A better option is **Linda de Taxco** (Plaza Borda 4 and 5, www.lindadetaxcojewelry.com). Besides silver you can purchase items with unusual mixtures of silver and ceramics, or silver, brass, copper, and ceramics.

Pineda's Taxco (Plaza Borda 1, www.pinedas taxco.com), right next to Santa Prisca, showcases the work of Bruno Pineda and brothers, with high-quality workmanship and original designs.

Among the many other good shops is **Platería Evelyn** (Plazuela de San Juan 15).

Inveterate jewelry shoppers will find many bargains by shopping around over the course of a couple of days.

HOTELS

Budget travelers will not find a whole lot of options in Taxco, as the hotels cater mainly to mid-range and upmarket visitors. It's a good idea to make reservations, as rooms can sometimes be scarce. Parking can be a hassle in Taxco, so if you're driving, look for a hotel with a parking lot.

$30-50

Hotel Casa Grande (Plazuela de San Juan 7, 762/622-0969, $20 s, $35 d) offers 23 clean rooms with phones and TVs. Ask for a quiet room on one of the higher floors or at the back. The hotel's restaurant and bar, **La Concha Nostra,** overlooks the plaza, which makes up for the softish beds and slightly funky bathrooms. Tacos, pizzas, and quesadillas are all good.

Posada de Los Castillo (Juan Ruíz de Alarcón 7, 762/622-1396, $42 s, $47 d) is a finely restored mansion from the colonial era with 15 rooms—a great place to stay in the center of town. There are plants, flowers, and handpainted murals every place you look. A statue of La Virgen de Guadalupe guards the stairwell.

Hotel Los Arcos (Juan Ruíz de Alarcón 4, a block down the hill from Plaza Borda, 762/622-1836, $38 s, $44 d, $50 t) was originally built as a monastery in the 16th century. The hotel is decorated with plenty of tile and has a great rooftop terrace. The 21 rooms, each with private bath, are simply furnished and have comfortable beds facing a verdant interior courtyard.

Hotel Posada Lucy (Carlos J. Nibbi 8, 762/622-1780, $35 d, $60 q), a few streets north of the Plazuela de San Juan, offers 30 rooms with adjoining baths between them. Pleasant gardens surround the narrow rooms. Parking is available.

Hotel Santa Prisca (Cena Oscura 1, on Plazuela de San Juan a couple of blocks west

handicrafts for sale in front of the colonial-era Iglesia Santa Prisca

COURTESY OF CONSEJO DE PROMOCIÓN TURÍSTICA DE MÉXICO/BRUCE HERMAN

of Plaza Borda, 762/622-0080, $35 s, $50 d) has 30 small but comfortable rooms around a patio and fountain. Grab one of the many English-language books from the library and enjoy a drink at the hotel's hole-in-the-wall bar. A section of the hotel is newer, with larger rooms and rambling junior suites. The dining room serves decent food.

Hotel Melendez (Cuauhtémoc 6, 762/622-0006, $37 s/d, $45 t) is home to 32 brightly decorated rooms surrounding an interior courtyard. Kitschy painted butterflies hover beside iron balconies in some of the rooms; other rooms open onto seating areas.

A beautiful garden surrounds **Hotel Posada San Javier** (Ex-Rastro 6, 762/622-3177, $46 s, $49 d, $ 52 t), with a swimming pool as centerpiece. This villa-style hotel features three terraces and quaint rooms, as well as spacious suites at reasonable prices. Parking is available.

EXCURSIONS

$50-75

Hotel Agua Escondida (Plaza Borda 4, 762/
622-0726, $60 s, $75 d, $90 t without TV; $57
s, $72 d, $87 t with TV) enjoys a great location right on the Plaza Borda. The 50 rooms
are painted with decorative garden motifs, and
many now offer cable TV. Amenities include a
rooftop terrace and snack bar, adjacent restaurant, video arcade, and a pool. Expect a crowd
on weekends.

Hotel Victoria (Carlos Nibbi 5 and 7,
762/622-0004, $58 s/d, $80 t) has some of the
best views of Taxco and is only a five-minute
walk from Santa Prisca. The 60 spacious rooms
have cable TV and private bath. There is a private dining room apart from the pleasant restaurant, which offers great views. Parking is
available, and pets are allowed.

$75-110

Hotel de la Borda (Cerro del Pedregal 2, opposite the junction of Av. Kennedy and Calle La
Garita, 762/622-0025, www.hotelborda.com,
$85 s, $95 d, $100 t) is where JFK and Jackie
honeymooned, enjoying panoramic views from
its large-windowed suites. Restored to its former
glory, it offers 120 large clean rooms and suites
with charming balconies, a restaurant, a large
sparkling pool with a view, and free parking.
The themed Revolución bar offers the classic
"Berta" town specialty and other cocktails.

Over $110

Hotel Posada de la Misión (Cerro de la
Misión 32, just off Av. Kennedy, 762/622-0063
or 762/622-5519, www.posadamision.com,
$160 s, $180 d) has 150 colonial-style rooms
with private baths, and suites with fireplaces
are available. On the premises you'll find one
of the town's most elegant restaurants, an
open-air chapel, banquet hall, silver workshop, large pool and gardens (adorned by Juan
O'Gorman's 1956 mural dedicated to the last
Aztec emperor Cuauhtémoc), beauty salon, and
shops. Parking is available, and ask about tours
to ex-haciendas by horse-drawn cart. Room
prices include breakfast.

Best Western Hacienda del Solar (off

México 95 south of town, opposite the tourist information office, 762/622-0587, $160 d)
is an intimate hotel surrounded by beautiful
views of the surrounding mountains. Balcony
rooms and suites are available. Amenities include a pool, tennis court, gourmet restaurant
La Ventana de Taxco, and strolling musicians.
Children under 12 are not allowed.

The 156-room **Hotel Monte Taxco** (762/622-
1300, www.montetaxco.com.mx, $155 s/d, $175
t) has a choice location, perched on the top of a
bluff on the north end of town near México 95.
The hotel offers guests (and nonguests) a nine-
hole golf course, tennis courts, horseback riding,
steam baths and massage, a fitness center, three
restaurants, bars, and a club.

PRACTICALITIES
Information and Services

Taxco has two tourism offices: the state
tourist office (762/622-2274, Mon.–Fri.
9 A.M.–3:30 P.M., Sat. 9 A.M.–1 P.M.) and the
federal tourism office (762/622-0798, daily
9 A.M.–7 P.M.). Both are on Avenida de los
Plateros (Avenida John F. Kennedy), but the
latter is closer to the center, just 50 yards from
the Hotel Posada de la Misión.

One extremely thorough (literally A to Z)
website on Taxco, in English, is www.taxco-
today.com, and another good source is www
.taxcolandia.com.

For medical attention, call the Red Cross
(762/622-3232); Hospital Adolfo Prieto
(762/622-0121); or Clínica Santa Cruz
(Av. Plateros in front of the Seguro Social,
762/622-3012). The latter has doctors who
speak English.

The post office (Mon.–Fri. 8 A.M.–7 P.M.,
Sat. 9 A.M.–1 P.M.) has a branch below the
ayuntamiento, or town hall, on Benito Juárez.

The **Centro de Enseñanza para
Extranjeros** (762/622-0124, www.cepe.unam
.mx), a branch of Universidad Nacional
Autónoma de México (UNAM), offers six-
week intensive Spanish courses. Food and accommodations are extra, but the school can
often set up rooms with local families. Call
for starting dates.

Banco Santander and HSBC have 24-hour ATMs and cash travelers checks during normal banking hours. Banco Santander is on Calle San Agustín between Plaza Borda and Plazuela de San Juan, while Bital is in Plaza Borda next to the Iglesia Santa Prisca.

There are several Internet cafés within a stone's throw of Plaza Borda. Try **La Estación** (on Cuauhtémoc, just 50 meters from the square, 10 A.M.–midnight). Another is **E Zone** (Callejón Las Delicias 3, Mon.–Sat. 10 A.M.–10 P.M.).

Getting There and Away

Taxco has two bus stations, both on Avenida de los Plateros (Avenida John F. Kennedy). The **Estrella Blanca/Flecha Roja station** (762/622-0131), near the intersection of Calle Santa Ana about halfway through town, runs first-class buses to Terminal Tasqueña in Mexico City more than 10 times daily, $11; to Acapulco once daily, $17; and to Cuernavaca frequently, $6. Frequent and less-expensive second-class buses go to the same destinations, as well as Toluca and Chilpancingo.

More comfortable and organized, **Estrella de Oro** (near the exit to Acapulco, 762/622-0648) offers 6–10 first- and second-class buses to the same destinations for about the same prices. Buses also stop at the Hotel Posada de la Misión, which has a small ticket office (6:30 A.M.–8 P.M.) in the lobby.

NEAR TAXCO
Parque Nacional Las Grutas de Cacahuamilpa

These extremely impressive caves comprise 15 interconnected chambers spanning 12 kilometers. About two kilometers are accessible to casual tourists, with concrete footpaths and dim overhead lighting—a flashlight wouldn't hurt, though, to help see places the lighting doesn't reach, and also because power cuts are not unknown! Several of these "rooms" are quite massive—fully 70 meters tall and equally wide, filled with stalactites, stalagmites, and other stone formations. Guided tours leave every hour 10 A.M.–5 P.M. and

cost $3, $2 for kids up to 12 years old. You must go with a guide, but not all guides speak English. Often it's very crowded, especially on weekends, although the caves are vast enough and the path easy enough to follow that escaping from the group is safe and easy. For a side trip, take the path branching to the right before arriving at the mouth of the caves, which leads to a place where the river flows into a 60-meter cave entrance. Minibuses (*combis*) marked Las Grutas leave from in front of the Taxco terminal to the caves roughly every hour throughout the day and cost $1.50 for the approximately 50-minute trip. If you're driving, take the highway east out of town toward Toluca and Cuernavaca, turn north on México 55 (toward Ixtapan de la Sal and Toluca), then watch for the marked turnoff, about 30 kilometers from town.

Ixcateopan

This beautiful mountain village, whose winding streets are hewn out of local marble stone, is held to be the birthplace of Cuauhtémoc. The last Aztec leader was tortured and killed by Cortés's men in Tabasco, but local myth has it his bones were secretly brought home and buried here. A much publicized excavation last century uncovered some charred remains, and these are now displayed in a church, **La Iglesia de la Asunción,** that has been converted into a small museum. While controversy remains as to the veracity of these lugubrious artifacts, you are advised to suspend disbelief and enjoy the mythology while here.

The other attraction, related in matters of pre-Hispanic pride, is **Museo de la Resistencia Indígena** (information in Taxco, 762/622-3927), or the Museum of Indigenous Resistance. This treasure trove of information on the conquest of New Spain is presented from the Indian point of view.

The best day to visit is on a Sunday, when the local market brings together the best of regional produce, from rare wild mushrooms to unusual sweet breads and *pulque,* a weirdly viscous fermented cactus alcohol. Ixcateopan has one of the oddest regional delicacies, *tortas de nieve* (ice-cream bread rolls) sold on the main street leading up to the church.

Ixcateopan is roughly 25 kilometers west-southwest of Taxco as the crow flies, but a lot longer over the windy, bumpy mountain roads.

Combi buses run daily between Ixcateopan and Taxco every 25 minutes until 7 P.M. from a bus stop opposite Taxco's Estrella de Oro station. The journey takes just under two hours and costs $3.

Toluca and Vicinity

The capital of the state of Mexico, Toluca, lies 67 kilometers west of Mexico City. Perched in the mountains at an elevation of 2,680 meters, it's the country's highest state capital. Toluca is a large and growing industrial city not frequented by tourists, but the city center does have a few buildings and parks from its colonial past.

SIGHTS

Most of Toluca's sights of note are clustered around the broad, open Plaza de los Mártires or the adjacent Plaza Garibay and can easily be visited on foot. A block south of the Plaza de los Mártires, right behind the cathedral, are the *portales* (arched colonnades) where Tolucans come to eat, shop, and pass the time of day. The square boasts the most *portales* of any city in Mexico. The principal *portal,* with 44 arches, is **Portal Madero,** which runs in front of Avenida Hidalgo. **Portal Constitución,** on the east side, has 38 arches, and **Portal Reforma,** the smallest of the three, with 36 arches, is on the west side. Between the *portales* and the cathedral is a small hidden square, with a simple round chapel in the middle.

Plaza de los Mártires

Several colonial buildings, most built of the local dark volcanic stone, face the central plaza, including the **Catedral de la Diocesis de Toluca,** begun in 1573 and finished in 1797. The church is one of the largest in the country and sports a rather severe neoclassical facade. Facing the principal altar on the right side is a *portada* (entranceway) leading into a separate but adjacent church. Other buildings in the plaza include the adjacent neoclassical **Palacio Municipal,** and, on the far side, the

18th-century **Templo de la Santa Veracruz.** Half a block west is the visually interesting modern **Teatro Morelos,** a brick cube ringed by copper arches.

Cosmo Vitral Jardín Botánico

This botanical garden (Tues.–Sun. 9 A.M.– 5 P.M., $2), at the eastern end of Plaza Garibay, lies within the walls of a 19th-century market building sporting 54 stained-glass panels. The panels—created by Leopoldo Flores over a period of three years—portray the story of humanity. The blazingly colorful glass art makes a fine backdrop for the garden's 400 different species of plants and flowers from Mexico, Central and South America, Africa, and Asia.

Museums

Eight kilometers west of the city center, the Centro Cultural Mexiquense (Mexican Cultural Center) is an impressive complex holding three museums that contain some of the state's finest exhibits: **Museo de Antropología, Museo de Culturas Populares,** and **Museo de Arte Moderno** (Blvd. Reyes Heroles 302, Tues.–Sun. 9 A.M.–5 P.M., $2 for all three museums). The creatively designed buildings (the art museum looks like a spaceship sunken into the earth) comprise one of the finest cultural institutions in the country. Among the highlights are a huge, colorful "tree of life" from Metepec and artwork by famed Mexican painters such as Siqueiros, Rivera, and Orozco. English-speaking guides are available. Get there via bus (Línea 2 de Marzo) or taxi. Opposite the complex is the imposing Tec de Monterrey University Toluca campus.

EXCURSIONS

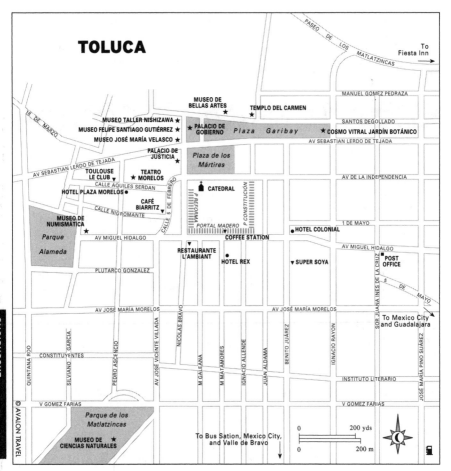

On Calle Santos Degollado, find the 16th-century **Templo del Carmen** and, just to its west, the **Museo de Bellas Artes** (722/215-5329, Tues.–Fri. 10 A.M.–6 P.M., Sat.– Sun. 10 A.M.–3 P.M., \$1), which houses paintings and sculptures from the 16th to the 19th centuries. Around the corner on Nicolás Bravo are three small art museums: **Museo Felipe Santiago Gutiérrez, Museo José María Velasco,** and **Museo Taller Nishizawa** (Tues.–Sun. 10 A.M.–6 P.M., free).

Other museums (of limited interest to casual tourists) include the **Museo de Numismática**

(Hidaglo Pte. 506, 722/213-1927), about currency and money, and **Museo de Ciencias Naturales** (Parque de los Matlatzincas), a natural history museum.

RESTAURANTS

For snacks, head to the *portales* in the city center, where you'll find a couple of bakeries and plenty of vendors selling tamales and *atole* (a sweet, warm corn drink).

If you're looking for fresh juice, a *torta,* or a *comida corrida,* the health-food restaurant chain **Super Soya** (Juárez 111, half a block off Hidalgo, Mon.–Sat. 8 A.M.–9 P.M., Sun. 10 A.M.–7 P.M.) is a good option.

Coffee Station, in the *portales,* is an American-style café with espresso drinks, salads, croissants, yogurt, and baguette sandwiches at mid-range prices.

Café Biarritz (Nigromante 200, facing the side of the cathedral, 722/214-5757, Mon.–Fri. 8 A.M.–11 P.M., Sat.– Sun. 8 A.M.–8 P.M.) is a good and inexpensive diner-type café with a large menu of standard Mexican meals, as well as fish and seafood. Similar is **Restaurant L'ambiant** (Hidalgo 231, opposite Portal Madero, 722/215-3393, daily 9 A.M.–9:30 P.M.), with odd bluish lighting (the "ambiant," perhaps?).

Toluca is known for its excellent cuts of meat and sausage, and one good place to give them a taste is **Las Costillas de Venustiano** (V. Carranza 201, at Aldama, several blocks south of the town center, 722/270-4036, daily noon–2 A.M., mains $5–12). An unpretentious place with tables in front of a big grill and TVs invariably showing a soccer match (especially if the beloved Diablos Rojos of Toluca are playing), it serves an excellent *arrachera* (flank steak) plate with beans, guacamole, and tortillas for $11. Also on offer is a variety of tacos and *alambres* (meat stir-fry), as well as the *chorizo mero toluca campeón,* a sausage named in honor of the soccer team's championship victories.

For a cold beer and a game of pool, chess, or backgammon, check out **Toulouse Le Club** (at the corner of Aquiles Serdán and Pedro Ascencio, two blocks west of the cathedral, Mon.–Sat. until midnight, Sun. until 10 P.M.). This relaxed spot is welcoming for old and young alike, and women will also feel comfortable.

HOTELS

$15-30: At the **Hotel Rex** (Matamoros Sur 101, 722/215-9300, $22 s/d), you'll find 40 basic, unremarkable rooms.

$30-50: Two blocks east of the *portales,* **Hotel Colonial** (Hidalgo Ote. 103, 722/215-9700, $35 s, $40 d) is about the best low-priced option. The hotel's 33 spacious rooms, each with TV and telephone, have high ceilings and wooden floors. Beware of rooms facing the street, as they can be noisy. Parking is available. At a higher price and comfort level, though in an unattractive modern building, **Hotel Plaza Morelos** (Aquiles Serdán 115, 722/215-9201, $46 s, $50 d) is next to the Teatro Morelos, in the town center. The 57 rooms, though a bit small, are clean and carpeted. Each has a TV and telephone. A parking lot and restaurant are downstairs.

Over $110: High-end rooms can be found at **Hotel Fiesta Inn** (Paseo Tollocan Ote. 1132, 722/276-1000, www.fiestaamericana.com, $140 s/d, $188 junior suites), with 140 rooms and four suites with all the amenities, as well as an indoor pool, gym, restaurant, meeting rooms, and a business center.

PRACTICALITIES
Information and Services

The state tourism office (Av. Robert Bosch and Av. 1 de Mayo, 722/275-6881 or 722/275-6880, Mon.–Fri. 9 A.M.–6 P.M.) is in the city's industrial zone behind the Nestlé factory. They are not prepared to deal with the general public and it is not worth the effort it takes to get there.

The main post office (Mon.–Fri. 9 A.M.–5 P.M., Sat. 10 A.M.–2 P.M.) is at the corner of Hidalgo and Sor Juana Inés de la Cruz.

Getting There and Away

Flecha Roja (722/217-0285) and **Caminante** (722/217-0152) both offer buses between Toluca and the Terminal Observatorio in Mexico City every five minutes 5 A.M.–9 P.M. for $5. Caminante also has direct buses to and from the Mexico City airport 17 times daily for $10 (4 A.M.–8 P.M.). **Primera Plus** (722/217-3485) runs buses to Morelia, six times daily, second class ($16); Guadalajara, six times daily, first class ($37); and Querétaro, every hour, first class ($15). **Transportes Frontera/Estrella Blanca** (722/217-1174) sells tickets for Taxco ($9) and Acapulco ($30) on Primera Clase; to Monterrey ($64) and Nuevo Laredo ($80) on Turistar Ejecutivo; and to Monterrey ($60) and Nuevo Laredo ($74) on regular first-class Futura buses. **ETN** (722/217-7308) runs luxury buses to Guadalajara ($55), San Luis Potosí ($35), and Querétaro ($20); all twice daily. It also has 20 buses a day to Mexico City's Observatorio station ($5.50).

México-Toluca-Zinacantepec y Ramales (722/217-1596) has frequent buses throughout the day to Valle de Bravo ($5). **TMT** runs frequent buses to El Oro ($7). **Tres Estrellas del Centro** has frequent buses to Teotenango ($1), Ixtapan de la Sal ($4.50), and Malinalco ($5).

Once in Toluca, look for buses marked Centro if you're heading into the city center. To get back to the bus terminal, catch one of the buses on Morelos (near Juárez, two blocks from the *portales*) marked Terminal. The terminal is about two kilometers southeast of the town center. A taxi to/from the center costs $2.

To leave the center of town by car, take Avenida Benito Juárez until it dead-ends into Paseo Tollocan, which exits toward Mexico City to the left (east) or to Valle de Bravo to the right (west).

NEAR TOLUCA
Teotenango Archaeological Site

The ominous-looking hilltop complex of Teotenango (Tues.–Sun. 9 A.M.–5 P.M., $2), 25 kilometers south of Toluca, was established first by the local Teotenanca tribe, who were conquered by the Matlatzinca people in A.D. 1200. The Matlatzincas (whose name means "net-users" in Náhuatl, a reference to the people's frequent use of fishing nets) were in turn defeated by the Aztecs in 1477. One of the more fascinating artifacts found was a stone jaguar eating the sun, thought by some archaeologists to depict a solar eclipse. Other structures include a large ball court and several large, squat temples. At the bottom of the hill, where you pay your admission, you'll pass a small museum holding some of the artifacts found during restoration.

The site is just under a kilometer from the town of Tenango de Arista (also known as Tenango del Valle), which is serviced by frequent buses from Toluca ($10 with Tres

© CHRIS HUMPHREY

a church among cornfields in Teotenango

Estrellas del Centro) and easily reached by bus-and-taxi combination. From Tenango tourists may either walk or take a $1.50–2 taxi to get to the ruins. The town itself is a pleasant place to wander around for an hour or so to get a taste of rural life in the region. It's also known for its excellent *barbacoa* (lamb barbecue) and *carnitas* (pork), which can be found in several restaurants or at the local market.

◖ Nevado de Toluca

The 4,691-meter Nevado de Toluca, sometimes called by its Náhuatl name, Xinantecatl (zee-nan-te-KAHT-el), is an inactive volcano with two small lakes in its crater. It is the fourth-highest mountain in Mexico. Tourists can drive up into the crater on a dirt road offering spectacular views, as long as it's not snowing (hence the name, *nevado,* which roughly translates to "snowy one"). From the crater it's another 500 meters or so of scrambling up to the actual crater rim. The 2- to 4-hour hike around the crater rim can be fun, but it is exposed and the trip entails scrambling up lots of boulders and scree, so don't undertake it lightly. The really daring can climb part way around the rim and plunge down the steep scree slopes into the crater, sliding meters with each step and descending in just moments what it took so long to slog up. The best sliding chutes are from between the two highest points on the crater rim. Those who agree with Falstaff on discretion being the better part of valor can content themselves with hiking an hour or less up to the crater rim for the fantastic views (weather permitting).

If possible, come during the week, as the crater turns into a mob scene on some weekends, with competing radios, football games, and even a couple of taco stands. The weather is very changeable up on the mountain, so come prepared for anything from sunburn-level sun to freezing cold, snow, and high winds. The mornings usually have the best views, and if you're lucky, you can see all the way across Mexico City and spot Popocatépetl, Ixtaccíhuatl, and Pico de Orizaba in the distance.

In the late 1990s a Mexican development company had grandiose plans of building a ski resort on the mountain, but such ideas were put on hold by the local campesinos, who have part controlling rights of the forest. Apparently they feared that the necessary artificial snow-making would destroy their crops, or perhaps they just didn't like the idea of chopping up their mountain. At any rate, would-be Mexican skiers shouldn't expect to buy their season pass just yet.

To reach Nevado de Toluca by car, take México 134 heading west from Toluca. At Km 19, in the midst of pine forest, take México 3 south toward Texcaltitlán. Continue 7.3 kilometers, with great views of the volcano, to the dirt road turning left up the mountain, just past the village of **Raíces.** From this turn, it's another 19 kilometers of dirt road east to the crater, first through pine forest, and then above the tree line. Buses to Texcaltitlán and Sultepec can drop you at the turnoff, where you can hitch up on weekends. During the week there's very little traffic.

Part of the way up the road you'll pass a large *albergue* (hostel) with 200 bunk beds, hot water, and a kitchen. It's noisy on weekends but certainly cheap at $5 per night. Camping is allowed anywhere on the mountain except in the crater, but be sure to come well prepared for the cold.

El Oro

Right on the border with the state of Michoacán, 94 kilometers northwest of Toluca via Atlacomulco, is this old mining town nestled into a hillside. Missionaries from the nearby Rancho de Guadalupe found chunks of gold around 1700, but it wasn't until the late 19th century that large-scale mining began, much of it undertaken by foreign miners. Although not a major destination for tourists, it's worth a day trip if you're interested in an offbeat place. There are no hotels to stay in in town, so plan on returning to Toluca or Mexico City by the end of the day.

The very friendly folks at the local tourist office, in the white and red **Palacio Municipal** (711/125-0036 or 711/125-0099, ext. 26, Mon.–Fri. 9 A.M.–5 P.M., Sat.–Sun. 10 A.M.–4 P.M.) will happily take you on a tour of the town themselves if they aren't too busy, as they are eager to promote El Oro as a tourist destination. Main sites include the *palacio* itself, built in 1910, with an elegant old meeting hall on the top floor. Around the corner is the ornate **Teatro Juárez** (daily 9 A.M.–5 P.M.), with four columns in front of its stone facade. The public is welcome to wander around; ask the workmen to turn the lights on for you if they are off. Several other buildings dating from the town's heyday are worth a look, including the old **Oro Club,** now housing a BBVA bank. In the old railway station, a block uphill from the theater, is a collection of artisans selling their wares, including ceramics and woodwork.

A 10-minute walk above town is the **Museo de la Minería del Estado de México** (Tues.–Sat. 10 A.M.–6 P.M., Sun. 10 A.M.–3 P.M., free), with lots of weird old mining gear, photos of the town during the mining boom, and rusted sculptures of two heroic-looking miners and a woman sitting outside. During the week there's often no one around at all. Views over the town are good from the museum, making it a good excuse for a walk even if the exhibits don't do much for you.

A couple of kilometers outside of town is the **Presa Brockman,** a small lake created by a dam, popular among locals as a place to picnic on weekends.

Several unpretentious eateries in town offer good food. One of the better ones is **Los Girasoles** (one block up from the theater, on the 2nd floor of a building formed by a fork in the road, Tues.–Sun. 8 A.M.–8 P.M., mains $4.50), run by a friendly matron who takes good care of her clients with very tasty *comidas corridas*. Downstairs is a bakery.

TMT and **Caminante** buses run several times a day between El Oro and Toluca ($7) and Terminal Observatorio in Mexico City ($10).

Tlalpujahua

Just over the border in the state of Michoacán, just a 15-minute drive (or 25-minute bus ride) from El Oro, is this picturesque colonial village,

well worth a visit to enjoy the relaxed *pueblo* atmosphere and clean mountain air. There's not much in the way of sights per se, but it's fun to stroll the cobbled streets, admire the colonial buildings, or take a hike in the surrounding forest hills. If hunger pangs strike, be sure to stop for a bite at **La Terraza** (Allende 10), appropriately named for the terrace on which it is situated, with lovely views over town. The enchiladas, mole, and other Mexican snacks are tasty, and they even serve a decent cappuccino.

IXTAPAN DE LA SAL

Thermal springs are the attraction at Ixtapan, a low-key spa/resort of about 25,000 people, 117 kilometers from Mexico City. The mineral baths scattered around town have made Ixtapan a favored weekend getaway for people from Mexico City, Toluca, and Cuernavaca. All the locals will cheerfully tell you that the water is radioactive and can cure whatever ails you. More scientifically, the water comes out of the spring at 40.8°C, with a salt and mineral content of almost 10,000 parts per million. If your hotel doesn't have private baths, you can take a dip at the **Ixtapan Spa** (Mexico City 55/5254-0500, www.ixtapan.com.mx, daily 8 A.M.–7 P.M.), right at the entrance to town coming in from Toluca, with pools ranging between 32°C and 38°C, as well as regular swimming pools, for $14 adults, $6 kids under 10. The **Balneario Municipal,** at the corner of Allende and 20 de Noviembre in the center of town, charges a mere $2.50 for a hot bath or $8 for a massage.

Between Ixtapan and Toluca, the highway passes very lovely stretches of countryside, with many hillside towns specializing in growing flowers. Two towns worth a visit if you're coming by car are Santa Ana and Tenancingo.

Restaurants

Check out the string of restaurants on Avenida Juárez Norte between the Ixtapan Spa and town. One good one is **Restaurante Los Arcos** (daily 9 A.M.–8 P.M., mains $4–8), where you can get a filling set three-course meal for $6, or order entrées from the menu.

Hotels

Hotels in Ixtapan tend to be of the all-inclusive variety, offering package rates that include room, meals, and spa services.

$15-30

One of the less-expensive places in town is **Hotel Mari's** (right across from the municipal spa at Allende 7, 721/143-0195, $25 s/d), a family-run place with its own restaurant. There is double or triple occupancy only, unless there are not many visitors in town and you can negotiate. Breakfast is an extra $4.

$30-50

Hotel Don Isidro (Av. Juárez Norte, one street down from the Ixtapan Spa, 721/143-0315, $30 s, $40 d) is also a decent mid-range option.

$75-110

Hotel Casa Blanca (Juárez 615, 721/143-0036, $75 d with three meals) has a warm (not hot) pool and a restaurant that stays open all day. Rooms are spread around the one-level complex, with tropical plants everywhere.

Over $110

An upscale hotel outside of town, **Rancho San Diego** (Mexico City 55/5254-7491, Ixtapan 721/143-4000, www.ranchosandiego.com.mx, $175 d with private mineral bath, $155 d without, a bit less during the week) offers all-inclusive stays with plenty of activities to keep you entertained, such as tennis, rappel, waterslides, mountain biking, or just relaxing on the many patios and enjoying the atmosphere. The complex is interestingly designed, with modern-style buildings painted in earth tones with wood beams.

Ixtapan de la Sal Marriott Hotel and Spa (Morelos s/n, Fraccionamiento Bugambilias, 721/143-2010, www.marriott.com, $119 s/d and up) offers newly remodeled rooms including flat-screen TVs and iPod connections. The spa includes treatments based on the Aztec and Náhuatl cultures, and the hotel also offers tennis courts, swimming pools, and facilites for kids.

Practicalities

Tres Estrellas del Centro runs buses between Terminal Observatorio in Mexico City and Ixtapan de la Sal every hour 7 A.M.–7 P.M. ($9), and to Toluca ($5).

Tourist information can be found at the bus station, 1.5 kilometers from town on the road toward Taxco.

For information on Ixtapan and the surrounding areas, either visit or call the local tourist office (near Hospital General on highway to Tonatico, 721/141-1450).

Las Grutas de la Estrella

Past Ixtapan, about 17 kilometers down the road toward Taxco, is the turnoff to Las Grutas de la Estrella (Tues.–Sun. 10 A.M.–4 P.M. $2), or "Star Caves," carved out of a limestone mountain by millennia of rushing water. Take a wander in an impressive series of caverns and side chambers, replete with bizarre rock formations. Through parts of the cave rushes the Río Zapote, which in the height of the rain season can flood the caverns. The caves were first explored thoroughly in 1956, revealing an altar to Tlaloc and other pre-Hispanic artifacts. To get there by bus, take a Tres Estrellas bus from Ixtapan toward Taxco and get off at the turnoff for the caves ($2).

◖ MALINALCO

Set amidst dramatic scenery in a remote corner of the mountains between Toluca and Cuernavaca, Malinalco is well worth the trip just to see this region not oft-visited by foreign tourists, as well as to check out the 16th-century convent in the center of town and the impressive archaeological site on a hill just outside. Because of its natural beauty and bucolic ambience, Malinalco has become a popular spot for Mexico City residents to have a weekend home.

Malinalco was a strategic spot dominating a mountain pass and was not conquered by the Aztecs until shortly before the arrival of the Spaniards. The Aztec ruins are thought to have been a means of impressing the local population with the empire's dominance. After the Spanish conquest, a mission of seven Augustinian monks made their way to Malinalco in 1540 to begin evangelization of what was considered an important region. Malinalco also served as a strategic site during the Mexican Revolution, when it was used as a base by Zapata's troops.

Ex-Convento de la Transfiguración

Dominating the center of town is this impressive Augustinian monastery dating from the 1540s. Similar in style to the convent in Tepoztlán, the church itself (dedicated to San Salvador) is unadorned and fortresslike, while the cloister to the side is in two levels around an open garden. Decorating the walls of the cloister are very beautiful murals of flowers and animals. Visitors are free to wander around both the church and the cloister at no charge. Note an obviously pre-Hispanic carved rock sitting on a stump in front of the church.

Malinalco Archaeological Site

This famous temple complex sits on a bluff about one kilometer west of the town of Malinalco, all uphill on a dirt road. The small but impressive site (Tues.–Sun. 9 A.M.–5:30 P.M., $3, $3 more for video camera) was built by the Aztecs starting in 1501, although archaeologists believe they built on a preexisting temple. The six monuments are carved directly out of the mountain rock, which was the only time the Aztecs used this technique. The principal structure is the **Temple of the Eagle,** thought to have been where Eagle and Tiger Aztec warriors were initiated into their cult. Two carved ocelots flank the steep stairway up to the circular temple, which has a carved eagle in the center and jaguars around it. Views from the ruins across the town and surrounding countryside are magnificent. The long stairway up to the ruins is a bit of a slog, but it's broken up with interesting write-ups (in three languages: English, Spanish, and Náhuatl) on the site itself and local history, culture, and environment.

Visible from the stairway up is **Rincón de San Miguel,** a small chapel with pre-Hispanic ruins to one side, tucked into a narrow valley below. This is the where the town holds its

© CHRIS HUMPHREY

trimming flowers for holiday decorations in the Ex-Convento de la Transfiguración

annual festival on September 29. According to the guards at the main ruins, the hillsides around Malinalco are littered with unexcavated ruins. If you'd like to take a walk in the hills, one place to go is up the cobblestoned road past the turnoff to the ruins, which soon becomes a footpath across the mountains to the town of Tenancingo, about 15 kilometers away.

Restaurants

Calle Guerrero, leaving from the small square in front of the church up toward the archaeological site, has several good restaurants. One of the best is **Las Palomas** (Guerrero 104, 714/147-0122, Mon.–Thurs. until 6 P.M., Fri.–Sat. until 11 P.M., Sun. until 8 P.M., mains $3–7), with tables around a small garden. Specialties include trout cooked with *epazote* (a pungent herb also known as Mexican tea) and *hoja santa* (herb) spices and chicken breast with cheese and plum sauce. Prices are reasonable, and quality is very good. Another popular place is **Los Miranda,** three blocks up from the square on Calle San Juan.

Two kilometers south of town is a large trout farm, where you can fish if you like or buy a tasty cooked trout from one of the several small restaurants nearby.

Hotels

One low-priced spot right in the center of town is **Hotel Santa Mónica** (Hidalgo 109, 714/147-0031, $20 s/d, or $35 for two double beds with TV), with simple rooms around a garden courtyard. Prices are a bit less during the week.

Not as good a deal, but acceptable in a pinch, is **Posada Familiar** (just down from the convent on Av. Juárez, 714/147-0354, $25 s, $30 d), with clean rooms but somewhat lumpy beds. It has an inexpensive *comedor* also.

Practicalities

Tres Estrellas del Centro (Mexico City 55/5264-3739) runs buses between Malinalco and Toluca ($5) and Terminal Observatorio in Mexico City ($8) regularly throughout the day.

The quickest route to drive to Malinalco from Mexico City is to take the Toluca highway and turn south at La Marquesa, following signs to Chalma. You'll also see signs to the Club de Golf Malinalco. The drive takes 1.5–2 hours. It's also possible to drive from Malinalco to Cuernavaca through beautiful, wild mountain country, but the road is in poor condition, so expect to go slowly.

Tourist information can be found in the small office right on the higher of the two downtown squares (daily 9 A.M.–4 P.M.).

Near Malinalco

CHALMA

About 11 kilometers east of Malinalco, set amid forests and gorges, is the church of **Nuestro Señor de Chalma.** The 16th-century sanctuary was built at the site of an ancient sacrificial center, after the "miraculous" appearance of a crucifix on the site in 1533. The church is one of the most venerated pilgrimage sites in Mexico.

Valle de Bravo

Beautiful Valle de Bravo—often shortened to "Valle"—lies 147 kilometers west of Mexico City and 84 kilometers west of Toluca and serves as a playground for wealthy city dwellers who flock here on weekends. Perched on a hillside above Lago (Lake) Avándaro, the ex-colonial town is crisscrossed by serpentine cobblestone streets lined with whitewashed stucco houses topped with red-tile roofs and draped with brilliant flowers and bougainvillea.

Lago Avándaro is actually a dammed reservoir created in the 1940s across a former river valley, measuring three kilometers across by seven kilometers wide, and is invariably dotted with dozens of small yachts and motor boats skimming the cool waters, particularly on weekends.

The gorgeous surrounding pine-forested mountains make a great outdoor venue for hikers, mountain bikers, and nature lovers in general. Thermal conditions over the lake and

nearby countryside make the area one of the premier locations in Mexico for hang gliding and paragliding. And in the hills right above town is a butterfly reserve, one of the best places in Mexico for visitors to see the migrating monarch butterflies during the winter.

Orientation

Valle is divided into two distinct sections, the main center of town up on the hilltop around Plaza Independencia, and a second neighborhood down on the lakeshore and toward the road exit to Avándaro and Toluca. Most of the less-expensive hotels, bike shops, government offices, the market, the bus station, and many restaurants are in the center of town. Down at the docks are a few of the better and more expensive restaurants, a couple of sport shops, and of course the lake. Visitors without wheels may find themselves trudging up and down the steep but short hill between the two with

EXCURSIONS

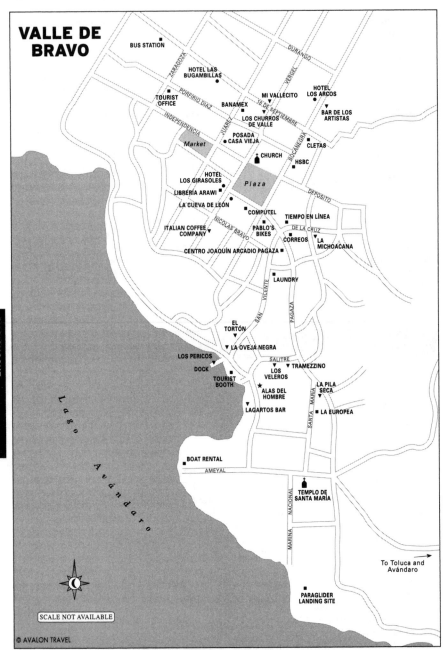

regularity, or you can flag down a passing cab for about $3, or $0.50 cents if you share (ask if the taxi is a *colectivo* before you get in), which is common practice in Valle. From the dock, a small road follows the lakeshore north, bypassing the town center.

The road leading downhill to the dock from the plaza will eventually take you to the main exit toward Toluca. Just outside of town, a road branches off to the right, leading to **Avándaro,** where many wealthy families maintain holiday homes. Leaving town in the other direction, to the north, a secondary highway passes the Avándaro dam and takes a longer and windier route back to Toluca.

SIGHTS

Valle doesn't have much in the way of tourist sights in town per se. The **Centro Joaquín Arcadio Pagaza** (Pagaza 201, Tues.–Sat. 10 A.M.–6 P.M., Sun. 11 A.M.–7 P.M., free) frequently hosts small exhibitions by Mexican and international artists. A couple of blocks below the plaza, the Centro was once the home of Joaquín Arcadio Pagaza (1834–1918), a famed Mexican poet and translator born in Valle de Bravo.

RESTAURANTS

If you visit Valle during the week, note that many restaurants are open only Thursday through Sunday, which means your options will be a bit limited on other days. Generally the less-expensive eateries are clustered around Plaza Independencia, while the more pricey restaurants are found down toward the docks.

If you're renting a place in Valle and are looking for supplies, the first place to start is of course the market, one block from the plaza at the corner of Juárez and Porfirio Díaz. For more luxury goods, including a great selection of wines, cheeses, and other expensive treats, head to **La Europea** (Santa María 114, 726/262-2549, daily 10 A.M.–6 P.M., until 10 P.M. weekends), down near the lake.

Coffee and Sweets

The **Italian Coffee Company** (Coliseo 104, daily 10 A.M.–10 P.M.), a chain coffee shop that

started in Puebla, has a place a block above the plaza, with coffee, sweets, and a decent ham-and-cheese croissant for a light breakfast.

Italian

Tramezzino (Salitre 104C, 726/262-4082, Fri. 4–11:30 P.M., Sat. 1–11:30 P.M., Sun. 1–7 P.M., $11 medium pizza, $20 large) serves very tasty pizzas and pastas in a spacious, upscale (though still relatively informal) dining room and courtyard that fills up regularly on weekends with out-of-town visitors. They also deliver.

Mexican

La Michoacana (Calle de la Cruz 10, just off Pagaza, 726/262-1625, daily 8:30 A.M.–11 P.M., mains $4–8), not to be confused with the ice-cream shop on the plaza, serves great traditional Mexican dishes such as *sopa de tortilla* (tortilla soup), *cecina* (a type of flattened beef), trout, and for the adventurous, *gusanos de maguey* (cactus worms). Meals are moderately priced, and the dining room's windows offer fine views overlooking the town and lake.

A very good, inexpensive local eatery is **Los Churros de Valle** (corner of 16 de Septiembre and Vergel, two blocks from the plaza), with a small but tasty menu, much of it made with ingredients from the owner's farm. Specialties include a great artichoke dip, hearty soups, and of course the namesake churros, a sugary pastry served with hot chocolate.

Right across the street is another good place for inexpensive meals, **Mi Vallecito** (daily 9 A.M.–10 P.M.), serving quesadillas, trout, beef dishes, and buffet meals.

Serving the best inexpensive food down by the lake is **La Oveja Negra** (726/262-0572, Tues.–Sun. 9 A.M.–7 P.M., mains $2–6), in front of the town dock. Breakfasts, including some creative egg dishes, run $2–4, while a variety of entrées—pasta, meats, shrimp, and salads—cost a bit more.

Seafood

Just about every restaurant in town serves the locally famous *trucha*, or trout. One popular low-budget place is **La Cascada,** a small restaurant on

© LUCAS DE BEAUFORT

colonial houses on winding streets in Valle de Bravo

the road between Valle de Bravo and Avándaro, on the roadside next to a waterfall.

A much more upscale spot is **Los Veleros** (Salitre 104, 726/262-0370, Fri.–Sun. 1 P.M.–midnight, mains $9–15), an exceptionally fine restaurant specializing in seafood (but also serving salads and meat dishes) in a beautiful old house. Diners may sit either in one of the interior rooms, decorated with pictures and drawings of sailboats, or on one of the outdoor balconies overlooking the lawn and garden.

If you like waterborne dining, **Los Pericos** (at the municipal dock, Thurs.–Tues. 8 A.M.–10 P.M., 726/262-0558) specializes in fish and seafood. You pay a little extra for swaying about while you eat, but the views across the lake are worth it.

Tacos, *Tortas*, and Snacks

At the southeast corner of the Plaza Independencia, on Bocanegra at Pagaza, two stalls offer excellent stand-up fare, perfect for breakfast or a mid-morning snack. A great way to start your day from around 8:30 A.M.

is the fresh *jugo de naranja con piña* (orange with pineapple juice) with *barbacoa de puerco* (steamed pork). Less than a dollar will get you a big dollop on a double tortilla. Note that the makeshift stall closes when food sells out, which happens well before Mexican lunchtime begins, so get there before midday to avoid disappointment.

Several small stands in the market, one block from the plaza, sell inexpensive breakfasts and *comidas corridas* daily until 5 P.M.

For another option open from 2:30 P.M. until late, head to El Callejón del Arco one block west of the main church near the corner of Independencia and Juárez near to the market. This is a little cobblestone street that everyone knows as *el callejón del hambre* (hunger alley) because of the wonderful beef tacos cooked up here on makeshift stands for under $1 a serving. For some of the finest *tacos de barbacoa* you're likely to find, go to the first stall on the right as you enter the market, where you'll see a crowd gobbling down this local specialty either *sencillo* (single) or *con copia* (literally, "with copy," i.e., with two tortillas) daily while supplies last.

El Tortón, on Plaza Independencia next to Posada Girasoles, whips up decent ham, chicken, or sausage *tortas* for $1.50. It also has a stand down by the dock.

La Michoacana (on Plaza Independencia opposite the church) is the place for fruity ice-lollies, some of the best being *zarzamora* (blackberry) and *zapote* (a sweet, inky black fruit). The custom is to go and pick up a bag of *campechanas* (thin sugary pastries) sold on every corner of the *zócalo* and stroll around, taking alternate bites of ice and pastry.

NIGHTLIFE

La Pila Seca, at the corner of Pagaza and Santa María, near the entrance to town, is a chilled-out bar with good music and comfortable places to sit. It's popular with the alternative crowd living in or visiting Valle. A similar spot is **Bar de los Artistas** (Bocanegra 303), a couple of blocks off the plaza. It's slightly more upscale but still relaxed and sometimes has live music.

Lagartos Bar (Fray Gregorio J. de la Cuenca 6, 726/262-6691) offers live music on Saturday nights, when it is open until midnight. It is a good place to meet people, providing a friendly atmosphere for a drink and a snack, especially around dusk most evenings.

ARTS AND LEISURE

With its large reservoir and encircling mountains, Valle is an outdoor recreation haven. While most Valle visitors live in Mexico and have their own gear, some rental equipment is available.

Festivals and Events

The town's two major festivals are the **Fiesta de la Santa Cruz** (May 3), better known locally as *la feria de Santa María,* and the **Fiesta de San Francisco** (October 4). These events maintain many old Mexican traditional games and dances, as well as elaborate fireworks. If you plan to come on these dates, or on a weekend, make hotel reservations well in advance.

Water Sports

The going rate to rent motorboats on the lake is about $30 for an hour's touring, or $50 to go waterskiing (skis included). However, an affordable treat ($20, seating 8 people) is to hire a speedboat at **Los Pericos** (726/262-0558), the first of Valle de Bravo's two floating restaurants. Fishing trips (perch and bass are plentiful) can also be arranged. To find a pilot, continue past the municipal dock south on the main street and look for a turnoff to the right leading down to a small marina. Be prepared to negotiate.

With a regular stiff breeze and just enough room to get up to full speed, Lago Avándaro is popular for small racing yachts and holds frequent regattas. While boat rentals are not easy to come by, it is possible to take racing classes if you're going to be in the area for a few weeks. The **Club Vela Santa María** (Marina Nacional 201, 726/262-1012, in Mexico City 55/5606-4778, www.cvsm.info) offers classes in single-mast, twin-sail Ventura 21-footers for $80 per class, four classes minimum.

Mountain Biking and Hiking

The pine forests and hills spreading in all directions from around Lago Avándaro are idyllic for taking long hikes or mountain bike rides along old dirt roads or narrow trails. The countryside in this area is generally safe, but robberies have occurred, so stay aware and don't head off alone. When in doubt, ask for information at the bicycle shops or at the municipal tourism office, where you can also arrange biking or hiking guides.

If you're just after a short stroll and a view of town, walk up Calle Depósito, off Bocanegra behind the church, which leads up to a fine lookout spot in the trees. Another good walking destination is to **La Peña,** a rocky outcrop jutting up right from the lakeshore on the northern end of town. On your way up to the rocky peak (with great 360-degree views over the lake and surrounding area), you can take a look at some of the mansions of wealthy Mexicans, some of which have very interesting architecture. Local rock climbers have set up a few routes at the top of La Peña.

MIGRATION OF THE MONARCHS

The migration of millions of monarch butterflies over 2,000 miles or more from the United States to their winter homes in Central Mexico is one of the great natural wonders of the animal world. Seeing them in their nesting zones on a dozen mountainsides in Michoacán and the state of Mexico, turning the pine forest into a shimmering mirage of gold and black, is an experience not to be missed if you're there between November and March.

Monarch butterflies (*Danaus plexippus*) are native to North and South America. The North American subspecies, *Danaus plexippus plexippus*, is divided into two main populations by the Continental Divide. Those west of the Rocky Mountains flutter off to about 25 nesting sites along the coasts of California for the winter, while those east of the Rockies winter either in Florida (where there's also a year-round population – the smart and lazy crowd) or take the long voyage down to Mexico to flee the cold.

The journey south to Mexico begins from summer breeding grounds, which stretch across a wide swath of eastern and central United States and Canada. The monarch resides in patches of wild milkweed plants, which provide their nourishment as well as a toxin called cardenolides, which render the butterflies poisonous to many would-be predators. Monarch eggs hatch after about four days, followed by the roughly two week larval stage, which is when most of their growth occurs, and then finally the pupae stage, when they transform into adult butterflies.

Nonmigrating monarchs live only a few weeks, meaning two or three generations pass during the course of the summer. The migrating monarchs, born in the early fall, live far longer, as much as nine months, redirecting part of their life energies from breeding to sustaining their bodies during their voyage.

How exactly the tiny monarchs, spread across such a huge area, convene into migrating convoys of millions and navigate their way to an area of only about 20 hectares in Central Mexico, two or three thousand miles from their birthplace, "may be one of the most compelling mysteries of animal ecology," as scientists Karen Oberhauser and Michelle Solensky put it. A myriad of theories have been put forth on monarch navigation – including visual clues, like river valleys or mountains; following the earth's magnetic fields with an internal compass; using the sun, moon, or stars, infrared energy perception, internal circadian clocks; or some combination of them all.

However they manage it, around November 1, the monarchs begin arriving in Central Mexico. Because the date coincides with the Mexican Day of the Dead festival, local traditions have long believed the monarchs to be the spirits of dead children returning home. The butterflies first spread out around mixed forests at lower elevations, then gradually over the course of the month congregate in a dozen nesting sites located at around 3,000 meters in dense stands of oyamel fir trees. Favored locations for nesting sites are relatively steep hillsides, invariably with a southerly or southwesterly exposure, and often near a small stream. Exactly how to count how many butterflies are nesting in a given site is still a matter of debate among scientists, but 10 million per hectare is a frequently used estimate.

In early March, those who survive the winter begin dispersing and fluttering north, but in less dense groups than when they came down. Often the butterflies mate right before leaving Mexico, then lay their eggs and die in the southern United States, leaving it to their offspring to reach the summer nesting sites by May.

Monarch populations have fluctuated dramatically in the 12 years since they have been tracked systematically. The winter of 2004-2005 was particularly bad, with 75 percent fewer butterflies than the previous year, according to a study by the World Wildlife Foundation and the Mexican government. The government, long stung by criticism of its record in protecting the butterfly habitat, promptly put most of the blame on the loss of butterfly habitat in the United States and Canada.

Although the loss of U.S. summer breeding grounds are unquestionably a major problem, the situation in Mexico is more critical due to the extreme concentration of the monarch habitat – across just a dozen mountaintops in a very limited area. Here the dense oyamel forest on which the monarch depends is being steadily whittled away at by poor campesinos, who are logging to feed their families. According to one study, 44 percent of the dense, mature forest in the area frequented by the monarchs was destroyed between 1971 and 1999. The government created a reserve in 1986, and then expanded it in 2000 to a current size of 56,259 hectares, but with limited patrolling and the constant pressure of poverty, logging continues. Other creative NGO-led efforts include setting up a system to pay those with logging permits not to log. However, payments of only about $150 a year per family are not likely to put an end to the problem, as the frequent whine of the chainsaw in the forests attests.

The forest doesn't even have to be totally destroyed to become compromised as a shelter for the fragile butterflies. The removal of just a few trees is enough to break the forest canopy, opening the front door to rain and cold in the middle of winter. Particularly harsh storms in the region, like those during the winter of 2001-2002, have killed as much as 80 percent of the population of some winter sanctuaries.

Tourists should be sure to use local guides, and don't begrudge the cost! These guides are literally the first line of defense for the monarchs. Mexicans generally love the butterflies as much as the many entranced foreigners, but even a superficial look around the surrounding countryside villages reveals that these are very poor areas indeed, sustained mainly by meager farming and remittance from the many local people who've traveled to Mexico City or the United States for work.

While government proclamations to create the reserve (out of, locals never tire of pointing out, communal lands they had owned for centuries) may be well intentioned, the only real way to save the forest homes of the monarchs is to make it worth the while of the people who live there. Visitors like you and I can have a greater impact than any environmental campaign, simply by paying a decent price for a guide into the reserve, and enjoying some food or a drink at a campesino-owned roadside eatery near the reserve.

A great spot for a longer hike or bike ride is the ridgeline directly behind town. The easiest way to get up into the forest is to follow Calle Bocanegra from behind the church straight out of town without making any turns. After the road leaves town, it heads uphill and eventually turns to dirt. Look for a well-beaten trail on the right side just before reaching a crest in the road, about one kilometer from where the pavement stops. This trail follows the ridge several kilometers south, with the town and lake to your right, and eventually arrives at **La Torre**, a peak used as a takeoff point for hang gliders and paragliders. Before the trail reaches La Torre, several other trails descend to the right back into town. From La Torre a dirt road winds about 14 bumpy kilometers through forest and farmland back to the main highway coming into Valle from Toluca, about five kilometers above town. To find the turnoff to this road (used by all the paragliders on their way to launch) coming from Valle, look for a dirt road on the left about 200 meters below the Pemex station, signposted S.M. Acatitlán.

Another fine area for getting into the woods is past the **Velo de Novia** (Bridal Veil), a 35-meter waterfall in Avándaro. To get there, take the road to Avándaro, pass through the small town center, and follow signs for Avándaro Spa. After passing the *glorieta* (traffic circle), look for a street to the right called Vega de Valle. Follow this a few hundred meters until you see a dirt lot on the right with a few food stands. If you have a car, park here and follow trails walking down to the waterfall or continuing around the lake. A regular taxi from Valle to the entrance to Velo de Novia will charge $3, while *colectivos* run $1.

Many longer trips are available in the surrounding mountains. One great multihour bike ride is to get driven up to the highest point on the highway heading back from Valle de Bravo toward Toluca, before the road descends to meet the Toluca–Zihuatanejo highway; take a left-hand turn at a dirt road heading into a broad open meadow, called **Corral de Piedra**. From here trails and dirt roads wind way down the mountains through forest and remote farmland all the way back to Valle de Bravo.

Should you prefer to go on an organized trip rather than plunge off into the wilds on your own, or if you need to rent a bike, two shops operate in Valle. **Cletas** (16 de Septiembre 200, 726/262-0291, daily 10 A.M.–8 P.M.) rents bikes for $5 per hour or $20 a full day, or takes people on 2- to 4-hour rides for $15 per person (bike rental not included). The friendly owner Carlos Mejía speaks a little English and will give bikers tips on where to go. He'll also give your bike a quick tune-up.

A block down from the plaza, **Pablo's Bikes** (Pagaza 103, 726/262-3730, www.pablosbikes .com, Mon.–Wed.10 A.M.–3 P.M. and 4–8 P.M., Fri.–Sun. 10 A.M.–8 P.M.) rents bikes at similar prices ($5 per hour, $25 per day) and also organizes rides.

Monarch Butterfly-Watching

Valle de Bravo was receiving seasonal vacationers for quite some time before Mexico City residents started showing up. Flocks of millions of monarch butterflies (*mariposas monarcas*) fly down from Canada annually to spend the winter in the western part of the state of Mexico and nearby Michoacán. Walking through forests covered with a brilliant blanket of brightly colored, constantly moving butterflies is a magical experience, not to be missed if you're in the area from December to February. At last count the monarchs wintered at 57 separate sites on the slopes of 11 volcanoes in central Mexico.

As the forests that provide winter homes for the monarchs are increasingly threatened by logging, the Mexican government has created a series of protected areas. One reserve is about 20 kilometers from Valle de Bravo, near Los Saucos, a small roadside village. Keep an eye out for **Restaurant Las Tres Vírgenes**—that's Los Saucos. Just beyond the village toward Toluca, on weekends during the butterfly season, you'll see men with horses on the side of the road; they

monarch butterflies

© LUCAS DE BEAUFORT

of forested mountainside literally blanketed in butterflies, to the point where it's hard to actually see the trees they are covering. If you sit still long enough, they'll start covering you, too!

Flying

While the thought of leaping into space and expecting to fly gives some of us visions of Icarus's ill-fated jaunt, hundreds of apparently sane people do just that each year from **La Torre,** the rocky peak behind Valle de Bravo. The equipment is of course much improved from the days of swan feathers and wax: Modern wings of choice are either stiff-wing hang gliders or the newer paraglider, a type of soaring parachute. The debate continues to rage over which one is safer, but there's no doubt that paragliding is easier to learn and the equipment is more compact and convenient to transport, and thus more popular with beginners.

Near the lake, **Alas del Hombre** (Plaza Valle, Local 22 and 24, Fray Gregorio J. de La Cuenca, 726/262-6382 or 726/262-0934, www.alas.com.mx) has nearly 30 years of experience flying around Valle de Bravo and elsewhere in Mexico. They offer courses for both hang gliding and paragliding, tandem flights, and guided tours—all with certified instructors. A 30-minute glide down in a tandem with an instructor costs $130 on weekends and $100 during the week (minimum age seven). Take a windbreaker, sports shoes, and a camera. There are also weeklong courses for those planning to stay in town for a while. The basic introductory paragliding course includes eight days of training over four weekends and costs $1,100–1,500 per person, depending on how many people sign up for the course.

One U.S./Mexican company that runs hang gliding and paragliding trips to Mexico is **Fly Mexico** (U.S. 512/467-2529 or 800/861-7198, in Valle de Bravo 726/262-0579, www.flymex .com); courses cost $895 (paragliding) or $1,195 (hang gliding) for one week, all included except airfare. Student trips cost more if you're not a certified flier already.

are offering inexpensive visits to the reserve. A 1.5-hour trip will set you back $20 for a guide and $15 for a horse (if you want one)— considerably less expensive than the better-known sanctuaries in Michoacán.

The Valle de Bravo municipal tourism office (Porfirio Díaz and Zaragoza, three blocks northwest of the plaza, 726/269-6200, www .avalledebravo.com, Mon.–Fri. 9 a.m.–7 p.m., Sat. 9 a.m.–2 p.m.) can also set you up with guides. Longer trips in the forests can be arranged without difficulty. If you don't see anyone on the road, ask in Los Saucos for a guide. The best month to visit is January, when the southward migration is mostly complete; during the week the sanctuaries are much less crowded (with people, that is). In years when there are more butterflies than normal, you'll see clouds of monarchs all the way down along the highway itself, along with local policemen waving cars to slow down as they pass through the area. And up in the forest, at "butterfly central," the sight is really staggering: about an acre

EXCURSIONS

Paragliding is one of Valle de Bravo's many recreation possibilities.

HOTELS

While Valle doesn't have a huge selection of hotels, there are a number of good inexpensive options and a few lovely high-priced spreads. Rates are sometimes lower during the week. Reservations are a good idea if you plan to visit on a weekend or holiday.

$15-30

The best low-priced place to stay in town is **Hotel Los Girasoles** (right on the main square at Plaza Independencia 1, 726/262-2967, $40 s/d weekends, $30 s/d weekdays). The hotel is small, but the brick and plaster rooms are quite spacious and spotless, with nice powerful showers to boot. It's a good deal.

$30-50

An excellent mid-range option, with not much in the way of amenities but lots of character, is **Posada Casa Vieja** (Juárez 101, 726/2620338, rooms start from $47 weekends, less during the week). In a converted hacienda built more than 200 years ago and run by descendants of the original owners, the whitewashed rooms with wooden roofs and brick floors (no phones) spread around a tree-filled courtyard and are surprisingly affordable. If you come during the week it's less expensive, and you might even have the place to yourself. Parking is available.

Hotel las Bugambilias (Av. 16 de Septiembre 406, 726/262-1966, $40 d) offers clean but very small rooms in a motel-like complex with parking.

$50-75

Right on the plaza, **La Cueva del Leon** (Plaza Independencia 2, 726/262-4062, $73 d, $110 king-sized) features 14 rooms around a small interior courtyard filled with lots of hanging plants. The brightly painted rooms, with lots of pink trim, all have air-conditioning and color TVs. King-sized rooms have whirlpool tubs. The attached dining room has mediocre food (for the price) but a nice small balcony overlooking the square.

Over $110

The most upscale place in the center of town is **Hotel Los Arcos** (Bocanegra 310, 726/262-0042 or 726/262-0168, $110 s/d). There are 24 wood-beamed rooms and suites, each equipped with TV and working fireplace, around an interior garden area with a small pool.

An activity-oriented "therapy center" is the plush **Avándaro Golf and Spa Resort** (Vega del Río s/n, 726/266-0200 or 726/266-0370, Mexico City 55/5282-1212, www.hotel avandaro.com, $155 s/d, up to $445 for Suite Monarca). Composed of a hotel, health complex, and 18-hole golf course, the resort is secluded amid the pine forests in the town of Avándaro, southwest of Valle de Bravo. Rooms are spacious and bright, and the facilities include a palatial pool, seven tennis courts, a full spa, and the golf course. Guests must still pay an additional $18 to use the spa or $180 for the golf course, while the pool is included in room price. Nonguests may pay $18 to use the spa but are not allowed in the pool or on the golf course.

The adventure travel company Río y Montaña runs a forest lodge, **Rodavento** (Km 3.5 Valle de Bravo Los Saucos, 726/251-4182, Mexico City 55/5292-5032, www.rioymontana .com, $1,300–1,800 for 5–7 days, all included, double suite for $330 per night) above Valle de Bravo. Here tourists can take part in a number of different outdoor activites, including kayaking, paragliding, mountain biking, or just enjoying the greenery. The hotel is kind of an updated cabin-style construction out of brick and wood; it integrates well into the forest surroundings. Rooms are comfortable and well kept. Check out the *temazcal*, where you can sweat out your toxins in a traditional indigenous sauna and follow it up with a massage. Although they are geared toward longer stays, they will sometimes accept clients for one or two nights, depending on how busy they are.

PRACTICALITIES
Information and Services
For information, tourist maps, and pamphlets, stop in at the very helpful and friendly **Municipal Tourism Office** (Porfirio Díaz and Zaragoza, three blocks northwest of the plaza, 726/269-6200, www.avalledebravo.com,

Mon.–Fri. 9 A.M.–7 P.M., Sat. 9 A.M.–2 P.M.). The tourism office also has a module on the lakeside (daily 10 A.M.–6 P.M.).

The Valle post office (Mon.– Fri. 9 A.M.– 4 P.M.) is on the corner of Pagaza and Calle de la Cruz, a block down from the plaza toward the dock.

Computel (on the plaza opposite the side of the church, daily 7 A.M.–8:30 P.M.) offers long-distance phone and fax service.

Internet service is available at many places around town, including **Tiempo en Línea** (Calle de la Cruz 100, Mon.–Sat. 10 A.M.–9 P.M., Sun. noon–7 P.M., $1.60 an hour), a block below the plaza on Pagaza.

Banamex, HSBC, and BBVA, all within two blocks of the plaza, change dollars and travelers checks, and each has an ATM. On Saturday the banks are open 10 A.M.–2 P.M. only.

On San Vicente, a couple of blocks down from Pagaza toward the lake, is an inexpensive, no-name laundry service (Mon.–Sat. 9 A.M.–2 P.M. and 5–8 P.M.).

Librería Arawi (Coliseo 101, 726/262-2557, daily 9:30 A.M.–3 P.M. and 5–9 P.M.), on the plaza, sells magazines and newspapers, some in English.

The police can be reached, if you can believe it, via a lawyer's office (726/262-1126).

Clínica Santa Fe (Nicolás Bravo 203, 726/262-0018), a block south and west of the plaza, offers 24-hour medical attention. The Cruz Roja ambulance service can be reached at 726/262-0391. Farmacia Santa Juanita (Nicolás Bravo 103 at San Vicente, 726/262-1065) is open 24 hours a day.

Getting There and Away
Two roads leave Valle de Bravo to Toluca, the windier and slower México 48 and the faster and more scenic México 134, which passes near Nevado de Toluca. Be prepared for lots of traffic on weekends.

Zinacantepec (16 de Septiembre just past Zaragoza, 726/262-0213) runs buses once an hour from Valle de Bravo to Toluca and Terminal Observatorio in Mexico City between

6 A.M. and 6 P.M., charging $5 to Toluca (one hour and 45 minutes) and $8 to Mexico City (two hours and 45 minutes). It also runs two direct buses to Mexico City per day, leaving in the afternoon ($11).

Collective taxis running between Valle and Avándaro leave regularly from Pagaza, right next to the plaza, for $1, while other taxis go to Colorines across the dam from Avenida 16 de Septiembre, just off Juárez, also for $1.

Popocatépetl and Ixtaccíhuatl

The second- and third-highest mountains in Mexico, Popocatépetl (5,465 meters) and Ixtaccíhuatl (5,230 meters) form the southeastern lip of the Valle de México. On clear days in Mexico City, the two snowcapped peaks can be seen in the distance from a number of tall buildings in the city center.

Until a decade ago, climbing Popo was probably the most popular mountaineering adventure in Mexico. In December 1994, however, the formerly dormant volcano began intermittently belching clouds of smoke and ash. The peak is still off-limits to climbers. For updated information on the volcano's activity, visit the website www.cenapred.unam .mx/mvolcan.html.

The Paso de Cortés, between the two volcanoes, is a destination in itself for the brisk air and amazing views. It's also the take-off point for an Ixtaccíhuatl climb and is reached by driving or busing 48 kilometers from Mexico City to Amecameca, a large town at the base of the mountain. Driving from Amecameca to the pass, you will pass an army checkpoint and may be asked to show some identification.

PASO DE CORTÉS

Visitors not interested in climbing might like to wander the many trails around the Paso de Cortés between the two peaks. Be sure to bring plenty of warm clothing, as it can be bitter cold and windy. The pass is so called because Cortés came through here from Cholula on his way to conquer the Aztec capital of Tenochtitlán. On the way, two of the Spanish soldiers reputedly climbed up Popo and descended into the crater to get sulfur for gunpowder (apparently not a big deal for those

unbelievably hardy conquistadors), which would make them the first recorded climbers to scale the mountain.

On weekends, several food stands offer quesadillas and other snacks at the parking lot in the pass, and a visitors center can provide some information on the volcanoes. The **Albergue Alzomoni**, by the radio towers just off the dirt road leading to La Joya, rents beds for $2 a night, with very minimal facilities (reserve with CONANP offices in Amecameca, 597/978-3829). The lodge, atop a hill with great views of both peaks and the valleys below, can be crowded on weekends.

Practicalities

Although no buses drive the 30-kilometer potholed road to the Paso de Cortés from Amecameca, taxis in Amecameca are accustomed to taking up weekenders for a negotiable fee, usually around $15 per car. If you did bring a car and don't mind a few bumps, consider continuing down the dirt road on the far side from the pass—it leads down through the forest to Cholula (46 kilometers) and on to Puebla (10 kilometers farther), where you can take the highway back to Mexico City. Driving up through Amecameca, enjoying the views at the pass, and returning to Mexico City via Cholula makes a great day trip. Sometimes, however, the road between the pass and Cholula is closed to regular traffic due to volcanic activity.

CLIMBING IXTACCÍHUATL

Ixtaccíhuatl is still open for climbing and presents more of a challenge than Popo did. While the single cone of Popo required a steep hike of four to seven hours to reach the peak, the most

© CHRIS HUMPHREY

climbing Ixtaccíhuatl, with Popocatépetl in the background

common route up the broken, jagged Ixta, replete with false summits along the way to test your resolve, takes a solid seven to ten hours.

The description here is only a general overview of what the route is like, and does not pretend to serve as a step-by-step guide. Climbers should take a certified guide. The climb, while not particularly difficult in a technical sense, is nonetheless extremely dangerous for getting lost on the vast mountain terrain and getting caught unprepared in bad weather. Only very experienced and well-prepared climbers should attempt the route without a guide. Whether you go with a guide or not, it's very important (and legally required) to register with the Amecameca offices of CONANP (Plaza de la Constitución 9B, 597/978-3830), the National Commission for Protected Areas, which administers the Izta–Popo park and is in charge of organizing rescue teams in case of emergency. Usually someone in the office speaks English.

For more detailed route-finding information on Ixtaccíhuatl or other Mexican volcanoes, buy a copy of R. G. Secor's guide, *Mexico's Volcanoes,*

3rd edition (Seattle: The Mountaineers, 2001). The official government website (in Spanish) contains excellent updated information and maps: http://iztapopo.conanp.gob.mx.

La Joya Route

By far the most frequented route up Ixta begins at La Joya (4,000 meters), a dirt parking lot perched on the southern flank of the mountain, reached by a seven-kilometer dirt road from the Paso de Cortés. The road is passable by passenger car most of the year but can get treacherous in the rainy season. No buses go to either the Paso de Cortés or La Joya, so if you don't have wheels, you'll have to hire a taxi in Amecameca ($24 per carload).

In profile Ixta looks something like a sleeping woman, and climbers have labeled parts of the mountain accordingly. The La Joya climb starts at "Los Pies" (the feet) and continues up "Las Piernas" (the legs) to the brutally steep "Rodillas" (knees). From there it crosses the snowfields of "La Barriga" (the belly) at a gentler grade to reach the mountain's summit atop "El Pecho" (the breast). Although it's not so steep, the last stretch across the icefields is really a rude shock for most people, who frequently give everything they have up Las Rodillas, thinking the summit is not much further. It's also extremely bright when sunny, so hopefully you thought to bring your sunglasses, or you might have to turn back. From El Pecho, the views down onto the rock formation of "La Cabeza" (the head) and the surrounding countryside are spectacular.

One popular schedule for climbing is to arrive at the parking lot at La Joya in the afternoon or evening, sleep until around 2 A.M. in your car or a tent, then climb most of the way up in the darkness, arriving at the peak sometime between 8 and 11 A.M. and returning to the parking lot in the early afternoon. Leaving at this ungodly hour provides spectacular sunrise views and ensures that the ice on the peak is hard, making it easier and safer to cross. The drawback for this schedule is the possibility of losing your way in the dark if you're unsure of the trail.

If no one in your group has been on the

EXCURSIONS

mountain before, or if you just think getting up so early is for the birds, leave La Joya in late morning or early afternoon and spend the night about halfway up the mountain (at 4,750 meters) in a pair of climbing huts just below the Knees. Although rudimentary, the huts are protected from the elements and will keep you warm enough if you have a good sleeping bag and pad. They can get crowded on weekends in the dry season, so if you go then, it's better to have a tent on hand, just in case. Another consideration is the altitude—if you're not acclimated, it's often better to knock out the climb in one shot rather than try to sleep at the huts, where the thin air can make for a miserable night.

Although the trail is well worn, it zigzags back and forth across a long ridge leading northward up to the summit—sometimes on the Mexico City side of the mountain, sometimes on the Puebla side—and can at times be difficult to spot among the jumble of rocks and gravel. Go slowly and avoid energy-consuming detours.

Should you have no particular desire to go to the summit, a hike halfway up to the huts (either spending the night or returning the same day) crosses over only dirt and rock, not ice, and requires no special climbing equipment. The hike is still very arduous, especially with the altitude, and takes five to eight hours round-trip.

Equipment and Safety Precautions

If you hike Ixta in the dry season (December to April), you can generally get away with just bringing an ice axe for emergencies, as the only stretches of ice you'll have to cross are mostly flat. The rest of the year you'll also need crampons. A rope is generally not needed. Check with a climbing shop in Mexico City for current snow conditions. As with any mountain climb, keep a close eye on the weather, and come prepared with waterproof, warm clothes in case things take a turn for the worse.

Visiting climbers may be disheartened to see Mexicans young and old tromping gleefully past them on the trail, while they rest, wheezing, against a convenient rock. But don't forget, most of these locals live in Mexico City

(which has an elevation of 2,240 meters) and are well acclimated. Don't fly in from sea level or thereabouts and expect to hike up to the peak without a care. Even those who have spent some time in Mexico City may get struck by a splitting headache, fierce vomiting, and possibly worse. Should these symptoms befall you, the quickest remedy is a fast descent. Drinking plenty of water while climbing can help keep altitude sickness at bay.

Though not a technically challenging climb, this is a very large mountain and should not be taken lightly—don't go unless you have some experience climbing or you're with an experienced group leader. **Socorro Alpino** has a rescue crew at La Joya on weekends in case of problems, and someone is always around who can call for help at the ranger station at the Paso de Cortés. The closest medical help is the hospital at Amecameca.

To rent basic mountaineering gear for a climb, go to **Deportes Rubéns** in Mexico City (Venustiano Carranza 17, 55/5518-5636, www.dscorp.com.mx/rubens, Mon.–Sat. 10 A.M.–7:30 P.M.). They rent rather worn ice axes and crampons, but no boots, for $11 a set per weekend, plus a $42 cash or voucher deposit. The store sells a decent selection of outdoor clothing, backpacking supplies, and some climbing gear, both Mexican and imported. Two better shops with much higher-quality gear, for sale only, are **El Séptimo Grado** (Fernando Montes de Oca 61, Col. Condesa, 55/5553-3777, www.elseptimogrado.com) and **Vertimania** (Patriotismo 899, Col. Mixcoac, 55/5615-5229, www.vertimania.com.mx).

Guides

Colorado Mountain School (341 Moraine Ave., P.O. Box 1846, Estes Park, CO 80517, U.S., 970/586-5758 or 888/267-7783, www.totalclimbing.com) offers a package trip from the United States to climb Ixta and Pico de Orizaba. An 11-day two-peak trip costs $2,450 per person.

One Mexican guide group that offer less-expensive trips up Ixta is **Río y Montaña** (55/5292-5032 or 55/5292-5058, www.rioy

montana.com), with two-day trips running about $250 per person. Río y Montaña organizes all sorts of adventure trips around Mexico, including their popular rafting trips to Veracruz. A smaller outfit is **Teporingo's Expediciones** (on the plaza in Amecameca, 597/978-0349, teporingo_ex@yahoo.com.mx), which specializes in hiking, mountaineering, and mountain bike trips in the volcanoes of central Mexico.

Practicalities

Get on the Puebla highway leaving Mexico City, then take the turnoff marked Cuautla–Amecameca. After going through a $1.50 toll, a secondary highway continues 22.5 kilometers to Amecameca. One kilometer beyond Amecameca, a road turns left (east) and snakes its way 30 kilometers up the mountain to the Paso de Cortés, accessible by either car or taxi from Amecameca. By bus, ride from Terminal TAPO in Mexico City to Amecameca and take a taxi (see the *Amecameca* section for details).

Elsewhere on Ixta

The pine-forested flanks of Ixta are crisscrossed with dirt roads, giving access to the mountain from several different directions besides the Paso de Cortés.

On the Mexico City–Puebla highway, at the road's highest point above the Valle de México, 21 kilometers from the toll gate leaving Mexico City, is the roadside village of **Llano Grande,** where you'll see a couple of dozen food stands and stores. Look for an archway on the north side of the highway—a dirt road turns in here and continues 10 kilometers up the northern side of Ixta, where it runs into a large meadow at 3,350 meters, with a forestry research station managed by the Universidad de Chapingo. From here secondary dirt tracks continue up the side of the mountain to a second, higher meadow with fantastic views of the peak, as well as down toward Cholula on the east side and toward San Rafael and Amecameca to the west. The climbing routes up Ixta from here all go by the "Head" of the mountain and are more technical, so don't attempt them without a guide.

While the forests on this side of Ixta are lovely for hiking and mountain biking, don't park your car near the village of Llano Grande, as robberies and assaults have been reported. Instead drive all the way up the dirt road as far as the research station, and leave the car there, where it's generally safe. This is, nonetheless, a very remote area, so there is always some risk.

North of Amecameca, on the eastern side of Ixta, is the village of **San Rafael,** the take-off point for another approach to the summit. Robberies have been reported around San Rafael, so it's not advisable to venture over this way.

AMECAMECA

On the way to the Paso de Cortés from Mexico City is Amecameca (2,475 meters), a mountain town with clean brisk air (dress warmly). The market and picturesque town square, with the bright-red **Iglesia de la Asunción** on the east side, are fun to explore for an hour or two. It's also a good place to grab a meal or pick up supplies before heading up the mountain. The best season to visit the town is after the rains have finished, usually towards the end of October, until May, when the views are razor sharp. It is very cold at night in the winter months, so take coats and scarves.

Just west of town is a hilltop park known as **El Sacramonte** (Sacred Mountain), with two chapels on top. Each year on Ash Wednesday, the townsfolk carry a decorated image of Christ—supposedly made in 1521—in a candlelight procession from one of the churches to the nearby burial cave of Fray Martín de Valencia, who is said to have been the leader of the first group of missionaries to the area.

Another attraction just before arriving in town from Mexico City, on your left, is **Hacienda de Panoaya** (Km 58 Carr. Fed. Mex–Cuautla, 597/978-2670 or 597/978-2813, Tues.–Sun. 9 A.M.–7 P.M.), which has been converted into a museum, zoo, and restaurant complex. The museum contains a small volcano museum (Sat.–Sun. only, $2 adults, $1 children), and the restaurant serves good venison steaks.

Amecameca holds a **Feria de la Nuez** (Nut Fair) in August.

A tourism office (in the Presidencia Municipal, 597/978-0028 or 597/978-0345) provides visitor information and ideas for day trips or weekend visits.

The best place to get information on the volcanoes, and also very good for finding hiking, biking, or climbing guides, is the CONANP (Plaza de la Constitución 9B, 597/978-3830, http://iztapopo.conanp.gob.mx), the National Commission for Protected Areas, which administers the Izta–Popo park.

Practicalities

Transportes Volcanes runs buses every 15 minutes or so, 5 A.M.–10 P.M., between Terminal TAPO in eastern Mexico City and Amecameca; the fare is $2.80. Taxis from Amecameca's plaza to Paso de Cortés cost around $20 per carload, or $30 to La Joya (for climbing Ixta), although prices vary.

Puebla and Vicinity

The Spanish founded the city of Puebla in 1531 as an intermediate supply depot and resting point between the port of Veracruz and the Mexican capital. Puebla became an important trading center in the colonial era, and the route from Mexico City to the coast via Puebla is still one of the country's main commercial arteries.

The city was laid out in the neat grid pattern typically employed by the Spanish. The historic city center is full of ornate colonial buildings replete with magnificent stonework, gold leaf, and Puebla's distinct signature, **Talavera tile,** which decorates rooftops, church domes, walls, and much else besides. Those with an eye for architecture will enjoy the city's plentiful baroque churches and churrigueresque facades.

The **Cinco de Mayo** holiday, one of Mexico's greatest celebrations, originated in Puebla, when on May 5, 1862, a ragtag Mexican army beat back the invading French. The French were eventually victorious, but Mexicans still celebrate Cinco de Mayo as a day of national pride.

Today Puebla is the fourth-largest city of Mexico, with a population of about 1.5 million people. The city's colonial architecture provides a backdrop for bustling commerce, cafés, bars, shops, shoppers, museums, students, and scores of tourists. Agriculture, tourism, and the production of ceramics are major industries, and Puebla is also home to Mexico's Volkswagen factory, responsible for the *bochitos* (Beetles) seen all over Mexican roads, as well as the sleek new Beetle so popular in the United States. Tragically for those with a soft spot for the ubiquitous old *bochitos,* production has been discontinued, although there'll surely be lots of them still running for years to come.

More information about the city can be found at www.pueblacapital.gob.mx.

Orientation

Puebla was the first Mexican town built from a master plan rather than around an existing Indian city. With a few exceptions, streets running north–south are called *calles,* and those running east–west are called *avenidas.*

The intersection at the northwest corner of the *zócalo* forms the center of town for purposes of street labeling. Here, Avenida Reforma/Palafox (east–west) meets Avenida 16 de Septiembre/Cinco de Mayo(north–south, one of the exceptions mentioned above). Coming from the west, Avenida Reforma becomes Avenida Palofax east of this intersection. Coming from the south, Avenida 16 de Septiembre becomes Avenida Cinco de Mayonorth of this intersection.

Even-numbered *avenidas* lie north of Avenida Reforma/Palafox; odd-numbered *avenidas* lie to the south. On the west side of Avenida 16 de Septiembre/5 de Mayo, all *avenidas* are labeled with the suffix "Poniente" (west), abbreviated

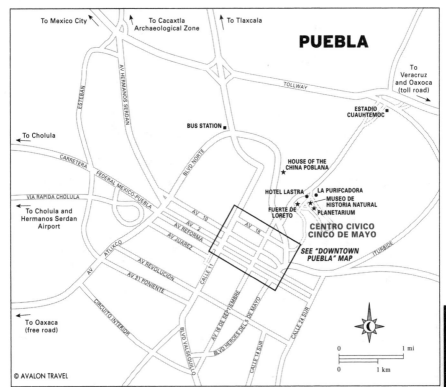

To Mexico City

To Cacaxtla
Archaeological Zone

To Tlaxcala

PUEBLA

AV HERMANOS SERDAN

ESTEBAN

TOLLWAY

To
Veracruz
and Oaxoca
(toll road)

BUS STATION

ESTADIO
CUAUHTEMOC

To Cholula

CARRETERA

BLVD NORTE

HOUSE OF THE
CHINA POBLANA

FEDERAL MEXICO-PUEBLA

VIA RAPIDA CHOLULA

LA PURIFCADORA

HOTEL LASTRA

To Cholula and
Hermanos Serdan
Airport

AV 10

MUSEO DE
HISTORIA NATURAL
PLANETARIUM

FUERTE DE
LORETO

AV 2

AV 18

ATLIXCO

AV REFORMA

CENTRO CIVICO
CINCO DE MAYO

AV JUAREZ

ITURBIDE

CALLE 11

SEE "DOWNTOWN
PUEBLA" MAP

AV REVOLUCION

AV 31 PONIENTE

AV

CIRCUITO INTERIOR

To Oaxaca
(free road)

BLVD VALSEQUILLO

AV 16 DE SEPTIEMBRE

BLVD HEROES DEL 5 DE MAYO

CALLE 11 SUR

CALLE 21 SUR

0   1 mi

0   1 km

© AVALON TRAVEL

to Pte.; on the east side, they're all labeled "Oriente" (east), shortened to Ote.

Even-numbered *calles* lie east of Avenida 16 de Septiembre/5 de Mayo; odd-numbered *calles* lie to the west. On the south side of Avenida Reforma/Palafox, all *calles* are labeled with the suffix "Sur" (south), while on the north side they're all labeled "Norte" (north), or Nte.

The historic section of town is bounded by Boulevard Héroes del Cinco de Mayoon on the east, Calle 11 on the west, Avenida 18 on the north, and Avenida 11 on the south. Most sites of interest to visitors are within easy walking distance of the central plaza. A few destinations, such as the Railway Museum, Uriarte Talavera, and the Ex-Convento de Santa Mónica, are a bit farther afield and are best visited by taxi or *colectivo*.

Taxis in Puebla do not use meters, so check the cost before you board. One taxi company you can call for a car is **Radio Taxi** (222/243-7059 or 222/243-7212).

SIGHTS
Plaza

The city center (call it the *zócalo,* the plaza, the Plaza de la Constitución, or the Plaza de Armas) faces the cathedral and is bordered on three sides by the original broad stone *portales* (arches). The buildings exhibit a variety of architectural styles from across the centuries: baroque, churrigueresque, neoclassic, herreresque, and Renaissance. The 16th-century arches lining the plaza house sidewalk cafés, restaurants, shops, and newspaper stands. The broad *zócalo*—once a bustling marketplace—is an

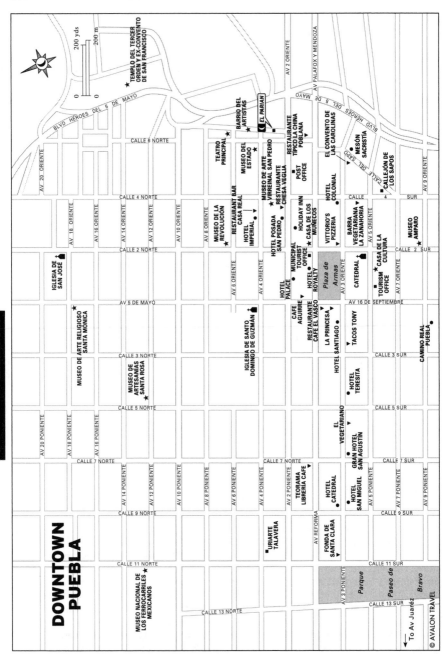

EXCURSIONS

DOWNTOWN PUEBLA

200 yds
200 m

TEMPLO DEL TERCER ORDEN Y EX-CONVENTO DE SAN FRANCISCO

BLVD. HÉROES DEL 5 DE MAYO

BARRIO DEL ARTISTAS

EL PARIAN

AV. 2 ORIENTE

AV. PALAFOX Y MENDOZA

BLVD. HÉROES DEL 5 DE MAYO

CALLE 6 NORTE

TEATRO PRINCIPAL

MUSEO DEL ESTADO

RESTAURANTE TIPICO LA CHINA POBLANA

EL CONVENTO DE LAS CAROLINAS

MESÓN SACRISTIA

AV. 20 ORIENTE

CALLE 4 NORTE

MUSEO DE ARTE VIRREINAL SAN PEDRO

RESTAURANTE CHESA VEGLIA

POST OFFICE

CALLEJÓN DE LOS SAPOS

CALLE DEL SAPO

AV. 18 ORIENTE

AV. 16 ORIENTE

AV. 14 ORIENTE

AV. 12 ORIENTE

AV. 10 ORIENTE

AV. 8 ORIENTE

MUSEO DE LA REVOLUCIÓN

RESTAURANT BAR CASA REAL

HOTEL IMPERIAL

HOTEL POSADA SAN PEDRO

HOLIDAY INN

CASA DE LOS MUÑECOS

HOTEL COLONIAL

CALLE

4

SUR

AV. 9 ORIENTE

CALLE 2 NORTE

VITTORIO'S PIZZERIA

BARRA VEGETARIANA LA ZANAHORIA

MUSEO AMPARO

IGLESIA DE SAN JOSÉ

HOTEL PALACE

MUNICIPAL TOURIST OFFICE

HOTEL ROYALTY

Plaza de Armas

CATEDRAL

TOURISM OFFICE

CASA DE LA CULTURA

AV. 5 DE MAYO

AV. 6 ORIENTE

AV. 4 ORIENTE

AV. 3 ORIENTE

AV. 5 ORIENTE

AV. 7 ORIENTE

MUSEO DE ARTE RELIGIOSO SANTA MÓNICA

IGLESIA DE SANTO DOMINGO DE GUZMAN

CAFE AGUIRRE

RESTAURANTE CAFE EL VASCO

LA PRINCESA

HOTEL SANTIAGO

TACOS TONY

AV. 16 DE SEPTIEMBRE

CAMINO REAL PUEBLA

CALLE 3 NORTE

MUSEO DE ARTESANÍAS SANTA ROSA

HOTEL TERESITA

CALLE 3 SUR

CALLE 5 NORTE

CALLE 5 SUR

AV. 20 PONIENTE

AV. 18 PONIENTE

AV. 16 PONIENTE

EL VEGETARIANO

CALLE 7 NORTE

CALLE 7 SUR

AV. 14 PONIENTE

AV. 12 PONIENTE

AV. 10 PONIENTE

AV. 8 PONIENTE

AV. 6 PONIENTE

AV. 4 PONIENTE

AV. 2 PONIENTE

TEORAMA LIBRERIA CAFE

HOTEL CATEDRAL

GRAN HOTEL SAN AGUSTIN

AV. 5 PONIENTE

AV. 7 PONIENTE

AV. 9 PONIENTE

CALLE 9 NORTE

HOTEL SAN MIGUEL

CALLE 9 SUR

URIARTE TALAVERA

FONDA DE SANTA CLARA

AV. REFORMA

CALLE 11 NORTE

CALLE 11 SUR

MUSEO NACIONAL DE LOS FERROCARRILES MEXICANOS

Parque

Paseo de

Bravo

AV. 3 PONIENTE

CALLE 13 SUR

CALLE 13 NORTE

To Av Juárez

© AVALON TRAVEL

COURTESY OF CONSEJO DE PROMOCIÓN TURÍSTICA DE MÉXICO/BRUCE HERMAN

Puebla's Catedral de la Inmaculada Concepción

island of tranquility with shady trees, benches, and a bandstand.

Catedral de la Inmaculada Concepción

On the south side of the *zócalo,* you can't miss the cathedral, considered one of the most beautiful churches in Mexico (no small compliment). The twin-towered and tile-domed cathedral, begun in 1575 by Francisco Becerra and completed in 1664, shows medieval, Renaissance, and baroque styles on the facade, and even a few neoclassical hints on the inside, for example Manuel Tolsá's marble and onyx altar. Inside, past the lovely carved wooden doors, visitors will find 14 gilded chapels filled with religious paintings, relics, and sculptures, as well as a 12-meter-high pipe organ.

One tale about the church says the enormous 8.5-ton bell was placed in the bell tower by angels. How else would it have gotten up to the top of the 73-meter tower? The second tower has no bell, because it was feared that the weight would cause the structure to sink into the ground. A tower tour is offered every day at 11 A.M.; English-speaking guides are usually available.

Casa de la Cultura and Biblioteca Palafoxiana

Formerly the archbishop's palace, the Casa de la Cultura (Avenida 5 Ote. 5, next door to the tourism office, 222/246-3186 or 222/232-4647) was built in 1597. The palace housed the colleges of San Pablo, San Pedro, and San Juan in the 17th and 18th centuries. In 1891 it became the Governor's Palace, and in 1973 it was reconstructed. Inside you'll find a movie room, exhibition space, workshops, and restrooms.

Up a flight of marble stairs to the 2nd floor is the **Biblioteca Palafoxiana,** one of the oldest libraries in the Americas. In 1646, Bishop Juan Palafox y Mendoza donated the first 5,000 volumes, including works of philosophy, theology, and history. The books cover a wide variety of scholars; many are in Greek and Latin, others in Hebrew and Sanskrit, and some were printed as early as the 15th century.

In 1773 Bishop Francisco Fabian y Fuero constructed the library, a parallelogram 43 meters long and 12 meters wide, covered by five domes on six Doric arches. Shelves of white cedar, divided into 2,472 sections, hold 50,000 volumes. Check out the revolving *atril*, or lectern, used to consult various books at once. It's an amazing, unique sight, something out of *The Name of the Rose* or *Harry Potter*, and well worth a visit.

Iglesia de Santo Domingo de Guzmán

Three blocks north of the plaza on Cinco de Mayolies what remains of a fine baroque Dominican monastery (daily 10 A.M.–12:15 P.M. and 4:30–8 P.M.), consecrated in 1690. Inside the exceptional **Capilla del Rosario,** the walls are covered with gilded ornate carvings, tiles, and cherubs.

Iglesia de San Cristóbal

Another baroque beauty—this one is on Calle 4 Norte at Avenida 6 Oriente. The interior is similar to that of the Capilla del Rosario; the elaborate relief figures are very well done but not gilded.

Other Churches

Puebla has around 60 churches, many dating from the colonial era. Church buffs might want to take a look at **Iglesia de San José** (nine blocks north of the plaza, at Av. 18 Ote. and Calle 2 Nte.) and the adjoining tile-domed **Capilla de Jesús.** The church's interior is inaccessible but worth a look from the outside.

The churrigueresque **Templo del Tercer Orden y Ex-Convento de San Francisco** (Av. 14 Ote. 1009, at Blvd. Héroes del 5 de Mayo) was begun in 1535 and completed in 1667. The principal dome is an eight-sided star. *La Virgen de la Conquistadora,* the statue of the Virgin that according to legend accompanied Cortés on his battles of conquest, is also here—an ominous sight for those who can imagine the scenes the small statue witnessed.

Other churches worth a visit are **Iglesia de la Compañía** (Av. Palafox at Calle 4 Sur), **Iglesia del Carmen** (Av. 16 de Septiembre at Av. 17 Ote.), and **Iglesia de la Santa Cruz** (Av. 14 Ote. and Calle 14 Sur), built at the site of Puebla's first Mass, held in 1530.

Museo de Arte Religioso Santa Mónica

This religious museum (Av. 18 Pte. 103 at 5 de Mayo, 222/232-0178, Tues.–Sun. 10 A.M.–4:30 P.M., $3) was founded as a convent in 1610. With the laws of the Reforma, promulgated by president Benito Juárez in 1867, the Catholic nuns of this convent literally went underground and remained hidden there until they were discovered in 1935. The building then was converted into a museum. Visitors can walk through narrow halls, winding stairways, hidden passages, and look through a secret window where the nuns watched Mass in the adjacent church. The museum entrance is through a private home, as it was when the convent was in operation. Kids will get a kick out of the velvet paintings with hands and faces that seem to change position when you view them from different angles, the neat spiral staircase, and the creepy cold crypt.

Museo Amparo

This restored colonial mansion (Calle 2 Sur 708, 222/246-4646, www.museoamparo.com, Wed.–Mon. 10 A.M.–6 P.M., $2.50), three blocks from the *zócalo,* showcases an extensive collection of pre-Hispanic and colonial art. The displays are labeled in Spanish and English, with push-button recordings (headsets cost $2). The museum's restaurant and shop are both very good.

Museo de Arte Virreinal San Pedro

Puebla's newest museum (Calle 4 Nte. 203, 222/246-6618, Tues.–Sùn. 10 A.M.–5 P.M., $3) is dedicated to colonial religious art. Housed in the former Hospital de San Pedro, the museum has a permanent exhibit of art from the many churches around the city, displayed in a fine two-story stone building around a courtyard with lovely exhibition spaces. Note several fine carved sculptures of saints, including the imposing San Cristóbal holding the baby Jesus.

© CHRIS HUMPHREY

Santo Domingo asks for some quiet at the Museo de Arte Virreinal San Pedro

One of the rooms traces the construction of the building itself (begun in 1556) and its operation as a hospital.

Museo Bello y González

José Luis Bello, a businessman who amassed a fortune, spent his riches on this seemingly endless collection of elegant furnishings and art from throughout Mexico, Europe, and Asia. The museum (Av. 3 Pte. 302, 222/232-9475, Tues.–Sun. 10 A.M.–5 P.M., $3, free Tues.) displays all manner of art and collectibles, including porcelain, glass, Talavera ceramics, wrought iron, religious vestments, clothing, locks, and even original sheet music by Beethoven. English-speaking guides are available.

Museo de Artesanías Santa Rosa

This museum (Calle 3 Nte. 1203, in the ex-convent of Santa Rosa, 222/232-7792, Tues.–Sun. 10 A.M.–4:30 P.M., $2) houses the Talavera-tiled kitchen with huge cauldrons and other earthenware utensils where legend has it that Dominican nun Sor Andrea de la Asunción created the first *mole poblano*. One of Mexico's most famed dishes, this mole has more than 25 ingredients, including a variety of spices, chiles, and chocolate. Mexican art is displayed on two floors, and a gift shop offers a selection of local handicrafts.

Museo del Estado Casa de Alfeñique

The intricate baroque facade of this building (Av. 4 Ote. 416, 222/232-0458, Tues.–Sun. 10 A.M.–5 P.M., $2) is a classic example of *alfeñique* architectural style, named for a white sugar candy made in Puebla. Built in 1790, it now houses the state museum, with old manuscripts related to Puebla history, ethnography on different indigenous groups in the state, and colonial clothing (including the original *china poblana* dress).

Casa de los Muñecos (House of Dolls) or Museo Universitario

The top floor of this house (Calle 2 Nte. at Av. Palafox) is famous for its facade. It is decorated with caricatures of the town fathers, who refused to let the owner add the 3rd floor. After going to Mexico City and getting the necessary permission, the owner exacted his vengeance on his opponents by making fun of them in stone. The building suffered extensive interior and exterior damage during an earthquake, but restoration is under way.

Barrio del Artista

Across the alley from the Teatro Principal, check out the Barrio del Artista, an exhibition hall that in former years housed the fabric spinners of the local clothing industry. Nowadays it's used by local artists as a workshop and selling space, and is open daily.

Zona Cívica del Cinco de Mayo

Three kilometers northeast of the *zócalo,* at Boulevard Héroes del 5 de Mayo, is a complex of parks and museums on the site of the Battle of Puebla, which gave birth to the Cinco de Mayo fiesta. The **Fuerte de Loreto,** built in 1821, was the center of the battle; 2,000 Mexicans

EXCURSIONS

led by General Ignacio Zaragoza defended the fort against an attack by 6,000 French troops. The fort is now a museum (Tues.–Sun. 10 A.M.–4:30 P.M., $2.50) that contains dioramas of the battle, photos, drawings, and paintings. Cinco de Mayo is celebrated here each year with a major military and school parade.

Also at the complex are a modern planetarium, a children's museum called Museo Imagina, and the Museo de Antropología (Tues.–Sun. 10 A.M.–4:30 P.M., $2.50 to each museum).

Museo Nacional de los Ferrocarriles Mexicanos

Choo-choo buffs should not fail to come to the railroad museum (Calle 11 Nte. 1005 at Av. 12 Pte., 222/246-1074 or 222/246-0395, Tues.–Sun. 10 A.M.–5 P.M., free) to study the collection of spiffed-up trains that have been put out to pasture. The antique steam engines and rail cars are open for visitors to examine and explore. Kids will have a ball climbing in and around the 50 rail cars, some of which have special bunk-bed lookouts where guards kept watch for *bandidos* (bandits). In some of the cars visitors find pictures and displays illustrating the history of Mexican trains since 1837.

Africam

At this zoo (222/281-7000 or 222/236-1212, Mexico City 55/5575-2731, www.africam safari.com.mx, daily 10 A.M.–5 P.M., $15 adults, $14 children 12 and under), about eight kilometers from town, you can take a safari ride through 6,075 hectares inhabited by wild animals, including giraffes, antelope, ostriches, rhinoceros, guacamayas, lions, pelicans, bears, hippos, chimpanzees, and blue-eyed Bengal tigers. A boat trip and llama rides for children break up the tour at a halfway area (called Mombasa). All of this is before you reach the children's area, which is prettily arranged in walkable segments that include a Bat Cave, a resplendent Butterfly House, cages of hopping toucans, and a good look at the tiger cubs. To make the most of a visit, take at least four hours, if not more. As Sunday is the busiest day, it's a good idea

to plan your visit for a Saturday or, if possible, during the week. Arrive early. Buses for Africam leave the Central Camionera (CAPU, north of the city at Calle 11 Nte. and Blvd. Atlixco) three times daily. A taxi to the park costs about $8, and they can sometimes be difficult to find returning, so best to arrange a return pickup at a pre-arranged time.

RESTAURANTS

Puebla is noted for its exceptional cuisine. In addition to mole, which everyone here will tell you was first made at the Santa Rosa convent (although natives of the southern state of Oaxaca might beg to differ), several other local specialties are worth a try. *Mixiotes* are made by wrapping barbecued meat (beef, pork, lamb, or goat) and spices in a maguey leaf (not edible) and steaming. *Tinga* is a meat (pork or chicken, usually) and vegetable mélange, sort of half salad, half stew, and delicious. *Chiles en nogada* consists of pork-stuffed green poblano chile peppers in a white sauce of crushed walnuts, decorated with pomegranate seeds. The patriotic colors of the dish (red, green, and white) make it popular around Independence Day, September 16. *Taco árabe* is a Middle Eastern version of the taco—pita bread wrapped around meat cooked on a spit.

Mexican

For an outdoor seat and a good strong cup of coffee, the **Cafe Aguirre** (Av. Cinco de Mayo 4, 222/242-0997, Mon.–Sat. 7 A.M.–10 P.M., Sun. 8 A.M.–6 P.M., mains $5–10) is a good choice any time of day. For a solid meal, try **La Princesa** (Portal Juárez 101, 222/232-1195, Mon.–Sat. 7 A.M.–10 P.M., Sun. 8 A.M.–6 P.M., mains $5–10), where the breakfasts, appetizers, and *comidas corridas* are all reasonably priced and hearty. The west side of the plaza has several restaurants, including **Restaurante Cafe El Vasco** (Mon.–Sat. 1–10 P.M., mains $5–12), specializing in Spanish dishes, including good Valencian paella.

The sidewalk café at **Hotel Royalty** (Portal Hidalgo 8, 222/242-0202, daily 7 A.M.–10 P.M., mains $7–15) is a relaxing spot for cocktails or a nice meal, though prices are slightly high.

Tacos Tony (Av. 3 Pte. 149, 222/232-0675, Wed.–Mon. noon–10 P.M., $2–3) is a good place to try one of Puebla's popular *tacos árabes,* an inexpensive and meaty treat.

Restaurant Bar Casa Real (Av. 4 Ote. 208, 222/246-5876, daily 8 A.M.– 10 P.M., later on weekends, mains $5–12), two blocks from the *zócalo,* is open for breakfast, lunch, and dinner and serves local specialties such as mole, *chalupas, chiles en nogada,* and a large selection of meats. Prices are moderate. On weekends (and some weeknights), live music is presented; shows start at 9 P.M.

Legendary **Fonda de Santa Clara** (Av. 3 Pte. 307, 222/242-2659, and Av. 3 Pte. 920, 222/246-1952, daily 8 A.M.– 10 P.M., mains $5–15) is a popular and often noisy restaurant serving traditional regional food. Try the *mixiotes, tingas,* or *mole poblano.* The adventurous can even order *gusanos de maguey en salsa borracha* (maguey worms in tequila sauce). The menu is available in English.

Restaurante Típico La China Poblana (one block south of El Parian at Calle 6 Nte. 1) offers a small storefront room with three tables next to the kitchen and a larger dining room in the rear. It's decorated with local plates, masks, clothing, and a life-sized China Poblana. The food is very good, but there's no written menu, so be sure to ask carefully. Double-check your order and the price if your Spanish is weak.

Plazuela de los Sapos, on the southeast side of the city's center, is another good arena for restaurants. The small plaza and its surrounding streets are home to several trendy restaurants and good, cheap eateries, as well as interesting home-furnishing shops to browse in. **El Resguardo de los Ángeles** (Calle 6 Sur 504, 222/246-4106, Tues.–Sun. 1–3 P.M. and 6–11 P.M.), **La Guadalupana Restaurante** (Av. 5 Ote. 605, 222/242-4886, Mon.–Sat. 9 A.M.–10 P.M.), and **La Bella Elena** (Calle 6 Sur 310, 222/242-0702) are a few of the nicer spots for drinks or dinner, all offering local and international dishes for $5–12.

The west side of town, Calle Juárez in particular, offers the city's largest array of high-end Mexican, European, and Asian restaurants. Cruise this strip in a taxi and you'll be sure to find what you're looking for if you've had enough of the historical district.

International

At **Vittorio's Pizzería** (Portal Morelos 106, 222/232-7900, daily 7 A.M.–midnight, $4–12), you can enjoy a cappuccino or espresso outside, or stay indoors if it's cold. If you haven't had a Mexican-style pizza yet, here's your chance. And if you haven't had your share of mole already, the restaurant offers a pizza version. The menu also includes pasta, salad, and *típico* (typical) fare, and food can be delivered.

Restaurante Chesa Veglia (Av. 2 Ote. 208, 222/232-1641, daily 1–11 P.M., mains $5–12) serves good Swiss food, including cheese, meat, and chocolate fondues.

La Cava (Av. Juárez 2302, 222/248-5839, mains $8–18) serves good-quality international (including pastas, salads, steak, and seafood) food in a mellow, refined ambience with good service.

Vegetarian

Two vegetarian restaurants run by the same group are close to the city center. **Barra Vegetariana La Zanahoria** (Av. 5 Ote. 206, 222/232-4813, daily 7 A.M.–9 P.M.) and **El Vegetariano** (Av. 3 Pte. just past Calle 5 Sur, daily 7 A.M.–9 P.M.) both sell veggie versions of fast food and Mexican specialties, as well as wheat germ and bulk health-food products.

NIGHTLIFE

La Cantina de los Remedios (Juárez 2504, 222/249-0843) is one of the most typical and popular drinking holes on Avenida Juárez, west of downtown. You may have to line up to get in on Thursday to Saturday night, and the bar will be crowded, but the atmosphere is kicking.

For a taste of the bohemian life in Puebla, visit **El Convento de las Carolinas** (Av. 3 Ote. 403). This gallery, live music venue, bar, and *antojería* (snack restaurant) is popular with the local literati as well as young people.

EXCURSIONS

La Leyenda Restaurant and Bar is more bar than restaurant and conveniently located right on the plaza. This hole-in-the-wall caters to a young crowd, and the music is invariably techno. There are lots of small rooms in which to comfortably ensconce yourself, and drinks are reasonable at $1–4.

Teorema Librería Cafe (Reforma at Calle 7 Nte., 7 A.M.–1 A.M.) is a bookstore and coffeehouse that transforms itself into a hip nightspot come dark. Don't forget your black turtleneck.

The rooftop terrace bar at Puebla's newest boutique hotel, **La Purificadora** (Callejón de la 10 Nte. 802, Paseo San Francisco, Barrio Alto, 222/309-1920, www.lapurificadora.com), draws the young-and-beautiful crowd. Weekend nights see a buzzing scene with DJs and cocktails. It's definitely not a budget option.

Both the Juárez area west of downtown and the road from Puebla to Cholula (eight kilometers) are home to several of the area's discos. Most don't get started until about 11 P.M. It's best to ask around to find out which discos are the current favorites.

ARTS AND LEISURE

Teatro Principal (Calle 6 Nte. at Av. 8 Ote., 222/232-6085) and **Teatro U.A.P.** (Calle 4 Sur 104) both offer performing-arts events. For a schedule, check at the tourist office.

Soccer packs in the locals during the season (September to December and January to May) at Estadio Cuauhtémoc (Calz. Ignacio Zaragoza 666, 222/226-2166, www.pueblafutbolclub.com), which has a capacity of just over 40,000. The local team, known as La Franja, spent two years in the second division, but was promoted back into the top flight league in the spring of 2007.

For **bullfights,** go to Plaza de Toros El Relicario (222/236-1868), near the fort in the Zona Cívica de Cinco de Mayo. The season is late November and December, and also during the city fair, in late April through May. It is also used as a venue for concerts and other events. A *lienzo charro* (Carretera Tehuacán Pte. 1032, 222/283-6308), or rodeo ring, holding 4,000 people hosts **charreadas**

(rodeos). *Charrería* is big in Puebla, and *charreadas* are held most Sundays.

For listings of events in Puebla, see www .todopuebla.com.

SHOPS

Puebla is an outstanding shopping city, filled with stores selling fine Talavera tile, pottery, onyx, handicrafts from surrounding regions, wool and cotton clothing, amate fiber paper, and a myriad of other artwork and handicrafts.

◖ El Parian

A former 18th-century clothing warehouse, El Parian (Calle 8 Nte. betw. Av. 2 and Av. 6 Ote.) today houses rows of shops selling all manner of handicrafts. If you're looking for good-quality Talavera and don't mind the price, check out **Centro de Talavera La Colonial** (Av. 6 Ote. 11, 222/242-2340). Also in the Parian, an up-and-coming workshop with factory tours for the public is **Talavera Armando's** (Av. 6 Ote. 408 at 6 Nte., 222/242-3455, 10 A.M.–6 P.M.).

Uriarte (Av. 4 Pte. 911, 222/232-1598, www .uriartetalavera.com.mx) is not in El Parian, but it is nonetheless one of the most famed Talavera shops in the city. The shop, which opened its doors in 1872, has excellent guided tours.

Amozoc

If you've always had the cowboy fantasy and want to indulge in all the accoutrements, take a short bus ride out to this small town, 17 kilometers due east of Puebla on the free highway to Tehuacán. Here you'll find superb craftsmen in dozens of shops fashioning what is reputed to be the finest ornamental silver and ironware for Mexican *charro* outfits. Particularly famous are the spurs, but they also make dagger handles, buckles, and *mancuernos,* which are chained brooches worn on clothing, saddles, and reins. Prices are not cheap, but the quality is excellent.

Markets

Callejón de los Sapos (Av. 7 Ote. and Calle 4 Sur, three blocks south and one block east of the *zócalo*) is a quiet antiques district during the week, but converts into a bustling flea market on weekends, especially Sundays. **Mercado Municipal** (Calle 11 Nte. and Av. 4 Pte.), a sprawling indoor market, is chockablock with all manner of foods from the region. Market days at a few of the surrounding cities can be an expedition of discovery. In **San Martín Texmelucan,** market day is Tuesday; in **Huejotzingo,** Saturday; in **Cholula,** Wednesday and Sunday; in **Tepeaca,** Friday; and in **Tehuacán,** Saturday. **Puebla** has a market day every day.

HOTELS
Under $15
With two branches in town, **Hotel Catedral** (Catedral 1 at Av. 3 Pte. 310, 222/232-2368 or 222/232-5089, and Catedral 2 a few blocks west on 3 Pte., 222/232-8416, $14 s/d) offers private and shared rooms and baths at cheap prices. Some of the rooms are cabin-style, with two stories and grubby makeshift kitchens.

$15-30
A better value is **Hotel Teresita** (Av. 3 Pte. 309, 222/232-7072, $18 s, $22 d), with 47 rooms with TV and tiled bathrooms.

Gran Hotel San Agustín (Av. 3 Pte. 531, 222/232-5089, $21 s, $24 d, with continental breakfast) is a friendly place with clean rooms.

Hotel San Miguel (Av. 3 Pte. 721, 222/242-4860, $23 s, $30 d) has a modern facade and a bright, clean lobby. The rooms are a little dank and on the monastic side but are good value for the increased cleanliness and security.

$30-50
A dramatic step up in quality is **Hotel Imperial** (Av. 4 Ote. 212, 222/242-4981, $38 s, $48 d). This spacious hotel has 65 large rooms, each with TV, telephone, and private bath. Amenities include a restaurant, pool table, parking lot, hot water all day, and bicycles for free use. Anyone carrying a copy of this guide (not a photocopy) gets a 30 percent discount, making it that much better a value. Breakfast is included.

Hotel Provincia Express (Reforma 141, 222/246-3557 or 222/246-3642, $34 s, $42 d) is on the main drag closer to the plaza and has very tidy rooms at great prices. The building dates to the 17th century and has lovely handpainted tiles and decorous hallways.

$50-75
Hotel Royalty (Portal Hidalgo 8, 222/242-0204, $46 s, $56 d) offers 45 rooms and an outdoor café under the *portales*. The hotel and café face the *zócalo* and make for a lively atmosphere. The colonial building's interior is lovely, although rooms are somewhat small.

At **Hotel Santiago** (Av. 3 Pte. 106, 222/242-2860, $38 s, $52 d), the staff may go a bit overboard in their use of cleaning products, but the sparkling rooms and sterilized bathrooms of this modern hotel are nothing to scoff at.

Hotel Colonial (Calle 4 Sur 105, 222/246-4612, $59 s, $69 d), a block from the plaza (and across from its own picturesque little square), is convenient for exploring downtown. The rooms are fairly large, and some have balconies, wood floors, and tile baths. The good restaurant has a gorgeous stained-glass ceiling. Parking is available.

You'll find nice rooms at the **Hotel Palace** (Av. 2 Pte. 13, 222/232-2430, $43 s, $58 d). King-sized rooms for just a few dollars more have better light and a street view.

$75-110
Hotel Lastra (Calzada de los Fuertes 2633, 222/235-9755, $85–160 s/d) has 66 pleasing rooms of differing sizes with spick-and-span bathrooms. It's located several minute's walk northeast of downtown near the planetarium.

Just one block north of the *zócalo* is **Hotel Posada San Pedro** (Av. 2 Ote. 202, 222/246-5077, $77 s/d, including breakfast). Housed in a 16th-century building, the hotel is a good mix of interesting architecture and modern amenities, such as the interior courtyard pool, hot tubs, restaurant, and bar.

Over $110
One of the more interesting high-end hotel options is **Mesón Sacristía** (Calle 6 Sur 304, 222/246-6084, www.mesones-sacristia.com,

$ 160s/d, $200 suites), in the vicinity of Los Sapos. Each of the hotel's eight rooms is individually appointed with fabulous antiques and collectibles such as a 1940s-era typewriter turned into a bedside lamp. An antiques store, the lovely Restaurante Sacristía, and Bar El Confesionario are all within the 18th-century building that houses the hotel. Live music plays evenings until midnight, except for Sunday.

Equally elegant is the sister hotel **Mesón Sacristía de las Capuchinas** (Av. 9 Ote. 16, 222/242-3554, www.mesones-sacristia.com, $160 s/d, $190 suites), a converted convent. Thick monastic walls ensure silence and privacy, and antiques are for sale. Rates for both hotels include à la carte breakfast and courtesy car wash.

The **Camino Real Puebla** (Av. 7 Pte. 105, 222/229-0909, toll-free in Mexico 800/901-2300, www.caminoreal.com, $215 and up), downtown, is not what you might expect if you've seen other hotels in the chain. There is no swimming pool or tennis courts here, just top-quality rooms in the late-16th-century Ex-Convento de la Concepción. Amenities include two restaurants and a bar; for alfresco eating and drinking, tables are placed outside on the central patio—a very pleasant place on a sunny day.

The **Holiday Inn** (Av. 2 Ote. 211, 222/223-6600, $175 s/d) has 78 remodeled rooms in an elegant old French-colonial building one block from the plaza. A white-linen restaurant (San Leonardo), bar, rooftop pool, and parking lot are on the premises. Rooms have hand-painted bed frames, and the lobby is decorated with antiques and Oriental rugs.

La Purificadora (Callejón de la 10 Nte. 802, Paseo San Francisco, Barrio Alto, 222/309-1920, www.lapurificadora.com, rooms start from $145) is the newest addition to Puebla's hotel scene and the brainchild of Grupo Hábita—responsible for Hotel Hábita and Condesa df in Mexico City. The hotel is a converted water purification factory northeast of downtown near the convention center, and successfully blends 19th-century architecture with modern design. The 26 rooms, identified by letters of the alphabet, are not huge, but the expansive floor-to-ceiling window or balcony door (depending on your floor) and transparent closets lend a feeling of light and space.

PRACTICALITIES
Information and Services

The state tourism office (Av. 5 Ote. 3, 222/246-2044, www.puebla.gob.mx, Mon.–Sat. 9:30 A.M.–8:30 P.M., Sun. 9 A.M.–2 P.M.) has a very friendly and helpful staff—many have a good command of English, and their love of the beauty and culture around them is evident. Maps and directions are cheerfully provided, and three-hour tours (in English) are available for around $40 (prices vary and are negotiable). It's better to use the official Sectur guides rather than the freelance guides who seek clients in the bus station and in downtown.

The municipal tourist office (Av. Palafox and Calle 2 Nte., Mon.–Fri. 9 A.M.–8 P.M., Sat. 9 A.M.–5 P.M., Sun. 9 A.M.–3 P.M.), in the Palacio Municipal on the plaza, can also be helpful with city information.

The post office (corner of Av. 5 Ote. and 16 de Septiembre, Mon.–Fri. 8 A.M.–8 P.M., Sat. 9 A.M.–1 P.M.) is in the Archbishop's Palace; it isn't well marked.

There is no shortage of Internet places close by. One is on Calle 2 Sur, between 5 and 7 Oriente ($1 per hour).

Several banks scattered about the center of town exchange both dollars and travelers checks and have ATMs. Try **BBVA** (Av. 3 Pte. 116) and **Banamex** (Av. Reforma 135). A *casa de cambio* (exchange booth) in the Pasaje del Ayuntamiento between Palafox and 2 Oriente is another good place if you don't feel like waiting in bank lines.

Hospital UPAEP (Av. 5 Pte. 715, 222/229-8100, ext. 1602, www.upaep.mx/hospital) is a hospital option. **Farmacia del Ahorro** (at 2 Nte. with 2 Ote., 222/231-3383) is the main chain of pharmacies in the center. One centrally located pharmacy is Farmacia Belén (Calle 4 Pte. 713, Centro, 222/242-2544).

Getting There and Away

The modern toll road (México 150D) goes from

Mexico City clear to Veracruz and avoids larger cities. To Puebla it is 120 kilometers—two hours by bus, and usually less if you are driving. There are two *casetas* (tollbooths) that charge about $6 and $4. The free road crosses the same mountain pass but can be difficult to follow leaving Mexico City, and it is also very congested. Coming into Puebla, the free road is slow as it passes through several towns, but it also gives an excuse to stop at the impressive monastery at Huejotzingo.

Rent a car from **Budget** (Av. Juárez 1914, 222/232-9108, www.budget.com) or **Easy Rent A Car** (7 Sur at 41 Pte., 222/243-9100 or 222/211-1413).

CAPU, the large Puebla bus station, is north of the city at Calle 11 Norte and Boulevard Atlixco. From the station, you can get to the city center on a *combi* marked Centro ($0.50) or a *sitio* taxi ($3). Ignore taxi touts. Here, first- and second-class buses depart for Mexico City's Terminal TAPO almost constantly, all day and night, with lines ADO, Cristóbal Colón, Estrella Roja, and Estrella Blanca (222/249-7561, $10 for first class, $7 for second class).

There are now hourly departures from Terminal Sur (Tasqueña) in Mexico City with **Cristóbal Colón** (55/5544-9008 in Mexico City). **Estrella Roja** (222/249-7099) runs the express bus direct from CAPU to the Mexico City airport (every hour 3 A.M.–6 P.M.) for $14. **ADO** (222/225-9001 or 55/5133-2424 in Mexico City) offers first-class buses to Jalapa ($12), Veracruz ($19), Mérida ($78), Cancún ($94), Oaxaca ($25), and elsewhere in the southeast of the country. **Cristóbal Colón** (222/249-7327 or 222/225-9007) runs first-class buses to Tuxtla Gutiérrez in Chiapas ($58). **Autobuses Unidos** (222/225-9004) offers first- and second-class buses to Veracruz ($19) and elsewhere. **Estrella de Oro** has frequent buses throughout the day to Cholula and Huejotzingo.

Tickets for ADO, Cristóbal Colón, and Autobuses Unidos, and many other bus lines throughout the country as well, can be bought at Ticketbus (55/5133-2424 in Mexico City or 800/702-8000 nationwide, www.ticketbus.com.mx). Buying tickets online is a very efficient way to go.

CHOLULA

This large town is just a few minute's drive from Puebla, and is fast becoming a sort of suburb of the larger city. But Cholula retains the laid-back, friendly rhythms of a rural lifestyle, surrounded by attractive countryside and farmland. It's also a university town, filled with lots of cheerful young folk, mainly Mexican but also a number of foreign students. Cholula has a long and important history in Mexico, and has numerous sites well worth taking a day or more detour from Puebla to visit.

The major population center in the region of Mexico where Cortés arrived was Cholula, and the Spaniards stopped here on their way between Tlaxcala and the Aztec capital in Tenochtitlán. The local leaders planned a secret revolt, which was discovered by Cortés's Tlaxcalan allies. The Cholulans paid with their lives, one of the more brutal and bloody episodes of the Spanish conquest. Cortés was so incensed by the Cholulans' almost successful ploy that he vowed to build a Catholic church in Cholula for each day in the year. He didn't quite make it, but there are at least 39.

Cholula was the base for the first Franciscan friars who came to convert the native people of New Spain. In 1524 the Franciscans established themselves on the former temple of Quetzalcóatl, where soon they began to build the Convent of San Gabriel, or San Gabriel's Friary (1540). This is still a functioning monastery—about 15 to 20 Franciscan monks still live in one part of the premises.

Cholula had, and still has, the largest ancient structure in the Americas, the Great Pyramid of Tepanapa. It covers 18 hectares, is 60 meters high, and has a volume of three million cubic meters. Cholula lies 10 kilometers (and about a 20-minute drive) west of Puebla.

The liveliest time to visit Cholula is on weekends, when you will catch the Sunday market and live music in restaurants on evenings. Even better, try to catch one of the town's many festivals, especially *la feria de San Pedro* (first two weeks of September), which includes *la bajada de la Virgen*, when the Virgin of Remedies is carried down from her church atop the pyramid and stays a night in each of the town's neighborhoods (normally from September 1 to 9). Other festivals are *la feria de San Andrés* (in the week around November 30) and the ritual of Quetzalcóatl (March 21).

Around the Zócalo

On the east side of the *zócalo* is the fortress-like **Ex-Convento y Iglesia de San Gabriel** (San Gabriel Monastery), with its Moorish look and 49 domes. The Franciscan ex-convent is one of the original 12 built after the conquest. Construction began in 1549 and was completed in 1571. During the 16th and 17th century, this was a major religious center, where massive baptism and confession ceremonies were held. Check out the entrance door, with 122 Roman nails, each a different design. On the north side of the *zócalo*, you'll find **Parroquia de San Pedro,** which dates to 1641. In 1986, the monks agreed for part of the building to be renovated and converted into the Franciscan Library. When the Anthropology Department of the Universidad de las Américas began the work on the library, they found the stairs outside (near the ramp, parallel with the arches) were actually part of the pyramid of Quetzalcóatl. This is located in the Portal de Peregrinos, or the Pilgrim's Arcade—a series of round arches to the north of San Gabriel's huge atrium, where the pilgrims slept before going to Mass. With 17 *portales,* it has the largest number of arches of any Portal de Peregrinos in the Americas. For more information, contact the library (222/261-2395) or the Universidad de las Américas (222/229-2084, www.udlap.mx).

Gran Pirámide de Tepanapa

If it weren't for the church sitting on top, you might never realize this large hill is actually the largest pyramid in the continent (by volume), with a base measuring 450 meters on each side. About the same age as Teotihuacán, the Great Pyramid of Tepanapa of Cholula was in use before the birth of Christ.

As was the custom in ancient Mesoamerican civilizations, seven structures were superimposed over the original pyramid. The whole process, from original pyramid to seventh structure, spanned 600 years. Because of the massive pyramid, Cholula was also referred to as Tlachihualtepetl (hill made by hand, in Náhuatl) in the past.

On the far side of the pyramid from the main road is the entrance to the Gran Pirámide de Cholula archaeological zone. The pyramid was first explored in 1931 and the archaeologist in charge decided to excavate two tunnels to prove that *el cerrito* (the little hill), as many still call it, was an archaeological monument. In the process, he also discovered altars with offerings, floors, walls, and buried human remains.

Guides are available at the pyramid (Calzada San Andrés at Calle 2 Nte., 222/247-9081, daily 9 A.M.–5:30 P.M., $3.50), and it's a good idea to hire one; you'll see and appreciate more than if you go it alone in this lighted, subterranean maze. The guides charge about $6. Excavations continue today. About eight kilometers of tunnels have been dug, but only a section is open to the public.

Follow the signs to the small site museum (half a block further down the road away from the *zócalo*), containing early chisels and blades, female fertility icons, and polychromatic ceramics, for which the area is famed. There is also a replica of the 50-meter-long mural of *The Drinkers* that depicts people drinking *pulque* in loincloths, headdresses, and masks. The mural is one of the largest in the continent, but the original, located in a large building on the **Gran Plaza** to the south of the pyramid, has been protected so that its colors are not further damaged by the elements, and is not open to public view. Information in English outlines pre-Hispanic funerary customs, the introduction in the Postclassic period (A.D. 800 to 1521) of the practice of human sacrifice, and the custom of cranial deformation. Entrance to the museum is included in the admission price. Use of a flash or video camera costs $3 more.

To get to the beautifully gilded **Capilla de la Virgen de los Remedios** (daily 1–5 P.M.), first built in 1594 and rebuilt after an earthquake in the mid-19th century, turn back the way you came and follow the steep path to the top of the hill. Early and late in the day the views of Popocatépetl are spectacular.

Restaurants

While not extravagant, the cooking in Cholula is wholesome and cheap, at least by Puebla and Mexico City standards. Service is also much more laid-back and friendly than in the big cities.

One block off the main street, **La Casona** (Av. 3 Ote. 9, 222/247-2776, Mon.–Sat. noon–8 P.M., mains $2–6) is an attractive restaurant filled with trees and flowers. Take a seat on the outdoor patio (or inside if the patio is full, as it often is on weekends) and enjoy a good-quality traditional Mexican meal.

La Pirámide (Morelos 416, daily 1–11 P.M.) is another popular spot with locals, offering moderately priced traditional regional food.

Café Enamorada (daily 9 A.M.–11 P.M.) and its adjacent shop frame the southwest corner of the *zócalo*; it's a good spot for outdoor dining. This side of the plaza is full of busy cafés, ice-cream parlors, and coffee shops.

The Italian Coffee Company (Portal Guerrero 9A, daily 9 A.M.–10 P.M.) has managed to find its way into this ancient city serving brownies, cakes, and cookies under the arches. There is also **Los Tulipanes** (daily 10 A.M.–10 P.M.), whose mushroom *antojitos* are not to be missed, and nearby **Restaurant-Bar Los Jarrones** (Portal Guerrero 7, 222/247-1098, daily 10 A.M.–10 P.M., mains $3–7) is a charming spot with tasty Mexican food. The breakfast buffet on weekends is a good bargain, and live music at night is loud but tuneful. Try the *cecina* (salty, thin beef), served with guacamole.

Just under three blocks from the pyramid, a pretty little restaurant, **La Lunita** (Av. Morelos, corner with 6 Nte., 222/247-0011, daily 9 A.M.–11 P.M., mains $7–12), provides welcome refreshment. Although prices are a little inflated, the *acamayas* (crayfish) are great when in season.

Tacos Tony (Morelos 212, 222/247-9196, Wed.–Mon. noon–10 P.M.) serves inexpensive *tacos árabes*, a regional style of taco in pita bread. For Mexican fast-food standards, fresh and hot in a bustling and industrious atmosphere, go to **Restaurante Güeros** (Av. Hidalgo 101, on a corner of the *zócalo*, 222/247-2188, daily 9 A.M.–midnight, mains $2–6). Here you can tuck into, or take away, tacos, *cecina, tacos árabes, tortas,* tostadas, flautas, *pozole,* pizzas, and fish.

Hotels

$15–30

The basic **Hotel y Bar Reforma** (Calle 4 Sur 101, 222/247-0149, $20 s/d, $35 d with two beds) has reasonably maintained rooms with private baths a block from the *zócalo*.

$50–75

Hotel Posada Señorial (Cinco de Mayo 1400, 222/247-0049, $52 s/d, $58 t) is a clean, pleasant spot just outside of town on the road back toward Puebla.

Villa Arqeológica (Av. 2 Pte. 601, 222/273-7900, U.S. 800/722-0697, www.come2clubmed.com/mexican_villas.htm, $87 s/d Sat.–Sun., $70 s/d during week) is one of the resorts in the Club Med–owned chain of hotels built near various archaeological zones in Mexico. It's about 15 minutes from the Great Pyramid and offers tennis courts, swimming, and a reasonably good French restaurant.

OVER $110

Hotel Quinta Luna (Calle 3 Sur 702, 222/247-8915, toll-free in Mexico 800/672-8669, www.laquintaluna.com, $160 standard room, $190 suite) is Cholula's newest and best hotel, housed in a converted 17th-century mansion just a five-minute walk from the *zócalo*. Six luxurious rooms are arranged around a central patio with fountain, where you can eat alfresco or inside. With traditional Mexican and nouvelle recipes, this is also the town's finest restaurant. One of the unusual attractions is the library, built with 17th-century wooden beams. Guests have access to the 3,000 books within (on design, economics, and Mexican artists, as well as a small collection of Spanish- and

EXCURSIONS

English-language literature). Each room has flat-screen television, DVD player, minibar, coffee service, and safety box. Rates include an à la carte breakfast.

Practicalities

The post office is at 7 Sur, between 5 Poniente and 7 Poniente. You can change money at the **BBVA** or **Banamex** (Av. Morelos on the *zócalo*), which each have ATMs, or nearby at **Casa de Cambio Azteca** (2 Sur, close to the center).

The **Municipal Tourist Office** (Calle 12 Ote. at 4 Nte., 222/261-2393, Mon.–Fri. 9 A.M.–7 P.M., Sat.–Sun. 9 A.M.–5 P.M.) has some information and usually someone on hand who speaks a bit of English.

One pharmacy in town is **Farmacia Nuestra Señora del Sagrado Corazón** (Av. Hidalgo 103B, 222/247-0398, daily 9 A.M.–10 P.M.).

Buses from CAPU bus station in Puebla to Cholula, Huejotzingo, and San Martín depart every 15 minutes (Estrella de Oro) or every half hour (Estrella Roja) between 5 A.M. and 9 P.M. Minibuses also leave Puebla from Avenida 2 Poniente at Calle 13 Sur, across from the Railroad Museum. Authorized taxis cost around $9 from CAPU to Cholula, and about $11 to return.

If you are driving from Puebla, take Avenida Juárez west, go halfway around the traffic circle (México 190 to Cholula), and continue for about 10 kilometers.

Near Cholula

Just south of Cholula, in the villages of **Santa María Tonantzintla** (also famed for its pottery) and **San Francisco Acatepec,** are two of the country's finest churches from the early colonial period.

West of Cholula, a dirt road heads to the town of **San Nicolás de los Ranchos** and continues up into the forest to reach the **Paso de Cortés,** between the volcanoes of Popocatépetl and Ixtaccíhuatl, about 30 kilometers from Cholula. From here a paved road continues down to Amecameca, and from there on to Mexico City or Cuautla. This road is passable in any decent passenger car—if you don't mind

a little dust—and the scenery is fantastic. At times the road is closed above San Nicolás due to volcanic rumblings by Popocatépetl.

◖ HUEJOTZINGO

Fourteen kilometers northwest of Cholula, on the free highway back to Mexico City (about half an hour's drive), is the dusty town of Huejotzingo, site of a 16th-century monastery dedicated to the Archangel Michael, one of the first built in Mexico and one of the best preserved as well. The mix of indigenous and Christian motifs in the carvings on the church and adjacent cloister are fascinating. Note the ominous carved skulls on the courtyard towers, known as *capillas posas.* Inside, the superb late-16th-century *retablo* (altarpiece) is considered one of the greatest of its kind in the New World. The monastery is open daily until 5 P.M.

The best times to visit Huejotzingo, if you want a spectacle, are the week around its saint's day—San Miguel, on September 29, which conveniently doubles up with a national cider festival—and carnival, in the early spring, which here culminates on Shrove Tuesday, featuring enactments of battles that combine indigenous history, colonial legend, and sheer fantasy.

Catch buses on the highway passing frequently for Cholula and Puebla, or go the Estrella Roja office (Nicolás Bravo 3, in the center of town near the monastery, 227/276-0213) for buses to and from the TAPO terminal in Mexico City. The roughly two-hour ride costs $4.

The same road to Huejotzingo branches left and leads to **Calpan,** a poor, rural village famed for the **Ex-Convento de San Andrés Calpan,** an outstanding colonial building. At the entrance you can see the details of the chord of San Francisco, carved carefully in stone, and inside are possibly the best-preserved *capillas posas* in the world. You can see St. Michael with his lance, stepping on the devil, the souls rising from their graves, and many indigenous motifs, including pre-Hispanic flowers and hearts cut open with ventricles on display.

Tlaxcala and Vicinity

Tlaxcala, the capital of the state of the same name, is a beautiful colonial city built on the site of the pre-Hispanic capital of the Tlaxcalteca people. This was the first major Amerindian city seen by Cortés and his band of conquerers as they marched toward the Aztec capital of Tenochtitlán in 1519. After fighting and losing to the Spaniards, the Tlaxcaltecas opted to join the conquerers in fighting the Aztecs, their hated enemies. Cortés and a group of Franciscan monks founded the colonial city in 1520. The first bishopric of the country was established here in 1527, and the chapels of the San Francisco convent were built in 1537. About 120 kilometers east of Mexico City, Tlaxcala still has a population of only around 50,000. Though not possessing the stunning colonial art and architecture of nearby Puebla, Tlaxcala has a number of interesting sites and is a relaxed place to escape the hectic city, well worth taking a day or two to visit to appreciate the small-town vibe.

Just outside of Tlaxcala is a rather unusual vacation retreat, a school offering one-week courses on traditional Mexican cooking, fusing indigenous, French, and Spanish influences. **Mexican Home Cooking School** (246/468-0978, www.mexicanhomecooking.com, $1,200 per person with all transport, lodging, food, and drinks included) offers highly recommended classes all year for up to a maximum of six people (no minimum) in the sunny kitchen of the hacienda-style home of the owners. Some of the recipes on offer include: trout stuffed with cheese and wrapped in *hoja santa* leaves, *pozole* (a spicy soup of pork, chicken, and corn), tamales (stuffed, wrapped cornmeal dough), banana cream pie, *chiles en nogada* (battered, stuffed chiles in walnut sauce), beef in *mole verde* sauce, and *sopa de tortilla.*

SIGHTS

One of Tlaxcala's charms is its compact size, large enough to contain several interesting sights and small enough to be easily navigated on foot or, at most, inexpensive taxi ride.

Plaza de la Constitución

In the center of the city, Plaza de la Constitución (also known as the *zócalo*) holds a 19th-century bandstand surrounded by flowers. The nearby octagonal fountain, topped by a carved stone cross, was given to the city in 1646 by Spain's King Philip IV. Adjacent is another large square, the Plaza Xicoténcatl.

Palacio de Gobierno

The 16th-century Palacio de Gobierno, on the north side of the plaza, has suffered a turbulent history. It was burned during an Indian uprising in 1692 and rocked by an earthquake 20 years later; only the lower part of the facade and interior arches remain of the original structure.

On the first floor are a series of murals by Tlaxcalan artist Desiderio Hernández Xochitiotzin, depicting the history of Tlaxcala since pre-Hispanic times. The work, begun in 1957, is still in progress; it was interrupted for years due to disagreements between Hernández and local politicos on the content of the mural. Hernández Xochitiotzin, now in his 70s, still has one section to complete.

There is a poignant anecdote of Hernández Xochitiotzin, a Tlaxcalan, going to Mexico City many years ago to see Diego Rivera's murals in the Palacio Nacional (in preparation for his work here). The guide sneered at him, saying he "did not give explanations to Indians," and as a response, these murals in Tlaxcala are accompanied by a text, in Spanish, and every section has a title also in Náhuatl.

Tours of the building (Mon.–Fri. 9 A.M.– 9 P.M.) are available; only flashless photography is allowed.

Parroquia de San José

Across the street from the Plaza de la Constitución, Parroquia de San José (Mon.–Sat.

EXCURSIONS

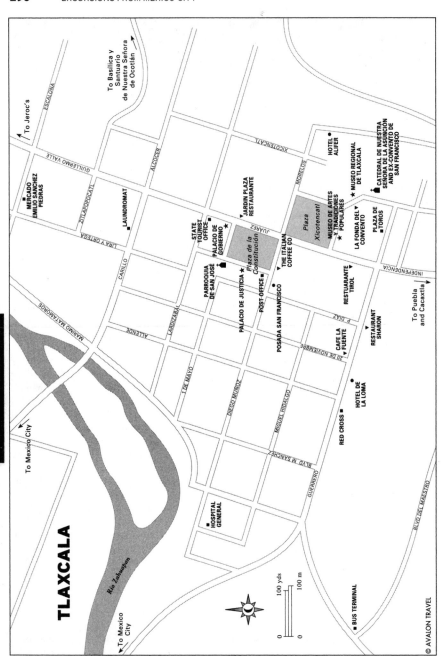

TLAXCALA

To Mexico City

Río Zahuapan

To Mexico City

To Jeroc's

To Basílica y Santuario de Nuestra Señora de Ocotlán

ESCALONA

GUILLERMO VALLE

ZITLAPOPOCATL

ALCOCER

XICOTENCATL

MERCADO EMILIO SANCHEZ PIEDRAS

LAUNDROMAT

LIRA Y ORTEGA

CARILLO

LARDIZABAL

ALLENDE

MARIANO MATAMOROS

JARDIN PLAZA RESTAURANTE

STATE TOURIST OFFICE

PALACIO DE GOBIERNO

Plaza la Constitución

JUAREZ

THE ITALIAN COFFEE CO.

PARROQUIA DE SAN JOSÉ

PALACIO DE JUSTICIA

POST OFFICE

POSADA SAN FRANCISCO

20 DE NOVIEMBRE

CAFE LA FUENTE

P. DIAZ

T. DE MAYO

DIEGO MUNOZ

MIGUEL HIDALGO

BLVD M SANCHEZ

GUERRERO

RED CROSS

HOTEL DE LA LOMA

HOSPITAL GENERAL

MORELOS

Plaza Xicotencatl

MUSEO DE ARTES Y TRADICIONES POPULARES

LA FONDA DEL CONVENTO

PLAZA DE TOROS

RESTUARANTE TIROL

RESTAURANT SHARON

INDEPENDENCIA

To Puebla and Cacaxtla

HOTEL ALIFER

MUSEO REGIONAL DE TLAXCALA

CATEDRAL DE NUESTRA SEÑORA DE LA ASUNCIÓN AND EX-CONVENTO DE SAN FRANCISCO

BLVD DEL MAESTRO

BUS TERMINAL

0 100 yds
0 100 m

© AVALON TRAVEL

6 A.M.–8 P.M., Sun. 7 A.M.–8 P.M.) dates from early in the 17th century. The Bishop of Puebla dictated the original design, including the mortar images, tiled facade, and lone tower. The dome was damaged in an 1864 earthquake, and the resulting cracks were covered over with the tiles. No flash photography is allowed. Masses go on much of Sunday morning.

Catedral de Nuestra Señora de la Asunción

The cathedral (Mon.–Fri. 6 A.M.–2 P.M. and 4–8 P.M., Sat. 6 A.M.–7:30 P.M., Sun. 6 A.M.–8:30 P.M.) is part of the complex of the Ex-Convento de San Francisco, which began construction in 1520. Among the interesting details in the church are heavy cedar crossbeams decorated with stars and the wrought-iron gate of the Virgin's Chapel. In the Capilla de la Tercer Orden is the stone baptismal font first used in 1520 to baptize the four rulers of Tlaxcala. No flash photography is allowed.

Museo Regional de Tlaxcala

Next to the cathedral in the old cloisters of the Ex-Convento de San Francisco, this museum (Tues.–Sun. 10 A.M.–5 P.M., $3.50) contains exhibits from pre-Hispanic to the independence era, as well as a bookstore and library. Exhibits include a *chac mool* (sculpture of the ancient Maya god) and the original state constitution. Tours are available.

Museo de Arte de Tlaxcala

This modest little art museum (Plaza de la Constitución 21, 246/462-1510, www.mat .org.mx, Tues.–Fri. 10 A.M.–5 P.M., $3.50) has three oil paintings and five engravings by Frida Kahlo, collected by a poet friend of hers named Miguel Nicolás Lira. The museum also has temporary exhibits of Mexican art over the centuries, with a special emphasis on artists from Tlaxcala.

Basílica y Santuario de Nuestra Señora de Ocotlán

On a hill above the city is this high baroque church (daily 7 A.M.–7 P.M.), with ornate sculptures of the 12 apostles, seven archangels, and other religious figures, framed by plaster columns. Note the star-shaped stained-glass window above the choir depicting the Immaculate Conception. Ask permission before taking pictures.

Plaza de Toros

Dating from the early 19th century, the town bullring (daily 10 A.M.–10 P.M. for touring), just off Independencia on Calle Capilla Abierta, is Mexico's oldest existing *plaza de toros.*

Museo de Artes y Tradiciones Populares (Casa de las Artesanías)

In this living museum (Av. Emilio Sánchez Piedras 1, 246/462-2337, Tues.–Sun. 10 A.M.– 6 P.M., $1), some artisans are on display along with the folk art produced. Exhibits highlight the traditional lifestyle of the region's Amerindian people and include an Otomí kitchen complete with three stone *tlecuil* (stoves) and large cooking vessels, a typical bedroom, designs for *huipiles* (blouses) and *titixtle* (woolen dresses), a *cuexcomate* (for storing corn), and a working *temazcal* (sauna).

Upstairs Otomí women spin wool into yarn using traditional methods and use different types of looms to make sweaters, blankets, jackets, and rugs. Another display shows the making of *pulque,* a regional drink of fermented cactus juice. Throughout the museum are exhibits of local costumes and masks.

In the store downstairs you'll find lots of information about Tlaxcala, including some in English, and local crafts, such as Talavera and walking sticks. A small restaurant offers visitors a taste of traditional Tlaxcalteca cuisine, including *mixiotes, pulque, escamoles,* and *gusanos de maguey.*

Santa Ana Chiautempan

This small town, six kilometers east of Tlaxcala, is famous for its woolen textiles and makes a good afternoon outing. After a round of shopping, stop for a look at Santa Ana's two colonial churches, the **Iglesia de Nuestra Señora**

Santa Ana Chiautempan, built in 1588, and the **Parroquia de Santa Ana,** finished at the end of the 17th century.

RESTAURANTS

Those who enjoy regional cuisine will have no problems eating very well in Tlaxcala, and at very reasonable prices. Specialties include *mixiotes, chiles rellenos al pulque, sopa de haba con nopal* (bean and cactus soup), and *pollo Tocotlan* (Tocotlan-style chicken).

The restaurant at **Hotel de La Loma** (mains $3–5) is a good spot to try delicious regional cuisine. For an interesting taste sensation, try *chamorro al pulque,* pork knuckle prepared with *pulque.*

Facing the plaza and shaded beneath the Arcos de Hidalgo are several lovely restaurants with outdoor dining as well as cozy indoor tables. **Los Portales** (Plaza de Constitución 8, 246/462-5419, mains $4–8, daily 8 A.M.–11 P.M.) is an attractive hideaway behind the restaurant Los Portales and specializes in a *filete de res con huitlacoche* (beef steak smothered in corn fungus sauce) for $6 or *sopa de habas con nopal* ($2.60). Next door is **Gran Cafe del Zócalo** (daily 7 A.M.–10 P.M., mains $4–6), where the prices and setup are less fancy but the cuisine is similar.

For regional versions of familiar dishes, try the *quesadillas cacaxtla* or the *spaghetti tlaxcalteca* at **Jardín Plaza Restaurante** (daily 8 A.M.–10 P.M., mains $4–8), in the center of the Arcos.

Just off the square and not far from the bullring is **Restaurante Tirol** (Independencia 7A, Mon.–Sat. 7 A.M.–4 P.M., mains $3–6), recommended by one reader for its charmingly decorated tables facing the street and superb breakfasts (with fruit and juice) and *comidas corridas* for about $4. Service is snappy.

La Fonda del Convento (Calzada de San Francisco, 246/462-0765, daily 7 A.M.–9 P.M.) is an attractive and intimate restaurant on a cobblestone street downtown. It offers regional cuisine and is open for breakfast.

Restaurant Sharon (Guerrero betw. Porfirio Díaz and Juárez, mains $4) has an excellent *comida corrida* for $4, as well as *queso fundido* and *pozole* for $2.

For a good cup of coffee and a snack break, head to **Cafe La Fuente** (Guerrero at 20 de Noviembre). The small café is upstairs from the gift shop El Regalito. Another option for coffee is **The Italian Coffee Company,** at the southern end of the *zócalo,* where you can buy gourmet coffees and sweets to sip there or take away.

ARTS AND LEISURE
Balnearios

Dotting the countryside around Tlaxcala are many small *balnearios,* or swimming spas, which make good places to cool off. They're usually crowded with Mexican families on weekends, so try to go during the week.

A few near Tlaxcala are **Zacatelco** (18 km out of Tlaxcala by way of México 150 and 119), **Palo Huérfano** (16 km from Tlaxcala via 150 and 119, 246/461-0268), **Los Pinos** (six km from Tlaxcala via 150 and 119, in Santa Ana Chiautempan), and **Santa Lucía** (16 km from Tlaxcala via 150 and 119).

For more information about these *balnearios,* ask at the tourist office.

Regional Fiestas

Fiestas de la Virgen de Ocotlán take place on the first and third Mondays in May. On August 15 look for **Fiesta de la Virgen de la Asunción,** one of the biggest events in the state. The **Feria de Tlaxcala** comes to town the last week of October through the first week of November.

Tlaxcala's colorful carnival (at the beginning of Lent) is famous nationwide, with hundreds of Tlaxcaltecans donning masks and outlandish costumes to join in ancient dances on Shrove Tuesday and the weekends before and after. Dates change from year to year, but the event is always in February or March.

Also renowned throughout the country is the annual running of the bulls in the town of Huamantla, 50 kilometers from Tlaxcala. This Mexican version of the famed Pamplona festival, called the **Huamantlada,** takes place in late August and is great fun to attend (but stay out of the bulls' way!).

SHOPS

Bazar del Claustro (Plaza Xicoténcatl 8) is a great place to browse for art, jewelry, and other collectibles, although prices can be high. **Museo de Artes y Tradiciones Populares** sells the high-quality textile work of its artisans, but you might find the same quality at a lower price in the town of Santa Ana Chiautempan. **Mercado Emilio Sanchez Piedras,** a standard town market for food and other necessities, is on the corner of Lira y Ortega and Escalona, four blocks north of the *zócalo.*

For high-end browsing, **La Tlaxcalteca Tendajón Cultural** (Tues.–Sun. 10 A.M.–8 P.M.) is amid the row of restaurants beneath the Arcos de Hidalgo on the plaza. Regional music, books, lithographs, textiles, carved wooden sculpture, and reproduction silver pieces are sold here.

HOTELS
$15–30

Hotel Alifer (Av. Morelos 11, off Independencia, 246/462-5678, $30 s/d) has rooms of varying sizes, each with double beds, a writing desk, marble-tiled bath, and cable TV. Other amenities include a restaurant/bar and parking.

$50–75

Hotel de la Loma (Av. Guerrero 58, 246/462-0424, $35 s, $45 d) is small and pleasantly hidden at the top of a long and winding staircase facing the street. The 25 rooms—some with a view overlooking the city—are comfortable and well lit. The restaurant serves inexpensive regional food as well.

Jeroc's (Blvd. Revolución 4-Bis, 246/462-1577, $66 s, $75 d), a 10-minute drive outside of downtown, offers modern clean rooms with double beds, TVs, and stereo music; the common areas include a pool, tennis courts, gym, conference room, restaurant, and disco.

$75–110

Posada San Francisco (Plaza de la Constitución 17, 246/462-6022, www.posadasanfrancisco.

com.mx, $95 s, $100 d) faces the *zócalo* and is a large, roomy building with interior courtyards and all the amenities, including a good restaurant—**Piedras Negras**—a billiards room, tennis courts, a boutique, a library, and the **Bar Rancho Seco.**

Mision Tlaxcala (10 km out of town on the highway to Apizaco, 246/461-0256, www.hoteles mision.com.mx, from $100 s/d including breakfast) is a remodeled version of what used to be the Cascada Inn and Spa. Amenities include tennis courts, heated pool, and room service.

Hotel Escondida, Hacienda Soltepec (Km 3 Carr. Huamantla–Puebla, 247/472-1466 or 247/472-3110, www.haciendasoltepec.com, $82 d, $92 suites at weekends, from $68 during the week) is in Huamantla, 51 kilometers from Tlaxcala, and is definitely worth looking into for a quiet retreat. Named for the 1957 María Felix film shot here, this extraordinary hotel lies within view of the Malinche volcano. Inside the stately hacienda you'll find a gleaming gym, large indoor heated swimming pools, steam bath, two squash courts, and a juice bar, as well as 12 rooms and one of the best restaurants in the state.

PRACTICALITIES
Information and Services

The state tourist office (246/465-0960 or 246/465-0968, toll-free within Mexico 800/509-6557, www.tlaxcala.gob.mx/turismo) is just off the *zócalo* at the corner of Juárez and Lardizabal. A friendly and helpful staff will give you information and maps.

The post office is on the Plaza de la Constitución. Long-distance phones are available at Avenida Juárez 56C (8:30 A.M.–8 P.M.) and under the *portales* at the plaza.

Banamex is at Plaza Xicoténcatl 8, and BBVA is at Avenida Juárez 54.

Get your duds cleaned at a **no-name laundry** (Alcocer 30, about two blocks north of the Plaza de la Constitución, Mon.–Fri. 8 A.M.–4 P.M. and 5–7 P.M., Sat. 8 A.M.–3 P.M.).

The **Red Cross** (Allende betw. Guerrero and Hidalgo, 246/462-0920) offers 24-hour ambulance service. Other medical services can be obtained at **Hospital General** (Av. de La Corregidora, 246/462-0357).

Getting There and Away

From Mexico City take the highway to Puebla and turn off before Puebla toward Tlaxcala. Driving time is roughly 90 minutes, depending on traffic leaving Mexico City. An alternative scenic route, probably an hour longer depending on traffic, is to follow México 136 east out of Texcoco.

The **central bus station** is a kilometer from the Plaza de la Constitución. Buses to Mexico City (Terminal TAPO) are with ATAH (55/5542-8689 in Mexico City), which has a bus every hour and a half or so 6 A.M.–8 P.M., charging $10 for the two-hour ride. Buses to Puebla and Jalapa-Veracruz leave often throughout the day with ADO (241/417-0085). Minibuses to Apizaco and Huamantla can be found outside the Casa de las Artesanías or in the market.

CACAXTLA AND XOCHITÉCATL

A small hilltop ruin, Cacaxtla was for years not considered an important site. But in 1975, locals found an immense mural showing a man painted black and dressed as a bird in a polychrome panorama filled with details. The mural caught the attention of representatives of the Instituto Nacional de Antropología e Historia. Using clues from murals and ruins, archaeologists have been busily piecing together what life was like in the 1,100-year-old culture. A few years later, searching for more murals, archaeologists uncovered the related but much older site of Xochitécatl.

The People of Cacaxtla

The archaeological site lies 130 kilometers east of Mexico City, a strategic junction point between traders from the Mayan coastal regions and the central highlands, dominated until A.D. 750 by the city of Teotihuacán. The inhabitants of the region are thought to have been originally Chontal Maya from the Gulf Coast, near the border of present-day Veracruz and Tabasco, who migrated into the highlands shortly before the time of Christ. After they populated several of the valleys around what is today Puebla and Tlaxcala, Cacaxtla rose some time around A.D. 300 as the capital of the region.

Cacaxtla is believed to have ruled over about 200 rural towns and villages, each controlled by a local strongman, or *cacique*. Perhaps because of competition among these many different local leaders, Cacaxtla society was extremely warlike, with the warrior as the most exalted figure in society. These traits are readily apparent when examining the spectacular battle mural. Some believe it may have been an invasion from Cacaxtla that finally toppled the rulers of Teotihuacán and put that city to the torch around A.D. 750. Cacaxtla slid into decline around A.D. 1100.

During its heyday, the white-stuccoed hilltop acropolis looming over the surrounding countryside must have been a striking sight. The ceremonial center measures roughly 1.7 kilometers long by just under a kilometer wide, and contains various platforms, pyramids, palaces, and other buildings. While the structures are impressive to modern visitors—particularly the **Gran Basamento** (Great Base, now covered with a metal roof), **Templo Rojo** (Red Temple), and **Building A**—the real attraction is unquestionably the amazing murals decorating the walls.

Scholars believe that murals once covered most of Cacaxtla's exterior, and that they were painted somewhere between A.D. 750 and 850. Motifs common to both Mayan lowland painting and also to those used in nearby Teotihuacán point to Cacaxtla's position as an intermediary of sorts between these two stronger cultures. The brilliant colors of the murals, depicting all sorts of people and creatures, remain shockingly bright considering the intervening centuries.

The largest and most impressive of Cacaxtla's murals, the ***Battle Mural*** (on the north wall of the North Plaza) displays 48 warriors divided into two groups. Those dressed like jaguars appear to be the victors of a battle over those dressed as birds, who are shown wounded or already dead, in gory detail. It's uncertain whether the mural depicts the fighters of Cacaxtla defending against invaders, invading a foreign place themselves, or some other as-yet-unknown event.

Practicalities

The sites are open seven days a week 10 A.M.–6 P.M.; admission is $4. A snack shop and restrooms are at the entrance to Cacaxtla. Avoid Sundays, as it is free for Mexicans and very crowded. During the week the site is very quiet.

Cacaxtla-Xochitécatl is 19 kilometers southwest of Tlaxcala near the town of San Miguel de Milagro. From there take the Nativitas bus from the central bus station. You will find taxis and *colectivos* that will take you to the site. Be prepared for a lot of walking around when you get there, and try to arrive as soon as the site opens.

If you're driving from Tlaxcala city, head toward Puebla on the free highway, which leaves town from near the bus terminal, and follow signs to Nativitas. Once you pass Nativitas, look for a sign about two kilometers out of town; the road will go to the right and is quite bumpy. Though the distance isn't great, many *topes* (speed bumps) slow you down.

From Mexico City the site is less than two hours' drive. Take the *autopista* (fast highway) to Puebla, and turn off to your left when you reach the factory of Santa Juliana. Signs first point to Xalmimilulco, then you take a right in San Rafael, after which there are clear signposts. From Puebla it is no more than a half hour's drive.

LA MALINCHE

One of the best hiking areas in central Mexico is Volcán La Malinche (4,462 meters), Mexico's fifth-highest mountain. This extinct volcano is blanketed by thick forest protected as **Parque Nacional La Malinche.** Locals usually refer to the mountain by the indigenous version of the name, Malintzi (the "n" is silent). Climbing the peak makes an excellent hike for those who want to experience the high mountains of central Mexico without dealing

with ropes, crampons, and glaciers, and it is also a perfect acclimatization hike for those looking to tackle the higher mountains of Pico de Orizaba or Ixtaccíhuatl.

The trail begins easily, heading up through lovely forest before coming out onto grassy fields below the peak. The last stretch up the sandy, exposed flanks of the mountain is tougher going. Allow three to four hours one-way. The views from the peak are stupendous, as the mountain lies between Popo and Ixta to the west and Pico de Orizaba to the east.

All visitors to the park must pay a $1 admission. The park is open daily 9 A.M.–5 P.M.

Camping

Camping is allowed in the forest above the camp for free, or in the camp itself for $2.50 per person. Cabins at the camp, run by the Mexican Social Security Institute (IMSS), cost $50 for a basic cabin sleeping six, or $80 for a cabin sleeping nine. Reservations (necessary for the cabins, but not for camping) can be made by phone, in Spanish, at 246/462-4098 or 246/461-0700, ext. 677, or by going on the IMSS website at www.imss.gob.mx/vacaciones and clicking the link "Malintzi."

Practicalities

Travel east from Apizaco (which is northeast of Tlaxcala) on México 136 about 13 kilometers to a signed junction directing you to Campamento IMSS La Malintzin. The paved road leads to a camp on the side of the mountain, at about 3,100 meters. Drivers will have to pause at a little road block, manned by the Coordinación General de Ecología de Tlaxcala, and write down their names and explain the purpose of their visit. From the camp, continue 4.7 kilometers to the road's end at the trailhead, where there are the ruins of a building. You may want to leave your vehicle at the camp and walk up the last stretch of road, as some cars have been broken into at the trailhead, although it adds a good hour's walk each way. Driving from Puebla, take the Highway 150 Puebla–Amozoc, and then Highway 129 to Huamantla, and from there Highway 136

MYSTERIES OF XOCHITÉCATL

Unearthed less than two decades ago, steeped in mystery and deeply entwined with local legend, the pre-Hispanic ruins of Xochitécatl in the state of Tlaxcala can provide one of the most rewarding visits to an archaeological site within a reasonable distance from the capital. The ruins reemerged into the blinding sunlight of this region because archaeologists hoped to find murals similar to those at neighboring Cacaxtla.

They didn't find any impressive polychrome murals, but they found an unusual spiral structure, two lava stone tubs, and a pyramid – perfectly aligned with the Malinche volcano – whose steps were adorned with clay figurines. Curiously, all these figures are female, from babies in baskets to elderly dames with visible crow's feet. There are even pregnant women with holes in their inflated bellies in which little clay fetuses have been inserted.

Unlike its neighbor, Xochitécatl dates from the late Preclassic period, peaking in around 800 B.C. and continuing to be used until around 400 B.C. Then it was inhabited again – no one knows if by descendents of the same ethnic group, or if by newcomers – at the same time as Cacaxtla, in the Epiclassic period (circa A.D. 600-900).

The archaeologist who excavated the site, Dr. Maricarmen Serrapuche, thought the second occupation was by the original group that remembered the sacred place of their ancestors. "But the majority now hold that it was by the Olmec-Xicalanca people, who are believed to have built Cacaxtla," explained Catalina Barriendos, author of a thesis on the Preclassic period of Xochitécatl. "The important thing is we know in the second occupation, the two sites were united."

As with Teotihuacán, no one knows why the site was abandoned, but one reasonable theory is that activities of the Popocatépetl volcano, nearby to the south, could have temporarily stunted the productivity of the fields. It is known that there was some kind of eruption between 100 B.C. and A.D. 100, Barriendos said, and this may have caused mudslides, causing the agricultural population to leave.

Visitors should make their first stop the Museo del Sitio, displaying small clay figurines of images of women – some pregnant, others ancient – which were part of a large offering found on the steps of this site's large pyramid, known as the Pirámide de Las Flores (*xochitl* is Náhuatl for "flower," and *técatl* means "lineage"). Outside the museum there is a very odd assortment of statues and

toward Apizaco, and keep an eye out for the signposted turnoff to the park.

To get to La Malinche without a car, catch a bus to either Apizaco or Huamantla, and from there hire a taxi. The price should be $10 one-way, and usually it's no problem to arrange to be picked up. On weekends a bus winds its way around the volcano on bumpy dirt roads and down to the bus terminal in Puebla. Times vary, but the last one usually heads down around 5 P.M.

TOWARD VERACRUZ
Huamantla

East of Apizaco past La Malinche is Huamantla, a midsized agricultural town. Most of the

year there's not a lot to attract tourists to Huamantla apart from the attractive 16th-century Franciscan monastery, but every August the town holds the largest "running of the bulls" festival in Mexico over the course of two weeks. Try to get there before the morning of the 15th to see the elaborate and colorful sand paintings that local residents use to decorate the streets before the religious processions begin. For more information on the festival and the town, visit the municipal website (www.huamantla.gob.mx).

Tlaxco

Turning north from Apizaco on the road to Zacatlán (instead of continuing east to heads, including a frog looking upwards to the sky, a serpent's tongue, and a head with a lopsided mouth.

"The frog is clearly associated with water," Barriendos said, "and research has showed that facial paralysis, and its cure, was the domain of the water gods."

Water has retained a sacred vale in the surroundings, according to Barriendos, who gives the example of the village of San Miguel de Milagro, on the slopes below Cacaxtla, where people come on pilgrimages to the *santuario* (small church) whose well provides holy water with healing properties.

On the pyramid that faces south, called El Pirámide del Serpiente, is a first monolithic (made of just one stone) tub, which has a drainage hole. It is thought this was used to collect rainwater used in ritual cleansing. The other tub, at the foot of the Pyramid of the Flowers, also has a drainage hole pointing in the same direction, toward Popocatépetl and Ixtaccíhuatl volcanoes, leading Barriendos to think that even the drainage of the water was part of the site's ritual function.

"People here still have a legend that a large serpent lives in the hill of Xochitécatl. Workers say they have seen or heard it and have left in fear. It lives in a cave inside the hill and

has gold scales," Barriendos said, adding that she has seen small rattlesnakes in the area but nothing so monstrous. "Sometimes it leaves and goes to the Ixta or Malinche volcanoes, both female mountains."

Another potent local legend tells of a *hacendado* (landowner) who fell in love with a beautiful Indian woman who washed her clothes on the other side of the river. He persuaded her to elope and waded across to take her home, but as he carried her back through the water, he realized she had turned into a giant snake, which he dropped and fled. There are two versions of the ending, that he killed the snake, and that she – in her human form – continued to reappear at the edge of the river, washing.

"In either version, the serpent is clearly a woman, Cihuacoatl, the snake goddess," Barriendos said.

The mysteries of this unique sacred place remain far from resolved, but the interaction with living folk invests Xochitécatl with power and intrigue. In addition it is a comfortable site to visit, without too much arduous climbing and with a number of benches set beneath trees so visitors can rest in the shade.

–Contributed by Barbara Kastelein, a free-lance journalist and travel writer living in Mexico City.

EXCURSIONS

Huamantla and Jalapa), a secondary road leads to Tlaxco, about a 30-minute drive from Apizaco across the high plains of Tlaxcala. The town itself is nothing stupendous, but it's a picturesque little Mexican town with an attractive church. The town is well known for its *requesón* and *tenate* cheeses; ask around for where to buy some. Nine kilometers west of town on the road toward Hidalgo is the **Hacienda Xochuca,** an old-style ranch that still produces *pulque,* a curious fermented cactus drink for which Tlaxcala and Hidalgo are well known. About 15 kilometers on the road toward Puebla you'll enter the Sierra de Tlaxco, a forest-covered range with some campsites and hiking. By public transport, catch a bus here

every hour throughout the day with ATAH from the Terminal TAPO in Mexico City ($9), or from Tlaxcala.

Chignahuapan

On the far side of the Sierre de Tlaxco, right at the edge of where the central plateau ends and begins to drop off down steep canyons to the coast, is Chignahuapan, a small town 65 kilometers from Apizaco. Perched in the very top of one of these canyons five kilometers from town is the **Hotel Baños Termales de Chignahuapan** (797/971-0313 or 797/971-0792, www.termales chignahuapan.com.mx, $85 per person), a spa hotel built around a gushing thermal hot spring. The hotel has 75 rooms in two buildings. The rooms are a little faded, but each has its own large bath fed directly from the spring (too hot by itself, you'll have to mix it with the cold for it to be bearable). Down below, built along the river, is a big public pool, as well as a smaller pool and whirlpool tub reserved for guests. The prices might seem steep, but they include three meals, and the restaurant food is hearty and well cooked. If you're not a guest, the public pools cost $6 per person for the day and are open until 10 P.M.

If you'd like to stretch your legs between lazing about in the hot springs, take a hike up the hillside above the hotel. A good place to start is the high point of the dirt road from town. Just pick a likely-looking trail and head upward. You'll go through small mountain farms owned by humble campesinos who are very friendly, especially if you say *buenos días* with a wave and smile. Further up are patches of forest, and up higher you'll have great views over the landscape. Keep an eye out for the huge maguey cacti all over the place.

If you're without a car, you can catch buses here several times daily from Tlaxcala, or take a bus from Mexico City to Zacatlá, Puebla, from the Terminal del Norte, and get off at Chignahuapan.

BACKGROUND

The Setting

GEOLOGY

Mexico City takes up half the surface area of the roughly 3,100-square-kilometer Valle de México, a unique land formation in the center of Mexico's volcanic central highlands. Technically not a valley—as it has no natural drainage—the basin is completely ringed by mountains. The worn down, low hills to the north rose 30 million years ago and were followed later by the steep-walled ridges on the east and west. A row of volcanoes to the south first erupted around two million years ago, thus sealing off the basin entirely. Several of Mexico's highest peaks—Popocatépetl (5,465 meters), Ixtaccíhuatl (5,230 meters), Ajusco (3,930 meters), Volcán Tláloc (3,690 meters), and Cerro Pelado (3,670 meters)—rim the valley to the south and southeast.

The valley floor, more than half of which was once covered by a series of broad, shallow lakes, varies between 2,100 and 2,400 meters in altitude and extends roughly 120 kilometers north to south, depending on where you measure from (the northern boundary is a bit vague), and between 40 and 70 kilometers from east to west. While mostly flat, the valley is punctuated by several anomalous mountains, mainly volcanic in origin, such as Cerro de la Estrella, Cerro Chapultepec, and Cerro Tepeyac.

The Valle de México is very active seismically and experiences frequent earthquakes, most of which are generated from the movement of geologic plates toward Mexico's Pacific coast. Because of the interaction between earthquake wave movement and the valley's weak subsoil, Mexico City sometimes feels the effects of a coastal quake more than places closer to the quake's actual epicenter. Such was the case in the deadly 1985 earthquake, the epicenter of which was more than 160 kilometers away.

HYDROLOGY

One of the most vexing problems that people settling in the Valle de México have had to deal with throughout its history is the complex water system. Before humans began making their modifications (originally under the Aztecs), five interconnected lakes in the valley fluctuated dramatically in size throughout the year, depending on rainfall and evaporation rates. The highest of the lakes, Chalco, had the freshest water, while Texcoco, the largest and lowest-lying, was the saltiest.

This constant fluctuation in water levels was a problem for the Aztecs. Because all the best land on the lakes' shores had already been taken by the time they arrived, they settled on an island near the center of the lake. Thus when lake levels rose, their territory shrank on all sides. In the late 15th century, Nezahualcóyotl, the poet-king of neighboring Texcoco and an Aztec ally, oversaw the construction of a massive dike dividing Lake Texcoco into two halves, one salty and one fresh, as a means of controlling the annual floods. In addition, a network of canals was built for drainage control and transportation.

As part of his final assault on Tenochtitlán in 1521, Cortés ordered the breaching of the dike to flood the Aztec city. The water level was not high enough at that point to cause the damage he'd hoped for, but in the long run Cortés may have been more successful than he had planned. The Spaniards, not understanding the complexities of the ecosystem, left the dike in ruins when they rebuilt the city, and as a result saw their new colonial capital flooded repeatedly over the next few centuries. After several heavy rainy seasons, the entire city remained underwater constantly for five years in the early 17th century, forcing many inhabitants to abandon their palaces and live temporarily on higher ground at the edge of the valley.

Thus a public works project was initiated that has continued unabated to this day, digging ever bigger tunnels and canals to completely drain the valley. Although successive colonial governments dug drainage canals, it was not until 1900, with the construction of the Gran Canal de Desagüe (Great Drainage Canal) under the administration of Porfirio Díaz, that the waters of Lago Texcoco were finally emptied almost entirely.

Currently the only major bodies of water in the valley are small tracts of Lago Xochimilco in the south, the lakes in Chapultepec, and the much reduced remnants of Lago Texcoco northeast of the city, in the state of Mexico. The dozen or so rivers that once flowed into the valley mainly from the western mountains—such as Río Mixcoac, Río de la Piedad, Río Tacubaya, and Río Churubusco—still exist but are canalized and sealed under major avenues, eventually draining into one of the five canals on the east side of the city, which in turn flow out of the valley to the northeast.

While only a few patches of lake still exist, flooding remains a yearly occurrence in many parts of the Mexico City metro area during the April–October rainy season.

The results of all this drainage can be seen in the capital's uneven streets and settling architecture. Because much of the valley's groundwater has been siphoned off, the sandy, unstable soil has sunk dramatically (about 7.5 meters in the last century, currently 15 centimeters a year in places), leaving many downtown buildings comically contorted as different parts sink at different rates. City air is also affected; the dried lakebeds in the northeast part of the valley create swirling clouds of dust that are swept up into the atmosphere and moved to the southwest, directly across the city, by the prevailing winds, worsening the air pollution.

CLIMATE

Although Mexico City straddles the 19th parallel North, thus placing it squarely in the tropics, its 2,240-meter elevation can add a chill to the air, particularly during the December–February winter months, and at times during the summer rainy season due to the cloudy weather. Nights and early mornings can be chilly throughout the year. Generally the city has one of the mildest climates in Mexico—pleasant during the day and comfortable for sleeping at night.

The rains usually begin in April or May and continue sporadically until October. They often abate for two or three weeks in August, usually before the coming of the fall hurricane season. The violent high winds that lash Mexico's coasts during the frequent annual storms do not usually make it to Mexico City, but they can leave skies gray and rainy for days at a time, and sometimes flooding occurs.

Rain levels average 700–1,300 millimeters per year in the southwest mountains, and 400–600 millimeters per year in the more arid central and northern parts of the valley.

Temperature also varies depending on location, ranging from 12°C on average in the western mountains to 16°C in the center of town. The hottest months of the year are usually April and May, when temperatures sometimes hit 30°C in the day, while the coldest are December and January, with daytime temperatures averaging 14°C. Humidity is low to moderate, except during the rainy season.

ENVIRONMENT

With its 18-million-plus population, Mexico City has a well-deserved reputation for being overcrowded and polluted. Long gone are the days when Carlos Fuentes could title his novel *Where the Air Is Clear*. Despite the understandably apocalyptic and fatalistic attitude many *chilangos* take toward their city's environment, there has been some progress in recent years, although it's barely begun to redress the existing problems.

Mexico City hosts a number of environmental groups dedicated to raising environmental awareness. Mexican Conservation Learning Network (www.imacmexico.org) is the country's leading clearest house on environmental matters, with news and publications in Spanish.

Air Quality

Mexico City measures its Metropolitan Air Quality Index (Índice Metropolitana de Calidad de Aire, or IMECA) every hour every day. According to collected stats, air pollution is usually worse on the southern edge of town because the prevailing winds are from the north and the air is trapped by the Sierra Ajusco to the south. The winter months are the worst months for air pollution in the Valle de México, because of fewer and lighter air currents. Cooler air temperatures create thermal inversions, which keep car exhaust and industrial emissions hovering just above ground level, often causing respiratory, eye, and throat irritations.

The United Nations' World Health Organization classifies Imeca readings of more than 100 points as Unsatisfactory, readings of more than 200 points as Bad, and readings of 300 Dangerous. When the Imeca breaks 200 points, the city orders all outdoor activities for primary, secondary, and preschool canceled, as the young are more susceptible to the ill effects of bad air. You can track the daily Imeca readings in most local newspapers or online at www.sma.df.gob.mx/simat (the Mexico City environmental secretariat's air quality monitoring office). You can also see the most recent reading on the home page of the city government, www.df.gob.mx.

Anecdotal and statistical evidence suggests that although Mexico City's air is still extremely poor, it is improving. In 2006, air quality was above 100 points for 233 days, compared to 306 in 2000, and the number of emergencies (*contingencias*) has dropped as well. For recent reports (in Spanish) on air quality, look at the website for the Mexico City Secretaría de Medio Ambiente (Environment Secretariat) at www.sma.df.gob. mx. A report by the national environmental authorities states that the Mexico City area has gone from being among the top three worst air qualities in the world in the 1980s to 14th place in 2007, one better than Beijing.

The single biggest contributor to D.F.'s

haze is the automobile, which accounts for an estimated 85 percent of detectable smog. The Hoy No Círcula program, which is supposed to ensure that every registered vehicle stays off the roads at least one day a week, has by some accounts exacerbated the problem, by giving an incentive for wealthier people to simply by a second or third vehicle. However, exemptions from the program for newer, cleaner vehicles and tighter emissions inspection programs and incentives for trucks and buses to upgrade their vehicles have definitely helped in recent years.

Dr. Mario Molina Pasquel, the Mexican scientist who won the 1995 Nobel Prize for Chemistry, has been working on a plan to reduce particulate matter (PM10) levels, one of the leading pollution causes of health problems, but he's fighting a hard battle. The plan entails convincing Pemex to recalibrate its refineries to reduce sulfur in fuel emissions, in particular diesel, and implementing new large-capacity, low-polluting buses on dedicated lanes. The government is moving ahead with the bus part of the plan (witness the new Metrobús along Av. Insurgentes), but time will tell if Pemex can be convinced to change its fuel production techniques. The $3 billion cost of refinery upgrading is meant to be paid for by a fuel tax. Pemex has stated that by the end of 2008, it will have lowered the sulfur content of its fuels from 500 parts per million to 30 parts per million. Molina believes that because much PM10 pollution comes from trucks traveling to Mexico City from across the country, only a national-level solution to emissions, rather than only local measures, would have any significant effect.

Needless to say, the air quality is still very far from ideal in Mexico City, and can come as a physical shock to those accustomed to cleaner environments. Those who are more sensitive to air conditions may find that on bad air days in Mexico City their throats and eyes become irritated. This is a particular concern for younger children, especially those with asthma or other respiratory problems. One way to mitigate these problems is to stay inside during the height of the day, when air quality is usually at its worst.

Water

The city has a seemingly unquenchable thirst for water. Most of the city's water supply is pumped from aquifers beneath the city. The removal of the groundwater has caused some of the buildings to sink more rapidly than usual. The water table has dropped by 32 meters, and the city itself has sunk by seven meters since 1940. The city consumes 3.5 million cubic meters of water every day, twice the level of many industrialized countries, and up to a quarter of the city's water supply is lost through leaky pipes before it reaches household taps.

Because of the dwindling aquifers, about 20 to 30 percent of the city's water is pumped uphill 1,000 meters from the Lerma and Cutzamala Rivers, 100 kilometers to the west. As a result, not only is the Mexico City water table dropping, but water shortages are increasing all around central Mexico as a result of supplying the needs of the capital.

A reforestation program along the banks of the dwindling Lago de Texcoco has helped to cut back on dust and to recycle carbon dioxide, and it may also speed efforts to reclaim more rainwater in the lake basin. More creative, low-tech measures begun include digging 600 absorption wells in the southern mountain parts of Tlalpan, Milpa Alta, Xochimilco, Magdalena Contreras, and Cuajimalpa *delegaciones*. These will collect rainwater and funnel it underground, which will both reduce the risk of flooding and help replenish the subterranean aquifers. A total of 2,000 wells—each costing only $9,000—had been dug by 2008.

Sewage is disposed of out of town, much to the frustration of outlying communities. Built in 1900, the Gran Canal de Desagüe (Great Drainage Canal) project drove a pipeline through the northern hills to carry human waste, garbage, and floodwater outside the valley. At the beginning of the century, gravity was sufficient to pull the putrid black waters out of town. But as the city began to sink, 11 pumping stations were constructed. Today, another deep drainage system is under construction.

History

Mexico's history is far too gloriously complex and rich to do justice to in these pages. This section offers an overview of the evolution of Mexico City itself, rather than the entire country—although considering the capital's importance, the two often overlap.

PRE-HISPANIC HISTORY
First Arrivals

Mexico's earliest human inhabitants arrived slowly via the Bering Strait land bridge (which at the time spanned the Asian and North American continents) between 50,000 and 25,000 B.C. Descendants of Asia's late Paleolithic epoch, these nomadic hunter-gatherers dispersed throughout North America seeking food and benign natural conditions. No evidence of any sociocultural organization survives, although remains of hunted mammoth, mastodon, giant bison, and antelope near Puebla suggest humans arrived this far south by 24,000 B.C.

The First Inhabitants of the Valley

Groups of nomads are thought to have first found their way into the Valle de México sometime around 20,000 B.C. The advantages of an abundant water supply and the surrounding wall of the mountains—which served both as a natural defense and as a barrier for keeping game near at hand—must have made the valley an appealing place for these wandering bands to settle down and build small villages.

But this very appeal led to the extinction of the valley's large game between 9000 and 8000 B.C. Over the next several thousand years, the valley's population grew to rely on gathering fruits and grains, especially maize, until the third millennium B.C., when fully agricultural societies established themselves.

As in other parts of the world, this agricultural revolution created profound changes in social organization. Between 1500 and 650 B.C., villages around the edge of the valley's

lakes grew in size, particularly in the northeast and in the south. The first full-fledged city to develop was Cuicuilco, centered around a pyramid site that can still be seen at the junction of Insurgentes Sur and Periférico Sur. By 100 B.C. a second city was growing at Teotihuacán in the north, the location of several freshwater springs which permitted irrigated agriculture.

The incipient rivalry between the two cities was dramatically cut short sometime in the second century A.D., when Volcán Xitle blew its top and covered Cuicuilco and much of the southeastern part of the valley with beds of lava. Following Cuicuilco's fiery demise, the population of Teotihuacán increased sharply, reaching a height of perhaps 200,000 in A.D. 750. Through a combination of excessive logging and overintensive agriculture, the productivity of the once fertile valley began to decline (visitors today will see a barren and arid landscape), and the final blow was dealt by successive invasions by northern warrior tribes.

The Toltecs

Just before the end of the first millennium, the Toltecs—a culturally hybrid group dominated by Amerindians from northern Mexico—established a fortified capital at Tula in present-day Hidalgo, just north of Mexico City. Between A.D. 900 and 1200, Toltec centers developed as far north as Zacatecas and as far south as Guatemala; Toltec influence apparently extended to the post-Classic Maya architecture at Chichén Itzá as well.

The Toltec civilization never reached the heights achieved by Teotihuacán and slipped into decline after A.D. 1200. After suffering successive invasions by warrior tribes from the north, Tula was abandoned in the 13th century.

The Aztecs

In the wake of Tula's fall, control of the valley was divided between several competing communities, with population centers of

10,000–20,000 at Texcoco, Azcapoltzalco, Tacuba, and Xochimilco, as well as dozens of smaller towns. Into this mix arrived yet another northern tribe, the Aztecs, in the mid-13th century. The fiercest warriors Mexico has ever known, the Aztecs claimed to come from an island in the north called Aztatlán or Aztlán (Place of Herons), thought to be on the coast of modern-day Nayarit. According to Aztec chronicles, their war god Huitzilopochtli led them to the valley after a century of wandering and gave the tribe a new name, México.

Receiving a cold reception from the tribes already living around the lake, the Aztecs first settled on the insect-infested Cerro Chapultepec in A.D. 1280 and tried to ingratiate themselves to the neighboring Tepanecs by serving as mercenaries. They quickly developed a reputation as bloodthirsty warriors. Around 1300 the Culhuacán, rivals of the Tepanecs, defeated the Aztecs in battle and took the survivors as slaves. After serving for 25 years as Culhuacán mercenaries, the Aztecs were eventually granted their freedom. In a telling sign of their vengefulness and brutality, they tricked the Culhuacán leader into giving them one of his daughters to marry their own ruler. At the Aztec "wedding" ceremony, the guest leader was greeted by the sight of the Aztec high priest wearing the flesh of his daughter.

Still weaker than the Culhuacán, the Aztecs fled to an uninhabited island named Tenochtitlán, in the center of the lake, rather than risk a war they might lose. Legend has it that the sight of an eagle perched on a cactus, a snake in its beak, was the fulfillment of Aztec prophecy, which convinced the tribe to settle there for good. Historians cite the island's natural defenses and the existence of several small freshwater springs on the island as more prosaic reasons.

For a time the Aztecs returned as soldiers for their former Tepanec masters, but the fourth Aztec king, Itzcoatl, overthrew the Tepanecs in 1428 and, along with the leaders of nearby city-states Texcoco and Tlacopán, established the Triple Alliance to rule over the valley. Aztec hegemony in the alliance was implicit from the start and grew stronger over the next century.

Under Itzcoatl's mid-15th-century successors, all historical records belonging to other tribes were destroyed to cement the Aztec perspective of the Valle de México, which revered the Toltecs as their spiritual ancestors and downplayed their nomadic past. Moctezuma I (1440–1469) embarked on an expansionist program that brought the Huastec and Mixtec regions under Aztec control, and under Aztec monarch Ahuitzotl (1486–1502) all of central Mexico fell under Aztec sway, except for the fierce and copper-equipped Tarascan warriors of Michoacán and the doughty Tlaxcaltecas to the east, who would later prove key in the Spanish conquest.

Far from tempering their bloody ways as they grew in power, the empire Aztecs took their formerly modest practice of human sacrifice and occasional cannibalism to staggering heights. Historians continue to argue about the accuracy of the incredible number of victims Spanish chroniclers reported killed in single ceremonies (in the tens of thousands), but the Aztecs unquestionably sacrificed on a huge scale, reputedly believing it necessary to feed the sun with blood so it would rise each day.

Conquered by such a culture, vassal states obeyed the Aztecs from fear rather than loyalty. Tribute demanded by the Aztecs included gold, copper, gemstones, jade, amber, rubber, jaguar skins, tropical feathers, and chocolate. Apart from these material goods, other tribes were required to send victims for sacrifice. Even nominal Aztec enemies such as the Tlaxcaltecans and the Cholulans were forced into mock battles known as "flower wars," in which soldiers were rarely killed; instead they were taken as prisoners to have their hearts ripped out a few days later by Aztec priests.

The glittering city of Tenochtitlán was the heart of the great empire, an island command center measuring roughly three kilometers square and linked to the mainland only by four causeways that could be easily blocked from attack. Adjacent to Tenochtitlán, and eventually linked to it by continual landfill projects, was

sculpture detail from the Templo de Quetzalcóatl, Teotihuacán

© ELENA PAPPAS

the smaller island of Tlatelolco, the empire's principal market center.

Tenochtitlán was laid out in an orderly grid pattern and crisscrossed by a system of canals, which allowed for drainage during the flood season and also provided the principal means of transportation. The Spanish conquistadors (mostly young provincials with limited educations) who saw Tenochtitlán before they destroyed it were in utter awe of the pervasive cleanliness and order.

As the conquistador Bernal Díaz del Castillo put it in his book, *The Conquest of New Spain:*

> ... we were struck with admiration and said that it all seemed like enchanted things from the book of Amadís, seeing the great towers and buildings which they had built in the water all made of plaster and stone, and some of our soldiers asked if what they saw was a dream, and how marvelous it was the things that I write about here, because it made one amazed. I don't know

how to describe it, seeing things never heard of, never even dreamed of.

In 1519, with a population of perhaps 250,000, Tenochtitlán was arguably the greatest city on earth.

SPANISH CONQUEST AND COLONIZATION
The Spanish Entrada

In the wake of Columbus's momentous voyage in 1492, the Spaniards quickly took over several Caribbean islands, principally Hispaniola and Cuba. In 1518, Cuban Governor Diego Velázquez chose a 34-year-old Spaniard named Hernán Cortés from Medellín, a town in the poor province of Extremadura, Spain, to lead what was intended as a reconnaissance expedition to the Mexican coast.

Cortés, who at the time was working as a secretary for Velázquez, had other ideas in mind. The expedition of 530 soldiers landed in what is now the Gulf Coast state of Veracruz on April 20, 1519. After destroying his ships and convincing his men to risk all for glory, he made his way over the next several months to Tenochtitlán, gathering Aztec enemies as his allies along the way. According to many accounts, the superstitious Aztec Emperor Moctezuma II apparently became convinced that Cortés was the embodiment of the plumed serpent god Quetzalcóatl, who according to legend would return from the east. Because of this, or perhaps because of Cortés' clever diplomacy through Aztec messengers, Moctezuma eventually allowed the Spaniards into his city as protected guests when they finally arrived at Tenochtitlán in November of 1519. Through sheer force of personality and a series of psychological tactics, Cortés assumed a bizarre sort of mental control over Moctezuma, who was soon doing the bidding of the Spaniards and keeping them safe from an increasingly restive and angry Aztec elite.

While Cortés was away on an expedition to the coast to fight off a group of rival conquistadors who had sailed from Cuba, the less subtle Pedro de Alvarado led a slaughter of Aztec nobility who were performing a ceremony that apparently he didn't like the looks of. Cortés hastened back, but the damage was done, and the already unhappy populace rallied to expel the Spaniards from the city on July 1, 1520, known as the *noche triste* (sad night).

Cortés had hoped to hand over Tenochtitlán intact, as a sparkling jewel to the Spanish crown, but after several months of regrouping their forces, organizing allies around the valley, and building a flotilla of lake boats, the conquistadors mounted a brutal 90-day siege and then invaded the city. The Aztecs, already weakened by the diseases brought by the Spaniards and starving to death, fought to the bitter end under the iron leadership of a young warrior named Cuauhtémoc, who is today a national hero in Mexico.

To take the city, the conquistadors were forced to destroy it block by block, eliminating the high redoubts from which the Aztecs flung down rocks and spears, until eventually the remaining defenders, refusing to surrender, were killed in the main plaza of Tlatelolco.

Cuauhtémoc was captured, tortured to reveal hidden stashes of gold (of which none remained—the Spaniards lost most of it during the *noche triste*), and was later executed by Cortés on a pretext.

Nueva España

Facing the rubble of Tenochtitlán, Cortés contemplated establishing the new colonial capital on the edge of the lake, but in the end chose to rebuild the old Aztec city, partly for defensive reasons, but also for the symbolic significance: in many ways, the Spaniards aimed to merely replace the Aztecs as the rulers of the already existing empire system. So under the direction of Alonso García Bravo, a new city was laid out atop the old, utilizing much of the original Aztec street plan.

While the new conquerors often rationalized their right to rule Mexico on the grounds that they were converting the natives to Christianity, missionary zeal was hardly their only motive. Early Aztec gifts of gold and silver had tantalized the treasure-seeking Spaniards, and silver strikes in Taxco in 1522 presaged the fabulously rich mining industry that would form the basis of the colonial economy, and in fact that of all Europe as well.

All of the immense quantities of silver mined in New Spain passed through *la ciudad de México*—as the capital was soon called—on its way back to Spain. On top of this, the Mexico City merchants had an official monopoly on all trading in the colony. As a result of these convenient, royally granted advantages, the city grew immensely wealthy and came to be known throughout Europe as *la ciudad de los palacios* (the city of palaces).

With the decline of the silver industry, Mexico City stagnated in the late 17th and early 18th centuries, but the last decades of the 18th century saw a burst of reformist zeal under the new Bourbon kings, who appointed a series of activist viceroys, the colonial governors. Viceroy Conde de Revillagigedo ordered the creation of a master plan for the city's development, calling for all manner of urban improvements—including an overhaul of basic infrastructure such as sewage and street lighting and building new tree-lined avenues outside downtown (such as La Viga and, later, Paseo de Bucareli).

MEXICO CITY AFTER INDEPENDENCE
Independence and Early Instability

Mexico's struggle for independence from Spain began on September 16, 1810, when Padre Miguel Hidalgo y Costilla gave his famous *grito de la independencia* (independence shout) from a church in Dolores, Guanajuato. Mexico City, which depended on the colonial trade monopoly for its living, remained a royalist holdout during the struggle, firmly opposed to independence. Hidalgo's anarchic rebellion, with racial and class overtones, was quickly put down, and independence was not consummated until royalist officer Agustín Iturbide switched sides and cut a deal with rebel Vicente Guerrero in 1821. Iturbide was appointed emperor of the new republic, but his reign lasted only two years before he was overthrown by another junta that established a federal republic called Los Estados Unidos de México—the United States of Mexico—in 1824. Under this republic, named for the México (Aztec) tribe originally defeated by the Spanish, the 22 provinces of New Spain were divided into 19 states and four territories.

Over the next six years the Mexican republic endured two more coups; it wasn't until 1829 that all Spanish troops were expelled from Mexico. In 1833 Antonio López de Santa Anna, a megalomaniac opium-addicted general in charge of enforcing the expulsion of Spanish troops, seized power and revoked the Constitution of 1824. Mexico in many ways was cursed by Santa Anna, who was a brilliant, charismatic general but utterly uninterested in the difficult tasks of administering a new nation. Santa Anna was in and out of power for the next decade, switching sides repeatedly between the feuding liberals and conservatives. The former favored reining in the power of the church and proceeding with modernist reforms, while the latter felt that the only way

for the country to survive was to maintain the social structure with a strong church and central government.

While Mexico was engrossed in this bitter in-fighting, its neighbor to the north was increasing its control on the Mexican territory of Texas and eyeing other territories covetously. In 1847, on a flimsy pretext, U.S. president James Polk ordered the invasion of Mexico, which ended with the U.S. occupation of Mexico City for 10 months. It was during the battle for Mexico City that six young military cadets, defending the Castillo de Chapultepec from the invading *yanquis,* reputedly leapt to their deaths from the castle ramparts rather than surrender. For their quixotic heroism, the six are remembered in Mexican history as the Niños Héroes, the Child Heroes. As a result of the unequal and unjust war, Mexico ceded almost half of its territory to the United States.

Juárez and Maximilian

Santa Anna returned to power after the war, but he was finally overthrown in 1855 by a Zapotec lawyer named Benito Juárez. The new president and his liberal allies promulgated a constitution in 1857 and passed laws restricting the financial powers of the Church; all Church property save for actual places of worship had to be sold or otherwise relinquished. These actions infuriated conservatives and, not surprisingly, the Church, and led to the War of Reform, with self-appointed governments in Mexico City and Veracruz vying for national authority. A reactionary opposition group took control of Mexico City, and fighting continued until 1861, when the liberals won and Juárez was elected president.

Once in power, Juárez promptly enacted the Reform Laws, dispossessing the Church of its property, a turn of events that would change the face of Mexico City. Much of the downtown area was at that time covered by large monasteries and convents, including San Agustín, San Francisco, Santo Domingo, and La Merced. After seizing the properties, city officials demolished parts of these religious compounds, running new streets through and

The Casa Lamm in the Roma is an example of a European-style mansion built by Mexico's elite during The Porfiriato.

walling off the old churches. While remnants of the old convents and monasteries still stand, none in the Centro Histórico are intact.

Between 1863 and 1867, Mexico was governed by Austrian Emperor Maximilian, installed by an invading French army and supported (initially at least) by Mexican conservatives. Maximilian's rule was brief: once he had alienated his conservative supporters by well-intentioned but half-baked liberal reforms, they withdrew their backing, and the liberal rebels under Juárez defeated his armies and executed Maximilian. But the modernist-minded emperor made a lasting mark on the city. Unhappy with the cold, gloomy palace on the Zócalo, Maximilian and his wife moved to and remodeled the Castillo de Chapultepec, now a popular tourist sight. To link the new palace with downtown, the Paseo de la Reforma (originally the Paseo de la Emperatriz), now the city's broadest boulevard, was laid out. He also overhauled the Zócalo itself, decorating it with trees, benches, and a Parisian-style kiosk.

MODERN MEXICO CITY
The Porfiriato

Juárez defeated the hapless Maximilian in 1867 and again took power, governing Mexico until his death in 1872, when political opponent Porfirio Díaz succeeded him. Díaz thoroughly dominated Mexico for the next 28 years, governing with a brutal and efficient authoritarianism, modernizing the country's education and transportation systems, and opening the doors wide for foreign investors and speculators.

Although originally from rural Oaxaca, Díaz became so attached to Mexico City's pomp and ceremony that by the end of his regime he rarely left the city, a factor that left the formerly wily ruler out of touch with the country as a whole. He spent lavishly on city infrastructure, overhauled the police force, and did his best to convert the wealthy neighborhoods on the western side of the city into little pockets of Europe. The poor shantytowns to the east were ignored entirely, except when he unleashed the police on their inhabitants whenever they ventured into the "good" parts of town.

It was under Díaz that Mexico City began to systematically expand beyond the Centro Histórico. The first neighborhoods established outside downtown were Guerrero and San Rafael, north and west of the Alameda, in the 1850s and 1860s. Under Díaz, this trend accelerated, first with the development of San Cosme and Santa María de la Ribera farther west, and later Juárez and Cuauhtémoc on either side of the newly chic Paseo de la Reforma, and the Colonia Roma just to the south.

Interestingly, this division of the city between the wealthy west and poor east has continued to the present day. The likeliest explanation for the split, which began early in the colonial era, is that the elite were trying to keep as far away as possible from the floodwaters of Lago Texcoco, which lay on the east side of the city.

The Mexican Revolution

By the early 20th century, it was obvious that the gap between rich and poor was increasing, caused by the extreme pro-capitalist policies of the Díaz regime and the lack of a political voice for workers and peasants. Following the annulment of elections won by opposition candidate Francisco I. Madero in 1910, the Mexican Revolution unleashed itself upon the country, and 10 years of warring between different factions followed, until Sonoran General Álvaro Obregón established control in 1920.

As during the independence wars, Mexico City remained on the side of the conservatives throughout the conflict. The populace gave no sign of rising to defend Madero when General Victoriano Huerta staged a coup d'état and had the liberal president executed in early 1913. In retaliation for this apathy, when guerrilla leader Pancho Villa took the capital (which he loathed) in 1915, he staged an elaborate ceremony to shame the city elite, forcing them to rename Plateros, the wealthiest street in the Centro, to Francisco I. Madero, in honor of Villa's slain hero.

Mexico City Under the PRI

Despite its antirevolutionary inclinations, there was never any doubt that the city would remain the heart of Mexico's political, social, and economic life. With the creation of a stable, single-party government under the Institutional Revolutionary Party (PRI), the capital embarked on a new path of explosive growth that has continued to the present day.

After the rule of General Álvaro Obregón (1920–1924) and General Plutarco Elias Calles (1924–1934), Lázaro Cárdenas was elected president in 1934. Cárdenas, a mestizo with Tarascan Indian heritage, was handpicked by Calles, who hoped to remain the power behind the throne, but he was quickly disabused of this notion. Cárdenas instituted the most sweeping social reforms of any national leader to date, effecting significant changes in education, labor, agriculture, and commerce. Because of his humble ways and his evident desire to improve the lot of the average Mexican, he is revered to this day throughout the country.

Cárdenas didn't devote a lot of attention to Mexico City in his reformist drive, but the reforms themselves would end up having a major impact on the capital. The new offices created to manage the myriad new programs would eventually lead to the Mexican "super state," a massive, bloated bureaucracy located entirely in Mexico City: "The dreams of the revolution, converted into a nightmare of centralization," as one historian put it.

Further catalysts to growth came from falling investment in the countryside and from policies encouraging all manner of new industry to spring up in Mexico City. Rather than trying to locate these factories outside of the city, successive governments actively encouraged them to stay, offering tax breaks and promising to build necessary infrastructure if industries would locate in northern suburbs such as Naucalpan, Azcapotzalco, Tlanepantla, and Ecatepec.

The lack of jobs in the countryside and the new industry in Mexico City kicked off waves of migration to the capital, which doubled the population in 20 years, from 906,000 in 1920 to 1,757,000 in 1940. To cope with its new residents, the city expanded in all directions. And as is immediately apparent when you fly over Mexico City, this expansion took place with very little planning or forethought. The government turned a blind eye to the impromptu settlements set up by rural immigrants, which would eventually become entire cities in their own right, and freely gave out permits to build new, upscale neighborhoods for the wealthy. First Colonia Condesa was the "in" place in the 1930s, and it was soon followed by Polanco and Lomas farther west in the 1940s.

The Post-World War II Boom

The dynamics of centralization and rural migration accelerated in step with Mexico's economic growth levels during and after World War II. The construction of the new national university complex in the south of the city in the early 1950s, and the expansion of Avenida Insurgentes to connect it to the city center, led to the buildup of the entire southwestern quadrant of the city in just a few short years. Wide open fields south of Roma were quickly converted into the Del Valle and Nápoles neighborhoods. In the early postwar years the formerly outlying villages of Mixoac, San Ángel, Tacuba, Tacubaya, and Coyoacán were formally incorporated into the city limits.

To the north, the industrial areas promoted by the government spurred the building of ever-greater numbers of houses, to the point where the remaining open land between them and the city itself soon disappeared entirely as the *mancha urbana* (urban stain) spread across the entire valley. When the middle-class suburb Ciudad Satelite was built with great optimism in the late 1950s, it was surrounded by open land, but in the intervening years the city gobbled it up completely, sprawling all the way to Tepozotlán, by the entrance of the tollway to Querétaro.

The poor, rural immigrants flooding into the city didn't have money to buy property or houses, and so they simply erected shantytowns in the less desirable, eastern side of the valley, once under the waters of Lago Texcoco. Over the years these *ciudades perdidas* (lost cities) have converted into increasingly permanent cities themselves, with infrastructure and local government. The classic *ciudad perdida* is Ciudad Nezahaulcóyotl (Ciudad Neza for short), which saw its population increase from 65,000 in 1960 to 650,000 in 1970 to 1,233,868 in 1995, making it one of the largest cities in the country.

Immigration has fallen off somewhat in recent years, and city and federal governments make a lot of noise about controlling city growth, but the overall dynamic appears to have changed little. If anything, the changes under way due to NAFTA and the privatization of the communal farms will only drive more people out of rural Mexico, and if these migrants can't get to the United States, they'll come to Mexico City.

One example of the continuing relentless city growth can be seen in Chalco, in the southeastern corner of the valley. Still a farming community with miles of open fields, Chalco is now being "colonized" by immigrants from Ciudad Neza, and urban researchers say it's just a question of a few years before new roads are built, power lines are put in, and the new communities are regularized.

Government and Economy

GOVERNMENT
Colonial Era

During the Spanish colonial era, Mexico City was governed as an *ayuntamiento,* the traditional Spanish form of town council. While subservient to the royal authorities, the *ayuntamiento* was a power to be reckoned with in colonial affairs.

The capital government became a *municipio* (roughly equivalent to a county in Anglo-American administrative systems) after independence from Spain, and was declared the official seat of the federal government. City authorities managed to maintain a limited autonomy throughout the turbulent decades until the arrival of Porfirio Díaz, who centralized its authority (along with the rest of the country's) in his hands.

Under the PRI

In 1928, the revolutionary government of president Álvaro Obregón revoked the city's status as a *municipio,* creating the Distrito Federal, whose mayor was appointed directly by the president. The new entity encompassed what was previously the *municipio* of México and several outlying communities, converting them into 16 *delegaciones,* so named because their leaders were delegated by the federal government.

While these centralizing reforms were ostensibly intended to help modernize the city, in reality they created a bloated, incredibly inefficient, and numbingly corrupt bureaucracy. Taking care of any sort of *trámite* (official procedure) was an exercise in frustration, unless you were willing to pay the *mordida* (literally, "the bite," a bribe) to speed up matters. Any kind of government contract became an opportunity for graft. The entire patronage system was managed by the long-ruling Institutional Revolutionary Party (PRI).

After seven decades as a badly managed appendage of the federal government, Mexico City's political reform began in 1989 with the birth of the Asemblía de Representantes del Distrito Federal (ARDF), housed in the old federal Congress in the Centro. After arduous negotiations, the city took its first step in modern democracy by voting for the first full elections of the assembly and mayor on July 6, 1997.

The PRD in Government

The election was a watershed. With 47 percent of the vote, Cuauhtémoc Cárdenas won by almost double the number of his closest competitor, the PRI's Alfredo del Mazo (25 percent). Carlos Castillo Peraza of the center-right Partido Acción Nacional (PAN), who was early on thought to be the likely winner, finished with a distant 15 percent.

And on top of that, Cárdenas's leftist Partido de la Revolución Democrática (PRD) swept every single assembly district in direct vote. The PRI, PAN, and the smaller parties were able to capture seats only by proportional representation. With this overwhelming mandate, joyously expressed in the victory celebration in the Zócalo on election night, Cárdenas's possibilities seemed limitless.

But the euphoria evaporated quickly. Given only a shortened term of three years and facing a city with an array of complex problems, the Cárdenas administration was bound to fall short of public expectations. While the new government, filled with idealistic young reformers, clearly made some efforts to clean up bureaucracy in the *delegaciones* and fight corruption in the police, it did not manage to seize its golden opportunity as dramatically as it might have. Cárdenas's dour, uncommunicative style did not help the city government's poor public image.

In the 2000 elections, when the PRI finally lost the presidency after seven decades in power to Vicente Fox of the National Action Party (PAN), the PRD again easily won in Mexico City under Andrés Manuel López Obrador, irreverently known as *el peje lagarto,* "the alligator mayor," because of his origins in the coastal state of Tabasco. A fiery leftist politico who made his name fighting the PRI in Tabasco (although, like many of the PRD old guard, he started in the PRI and left only when he did not get a post he desired), López Obrador had a mixed record running the city. As with Cárdenas, he used his position as mayor to set himself up for a run for president in 2006.

The mayor scored political points through a program offering increased pension payments to the elderly poor and by building a second story along a congested stretch of the Periférico highway. Some progress has been made on corruption and crime, the two issues Mexico City residents are most concerned about. But the success or failures of López Obrador in Mexico City ended up being overshadowed by the controversial 2006 election, which he lost by a razor-thin margin to the PAN's Felipe Calderón. The ensuing protests by López Obrador paralyzed parts of the city for months, although they have since eased.

The same 2006 elections saw the victory of Marcelo Ebrard as Mexico City mayor. Ebrard, now with the PRD, began his career in the 1980s with the PRI under then-mayor Manuel Camacho, and briefly served as a deputy for the Green Party and then as an independent before joining the López Obrador team. In the late 1990s when he served in Congress and I worked as a journalist in Mexico City, I interviewed him several times and came away with the impression that he was a non-ideological problem-solver, and this is borne out by his current reputation. As one newspaper wrote after his election, "He looks like a conservative, talks like a leftist, thinks like a centrist, and decides like a businessman." After the polarizing tenure of López Obrador, *chilangos* seem to welcome this pragmatism—his approval ratings were higher than 60 percent at last report.

ECONOMY

As it has for centuries, Mexico City controls a far larger share of the country's economy than any other region. At last report, the city accounted for about one-third of Mexico's entire gross domestic product. During the colonial era, the wealth came primarily from the monopolies held by Mexico City merchants on imports and exports between the colony and Europe. After independence from Spain, but especially under the rule of the PRI since the revolution, a large part of the country's new industry was located in the city, which only accentuated the already-growing dominance of the capital.

Since the 1950s, Monterrey and Guadalajara have been developing industrial bases of their own, and in more recent decades, cities such as Puebla, Querétaro, Aguascalientes, and Toluca have started industrializing as well. Mexico City completely controls the financial sector, as it is home to the stock exchange and all major banks and insurance companies, and it plays a major role in the service economy. As it is the location of essentially all federal government offices, government jobs are also a major factor in the economy.

Employment and Wages

Because Mexico City is such a magnet for migrant workers from the countryside, it has a higher unemployment rate than the national average, despite the city's overall economic strength. The official unemployment figures—6.2 percent in 2007—don't even come close to reflecting reality. With such a high proportion of the population participating in an informal, unregistered economy, accurate numbers are extremely difficult to come by.

Fully three quarters of Mexico City's jobs are in the service and commerce sectors, while just under a quarter are in industry and manufacturing. The retail sector accounts for 20 percent of employment, followed by transport at 8 percent and wholesale commerce at 7 percent.

Wages tend to be higher than the national average. The city is in the highest of the three national minimum wage brackets, with a daily minimum wage of just over $5.

No look at the Mexico City economy would be complete without mentioning the legendary armies of *ambulantes,* the informal street vendors seen all over the city, their wares spread out on the sidewalk. Guesses on the number of city *ambulantes* vary wildly, but they certainly number in the tens of thousands. As they have for generations, many new immigrants to the city begin their new urban lives hawking their modest wares from any street corner not already occupied by another seller.

For years the *ambulantes*—organized into disciplined groups that voted for the PRI and could be relied on to show up at progovernment rallies—were protected by the city police, despite the occasional crackdown. But driven in part by a desire to clean up the downtown area, and also because of the severe increase in *ambulantes* in the wake of the 1994–1995 crisis, city authorities have begun regular patrols to evict the vendors. These have stepped up in the last few years, such that the Centro has far fewer *ambulantes* than it did in past years.

People and Culture

POPULATION

Accurate population statistics for Mexico City are notoriously difficult to obtain. The Mexican government 2005 census put the population of Mexico City proper at 8.7 million, which makes it the 12th-largest city in the world. If you include the more densely populated *municipios* immediately adjacent to D.F. in the state of Mexico, then the number rises to 18.8 million. These are the most up-to-date official numbers; and any more current numbers you see are only estimates.

According to the most recent statistics from the government's Institute of Statistics, Geography, and Information (Instituto de Estadísticas, Geografía e Información, or INEGI), the Federal District's population density averages about 5,600 people per square kilometer. Figures for the individual 32 states vary considerably, ranging from very low rates in the states of Baja California Sur, Chihuahua, Sonora, Campeche, Durango, and Coahuila (each with fewer than 15 inhabitants per square kilometer) to the state of Mexico, where there are 571 inhabitants per square kilometer. Compare with Mexico's overall average density of just 48 per square kilometer, and you'll get an idea just how intensely urbanized the city is, although it's less packed than Hong Kong (6,364 per square kilometer).

INEGI claims that the total population of Mexico stands at 103 million, which means that the D.F./México metro area harbors approximately 18 percent of the nation's inhabitants, making Mexico City meet the classic sociological definition of a primate city, i.e., one in which more than 10 percent of a nation's inhabitants live. Economic factors such as Mexico City's disproportionate share of national wealth (around 35 percent) and the fact that a preponderance of goods produced in the country as a whole end up in Mexico City complete the definition of urban primacy.

Mexico City's growth has slowed considerably since the 1970s, when its population was expanding at an average rate of 4.5 percent per annum. The city's population in 2000–2005 grew at only 0.2 percent each year, well below both the national annual rate (1 percent). Only the state of Michoacán, with a huge out-migration to the United States in search of work, has a lower growth rate.

Interestingly, the slowing overall growth masks two distinct trends: All the population growth of the past 30 years has been in the outer edges of Mexico City, while the population of the inner core has been declining steadily. The combined population of the Cuauhtémoc and Miguel Hidalgo *delegaciones* dropped from 1.5 million in 1960 to 850,000 today. By contrast, the outer edges of the city are still growing, while the adjacent areas outside the city limits are growing faster still.

Anecdotal newspaper stories suggest that for the first time the city's population may be flattening out, or even declining. While this

WHO'S BIGGER?

It is often said that Mexico's capital is "the largest city in the world," yet after a relatively exhaustive research into existing records, I could find no set of statistics that would back this claim. According to the 2005 census, the population of the city proper is 8,720,916, which makes it the 12th most populous city in the world. Shanghai is first, with 15.4 million, and Buenos Aires is the largest in Latin America, with 11.6 million.

Considering urban area rather than strictly city limits, a study published by World Gazetteer (www.world-gazetteer.com) for 2007 listed Tokyo in first place with a whopping 37 million, Mexico City in second place with 22.752 million, and New York just behind in third with 22.747 million.

Another authoritative source, the United Nations Center for Human Settlements (HABITAT), has a different ranking. According to this report, Mexico City contained an estimated 11.2 million in 1975 – ranking it number four for that year – and was expected to reach 19.2 million by the year 2015. This latter projection would bring Mexico City down to a standing of 10th for that year. In first place for both HABITAT lists, again, was Tokyo (19.8 million in 1975; 26.4 million in 2015).

The apparent discrepancies among all these estimates can be explained by the fact that different organizations are tracking different statistical entities, from the 16 *delegaciones* of the Distrito Federal all the way to the entire Valle de México, which measures roughly 120 by 65 kilometers, or more than 7,000 square kilometers.

A middle-ground approach says that *la Ciudad de México* – or Zona Metropolitana de la Ciudad de México (ZMCM) – covers the Distrito Federal plus 21 *municipios* (a *municipio* is roughly equivalent to "county" in Anglophone countries) in the adjacent state of Mexico. Using this definition, the Mexican Instituto Nacional de Estadística, Geografía e Informatica (INEGI) estimates the entire metro area to be at 18.8 million, a number that many independent observers consider the most realistic.

has yet to be confirmed by census figures, it is true that an increasing number of younger professionals are moving to nearby cities like Querétaro and putting up with the long commute to escape the stressful life of the city. News reports from 2004 put the number of out-migrants at 100,000 per year.

Other interesting demographic facts are that Mexico City has the oldest average age of population—29 years—in the country, as well as the second-highest life expectancy, at 75.8 years.

Mestizaje

In Spanish colonial Mexico City, the most privileged class was the *peninsulares,* pure-blooded Spaniards born in Spain (known pejoratively as *gachupines*), followed by *criollos,* pure-blooded Spaniards born in Mexico; mestizos, those of mixed Indian-Spanish blood born in Mexico; and *indios,* pure-blooded Indians. In many cases the Spanish lumped together *indios* and mestizos as *indígenas*. One of the ironies of the colonial caste system was that "pure-blooded" Spaniards were themselves descended from a 700-year mixing of Moors and Iberians, the conquerors and the conquered—a pattern the Spaniards repeated in the New World.

The caste system still exists in a subtler and more simplified form throughout Mexico today. The national government recognizes *mestizaje* (mestizoism, or "mixing") as the root cultural characteristic of Mexico, yet distinguishes between two kinds of mestizos, the *indomestizos* of the south, "in whom indigenous characteristics predominate," and the *euromestizos* of the north, "in whom European traits prevail." Also recognized are smaller groups of *afromestizos* from the south gulf coastal regions, particularly Veracruz, where toward the end of the colonial era the Spanish imported African slaves to fill labor shortages caused by the rapidly shrinking local population.

According to the Mexican government, mestizos represent roughly 55 percent of the population of the whole nation. Caucasians are believed to represent another 14 percent; with 6 percent *indígenas,* that leaves 25 percent of the nation unaccounted for. Many other independent estimates place the indigenous population at around 10 percent of the national population, but of course these categorizations are inexact attempts to capture a fluid social reality.

Representatives of virtually all 56 Amerindian groups recognized by the government can be found in Mexico City, along with many of the 90 officially cataloged native languages. Altogether around 100,000 inhabitants of the Mexico City metro area speak Amerindian languages, more than in any other city in the Americas.

Most numerous are the Nahua or Nahuatl-speaking people of Puebla, Veracruz, Hidalgo, Guerrero, Tlaxcala, Morelos, México, and San Luis Potosí. Most often described as progeny of the Aztecs, today's Náhuatl speakers are actually descendants of a number of disparate tribes whose individual languages were lost to the lingua franca of the Valle de México.

While Indian values are publicly extolled, in practice almost anything labeled *indio* is considered low caste. Political and economic power remains concentrated in the hands of an elite group of "pure" European descent, a social stratum sometimes referred to as the "Thousand Families."

RELIGION

Between the 16th and 19th centuries, Spanish missionaries indoctrinated the original inhabitants of the Valle de México in the ways of Roman Catholicism. That Catholicism is now the nation's majority religion is an amazing achievement, considering it was laid over a vast variety of native belief systems in existence for thousands of years. About 90 percent of the population call themselves Catholics; Mexico is the second-largest Roman Catholic nation in the world after Brazil.

Mexico's Protestant population consists

> ## DID YOU KNOW?
>
> **Population of Mexico City urban area, best estimate:** 18.8 million
> **Number of registered cars and buses in the city:** 2.6 million
> **Daily driving trips within the city:** 29.2 million
> **Number of hotel rooms:** 25,000
> **Hospitals:** 344
> **Museums:** 161
> **Art galleries:** 106
> **Streets:** 90,000

mostly of Indians in the South missionized by North Americans in the 19th and 20th centuries. There are very few Protestants in Mexico City, which is considered the nation's most stalwart Catholic base after Guadalajara. Although many Spanish Jews arrived in the early days of European migration to Mexico, the Spanish Inquisition forced most to convert to Catholicism. A wave of immigration from the Middle East in the early 1900s established a Jewish community in Mexico City that remains strong, as well as a smaller but also powerful Arab contingent, mainly from Lebanon and Syria. The Mexican Constitution of 1917 guarantees freedom of religion; Church and State are strictly separated.

Mexico City roughly follows the national trends with regards to religion—just over 90 percent of the population identified themselves as Catholic in the most recent census, with 3.6 percent evangelical protestant, 1.3 percent as "biblical non-evangelical," and 2.9 percent as non-religious.

Mexican Catholicism

Mexican Catholics tend to be devout practitioners of their faith. Mexican Catholicism, however, has its own variations that distinguish the religion from its European predecessors. Some differences are traceable to preexisting Indian spiritual traditions absorbed by the Catholic faith, and as such are localized according to tribe.

© GUILLAUME COPART MULLER/WWW.GCMPHOTO.COM

Mexico is an overwhelmingly Catholic country.

One religious icon common to all of Mexico—even those who aren't particularly religious—is the Virgin of Guadalupe cult, which began in 1531 when a dark-skinned Virgin Mary appeared before Juan Diego, an Aztec nobleman formerly named Cuauhtaoctzin, in a series of three visions at Tepeyac, near Mexico City, previously a sacred Aztec site dedicated to the goddess Tonantzin. According to legend, in the third vision the Virgin commanded Diego to gather roses and present them to the local bishop, requesting that a church be built in her honor. When the devout Diego unfolded his rose-filled cloak, both he and the bishop beheld an image of the dark-skinned Virgin imprinted on the garment. This was deemed a miracle, and church construction commenced at once.

Today, many Mexican churches are named for Our Lady of Guadalupe, who has become so fused with Mexican identity that the slogan *¡Viva Guadalupe!* is commonly used at political rallies. The affectionate Mexican nickname for Guadalupe is La Morenita, "Little Dark One." She has become, as Mexican American cultural commentator Richard Rodriguez puts it, the "official private flag of Mexico," and one way in which Catholicism has been absorbed by native cultures rather than vice versa. The official feast day for Guadalupe, December 12, is fervently celebrated in Mexico City and throughout the country. (For more information, see the entry on the Basílica de la Virgen de Guadalupe in the *Sights* chapter.)

Mexican Saints

The legion of saints worshiped in Mexico runs the gamut of Catholic history. Three native saints warrant special mention. San Felipe de Jesús (1527–1597), a Franciscan friar, became Mexico's first Catholic martyr when he was killed while performing missionary work in Nagasaki, Japan. His martyrdom was officially recognized by the Church in 1627, and in 1629 Mexico named him the patron saint of the *virreinato* (the viceroyalty, i.e., the Spanish administration in Mexico). Santa Rosa de Lima

© GUILLAUME COPART MULLER/WWW.GCMPHOTO.COM

statues in a cemetery, state of Hidalgo

(1586–1617), a Dominican nun, was canonized as a saint in 1671 and thus became the first *santa americana* (American female saint) within the Catholic tradition. After years of controversy, Juan Diego, the Aztec nobleman who saw the vision of the Virgen de Guadalupe, was declared a saint in 2002.

LANGUAGE

Mexico is the largest Spanish-speaking country in the world. The type of Spanish spoken in Mexico is usually referred to as Latin American Spanish, in contrast to the Castilian Spanish spoken in Spain. Still, the Spanish here differs significantly from that of even other Spanish-speaking countries in the Western Hemisphere. Many Anglicisms have crept into the Mexican language. For example, the common Latin American Spanish term for car is *coche,* but in Mexico you'll often hear *carro.*

While English is occasionally spoken by merchants, hotel staff, and travel agents in the Centro and in wealthier suburbs, first-time visitors are often surprised by how little English one

hears in Mexico City compared to what might be encountered at popular beach resorts in Mexico. Outside areas of the city frequented by tourists, it's relatively rare to encounter anyone who speaks more than a few words of English.

Hence it's incumbent upon the visitor to learn at least enough Spanish to cope with everyday transactions. Knowing a little Spanish will not only mitigate communication problems, it will also bring you more respect among *capitalinos,* who quite naturally resent foreign visitors who expect Mexicans to abandon their mother tongue whenever a gringo approaches. Out of courtesy, you should at least attempt to communicate in Spanish whenever possible. (See the *Spanish Phrasebook* for a list of useful words and phrases and for a guide to pronunciation. Also see the information on Spanish language courses in Mexico and recommended reference works.)

Mexican Spanish, and especially Mexico City Spanish, is extremely rich with slang expressions, unique tones of voice, and hilarious wordplay. It is unquestionably one of the richest types of Spanish spoken anywhere, and one that is immediately recognizable to any other Spanish-speaker (who usually reacts with a smile), both because of its distinct character and also because of the prevalence of Mexican television and movies throughout Latin America. (See the *Chilango Slang* phrasebook for more details.)

The Arts

Mexico has one of the richest cultural traditions of any country in the Americas, if not the world. The gumbo resulting from the country's complex history is evidenced constantly, from the dozens of indigenous languages still spoken by 10 percent of the population to the little sugar skeleton candies you'll see everywhere for Día de los Muertos (November 1). Thus it comes as no surprise that Mexico has an extraordinarily strong tradition of literature, music, and arts, much of which has been concentrated in Mexico City.

LITERATURE

Elaborate hieroglyphic books and a priest-dominated literary tradition existed in the New World before the arrival of the Spaniards. But many scholars consider the fantastic chronicles of newly arrived Spanish soldiers, explorers, and priests as the first flowering of a truly Mexican literature, early expressions of what would become enduring Mexican themes: being caught between Indian and European worlds, and the fall from (or destruction of) an Edenic paradise.

Two examples of this genre, widely available in English translation, make for compelling reading. Bernal Diaz del Castillo's *Conquest of New Spain* is the memoir of a foot soldier in Cortés's military campaign against the Aztec empire. With just 400 men, superior weaponry, horses, and the help of Indian tribes in thrall to the Aztecs, the Spaniards marched into Tenochtitlán, the heart of the empire, and triumphed against an army numbering in the tens of thousands.

A very different view can be found in Bartolomé de las Casas's *Brevísima relación de la destrucción de las Indias* (Brief Account of the Devastation of the Indies), which details the astounding brutality that the invaders visited upon the people of what was then called the New World. De las Casas, a priest who accompanied many expeditions, raised the first voice of protest against Spanish destruction of native peoples and cultures.

The colonial era produced many authors who tried to imitate the prevailing styles in Europe. One colonial-era writer whose work has outlived that of most of her contemporaries is Sor Juana Inés de la Cruz, a remarkable nun, poet, and playwright. Her *Repuesta* (The Reply), a reply to a bishop who censured her and wrote of how women's role in the Catholic church should be severely limited, has become a feminist classic and is available in English translation, often accompanied by her poems, the best known of which is *Primer Sueño* (First Dream).

Modern Mexican writers—including Juan Rulfo, Octavio Paz, Carlos Fuentes, Mariano Azuela, Agustín Yáñez, Elena Poniatowska, and Rosario Castellanos—enjoy success outside of Mexico as well as in their native land. Rulfo's *Pedro Páramo,* published in 1955, is a hallucinatory novel of a man's return to the small town of Comalá, which is a real place in the state of Colima but in the book is a town of ghosts. Some consider it Latin America's first magical realist novel. Paz's *Labyrinth of Solitude* comprises classic essays that address the mysteries of Mexican identity. Poniatowska's *Massacre in Mexico* is an account of the 1968 killings of protesting Mexico City students by government troops. All are available in English translation. Another excellent observer of Mexican character and society is Carlos Monsiváis, whose *Rituales del Caos* is a collection of essays on life in Mexico City; it's available in Spanish only.

Two Colombian writers long residing in Mexico City, Gabriel García Marquéz and Álvaro Mútis, have garnered international acclaim for their fiction, which is set in Latin American locales and imbued with a distinctly Latin perspective. The fact that these two literary stars have chosen to live and write in Mexico City says much about the capital's intellectual environment. Both have works available in English translation.

Paco Ignacio Taibo II writes detective novels set in Mexico City, often from the bicultural view of a character or characters who move back and forth between Mexico and the United States. Taibo novels available in English translation include *An Easy Thing, Four Hands, Just Passing Through, Some Clouds,* and *No Happy Ending.*

Of the many current Mexican writers, Guillermo Fadanelli is definitely worth a read, if your Spanish is up to it. His gritty, realistic, and funny novels and stories are set in contemporary Mexico City. Two of his better-known works are *¿Te veré en el desayuno?* and *La otra cara de Rock Hudson.* José Emilio Pacheco's novella *Las batallas en el desierto,* set in the Roma neighborhood of Mexico City, is a great read and is easy to follow, even if your Spanish is not excellent. Other current fiction writers include Sara Shefkovich, Mario González Suárez, Mario Bellatin, Mauricio Montiel, Norma Lazo, and Ignacio Padilla. Padilla's 2000 novel *Amphytrion* (translated in English under the title *Shadow Without a Name*), got a lot of attention but has nothing to do with Mexico: It's set in Europe during World War I, where two strangers exchange identities as a result of a chess game on a train.

One great novel that takes place mainly in Mexico City is *Los Detectives Salvajes,* by Chilean expatriate Roberto Bolaño (who died in 2003). It's about a group of idealistic (or just weird) young poets in D.F. who call themselves the *real viceralistas,* and it offers a great portrait of one of the many subcultures of the city.

Works by all of these authors can be found in many Mexico City bookstores. Two good ones are Librería Gandhi, on the Alameda and in Coyoacán, and El Péndulo, in Condesa and the Zona Rosa. (See the *Shopping* chapter for more details.)

MUSIC
Rancheras, Corridos, and Boleros
The most popular song forms among the middle class and among the older generation in Mexico City are *rancheras* (similar to American country and western), *corridos* (Mexican ballads), and boleros (based on a traditional Andalusian form)—sometimes collectively known as *bohemio* (bohemian). This music become very popular in the 1940s and 1950s, with *trío* bands such as Los Panchos and Los Diamantes.

Grupera
This is the latest name for a musical genre that basically has northern Mexican origins. The name itself refers to music performed by large ensembles blending the *ranchera*-and-polka *música norteña* of groups such Los Tigres del Norte with Sinaloan *perrada* or *tambora sinaloense.* The latter is a type of brass-and-drum band music originally brought by German immigrants to south Texas in the mid-1800s, but adopted and adapted in northern Mexico and especially Sinaloa to become the "music of the people" when string music was still for the elite; during the 1910–1920 Mexican Revolution it became a rallying soundtrack for the *constitucionalistas.*

The immense popularity can be explained not only by the cheerful horn and accordion instrumentation (brass carries the quality most cherished by the Mexican mainstream, *alegría,* or joy), but—because today's *grupera* lyrics reflect the daily lives and sentiments of Mexican peasants—sometimes with a political edge. *Norteña* lyrics often chronicle the tragedies and triumphs of *mota* (marijuana) and *coca* (cocaine) *narcotraficantes* (drug runners) and illegal immigrants to the United States on the run from law enforcement and the Border Patrol (*la migra*). Some *grupera* songs have been

Mariachis strike up a tune in Plaza Garibaldi.

COURTESY OF MEXICO TOURISM BOARD/CARLOS SÁNCHEZ

banned by the Mexican government and can be heard only from bootleg tapes that circulate at cantinas or local fiestas.

Rock en Español

Although lyrically descended from Latin American *nuevo canto* folk/rock music (sometimes called *musica de protesta* for the political environment in which it grew popular), *rock en español* takes its major musical inspiration from Anglo-American rock and Anglo-Jamaican ska. With Mexico City the premier center for the movement, this international genre has spread all over Latin America, particularly to Argentina and Brazil. *Rock en español,* also known as La Nueva Onda (The New Wave), began reaching critical popular mass in the mid-1980s.

In the late 1980s, Botellita de Jeréz (Little Bottle of Sherry) and Maldita Vecindad (Cursed Neighborhood) began blending ska, punk, rock, jazz, and traditional Mexican elements. Maldita Vecindad's first major hit was "Mojado" (Wetback), a tribute to transborder Mexican workers.

Also popular is rock fusion/art group Café Tacuba, a band that mixes alternative rock sounds with ska and some Amerindian instrumentation and inspired live performances. Santa Sabina adds a hint of Latin jazz improvisations to the mix, giving the band an art-rock feel. Most of the major groups working in this medium come from D.F. or the state of Mexico, except for some like ¡Tijuana No! and Kinky, from Monterrey. Former ¡Tijuana No! singer Julieta Venegas has now branched out on her own, and, with her four albums (*Aquí, Bueninvento, Sí,* and *Limón y Sal*) has established herself as a talented singer-songwriter.

Two Mexican rap/rock bands very popular in recent years are Control Machete and Molotov. Control Machete's "Sí Señor" was the theme song to a Levi's ad shown in the United States a few years back, depicting a wobbly-legged young tough with a walkman ambling through the streets of some Mexican city. Molotov's tune "Frijolero" is hilarious with a hard edge, making fun of gringos and illegal immigrants equally. Other Mexican rock groups still playing in

Mexico include the venerable El Tri (kind of a Mexican Rolling Stones), CuCa, Maná, Los Jaguares, Caifanes, Plexo Solar, La Castañeda, La Barranca, El Sr. González, La Lupita, Amantes de Lola, Fobia, Víctimas del Doctor Cerebro, Plastilina Mosh, Mauricio Garces, and Kinky.

Música folklórica

Folkloric and ethnic folk music has its roots at the local level in Mexico's rural areas, with differing *son* or song forms and instrumentation tied to particular regions of Mexico, such as the *sandunga* in Oaxaca, *jarabe* in Jalisco, *jarana* in Yucatán, *danzón* in Veracruz, or *huapango* in Tamaulipas and San Luis Potosí. Such song forms are for the most part restricted to regional festivals or small bars in rural areas, and are not often heard in Mexico City.

A Mexican record label called Discos Corasón (www.corason.com) produces an excellent series of tapes and CDs focusing on folkloric music of Mexico and the Caribbean. Corasón's three-CD set *Antología del Son de México* (Anthology of Mexican Folk Music) is a good place to start. The company was started in an apartment in the Condesa back in the 1990s by two Mexicans who were obsessed with traveling around the country and making recordings of traditional music. Their passions soon diversified to throughout the Caribbean, and they have built a wonderful collection. Discos Corasón recorded many of the old Cuban greats, and it was through their efforts that Ry Cooder ended up hearing them and helping make the phenomenal Buena Vista Social Club album.

MODERN ART

Postrevolutionary nationalism in Mexico inspired grand works of art in painting and mosaics on the walls of public buildings throughout the nation. Often containing social and political criticism, Mexican murals have become one of the most imitated visual art forms in the Americas. Among the country's most famous muralists are José Clemente Orozco, Diego Rivera, Davíd Alfaro Siqueiros, Jean Charlot,

Rufino Tamayo, and Juan O'Gorman. One of the best places to see murals by different artists in the same location is at the Antiguo Colegio de San Ildefonso in the Centro (see the *Sights* chapter for details).

Serving as a bridge between the highly symbolic and often political art of the early 20th century and the more representational art of younger artists are two older contemporary Mexico City painters, Gunther Gerzso and José Luis Cuevas. Gerzso abandoned symbolism for intensely abstract works that today are highly collectible. Cuevas rebelled against the idea that art had to serve a higher moral or political purpose and instead has invested his talents in intensely personal explorations in concept, technique, and media, producing everything from labeled vials of his own semen to elaborate metal sculptures.

Currently extremely popular on the international art scene is the Oaxaca School of painters, a movement that was kicked off by Rufino Tamayo in the 1950s and continues to the present day with the whimsical, dreamlike works of Francisco Toledo. Others from Oaxaca include Rodolfo Morales, Jorge Barrios, and Alejandro Santiago.

ARCHITECTURE

Architectural styles in Mexico City vary from ancient Aztec pyramids to flamboyantly colored cubist high-rise office buildings. **Colonial architecture** in the capital extends from simple early-16th-century churches to the highly ornate late baroque or churrigueresque styles that flourished in the 18th century. The **baroque** period in Spanish church architecture was a response to the Protestant Reform and formed part of a Catholic religious movement known as the *contrareforma,* during which many Catholics felt a strong need to elaborate on the mysteries of their faith. The baroque style permitted artists to experiment more freely with ornamentation, developing the twisted Solomonic column in the 17th century and the *estípite* (sections of columns and ornamentation layered vertically) in the 18th century.

As Mexican nationalism surged toward the end of the 18th century, government buildings adopted a more restrained, French-influenced **neoclassic style,** also known as republican style. For colonial and neoclassic architecture, the Centro Histórico is far and away the best district for touring, followed by Coyoacán and San Ángel.

For a taste of **art deco** architecture, take a couple of hours to tour around the Condesa neighborhood, particularly around Parque México, which began its boom in the 1930s. Across Avenida Insurgentes in the Roma are scores of century-old mansions built in homage to the Parisian styles to which the owners aspired. Paseo de la Reforma, Polanco, and Chapultepec showcase styles of **modern architecture** created by such renowned 20th-century architects as Ricardo Legoretta, Luis Barragán, and Pedro Ramírez Vásquez.

Food

No write-up of Mexican culture could be complete without a lengthy, hunger-inducing description of the magnificent culinary delights for which the country is famous throughout the world. What follows is merely intended to give a taste, as it were, of the myriad pleasures of Mexican food, with more suggestions for further culinary explorations. A comprehensive review would require years of (admittedly very pleasurable) research and an entire book, or series of books, in which to expound upon all its variations. You'll find a dozen such books at any decent library or bookstore, and even more cookbooks. For those Americans who have never been to Mexico, or only to tourist areas, don't expect to find any burritos around here, or fajitas, or tacos stuffed with everything but the kitchen sink—those are northern Mexican specialties that have been adopted (and modified) with gusto by Tex-Mex restaurants in the States. Mexico City cuisine is far-ranging and constantly changing, but it is definitely not Tex-Mex.

Breakfasts

The most common *desayuno* for the majority of Mexicans is simply *pan dulce* and/or *bolillos* (torpedo-shaped, European-style rolls) with coffee and/or milk. Cereal is also sometimes eaten for *desayuno,* e.g., *avena* (oatmeal), *crema de trigo* (cream of wheat), or *hojuelas de maíz* (corn flakes). A favorite *desayuno* on the run is a *tamal* (steamed corn meal stuffed with a bit of meat or cheese) and a cup of *atole,* a hot corn-based drink, sold in the morning throughout the city by street vendors out of big steel containers. Another economic choice is *molletes,* a split *bolillo* spread with mashed beans and melted cheese, served with salsa on the side.

The heavier eggs-and-frijoles dishes known widely as "Mexican breakfasts" in the United States and Canada come in a variety of ways, including *huevos revueltos* (scrambled eggs), *huevos duros* (hard-boiled eggs), *huevos tibios* (coddled eggs, not soft-boiled, as sometimes translated), *huevos escafaldos* (soft-boiled eggs), *huevos estrellados* or *huevos fritos* (eggs fried sunny-side up), *huevos a la mexicana* (eggs scrambled with chopped tomato, onion, and chile), *huevos rancheros* (fried eggs served on a tortilla), and *huevos divorciados* (two *huevos estrellados* separated by beans, each egg usually topped with a different salsa). One of the most filling *desayunos* is *chilaquiles,* tortilla chips in a chile gravy with crumbled cheese on top, a favorite hangover remedy. Eggs and/or chicken can be added to *chilaquiles* as options.

Main Dishes

The main dish, or *el plato fuerte,* of any meal can be a grander version of an *antojito,* a regional specialty (*mole poblano,* for example), or something the *cocineros* (cooks) dream up themselves. Typical entrées are centered on meats, seafood, or poultry. Common meats include *carne de res* (beef), *puerco* (pork), and

© DEB DUTCHER

street snacks for sale on the Zócalo

cabrito (kid goat). *Venado* (deer) and *conejo* (rabbit) are often found in rural areas in central Mexico but less so in the city itself. Poultry dishes include *pollo* (chicken), *pavo* or *guajalote* (turkey), and, less frequently, *pato* (duck) and *codorniz* (quail).

All of these can be cooked in an astonishing variety of ways in Mexico City, with literally hundreds of different kind of salsas and preparation techniques. Both chicken and beef are often prepared *a la mexicana,* with chopped tomatoes, onions, and serrano chile peppers. The name is because the colors of the three vegetables match those of the national flag. Another popular meat dish is a *tampiqueña,* a cut of beef surrounded by a full plate of guacamole, frijoles, fried cheese, and an *enchilada. Puntas de res* are beef tips, frequently served in a smoky hipotle sauce. *Arrachera* denotes a flank steak, more tender and of better quality (and hence a bit more expensive) than regular beef. *Milanesa* is any kind of breaded meat, frequently pork or beef but sometimes chicken or veal as well.

Some of the best-known Mexican specialties are the many varieties of mole (MO-lay), thick brown sauces from the states of Puebla and Oaxaca usually served over chicken or turkey. The sauce is typically made from a lengthy list of ingredients that may include unsweetened chocolate, sesame seeds, and chiles. A similar but green-hued sauce made with pumpkin seeds is called *pipián.* Both are ancient dishes dating to Mexico's pre-Hispanic cultures.

Another Puebla specialty is *chiles en nogada,* big poblano chiles stuffed with a mix of shredded beef, raisins, olives, and almonds and bathed in a cream-and-nut sauce. Chiles rellenos are similar but stuffed with rice and/ or cheese and fried in a bean sauce. From the southern Yucatán state come dishes like *cochinita pibil,* a way of cooking tender pork with oranges, garlic, and cumin. A favorite in the central Mexican highlands is *barbacoa* (barbecued lamb, or sometimes pork).

Seafood runs the gamut, from succulent *huachinango* (red snapper) from the coast to *trucha* (trout) from mountain streams near the city. Fish can be cooked myriad ways, including *al mojo de ajo* (with garlic), *empanizado* (breaded), *empapelado* (in foil), *a la veracruzana* (with a tomato and olive sauce), or just plain old *frito* (fried). *Camarón* (shrimp) and other shellfish are often served as *cocteles* (cocktails, steamed or boiled and served with lime and salsa), *en sus conchas* (in the shell), as ceviche (raw fish or shellfish marinated in lime juice, onions, and chiles until "cooked" by the acidic juices), or many other ways. Upscale restaurants sometimes cook shrimp in a tequila sauce.

Vegetables and salads are very common in Mexico, and much of what you'll see is exactly what you'd find at home, only usually a whole lot more flavorful, since most Mexican produce isn't industrially farmed (not yet at least). A few vegetables you might not have seen before include the light and delicate *flor de calabaza* (squash flower), dark green and chewy nopal (cactus petals), and trufflelike delicate *huitlacoche* (sometimes spelled *cuitlacoche*), a blue-black fungus that grows on fresh corn. *Maiz* (corn) is the grain of choice in Mexico (not wheat), and apart from serving as the basis for many foods, *elotes* (ears of corn) are often sold hot and fresh by street vendors, topped with mayonnaise and chile pepper if you don't ask otherwise. *Chayote* is a native vegetable that looks sort of like a pear and is frequently used as the base for a cream soup.

Tortillas

A Mexican meal is not a meal without tortillas, the round, flat pancakelike disks that are eaten with nearly any nondessert dish, including salads, meats, seafood, beans, and vegetables. Many foreigners may have an automatic desire to fill a tortilla full of their main meal and eat it like a burrito. Think again. The idea is to grasp a utensil in one hand and the tortilla with the other, and after having a bite of the main meal, have a bite off the end of the rolled-up tortilla.

Both corn and wheat tortillas are consumed in great quantity, although *capitalinos* clearly have an overall preference for corn tortillas. Some Mexicans claim meat and poultry dishes taste best with flour tortillas while vegetable dishes

go best with corn. Restaurants sometimes offer a choice of the two; if you order tortillas without specifying, you may get *"¿De harina o de maíz?"* (Flour or corn?) as a response.

Incidentally, a tortilla has two sides—an inside and an outside—that dictate which direction the tortilla is best folded when wrapping it around food. The side with the thinner layer—sometimes called the *pancita,* or belly—should face the inside when folding the tortilla. If you notice the outside of your tortilla cracking, with pieces peeling off onto the table, you've probably folded it with the *pancita* outside instead of inside.

Bread and *Pan Dulce*

The most common bread (*pan*) you'll encounter is the *bolillo* (little ball), a small torpedo-shaped roll, usually rather hard on the outside. *Pan telera* ("scissor bread," so named for the two clefts on top) resemble *bolillos* but are larger and flatter; they're mainly used for making *tortas,* the ubiquitous Mexican sandwich.

Sweetened breads or pastries are known as *pan dulce* (sweet bread). Common types of *pan dulce* include *buñuelos* (crisp, round, flat pastries fried and coated with cinnamon sugar), *campechanas* (flaky, sugar-glazed puff pastries), *canastas* (thick, round, fruit-filled cookies), *capirotada* (bread pudding), *cortadillos* (cake squares topped with jelly and finely shredded coconut), *cuernitos* (small crescent rolls rolled in cinnamon sugar), or just straight-ahead *galletas* (cookies), to name a few.

Salsas and Condiments

Any restaurant, café, *cafetería, lonchería, taquería,* or *comedor* will offer a variety of salsas. Sometimes only certain salsas are served with certain dishes, while at other times one, two, or even three salsas are stationed on every table. Often each place has its own unique salsa recipes—canned or bottled salsas are rarely used. The one ingredient common to all salsas is chile peppers, varying in heat from mild to incendiary.

There are as many types of salsas as there are Mexican dishes—red, green, yellow, brown, hot, mild, salty, sweet, thick, thin, blended, and chunky. It would take a separate book to describe them all. The most typical is the *salsa casera* (house salsa), a simple, fresh concoction of chopped chiles, onions, and tomatoes mixed with salt, lime juice, and cilantro. This is what you usually get with the free basket of *totopos* (tortilla chips) that are served at the beginning of many Mexican restaurant meals. Another common offering is *salsa verde* (green salsa), made with a base of tomatillos, a small, tart, green tomato-like vegetable. Some salsas are quite *picante* (spicy hot), so it's always a good idea to test a bit before pouring the stuff over everything on your plate. Smoky chipotle salsas are often an interesting change from the hotter stuff.

Sliced, pickled chiles and carrots are sometimes served on the side as a condiment, especially with tacos and *tortas,* and are called *rajas.* In Mexico City's few Sonoran restaurants you may see a bowl of *chiltepines* (sometimes spelled *chilpetines* or *chiles pequines*), small, round fiery red peppers. The kick of the *chiltepín* is exceeded only by that of the habanero, the world's hottest pepper and a regular table condiment at restaurants featuring dishes from the state of Yucatán.

Salt (*sal*) is usually on the table, although it's rarely needed, since Mexican dishes tend to be prepared with plenty of salt. Black pepper is *pimienta negra,* and if it's not on the table it's normally available for the asking. *Limones* are not lemons but limes (and counterintuitively enough for English-speakers, lemon is *lima*!), and they are served in almost all but the most upscale restaurants. Apart from adding flavor, lime juice is also an excellent anti-bacterial, so if you're dubious about the cleanliness of your tacos, squeeze a lot of limes over them.

In *taquerías,* guacamole (mashed avocado blended with onions, chiles, salt, and other optional ingredients) is frequently served as a condiment. In restaurants it may be served as a salad or with tortilla chips. "Guacamole" sometimes refers to a very spicy paste of tomatillos and green habanero chiles that may resemble avocado guacamole—always taste before heaping it on your plate.

Cheese

Mexicans produce a great variety of cheeses. Among the most commonly used are *queso cotijo* (also called *queso añejo*), *queso chihuahua* (called *queso menonita* in the state of Chihuahua), *queso manchego, queso oaxaqueño,* and *queso asadero.*

Queso menonita or *queso chihuahua* (Mennonite or Chihuahuan cheese) is a mild, white cheddar produced in wheels by Mennonite colonists in Chihuahua and Durango. *Queso manchego* imported from Spain (called *tipo manechego,* or "manchego style," when made in Mexico) is similar but usually softer. *Queso asadero* (grilling cheese) is a braided cheese somewhat similar to Armenian string cheese, made by combining sour milk with fresh milk. *Chihuahua* is a common ingredient in dishes stuffed with cheese, such as enchiladas or chiles rellenos, that won't receive high, direct heat. *Asadero* melts well at high temperatures without burning or separating, and as such is well suited to *chile con queso* (hot, blended chile-cheese dip), *queso fundido* (hot melted cheese topped with chorizo or mushrooms), and other dishes in which the cheese is directly exposed to high heat. *Queso oaxaqueño,* also called *quesillo,* is a lump-style cheese similar to *asadero* but a little softer—close to mozzarella. It's popular in *tortas.*

Cotijo or *añejo* is a crumbly aged cheese that resists melting and is commonly used as a topping for enchiladas and beans; the flavor and texture is somewhat like a cross between feta and parmesan.

Occasionally you'll also come across *panela,* an extra-rich cheese made from heavy cream, usually sliced and served as a side dish all its own.

Soup

The general menu term for soup is *sopa,* although a thick soup with lots of ingredients is usually a *caldo.* Frequently a *crema,* or cream of vegetable soup, is one of the soup options with a *comida corrida.* Menudo—a soup made with hominy (*nixtamal*), cow's feet, and stomach (or, less commonly, intestine) in a savory, reddish-brown broth served with chopped onions, chiles, and crumbled oregano—is seen throughout Mexico and is highly prized as a hangover remedy. Mexico City has its own version of *menudo, pancita* (little stomach). *Pozole*—eaten since Aztec times, when it was known as *pozolli*—is a thick stew made with a much lighter-colored broth and filled with corn and some kind of meat.

Other tasty soups include *sopa de tortillas, sopa azteca,* and *sopa tlapeña,* all featuring varying combinations of artfully seasoned chicken broth garnished with *totopos* (tortilla wedges) and sliced avocado. *Sopa de hongo* (mushroom soup) is a favorite at the many village restaurants in the mountains around Mexico City.

Vegetarian Options

It's difficult but not impossible to practice a vegetarian regime in Mexico City. Lacto-vegetarians can eat quesadillas—but ask for corn tortillas, which do not contain lard (most flour tortillas do)—or *enchiladas de queso* (cheese enchiladas). With some luck, you'll stumble across restaurants that can prepare a variety of interesting cheese dishes, including *queso fundido con champiñones* (melted cheese with mushrooms, eaten with tortillas) and quesadillas made with *flor de calabaza.* Some places make beans without lard (*sin manteca*), but you'll have to ask to find out. Many Mexico City restaurants offer pizza, usually offered in vegetarian versions (often called *pizza margherita*). You'll also find vegetarian/health food stores (usually called *tiendas naturistas*) with small dining sections as well as bulk foods.

Ovo-lacto vegetarians can add egg dishes and flan to their menus. Vegans for the most part will do best to prepare their own food. Look for shops with signs reading *semillas* (seeds) to pin down a good selection of nuts and dried beans. Of course you'll find plenty of fresh fruits and vegetables in markets and grocery stores. The ever-present fruit juice stands are a great place to get all sorts of fruit combinations, along with carrots, beets, granola, and whatever else you feel like throwing in.

Mexican Drinks

Apart from the usual array of soft drinks and alcohols, Mexico has a number of unique beverages well worth sampling during your stay. *Licuados* are similar to American smoothies—fruit blended with water, ice, honey or sugar, and sometimes milk or raw eggs to produce something like a fruit shake. One of the great joys of traveling or living in Mexico is to wander to a nearby street-corner *licuado* stand and order a mix with whatever fruits strike your fancy for under $1. In Mexico, *tuna* (not the fish, but the prickly-pear cactus fruit) *licuados* are particularly delicious. Other tasty and nutritious additives include oats (*avena*) and wheat germ (*germen de trigo*). Most places that make *licuados* also offer fruit juices such as orange juice (*jugo de naranja*) or carrot juice (*jugo de zanahoria*).

Aguas frescas are the colorful beverages sold from huge glass jars in markets and occasionally on the streets. They're made by boiling the pulp of various fruits, grains, or seeds with water, then straining it and adding large chunks of ice. *Arroz* (rice), *horchata* (melon-seed), and *jamaica* (hibiscus flower) are three of the tastiest *aguas*. *Licuados* and *aguas frescas* are often sold from colorful storefronts invariably named La Flor de Michoacán or La Michoacana.

Local soft drinks include Boing and Jarritos, as well as an apple-flavored soft drink called Manzanita. Less common, but very good, is Peñafiel, a flavored mineral water drink.

Coffee is everywhere in Mexico (they grow lots of it in Veracruz and Chiapas), but a particularly Mexican version of the brew is *café de olla* flavored with cinnamon, clove, or other spices. *Café con leche* is the Mexican version of café au lait (coffee and hot milk mixed in near-equal proportions). Also common is a *café cortado,* an espresso "cut" with milk, similar to a macchiato. *Café con crema* (coffee with cream) is not as available; when it is, it usually means nondairy powdered creamer.

Centuries ago, Mesoamericans mixed honey and spices with a bitter extract of the cacao bean to produce a warm chocolate drink popular among the upper classes.

Today hot chocolate is still commonly found on Mexican menus. It's usually served very sweet and may contain cinnamon, ground almonds, and other flavorings. *Atole,* a thick corn-based hot drink also derived from Aztec times, is commonly served by street vendors to accompany *tamales.*

Desserts and Sweets

The most popular of Mexican desserts, or *postres,* is a delicious egg custard called *flan.* It's listed on virtually every tourist restaurant menu, along with *helado* (ice cream). Other sweet alternatives include pastries found in *panaderías* (bakeries) and the frosty offerings at *paleterías.* Strictly speaking, a *paletería* serves only *paletas,* fruit-flavored ice on sticks (like American popsicles but with a much wider range of flavors), but many also serve *nieve* (literally, "snow"), flavored grated ice served in bowls or cones like ice cream.

Another street-vendor sweet is churros, a sweet fried pastry that's something like a doughnut stick sprinkled with sugar and cinnamon. To complete the full sugar dose, dunk it in a glass of hot chocolate. If this sounds even slightly appealing, you must visit the Churrería El Moro, on Eje Central between Uruguay and V. Carranza, where you'll find the city's best churros 24 hours a day.

ESSENTIALS

Getting There

AIR
Aeropuerto Internacional Benito Juárez

Mexico City's airport (www.aicm.com.mx), in the eastern part of the city near the exit toward Puebla, has two terminals, domestic and international. As you enter from the Circuito Interior, the domestic terminal comes first. Both terminals have been totally overhauled, with the completion of a second floor now stocked with numerous restaurants, shops, and services. The largest area for eating is on the 2nd floor above the international terminal, and a second dining court is located past security, also in the international terminal.

Travelers will also find many newsstands, ATMs, and money-exchange booths. One of the latter, Tamibe, in the arrival hall for international flights, is open 24 hours. Also in the international terminal is a 24-hour Servitel telephone office for long-distance calls, and an expensive Internet shop, also open 24 hours a day. The cheapest way to make local phone calls is to buy a Ladatel card at a newsstand and use one of the many Ladatel phones in the terminal. For general airport information, call 55/5571-3600. Both Conaculta (the government culture institute) and INEGI (the government map and information service) have stores in the domestic terminal on the ground floor.

Conaculta has a few pulp novels in English, but all other books are in Spanish. On the other side of security in the international terminal are many gift shops (with T-shirts, jewelry, etc.), eateries, and newsstands.

Inside the domestic terminal, a wall between Gates B and C features a mural (thoroughly ignored by the thousands of travelers swarming below it every day) by Juan O'Gorman illustrating the history of flight, from an Aztec nobleman eyeing the wings of a bat with curiosity to the Wright brothers and Charles Lindbergh.

A new terminal near the Hangares Metro station (on the opposite side of the runways from the existing one) was scheduled for completion in 2008. Check the website (www .aicm.com.mx) for exact information on specific airlines and flights.

Despite the ongoing expansion, the airport is well past its capacity. The government plan to open a new airport not far northeast of the current location was stopped due to protests, and the whole issue got lost in a swamp of politics from which it appears unlikely to emerge. Instead, nearby regional airports like Toluca, Puebla, and Querétaro are gearing up for international traffic. Continental inaugurated the first international nonstop flights from Houston to Toluca and Puebla in 2004.

Airlines

The principal domestic airlines flying from Mexico City to other destinations in the country include Aero California (Paseo de la Reforma 332, 55/5207-1392 or 800/237-6225, www.aerocalifornia.com); Aeromar (Paseo de la Reforma 505, ground floor, 55/5133-1111 or 800/237-6627, www.aeromar.com .mx); AeroMexico (Paseo de la Reforma 80, 55/5133-4000 or 800/021-4010, www.aero mexico.com); Aviacsa (Paseo de la Reforma 195, 800/284-2272 or 55/5482-8280, www .aviacsa.com.mx); and Mexicana/Aerocaribe (Paseo de la Reforma 312, 55/2881-0000 or 800/801-2010, www.mexicana.com.mx).

The following airlines service the North American market (phone numbers are for dialing from Mexico): Air Canada (55/5208-1883, www.aircanada.com); American Airlines (800/904-6000 or 55/5209-1400, www .aa.com); Continental Airlines (55/5283-5500 or 800/900-5000, www.continental.com); Delta Airlines (55/5279-0909 or 800/123-4710, www .delta.com); Northwest Airlines (55/5279-5390 or 800/907-4700, www.nwa.com); United Airlines (55/5627-0222 or 800/003-0777, www .ual.com); and US Airways/AmericaWest (www .usairways.com/awa).

To fly elsewhere in Latin America, contact Aerolineas Argentinas (55/5523-7154 or 800/123-8588, www.aerolineas.com.ar) for Argentina; Lan Chile (55/5566-5211 or 800/123-1619, www.lanchile.com) for Chile or other South American destinations; Lloyd Air Boliviano (55/2599-1180 or 55/5559-9269, www.labairlines.com.bo) for Bolivia; Taca (55/5553-3366 or 800/400-8222, www .taca.com) for Central America; and Varig (55/5280-9192 or 800/907-8800, www.varig .com) for Brazil.

To Europe and Asia, contact Air France (55/5627-6060, www.airfrance.com.mx); Air New Zealand (55/5208-1708, www.airnz .co.nz); Alitalia (55/5533-1240, www.alitalia .it); British Airways (www.britishairways.com); Iberia (55/1101-1515, www.iberia.com); Japan Air Lines (55/5242-0150 or 5242-0154, www .jal.com); KLM (www.klm.com); Lufthansa (55/5230-0000, www.lufthansa.com); Qantas (www.qantas.com.au); and Swiss International Airlines (877/359-7947, www.swiss.com).

Arriving

When flying into Mexico City, your first airport stop is immigration, where you will fill out a tourist card if you don't already have a Mexican visa. While tourists are eligible to stay for six months, immigration agents will arbitrarily stamp the card with as many days as they feel like (often 60 days), meaning you'll have to go to an immigration office to renew it if you plan to stay longer. However, if before they've had a chance to stamp your card, you say authoritatively *"Ciento ochenta días, por favor"* ("One hundred and eighty days, please") they'll usually give it to you. Once they start writing, don't bother to say it, as they apparently never rewrite a card once they've already started.

After immigration, you'll proceed downstairs to collect your luggage from baggage claim and pass through the customs station, where you may be randomly chosen for inspection.

If you are waiting to meet someone arriving on an international flight, be prepared to wait an hour or so (occasionally less, often more), along with a hundred or so others outside the glass doors past the customs checkpoint. While the bar at the Freedom restaurant looks like a great vantage point to wait for someone, the staff will only let you sit there if you order a meal.

Departing

Almost all departing international flights leave, logically enough, from the international terminal, but a few leave from the domestic terminal if the plane has a stopover in another city (such as Guadalajara or Cancún) while flying out to another country. Check with your airline by phone beforehand to be sure. When you depart Mexico, be sure to bring the tourist card you were given when you entered the country, as you will be asked for it before leaving the country. If you don't have it, expect to pay a fine and have some hassles.

It's very important to leave enough time when departing from the Mexico City airport, as the lines to check in can be very lengthy at times, as can the second line upstairs to go through security before heading out to the gate. The security officials are entirely unsympathetic to pleas of those who are close to missing their flight and want to go to the front of the line.

The duty-free shops in the international terminal have a large selection of tequila, cigars, and other consumer goods. There's also a food court toward the domestic terminal end, as well as a couple of small eateries in the international terminal.

To and From the Airport

TAXI

No city buses service the airport, making taxis the only option besides the Metro to get into town. Tourists should use only the authorized airport taxi service. They are not cheap compared to other taxis in Mexico City, but there's not much alternative, as street taxis are not available without taking a long walk (and are not recommended to take near the airport for safety reasons). Buy a ticket from the taxi service window, in the international terminal right where passengers are let out after the customs checkpoint. There are two windows: Be sure to go to the one with regular taxis, not the large Suburban vans that are considerably more expensive—the window attendants have been known to refrain from sharing this fact with foreign tourists. These vans are a reasonable option if you have a large group of people or a whole lot of luggage.

Fares are based on how far your destination is from the airport—a map next to the window tells you which zone you're going to (assuming you know the city well enough to find it). Regular taxis costs $14 to the Centro; $14 to the Alameda area, Roma, and part of Paseo de la Reforma; $16 to Condesa or the Zona Rosa; $20 to Polanco or Coyoacán; and $22 to San Ángel or farther west along Paseo de la Reforma.

Chauffeured cars (seating four) and vans (seating eight) are also available to nearby cities such as Pachuca ($70 car, $75 van), Toluca ($75 car, $85 van), and Puebla or Cuernavaca ($80 car, $90 van).

METRO

If you're arriving in Mexico City between 6 A.M. and midnight and don't have a lot of baggage, you could conceivably take the Metro into town from the Terminal Aéreo station, a 15-minute walk up the sidewalk from outside the domestic terminal (not well-signed). It's a lengthy ordeal, but saves a $14–17 taxi ride for those pinching their pesos.

BUS

Several bus companies offer direct routes from the airport to the nearby cities of Toluca, Pachuca, Puebla, Cuernavaca, and Querétaro. To get to the bus station, go to the 2nd floor of the international terminal near Gate E, and walk over the crosswalk. The ticket counters are on the far side. Buses run every half hour or so throughout the day to these destinations.

DRIVING

The airport is just off the eastern side of the Circuito Interior ring highway, which is easily accessible from most major neighborhoods in the center, west, and south of the city. The best route from most neighborhoods frequented by tourists is the Viaducto, an east–west highway across the center of the city that has an exit onto the Circuito just south of the airport. However, the turn off the Viaducto to the Circuito in the direction of the airport is badly marked and easy to miss, so beware—it's a left-hand exit. The airport exit from the Circuito is clearly marked. The entrance road first passes between the domestic terminal (on the right) and the domestic parking terminal (on the left). Another 500 meters beyond on the right side is the international terminal, with its parking lot just beyond, also on the right side. Returning to the city, just loop back around to the left past the international terminal and either bear to the right to get on the Circuito heading north or stay in the middle and cross over the Circuito to the southbound side. Go southbound to get to the Viaducto—again, the turnoff is a bit tricky. Taking the Circuito northbound is a quicker route to get to Polanco and nearby neighborhoods.

BUS

Mexico's top-notch bus system has dozens of competing companies offering first- and second-class buses throughout the country at very reasonable prices. First class has more-comfortable seats, fewer stops, and, whether you like it or not, videos. The screens are usually spaced every four or five seats, so request a seat as far as possible from one if you don't want to watch. Second-class buses are 20 to 40 percent cheaper, but they're not as comfortable and always take longer, as they stop at seemingly every town on the route.

For trips to nearby major cities (such as Puebla, Toluca, Cuernavaca, or Guadalajara), there's usually a departure every 15 minutes or so throughout the day, so travelers can safely show up at the bus station whenever is convenient and not have to wait very long. If you are going to destinations with less frequent service, want a particular seat, or are traveling during the holidays, it's best to get your ticket beforehand. The easiest way to do this for most bus lines is through **Ticket Bus** (55/5133-2424 or from outside Mexico City toll-free 55/800/702-8000, www.ticketbus.com.mx), a central reservation service for basically all of the main bus lines in Mexico. Most bus companies now encourage all sales through Ticket Bus instead of by contacting them directly. It has nearly 40 offices around the city where you can go to buy tickets. Some convenient ones are: Isabel la Católica 83, in the Centro, 55/5709-9985; Paseo de la Reforma 412, near the Diana monument, 55/5207-9437; and Puebla 46, in the Roma, 55/5511-2916. Alternatively, although less convenient, you can go to the bus station and buy a ticket the day before your departure. For smaller bus lines to less-frequented destinations, you may have to go to the terminal itself a day beforehand. (For the Mexico City telephones of several of these bus lines, see the *Excursions from Mexico City* chapter, but reservations with small companies are iffy, even if you can get through on the phone, which is rare.)

First-class bus companies include Omnibus de Mexico (55/5719-2397 or 800/765-6636, www.omnibusdemexico.com.mx) for Northern and Central Mexico; Estrella Blanca/Turistar (55/5729-0807 or 800/507-5500, www.estrellablanca.com.mx) for Northern, Central, and Western Mexico; Primera Plus/Flecha Amarilla (55/5985-2329 or 800/375-7587, www.flecha-amarilla.com) for Western and Central Mexico; Estrella de Oro (55/5549-8520 or 5549-8521, www.estrelladeoro.com.mx) for Cuernavaca, Acapulco, and Taxco; ADO (www.ado.com.mx) for southeastern Mexico; and Cristóbal Colón (www.cristobalcolon.com.mx) for Oaxaca and Chiapas.

Luxury bus line ETN (www.etn.com.mx) offers very comfortable reclining seats and nonstop rides at a premium cost, but it's worth it for a long haul. ETN serves north-central

Mexico. Another luxury line, this one serving Oaxaca, Chiapas, Veracruz, and other parts of the southeast, is UNO (www.uno.com.mx).

For connections to destinations within the United States, call Greyhound (Amores 707-102, Colonia Del Valle, 55/5543-1511 or 800/710-8819, www.greyhound.com.mx).

Terminals

Mexico City has four intercity bus terminals at the four main highway exits out of the city, corresponding to the cardinal points of the compass. Each is accessible by Metro, and all have authorized taxi services on arrival. It's always better to take an authorized taxi than the ones on the street, because bus stations are prime scouting sites for taxi thieves.

Terminal Central del Norte (North Terminal, Av. de los Cien Metros 1907): Take Metro Line 5 to Terminal Norte station. From this station, there's bus service to Querétaro, San Miguel de Allende, Guanajuato, Zacatecas, Chihuahua, Monterrey, and Tijuana.

Terminal Central del Sur (South Terminal), also known as Terminal Tasqueña (Av. Tasqueña 1320): Take Metro Line 2 to Tasqueña station. This terminal offers buses to Cuernavaca, Acapulco, Taxco, and Ixtapa/Zihuatanejo.

Terminal Poniente (Western Terminal, Av. Sur 122): The Metro stop is Observatorio at the western end of Metro Line 1. From this station there are departures to Toluca, Valle de Bravo, Morelia, Guadalajara, and Puerto Vallarta.

Terminal Oriente (Eastern Terminal), also known as Terminal TAPO (Calz. Ignacio Zaragoza 200): Take Metro Line 4 to the Morelos station or Line 1 to San Lázaro station. Buses depart to Puebla, Veracruz, Mérida, Cancún, Palenque, San Cristóbal de las Casas, and Tapachula.

Note: Buses leave directly from the international airport for Toluca, Pachuca, Puebla, Cuernavaca, and Querétaro frequently throughout the day, which may be convenient for some travelers who wish to bypass Mexico City for these destinations. (See the earlier *To and From the Airport* section for more details.)

CAR

From the United States, Mexico City can be reached in 12–48 hours of reasonably sane driving, depending on which route you take. The shortest route (about 12 hours) is to cross the border at Laredo, Texas, taking México 85 to Monterrey, then México 57 on to Saltillo, San Luis Potosí, and Querétaro, all on good highway and almost entirely free of tolls. Other, longer routes extend from Ciudad Juárez on México 45 through Chihuahua, then México 49 on to Gómez Palacio, Zacatecas, and San Luis Potosí (two days, best broken for the night somewhere between Zacatecas and Saltillo); the northwest highway from California and Arizona (México 15) passes through Hermosillo, Mazatlán, Tepic, and Guadalajara (Tepic or Mazatlán are about a day's drive from D.F.).

In many places along Mexican highways drivers can choose between the free (*libre*) or the toll (*cuota*) road. The toll highways can be pricey, but the pavement is excellent and traffic is much lighter than on the congested free roads. However, some free roads, especially in the northern deserts, are wide open and fast, and if you get to know which ones are good you can save a chunk of money without sacrificing much time. But don't drive on the free roads at night if you can avoid it; if you do, be cautious.

The highways connecting Mexico City to Guatemala (via Tapachula, 16–20 hours of driving) and Belize (via Chetumal, 20–24 hours of driving) are in worse condition than the northern roads and should be driven only during the day.

Try to avoid arriving in Mexico City on Sunday afternoon and evening, as the highways are invariably jammed with weekenders heading home. Conversely, Friday afternoon is about the worst time to try to leave the city.

Insurance

It's very important to carry a Mexican liability insurance policy on your vehicle when driving in Mexico. No matter what your own insurance company may tell you, Mexican authorities don't recognize foreign insurance policies for private vehicles in Mexico.

At least minimum liability vehicle insurance is now required by law in Mexico. Without it, a minor traffic accident can turn into a nightmare. Short-term—as little as one day's worth—insurance can be arranged at any of several agencies found in nearly every border town between the Pacific Ocean and the Gulf of Mexico.

One of the most popular, and reliable, Mexico insurers is **Sanborns Mexico Insurance** (P.O. Box 310, McAllen, TX 78505, 55/956/682-6677 or 800/222-0158, fax 956/686-0732, www.sanbornsinsurance.com), which has offices in or close to virtually every town along the U.S.-Mexico border except Tijuana and some of the smaller border crossings. Sample coverage for a vehicle insured at a value of $20,000-25,000—plus $50,000 property damage, $80,000 liability, and medical payments of $2,000 per person (up to $10,000 per occurrence)—costs around $12 per day or around $800 per year to drive anywhere in Mexico.

For long-term visits, better deals can sometimes be negotiated from other sources, especially for drivers who will be making more than one trip into Mexico each year. Some agencies in Mexico offer annual policies in which you're only charged for those days you're actually in Mexico. Of course, this requires a trip south of the border to obtain such a policy in the first place, so you'll need a day or two's worth of border insurance for the trip. Whichever policy you choose, always make photocopies of the policy and keep originals and copies in separate, safe places.

Driving To and From Querétaro

Take Paseo de la Reforma west out past Chapultepec to the Periférico, turn north on the Periférico, and follow it all the way past Satélite and Tlanepantla, keeping an eye out for Querétaro signs. It's also possible to follow the Eje Central north from downtown, but this is sometimes more complicated and with more traffic. Returning to the city, stay on the Periférico around the northwest side of the city and either get off at Paseo de la Reforma (for Polanco, the Zona Rosa, and the Centro) or continue farther south on the Periférico for San Ángel and Coyoacán.

Driving To and From Toluca

Paseo de la Reforma and Avenida Constituyentes (a major avenue parallel to Reforma but farther south) both lead directly to free and toll highways to Toluca. The toll road costs $5 for the 10-mile stretch to La Marquesa (one of the most expensive tolls in the country for the distance), where it meets back up with the free road. If you're not in a rush, take the free road and save your pesos. Coming in from Toluca, keep an eye out for signs directing you to Reforma (for Polanco, Paseo de la Reforma, or the Centro Histórico) or Constituyentes (for Condesa, Roma, or anywhere in the south of the city).

Driving To and From Cuernavaca

Both Avenida Insurgentes and Calzada Tlalpan (the southern extension of Pino Suárez, the road on the east side of the Zócalo) lead directly to both the free and toll highways to Cuernavaca. Tlalpan is usually faster as there are more lanes and less stop lights. The Periférico ring road also connects with the highway exit in the south part of the city. The $6.50 toll highway to Cuernavaca bypasses the windy, scenic, and slow free road. Returning to Mexico City, watch for a major road junction as you come out of the hills and enter the valley, the right-hand fork leading to Tlalpan and downtown, and the left-hand one to Insurgentes, San Ángel, Coyoacán, Roma, and Condesa.

Driving To and From Puebla

Navigating your way from the Centro through to the market neighborhoods to the eastern exit of the city is no simple task. It's often easier to head south along Pino Suárez and Tlalpan, turn off on the Viaducto Miguel Alemán heading east, and follow the signs to Puebla. It's also possible to follow Avenida Chapultepec east (farther along, it's called Avenida Fray Servando) to Calzada Izazaga and the highway to Puebla, but a couple of turns are confusing, and traffic is usually bad. From the west and south of the city, take Viaducto Miguel Alemán.

Returning to the city, paradoxically, it's a bit of a trick to find the entrance to the Viaducto, whereas following Izazaga and then Fray Servando into the city center is fairly straightforward. Once you learn the Viaducto entrance, however, it's the quickest way to get into most of the center, south, and west parts of the city.

The toll road to Puebla costs $5 and allows you to avoid all the curves and slow trucks on the free highway.

Driving To and From Teotihuacán and Pachuca

Getting out on the highway to the ruins northeast of Mexico City, as well as to Pachuca, couldn't be simpler: Just get on Avenida Insurgentes north and keep going straight. At the first tollbooth, Pachuca drivers stay to the left, while those going to Teotihuacán stay to the right. Coming back is just as easy.

TRAIN

At last report, there was no passenger train service operating out of Mexico City. The last routes, to Tlaxcala and Veracruz, have been discontinued. If for some reason you need to get to the train station anyhow, it is on Avenida Insurgentes Norte in Colonia Buenavista (Metro station Buenavista).

The federal government announced in 2004 that it would support the construction of a proposed high-speed train linking Mexico City to Guadalajara via the thriving *Bajío* cities of Querétaro, Celaya, and León. The total trip would take roughly 2.5 hours at 250 kilometers per hour for $90, if all goes as planned (a big if!), making it a great improvement over the 6.5-hour, $55 bus ride. It will, however, take several years to build, so make do with the bus or fork out $140 for the plane ride in the meantime.

Getting Around

Getting around Mexico City is cheap, efficient, and—with a little caution—safe. Within each neighborhood, walking is the best way to see everything; attractions are usually concentrated in each of the city's most popular areas.

To cover more ground, the options available include bus, taxi, and Metro. Those who have their own wheels will find negotiating the city not as daunting as might be expected, unless they're unlucky enough to be caught in one of the political demonstrations that frequently snarl the city center.

BUS

The most common of Mexico City's several bus types is the *pesero,* a medium-sized, box-shaped bus painted white and green. Fares ($0.20–0.50) depend on how far along the route you are going—ask and pay when you get in. To signal a stop, push the button above the rear door, and if that doesn't work, call out *"baja, por favor"* (stop, please) in a loud voice. *Peseros* tend to stop anywhere, not just

designated stops. These buses can be extremely crowded during peak hours, and pickpockets are common, so watch out if you're standing.

To find the right bus for your destination, start by looking at the placards posted in the front window. Only the end of the route is listed, so you most likely will have to ask drivers if they are going your way, and if not, which bus you should take. At the end of each Metro line, huge corrals of *peseros* and smaller VW-bus *combis* depart for destinations around the edge of the city.

Mexico City has a dedicated bus lane each way along Avenida Insurgentes for the **Metrobús,** larger buses that stop only at designated stations along the route. *Peseros* have been banned from Insurgentes. This bus system—modeled after the Transmilenio project in Bogotá, Colombia—has eased traffic on this critical Mexico City artery. To use the Metrobús, go to one of the stations along Insurgentes (accessed via crosswalks at stop lights) and buy a card using the easy instructions on the vending box. Uniformed guards are at most stations, and they are invariably happy to help if you are confused about the procedure. The cards cost a 20-peso minimum ($2), and can be recharged when needed. Each ride is $0.35, no matter how much distance you travel. Swipe the card through the turnstile on the way in, and get off at whatever station you like. During times of heavy traffic, the Metrobús is often faster than a taxi. Buses are quite crowded during rush hours, to the point where you may have to let a couple pass by before one comes with room to get on.

The Metrobús run from Indios Verdes in the north as far as San Ángel in the south. However construction was well underway to extend the service further south, past UNAM all the way to Tlalpan, and that should be completed by the time this book is printed. As well, a second Metrobús line was under construction running from Tacubaya in the west 20 kilometers across the city to Tepalcates in the east, beyond the airport, with 33 stations; that line also should be completed by the time this guide is printed. In all, the city plans to eventually build 10 Metrobús lines, for a total of 247 kilometers of dedicated bus lanes.

Note: Women will be pleased to hear that in early 2008 the Mexico City government began experimenting with female-only buses on a few routes (15 in 2008). They are easily visible with the wonderfully cliché bright pink placards in the front window.

METRO

Many visitors, expecting the worst, find themselves pleasantly surprised by Mexico's clean and efficient Metro system. At a cost of $0.25 per ride, the 11 lines (*líneas*) of the Metro move an average of five million people around the city each day. Just about all of the city's major sites, hotels, bus stations, and the airport are accessible from the system.

The Metro stations are well lit, fairly clean, and generally safe. Directions are indicated by the last stops at each end of each line, so you must know where you want to go in between these stops. Metro maps are posted on the walls of all stations. Signs marked Correspondencia indicate the walking route to take to transfer train lines—look for the name of the station at the end of the line in the direction you are going. For example, if you go into the Zócalo station and want to ride to Metro Revolución, go in the direction of Cuatro Caminos and get off at the Revolución station. There is no charge to transfer lines as often as you like, as long as you don't leave the Metro system. Try to buy several tickets in advance if you're going to use the Metro, as lines at ticket booths can sometimes be very long. Operating hours vary slightly according to day of the week and the line, but they're roughly 6 A.M.–midnight, or until 1 A.M. Saturday night.

For destinations beyond the reach of the Metro system, get off at the station farthest out in the direction you're going, then go outside where fleets of *microbuses* are parked and ask which one to take.

A *tren ligero* (light rail train) extends Metro service into the southern part of the city, from the Tasqueña Metro station as far south as Xochimilco. Annoyingly, a different sort of ticket is required for the *tren ligero,* requiring another wait in line at the ticket booth.

For more information about the Metro, see its website, www.metro.df.gob.mx.

Customs and Safety

Metro users are not known for their politeness, with people getting in at stations often shoving past others trying to get off. British travelers will no doubt be infuriated by the local habit of standing on both sides of the escalators, thus blocking those who are trying to walk. Mexicans who find their path blocked, however, stop walking and wait for the end of the ride with the resigned aplomb for which Mexico City is legendary; they don't even consider asking the person in front to move.

Foreign women, particularly those unaccompanied by a man, can expect plenty of looks at the least and very possibly some groping if the train is crowded—many female travelers avoid using the Metro if they're alone because of all the tiresome unwanted attention. At peak hours in some stations, the front couple of cars may be designated for women and children only—look for special roped-off lines, marked with signs. Pickpockets are also not unknown on the Metro—after taxi robberies, probably the most common form of crime foreigners will run across is having their wallet snitched on the Metro.

These annoyances aside, the Metro is generally safe and easy to use, particularly if you don't try to use it during the morning and afternoon rush hours (7–9 A.M. and 6–9 P.M.).

TAXI

Taxis in Mexico City come in two varieties: roving taxis hailed from the street, and various *sitio* taxi companies, based at a certain station and reached by telephone.

Street Taxis

The most common are the red-and-white four-door sedans, and less frequently the old green-and-white Volkswagen Beetles, which are being phased out. All are equipped with taxi meters (*taxímetros*). Metered taxis hailed from street corners in Mexico City have a bad reputation, and not without reason. Armed muggings, though not as common, still do occur, and foreigners are unquestionably a high-risk group. It's not recommended to take street taxis unless you really have to. Expats who get to know the city well, and have a good command of Spanish, may feel more comfortable taking street cabs, but even most expats avoid them, and tourists should as well. Better to take a *sitio* taxi (described next).

Should you decide to take a street taxi or end up in a situation where it's the only transport available, check that the driver has a *tarjetón,* or identification card, keep the window rolled up and door locked (most robberies involve an accomplice jumping in when the taxi stops), and give clear directional instructions to the driver. Also be sure the driver turns on the meter as soon as you start driving. If possible, try to have small bills when taking rides around town, as taxi drivers often don't have change. Tipping is not expected.

After 10 P.M. taxis are legally allowed to charge 20 percent above the meter reading. Some have special meters with a night setting, while with others you simply have to calculate the extra amount—ask when you get in. If it's late, taxi drivers may refuse to turn on their meter and will instead want to negotiate a price. Although this is technically illegal, it's common practice. Also, all rides going outside the city limits into the state of Mexico cost extra. Note the amount the meter reads when leaving the Distrito Federal—all charges incurred after entering the state of Mexico are doubled, then added to the amount accumulated on the meter while still in D.F.

Sitio, Radio, and Hotel Taxis

If you need to take a taxi in the city after dark, or you need one during the day and don't want to risk a street cab, a safer alternative is a *sitio* (pronounced SEE-tee-yoh) taxi. These are taxis attached to a permanent taxi stand, or *sitio.* You'll find taxi *sitios* all over the city, and you can recognize them by a short line of taxis, all painted the same color, with the name of the *sitio* emblazoned on the side. Often a curbside kiosk stands nearby where dispatchers log the taxis in and out.

Radio-dispatched *sitios* reached by telephone, with service to and from anywhere in the city, are considered to be the safest of all. Some are expensive, while others are very reasonable—check how the fare is calculated when you call. Sometimes it's a flat fee per route, sometimes it's a taxi meter plus a certain amount, and sometimes it's by kilometers. If you plan on using a lot of *sitio* taxis, it's not a bad idea to buy a Ladatel telephone card, so you can call them from public telephones. Below are a few well-established and generally reliable radio taxi companies.

Taxi Mex (55/5519-7690 or 55/9171-8888, www.taximex.com.) is a reliable *sitio* service charging the *taxímetro* plus $1.25 during the day; add another 20 percent after 10 P.M.

Servitaxi (55/5516-6020) has taxis charging according to the taxi meter plus $2. Call the central operator and they will radio for

© CHRIS HUMPHREY

Sadly, the days of the beloved *bocho* street taxi, as Volkswagen Beetles are known here, are fast coming to an end in Mexico City.

the nearest taxi, or call one of the neighborhood bases: Centro (55/5526-2300), Reforma (55/5566-1060), Polanco (55/5282-1428), Condesa (55/5553-5059), Insurgentes Sur/Del Valle (55/5687-8819), Coyoacán and Mixcoac (55/5534-3861), and Roma (55/5574-7356).

A very good taxi service using unmarked cars and charging by kilometer (rather than with a taxi meter) is **Radio Elite** (55/5660-1122 or 55/5651-2161).

Most high-end hotels have a cab service; these are the most expensive cabs, but they're quite safe, and fares are usually posted. The cars are usually unmarked, four-door Fords, and the drivers often speak some English (some are licensed guides as well). There may also be a taxi *sitio* near your hotel; ask the doorman to point one out.

Cars with Drivers

If you plan on driving around the city a lot and don't want to deal with taxis, or you are looking for a private driver for any other reason, one

excellent and reliable company is **Limorent** (55/5277-2304), which will provide an English-speaking driver (on request) and a car fitting four for $280 for an entire day. Longer and shorter rentals can also be arranged.

Two other companies offering chauffeur service around the city and elsewhere, with bilingual drivers, are **Transportación Turística y Ejecutiva Chapultepec** (55/5516-0850 or 55/5516-0770, www.mexicolimorent.com.mx) and **Arguba** (55/5523-2973 or 55/5687-0617).

CAR

Driving in Mexico City is certainly not for the faint of heart. Nevertheless, those who have driven in other large, chaotic cities will find Mexico City negotiable, as long as proper caution is taken and a few basic principals are kept in mind.

One essential factor to peaceful driving in the city is to choose your hours carefully. Mornings (8–10 A.M.) can be very congested, while midday traffic is usually fairly reasonable

WASHING YOUR DUDS

If you're tired of trying to wash those blue jeans in your sink (nightmare job) and want to have someone else clean the grime out of your clothes, you'll be pleased to hear getting your washing done in Mexico City is easy and inexpensive. Coin-operated laundries are not common in Mexico – instead you normally drop your clothes off and pick them up either later that same day or the following day. Usually prices are charged in kilos, with a minimum of three kilos for wash, dry, and fold. If your clothes need special treatment, be sure to tell the owners first.

Below are three places I've found to be reliable. There are many more in every *colonia* in the city, and many hotels will wash clothes for a fee also.

Lavandería Automática Edison, Edison 91, near Monumento a la Revolución, Mon.-Fri. 10 A.M.- 7 P.M., Sat. 10 A.M.-5 P.M.

Lavandería Del Río, Jalapa 99, Col. Roma, 55/5511-2538, Mon.-Sat. 8 A.M.-7 P.M., Sun. 8 A.M.-2 P.M., $4 for three kilos

Lavandería Karina, Mesones 42, Col. Centro, Mon.-Sat. 10 A.M.-6 P.M.

until around 4 P.M. During the week, late afternoon and early evening are the worst, particularly on the main commuter routes in and out of the city and in the Centro. Traffic begins to dissipate around 9 P.M., or earlier in the city center. The worst traffic of all is Friday afternoon, and even worse still if it's a *viernes quincena,* a Friday that coincides with the twice-monthly payday. Unpredictable demonstrations in various parts of the city—but particularly on Paseo de la Reforma, on Paseo Bucareli, and in the city center—also regularly tie up traffic.

Navigation

As might be expected, learning your way around an urban area of several million inhabitants can be a bit confusing, but being familiar with a couple of major avenues can help you stay oriented. Avenida Insurgentes is the longest boulevard in the city and is a major north–south route crossing Mexico City. To the northeast, Insurgentes takes you to the exit for Pachuca and Teotihuacán, while to the south it continues past San Ángel to UNAM and the exit to Cuernavaca and Acapulco.

Paseo de la Reforma is a broad avenue punctuated by large traffic circles (called *glorietas*) running northeast–southwest. Originally Reforma ran between the Alameda and Chapultepec, but now it extends west to the exit to Toluca and northeast to the Basílica de Guadalupe.

The city is circled by two ring highways, the inner Circuito Interior and the outer Periférico. The Circuito makes a complete loop, although it changes names (Río Churubusco, Patriotismo, Revolución, and Circuito Interior) along the way. The Periférico, however, extends only three-quarters of the way, with the northeast section (between the highway exits to Querétaro and Puebla) unfinished.

Cutting across these two loops is a grid of *ejes,* axis roads running in one direction with traffic lights (somewhat) timed, either east–west or north–south. *Ejes* are numbered and given a reference of *norte* (north), *sur* (south), *oriente* (east), and *poniente* (west). Hence the Eje 2 Norte is the second east–west road north of the center of the city, and the Eje 3 Norte runs parallel to it, several blocks north, etc. Other important roads that are not technically *ejes* are the east–west Viaducto Miguel Alemán and the south-to-center Avenida Tlalpan, both of which are major two-way arteries with few stoplights.

Finding specific addresses in the city can be tricky. The best tool is the *Guía Roji,* a bright-red book of maps and indexes of the city. It can be found in Sanborns and is sold on many street corners for $8. They also have maps available online at www.guiaroji.com.mx. When driving, don't expect to see street signs placed in logical places, and be ready to ask for directions frequently. And always try to know the name of the *colonia* (neighborhood) where your destination is located.

© GUILLAUME COPART MULLER/WWW.GCMPHOTO.COM

Mexico City residents like to joke that they should hang garlic at every traffic intersection, to improve circulation.

Hoy No Circúla

In an effort to reduce the number of cars driven in the city, hence reducing air pollution, the city enforces a ban on each vehicle one day during the week based on the final digit of its license plate, a program known as *"Hoy No Circula"* (literally, Don't Drive Today, but often translated as Day Without a Car). Foreign-registered cars are not exempt from the program. Failure to comply can result in fines of up to $80, or less if you are inclined to negotiate with the police officer who catches you. The ban is enforced 6 A.M.–10 P.M. five days a week. The schedule is as follows:

Monday: No driving if final digit is 5 or 6
Tuesday: No driving if final digit is 7 or 8
Wednesday: No driving if final digit is 3 or 4
Thursday: No driving if final digit is 1 or 2
Friday: No driving if final digit is 9 or 0
Saturday and Sunday: All vehicles may drive.

Local cars are required to have a decal bearing either a "0," "1," or "2." A "0" means the car is exempt from any days off, regardless of the license number, because it has passed emissions tests. A "1" requires the car to not circulate on one day, regardless of the conditions; and a "2" means the car cannot circulate on two days of the week during a pollution alert. Foreign-registered cars are not required to have these decals or to pass emissions inspections, but they are required to follow the Hoy No Circula schedule listed above.

Drive to Survive

The best advice I can offer for how to survive the roads of Mexico City is to remain watchful and alert at all times. Expect anything to happen. Most drivers usually follow the rules of the road (at least in a general sense), but you can't always rely on that. Drivers will pull out at inopportune moments, cut across in front of you to make a turn, drive the wrong way down a one-way street—all the while fully assuming you will get out of their way. Many intersections on side streets don't have stop signs in either direction, and the decision of who goes first seems to be whichever one appears more determined. In the many *glorietas* (traffic circles), the standard rule of the person in the circle having right-of-way does not pertain. Expect drivers to come barreling into the circle without even looking to their left to check traffic. Aggressive driving is not a tendency but a basic necessity. For example, the quaint notion of taking turns when two lanes merge is laughable here, and if you're on a highway entrance ramp in rush hour, you just have to jam the front of your car in and make them give room, or you'll never get in the lane.

Mexico City drivers are aggressive in general, but some are worse than others and bear watching out for. The *pesero* bus drivers, in particular, are legendary for swinging their green-and-white machines around the streets with great abandon, expecting everyone to get out of their way. Be prepared for taxis to slow down unexpectedly and veer across several lanes to pick up a potential passenger. Perhaps worst of all are the armored cars—high-speed tanks, really—piloted by sunglass-wearing toughs who think that because they are driving money and guns they are free to chug through red lights, make illegal U-turns, and perform all sorts of other lovely stunts.

Traffic control has improved noticeably in Mexico City. Transit police have become much more attentive to enforcing traffic rules and speeding the flow of cars, such as stopping left turns off of major avenues which would block two lines of traffic as turners await their chance to cross. Drivers even actually stop for zebra-stripe crosswalks on Paseo de la Reforma for pedestrians—a small thing, but unthinkable not that long ago. Another improvement is much better placed street signs, which is very helpful in navigating the city.

Officials

If your car has foreign plates, you may attract an inordinate amount of attention from Mexico City's various police forces, particularly the brown-uniformed *tránsito* police—either on foot, in patrol cars, or on venerable, stylish (and sometimes barely functioning) Harley-Davidson motorcycles. If your car is in Mexico legally, the papers are in order, and you haven't broken the law, all will be well. Insist that you have done nothing wrong, and you should be allowed to go on your way.

If you did break the traffic rules in some way (or even if you didn't but had the bad luck of running into a greedy cop), you may find yourself being threatened with going to the *delegación*, the precinct house, if you don't pay a "fine" there and then. How you react to this will depend on your own moral compass, as well as how much of a hurry you are in. Fed up with the perennial corruption of the police, some Mexicans have taken to refusing to pay bribes (known as *la mordida*, "the bite"). Foreign visitors may well wish to take this road also—it's certainly the scrupulous thing to do. And because you are a foreigner, and also because the policeman will not want to bother taking you down to the *delegación*, you may well be let off with just a warning. Certainly

if you are confident of having done nothing wrong, insist on being taken to the *delegación*, and chances are very good you will be allowed to go. If you did do something wrong, or don't want to risk going to the *delegación* for whatever reason, you should be able to get away from basic traffic violations with a 50- or 100-peso note ($5–10) or less, depending on your negotiating talent. Actually going down to the *delegación* is a several-hour ordeal.

In 2007, the city put in place a new point system for traffic infractions, rather then the old draconian practice of removing license plates and sending cars to the *delegación* (or, more commonly, threatening to do so to extract a bribe). Although only just beginning, the system seems to be having an effect on driver and police behavior. It's not a magic cure certainly, but there seems less incentive for corruption.

More serious than the *tránsitos* are the Policía Fiscal Federal, the Finance Secretariat police, who drive new-model blue pickup trucks and sometimes pull over foreign cars to check that their papers are in order. Again, if the papers are all fine and up to date, you'll have no problems whatsoever. If they are not, however, the car will be impounded, and you will go through a lengthy ordeal to get it out again. Don't think about offering *mordidas* to these guys, as it will just get you into more trouble.

Another official service on the streets of the city is Apoyo Vial ("Road Support"), men and women in bright-yellow uniforms driving motor scooters. Funded jointly by the city and federal governments, Apoyo Vial helps out with emergency breakdowns, traffic accidents, and directing traffic in congested areas. Their services are free.

Parking

Parking is an entire industry in Mexico City, employing many thousands of men (and occasionally women or children) who watch over certain stretches of sidewalk. As you pull up to park, they will hustle over and wave you into the spot with enthusiastic whistling and gesticulating. When you leave, they will again wave you out and expect a small tip in return. This can vary from $0.50 for a short stay in a normal area, up to $2–3 for spots near crowded parts of the city or during events. The custom is to merely acknowledge them when you park your car, and then when departing get in, have them guide you out of the spot, and then you roll down your window and hand them the coins as you drive off. While they have no particular right over that part of the sidewalk and probably wouldn't do anything if you didn't pay on leaving, the general custom is to pay them. And they do in fact generally watch out for your car.

The next rung up the parking ladder is the *estacionamiento,* a type of parking lot found all over the city. Pull in, give the attendant your keys in return for a ticket with the time punched on it, and pay (usually $0.75–1.50 an hour). Don't leave valuables in the car. The attendant will expect a small tip of a couple of pesos after he drives the car up for you to leave.

Outside crowded clubs, bars, and restaurants, clients frequently leave their cars with a valet for $2–5.

Parking meters, called *parquímetros,* are installed only in a few areas of the city, particularly around the Zona Rosa and Paseo de la Reforma. Should the meter expire, the parking cops will eagerly slap a "boot" onto your wheel, which is costly and time-consuming to have removed.

Car Rentals

You'll find many car rental offices throughout the city and in the airport. Also, many agencies have rental desks in the bigger hotels. The major agencies are generally expensive compared to U.S. prices. A small car with unlimited mileage will run $50–80 a day, sometimes less if you shop around or have some kind of discount. Major U.S. companies operating in Mexico include **Avis** (branches at the airport, Campos Eliseos 218 in Polanco, and Paseo de la Reforma 308, 55/5533-1336, nationally 800/288-8888, www.avis.com. mx); **Budget** (at the airport, 55/5784-3011 or 55/5784-3118; Atenas 40 just behind the Fiesta Americana on Reforma, 55/5566-8815, nationally 800/700-1700, www.budget.com. mx); and **Dollar** (at the airport, 55/2599-1111, www.dollar.com).

Some of the best car rental bargains are arranged before you leave home. It's always worth checking for discounts linked to airline mileage clubs and Costco/Price Club cards.

Many local rental agencies offer cars at lower prices than the U.S. agencies. One agency I've used several times is **Casanova Renta de Automoviles** (Chapultepec 442, right near Metro Sevilla, 55/5514-0449 or 5207-6007; Patriotismo 735, in Colonia Mixcoac, 55/5563-7606, www.casanovarent.com.mx), offering a no-frills (not even a cigarette lighter!) Nissan Tsuru (a simple four-door sedan) for around $40 a day with 200 kilometers mileage, or $45 with unlimited mileage, or $30 a day for a smaller Chevy. The agency is used to dealing with foreign renters, and someone who speaks English is always on hand. Another local agency is **Fresno Rent A Car** (at the airport, 55/5784-4030 or 5785-3951; Dr. Andrade 246, in the Centro, 55/5588-3809; Monterrey 324, in the Roma, 55/5584-2443). There are many more in the yellow pages, and it's worth calling around to compare rates. Be sure to carefully check all the details of mileage costs and liability before making any rental.

Visas and Officialdom

TOURIST PERMITS AND VISAS

For more detailed information than that supplied here regarding visa requirements, in English, go to the web page of the Mexican Foreign Relations Secretariat at www.sre.gob.mx/english, and then look under the "Services" dropdown menu.

Tourist Permits

Citizens of the United States or Canada (or of 38 other designated countries in Europe and Latin America, plus Singapore) visiting Mexico solely for tourism are not required to obtain a visa. Instead they must carry validated tourist cards (*forma migratoria turista*, or FMT). Although you can get FMTs at any Mexican consulate, it's not necessary to arrange them before going to Mexico—just show up at the airport or the border, and it will be taken care of with minimal hassle. The tourist card is valid for stays of up to 180 days and must be used within 90 days of issue. Your card becomes invalid once you exit the country—you're supposed to surrender it at the border—even if your 180 days hasn't expired. If you'll be entering and leaving Mexico more than once during your trip, you should request a multiple-entry tourist card, available from Mexican consulates only. To obtain the FMT you need a valid passport.

Once you cross the border or land at the airport in Mexico City, your tourist card must be validated by a Mexican immigration officer. You can arrange this at any *migración* office in Mexico (many *municipio* seats have them), but it's accomplished most conveniently at the border crossing itself. At airports you pass through immigration, where an officer stamps your paperwork with the date of entry and the number of days you're permitted to stay in Mexico.

The Mexican government collects a 250-peso fee (around $25) from all tourists entering the country. If you fly in, this fee is tacked on to your airfare. If you arrive by land, you can pay this fee at any bank in Mexico. The bank issues a receipt, which you must show when you leave the country.

Mexican regulations used to require children under the age of 18 crossing the border without one or both parents to carry a notarized letter granting permission from the absent parent or both parents if both were absent. This regulation is no longer in effect, but it's best for unaccompanied minors or minors traveling with only one parent to be prepared for all situations with notarized letters. In cases of divorce, separation, or death, the minor should carry notarized papers documenting the situation.

In reality, minors with tourist cards are rarely asked for these documents. Children under 15 may be included on their parents' tourist card, but this means that neither the child nor the parents can legally exit Mexico without the other.

Tourist Visas

Tourists from countries other than the 40 countries for which no visa is necessary need to obtain tourist visas in advance of arrival in Mexico. If you apply in person at a Mexican consulate, you usually can obtain a tourist visa on the day of application, although for some countries it can take a couple of weeks. Requirements include a valid passport, a round-trip air ticket to Mexico, three photos, and a visa fee of $29.

Foreign visitors who are legal permanent residents of the United States do not need visas to visit Mexico for tourism. A free tourist card can be obtained by presenting your passport and a U.S. residence card to any travel agency or at the airport or border crossing.

Non-Immigrant Visas

Citizens of Mexico's NAFTA (North American Free Trade Agreement) partners, the United States and Canada, are not required to obtain a visa to visit Mexico for business purposes. Instead you can receive a free NAFTA business permit (*forma migratoria nafta*, or

FMN), which is similar to a tourist card, at the point of entry (border crossing or airport); it's valid for 30 days. At the port of entry (the Mexico City airport if you arrive by air), you must present proof of nationality (a valid passport or original birth certificate, plus a photo identification or voter registration card) and proof that you are traveling for "international business activities," usually interpreted to mean a letter from the company you represent, even if it's your own enterprise.

Those who arrive with the FMN and wish to stay over the authorized period of 30 days must replace their FMN with an FM-3 form at an immigration office in Mexico. The FM-3 is valid for a period of up to one year, for multiple entries, and may be extended. Note that the FMN is not valid for anyone working during their time in Mexico, for either a foreign or Mexican company.

Citizens of non-NAFTA countries who are visiting for business purposes must obtain an FM-3 visa endorsed for business travel, which is valid for one year. An FM-3 is also required for students, although the requirements are somewhat different for each class of FM-3 visa.

Visitors to Mexico coming as part of human rights delegations, as aid workers, or as international observers should check with a Mexican embassy about the current regulations.

Overstays

If you overstay your visa and are caught, the usual penalty is a fine of $50 for overstays up to a month. After that the penalties become more severe. When leaving the country by airport, you will be required to show your FMT, and if you don't have it, will have to pay a fine. When crossing a land border, it's rare that a Mexican border official asks to see your FMT or visa. Having expired papers if you get into any trouble with the police while in Mexico will further complicate your situation, so the best policy is to stay up-to-date in spite of the apparent laxity of enforcement.

Pets

Dogs and cats over three months of age may be brought into Mexico if each is accompanied by a vaccination certificate that proves the animal has been vaccinated or treated for rabies, hepatitis, pip, and leptospirosis. You'll also need a health certificate issued no more than 72 hours before entry and signed by a registered veterinarian. Upon arrival in Mexico, bring the pet and documents to the animal health inspection authorities, found at all points of entry into the country (including airports). Here you will be issued an import animal health certificate for the pet. This certificate is free for one or two pets, but if you are traveling with more than two pets, expect to pay a fee of $120 per additional pet.

Visitante Rentista and Inmigrante Rentista Visas

FM-3 visas may be issued to foreigners who choose to live in Mexico on a "permanent income" basis. This most often applies to foreigners who decide to retire in Mexico, though it is also used by artists, writers, and other self-employed foreign residents. With this visa you're allowed to import one motor vehicle as well as your household belongings into Mexico tax-free.

The basic requirements for this visa are that applicants must forgo any kind of employment while living in Mexico and must show proof (bank statements) that they have a regular source of foreign-earned income amounting to at least $1,000 per month (plus half that for each dependent over the age of 15; e.g., $1,500 for a couple). A pile of paperwork, including a "letter of good conduct" from the applicant's local police department, must accompany the initial application, along with an immigration tax payment ($60) and various applications fees totaling about $75.

The visa must be renewed annually, but the renewal can be accomplished at any immigration office in Mexico. After five years in Mexico, you have to start over again or move up to the FM-2, or *inmigrante rentista* visa, which has higher income requirements and signifies an intent to stay longer. After five years on an FM-2, an *inmigrante rentista* is eligible to apply for *inmigrado* status, which confers all the rights of citizenship (including employment in Mexico), save the rights to vote and hold public office.

Many foreigners who have retired in Mexico manage to do so on the regular 180-day tourist visa; every six months they dash across the border and return with a new tourist card (issued at the border) on the same day. This method bypasses all the red tape and income requirements of the retirement visa. If you own a home in Mexico, however, some local immigrations officials may interpret the law to mean that you must have an FM-2 or FM-3 visa—not an FMT or tourist visa—to be able to stay in that home for any period of time whatsoever. Although it's clear from a straight reading that Mexico's immigration laws do not require any special visas for home ownership, each immigration district behaves like an individual fiefdom at the mercy of the local immigration chief.

Monthly income requirements for both *rentista* visas are keyed to the Mexican daily minimum wage (400 times minimum wage for the FM-2, 250 times for the FM-3), hence figures may vary according to the current dollar–peso exchange rate.

CUSTOMS
Entering Mexico
Officially, tourists are supposed to bring only those items into Mexico that will be of use during their trip. This means you can bring in practically anything as long as it doesn't appear to be in large enough quantities to qualify for resale.

Technically speaking, you're not supposed to import more than one still camera, one movie camera, and one video camera, and no more than 12 rolls of film or blank videocassettes for each. Anything more is supposed to require permission from a Mexican consulate. In everyday practice, however, Mexican customs officials rarely blink at an extra camera or two. Professional photographers and others who would like to bring more cameras and film into Mexico can apply for dispensation through a Mexican consulate abroad.

Regarding audio equipment, you're limited to one CD disc player and one audio cassette player (or combo), one MP3 player, and up to 20 CDs or recording cassettes. Other per-person limitations include one musical instrument, one tent and accompanying camping gear, one set of fishing gear, two tennis rackets, five "toys," and one sailboard.

Other limits are three liters of liquor or wine, two cartons (20 packs) of cigarettes, 25 cigars, or 200 grams of tobacco.

Other than the above, you're permitted to bring in no more than $300 worth of other articles. You will be subject to duty on personal possessions worth more than $300, to a max of $1,000, except for new computer equipment, which is exempt up to $4,000.

Returning to the United States
Visitors returning to the United States from Mexico may have their luggage inspected by U.S. customs officials. The hassle can be minimized by giving brief, straight answers to their questions (e.g., "How long have you been in Mexico?" "Do you have anything to declare?") and by cooperating with their requests to open your luggage, vehicle storage compartments, and anything else they want opened. Sometimes the officers use dogs to sniff luggage and/or vehicles for contraband and illegal aliens.

Nearly 3,000 items—including all handicrafts—made in Mexico are exempt from any U.S. customs duties. Adults over 21 are allowed one liter (33.8 fluid ounces) of alcoholic beverages and 200 cigarettes (or 100 cigars) per person. Note that Cuban cigars may not be imported into the United States, and customs will confiscate the cigars if discovered. An estimated 9 out of 10 cigars sold as Cubans in Mexico are fake anyway, so it's not worth the hassle. All other purchases or gifts up to a total value of $400 within any 31-day period can be brought into the U.S. duty-free.

The following fruits and vegetables cannot be brought into the United States from Mexico: oranges, grapefruits, mangoes, avocados (unless the pit is removed), and potatoes (including yams and sweet potatoes). All other fruits are permitted (including bananas, dates, pineapples, cactus fruits, grapes, and berries of all types).

Other prohibited plant materials are straw (including packing materials and items stuffed with straw), hay, unprocessed cotton, sugarcane, and any plants in soil (this includes houseplants).

Animals and animal products that cannot be imported include wild and domesticated birds (including poultry, unless cooked), pork or pork products (including sausage, ham, and other cured pork), and eggs. Beef, mutton, venison, and other meats are permitted at up to 50 pounds per person.

Returning to Canada

Duty-frees include 200 cigarettes (or 50 cigars or 250 grams of tobacco) and 1.14 liters of booze. Exemptions run from C$20 to C$500 depending on how long you've been outside Canada. To reach the maximum exemption of C$500, you must be gone at least one week. Because Canada is also signatory to NAFTA, customs legalities will continue change.

Returning to the U.K.

Duty-frees include 200 cigarettes (or 50 cigars or 250 grams of tobacco) and one liter of beverage with an alcoholic content of over 22 percent or two liters under 22 percent, plus two liters of wine. The total exemption runs £136.

Returning to Australia

Duty-frees include 200 cigarettes (or 250 grams of tobacco, including cigars) and one liter of alcohol. The total exemption runs $400.

Customs Regulations

Customs regulations can change at any time, so if you want to verify the regulations on a purchase before risking duties or confiscation at the border, check with a consulate in Mexico before crossing, or look on the customs website (in Spanish): www.aduanas.sat.gob.mx.

As NAFTA proceeds with scheduled decreases in trade tariffs among the United States, Canada, and Mexico, expect a steady loosening of customs regulations in all directions until 2009, when all import tariffs are supposed to be erased.

CONDUCT AND ETIQUETTE
Time and Appointments

Of the many stereotypes of Mexican culture, the one about the Mexican sense of time being highly flexible is probably the most accurate. The reasons are too numerous and complex for the context of this book; read *The Labyrinth of Solitude,* by Octavio Paz, for a glimpse of an explanation. That said, it's important to realize that the so-called *mañana* attitude is nothing more than a generalization; in many cases Mexican individuals are every bit as punctual as Americans, Canadians, or northern Europeans—especially when it comes to doing business with them.

If you make an appointment with a Mexican for dinner, a party, or other social engagement, the actual meeting time may end up being an hour or so later than actually scheduled. As with business engagements, if the person involved has dealt frequently with Americans, Canadians, or northern Europeans, this might not always be the case. But even then, 20 or 30 minutes late is considered actually more polite than arriving at the indicated hour. Also, Mexicans will typically accept an invitation rather than decline, even if they don't plan to attend the scheduled event. Within the Mexican social context, it is ruder to refuse an invitation than not to show up. To avoid disappointment, prepare yourself for any of these scenarios.

When hiring any sort of guide, you can expect a modicum of punctuality—Mexicans in the tourist industry usually adapt themselves to the expectations of American and European tourists.

La "Hora" de la Comida

The stereotypical siesta, where everyone goes off to sleep for a couple of hours in the afternoon, is fast becoming a thing of the past throughout Mexico. Nevertheless, a vestige of the siesta is preserved in the operating hours

EMBASSIES IN MEXICO CITY

Argentina
Blvd. M. Avila Camacho 1, 7th floor
Lomas de Chapultepec
55/5520-9430 or 55/5520-9431

Australia
Rubén Dario 55
Polanco
55/5531-5225
www.mexico.embassy.gov.au

Austria
Sierra Tarahumara 420
Lomas de Chapultepec
55/5251-0806
www.embajadadeaustria.com.mx

Belgium
A. Musset 41
Polanco
55/5280-0758 or 55/5280-1133

Belize
Bernardo de Gálvez 215
Lomas de Chapultepec
55/5520-1346 or 55/5520-1274

Bolivia
Insurgentes Sur 263, 6th floor
Roma
55/5564-5415 or 55/5264-6169

Brazil
Lope de Armendariz 130
Lomas de Virreyes
55/5202-7500

Canada
Schiller 529
Polanco
55/5724-7900
www.dfait-maeci.gc.ca/mexico-city

Chile
Andres Bello 10, 18th floor
Polanco
55/5280-9682 or 55/5280-9689

Colombia
Paseo de la Reforma 379
Lomas de Chapultepec
55/5525-0277
www.colombiaenmexico.org

Costa Rica
Río Po 113
Cuauhtémoc
55/5525-7764 or 55/5525-7765

Cuba
Av. Presidente Masaryk 554
Polanco
55/5280-8039
www.embacuba.com.mx

Czech Republic
Cuvier 22
Anzures
55/5531-2544

Denmark
Tres Picos 43
Lomas de Chapultepec
55/5255-4145

Dominican Republic
Guatemala 84
Centro
55/5522-7409

Ecuador
Tennyson 217
Polanco
55/5545-3141 or 55/5250-4999

El Salvador
Temistocles 88
Polanco
55/5281-5723

Finland
Montes Pelvoux 111
Polanco
55/5540-6063
www.finlandia.org.mx

France
Campos Eliseos 339
Polanco
55/5282-9700 or 55/5282-9840
www.francia.org.mx

Germany
Lord Byron 737
Polanco
55/5283-2200
www.embajada-alemana.org.mx

Greece
Sierra Gorda 505
Lomas de Chapultepec
55/5596-6333 or 55/5202-2310

Guatemala
Av. Explanada 1025
Lomas de Chapultepec
55/5520-9249 or 55/5540-7520

Honduras
A. Reyes 220
Hipódromo Condesa
55/5211-5747 or 55/5515-6689

India
Musset 325
Polanco
55/5531-1002 or 55/5531-1085

Israel
Sierra Madre 215
Lomas de Chapultepec
55/5201-1500 or 55/5201-1555
Italy
Paseo de las Palmas 1994
Lomas de Chapultepec
55/5596-3655
www.embitalia.org.mx
Jamaica
Schiller 326, 8th floor
Polanco
55/5250-6804
Japan
Reforma 395
Cuauhtémoc
55/5514-5459
www.embjapon.com.mx
Netherlands
Vasco de Quiroga 3000
Santa Fe
55/5258-9921
New Zealand
J. Luis Lagrange 103
Polanco
55/5283-9460
Nicaragua
Prado Norte 470
Lomas de Chapultepec
55/5540-5625
Norway
Virreyes 1460
Lomas de Chapultepec
55/5540-3486 or 55/5540-3487
Panama
Horacio 1501
Polanco
55/5557-6159 or 55/5557-2793
Paraguay
Homero 415, 2nd floor
Polanco
55/5545-0405 or 55/5545-0403
Peru
Paseo de la Reforma 2601
Lomas de Reforma
55/5259-0239 or 55/5570-2443
Philippines
Sierra Gorda 175
Lomas de Chapultepec
55/5202-8456
Portugal
Alpes 1370
Lomas de Chapultepec
55/5520-7897

Romania
Sófocles 311
Los Morales
55/5280-0197 or 55/5280-0447
Serbia
Av. Montañas Rocallosas 515 Ote.
Lomas de Chapultepec
55/5259-1332 or 55/5520-2523
Slovac Republic
Julio Verne 35
Polanco
55/5280-6544 or 55/5280-6451
South Africa
Andres Bello 10
Polanco
55/5282-9261 or 55/5282-9262
Spain
Galileo 114
Polanco
55/5282-2974 or 55/5282-2982
Sweden
Paseo de las Palmas 1375
Lomas de Chapultepec
55/5540-6393
Switzerland
Paseo de las Palmas 405, 11th floor
Lomas de Chapultepec
55/5520-3003
Turkey
Monte Libano 885
Palmas
55/5282-5043
United Kingdom
Río Lerma 71
Cuauhtémoc
55/5207-2449
www.embajadabritanica.com.mx
United Nations
Av. Presidente Mazaryk 29
Polanco
55/5250-1231
United States
Reforma 305
Cuauhtémoc
55/5080-2000
www.usembassy-mexico.gov
Uruguay
Hegel 149, 1st floor
Polanco
55/5254-1163 or 55/5531-0880
Venezuela
Schiller 326
Polanco
55/5203-4233 or 55/5203-4435

for offices and small businesses, which are typically closed 2–4 P.M. or 3–5 P.M. The first hour is reserved for *comida,* the midday meal, while the second hour is for relaxing or taking care of personal business. While to Americans and Canadians two hours may seem like a long lunch hour, the fact is that Mexican offices and businesses generally stay open later than in the United States or Canada, until 7 or 8 P.M.

No matter what hours are posted for small businesses, the actual opening and closing times may vary with the whims of the proprietors. This is also true for tourist information offices. Banks usually follow their posted hours to the minute.

Terms of Address

Mexicans frequently use titles of respect when addressing one another. At a minimum, *"señor"* will do for men, *"señora"* for married women, and *"señorita"* for unmarried women or girls.

Professional titles can also be used for variety and to show additional respect. *Maestro* (master) or *maestra* (mistress) are common and can be used to address skilled workers (cobblers, auto mechanics, seamstresses, etc.) and any teacher except those at secondary schools and colleges or universities, who are *profesores* (men) or *profesoras* (women).

College graduates are *licenciado* (men) or *licenciada* (women), while doctors are *doctor* or *doctora.* Some other professional titles include *arquitecto* (architect), *abogado* (attorney), *ingeniero* (engineer), and *químico* (chemist).

Body Language

Mexicans tend to use their arms and hands more during verbal communication than do their American, Canadian, or northern European counterparts. Learning to read the more common gestures can greatly enhance your comprehension of everyday conversations, even when you don't understand every word being spoken.

One of the more confusing gestures for Americans and Canadians is the way Mexicans beckon to other people by holding the hand out, palm down, and waving in a downward motion. Holding the palm upward and crooking the fingers toward the body—the typical American or Canadian gesture for "come here"—is a vaguely obscene gesture in Mexico.

Extending the thumb and forefinger from a closed hand and holding them about a half-inch apart means "a little bit" in the U.S. and Canada, but in Mexico, it usually means "just a moment" or "wait a minute" (often accompanied by the utterance *"momentito"*). The wagging of an upright forefinger means "No" or "Don't do that."

Mexicans commonly greet one another with handshakes, which are used between the sexes and among children and adults—in fact, with everybody. Mexican males who are friends will sometimes greet one another with a handshake, followed by an *abrazo* (embrace), and completed with another handshake, and urban women may kiss one another on the cheek. Foreigners should stick to the handshake until they establish more familiar relationships. Handshakes are also used upon parting and saying farewell.

Dress

Mexicans are relatively tolerant of the way visitors dress. Nonetheless, invisible lines exist that—out of respect for Mexican custom—shouldn't be crossed. In Mexico City almost no one ever wears shorts; although this is mainly because of the cool year-round climate, it also demonstrates that *capitalinos* tend to be more formal in dress than Mexicans in many other cities, especially those on the coast.

Upon entering a church or chapel in Mexico, men are expected to remove their hats. Many Mexican males will also remove their hats when passing in front of a church. More tradition-minded Mexican women will cover their heads when inside a church, but younger women usually don't, and foreign females aren't expected to. Shorts, sleeveless shirts/blouses, sandals, or bare feet are considered improper dress for both men and women in churches, even for brief sightseeing visits.

Tips for Travelers

STUDYING IN MEXICO
Spanish Language and Mexican Culture

Mexico City is an excellent place to study Spanish. In the first place, the level of spoken Spanish in the city is among the highest in the country, and just as important, it's a very friendly and open city, where Mexicans generally don't hesitate to speak to strangers, whatever their nationality. This isn't necessarily the case in other state capitals in Mexico.

Since 1921, the Universidad Nacional Autónoma de México (UNAM) has operated the Centro de Enseñanza para Extranjeros (CEPE), a special division of the university dedicated to teaching Mexican history, culture, and language. The programs enjoy a very good reputation and are divided among six departments: Spanish, Art History, History, Social Sciences, Literature, and Chicano Studies. The popular Spanish courses generally run three hours per day. Sessions run year-round, although the summer session, which combines language with cultural and historical studies, is the most intensive. A sampling of courses offered in the summer session include Mexican Art, Popular Culture in Xochimilco, Traditional Medicine in Xochimilco, Traditional Mexican Dance, 20th-Century Mexican Theater, History of Modern and Contemporary Mexico, History of Science in Mexico, Myth and Rationality in Contemporary Mexico, Mexican Literature, Contemporary Mexican Women Writers, Images of Mexico through Literary Texts, and Chicano-Latino Community in the United States.

UNAM also runs special training programs for teachers of Spanish as a Second Language (SSL). For all courses, tuition is reasonable, and CEPE can arrange housing either with local families or in dormitories. For further information contact CEPE-México (Apartado Postal 70–391, Ciudad Universitaria, 04510 México D.F., 55/5622-2470, www.cepe.unam.mx).

UNAM/CEPE also has a branch in Taxco (CEPE-Taxco, Ex-Hacienda El Chorrillo, Apartado Postal 70, 40200 Taxco, Gro., México, tel./fax 762/622-0124).

Universidad La Salle (Benjamin Franklin 65, Col. Condesa, 55/5728-0500, www.ulsa.edu. mx) offers good, inexpensive Spanish group classes and is closer to the center of the city than UNAM.

International House Mexico City is run by Language Link of Peoria, Illinois (800/552-2051, fax 309/692-2926, www.langlink. com). Programs include classes in the Colonia Condesa and, if desired, homestays with a Mexican family.

The city of Cuernavaca, an hour's drive south of Mexico City, is a very popular place for foreigners to take intensive Spanish courses for several weeks. (For more information, see the *Excursions from Mexico City* chapter.)

For a learning experience more oriented toward art and culture, consider taking one of the couple of dozen university-level courses each year on art, literature, music, politics, and society at the **Casa Lamm** (Álvaro Obregón 99 at Orizaba, 55/5514-4899, www.lamm.com. mx). Courses cost $200–800 per four-month semester. A program of guided visits to 10 different art galleries in the city over the course of a semester costs $250. Visit their website or call for more information.

EMPLOYMENT IN MEXICO CITY

A great many foreigners find themselves looking for ways to get by in Mexico City for a couple of months or a couple of years. Because it is one of the principal capitals of the Americas, and because it is uniquely linked to the United States economy through NAFTA, Mexico City is brimming with business activity. Would-be residents could try contacting their embassy and asking if they have information on work opportunities in Mexico. The U.S. Chamber of Commerce (Lucerna 78, near Paseo de la

Reforma, 55/5141-3800, www.amcham.com.
mx) maintains some information on jobs with
U.S. companies in Mexico.

Teaching English

The most popular way of making cash for
footloose visitors is teaching English at one
of the literally hundreds of English schools
in Mexico City. Hours are flexible, and pay is
usually around $7–10 an hour. The trick is to
put together enough hours to make a decent
living and to make sure the school pays you
regularly (some are notoriously shifty in this regard). A livable, though hardly luxurious, wage
is $1,000–1,200 a month.

While some schools require a TEFL
(Teaching English as a Foreign Language)
certificate, most do not. Schools generally pay
certified teachers better, and often they are able
to arrange private classes on the side.

Angloamericano (55/5658-6700 or 55/5659-
2148, www.angloamericano.com.mx), which
has schools in Polanco, Coyoacán, and Satélite,
has received decent reviews from foreign teachers. Apart from English, it sometimes needs
teachers for French, German, and Italian.

Harmon Hall (55/5211-2020, www.harmon-
hall.com) has schools all over the city (in fact,
all over the country) and is always looking for
teachers, but its pay scale is among the lowest.

To find others, just open the yellow pages
and start calling around. Beware that at some
of the smaller schools, payment can sometimes
be unreliable.

Journalism

As the number-one media center in Latin
America, Mexico City can be an excellent place
to get a start as a reporter. The favored place
for inexperienced writers to get a foot in the
door used to be *The News,* an English-language
daily established in 1950 by the Mexican publishing company *Novedades.* When *Novedades*
closed its doors in 2003, so did *The News,* to
the nostalgic chagrin of many a veteran, my-
self included. But in October 2007 it began
printing again as a daily, this time as an independent newspaper not affiliated with another

company. Hopes are up that it will continue—
there's certainly a market for it, as the newspaper was profitable up to when *Novedades* closed
down. At last check their website (www.the-
news.com.mx) was not yet up and running, is
expected to be soon, and the paper would be a
great option for budding journalists looking to
get a start abroad. *Latin Trade* (www.latintrade.
com), *Latin Finance* (www.latinfinance.com),
and many other outlets are still frequently on
the lookout for freelance writers, especially if
they can cover business news.

Mexican newspapers are often in the market for part-time translators. If your Spanish is
good (and it better be if you want to translate!),
pick up copies of all the major newspapers and
start calling around.

APARTMENTS

Compared to large cities in Europe and
America, housing in Mexico City is reasonable in price. Wealthier residents tend to live
in Polanco and farther west along Paseo de la
Reforma, in the Bosques and Lomas neighborhoods. San Ángel and Coyoacán are also more
upscale, though not as much, while Roma and
Condesa are favored by younger expatriates
who can afford the steadily rising rents. Del
Valle, south of Roma along Insurgentes, is also
a quiet residential neighborhood with many
apartment buildings. Colonia Cuauhtémoc,
north of Paseo de la Reforma, has both inexpensive and higher-end apartments. Real
penny-pinchers (or those fascinated with relentless urbanity) might consider checking out
the many old, lovely buildings in the Centro.

Rents for a mid-range two-bedroom apartment in the Condesa/Roma/Cuauhtémoc
areas run around $800–1,600 a month, while
Polanco apartments easily run $2,000–3,000.
In the Centro, decent places can be found for
as low as $300–700.

Word of mouth is the best way to find a good
apartment, but failing that, the ads in *Segunda
Mano* (a weekly classifieds publication) will
give you plenty of places to start. The daily
ads in *El Universal* are also extensive. Another
good technique is to choose a neighborhood

you want to live in and prowl the streets looking for *se renta* signs on buildings.

Red Tape

Most apartment contracts in Mexico City are fairly standard affairs, usually just a template bought at a local stationery store with the names, dates, and numbers filled in. Contracts usually extend by the year, although most landlords are amenable to shortening it if you notify them well in advance, and especially if you arrange for someone to take your place. If not, you may lose your deposit.

Landlords commonly request first and last months' rent, as well as an unusual requirement: a *fiador,* someone who owns property in Mexico City who is willing to sign a paper making themselves responsible for the rent if you do not pay.

Needless to say, many foreigners have a hard time finding a *fiador.* The options are twofold. The best plan is to try to convince the landlord that you are a responsible person, perhaps offering to pay a couple of months ahead of time. Long accustomed to Mexican tenants who go for months without paying (and who are very difficult to evict under Mexican law), landlords are often very well disposed toward potential non-Mexican tenants, as they have a reputation for paying on time. Thus they may sometimes waive the *fiador* requirement.

However, if the landlord is rigid, or if a real estate company (rather than an individual) is managing the apartment, the only option if you don't have a *fiador* is to buy a *fianza,* or a bond, from a local bank, which serves as your guarantee. The amount of the bond depends on the apartment rent but will run at least a few hundred dollars.

Utilities

Usually water is included in the rent, while tenants pay for electricity. This minimal fee can be paid at local banks if paid before the due date but only at the offices of Luz y Fuerza del Centro if you're late. It can take several days to reconnect after being cut off.

Water heaters and stoves invariably run on gas, which is either supplied from a tank attached to your building (in which case you will be charged each month) or sold in 30-kilo tanks ($17) to individual tenants from gas trucks that circulate a couple of days each week.

If a phone line is already installed, you will often have to buy it from the previous tenant or the landlord (usually $100–200). If the apartment has no line, you'll have to go down to the local TelMex office, wait in line for an hour or two, and pay $150 to get a new personal telephone line or $300 for a commercial telephone line. Company workers will usually come to your apartment one or two weeks later to install the line. While TelMex has a monopoly on local service, clients may choose among several long-distance providers.

Health and Safety

By and large, Mexico City is a healthy place. Sanitation standards, particularly in the areas most tourists are likely to visit, are relatively high compared to many other parts of Latin America.

FOOD AND WATER

Visitors who use common sense will probably never come down with food- or water-related illnesses while traveling in and around Mexico City. The first rule is not to overdo it during the first few days of your trip—eat and drink with moderation. Shoveling down huge amounts of tasty but often heavy Mexican foods along with pitchers of margaritas or Mexican beer is liable to make anyone sick from pure overindulgence. If you're not used to the spices and different ways of cooking, it's best to ingest small amounts at first.

Second, take it easy with foods offered by

street vendors, because this is where you're most likely to suffer from unsanitary conditions. Eat only foods that have been thoroughly cooked and are served either stove-hot or refrigerator-cold. Many visitors eat street food without any problems, but it pays to be cautious, especially if it's your first time in Mexico. One rule of thumb is to eat street food only where you see a lot of other clients, which is a good indication of quality and also means there's a lot of turnover, so the food isn't sitting around a long time. Squeezing lots of the ever-present limes over food also helps kill germs.

Hotels and restaurants serve only purified drinking water and ice, so there's no need to ask for mineral water or to refuse ice. Tap water, however, should not be consumed except in hotels that have a water-purification system—if so, you'll be informed by a notice over the washbasin in your room. Just about every grocery or convenience store sells bottled purified water (*agua purificada*). Water-purification tablets, iodine crystals, and water filters aren't necessary for Mexico travel unless you plan on extensive camping.

Turista

People who've never traveled to a foreign country may undergo a period of adjustment to the new gastrointestinal flora that comes with new territory. There's really no way to avoid the differences wrought by sheer distances. Unfortunately, the adjustment is sometimes unpleasant.

Mexican doctors call gastrointestinal upset of this sort *turista* because it affects tourists but not the local population. The usual symptoms of *turista*—also known by the gringo tags "Montezuma's Revenge" and "Aztec Two-Step"—are nausea and diarrhea, sometimes with stomach cramps and a low fever. Eating and drinking in moderation will help prevent the worst of the symptoms, which rarely persist for more than a day or two. If it's any consolation, Mexicans often get sick the first time they go abroad too.

Some Mexico travelers swear by a preventive regimen of Pepto-Bismol, begun the day before arrival in the country. Opinions vary as to how much of the pink stuff is necessary to ward off or tame the evil flora, but a person probably shouldn't exceed the recommended daily dose. Taper off over the second week, until you stop using it altogether.

If you come down with a case of *turista,* the best thing to do is drink plenty of fluids. Adults should drink at least three quarts or liters a day, a child under 37 kilograms at least a liter a day. Lay off tea, coffee, milk, acidic fruit juices, and booze. Eat only bland foods—nothing spicy, fatty, or fried—and take it easy. Pepto-Bismol or similar pectin-based remedies usually help. Some people like to mask the symptoms with a strong over-the-counter medication such as Imodium AD (loperamide is the active ingredient), but though this can be very effective, it isn't a cure. Only time will cure traveler's diarrhea.

If the symptoms are unusually severe (especially if there's blood in the stools) or persist for more than one or two days, see a doctor. It could be a case of amoebic or bacterial dysentery. Most hotels can arrange a doctor's visit, or you can contact a Mexican tourist office or your consulate for recommendations.

SUNBURN AND DEHYDRATION

Sunburn probably afflicts more Mexico visitors than all other illnesses and injuries combined. The sunlight can be very strong at the Valle de México's elevation, especially if you go to high mountain areas and have fair skin. For outdoor forays, sun protection is a must, whatever the activity. The longer you're in the sun, the more protection you'll need.

It's also important to drink plenty of water and/or nonalcoholic, noncaffeinated fluids to avoid dehydration. Alcohol and caffeine—including the caffeine in iced tea and colas—only increase your potential for dehydration. Symptoms of dehydration include darker-than-usual urine or inability to urinate, flushed face, profuse sweating or an unusual lack thereof, and sometimes a headache, dizziness, and general feeling of malaise. Extreme cases of dehydration can lead to heat exhaustion or even heatstroke, in which the victim may become delirious and/

or convulse. If either condition is suspected, get the victim out of the sun immediately, cover with a wet sheet or towel, and administer a re-hydration fluid that replaces lost water and salts. If you can get the victim to a doctor, all the better—heatstroke can be very serious.

ALTITUDE SICKNESS

Some visitors who fly into the 2,240-meter (7,347-foot) Mexico City airport experience mild altitude sickness shortly after arrival. Symptoms include headache, shaky stomach, breathlessness, and general malaise. The body needs time to acclimate to the change in baro-metric pressure and lesser amounts of oxygen. Those afflicted need to take it easy for a while: no running, no climbing pyramids, no alcohol. The city's polluted air may exacerbate symptoms. Those with medical problems relating to the heart or lungs should probably consult with a doctor before even considering a trip to Mexico's higher climes. Some people find it takes them two or three days to fully adjust to the elevation when flying in from places at or near sea level.

Altitude sickness strikes some people at elevations as low as 1,600 meters. Others don't feel a thing until they reach much higher elevations. Above 3,000 meters, acute mountain sickness (AMS) can occur—headache, loss of appetite, lethargy, shortness of breath, and insomnia are all pronounced. You're not likely to experience AMS unless you climb the higher volcanoes outside Mexico City. If you think you've been stricken, descending at least 300–600 meters should result in immediate relief. You can usually avoid AMS with a slow, step-by-step ascent. The climber's adage is to sleep no more than 300 meters higher than the place you slept the night before.

MEDICAL ASSISTANCE

The quality of basic medical treatment, including dentistry, is relatively high in Mexico City; ask at a tourist office or at your embassy for recommendations. Large hotels usually have a doctor on staff or a list of recommended physicians in the neighborhood.

Polanco is the best area for private medical clinics, where a consultation will run $25–60. Another good option is to call the Hospital ABC, which has a referral service for quality doctors of different specializations.

An ambulance may be summoned via Cruz Roja (Red Cross) by dialing 065 or 55/5557-5757.

Hospitals

Hospital American British Cowdray (ABC) (Calle Sur 136, No. 116, 55/5230-8000 or 55/5230-8161, www.abchospital.com), at the corner of Avenida Observatorio, south of Bosque de Chapultepec in Colonia Las Américas, is considered the best hospital in the city, and prices are accordingly high.

Another well-regarded hospital is **Hospital Español** (Ejército Nacional 613, Polanco, 55/5255-9700 for ambulances and 55/5255-9600 general information, www.hespanol.com).

Emergency Evacuation

Several American companies offer emergency 24-hour airlift service (accompanied by licensed physicians and nurses) from anywhere in Mexico to U.S. hospitals. Two of the longer-running operations are **Air Evac Services, Inc.** (2630 Sky Harbor Blvd., Phoenix, AZ 85034, toll-free in U.S. and Canada 800/321-9522, www.airevac.com) and **Advanced Aeromedical Air Ambulance Service** (P.O. Box 5726, Virginia Beach, VA 23471, 757/481-1590 or toll-free in U.S. and Canada 800/346-3556, www.aeromedic.com).

SAFETY CONCERNS

Until the 1980s, Mexico City enjoyed a reputation for being one of the safest large cities in the Americas. The image suffered a reversal after the economic crisis of 1994–1995, when the peso plummeted, unemployment soared, and some urban residents began resorting to robbery as a way to make up income short-falls—or to lash out at the crisis, if you take the psychological explanation. In both cases, before and after 1994–1995, the image was exaggerated. Mexico City was never as free from

policias charros (cowboy cops) in the Alameda, with Hotel de Cortés in the background

©CHRIS HUMPHREY

crime as, for example, Tokyo or Zurich, and nowadays it's nowhere near as bad as Nairobi or Bogotá, not to mention most large metropolitan areas in the United States.

To put things into perspective, FBI statistics indicate that Washington, DC, by comparison has a crime rate 230 percent above Mexico City's, while Los Angeles crime indices are 94 percent higher, New York's 63 percent higher, and Detroit's 292 percent higher. On the other hand, there is general agreement that crime increased substantially (most experts estimate a 35 percent increase) since the 1994–1995 economic crisis and has improved marginally if at all since the new opposition-led administrations after 1997.

Precautions

In general, visitors to Mexico City should take the same precautions they would when traveling anywhere in their own countries or abroad. Keep money and valuables secured, either in a hotel safe or safe deposit box, or in a money belt or other hard-to-reach place on your person.

Keep an eye on cameras and purses to make sure you don't leave them behind in restaurants, hotels, or campgrounds. At night, lock the doors to your hotel room and vehicle. Don't take taxis from the street; instead call an inexpensive *sitio* to pick you up—that alone will considerably reduce your chances of getting mugged, since street-taxi holdups are the most common way by far for foreigners to be robbed.

Take extra caution after dark, when certain districts that are safe during the daytime—such as the Centro Histórico—become a little riskier. Walking alone in the less-populated streets of the historic center after 9 P.M. is not a great idea. Even more dicey are the run-down neighborhoods north, northwest, and east of the Centro Histórico. Polanco, the Zona Rosa, the Roma, and the Condesa all seem to fare better after dark, though even in these areas you should stay alert. Stick to well-lighted areas and keep a steady, determined-looking pace. The centers of San Ángel and Coyoacán are relatively safe to walk around both day and night.

It's a good idea to carry limited cash and

credit cards—no more than you need for an outing—when moving about the city. Don't wear expensive-looking clothes or jewelry. If confronted by someone intent on robbing you, don't resist. The only instances of violence I've heard about occurred where the robbery victims tried to resist. Most Mexican thieves are simply out for quick cash, and are not nearly as likely to harm a victim as muggers in the United States are.

If you'll be using ATM machines as a source of cash, using off-street machines, such as those found inside many department stores (including Sanborns), is a good idea.

When riding the Metro or public buses, watch out for pickpockets, particularly when these modes of transport are crowded.

Help

The city's emergency telephone number for reporting criminal acts, 060, is designed to facilitate the reporting of crimes committed against tourists and residents alike. When an individual calls this number, a representative of the Ministerios Públicos Moviles (Mobile Justice Department) reports to the scene of the crime or, when tourists are involved, to their hotel to register the complaint. Tourist assistance, 078, can also be useful.

One city attorney general's office (where crimes are reported and investigated, in the Mexican legal system) accustomed to dealing with foreigners is the **Ministerio Público** (Amberes 54 at Londres, 55/5345-5382), right in the heart of the Zona Rosa. The staff here can help in English, French, or German. They are open daily 9 A.M.–5 P.M. Another Ministerio Público office for tourists closer to the Centro is located at Victoria 76, three

blocks south of the Alameda (55/5346-8881, daily 9 A.M.–7 P.M.). These are the offices to go to for reporting robberies or other crimes.

Legal Matters

All foreign visitors in Mexico are subject to Mexican legal codes, which are based on Roman and Napoleonic law updated with U.S. constitutional theory and civil law. The most distinctive features of the Mexican judiciary system, compared to Anglo-American systems, are that the system doesn't provide for trials by jury (the judge decides) nor writs of habeas corpus (though you must be charged within 72 hours of incarceration). Furthermore, bail is rarely granted to an arrested foreigner—for many offenses, not even Mexican nationals are allowed bail. Hence, once you're arrested and jailed for a serious offense, it can be very difficult to arrange release. The lesson here is: Don't get involved in matters that might result in your arrest. This primarily means anything having to do with drugs or guns.

The oft-repeated saw that in Mexico an arrested person is considered guilty until proven innocent is no more true south of the border than north. As in Canada, the United States, and most of Europe, an arrested person is considered a criminal *suspect* until the courts confirm or deny guilt. You have the right to notify your consulate if detained.

If you get into trouble with Mexican law, for whatever reason, you should try to contact your consulate in Mexico. Sectur and state tourist offices can also help in some instances. These agencies routinely handle emergency legal matters involving visiting foreigners; you stand a much better chance of resolving legal difficulties with their assistance.

Money

CURRENCY

The unit of exchange in Mexico is the peso, which comes in paper denominations of 20, 50, 100, 200, and 500. Coins are available in denominations of 5, 10, 20, and 50 centavos, and 1, 2, 5, 10, and 20 pesos.

Prices

The N$ symbol (standing for "new pesos" to differentiate from pre-1993 "old pesos") is sometimes, though rarely these days, used for indicating peso prices. Much more common now is the $ symbol for pesos. While it's highly unlikely you'll ever confuse dollar and peso prices because of the differing values, you should ask when in doubt. In this book, I refer to all prices in U.S. dollar terms.

Because coins smaller than one peso are often scarce, payments are sometimes rounded off to the nearest peso or at least to the nearest 50 centavos. For a marked price of $8.55, for example, you actually have to pay only $8.50; for a $8.75 price you may have to pay $9. Any denomination over $50 is difficult to break, so change them at every opportunity to secure a good supply of smaller notes and coins.

Dollars vs. Pesos

A few commercial establishments in Mexico City will take U.S. dollars as well as pesos. Paying with pesos, however, usually means a better deal when the price is fixed in pesos; if you pay in dollars for a purchase quoted in pesos, the vendor can determine the exchange rate. If a bottle of boutique tequila, for example, is marked at $280, and the bank rate is $10 per dollar, you'll pay $28 for the tequila with pesos changed at the bank. However, if you ask to pay in dollars, the vendor may charge $30.

Devaluation

The Mexican peso has had a tumultuous history in the past 30 years, but since 1998, the currency has been remarkably stable, even gaining value at times, despite floating (relatively) freely in the international market. The combination of a floating currency, restrained government spending policies, and a strong, independent central bank have combined to avoid dramatic plunges in the currency's value. At last report, the peso was around 10.8 to the dollar.

CHANGING MONEY

In general, changing money is not at all difficult in Mexico City. The most hassle-free way to get pesos is with an ATM card; they are widely accepted in Mexican banks and invariably offer the best and most up-to-the-minute exchange rate. Almost all Mexican banks are now owned by foreign banks, meaning the ATMs are all connected to most international networks.

Banks

Banks that handle foreign exchange generally accept a wide range of foreign currencies, including the euro, English pounds, Japanese yen, and Canadian dollars. Either cash or travelers checks are accepted, though the latter usually guarantee a slightly better exchange rate. The main drawbacks with banks are the long lines and short hours—9 A.M.–3 P.M. Monday–Friday, but the foreign-exchange service usually closes about noon–12:30 P.M.

Casas de Cambio

The second-best exchange rate, generally speaking, is found at the *casa de cambio,* or private money-changing office. The *casa de cambio* (also called *servicio de cambio*) either knocks a few centavos off the going bank rate or charges a percentage commission. It pays to shop around for the best *casa de cambio* rates, as some places charge considerably more than others. The rates are usually posted; *compra,* always the lower figure, refers to the buying rate (how many pesos you'll receive per dollar or other foreign currency), while *vende* is the selling rate (how many pesos you must pay to receive a dollar or other unit of foreign currency). As with banks, the difference between the buying and selling rates is the moneychanger's profit, unless it charges a commission on top of it.

Moneychangers are usually open much later than banks; some even work evening hours, which makes them more convenient than banks. U.S. dollar currency is generally preferred, though many *casas* will also accept Canadian dollars, Euros, and other foreign currencies, as well as travelers checks.

One of the better *casas de cambio* in the Centro is **Casa de Cambio Plus** (Paseo de la Reforma 449, Mon.–Fri. 9 A.M.–7 P.M., Sat. 9:30 A.M.–1:30 P.M.). Another in the Centro Histórico is **Casa de Cambio Tiber** (Madero 265, Mon.–Fri. 9 A.M.–5 P.M., Sat. 10 A.M.–2:30 P.M.).

The bank exchange booths at the Mexico City airport offer regular bank rates and are open long hours (some stay open 24 hours), so the airport is a good place to change some money on arrival. You'll also find ATMs and *casas de cambio* in the airport.

Credit Cards, Debit Cards, and ATM Cards

Plastic money (primarily Visa and MasterCard, and to a lesser extent, American Express) is widely accepted at large hotels, restaurants catering to tourists or businesspeople, car rentals (you can't rent a car without a credit card), and shops in tourist centers. Usually card displays at the cash register or on the door will announce that *tarjetas de crédito* (credit cards) are accepted. If in doubt, flash one and ask *"¿Se aceptan tarjetas de crédito?"* (Do you accept credit cards?) or simply *"¿Está bien?"* (Is it OK?). A reference to *efectivo* means cash. Many shops and some hotels add a 3 to 6 percent surcharge to bills paid with a card.

Cash advances on credit card accounts—a very useful service for emergencies—are available at Mexican banks. Keep in mind, however, that most credit card companies charge a much higher interest rate for cash advances.

Many banks now accept MasterCard or Visa debit cards ("cash" or "check" cards), as well as international ATM cards. Using such cards to obtain pesos from ATMs in Mexico is a much more convenient way to carry travel funds than

using travelers checks. Some banks that issue ATM cards charge transaction fees for use of another bank's ATMs; check with your bank to see how much they are. Most Mexican banks now charge nominal fees for withdrawing cash from their ATMs using a card from another bank.

Travelers Checks

If you decide to bring travelers checks, **American Express** is the most recognized type you can carry. Should you lose your AmEx checks, or should you need to buy more, go to the American Express office (Paseo de la Reforma 350, México D.F. 06600, Mexico, 55/5207-7204 or 5207-7049, Mon.–Fri. 9 A.M.–6 P.M., Sat. 9 A.M.–1 P.M.). AmEx maintains a 24-hour hotline, 55/5326-3625, for reporting lost or stolen checks or credit cards.

MONEY MANAGEMENT
Estimating Costs

Inflation in Mexico is running under 5 percent per annum, and barring major international financial crisis, it will likely stay that way. This doesn't mean that there won't be any increase in prices by the time you arrive. A couple of phone calls to hotels for price quotes should give you an idea how much rates have increased, if at all; this difference can be applied as a percentage to all other prices for a rough estimate of costs.

Students and seniors can frequently obtain discounts on the admission to many tourist sites—be sure to ask, and have your credential in hand.

Tipping

A tip of 10 percent is customary at restaurants with table service unless a service charge is added to the bill (be sure to look). Tips are not expected at less-expensive lunch or snack restaurants. Luggage handling at hotels or airports warrants a tip of $0.50–1, or the equivalent in pesos, per bag. A few hotels maintain a no-tipping policy; details will be posted in your room. The tipping of chambermaids is optional according to Mexican custom—some guests tip, and some don't. Remember that these folks typically earn minimum wage; even a small tip may mean a lot to them.

Taxes

An *impuesto al valor agregado* (IVA, or value-added tax) of 15 percent is tacked onto all goods and services, including hotel and restaurant bills as well as international phone calls. Hotels add a further 2 percent lodging tax. Some hotel rate quotes include taxes, but to make sure, you might ask *"¿Se incluye los impuestos?"* (Are taxes included?).

Bank Accounts

For long-term stays in Mexico—six months or more—visitors might consider opening a Mexican bank account. Now that peso deflation has been virtually halted, a peso account seems quite safe. While the 1994–1995 devaluation devastated the banking system, no depositers ever lost their savings. Essentially all Mexican banks are now owned by foreign companies, and many offer dollar- and even euro-denominated accounts now.

Maps and Tourist Information

MAPS

The government statistics institute, **Instituto Estadísticas, Geografía e Información (INEGI)** (Balderas 71, 55/5512-8331, Mon.–Fri. 9 A.M.–8 P.M.; Patriotismo 711, 55/5278-1000, www.inegi.gob.mx), sells a variety of maps, as well as statistical yearbooks and other information resources. They also have a small store at the airport's domestic terminal.

Mexico City Maps

Most casual Mexico City visitors will find the maps in this guide adequate for their needs, although they may wish to pick up a free foldout map designed by the Mexico City Tourist Department for easier reference. The foldout pamphlet has maps of the Centro, Reforma/Chapultepec/Polanco/Condesa, San Ángel, Coyoacán, the Metro, and a broad sketch map of the entire city. It's well made, easy to read, and printed on fairly sturdy paper that will hold up better than most paper maps. You can pick them up at any of the tourist information booths around the city, if they haven't run out (see the sidebar *Tourist Information Booths* for addresses).

If you're planning to take up residence in the capital, you'll want to go a step further and get the thick *Cuidad de México Area Metropolitana* street atlas published by Guía Roji (www.guiaroji.com), which has a scale of 1:22,500 and costs around $10 if you buy it in D.F., or around $16–20 abroad. It covers every corner of the Distrito Federal and includes two complete indexes, one by street name and one by *colonia*. Guía Roji also publishes a simple two-sided folding street map ($4 in Mexico City, up to $9 abroad), *Ciudad de México*, with a scale of 1:30,000, but it's really not a very good map. Another Mexican-made sheet map of similar quality is Pronto's *Ciudad de México*, which costs about the same as the Guía Roji sheet map.

Highway Maps

Those planning to spend time on Mexico's back roads should buy a Mexican road atlas. The best available is the annual 127-page *Guía Roji por las Carreteras de México*, published in Mexico but available through Treaty Oak (P.O. Box 50295, Austin, TX 78763, 512/326-4141, www.treatyoak.com) and Map Link (25 E. Mason, Santa Barbara, CA 93101, 805/965-4402, fax 805/962-0884, www.maplink.com), as well as many travel bookstores abroad and in Mexican department stores. This atlas contains 38 double-page maps with a scale of 1:1,000,000 (1 inch equals 25 kilometers), along with color graphics to indicate forests and woodlands, deserts, and marshlands. Best of all, the atlas includes a fairly complete network of unpaved roads, villages,

TOURIST INFORMATION BOOTHS

Aeropuerto Internacional de la Ciudad de México
Llegada Nacional Local 9
55/5786-9002
Daily 7 A.M.-10 P.M.

Bellas Artes
Av. Juárez and Angela Peralta (betw. Bellas Artes and the Alameda)
55/5518-2799
Daily 9 A.M.-6 P.M.

Centro
West side of the Catedral
55/5518-1003
Daily 9 A.M.-6 P.M.

Chapultepec
In front of Anthropology Museum
Paseo de la Reforma
55/5286-3850
Daily 9 A.M.-6 P.M.

Terminal Observatorio
55/5272-8816
Daily 9 A.M.-6 P.M.

Terminal 100 Metros
Terminal de Autobuses del Norte
55/5719-1201
Daily 9 A.M.-6 P.M.

Terminal TAPO
55/5784-3077
Daily 9 A.M.-6 P.M.

Terminal Tasqueña
Door 3
55/5336-2321
Daily 9 A.M.-6 P.M.

Zona Rosa
Paseo de la Reforma and Florencia
55/5208-1030
Daily 9 A.M.-6 P.M.

and *ejidos*. Another plus is that the atlas includes 15 city maps.

Guía Roji also publishes state maps at 1:800,000 scale, simple to read and adequate for most purposes, and a well-updated booklet of maps covering the entire country.

Topographical Maps

Because differences in elevation often determine backcountry route selection, hikers, kayakers, mountain bikers, and off-road drivers should consider using topographical maps. You can obtain these in advance from Treaty Oak or Map Link in the United States, or in Mexico from INEGI.

TOURIST INFORMATION

Mexico City has its own tourist office, the **Secretaría de Turismo de la Ciudad de México** (Av. Nuevo León 56, 9th fl., Col. Hipódromo Condesa, 55/5286-9077, fax 55/5286-9022, www.mexicocity.gob.mx). For the most part this is an administrative office, so if it's information you need, you're better off visiting one of the several tourist suboffices (*módulos de información turística*) around the city and at the airport (see the sidebar *Tourist Information Booths* for addresses). These small offices usually stock a variety of free brochures, maps, hotel and restaurant lists, and information on local activities, and are staffed by Mexicans who are trained to handle visitor queries. Some speak very good English, others not.

The federal government also operates a national tourism secretariat, the **Secretaría de Turismo de México** (Av. Presidente Mazaryk 172, México, D.F. 11570, 55/5250-0151 or 55/5250-0123, in U.S. 800/482-9832, fax 55/5250-6610, www.mexico-travel.com). Again, this office isn't much good with walk-in requests, and they don't have information on the city itself, just the rest of the country. Their telephone service for general tourist information (dial 078), however, can be quite useful for answering basic questions.

Translators and Interpreters

- **AHPLA Institute** (Juan Escutia 97, Col. Condesa, 55/5286-9016, www.ahpla.com)

- **Berlitz de México** (Eugenio Sué 316, Col. Polanco, 55/5545-0644 or 55/5545-0650, www.berlitz.com.mx)

- **Koiné** (Bajío 335–104, Col. Roma Sur, 55/5264-6787 or 55/5564-5256, koine traductores@prodigy.com.mx)

- **Recursos Técnicos para Conferencias** (Eugenia 13–602, Col. Nápoles, 55/5543-5011 or 55/5543-3517)

- **Traducciones Willy de Winter** (Horacio 528–404, Col. Polanco, 55/5545-5764 or 55/5254-7446, willywinter@infosel.net.mx)

TIME, POWER, AND MEASUREMENTS
Time

Mexico City time coincides with central standard time in the United States and is six hours ahead of Greenwich Mean Time (GMT -6). Between the first Sunday in April and the last Sunday in October each year, Mexico City changes by one hour to central daylight saving time.

Time in Mexico is commonly expressed according to the 24-hour clock, from 0001 to 2400 (one minute past midnight to midnight). A restaurant posting hours of 1100–2200, for example, is open 11 A.M.–10 P.M. according to the 12-hour clock popular in the United States. Signs in Mexico may be posted using either system.

Business Hours

The typical small business will be open Monday to Friday (plus Saturday for retail businesses) 9 A.M.–2 P.M., then closed until 4 or 5 P.M., and then open again until 7 or 8 P.M. Official government offices typically maintain an 9 A.M.–7 P.M. schedule, with a 2–3 P.M. lunch hour.

Banks are open Monday to Friday 8:30 A.M.–3 P.M., but remember that the foreign exchange service usually closes about noon (probably to lock in the exchange rate before afternoon adjustments). A few competitive banks have extended their hours as late as 5 P.M.

Electricity

Mexico's electrical system is the same as those in the United States and Canada: 110 volts, 60 cycles, alternating current (AC). Electrical outlets are of the American type, designed to work with appliances that have standard double-bladed plugs. Small towns in some rural areas may experience brief interruptions of electrical service or periods of brownout (voltage decrease). In a few villages, gasoline-powered generators are the only sources of electricity and they may be turned off during the day.

Measurements

Mexico uses the metric system as the official system of weights and measures. This means the distance between Nogales and Mazatlán is measured in kilometers, cheese is weighed in grams or kilograms, a hot day in Monterrey is 32°C, gasoline is sold by the liter, and a big fish is two meters long. The conversion chart at the back of this book will help Americans make the conversions from pounds, gallons, and miles to kilos, liters, and kilometers when necessary.

Communications and Media

COMMUNICATIONS
Postal Service

The Mexican postal service is mostly reliable, though relatively slow. Average delivery time between Mexico and the United States or Canada for letters is about 10 days, while to Europe figure two weeks. Mail sent to Mexico from outside the country generally reaches its destination more quickly.

Most post offices (*correos*) in Mexico City accept general delivery mail. Have correspondents address mail in your name (last name capitalized), followed by "a/c Lista de Correos," the *colonia* name, and the postal code (e.g., Chris HUMPHREY, a/c Lista de Correos, Col. Condesa, México 06140 D.F., México). Mail sent this way is usually held 10 days. If you want your mail held up to 30 days, substitute the words "Poste Restante, Correo Central" for "Lista de Correos" in the address (e.g. Chris HUMPHREY, a/c Poste Restante, Col. Condesa, México 06140 D.F., México). Because delivery time is highly variable, it's best to use poste restante just to be safe.

In small towns and villages, residents often don't use street addresses, but simply write the addressee's name followed by *domicilio conocido* (known residence) and the name of the town or village. Even in large towns and cities, addresses may bear the name of the street without a building number (*sin número*, abbreviated as "s/n"), or will mention the nearest cross streets (e.g., *ent. Abasolo y Revolución*, "between Abasolo and Revolución").

The Mexican post office offers an express mail service called Mexpost. International rates are relatively high; a Mexpost express letter to the United States or Canada, for example, costs $16; to Europe, $20. Mexpost claims to deliver almost anywhere in Mexico within 48 hours and to major cities around the world within 72 hours. A Mexpost parcel cannot exceed 1.05 meters along any one dimension and cannot weigh more than 20 kilos. The **main MexPost center** (Netzahualcóyotl 109, 55/5709-9606), in the Centro, offers packing services.

All post offices are open Monday through Friday; hours and convenient locations are listed below:

- **Palacio Postal** (Eje Central Lázaro Cárdenas and Tacuba, opposite the Palacio de Bellas Artes, 9 A.M.–6 P.M.)

- **Zócalo** (Plaza de la Constitución 7, 9 A.M.–2:30 P.M.)

- **Zona Rosa** (Londres 208 at Varsovia, 9 A.M.–5 P.M., Sat. 9 A.M.–1 P.M.; adjacent MexPost office 9 A.M.–2 P.M. and 2:30–4 P.M., Sat. 9 A.M.–1 P.M.)

- **Colonia Cuauhtémoc** (Río Misisipi 58, 9 A.M.–3 P.M., Sat. 9 A.M.–1 P.M.)

- **Colonia Condesa** (Aguascalientes 161, 9 A.M.–5 P.M., Sat. 9 A.M.–1 P.M.)

- **Roma** (Álvaro Obregón 31, 9 A.M.–7 P.M., Sat. 9 A.M.–1 P.M.)

- **Polanco** (Galileo 245, 9 A.M.–5 P.M., Sat. 9 A.M.–1 P.M.)

- **San Ángel** (Dr. Gálvez 16, 9 A.M.–5 P.M., Sat. 9 A.M.–1 P.M.)

- **Coyoacán** (Higuera 23, 9 A.M.–5 P.M., Sat. 9 A.M.–1 P.M.)

Courier Services

Several courier services operate in Mexico City. In my experience, DHL and UPS seem to offer the lowest prices and best services. MexPost, the express delivery offered by the Mexican Postal Service, is less expensive and a bit slower. All of the couriers listed here offer packing service. Each of these central offices has many branches other than the ones listed below, and offer home pickup: DHL Internacional de México (Paseo de la Reforma 76, 55/5703-0484, www.dhl.com); Federal Express (Insurgentes Sur 899, Col. Nápoles, 55/5228-9904 or 800/900-1100, www.fedex.com); MexPost (Palacio Postal, Eje Central, Col. Centro, 55/5729-3500); UPS de México (Insurgentes Sur 667, 55/5543-5274, www.ups.com).

The courier Estafeta Mexicana (Hamburgo 213, Zona Rosa, 55/5270-8300) is an official agent of the U.S. postal service, which makes for reliable, lower-priced service to the United States.

American Express

AmEx cardholders can pick up mail at the American Express office (Paseo de la Reforma 350, México 06600 D.F., México, 55/5207-7204, Mon.–Fri. 9 A.M.–6 P.M., Sat. 9 A.M.–1 P.M.).

Telephone Services

The national telephone company, **TelMex,** was privatized in 1990 and has improved its services considerably since then. Local phone calls are relatively cheap, as are long-distance calls *within* Mexico. If you can find a working phone—many public phones seem permanently "out of order"—connections are usually good, though you may have to wait a while to get through to the operator during busy periods such as Sunday and holidays.

If you don't want to use a phone booth or a hotel phone (hotels usually add their own surcharges to both local and long-distance calls), you can make a call during business hours from a TelMex office or from a private phone office or *caseta de teléfono*, often set up in the corner of a local shop. Like hotels, private telephone offices add surcharges to calls.

Probably the best option to make local calls and long-distance calls within Mexico is the public pay phone service called **Ladatel** (acronym for Larga Distancia Teléfono), with phone booths where you can pay for local and/or long-distance calls with a *tarjeta de teléfono* (phone card) issued by TelMex. You can buy these cards in denominations of 20, 30, and 50 pesos at many pharmacies, convenience stores, supermarkets, bus terminals, and airports. Often only the 50-peso cards are available.

Unlike most of the rest of Central Mexico,

Mexico City has a two-digit area code (55) followed by an eight-digit phone number used when calling locally. To dial a Mexico City number from elsewhere in Mexico, call 01-55-5234-5678. All other locations covered by this book have a three-digit area code followed by a seven-digit local phone number. For example, to dial a number in Cuernavaca from Mexico City, call 01-777/318-1234.

If you have a calling card for Sprint, AT&T, Verizon, or Bell Canada, you can use it to make long-distance calls within Mexico or to another country. Each of these has its own access code for direct dialing.

To direct dial an international call via TelMex, dial 00 plus the area code and number for a station-to-station call, or 09 plus area code and number for a person-to-person or other operator-assisted call. Long-distance international calls are heavily taxed and cost more than equivalent international calls from the United States or Canada.

The appropriate long-distance operator can place a collect call on your behalf or charge the call to your account if you have a calling card for that service. If you try these numbers from a hotel phone, be sure the hotel operator realizes the call is toll-free; some hotel operators use their own timers to assess phone charges.

Since the deregulation of Mexican telephone service, several private U.S.-based long-distance phone companies have set up their own phone systems—not just the lines and service but actual pay phones—in Mexico to take advantage of undiscerning tourists. The English-language signs next to the phone usually read "Call the U.S. or Canada Collect or with a Credit Card" or "Just Dial Zero to Reach the U.S. or Canada." Often a company operates under several different corporate names in the area, charging at least 50 percent more per international call than TelMex, AT&T, Verizon, or Sprint—as much as $10–20 for the first minute, plus $4 each additional minute, even on weekends. A percentage of these charges usually goes to the hotel or private phone office offering the service. At most private phone offices, it's much cheaper to use TelMex (or a well-known international

TELEPHONE CODES

- **Long-distance operator (national):** 020
- **Time:** 030
- **Directory Assistance (national):** 040
- **Police, Red Cross, Fire:** 060
- **Tourist Assistance (national):** 078
- **Tourist Assistance (Mexico City):** 800/008-9090
- **International operator:** 090

Long-distance direct dialing from Mexico via TelMex:

- **station to station (in Mexico):** 01 + area code + number
- **person to person (in Mexico):** 02 + area code + number
- **station to station (U.S. and Canada):** 001 + area code + number
- **person to person (U.S. and Canada):** 09 + 1 + area code + number
- **station to station (other international):** 00 + country code + area code + number
- **person to person (other international):** 09 + country code + area code + number
- **non-international U.S. 800 number:** 001 + 880 + number (be aware these are not free calls when dialed from Mexico)

Access numbers for other long-distance companies:

- **AT&T:** 01-800/288-2872 or 001-800/462-4240
- **Sprint:** 01-800/234-0000 or 001-800/877-8000
- **Verizon:** 001-800/674-7000

To call Mexico direct from outside the country, dial your international access code + 52 + number. Example: to call the number 5155-0631 in Mexico City from the United States, dial 011 (international access code) + 52 (Mexico country code) + 55 (Mexico City code) + 5155-0631 (the phone number in Mexico City). The Mexico City area code 55 is the only two-digit area code in the regions covered by this book; all others are three digits.

company such as AT&T, Verizon, or Sprint), even if you have to pay a service charge on top of the rates, than to use these fly-by-night companies. If you're concerned about economizing, always ask which company is being used before you arrange an international call through a hotel or private phone office.

For international service, calling collect often saves hassles. In Spanish the magic words are *por cobrar* (collect), prefaced by the name of the place you're calling (e.g., *"a los Estados Unidos, por favor—por cobrar"*). This will connect you to an English-speaking international operator. For best results, speak slowly and clearly. You can reach an international operator directly by dialing 090.

Many international telecommunications companies now offer international prepaid calling cards that can be used at pay phones, and have very good international rates. One example is Verizon's World Traveler card.

About the cheapest way to make long-distance international calls is via the Internet, either using Skype or some other service. Stop in at any Internet café and ask what services are available.

Cellular Phone Rental

Renting a cell phone in Mexico City is an increasingly easy and affordable option for travelers spending a couple of weeks or more in the city. Probably the most expensive option is to rent a phone from shops often found in higher-end hotels, which will charge you a daily fee along with whatever air time you use. You will need a credit card for this.

A cheaper option, especially if you have an old cell phone you can use in Mexico (most common models work just fine), is to get a SIM card and a prepaid plan, where you pay ahead of time for the amount of minutes you use, rather then setting up a multi-month account. Most phone shops can unlock your phone, install a new card, and activate a new plan for $15 or $20, including 100 minutes credit. It's possible to use your current cell phone also, but you will have to take care of your SIM card and ID number, and have the phone reprogrammed before you leave Mexico City. You can also buy a cell phone in Mexico City for about $90, with call credit already on it. Cell phone shops (*tienda de teléfono celular*) are found all over the city; just ask around.

Whatever option you chose, be sure to shop around as prices for activation and phone plans vary widely. Some plans are much better for international calls than others.

Email and Internet Access

If you're bringing a computer and modem to Mexico with hopes of staying on the infobahn, online options are limited to a handful of local Internet service providers and a few international ones. Band rates can be slow, bottlenecked by low bandwidth and line interruptions in the Mexican phone system. With fiber optic on the way in many parts of the country, this is changing rapidly, though much depends on the kind of equipment installed at any given town linked with fiber optics. Most travelers will be confined to using dial-up connections from hotels.

For expats or those planning an extended stay in Mexico City, it's possible to set up an account with an Internet service provider for telephone or DSL connections on a monthly basis. America Online and AT&T offer local access phone numbers in Mexico. Mexico's TelMex/Prodigy is the most widely used local service, along with Cablevision (which also provides cable TV service). The TelMex DSL connections seem to be the fastest, but also cost the most—about $50 a month. The Cablevision cost is a bit less than half that, but the connection speed is about mid-way between dial-up and true high-speed access. Other less well-known services are available (the average cost is $10–20 a month), but most people prefer using AOL, AT&T, TelMex/Prodigy, or Cablevision over anything else available in Mexico so far.

A very convenient option for many travelers and businesspeople is the use of pre-paid Internet access cards, which you can then use through a dial-up modem from a computer connected to a regular telephone line (no wireless hotspots yet). The most well-known of this type of card is **Todito Card** (55/5447-8864 in Mexico City, www.toditocard.com), which can be activated either for a set amount of minutes—900 minutes is $10, for example, or 1.1 cents a minute, and it gets less expensive per minute the more you buy. Conversely, you activate the card to provide unlimited access for a certain number of days, which can be very useful for travelers; $5 is good for 6 days and $10 is good for 15 days, and 25 days goes for $15. Email service is available as well if you need it, and the service works in several dozen cities across Mexico. They can be purchased online before you travel, or in a number of chain stores like Oxxo, Gigante, Superama, and Liverpool.

Cybercafés where you can log on using public terminals to send and receive email or browse the Internet are found in all corners of Mexico City, at reasonable rates. Normally the cafés in more expensive neighborhoods or those frequented by tourists are (logically) pricier, while those catering to working-class Mexicans or students are very cheap.

Libraries

The **Biblioteca Benjamín Franklin** (Liverpool 31, Col. Juárez, 55/5080-2733, www.usembassy-mexico.gov/biblioteca, Mon.–Fri. 11 A.M.–7 P.M.) is an excellent library run by the U.S. embassy and open to anyone over 16 years of age. To check out books, you're required to show proof of residence in Mexico City and wait several days to get a card, but anyone is allowed to browse the periodicals or books.

The largest library in Mexico City, and indeed the entire country, is the **Biblioteca Nacional de México** (55/5622-6800, http:// biblional.bibliog.unam.mx, main collection daily 9 A.M.–8 P.M.) at the Centro Cultural Universitario at UNAM, in the south of the city. Anyone over 16 with a current photo identification is welcome to peruse the over one million volumes in the general collection, but only accredited researchers can access more specialized collections.

A literary collection on the history of Mexico and the Americas (in Spanish only) is located at the **Instituto Mora** (Plaza Valentín Gómez Farías 12, 55/5598-3777, www.institutomora.edu.mx, Mon.–Fri. 8 A.M.–7 P.M., Sat. 8 A.M.–3:30 P.M.) in Colonia Mixcoac.

MEDIA
Newspapers

Among the national Spanish-language dailies, *Reforma* is considered the "paper of record" of sorts in Mexico, although it's often accused of favoring the points of view of the business and social elite. *El Universal* is a close second in terms of readership, and is seen as somewhat less biased. *La Jornada* leans well toward the left, while *El Financiero* is oriented toward business and politics. You can buy these newspapers at any of the many street-corner newspaper kiosks around the city, with the exception of *Reforma,* which (because of a dispute with the newspaper union) is sold by vendors on street corners or in convenience stores only. Even if your Spanish is minimal, city newspapers are worth a glance for current information on museum exhibits and local cinema.

The venerable English-language paper *The News,* formerly published by *Novedades* publishers, shut down in 2003, and restarted as an independent paper in 2007, is now sold in newsstands in Mexico City and 18 other cities in Mexico. As in its previous incarnation, it runs a mix of locally reported stories on Mexican politics, business, and culture, mixed with international wire service news. *USA Today* and the *International Herald Tribune* are sometimes sold in hotel lobbies or bookstores.

Downstairs from the Club de Periodistas de México Prensa Nacional y Internacional (International and National Press Club), **La Torre de Papel** (Filomeno Mata 6A, Centro Histórico, Mon.–Fri. 9 A.M.–6 P.M., Sat. 9 A.M.–3 P.M.) sells more than 300 daily newspapers from around Mexico, plus about 50 from other countries (mainly the U.S. and Europe). In Polanco, **Coffee Bar** (the branch at the intersection of Temistocles and Presidente Mazaryk) has a similarly large selection. Newsstands at the airport carry the *New York Times,* the *International Herald Tribune,* the *Financial Times, El Pais* from Spain, and several Mexican newspapers.

The stores mentioned also carry many international magazines from the United States and Europe. Any Sanborns store is also a good place to look.

Magazines

In English, *Latin Trade* (www.latintrade. com) is heavily focused on business stories. The U.S. Chamber of Commerce puts out a magazine in Mexico City called *Business Mexico,* also heavily oriented toward business and finance; it's available in Sanborns around the city. In Spanish, *Proceso* (www. proceso.com.mx) is the leading muckraking magazine. Its stories on Mexican political machinations, though occasionally a bit over the top on the conspiracy theory, are often excellent. Two glossy weekly magazines are *Milenio,* which also has good international news stories, and *Cambio.*

A new style of magazine on the Mexico City magazine market is *Chilango,* with features and short stories about slices of city life, with a heavy slant toward the upscale, hipster crowd. The restaurant and entertainment listings in the back are the best of any magazine in the city.

Television

Mexican TV offers a mix of American dramas and sitcoms dubbed in Spanish and Mexico's own versions of the same formula. Mexico's famous *telenovelas*—soap opera series that run several months rather than several years—are exported all over Latin America.

Many hotels and motels maintain their own satellite dishes with as many as 50 channels from Mexico and the United States. CNN International is widely available. The main movie channels in Mexico City are Cine Latino (Spanish), USA Network (English), Fox (English), Multicinema (mixed), De Película (Spanish), Multicinema (mixed), and Cinema Golden Choice (English). For international sports, look for the Fox Sports or ESPN channels.

Radio

Mexico City boasts hundreds of AM and FM stations. Most of the music stations play Mexican Top 40, but for visitors interested in authentic *música mexicana*, there are several stations worth checking out. Morena 89.7 FM broadcasts traditional *romanticismo*, romantic songs by such crooners as Luis Miguel, Alejandro Fernández, Tania Libertad, and Juan Gabriel.

Radioactiva 98.5 FM is an alternative rock/Top 40 station presenting a mix of English and Spanish groups, with a greater emphasis on English. For *grupera*, La Zeta 107.3 FM is the one to listen to, and for *tropical*, try Sabrosita 100.9 FM. Radio Uno 104.1 FM plays salsa daily 3–4 P.M. and 9–10 P.M.

One of the better radio news programs with news 24 hours a day is Formato 21, 790 AM.

RESOURCES

Chilango Slang

The Spanish spoken in Mexico is lined with a rich vein of colloquialisms, slang expressions, and turns of phrase. Much Mexican slang used to come from working-class neighborhoods in the capital (especially Tepito), but nowadays there doesn't seem to be any particular neighborhood of origin. It remains, however, a singularly *chilango* (Mexico City) phenomenon, and is transmitted by the media to the rest of the country. In fact, because Mexican soap operas are by far the most popular in Latin America, people from other Spanish-speaking countries tend to understand a lot more Mexico City slang than would normally be expected.

A crucial aspect of understanding Mexican Spanish is the world of the *albur*, a sort of pun made at the expense of another. When a group of Mexican men are standing around talking, you'll notice one after the other is constantly taking turns trying to twist someone's last phrase into something that will crack everyone else up. The trick is to make everyone laugh, but using clever phrasing, never just a straight insult or put-down.

As in Cockney English, another trick is to use words that sound similar to well-known swear words, thus making the meaning more acceptable, and more humorous, in polite company.

Rare is the foreigner who masters local slang enough to take part in this generally good-natured word competition, but it's entertaining to try. Just don't be surprised when suddenly everyone is laughing at you, and you're not quite sure why. Nothing to be done but laugh along with them.

Glossary

aguafiestas a spoilsport, a killjoy
aguas watch out!
a huevo definitely, for sure
antro nightspot, club
a toda madre excellent
a todo mecate similar to a *toda madre*, but softer, as *madre* has a slightly vulgar connotation when used in this sense
banda people, as in *mucha banda*, meaning a lot of people
bicla bicycle
cabrón a jerk, a mean person
cámara same as *simón;* cool
cantar oaxaca to vomit
carnal good friend, literally "of the flesh"
chafa poor quality
chale multipurpose exclamatory interjection (such as really? wow! no way! right on!); often used as "*chale, mano*"
chamaco, chamaca little boy, little girl
chamba work
chavo, chava young man, young woman
chela beer
chesco soft drink
chido cool, right on
chilango someone from Mexico City
chingar to "screw" somebody, in both meanings of the word
chingo a whole lot
chingón really excellent
chon underwear, sometimes used as "*le tiro el chon*," meaning to give someone an opening to pick you up

chota police
chupar to drink
colonia neighborhood, in Mexico City (*barrio* is more common elsewhere in Latin America)
cuate buddy, good friend
cuero handsome, good-looking
de pelos excellent
desmadre a big mess, really screwed up
donas two
duques two
en un ratón in a while, a twist on *"en un rato"*
está cañón a tough situation, a twist on *está cabrón*, which means the same but is more vulgar
está del nabo, está de la fruta it sucks
está grueso literally "it's fat," meaning "wow, heavy, that's serious"
fajar to make out, to kiss
fresa literally "strawberry," meaning a prissy, a snotty rich kid
gabacho American
gachupín, gachupina derogatory word for someone from Spain
guácala gross
guacarear to vomit
guapachoso someone who likes tropical music
guarro, guarura bodyguard
güey dude, guy; common throughout Mexico, but used every other word by young *chilangos*, and even *chilangas*
hueva a drag, something boring or tedious
jefe, jefa father, mother
jetón asleep
la neta the best; also the truth, the real deal
la pura neta even better
la puritita neta better still
lana literally "wool," i.e., money
mamón stuck-up, arrogant person
mango attractive
mano short for *hermano* (brother) and the Mexican equivalent of "bro"
melón 1,000,000 pesos
un milagro 1,000 pesos
móchate pass it along already, give me one, or give me some (often *"móchate, güey"* or *"móchate, cabrón"*)
naco someone with bad taste
nave literally boat, but slang for car

ni madres no way, not a chance
no mames vulgar, meaning "no way, get out"; invariably said as *"no mames, güey"*
no manches means the same as *mames*, but twisted at the end to make it sound less crude
ojete a strong, vulgar insult
órale exclamation, "right on, wow"
pachanga big party
pachangear to go partying
pacheco stoned (i.e., smoking marijuana)
pedo literally "fart," but meaning either "drunk" (*"está bien pedo"*) or a problem, i.e., ¿que pedo? (what's the problem?) or *no hay pedo* (no problem)
pendejo vulgar, insulting adjective, i.e., "idiot"
perro as an adjective, something very difficult
perro as a noun, a guy who sleeps around a lot
pinche a vulgar adjective, i.e., *"¡Abre la pinche puerta!"* ("open the @#! door!")
pitufos literally "smurfs," meaning the blue-uniformed police
ponerse punk to get mad, as in *"no te pongas punk,"* "don't get mad"
¿que hongo? literally "what mushroom?," a play on ¿que onda?
que mal viaje what a drag, what a bad trip
¿que onda? what's up?
que oso literally "what a bear," but meaning "what a fool," i.e., "what a ridiculous spectacle, they're making of themselves"
¿que pasión? twist on ¿que pasó? what's happening?
¿que pedo? same as above
que poca madre "can you believe that?" but with an indignant tone
¿que te picó? literally, "what bit you?," meaning "what's the matter?" or "what's your problem?"
quiúbule also "what's up?"; usually *"quiúbule, cabrón"* or *"quiúbule güey"*
rajar a verb, meaning to back out of doing something, to bail
ratero a thief (literally, "ratter")
rayarse to be lucky
reventón big party
rola a tune, a song
se puso hasta atrás he/she got thoroughly drunk

se puso hasta las chanclas he/she got thoroughly drunk

simón a play on the word *sí* (yes), but more hip and current; combination of "I agree" and "right on"

taco de ojo someone attractive, nice to look at

tamarindos the *tránsito* police, with brown uniforms

tirar la onda try to hit on someone

tostón 50 pesos

trancazo a blow, a hard hit

tranzar to deceive somebody

tripas three

uñas one

varos *pesos* (i.e., *cero* "it costs 10 pesos")

vecindad a grouping of apartments around a single courtyard, common in working-class Mexico City neighborhoods

vientos "winds," right on

vientos huracanados "hurricane winds," excellent

Spanish Phrasebook

PRONUNCIATION GUIDE

Spanish pronunciation is much more regular than that of English, but there are still occasional variations.

Consonants

c as c in "cat," before a, o, or u; like s before e or i

d as d in "dog," except between vowels, then like 'th' in "that"

g before e or i, like the ch in Scottish "loch"; elsewhere like g in "get"

h always silent

j like the English h in "hotel," but stronger

ll like the y in "yellow"

ñ like the ni in "onion"

r always pronounced as strong r

rr trilled r

v similar to the b in "boy" (not as English v)

y similar to English, but with a slight "j" sound. When standing alone it's pronounced like the e in "me."

z like s in "same"

b, f, k, l, m, n, p, q, s, t, w, x as in English

Vowels

a as in "father," but shorter

e as in "hen"

i as in "machine"

o as in "phone"

u usually as in "rule"; when it follows a q the u is silent; when it follows an h or g it's pronounced like w, except when it comes between g and e or i, when it's also silent (unless it has an umlaut, when it is again pronounced as English w.

Stress

Native English speakers frequently make errors of pronunciation by ignoring stress; all Spanish vowels–a, e, i, o, and u–may carry accents that determine which syllable of a word gets emphasis. Often, stress seems unnatural to nonnative speakers–the surname Chávez, for instance, is stressed on the first syllable–but failure to observe this rule may mean that native speakers may not understand you.

NUMBERS

0 *cero*

1 *uno* (masculine)

1 *una* (feminine)

2 *dos*

3 *tres*

4 *cuatro*

5 *cinco*

6 *seis*

7 *siete*

8 *ocho*

9 *nueve*

10 *diez*

11 *once*

12 *doce*

13 *trece*

14 *catorce*
15 *quince*
16 *dieciseis*
17 *diecisiete*
18 *dieciocho*
19 *diecinueve*
20 *veinte*
21 *veintiuno*
30 *treinta*
40 *cuarenta*
50 *cincuenta*
60 *sesenta*
70 *setenta*
80 *ochenta*
90 *noventa*
100 *cien*
101 *ciento y uno*
200 *doscientos*
1,000 *mil*
10,000 *diez mil*
1,000,000 *un millón*

DAYS OF THE WEEK
Sunday *domingo*
Monday *lunes*
Tuesday *martes*
Wednesday *miércoles*
Thursday *jueves*
Friday *viernes*
Saturday *sábado*

TIME
While Latin Americans mostly use the 12-hour clock, in some instances, usually associated with plane or bus schedules, they may use the 24-hour military clock. Under the 24-hour clock, for example, *las nueve de la noche* (9 P.M.) would be *las 21 horas* (2100 hours).

What time is it? *Qué hora es?*
It's one o'clock *Es la una.*
It's two o'clock *Son las dos.*
At two o'clock *A las dos.*
It's ten to three *Son tres menos diez.*
It's ten past three *Son tres y diez.*
It's three fifteen *Son las tres y cuarto.*
It's two forty-five *Son tres menos cuarto.*
It's two thirty *Son las dos y media.*

It's six A.M. *Son las seis de la mañana.*
It's six P.M. *Son las seis de la tarde.*
It's ten P.M. *Son las diez de la noche.*
today *hoy*
tomorrow *mañana*
morning *la mañana*
tomorrow morning *mañana por la mañana*
yesterday *ayer*
week *la semana*
month *mes*
year *año*
last night *anoche*
the next day *el día siguiente*

USEFUL WORDS AND PHRASES
Mexicans and other Spanish-speaking people consider formalities important. Whenever approaching anyone for information or some other reason, do not forget the appropriate salutation—good morning, good evening, etc. Standing alone, the greeting *hola* (hello) can sound brusque.

Hello. *Hola.*
Good morning. *Buenos días.*
Good afternoon. *Buenas tardes.*
Good evening. *Buenas noches.*
How are you? *¿Cómo está?*
Very good. *Muy bien.*
And you? *¿Y usted?*
So-so. *Más o menos.*
Thank you. *Gracias.*
Thank you very much. *Muchas gracias.*
You're very kind. *Muy amable.*
You're welcome. *De nada* (literally, "It's nothing.")
yes *sí*
no *no*
I don't know. *No sé.*
It's fine; okay *Está bien.*
Good; okay *Bueno.*
please *por favor*
Pleased to meet you. *Mucho gusto.*
Excuse me (physical) *Perdóneme.*
Excuse me (speech) *Discúlpeme.*
I'm sorry. *Lo siento.*
Goodbye *adiós*

see you later *hasta luego* (literally, "until later")
more *más*
less *menos*
better *mejor*
much, a lot *mucho*
a little *un poco*
large *grande*
small *pequeño, chico*
quick, fast *rápido*
slowly *despacio*
bad *malo*
difficult *difícil*
easy *fácil*
He/She/It is gone; as in "She left," "He's gone" *Ya se fue.*
I don't speak Spanish well. *No hablo bien el español.*
I don't understand. *No entiendo.*
How do you say... in Spanish? *¿Cómo se dice... en español?*
Do you understand English? *¿Entiende el inglés?*
Is English spoken here? (Does anyone here speak English?) *¿Se habla inglés aquí?*

TERMS OF ADDRESS

When in doubt, use the formal *usted* (you) as a form of address. If you wish to dispense with formality and feel that the desire is mutual, you can say *Me puedes tutear* ("you can call me 'tu'").

I *yo*
you (formal) *usted*
you (familiar) *tú*
he/him *él*
she/her *ella*
we/us *nosotros*
you (plural) *ustedes*
they/them (all males or mixed gender) *ellos*
they/them (all females) *ellas*
Mr., sir *señor*
Mrs., madam *señora*
Miss, young lady *señorita*
wife *esposa*
husband *marido or esposo*
friend *amigo* (male), *amiga* (female)

sweetheart *novio* (male), *novia* (female)
son, daughter *hijo, hija*
brother, sister *hermano, hermana*
father, mother *padre, madre*
grandfather, grandmother *abuelo, abuela*

GETTING AROUND

Where is...? *¿Dónde está...?*
How far is it to...? *¿A cuanto está...?*
from... to... *de... a...*
highway *la carretera*
road *el camino*
street *la calle*
block *la cuadra*
kilometer *kilómetro*
north *norte*
south *sur*
west *oeste; poniente*
east *este; oriente*
straight ahead *al derecho; adelante*
to the right *a la derecha*
to the left *a la izquierda*

ACCOMMODATIONS

Is there a room? *¿Hay cuarto?*
May I (we) see it? *¿Puedo (podemos) verlo?*
What is the rate? *¿Cuál es el precio?*
Is that your best rate? *¿Es su mejor precio?*
Is there something cheaper? *¿Hay algo más económico?*
single room *un sencillo*
double room *un doble*
room for a couple *matrimonial*
key *llave*
with private bath *con baño*
with shared bath *con baño general; con baño compartido*
hot water *agua caliente*
cold water *agua fría*
shower *ducha*
electric shower *ducha eléctrica*
towel *toalla*
soap *jabón*
toilet paper *papel higiénico*
air conditioning *aire acondicionado*
fan *abanico; ventilador*
blanket *frazada; manta*
sheets *sábanas*

PUBLIC TRANSPORT
bus stop *la parada*
bus terminal *terminal de buses* or *central camionera*
airport *el aeropuerto*
launch *lancha*
dock *muelle*
I want a ticket to... *Quiero un pasaje a...*
I want to get off at... *Quiero bajar en...*
Here, please. *Aquí, por favor.*
Where is this bus going? *¿Adónde va este autobús?*
round-trip *ida y vuelta*
What do I owe? *¿Cuánto le debo?*

FOOD
menu *la carta, el menú*
glass *taza*
fork *tenedor*
knife *cuchillo*
spoon *cuchara*
napkin *servilleta*
soft drink *refresco*
coffee *café*
cream *crema*
tea *té*
sugar *azúcar*
drinking water *agua pura, agua potable*
bottled carbonated water *agua mineral con gas*
bottled uncarbonated water *agua sin gas*
beer *cerveza*
wine *vino*
milk *leche*
juice *jugo*
eggs *huevos*
bread *pan*
watermelon *sandía*
banana *plátano*
apple *manzana*
orange *naranja*

meat (without) *carne (sin)*
beef *carne de res*
chicken *pollo; gallina*
fish *pescado*
shellfish *mariscos*
shrimp *camarones*
fried *frito*
roasted *asado*
barbecued *a la parrilla*
breakfast *desayuno*
lunch *comida*
dinner, or a late-night snack *cena*
the check, or bill *la cuenta*

MAKING PURCHASES
I need... *Necesito...*
I want... *Deseo...* or *Quiero...*
I would like... (more polite) *Quisiera...*
How much does it cost? *¿Cuánto cuesta?*
What's the exchange rate? *¿Cuál es el tipo de cambio?*
May I see...? *¿Puedo ver...?*
this one *ésta/ésto*
expensive *caro*
cheap *barato*
cheaper *más barato*
too much *demasiado*

HEALTH
Help me please. *Ayúdeme por favor.*
I am ill. *Estoy enfermo/a.*
pain *dolor*
fever *fiebre*
stomach ache *dolor de estómago*
vomiting *vomitar*
diarrhea *diarrea*
drugstore *farmacia*
medicine *medicina*
pill, tablet *pastilla*
birth control pills *pastillas anticonceptivas*
condom *condón, preservativo*

Suggested Reading

ARCHITECTURE

Opher, Philip with Xavier Sánchez Valladares. *Mexico City: A Guide to Recent Architecture.* Ellipse, 2000. This handy pocket-sized guide is a good compendium of Mexico City's modern architecture.

DESCRIPTION AND TRAVEL

Barros, José Luis. *Encuentros en la ciudad de México.* Miguel Ángel Porrúa, Grupo Editorial 1997. Collection of historic writings on the capital by such illustrative figures as Hernán Cortés, Thomas Gage, Guillermo Prieto, Miguel León Portilla, early Catholic friars, and others. Spanish only.

Gerrard, A. Bryson. *Cassell's Colloquial Spanish: A Handbook of Idiomatic Usage.* New York: Macmillan, 1980. Not as out-of-date as the publication year might suggest, Cassell's explains common *vulgarismos* (slang) used in Mexico, Central America, and South America; *píldora,* for example, is recognized as "the pill" in Mexico, but it refers to cocktail frankfurters in Argentina.

Legorreta, Jorge. *Guía del Pleno Disfrute de la Ciudad de México.* Mexico City: Jorge Legorreta/Metrópolis, 1994. This thin spiralbound guide to city nightlife, written by Mexico City politician Jorge Legorreta and oriented toward *capitalinos* rather than tourists, is a gem. Sadly out of print, the *Guide to the Full Enjoyment of Mexico City* contains critiques and descriptions of many classic Mexico City restaurants, cafés, cantinas, *pulquerías,* cabarets, burlesque shows, dance halls, and other nocturnal pursuits. Spanish only.

Martinez, Ruben. *The Other Side: Notes from the New L.A., Mexico City, and Beyond.* Vintage Books, 1993. A stimulating account of the growing pan-Latino culture extending from Los Angeles to El Salvador, with plenty of pop culture information on Mexico City.

O'Reilly, James and Larry Habegger, eds. *Travelers' Tales Mexico.* San Francisco: Travelers' Tales, 1994. If you only read one piece of travel literature on Mexico, make it this one. Forty-eight essays by travel writers, natural historians, journalists, and ecologists present a kaleidoscopic view of Mexico's mystery, beauty, tragedy, and internal contradictions.

Ryan, Allen, ed. *The Reader's Companion to Mexico.* New York: Harcourt Brace and Company, 1995. Contains 26 literary excerpts from works on Mexico—the oldest dates to 1888, the latest 1985—published by Katherine Ann Porter, Graham Greene, Paul Theroux, Langston Hughes, Paul Bowles, D. H. Lawrence, John Steinbeck, and a number of lesser-known authors. A full chapter is devoted to essays on Mexico City.

FICTION

Burroughs, William. *Queer.* New York: Penguin Books, 1987. Set mainly in Mexico City during the Beat era, this autobiographical novel fictionalizes Burroughs's flight to Mexico to avoid drug charges in the United States.

Kerouac, Jack. *Mexico City Blues: 242 Choruses.* New York: Grove Press, 1990. Beat novelist and poet Kerouac often tried to mimic the cadences of jazz in his writing. This work arguably comes closer to that goal than anything else he ever published, and it is evocative of 1950s Mexico City.

Lida, David. *Travel Advisory.* New York: William Morrow & Company, 2000. A collection of 10 gritty short stories set in Mexico (several in Mexico City) from an American writer who divides his time between New York and Mexico. Mexico has a bitter history with *americanos* and an even longer history with *malinchismo,* and some of these stories expose—rather than ignore—this essential cornerstone of modern Mexican culture. Lida has an especially good ear for dialogue, which he reproduces partly in Spanish.

Lowry, Malcolm. *Under the Volcano.* New York: Reynal & Hitchcock, 1990. Although it only sold two copies in two years when originally published in Canada in 1947, Lowry's tale of the alcoholic demise of a British consul in Cuernavaca has become a modern classic, often lumped together with Paul Bowles *The Sheltering Sky* for its similarly bleak view of the post-war world.

Taibo II, Paco Ignacio. *Return to the Same City.* New York: Mysterious Press, 1996. Mexico City's favorite eccentric Marxist mystery writer resurrects his detective protagonist, Héctor Belascoarán Shayne. While chasing a Cuban arms/drug dealer through D.F., Shayne gives us an insider's glimpse of the city and his existential way of coping with it. The novel's 1993 predecessor, *No Happy Ending,* is also set in *la capital.* Others in the series include *An Easy Thing, Some Clouds,* and *Frontera Dreams,* among others.

Traven, B. *The Rebellion of the Hanged.* New York: Hill and Wang, 1972. The mysterious B. Traven, author of the more well-known *The Treasure of the Sierra Madre,* here chronicles Amerindian exploitation under Porfirio Díaz in another powerful work of fiction.

FOOD

Adair, Marita. *The Hungry Traveler: Mexico.* Kansas City: Andrews McNeel Publishing, 1997. A pocket-sized Mexican culinary lexicon, with plenty of references to Mexico City and nearby states.

DeWitt, Dave and Nancy Gerlach. *The Whole Chile Pepper Book.* Boston: Little, Brown and Co., 1990. Written by the editors of *Chile Pepper* magazine, this compendium of fact,

lore, and recipes is the definitive culinary guide to chiles.

Quintana, Patricia. *The Taste of Mexico.* New York: Stewart, Tabori & Chang, 1993. Written by one of Mexico City's most famous chefs, this is perhaps the most authentic Mexican cookbook available in English. Also available in Spanish as *El Sabor de México.*

Walker, Ann and Larry Walker. *Tequila: The Book.* San Francisco: Chronicle Books, 1994. This small but beautifully bound and printed book contains the definitive history of agave distillate, along with tips on tequila etiquette and recipes for cocktails, *antojitos,* salads, soups, entrées, salsas, and desserts. Humorous anecdotes and place descriptions add to the reading fun.

HISTORY AND CULTURE

Arnold, Caroline. *City of the Gods: Mexico's Ancient City of Teotihuacán.* New York: Clarion Books, 1994. Illustrated with color photographs, Arnold's readable outing explores the ancient metropolis and extrapolates how the daily lives of the Teotihuacanos might have been.

Bierhorst, John. *The Mythology of Mexico and Central America.* New York: William Morrow, 1990. A good introduction to Mexican mythology, particularly with regard to Mesoamerican cultures.

Caistor, Nick. *Mexico City: A Cultural and Literary Companion.* New York: Interlink Books, 2000. An interesting and extremely atmospheric account of different aspects of Mexico City history and culture, written by someone who is clearly fascinated with the city.

Coe, Michael D. *Mexico: From the Olmecs to the Aztecs.* New York: Thames and Hudson, 1994. This textbook by curator/university professor Coe provides a readable, well-illustrated summary of pre-Hispanic history in central and southern Mexico, wisely leaving the Maya for another volume.

Johns, Michael. *The City of Mexico in the Age of Díaz*. Austin: University of Texas Press, 1997. A well-written, well-researched, and ultimately fascinating chronicle of the capital during the rule of dictatorial president Porfirio Díaz.

Kandell, Jonathan. *La Capital: The Biography of Mexico City*. New York: Random House, 1988. A readable chronicle of Mexico's capital city that would have benefited from a sharper focus on the city itself rather than the larger issues in Mexican history that it tends to fall back upon.

Katz, Friedrich. *The Life and Times of Pancho Villa*. Stanford: Stanford University Press, 1998. The larger-than-life bandit revolutionary Villa is portrayed here in all his complexity in exhaustive detail.

Krauze, Enrique. *Biography of Power: A History of Modern Mexico, 1810–1996*. New York: HarperCollins Publishers, 1997. One of Mexico's most respected historians traces the course of Mexican history, principally through the actions of its leaders. Because of his focus on personality, Krauze falls short on portraying the country's social dynamics.

Lewis, Oscar. *The Children of Sanchez: Autobiography of a Mexican Family*. New York: Random House, 1979. A gritty anthropological account of the city, based on the lives of a family whose patriarch works as a waiter at the restaurant Café Tacuba.

Lida, David. *First Stop in the New World: Mexico City, the Capital of the 21st Century*. New York: Riverhead, 2008. Lida, who is also a fiction writer and has worked as a journalist in Mexico City for years, put together a great selection of essays and reportages about all sorts of unique subcultures in the megalopolis in this volume. Many of them are based on stories originally written for Mexico City newspapers and magazines.

Oppenheimer, Andres. *Bordering on Chaos: Mexico's Roller Coaster Journey to Prosperity.* Boston: Little, Brown and Co., 1998. *Miami Herald* reporter Oppenheimer has some engrossing anecdotes on the turbulent times of the Salinas and Zedillo era, though at times he seems overly concerned about illustrating his own involvement with the power brokers rather than focusing on the people and events themselves.

Oster, Patrick. *The Mexicans: A Personal Portrait of a People*. New York: Harper & Row, 1989. Reporter Patrick Foster presents 20 profiles of not-so-ordinary Mexicans, from a streetside fire-eater in Mexico City to a Sonoran *PANista*. Most of those profiled are Mexico City denizens. Despite a nearly overwhelming gloom-and-doom perspective, the essays provide hard information on Mexican politics and social schema.

Paz, Octavio. *The Labyrinth of Solitude: Life and Thought in Mexico*. New York: Grove Press, 1961. Paz has no peer when it comes to expositions of the Mexican psyche, and this is his best prose work.

Preston, Julia and Sam Dillon. *Opening Mexico*. New York: Farrar, Straus and Giroux, 2004. Preston and Dillon, former *New York Times* correspondents in Mexico, create an engrossing successor of sorts to Alan Riding's *Distant Neighbors,* starting in the mid-1980s but focusing principally on the *sexenio* of Ernesto Zedillo and the transition in 2000 with the victory of opposition candidate Vicente Fox.

Quiñones, Sam. *True Tales from Another Mexico: The Lynch Mob, the Popsicle Kings, Chalino, and the Bronx*. Albuquerque: University of New Mexico Press, 2001. An idiosyncratic and entertaining collection of stories from across Mexico, but particularly from the northern border regions.

Reed, John. *Insurgent Mexico*. New York: International Publishers, 1994. Famed American journalist Reed, of *Ten Days That Shook the World* fame, wrote this breathless, entertaining, and unabashedly biased first-hand account of time spent with Villa's troops in Northern Mexico during the Mexican Revolution.

Riding, Alan. *Distant Neighbors: A Portrait of the Mexicans.* New York: Vintage Books, 1986. Riding was the *New York Times* correspondent in Mexico City for six years, and when he finished, he wrote this excellent exposition of Mexican culture and history.

Rodriguez, Jeanette. *Our Lady of Guadalupe: Faith and Empowerment among Mexican-American Women.* Austin: University of Texas Press, 1994. Explores the Guadalupe myth as the most powerful female icon in Mexican and Mexican American culture and as a symbol of liberation for Mexican Catholic women.

Scarborough, Vernon and David Wilcox, eds. *The Mesoamerican Ballgame.* Tucson: University of Arizona Press, 1991. A well-researched history of the martial sport in all its gory details.

Simon, Joel. *Endangered Mexico: An Environment on the Edge.* San Francisco: Sierra Club Books, 1998. A superb collection of essays on Mexico's precarious environmental situation and the many social factors propelling it, written by a journalist who has traveled far and wide to get his information. The data is getting a bit out-of-date by now, but the anecdotes and overall story remain powerful.

Thomas, Hugh. *Conquest: Montezuma, Cortés, and the Fall of Old Mexico.* New York: Simon & Schuster, 1995. The definitive account of one of the greatest events in history: the meeting of the New and Old Worlds in Mexico in 1519. Detailed and extremely well written.

Womack, John. *Zapata and the Mexican Revolution.* New York: Knopf, 1970. This is considered the classic account of the legendary *caudillo del sur,* Zapata, and his role in the Mexican revolution. A must for anyone interested in understanding Zapata's mythic status in the Mexican pantheon of heroes.

Internet Resources

While a substantial number of English-speakers live in Mexico City, the Internet offers paltry resources in English about one of the world's largest megalopolises. Yet for those Mexicophiles who feel the need to stay on top of city politics and tourism, government offices offer content-rich websites for those with some command of Spanish.

Keep in mind that websites come and go, and URLs (universal resource locators, or World Wide Web "addresses") may change. More websites are included throughout the book on different topics.

Directorio de Comunicación Social
www.directorio.gob.mx

An excellent directory of the entire Mexican government: all branches, the federal and state level, and state-run companies. As well, the site maintains updated lists of foreign embassies, foreign journalists in Mexico, media (radio, television, and newspapers) from across Mexico, universities, and political parties.

Eco Travels in Mexico City
www.planeta.com

The award-winning Planeta.com site has a great selection of blogs and stories about travels in Mexico City, many with an ecological orientation.

Environmental Information in Mexico City
www.planeta.com/ecotravel/mexico/df/mexinfo.html

A frequently updated one-stop information center for anyone interested in environmental issues.

Instituto Nacional de Estadísticas, Geografía e Informatica
www.inegi.gob.mx

INEGI is the government statistical institute, and its website (although difficult to navigate) has a wealth of detailed information about the country's population, economy, environment, and much else besides.

Mexico City Art
www.arte-mexico.com

Online map of the city's many galleries and art museums and listings of current exhibitions and openings.

Mexico City Government
www.df.gob.mx

Mexico City's website is well designed and, best of all, there is a great deal of content. If you're interested in city politics and administration, here you can track down the addresses, phone numbers, and emails of the city's precinct leaders or participate in the online chat forums (www.df.gob.mx/foros/index.html) on topics including public security, tourism, and environmental affairs. Mixing thoroughness and creativity, the Mexico City website exemplifies what a government website can be. The only thing missing would be an email mailing list to provide press releases and announcements from specific departments.

Mexico City Government Tourism Office
www.mexicocity.gob.mx

The city's tourism office has a fairly fancy website with plenty of good links, although descriptions are limited. Check the Centro Histórico page (www.mexicocity.gob.mx/eng/enjoy/chistorico/index.asp) and the links for museums, theaters, cinemas, and walking tours. You'll also find the addresses for tourism *modulos* around the city (www.mexicocity.gob.mx/ven/modulos.php) and an archive of city statistics.

Mexican Embassy in Washington, D.C.
http://portal.sre.gob.mx/usa

This is the place to come for the latest Mexican visa information.

The Mexpat
www.mexpat.com

Oriented toward younger expats, especially those living in Mexico City, with lots of information on city events of interest to the expat community. They also have a lively forum.

Moon Handbooks
www.moon.com

Moon's website contains occasional excerpts from this book and other Moon titles, ordering information, an online travel newsletter with articles on Mexico, and links to various related sites.

Museos de México
www.museosdemexico.org

This excellent site contains descriptions and opening hours of every important art and history museum in the capital.

Newspapers

A number of Mexican newspapers are on the Internet. Reforma (www.reforma.com) is great, but you have to pay to access their site. El Universal (www.eluniversal.com.mx) is free and also good. The English-language newspaper *The News* has a website at www.thenews.com.mx.

Nongovernmental Organizations
www.laneta.org

This umbrella site has links to the extensive NGO community in Mexico.

Index

NO

P

Restaurants Index

Nightlife Index

Shops Index

Hotels Index

Acknowledgments

Thanks to all those *chilangos* and *chilango*-philes who helped provide information for this guide: Eugenio Aburto, Marco Alcaráz, Lucas de Beaufort, Cristian Borja Vega, Luis and Leoni Briones, Manuel Felix, Tara Fitzgerald, Fernando Flores, Alicia Fuentes, Rodrigo García-Verdú, Bibiana Gómez, Emilia Gómez, Seraphine Hauessling, Ana and Chris Leroy, David Lida, Sara Llana, Dr. Gerardo López Gómez, Barbara Kastelein, Guadalupe Paz, Fernando Ruiz, Andrea Semaan, Stephanie Schneiderman, and Ken Shadlen.

Thanks also to Rodrigo Rodríguez and Carlos Mackinley Grohmann at the Mexico City Secretaría de Turismo for all their excellent assistance, and to Luis Fuguemann at the Consejo de Promoción Turística de Mexico for helping arrange the use of their photos.

Thanks to several photographers for the generous use of their photos: Lucas de Beaufort, Guillaume Copart Muller (www.gcmfoto.com), Deb Dutcher, Emilia Gómez, Elena Pappas, and Aymara Tello Manzanares.

Special thanks to the readers who took the time to provide their feedback on the guide: Lianne Beltrán, Don Canepa, Stephen Dolainski, Tom Donalek (happy climbing), Dr. Connie Markey, M. Martin, Moira Nelson, Thomas Randall, Tony Rich, and Jeff Stuckman. There was more reader feedback, but in the course of moving cities, I managed to misplace pieces of it—my apologies to those who wrote in but are not mentioned here.

www.moon.com

For helpful advice on planning a trip, visit www.moon.com for the **TRAVEL PLANNER** and get access to useful travel strategies and valuable information about great places to visit. When you travel with Moon, expect an experience that is uncommon and truly unique.

HANDBOOKS | METRO | OUTDOORS | LIVING ABROAD

MOON MEXICO CITY

Avalon Travel
a member of the Perseus Books Group
1700 Fourth Street
Berkeley, CA 94710, USA
www.moon.com

Editors: Naomi Adler Dancis, Sabrina Young,
Annie M. Blakley
Series Manager: Erin Raber
Copy Editor: Amy Scott
Graphics Coordinator: Domini Dragoone
Production Coordinators: Amber Pirker,
Darren Alessi
Cover Designer: Domini Dragoone
Map Editor: Albert Angulo
Cartographer: Kat Bennett
Indexer: Greg Jewett

ISBN-10: 1-59880-083-3
ISBN-13: 978-1-59880-083-8
ISSN: 1541-9150

Printing History
1st Edition – 2000
4th Edition – September 2008
5 4 3 2 1

Front cover photo: Colorful paper cut-outs adorn an
adobe building; © Alamy/Kim Karpeles.
Title page photo: Catedral from the Zócalo; Courtesy
of Consejo de Promoción Turística de México/Bruce
Herman.

Interior photos: pg. 2, 3 (left and center), 4, 5 (bottom
right), and 9 (bottom): © Guillaume Copart Muller/
www.gcmphoto.com; pg. 3 (far right) and 7 (top):
Courtesy of Mexico City Secretería de Turismo/Aymara
Tello Manzanares; pg. 5 (top left), 6, 7 (bottom), 13,
and 14: Courtesy of Consejo de Promoción Turística
de México; pg. 5 (top right and bottom middle), 9, 10,
11, and 12 : © Chris Humphery; pg. 8 © Deb Dutcher;
pg. 15 and 16: © www.123rf.com.

Printed in the United States by RR Donnelley

KEEPING CURRENT

If you have a favorite gem you'd like to see included in the next edition, or see anything
that needs updating, clarification, or correction, please drop us a line. Send your
comments via email to feedback@moon.com, or use the address above.

MAP SYMBOLS

▤▤▤ Expressway	◖ Highlight	✗ Airfield
▤▤▤ Primary Road	○ City/Town	✈ Airport
▤▤▤ Secondary Road	◉ State Capital	▲ Mountain
┄┄┄ Unpaved Road	⊛ National Capital	✛ Unique Natural Feature
------ Trail	★ Point of Interest	🗇 Waterfall
·········· Ferry	• Accommodation	♠ Park
┼┼┼┼ Railroad	▼ Restaurant/Bar	⬭ Trailhead
▤▤▤ Pedestrian Walkway	■ Other Location	⛷ Skiing Area
▥▥▥ Stairs	⋀ Campground	

Golf Course, Parking Area, Archaeological Site, Church, Gas Station, Glacier, Mangrove, Reef, Swamp

CONVERSION TABLES

$$°C = (°F - 32) / 1.8$$
$$°F = (°C \times 1.8) + 32$$
1 inch = 2.54 centimeters (cm)
1 foot = 0.304 meters (m)
1 yard = 0.914 meters
1 mile = 1.6093 kilometers (km)
1 km = 0.6214 miles
1 fathom = 1.8288 m
1 chain = 20.1168 m
1 furlong = 201.168 m
1 acre = 0.4047 hectares
1 sq km = 100 hectares
1 sq mile = 2.59 square km
1 ounce = 28.35 grams
1 pound = 0.4536 kilograms
1 short ton = 0.90718 metric ton
1 short ton = 2,000 pounds
1 long ton = 1.016 metric tons
1 long ton = 2,240 pounds
1 metric ton = 1,000 kilograms
1 quart = 0.94635 liters
1 US gallon = 3.7854 liters
1 Imperial gallon = 4.5459 liters
1 nautical mile = 1.852 km

MAP INDEX

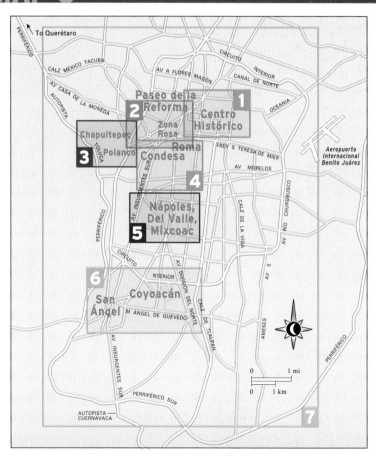

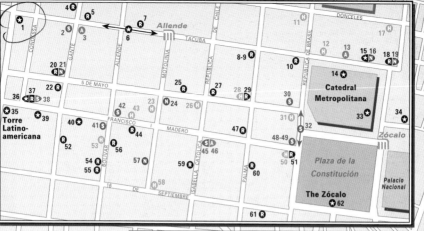

ⓡ RESTAURANTS

- 4 LOS GIRASOLES
- 5 TACO INN
- 7 CAFÉ TACUBA
- 8 LONCHERÍA VASCONIA
- 9 PANADERÍA Y PASTELERIA VASCONIA
- 10 MEXICO VIEJO
- 18 LA CASA DE LAS SIRENAS
- 20 ⓒ BAR LA ÓPERA
- 22 VEGETARIANOS DEL CENTRO
- 25 CAFÉ LA BLANCA
- 27 GILI POLLOS
- 29 CAFÉ EL POPULAR
- 37 SANBORNS
- 44 BISQUETS OBREGÓN
- 47 ⓒ EL CARDENAL
- 51 BEST WESTERN HOTEL MAJESTIC
- 52 CAFÉ EL PASSAJE
- 54 CAFÉ LA SELVA
- 55 SUPER SOYA
- 56 SALÓN CORONA
- 59 CASINO ESPAÑOL
- 60 EL REY DEL PAVO
- 61 SUPER SOYA
- 63 LA ÚNICA DE GUERRERO
- 69 SALÓN LA VICTORIA
- 82 HOSTERÍA SANTO DOMINGO
- 94 CAFÉ DEL PALACIO
- 99 FONDA SANTA ANITA
- 101 EL CARDENAL
- 114 MERCADO SAN JUAN
- 119 ⓒ CHURRERÍA EL MORO
- 120 EL DANUBIO
- 121 PASTELERÍA IDEAL

- 128 LA MASCOTA
- 130 COOX HANAL
- 147 EL EHDEN
- 148 AL ANDALUZ
- 149 FONDA DE DON CHON

ⓝ NIGHTLIFE

- 12 LA FAENA
- 16 CENTRO CULTURAL ESPAÑA
- 19 SALONES TEQUILA DE LA CASA DE LAS SIRENAS
- 21 BAR LA ÓPERA
- 24 BAR ZINCO
- 57 ⓒ PASAGÜERO
- 64 LA CASA DE PAQUITA LA DEL BARRIO
- 65 SALÓN LOS ÁNGELES
- 70 ⓒ SALÓN TENAMPA
- 71 PULQUERÍA HERMOSA HORTENSIA
- 78 SALÓN MÉXICO
- 79 CANTINA VIENA
- 80 LA PERLA
- 86 SALÓN ESPAÑA
- 92 ⓒ BALLET FOLKLÓRICO DE AMALIA HERNÁNDEZ
- 118 PULQUERÍA LAS DUELISTAS
- 124 PERVERT LOUNGE
- 129 LA MASCOTA
- 131 UPS & DOWNS
- 133 BUTTERGOLD

ⓢ SHOPS

- 2 CALENDAR STANDS
- 30 NACIONAL MONTE DE PIEDAD
- 32 PORTALES DE LOS MERCADERES
- 38 SANBORNS
- 41 AMERICAN BOOKSTORE
- 42 MINERALIA
- 45 MIXUP
- 48 ARTE MEXICANO PARA EL MUNDO
- 49 SOMBREROS TARDAN
- 68 ⓒ LA LAGUNILLA FLEA MARKET
- 91 CONACULTA BELLAS ARTES
- 98 ⓒ FONART
- 103 MUSEO NACIONAL DE ARTES POPULARES
- 107 LIBRERÍA GANDHI
- 110 ⓒ LA CIUDADELA

- 112 MERCADO SAN JUAN
- 117 LA EUROPEA
- 136 LIVERPOOL
- 137 PALACIO DE HIERRO
- 150 MERCADO LA MERCED
- 151 ⓒ MERCADO SONORA

ⓐ ARTS AND LEISURE

- 3 MUSEO DEL EJÉRCITO
- 13 ⓒ GALERÍA SCHP
- 46 MUSEO DEL ESTANQUILLO
- 75 MUSEO FRANZ MAYER
- 77 MUSEO NACIONAL DE LA ESTAMPA
- 81 ARENA COLISEO
- 89 MUSEO NACIONAL DE ARTE
- 96 LABORATORIO DE ARTE ALAMEDA
- 104 MUSEO NACIONAL DE ARTES POPULARES
- 134 MUSEO NACIONAL DE LA CHARRERÍA
- 144 MUSEO JOSÉ LUIS CUEVAS

ⓗ HOTELS

- 11 HOSTAL MEXICO CITY
- 12 HOSTEL CATEDRAL
- 17 ⓒ HOTEL CATEDRAL
- 23 HOTEL BUENOS AIRES
- 26 HOTEL GILLOW
- 28 HOTEL ZAMORA
- 31 HOLIDAY INN
- 43 TULIP INN RITZ MEXICO
- 50 BEST WESTERN HOTEL MAJESTIC
- 53 HOTEL PRINCIPAL
- 58 HOTEL LAFAYETTE
- 100 FIESTA INN
- 101 SHERATON CENTRO HISTÓRICO
- 105 HOTEL SAN FRANCISCO
- 106 HOTEL MARLOWE
- 108 HOTEL METROPOL
- 109 HOTEL FLEMING
- 111 HOTEL CONDE
- 115 HOTEL SAN DIEGO
- 125 HOSTAL AMIGO
- 126 HOTEL ISABEL
- 127 HOTEL MONTE CARLO
- 143 ⓒ HOSTAL MONEDA

✪ SIGHTS

2 LA ALAMEDA DE SANTA MARÍA
13 MONUMENTO A LA REVOLUCIÓN
14 MUSEO DE LA REVOLUCIÓN
25 PASEO DE LA REFORMA MONUMENTS

❑ RESTAURANTS

5 LA POLAR
7 RESTAURANTE EL DELFÍN
15 RESTAURANTE EL MIXTECO
17 MARISCOS DEL CAMARONERO
19 CANTINA LATINO
22 LA HABANA
29 MERCADO CUAUHTÉMOC
31 CAFÉ MANGIA
32 LES MOUSTACHES
33 DAIKOKU
34 QUEBRACHO
40 YUG
42 CHAMPS ÉLYSÉES
45 ANGUS
46 CORDON BLEU
48 SUSHI ITTO
48 LUAU'S
51 BOHEMIO'S
53 MERCADO INSURGENTES
55 FONDA DEL REFUGIO
56 TEZKA
58 LOS ARCOS

◑ NIGHTLIFE

8 LA FLOR ASURIANA
21 SALÓN PACÍFICO
35 CANTINA DE LOS REMEDIOS
37 LIVING
43 LIPSTICK
44 GAYTA
50 EL TALLER/EL ALMACÉN
52 BOHEMIO'S
57 VIP CABARETITO
61 BAR ARRABALERO

◎ SHOPS

3 MERCADO EL CHOPO
4 CENTRO ARTESANAL BUENA VISTA
49 CENTRO DE ANTIGÜEDADES PLAZA DEL ÁNGEL
54 MERCADO INSURGENTES

⬥ ARTS AND LEISURE

1 MUSEO DE GEOLOGÍA
6 MUSEO EL CHOPO
9 MUSEO SAN CARLOS
27 MUSEO CASA DE CARRANZA
62 ARENA MÉXICO

⬟ HOTELS

10 HOTEL OXFORD
11 CASA DE LOS AMIGOS
12 HOTEL EDISON
16 HOTEL CASA BLANCA
18 HOTEL CORINTO
20 HOTEL IMPERIAL
23 FIESTA AMERICANA
24 MI CASA
26 HOTEL MARIA CRISTINA
28 HOTEL BRISTOL
30 CASA GONZÁLEZ
36 FIESTA AMERICANA GRANDE
38 HOTEL MARQUIS REFORMA
39 HOTEL FOUR SEASONS
41 GALERÍA PLAZA
59 HOTEL DEL PRINCIPADO
60 HOTEL POSDA VIENA

SEE MAP 3

Parque
Chapultepec

0   400 yds
0   400 m

SANTA MARÍA
DE LA RIBERA

Alameda de
Santa María

La Alameda de
Santa María

Beunavista

San Cosme

Guerrero

SAN RAFAEL

Revolución

Museo de la
Revolución

Monumento a
la Revolución

Plaza de la
República

SEE MAP 1

Hidalgo

Alameda
Central

TABACALERA

Juárez

Jardín
del Arte

Monumento
de Colón

Monumento
Cuauhtémoc

Paseo de la Reforma
Monuments

ZONA
ROSA

Plaza José
María Morelos

Plaza de la
Ciudadela

Balderas

Cuauhtémoc

Insurgentes

Jardín
Dr. Ignacio
Chávez

SEE MAP 4

© AVALON TRAVEL

MAP 3

CHAPULTEPEC AND POLANCO

LOS MORALES
SECC PALMAS

POLANCO

PALMITAS

Parque
América

Plaza
Mazaryk

Parque "Lincoln"

MOLINO
DEL REY

Auditorio
Nacional

Lago
Mayor

La Feria

Segunda
Sección

Museo
Tecnológico

Lago
Menor

To Lienzo Charro

0   200 yds
0   200 m

⊙ SIGHTS

37	**MUSEO NACIONAL DE ANTROPOLOGÍA E HISTORIA**	51	BAÑOS DE MOCTEZUMA
47	ZOOLÓGICO DE CHAPULTEPEC	54	LA FERIA DE CHAPULTEPEC
49	MONUMENTO DE LOS NIÑOS HÉROES	56	MUSEO CASA BARRAGÁN
50	EL CASTILLO DE CHAPULTEPEC	59	LIENZO CHARRO
		61	CASA DE LA BOLA AND PARQUE LIRA

Ⓡ RESTAURANTS

1	**HACIENDA DE LOS MORALES**	23	THE COFFEE BAR
3	VILLA MARÍA	24	LAS TORTUGAS
7	IL PUNTO	27	RINCÓN ARGENTINO
8	L'OSTERÍA DEL BECCO	29	LOS ARCOS
13	KLEIN'S RESTAURANT	30	RESTAURANT TANDOOR
15	EL ZORZAL	31	LA HUERTA
16	YAMIL	32	LE CIRQUE
17	EL REY DEL TACO	40	JW GRILL
18	NON SOLO PASTA	42	AU PIED DE COCHON
19	CAFÉ LOS ASOMBROS	45	CAFÉ BISTRO MP
20	NANDA-YO	53	CAFÉ DEL LAGO
21	CHEZ WOK	58	CAFÉ DEL BOSQUE

Ⓝ NIGHTLIFE

11	BARFLY	44	HARD ROCK CAFÉ
25	EL ÁREA	46	AUDITORIO NACIONAL
33	MARÍA BONITA		

Ⓢ SHOPS

| 9 | TANE | 14 | LAS ARTESANÍAS |
| 10 | LA CASA DEL HABANO | 38 | PINEDA COVALIN |

Ⓐ ARTS AND LEISURE

2	GALERÍA ENRIQUE GUERRERO	36	MUSEO RUFINO TAMAYO
4	GALERÍA LÓPEZ QUIROGA	48	MUSEO DE ARTE MODERNO
5	GALERÍA ALFREDO GINOCCHIO	52	**CHAPULTEPEC PARK**
6	GOLD'S GYM	55	GALERÍA DE ARTE MEXICANO
12	CINEMEX CASA DE ARTE	56	MUSEO DEL NIÑO
28	MUSEO SALA DE ARTE PÚBLICO DAVÍD ALFARO SIQUEIROS	60	LIENZO CHARRO

Ⓗ HOTELS

22	CASA VIEJA	39	HOTEL NIKKO MÉXICO
26	HOTEL HÁBITA	43	PRESIDENTE INTER-CONTINENTAL MEXICO CITY
34	**CAMINO REAL MEXICO CITY**	41	JW MARRIOTT
35	FIESTA AMERICANA GRANDE		

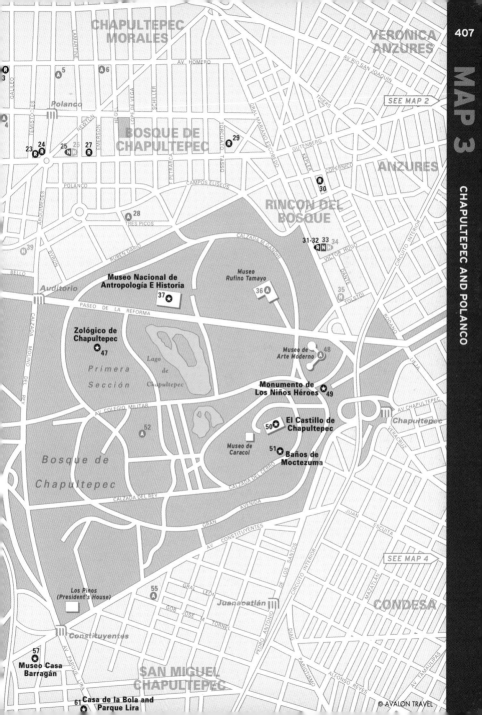

CHAPULTEPEC
MORALES

VERONICA
ANZURES

AV. HOMERO

Polanco

BOSQUE DE
CHAPULTEPEC

ANZURES

POLANCO

RINCON DEL
BOSQUE

TRES PICOS

CALZADA M. CANCHI

Museo
Rufino Tamayo

Museo Nacional de
Antropología E Historia

Auditorio

PASEO DE LA REFORMA

Zológico de
Chapultepec
47

Primera

Sección

Lago
de
Chapultepec

Museo de
Arte Moderno 48

Monumento de
Los Niños Héroes 49

AV. COLEGIO MILITAR

52

El Castillo de
50 Chapultepec

Chapultepec

Museo de
Caracol

51 Baños de
Moctezuma

Bosque de

Chapultepec

CALZADA DEL REY

CALZADA DEL CERRO

AVENIDA

SEE MAP 4

Los Pinos
(President's House)

55

Juanacatlán

CONDESA

Constituyentes

57

Museo Casa
Barragán

SAN MIGUEL
CHAPULTEPEC

61 Casa de la Bola and
Parque Lira

© AVALON TRAVEL

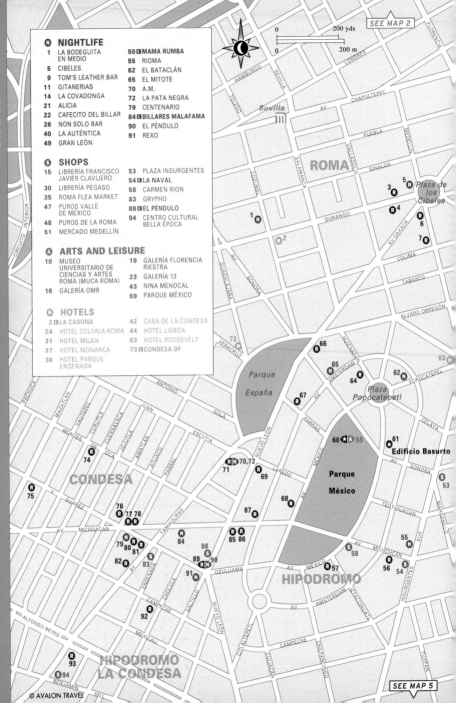

SEE MAP 2

SEE MAP 5

© AVALON TRAVEL

ROMA NORTE

Casa Universitária
del Libro

Around Plaza **17**
Río de Janeiro

Plaza
Río de
Janeiro

18 Colima 145

Tabasco 133

Casa Lamm

Plaza
Luis
Cabrera

Jardín
Dr Ignacio
Chavez

Jardín
Alexander
Pushkin

Hospital
General

Parque
de las
Americas

Mercado
Medellín

ROMA SUR

Centro
Médico

SEE MAP 1

◆ SIGHTS

12	CASA UNIVERSITÁRIA DEL LIBRO	20	TABASCO 133
17	AROUND PLAZA RÍO DE JANEIRO	28	CASA LAMM
18	COLIMA 145	60	PARQUE MÉXICO
		61	EDIFICIO BASURTO

◯ RESTAURANTS

3	TIERRA DE VINOS	57	CAFEMANÍA
4	CONTRAMAR	64	FLOR DE LIS
6	SUSHI KAITEN	66	BARRACUDA DINER
7	IXCEL	67	ROJO BISTROT
8	LA TECLA	68	LETTUZZE
13	LA COVADONGA	69	CAPÍCUA
25	LOS TAMALES EMPORIO	71	LA PATA NEGRA
27	CAFÉ D'CARLO	74	AJO Y CEBOLLA
29	RESTAURANTE LAMM	75	LAS ARRACHERAS
32	TACOS ÁLVARO O.	76	QUEBRACHO
33	*TORTA* STAND	77	LA BUENA TIERRA
34	CAFÉ PARIS	78	GARUFA
36	BISQUETS OBREGÓN	80	CAFÉ LA SELVA
39	LA AUTÉNTICA	81	CERVECERÍA
41	LA PIAZZA	82	VILLAGE CAFÉ
45	CAFÉ TAPANCO	85	FLORA LOUNGE
46	LA EMBAJADA JAROCHA	86	TAQUERÍA EL GRECO
		87	HOLA'S
52	MERCADO MEDELLÍN	89	CAFÉ LOS ASOMBROS
56	BISTROT MOSAICO	92	EL TIZONCITO
		93	EL ZORZAL

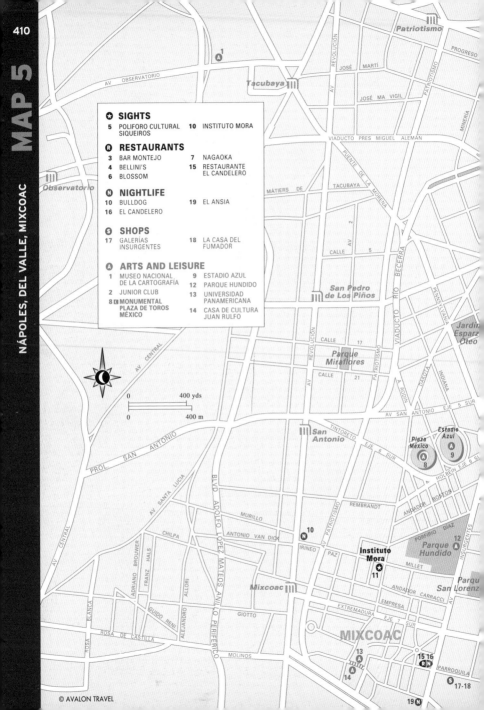

SIGHTS
5 POLIFORO CULTURAL SIQUEIROS
10 INSTITUTO MORA

RESTAURANTS
3 BAR MONTEJO
4 BELLINI'S
6 BLOSSOM
7 NAGAOKA
15 RESTAURANTE EL CANDELERO

NIGHTLIFE
10 BULLDOG
16 EL CANDELERO
19 EL ANSIA

SHOPS
17 GALERÍAS INSURGENTES
18 LA CASA DEL FUMADOR

ARTS AND LEISURE
1 MUSEO NACIONAL DE LA CARTOGRAFÍA
2 JUNIOR CLUB
8 MONUMENTAL PLAZA DE TOROS MÉXICO
9 ESTADIO AZUL
12 PARQUE HUNDIDO
13 UNIVERSIDAD PANAMERICANA
14 CASA DE CULTURA JUAN RULFO

0   400 yds
0   400 m

© AVALON TRAVEL

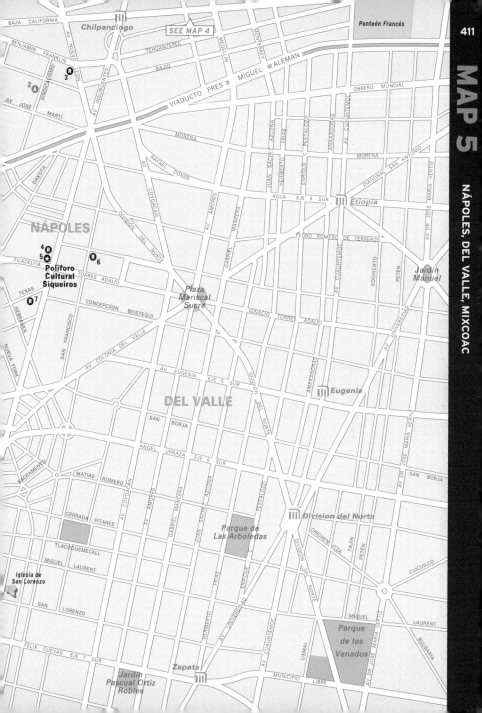

Barranca del Muerto

CONDOR

CALZ DESIERTO DE LOS LEONES

BLVD ADOLFO LOPEZ MATEOS ANILLO PERIFERICO

CORREGIDORA

LAS FLORES

GUSTAVO E. CAMPA

FELIPE VILANUEVA

ERNESTO ELORDUY

RICARDO CASTRO

PONCE

AV RIO MIXCOAC CIRCUITO INTERIOR

AV COYOACÁN

IZTACCÍHUATL

MORAS

FRANCIA

CAMELIA

MARGARITAS

MINERVA

HORTENSIA

AV INSURGENTES SUR

SAN ÁNGEL

JARDIN

AV LEÓN FELIPE

FRESNOS

AV ARTURO

SAN CARLOS

CALERO

13 R 14 A

12 S

5

RIVERA

ALTAVISTA

AV ALTAVISTA

PALMAS

ARCANO

REINA

AURELIANI

JUAREZ

25 S 26 A R R 27 28

HIDALGO

FRONTERA

JOSE MARIA DE TERESA

MARIA LUISA

AV REVOLUCIÓN

15 S A

RIO SAN ANGEL

PEDRO L. OGAZÓN

CAMINO AL DESIERTO DE LOS LEONES

16 S A 17 A

CRACOVIA

18 S

19 N

A LA PAZ

32 R R

31

30 ✪ **Ex-Convento del Carmen**

Casa del Risco

Plaza San Jacinto 29 ✪

Jardín del Arte

REVOLUCIÓN

AV INSURGENTES SUR

PROGRESO

PASEO DEL RIO

MIGUEL ANGEL DE QUEVEDO

Plaza San Luis Potosí

Jardín de La Bombilla

Parque Tagle

ARENAL

VITO ALESSIO ROBLES

AV PROGRESO

AV FRANCISCO SOSA

SALVADOR NOVO

Miguel Angel de Quevedo

DULCA OLIVA

CDA EPSILON

Parque Dos Conejos

CERRO DEL HOMBRE

CERRO DE LA LUZ

CERRO DEL AIRE

CERRO DEL AGUA

Viveros

Viveros de Coyoacán

AV UNIVERSIDAD

AV CD UNIVERSITARIA

FERROCARRIL

ALTAMIRANO

AV SAN JERÓNIMO

33 34 A 35
S A

Plaza Loreto

A 36

37 A

A 38 ✪

AV COPILCO

AV UNIVERSIDAD

PASEO DE LAS FACULTADES

Copilco

PEDRO ENRIQUEZ UREÑA

Universidad Nacional

Autónoma de México

CIRCUITO ESCOLAR

CIRCUITO ESCOLAR

PASEO DE LAS FACULTADES

CIRCUITO DE LA INVESTIGACIÓN CIENTÍFICA

AV A.D. MADRIGAL

TIZAPAN

0 — 400 yds

0 — 400 m

A 39-40

© AVALON TRAVEL

Universidad

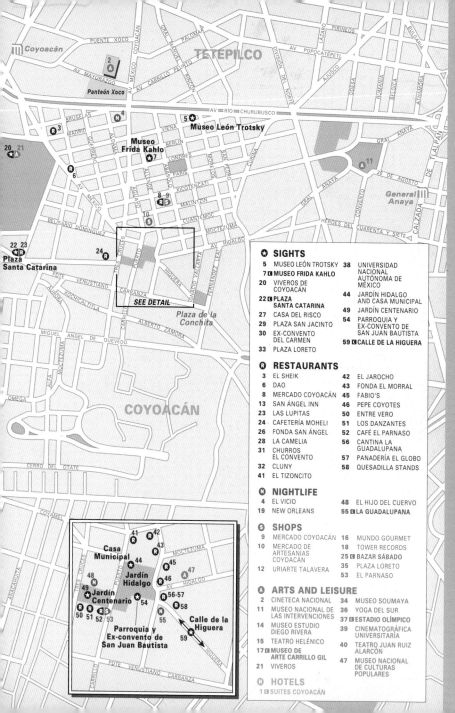

SIGHTS

5 MUSEO LEÓN TROTSKY	38 UNIVERSIDAD NACIONAL AUTÓNOMA DE MÉXICO
7 MUSEO FRIDA KAHLO	
20 VIVEROS DE COYOACÁN	44 JARDÍN HIDALGO AND CASA MUNICIPAL
22 PLAZA SANTA CATARINA	49 JARDÍN CENTENARIO
27 CASA DEL RISCO	54 PARROQUIA Y EX-CONVENTO DE SAN JUAN BAUTISTA
29 PLAZA SAN JACINTO	
30 EX-CONVENTO DEL CARMEN	59 CALLE DE LA HIGUERA
33 PLAZA LORETO	

RESTAURANTS

3 EL SHEIK	42 EL JAROCHO
6 DAO	43 FONDA EL MORRAL
8 MERCADO COYOACÁN	45 FABIO'S
13 SAN ÁNGEL INN	46 PEPE COYOTES
23 LAS LUPITAS	50 ENTRE VERO
24 CAFETERÍA MOHELI	51 LOS DANZANTES
26 FONDA SAN ÁNGEL	52 CAFÉ EL PARNASO
28 LA CAMELIA	56 CANTINA LA GUADALUPANA
31 CHURROS EL CONVENTO	57 PANADERÍA EL GLOBO
32 CLUNY	58 QUESADILLA STANDS
41 EL TIZONCITO	

NIGHTLIFE

4 EL VICIO	48 EL HIJO DEL CUERVO
19 NEW ORLEANS	55 LA GUADALUPANA

SHOPS

9 MERCADO COYOACÁN	16 MUNDO GOURMET
10 MERCADO DE ARTESANÍAS COYOACÁN	18 TOWER RECORDS
	25 BAZAR SÁBADO
12 URIARTE TALAVERA	35 PLAZA LORETO
	53 EL PARNASO

ARTS AND LEISURE

2 CINETECA NACIONAL	34 MUSEO SOUMAYA
11 MUSEO NACIONAL DE LAS INTERVENCIONES	36 YOGA DEL SUR
	37 ESTADIO OLÍMPICO
14 MUSEO ESTUDIO DIEGO RIVERA	39 CINEMATOGRÁFICA UNIVERSITARIA
15 TEATRO HELÉNICO	40 TEATRO JUAN RUIZ ALARCÓN
17 MUSEO DE ARTE CARRILLO GIL	47 MUSEO NACIONAL DE CULTURAS POPULARES
21 VIVEROS	

HOTELS

1 SUITES COYOACÁN

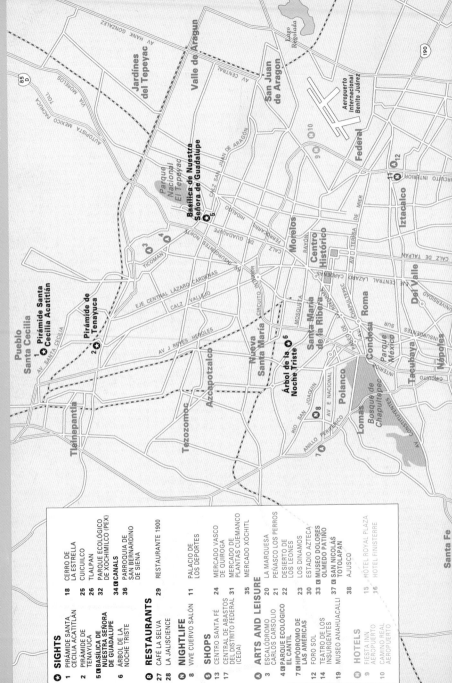

Lago Regolada

AV HANK GONZALEZ

Jardines del Tepeyac

Valle de Aragun

San Juan de Aragon

Aeropuerto Internacional Benito Juárez

Federal

VIA MORELOS

AUTOPISTA MEXICO PACHUCA TOLL

85 D

CIRCUITO INTERIOR

Iztacalco

Parque Nacional El Tepeyac

Basílica de Nuestra Señora de Guadalupe

Morelos

Centro Histórico

CALZ DE TLALPAN

Pueblo Santa Cecilia

Pirámide Santa Cecilia Acatitlán

Pirámide de Tenayuca

TICOMAN

EJE CENTRAL LÁZARO CÁRDENAS

CALZ VALLEJO

AV J REYES HEROLES

Del Valle

Roma

Santa María de la Ribera

Nueva Santa María

Árbol de la Noche Triste

Santa María

Condesa

Parque México

Tacubaya

Nápoles

Tlalnepantla

Tezozomoc

Azcapotzalco

Polanco

Lomas

Bosque de Chapultepec

RIO SAN JOAQUIN

AV E NACIONAL

ANILLO PERIFÉRICO

AV CONSTITUYENTES

Santa Fe

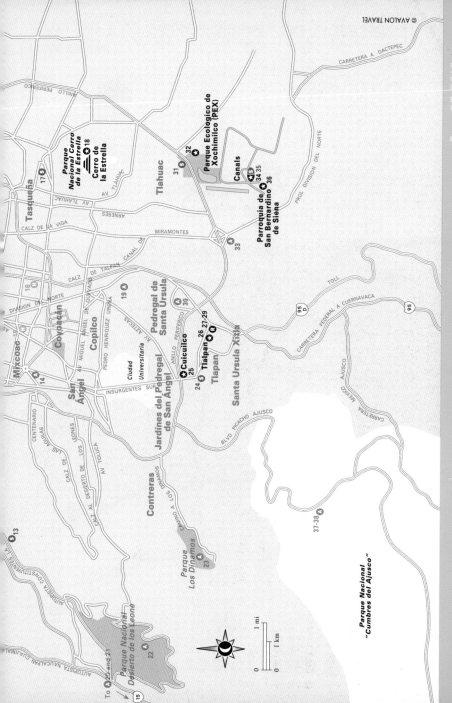

© AVALON TRAVEL

Parque Nacional Cerro de la Estrella

Cerro de la Estrella

18

17

Tasqueña

Tlahuac

31

32

Parque Ecologico de Xochimilco (PEX)

Canals

34 35

Parroquia de San Bernardino de Siena

36

33

MIRAMONTES

AV. TLAHUAC

ARNESES

CALZ. DE LA VIGA

Mixcoac

Coyoacán

Copilco

16

DIVISION DEL NORTE

AV. UNIVERSIDAD

AV. MIGUEL ANGEL DE QUEVEDO

PEDRO HENRIQUEZ UREÑA

CALZ. DE TALPAN

CANAL DE

14

San Angel

Ciudad Universitaria

INSURGENTES SUR

AV. AZTECAS

Pedregal de Santa Ursula

19

Jardines del Pedregal de San Angel

Cuicuilco

25

24

26 27-29

Tlalpan

30

Santa Ursula Xitla

ANILLO PERIFERICO

BLVD. PICACHO AJUSCO

LAS AGUILAS

CALZ. AL DESIERTO DE LOS LEONES

CENTENARIO

AV. TOLUCA

Contreras

CAMINO A LOS DINAMOS

Parque Los Dínamos

23

13

AUTOPISTA CONSTITUYENTES LA

Parque Nacional Desierto de los Leones

22

To 20 and 21

15

AUTOPISTA NAUCALPAN CUAJIMALPA

PROL. DIVISION DEL NORTE

CARRETERA A OAXTEPEC

TOLL

95 D

CARRETERA FEDERAL A CUERNAVACA

95

AJUSCO

CARRETERA MEXICO

37-38

Parque Nacional "Cumbres del Ajusco"

1 mi

0

1 km

0

SISTEMA DE TRANSPORTE COLECTIVO
Red del Metro

N

El Rosario · Tezozómoc · Ferrería · Vallejo · Instituto del Petroleo · Indios Verdes · Ciudad Az. · Plaza Aragón · Olímpica · Tecnológico · Múzquiz · Río de los Remedios · Impulsora · Nezahualcóyotl · Villa de Aragón · Bosque de Aragón · Deportivo Oceanía · Terminal Aérea · Hangares · Gómez Farías · Pantitlán · Agrícola Oriental · Canal de San Juan · Tepalcates · Guelatao · Peñón Viejo · Acatitla · Santa Marta · Los Reyes · La Paz

Aquiles Serdán · Azcapotzalco · Norte 45 · Lindavista · Deportivo 18 de Marzo · Martín Carrera · La Villa-Basílica · Talismán

Camarones · Autobuses del Norte · Potrero

Refinería · La Raza

Cuatro Caminos · Panteones · Tacuba · Cuitláhuac · Misterios · Bondojito · Consulado · Eduardo Molina · Aragón

Popotla · Tlatelolco · Valle Gómez · Canal del Norte

San Joaquín · Colegio Militar · Buenavista · Guerrero · Garibaldi · Lagunilla · Tepito · Morelos · Romero Rubio · Oceanía

Normal · San Cosme · Hidalgo · Bellas Artes · Allende · Flores Magón

Polanco · Revolución · Juárez · San Juan de Letrán · Zócalo · San Lázaro · Matzezuma

Auditorio · Cuauhtémoc · Balderas · Isabel la Católica · Pino Suárez · Candelaria · Balbuena

Sevilla · Insurgentes · Salto del Agua · Merced

Chapultepec · Niños Héroes · Doctores · San Antonio Abad · Fray Servando · Boulevard Pto. Aéreo

Constituyentes · Juanacatlán · Hospital General · Obrera · Zaragoza

Chilpancingo · Chabacano · Jamaica · Mixiuhca · Velódromo

Tacubaya · Patriotismo · Centro Médico · Lázaro Cárdenas · Santa Anita · Ciudad Deportiva · Puebla

Observatorio · La Viga · Viaducto · Coyuya · Canal de San Juan

Sn. Pedro de los Pinos · Etiopía · Xola · Iztacalco

Sn. Antonio · Eugenia · Villa de Cortés · Apatlaco

Mixcoac · División del Norte · Nativitas · Acuico

Insurgentes Sur · Zapata · Portales · Escuadrón 201

20 de Noviembre · Parque de los Venados · Ermita · Axomulco · Iztapalapa

Barranca del Muerto · Coyoacán · Eje Central · Mexicaltzingo · C. de la Estrella

Viveros · General Anaya · Via Lactea · Atlalilco · U.A.M. I

Miguel Angel de Quevedo · Tasqueña · Ganaderos · Const. de 1917

Copilco · Barrio Tula

Universidad · La Virgen · Calle 11 · Periférico Ote.

ESIME Culhuacán · Tezonco · Olivos · Nopalera · Zapotitlán · Tlaltenco

EL TREN LIGERO

En construcción · Tláhuac

Ciudad de México
Capital en Movimiento

SISTEMA DE TRANSPORTE COLECTIVO